W9-ANA-074

The Media of Mass Communication

SIXTH EDITION   2003 UPDATE

John Vivian
Winona State University

Boston   New York   San Francisco
o City   Montreal   Toronto   London   Madrid   Munich   Paris
Hong Kong   Singapore   Tokyo   Cape Town   Sydney

to Harold Vivian, my father,

who sparked my curiosity about the mass media at age 5 by asking what was black and white and read all over.

AND

to Elaine Vivian, my mother,

who nurtured this curiosity by keeping the house stocked with books, magazines and reading material of every sort.

Series Editor: Molly Taylor
Editor in Chief: Karen Hanson
Developmental Editor: Carol Alper
Editorial Assistant: Sarah McGaughey
Marketing Manager: Jacqueline Aaron
Editorial-Production Administrator: Annette Joseph
Photo Research: Katharine S. Cook and Omegatype Typography, Inc.

Editorial-Production Service: Omegatype Typography, Inc.
Interior Design: Carol Somberg
Composition Buyer: Linda Cox
Manufacturing Buyer: Megan Cochran
Cover Administrator: Linda Knowles
Cover Designer: Studio Nine
Electronic Composition: Omegatype Typography, Inc.

For related titles and support materials, visit our online catalog at www.ablongman.com

A previous edition was published under *The Media of Mass Communication*, Sixth Edition, copyright © 2002, 1999, 1997, 1995, 1993, 1991 by Allyn & Bacon.

CIP data not available at time of publication.

ISBN 0-205-37775-0

P
90
.V53
2003

Printed in the United States of America

10 9 8 7 6 5 4 3 2 1   VHP   07 06 05 04 03 02

Credits can be found on pages 509–510, which constitute an extension of the copyright page.

Contents

section one   The Mass Media

The mass media are the vehicles that carry mass messages. Television is a mass medium. So is the web—magazines too. In all, there are eight major mass media. An entire industry has been built up around each of these major media. This first section of your book includes an introductory chapter and then deals with each of these major mass media.

5   Recordings   101

6   Movies   127

■ **B O X E S** ■

7   Radio   153

■ **B O X E S** ■

8 Television 181

■ B O X E S ■

9 The Web 217

■ BOXES ■

section two   Mass Messages

The mass media carry all kinds of messages—earth-shaking news, frivolous horoscopes, _Ally McBeal,_ hard rock, Brahms and Reebok ads. This section of your book takes up some of the major forms of media messages. Mass messages are not unique to any media. News, for example, is as much at home in a newspaper as on the web and television. Public relations and advertising people don't limit themselves to any single medium to deliver their persuasive messages. To be sure, there are many other forms of mass media messages, but these are the major ones.

10   News   247

■ BOXES ■

section three — Mass Media Issues

This final section builds on what you learned in earlier sections about the mass media and about messages that media carry to their audiences. Every chapter is self-contained, so you can explore them in any order your instructor assigns. Each chapter is a springboard to improve your understanding and appreciation of the mass media and their role in every day of our lives as individuals and as a global society.

14 Mass Communication   347

15 Media Effects   365

16 Mass Media and Society 393

17 Global Mass Media 409

Features

■ MEDIA PEOPLE ■

■ MEDIA TIMELINE ■

Preface

When Fall 2001 classes began, mass communication students had the latest edition of *The Media of Mass Communication* in their hands. It was up-to-date. Some said it was the best edition in the history of the textbook, which was the most adopted one in the nation for beginning media courses. A few days later came September 11th. Everything changed, as commentators keep reminding us. The mass media were at the heart of what happened next, and they too were forever changed.

We watched, read and listened with unprecedented intensity. The media themselves went through torturous soul-searching about their underlying premises. Can news of such a dastardly attack on a civilian population be told in the detached, neutral voice of traditional journalism? In an instant advertisers yanked television commercials that had been applauded for poignancy, offbeat humor and effective pitches. Suddenly radio stations that had drifted away from news to all-music were carrying 24/7 news. Government went into a high propagandist gear. Public relations principles were put to use internationally, using media of all sorts to build world public opinion against terrorism.

September 11th was transformational. The new 2001 *MMC* sixth edition may as well have been from the previous century. The edition that had seemed to up-to-date the day before and in which both Allyn and Bacon, my publisher, and I took such pride was no longer good enough. Almost immediately we began work on this update.

Not only will you find the September 11th aftermath in this update. The revision gave us the opportunity to incorporate the latest information and analysis throughout the book. This includes the 2002 Stephen Ambrose plagiarism flap in the ethics chapter; the economic recession that sent Super Bowl XXXVI advertising rates plummeting; a public relations case study on Dean Kamen's Segway superscooter; and scholar James Campbell's landmark revisionist history on the Yellow Press. Throughout you will find the latest information and analysis so your learning is as current as it can be.

This new edition not only is a thorough update for a fast-changing field but is also significant in yet another way. An expanded companion web site, available free, is online at **www.ablongman.com/vivian.** You can take practice tests online and get immediate feedback. Exhaustive bibliographies, arranged with the most recent works first, can help with research papers. You will find special sections on media careers.

The web site is designed to take this edition to another level of "using the media to teach the media," our motto since the first edition. The printed material is the core of the content, while the web site provides the energy and excitement of the media itself.

We also have used the web to address our disappointment over the years that there was more to tell than the confines of a 500-page book could accommodate. Two new chapters, one on visual communication, the other on media roles within political systems, are on the book's Interactive Companion Website which is available via a CD-launcher if you purchased a new copy of this book. On this site, look for the Interactive Companion. It's where you can find web links, activities, video and audio clips plus additional practice tests designed to enrich and reinforce your learning experience.

How This Book Is Organized

This book has three sections, each intended to examine a different aspect of the mass media.

The Mass Media: Chapter 1, "Mass Media," provides a foundation for understanding the mass media and the dynamics that affect the messages that they transmit. The next eight chapters deal with each of the major mass media—books, magazines, newspapers, recordings, movies, radio, television and the web.

Mass Messages: Then come chapters on the major content forms disseminated by the media to mass audiences. These include news, public relations and advertising. A chapter on media research is also included.

Mass Media Issues: The rest of the book focuses on issues, including mass communication, media effects, the mass media and society, global mass media, media and governance, law and ethics.

Using This Book

This edition retains many of the popular features that have helped your predecessors master the subject.

- **Introductory Vignettes.** Chapters open with colorful descriptions about people who contributed significantly to the mass media or who exemplify important aspects of media operations.
- **Learning Goals.** Chapters begin with learning goals to help you guide your thoughts as you read through the chapters.
- **Study Previews.** Chapters include frequent summaries of the material in subsequent paragraphs. These study previews can help prepare you for the material ahead.
- **Running Glossary.** You will find glossary definitions in the margins, on the same page that the name or concept is introduced in the text.
- **Media Online.** The margins also contain hundreds of web addresses to guide your learning about the mass media beyond the textbook and the classroom.
- **Questions for Review.** These questions are keyed to the major topics and themes in the chapter. Use them for a quick assessment of whether you caught the major points.
- **Questions for Critical Thinking.** These questions ask you both to recall specific information and to use your imagination and critical thinking abilities to restructure the material.
- **Keeping Up to Date.** These sections list professional and trade journals, magazines, newspapers and other periodical references to help you keep current on media developments and issues. Most of these periodicals are available in college libraries.
- **Boxes.** Throughout the book, you will find four kinds of boxes that illustrate significant points. *Media People* boxes introduce personalities who have had a major impact on the media or whose story illustrates a major point of media history. *Media Abroad* boxes tell about practices in other countries to help you assess

your own country's media performance. The *Media Databank* boxes contain tables to help you see certain facts about the mass media at a glance. The *Media Timeline* boxes will help you see the sequence of important media events at a glance.

- **Web Sites.** You can go online for a great array of material designed especially to augment this edition (**www.ablongman.com/vivian**). The book's site includes review questions, glossaries, personality profiles, media abroad vignettes and even guidelines on how to build a media career, beginning with landing that first job. The additional Interactive Companion Website (available via the CD-launcher) includes bonus chapters and the Interactive Companion.

Supplements

INSTRUCTOR SUPPLEMENTS

INSTRUCTOR'S RESOURCE MANUAL (IRM).   This manual is designed to ease the time-consuming demands of instructional preparation, enhance lectures and provide helpful suggestions to organize the course. The IRM consists of helpful teaching resources and lecture enrichment including outlines, synopses, glossaries and an "at-a-glance" guide to the wealth of resources available in the package.

TEST BANK.   The test bank includes more than 2,200 multiple choice, true/false, matching, fill-in-the-blank, short answer and essay questions.

COMPUTERIZED TEST BANK.   The test bank is also available as an integrated suite of testing tools for Windows and Macintosh. Using the best-selling ESATEST III software, this computerized test bank allows instructors to edit, create and print tests using any combination of questions from the printed test bank.

INSTRUCTOR'S MULTIMEDIA RESOURCE CD-ROM.   This multimedia resource is designed to provide, in one convenient location, the wealth of materials offered by Allyn and Bacon to enrich your teaching of the introductory mass communication course. The Instructor's Resource Manual and Test Bank are provided here in their entirety in an electronic format. Also included are art images from the text, the entire PowerPoint package, the Interactive Companion (also available via the CD-launcher) plus two bonus online text chapters.

TEACHING TOOL FOR THE INTERACTIVE COMPANION.   This manual contains activities, teaching suggestions and test questions to help the instructor integrate the media assets in the Interactive Companion into his or her own teaching style and classroom environment.

THE ALLYN & BACON INTERACTIVE VIDEO PROGRAM.   Thirty specially selected news segments include commentary and on-screen critical thinking questions that deal with a variety of media issues and problems to help you bring media issues to life in your classroom. Includes an accompanying video user's guide.

POWERPOINT PRESENTATION PACKAGE.   This package consists of a collection of lecture outlines and graphic images keyed to every chapter in the text and is available on the web at **www.ablongman.com/ppt**.

ALLYN & BACON DIGITAL MEDIA ARCHIVE FOR COMMUNICATION VERSION 2.0. This collection of communication media images, video and audio clips, lecture resources and web links is available on CD-ROM for Windows and Macintosh and illustrates concepts in all areas of communication.

ALLYN & BACON MASS COMMUNICATION VIDEO LIBRARY. This library of videos, produced by Insight Media and Films for the Humanities and Sciences, includes full-length videos such as *Functions of Mass Communication, Making of a Newspaper, Illusions of News* and *The Truth about Lies.*

BLOCKBUSTER VIDEO GUIDE FOR INTRODUCTORY MASS COMMUNICATION CLASSES. This guide is intended to help teachers of mass communication use film and video to convey basic media concepts and historical facts or to illustrate complex media interrelationships.

ALLYN & BACON COMMUNICATION VIDEO LIBRARY. Contains a collection of communication videos produced by Films for the Humanities and Sciences (some restrictions apply).

STUDENT SUPPLEMENTS

CD-LAUNCHER TO INTERACTIVE COMPANION WEB SITE. This exciting new way to learn expands the traditional text by using the latest in multimedia. The Interactive Companion links the learning objectives established by the author to a wealth of media assets, including video and audio clips, web links, activities, and practice tests. Also featured are two bonus chapters, one on visual communication and one on media roles within political systems.

COMPANION WEB SITE PLUS. Revised and improved for the 2003 Update, this web site, available via the CD-launcher or at **www.ablongman.com/vivian,** features "Media in the News" text updates on current media developments. It also includes the following: links to media-related web sites, including those featured in the text's Media Online boxes; media profiles; timelines enhanced with links to related Internet sites; flashcards to review key terms; and a complete online study guide, including chapter objectives and practice tests. The "Careers in Media" section features links to various web sites to help students investigate media professions.

MEDIA LITERACY GUIDE. By Ralph Carmode of Jacksonville State University, this activity guide encourages your students to use critical thinking skills to develop an awareness and understanding of how and why media and their messages affect each of us.

MASS COMMUNICATION ON THE NET. By Ronald Roat, University of Southern Indiana, this booklet includes the basics of using the Internet, conducting web searches and critically evaluating and documenting Internet sources. It also contains Internet activities and URLs specific to the discipline of mass communication.

Acknowledgments

This book represents many new approaches for introducing students to the media of mass communication. The imaginative and far-sighted team at Allyn and Bacon deserves much of the credit for these innovations. When Bill Barke was editorial director, he chose to make this the most colorful and visually oriented text available for mass communication survey courses. Communication editor Steve Hull, who has a passion for the mass media, especially movies, and who shared Bill's commitment to make this book as colorful and interesting as the media themselves, organized the people and resources to see the project to completion. Joe Opiela, humanities editor, shepherded innovations that kept *The Media of Mass Communication* at the head of its field, including the accompanying web site.

Most of all, I am grateful to Karon Bowers, who took over as Allyn and Bacon's editor for the fifth edition. She knows the pulse beat of adopters, which helps me keep the book current with their needs. Just as important, Karon and her successor, Molly Taylor, continue the innovations that have marked *The Media of Mass Communication* since the beginning and aren't afraid to try innovations, like the extraordinary web accoutrements with this edition.

Since the first edition, *The Media of Mass Communication* has been noted for exceptional photos, tables and screen captures that underscore learning points. This edition outdoes its predecessors, thanks to the enterprise and imagination of Kate Cook at Allyn and Bacon and Anne Rogers and the team at Omegatype Typography, Inc. Forty percent of the photos are new, some as current as the 2000 Florida presidential recount and the 2001 XFL launch.

The greatest ongoing contributions have been those of Carol Alper, developmental editor. She not only has applied her lively imagination and good sense to the book's content but also has coordinated all the complexities of moving the manuscript to production.

With this level of support from the publisher, it's no wonder that more than 400 colleges and universities have adopted *The Media of Mass Communication*. Nor is it any wonder that Canadian editions, with my coauthor Pete Maurin, have been well received.

At Winona State University in Minnesota, several colleagues have been generous in sharing ideas from their teaching and reviewing portions of the manuscript. I especially want to thank Mike Cavanagh, whose web savviness and wit yielded continuing insights, and John Weis, who also read portions of the manuscript and made valuable suggestions.

Among the students who have written thoughtful suggestions that have shaped this edition are Niele Anderson of Grambling State University; Krislynn Barnhart, Green River Community College; Mamie Bush, Winthrop University; Lashaunda Carruth, Forest Park Community College; Mike Costache, Pepperdine University; Scott DeWitt, University of Montana; James Grades, Michigan State University; Dion Hillman, Grambling State University; Rebecca Iserman, Saint Olaf University; Scott Wayne Joyner, Michigan State University; Nicholas Nabokov, University of Montana; June Siple, University of Montana; and Candace Webb, Oxnard College. Matt Smith, son of Allyn and Bacon editor-in-chief Paul Smith, collected numerous examples of media effects on young people that have found their way into this new edition.

I also appreciate the thoughtful suggestions of colleagues who reviewed the manuscript in whole or in part:

Edward Adams, Brigham Young University
Ralph D. Barney, Brigham Young University

Thomas Beell, Iowa State University
Robert Bellamy, Duquesne University
ElDean Bennett, Arizona State University

Lori Bergen, Wichita State University

Bob Bode, Western Washington University

Kevin Boneske, Stephen F. Austin State University

E. W. Brody, University of Memphis

Joe Camacho, California State University-Sacramento

Patricia Cambridge, Ohio University

Dom Caristi, Iowa State University

Michael L. Carlebach, University of Miami

Meta Carstarphen, University of North Texas

Debbie Chasteen, Mercer University

Danae Clark, University of Pittsburgh

Jeremy Cohen, Stanford University

Michael Colgan, University of South Carolina

Ross F. Collins, North Dakota State University

David Donnelly, University of Houston

Thomas R. Donohue, Virginia Commonwealth University

Tom DuVal, University of North Dakota

Kathleen A. Endres, University of Akron

Glen Feighery, University of Nevada, Reno

Donald Fishman, Boston College

Laurie H. Fluker, Southwest Texas State University

Kathy Flynn, Essex County College in Newark, New Jersey

Ralph Frasca, University of Toledo

Mary Lou Galician, Arizona State University

Andy Gallagher, West Virginia State College

Ronald Garay, Louisiana State University

Steve Grommesch, Winona State University

Donna Halper, Emerson College

Bill Holden, University of North Dakota

Peggy Holecek, Northern Illinois University

Anita Howard, Austin Community College

Nancy-Jo Johnson, Henderson State University

Carl Kell, Western Kentucky University

Wayne F. Kelly, California State University, Long Beach

William L. Knowles, University of Montana

John Knowlton, Green River Community College

Sarah Kohnle, Lincoln Land Community College in Illinois

Charles Lewis, Mankato State University

Amy Lignitz, Johnson County Community College in Kansas

Larry Lorenz, Loyola University

John N. Malala, Cookman College

Maclyn McClary, Humbolt State University

Denis Mercier, Rowan College of New Jersey

Timothy P. Meyer, University of Wisconsin, Green Bay

Jonathan Millen, Rider University

Joy Morrison, University of Alaska at Fairbanks

Gene Murray, Grambling State University

Richard Alan Nelson, Kansas State University

Thomas Notton, University of Wisconsin-Superior

Terri Toles Patkin, Eastern Connecticut State University

John V. Pavlik, Columbia University

Sharri Ann Pentangelo, Purdue University

Deborah Petersen-Perlman, University of Minnesota-Duluth

Tina Pieraccini, SUNY-Oswego

Leigh Pomeroy, Mankato State University, Mankato

Thom Prentice, Southwest Texas State University

Hoyt Purvis, University of Arkansas

Jack Rang, University of Dayton

Benjamin H. Resnick, Glassboro State College

Ronald Roat, University of Southern Indiana

Patrick Ropple, Nearside
   Communications
Marshel Rossow, Mankato State
   University
Cara L. Schollenberger, Bucks County
   Community College
Quentin Schultz, Calvin College
Jim Seguin, Robert Morris College
Scott Shaw, Operations Manager,
   WIZM-AM, La Crosse, Wisconsin
Todd Simon, Michigan State University
Ray Sinclair, University of Alaska at
   Fairbanks
Karen A. Smith, College of Saint Rose
Mark Smith, Stephens College
Howard L. Snider, Ball State University
Penelope Summers, Northern Kentucky
   University

Larry Timbs, Winthrop University
John Tisdale, Baylor University
Edgar D. Trotter, California State
   University, Fullerton
Helen Varner, Hawaii Pacific University
Stephen Venneman, University of
   Oregon
Michael Warden, Southern Methodist
   University
Hazel G. Warlaumont, California State
   University, Fullerton
Ron Weekes, Ricks College
Bill Withers, Wartburg College
Donald K. Wright, University of South
   Alabama
Alan Zaremba, Northeastern University
Eugenia Zerbinos, University of
   Maryland

Keeping Current

To you, as a student, I want to emphasize that this book is a tool to help you become a more intelligent and discerning media consumer. If you plan on a media career, the book is intended to orient you to the courses that will follow in your curriculum. This book, though, is only one of many tools for staying on top of the subject for many years to come. A feature at the end of every chapter, "Keeping Up to Date," has tips on how to keep current even when your course is over.

Stay in Touch

Please feel free to contact me with questions and also ideas for improving the next edition. My e-mail is jvivian@winona.msus.edu. My address is Route 1, Box 32, Lewiston, MN 55952. My phone: (507) 523-2294.

May your experience with *The Media of Mass Communication* be a good one.

—John Vivian

John Vivian is a professor of journalism at Winona State University in Minnesota, where he has taught mass media survey courses for 20 years. Earlier he taught at Marquette University, the University of North Dakota, New Mexico State University and the University of Wisconsin centers in Waukesha and West Bend. He holds an honorary faculty appointment at the U.S. Defense Information School.

He is a past president of the Text and Academic Authors Association, and has been active in the Society of Professional Journalists and College Media Advisers.

His professional media experience began with his hometown newspaper in Kellogg, Idaho, and continued through college at Gonzaga University with United Press International and the Associated Press. After receiving a master's degree from Northwestern University's Medill School of Journalism, he returned to the AP in Seattle, Denver and Cheyenne. Besides Gonzaga and Northwestern, he has done advanced studies at Marquette University, the University of Minnesota and the University of North Dakota.

His work as an Army command information officer earned numerous Minaret, Fourth Estate and other awards. In college he was editor of the Gonzaga *Bulletin.* He was faculty adviser to the Marquette *Tribune,* and later founded the multicollege *Winona Campus Life* lab newspaper. He has edited numerous publications, including *The Academic Author,* and several online news sites, including Text and Academic Authors (http://taa.winona.msus.edu/TAA/index.html).

Vivian introduced his widely used college textbook, *The Media of Mass Communication,* in 1991. Vivian and coauthor Alfred Lawrence Lorenz of Loyola University in New Orleans wrote *News: Reporting and Writing,* a journalism textbook, in 1995. Vivian's scholarly, professional and trade articles have appeared in many publications, including *American Journalism, American Speech, Journalism Educator, Journalism History, Journalism Quarterly, Masthead* and *Newspaper Research Journal.* He also has written numerous encyclopedia articles.

The Media of Mass Communication by John Vivian has been awarded the Text and Academic Authors award for excellence. Affectionately called "the Texty," the award has been characterized as the Oscar for textbooks. The award is given to college textbooks in a broad range of academic disciplines that include communication, education and the performing and visual arts. The judges, all veteran textbook authors, evaluate books on four criteria: Is the book interesting and informative? Is the book well organized and presented? Is the book up to date and appealing? Does the book possess "teachability"? The judges gave *The Media of Mass Communication* perfect scores on all criteria. Said one judge: "By all measures, superior." John Vivian said he was especially pleased with the award because fellow textbook authors were the judges. "There is no more meaningful recognition than that which comes from peers," he said.

The Text and Academic Authors Association sponsors the Texty awards to promote excellence by identifying outstanding textbooks and other learning materials. TAA is the nation's leading organization for textbook authors. Its headquarters are at the University of South Florida-St. Petersburg.

The Media of Mass Communication was introduced in 1991 and quickly became the most-adopted textbook for introductory mass media and mass communication courses. The book's popularity has grown among college professors and their students with every new edition.

Running the Company Has Its Perks.   *For Sumner Redstone this includes hanging out with the likes of model Amber Valetta at Viacom's VH-1 fashion show.*

1

Mass Media

Sumner Redstone is full of stories. He will talk about growing up in a Boston tenement and about a habit of thriftiness that goes back to that time. He'll talk about buying a modest suburban house outside Boston for $43,000 many years ago and still having it.

But make no mistake: Redstone is one of our time's media super-moguls. He began inauspiciously in 1959 with a couple of drive-in theaters in the Northeast. Redstone built the company into an 1,100-screen enterprise. In 1989 Redstone bought Viacom, a little-known television production company that had been spun off by CBS. Redstone saw in Viacom a potential money machine to expand his empire. Within five years he had amassed enough cash and lines of credit to buy Paramount. The acquisition included not only the Hollywood studio and scores of other media interests but also Simon & Schuster, the world's largest book publisher at the time. Then he picked up the Blockbuster video chain. Next he masterminded a new television network, UPN.

At that point Viacom was a $26 billion company, a size beyond the ability of most of us to comprehend, but people hadn't seen anything yet. In 1999 Viacom plunked down $36 billion for CBS. The goal was to give Viacom's content-producing units, such as the Paramount studio, a significant new outlet for their products. Almost overnight, for example, Viacom's "Rugrats" was under consideration for CBS Saturday mornings.

Like many media moguls, Redstone is not as interested in content as in business. After acquiring Simon & Schuster as part of the Paramount deal, he never found the time to visit many of the book company's plants or offices. Instead, he was scanning bottom lines, looking for opportunities to enlarge the company. In 1998, for example, he sold all his Simon & Schuster textbook subsidiaries—half the company. He wanted the cash, and insiders said that he viewed the components of Simon & Schuster as expendable in the interest of raising more money for more acquisitions.

What does the story of Sumner Redstone tell us about the mass media today? One lesson is that no matter how compelling rags-to-riches stories may be, serious questions need to be asked about how media conglomerates function: What drives these companies? How are decisions made? As media consumers, are we being served well by the media content that these companies produce? Are these enormous companies contributing to a better society? Are they living up to their potential to do good things?

Sumner Redstone doesn't talk much about those issues. He would rather tell you about bottom lines. Or about the time a fire broke out in his ritzy Boston hotel room and how he hung from a windowsill, several floors up, until firefighters could rescue him. Or about the time . . .

This chapter—indeed, the entire book—is designed to give you the background to ask the right questions.

Importance of Mass Media

STUDY PREVIEW   Mass media usually are thought of as sources of news and entertainment. They also carry messages of persuasion. Important, though often overlooked, is how mass messages bind people into communities, even into nations.

Pervasiveness

Mass media are pervasive in modern life. Every morning millions of Americans wake up to clock radios. Political candidates spend most of their campaign dollars on television ads to woo voters. The U.S. consumer economy depends on advertising to create mass markets. American children see 30,000 to 40,000 commercial messages a year. With mass media so influential, we need to know as much as we can about how they work. Consider:

- Through the mass media we learn almost everything we know about the world beyond our immediate environs. What would you know about Kosovo or Pokémon or the Super Bowl if it were not for newspapers, television and other mass media?
- An informed and involved citizenry is possible in modern democracy only when the mass media work well.
- People need the mass media to express their ideas widely. Without mass media, your expression would be limited to people within earshot and those to whom you write letters.
- Powerful forces use the mass media to influence us with their ideologies and for their commercial purposes. The mass media are the main tools of propagandists, advertisers and other persuaders.

Media Databank

Media Consumption

People average 40 percent of their day and 60 percent of their waking hours with the mass media. These data, extracted from 2000 research from Veronis Suhler, show slight shifts over the years. Most notable are growth in time spent with the web and recorded music and shrinkage in time spent with television and radio.

	1997	2001	2003
Television	4.3 hours	4.4 hours	4.4 hours
Radio	3.0 hours	2.8 hours	2.7 hours
Records	0.7 hour	0.8 hour	0.9 hour
Newspapers	0.4 hour	0.4 hour	0.4 hour
Books	0.3 hour	0.3 hour	0.3 hour
Movies (including home video)	0.2 hour	0.2 hour	0.2 hour
Magazines	0.2 hour	0.2 hour	0.2 hour
Web	0.1 hour	0.4 hour	0.5 hour
Totals	9.2 hours	9.5 hours	9.6 hours

Information Source

The most listened-for item in morning newscasts is the weather forecast. People want to know how to prepare for the day. The quality of their lives is at stake. Not carrying an umbrella to work if rain is expected can mean getting wet on the way home, perhaps catching pneumonia, at worst dying. There used to be a joke that the most important thing the mass media did was to tell us whether a tornado was coming or whether the Russians were coming.

The heart of the media's informing function lies in messages called **news.** Journalists themselves are hard pressed to agree on a definition of news. One useful definition is that news is reports about things that people want or need to know. In the United States, reporters usually tell the news without taking sides.

Advertising also is part of the mass media's information function. The media, especially newspapers, are bulletin boards for trade and commerce. People look to supermarket advertisements for specials. Classified advertisements provide useful information.

Entertainment Source

The mass media can be wonderful entertainers, bringing together huge audiences not otherwise possible. More people cried at the movie *Titanic* than read any book about the tragedy. More people hear the Backstreet Boys on records or the radio than ever attend one of their concerts. Count the seats in Jimmy Buffet's bar in Key West, even calculate standing room only crowds, and contrast that with the audience for his signature "Margaritaville" in even one television appearance.

Almost all mass media have an entertainment component, although no medium is wholly entertainment. The thrust of the U.S. movie industry is almost all entertainment, but there can be a strong informational and persuasive element. Even the most serious newspaper has an occasional humor column. Most mass media are a mix of information and entertainment—and also persuasion.

news
Nonfiction reports on what people want or need to know.

Media Abroad

Mass Media and National Development

The United Nations gathers data on the number of television and radio sets around the globe. The data for these Western democracies and developing countries indicate correlations between media use, education and prosperity.

	Radios per 1,000 people	TV sets per 1,000 people	Literacy rate
Western Democracies			
United States	2,123	815	98%
Australia	1,280	486	100%
United Kingdom	1,146	435	99%
Canada	1,026	641	99%
Japan	620	907	99%
Developing Countries			
Ethiopia	191	2.3	62%
India	79	3.2	48%
Bangladesh	42	4.6	35%
Haiti	40	4.6	39%
Burkina Faso	26	5.3	18%

Persuasion Forum

People form opinions from the information and interpretations to which they are exposed, which means that even news coverage has an element of persuasion. The media's attempts to persuade, however, are usually in editorials and commentaries whose persuasive purpose is obvious. Most news media separate material designed to persuade from news. Newspapers package their opinion articles in an editorial section. Commentary on television is introduced as opinion.

The most obvious of the media messages designed to persuade is advertising. **Advertisements** exhort the audience to action—to go out and buy toothpaste, cornflakes and automobiles. **Public relations** is subtler, seeking to persuade but usually not to induce immediate action. Public relations tries to shape attitudes, usually by persuading mass media audiences to see an institution or activity in a particular light.

Binding Influence

advertisements
Messages intended to persuade people to buy.

public relations
Messages intended to win support.

The mass media can bind communities together by distributing messages that become a shared experience. On a global scale, this happened in the September 11th terrorist attack on the World Trade Center. Horrific images were burned into the collective consciousness of millions of people, giving them a common reference point that unified their resolve. It was a near-sudden unity unprecedented in human history.

The media can be a binding influence at many levels. The hometown weekly newspaper is something everyone in town has in common. In the same way, what subway riders in Philadelphia read on their way to work in the morning gives them something in common. A shared knowledge and a shared experience are created by mass media, and thus they create a basis for community.

The same phenomenon occurs on a national level. Stories on the 1986 Challenger space shuttle disaster bound the people of the United States in a nationwide grieving process. Coverage of the death of Princess Diana prompted a global dialogue on celebrity coverage. Stories on the dalliances of President Clinton and also of California Congressman Gary Condit helped us figure out what we as a society regard as right and wrong. The importance of mass media in binding people into nationhood is clear in every revolution and coup d'état: The leaders try to take over the national media system right away.

You might ask whether the media, in covering controversies, are divisive. The answer: No. Seldom do the media create controversy. They merely cover it. Thorough coverage, over time, helps to bring about societal consensus—sometimes for change, sometimes not. For example, most Americans once opposed legalizing abortion, but today, after exhaustive media attention, a majority consensus has emerged that abortions should be available legally. The same is true of many fundamental issues, such as gun control, racial integration and government budget priorities.

Collective Consciousness. Hundreds of images from the 2001 terrorist attacks on the World Trade Center are seared forever into the minds of people around the globe. Those powerful and evocative images, disseminated by the mass media, contributed to international resolve against terrorism.

Primary Mass Media

STUDY PREVIEW   The mass media fall into three categories based on the technology by which they are produced: print, electronic and photographic. The primary print media are books, magazines and newspapers. The primary electronic media are television, radio, sound recordings and the web. The one primarily photographic medium is movies.

Print Media

Books, **magazines** and **newspapers,** the primary **print media,** generally can be distinguished in the following four categories: binding, regularity, content and timeliness:

	Books	Magazines	Newspapers
Binding	Stitched or glued	Stapled	Unbound
Regularity	Single issue	At least quarterly	At least weekly
Content	Single topic	Diverse topics	Diverse topics
Timeliness	Generally not timely	Timeliness not an issue	Timeliness important

books
One-time, bound publications of enduring value on single topic.

magazines
Ongoing bound publications of continuing value with diverse topics.

newspapers
Unbound publications, generally weekly or daily, with diverse, timely content.

print media
Books, magazines and newspapers.

Media Timeline

Media Technology

1440s Primal Event
Johannes Gutenberg devised movable metal type, permitting mass production of printed materials.

1455 Books
Johannes Gutenberg printed the first of his Bibles using movable type.

1690 Newspapers
Ben Harris printed *Publick Occurrences,* the first newspaper in the English colonies.

1741 Magazines
Andrew Bradford printed *American Magazine* and Benjamin Franklin printed *General Magazine,* the first magazines in the English colonies.

1877 Recording
Thomas Edison introduced the phonograph, which could record and play back sound.

1888 Movies
William Dickson devised the motion picture camera.

1895 Radio
Guglielmo Marconi transmitted the first message by radio wave.

1927 Television
Philo Farnsworth invented the tube that picked up moving images for live transmission.

1969 Web
The U.S. Defense Department established the computer network that became the Internet.

Although these distinctions are helpful, they cannot be applied rigidly. For example, timeliness is critical to *Time* and *Newsweek,* even though they are magazines. Sunday newspaper supplements such as *Parade* are magazines but are not bound. Over the past 20 years, book publishers have found ways to produce "instant books" on major news events within a couple of weeks so that their topics can be timely. The *National Enquirer* has characteristics of both a newspaper and a magazine.

The technological basis of books, magazines and newspapers, as well as that of lesser print media such as brochures, pamphlets and billboards, is the printing press, which for practical purposes dates back to the 1440s. Print media messages are in tangible form. They can be picked up physically and laid down, stacked and filed and stored for later reference. Even though newspapers may be used to wrap up the leftovers from dinner for tomorrow's garbage, there also is a permanency about the print media.

Electronic Media

electronic media
Recordings, radio, television or web, whose messages are stored electronically for transmission and retrieval.

Television, radio and sound recordings flash their messages electronically. Pioneer work on **electronic media** began in the late 1800s, but they are mostly a 20th-century development. Unlike print messages, television and radio messages disappear as soon as they are transmitted. Although it is true that messages can be stored on tape and other means, usually they reach listeners and viewers in a nonconcrete form. Television is especially distinctive because it engages several senses at once with sound, sight and movement.

The newest mass medium, the web, combines text, audio and visuals—both still and moving—in a global electronic network.

Chemical Media

The technology of movies is based on photographic chemistry. Movies are a **chemical medium.** Although a lot of video production, including some prime-time television, is shot on videotape and stored electronically, Hollywood still makes movies on strips of transparent celluloid that are "pulled through the soup"—a technology that dates back to 1888.

In some respects, chemical technology is not only archaic but also expensive. Studios make as many as 6,000 copies of major releases and ship them from movie house to movie house in cumbersome metal boxes. The freight bill alone is astronomical. How much easier—and cheaper—it would be to transmit movies via satellite to movie houses, which would cut film and distribution costs perhaps 85 percent. Engineers working on digital electronic technology for movies have been stymied, however, in the attempt to match the image quality of film at a reasonable cost.

Eventually, as digital technology improves and costs come down, movies will shift from chemical to electronic technology. But don't hold your breath.

Mass Media Models

STUDY PREVIEW   Scholars have devised numerous ways to dissect and categorize the mass media. These include the hot-cool, entertainment-information, content-distribution, elitist-populist and pull-push models. Each offers insights, but all of them have shortcomings in explaining the mass media.

Hot-Cool Model

One model that helps to explain the mass media divides them into hot and cool categories. Books, magazines and newspapers are **hot media** because they require a high degree of thinking to use them. To read a book, for example, you must immerse yourself to derive anything from it. You must concentrate and tune out distractions. The relationship between you and the medium is intense—or hot. The same is true of magazines and newspapers, which require the audience to participate actively in the communication process.

In contrast, some media allow the audience to be less actively involved, even passive. These are **cool media.** Television, for example, requires less intellectual involvement than do the hot media. In fact, television requires hardly any effort. When radio is played mostly as background, it doesn't require any active listener involvement at all. It's a cool medium. Radio is warmer, however, when it engages listeners' imaginations, as with radio drama.

Are movies hot or cold? In some ways, movies are like television, with simultaneous visual and audio components. But there are essential differences. Movies involve viewers completely. Huge screens command the viewers' full attention, and sealed, darkened movie-house auditoriums shut out distractions. On a hot-cool continuum, movies are hot. What about a movie played at home on television? Cool.

Entertainment-Information Model

Many people find it helpful to define media by whether the thrust of their content is entertainment or information. By this definition, newspapers almost always are

chemical media
Underlying technology for movies is photographic chemistry.

hot media
Print media, which require intimate audience involvement.

cool media
Can be used passively.

considered an information medium, and audio recording and movies are considered entertainment. As a medium, books both inform and entertain. So do television and radio, although some networks, stations and programs do more of one than the other. The same is true with magazines, some titles being geared more for informing and some more for entertaining.

Although widely used, the entertainment-information dichotomy has limitations. Nothing inherent in newspapers, for example, precludes them from being entertaining. Consider the weirdest supermarket tabloids, which are newspapers but which hardly anybody takes seriously as an information source. The neatness of the entertainment-information dichotomy doesn't work well with mainstream newspapers either. Most daily newspapers have dozens of items intended to entertain. Open a paper and start counting with "Garfield" and the astrology column.

The entertainment-information dichotomy has other weaknesses. It misses the potential of all mass media to do more than entertain and inform. The dichotomy misses the persuasion function, which you read about earlier in this chapter. People may consider most movies as entertainment, but there is no question that Steven Spielberg has broad social messages even in his most rollicking adventure sagas. In the same sense, just about every television sitcom is a morality tale wrapped up in an entertaining package. The persuasion may be soft-peddled, but it's everywhere.

Dividing mass media into entertainment News and information categories is becoming increasingly difficult as newspapers, usually considered the leading information medium, back off from hard-hitting content to woo readers with softer, entertaining stuff. For better or worse, this same shift is also taking place at *Time* and *Newsweek*. This melding even has a name that has come into fashion: **infotainment.**

Although the entertainment-information model will continue to be widely used, generally it is better to think in terms of four media functions—to entertain, to inform, to persuade, and to bind communities—and recognize that all media do all of these things to a greater or lesser degree.

Content-Distribution Model

Many dynamics in mass media behavior today can be visualized in a model that divides media functions into message creation and message distribution. It's the **content-distribution model.** Some companies are heavily into creating content, like producing movies, publishing books and putting out magazines. Other companies are heavily into distribution, like operating movie houses, bookstore chains and cable systems. The heaviest players, including AOL Time Warner, News Corporation, Vivendi and Disney, are building stakes in both content creation and distribution. Consider these examples:

Media Company	Content Units	Distribution Units
AOL Time Warner	Cable News Network	Time Warner Cable
News Corporation	20th Century Fox	Sky Global
Vivendi	Vivendi Universal	Canal+
Disney	Disney Studios	ABC

Controlling both content creation and distribution, called **vertical integration,** was once considered a violation of U.S. antitrust laws. In 1948 the U.S. Supreme

infotainment
Melding of media role as purveyor of information and entertainment.

content-distribution model
Divides functions of media companies into a creation category, like producing a television program, to a distribution function, like delivering the program on a cable system.

vertical integration
A single corporation or individual's total control over production that can stifle competition. Example: An auto manufacturer that owns iron ore mines, steel plants, manufacturing plants and dealerships.

Court forced Hollywood studios to sell off their national movie-house chains. The Court ruled that controlling the movie business all the way from creation to final movie-house showing stifled competition. Later the Federal Communications Commission forbade the Big Three television networks to own the shows they aired. The commission's reasoning was the same, although the ban was relaxed in 1995 after cable channels and cut into the Big Three's one-time dominance.

In general, the government has backed off on the vertical integration issue. Some critics, including media commentator Steven Brill, blame politics: "Today's media landscape is filled with giants who are some of the key players in the modern Washington landscape of lobbying and campaign cash."

Whether Brill's cynicism is warranted, the fact is that giant media companies are scrambling to acquire the whole process from creation to distribution. Competition is severe. A glimpse into the dynamics occurred in 2000 when Time Warner dropped rival Disney's ABC television network from Time Warner cable systems. In this case a public outcry forced Time Warner to back off. More often, though, such cutthroat rivalry flies below most media consumers' radar. Even so, as the competition to own the entire mass media process intensifies, more confrontations like the Time Warner-Disney flap undoubtedly will erupt publicly. Viewing these confrontations through the content-distribution model helps to make sense of sometimes very confusing intercorporate feuds.

The worst downside of vertical integration is that the companies that own the entire process are inclined to favor internally produced products. When Steven Brill created the Court TV channel, for example, he felt forced to sell part of his company to three giant cable system operators, including Time Warner, to get his channel on the cable systems. In short, an outsider is disadvantaged. When an independent company tried to create a cable channel, the Classic Sports Network, major cable systems responded that they already were full up. The new independent channel disappeared. Meanwhile, Time Warner had no problem finding a channel for its own CNN/Sports Illustrated.

Elitist-Populist Model

An ongoing tension in the mass media exists between advancing social and cultural interests and giving broad segments of the population what they want. This tension, between extremes on a continuum, takes many forms:

- Classical music versus pop music.
- Nudes in art books versus nudes in *Playboy* magazine.
- A Salman Rushdie novel versus a pulp romance.
- A PBS documentary on crime versus Fox Television's "America's Most Wanted."

At one end of the continuum is serious media content that appeals to people who can be called **elitists** because they believe that the mass media have a responsibility to contribute to a better society and a refinement of the culture, regardless of whether the media attract large audiences. At the other end of the continuum are **populists**, who are entirely oriented to the marketplace. Populists believe that the mass media are at their best when they give people what people want.

The mass media have been significant historically in shaping social and cultural values. Media that are committed to promoting these values generally forsake the

elitists
They focus on media responsibility to society.

populists
Applaud media that attract a large following.

largest possible audiences. For years in New York City, the serious-minded *Times,* which has no comics, lagged in street sales behind the *Daily News,* a screaming tabloid that emphasizes crime and disaster coverage, loves scandals and sex, and carries popular comics. The *Times* can be accused of elitism, gearing its coverage to a high level for an audience that appreciates thorough news coverage and serious commentary. The *Daily News,* on the other hand, can be charged with catering to a low level of audience and providing hardly any social or cultural leadership. The *Daily News* is in the populist tradition.

A lot of media criticism can be understood in the context of this elitist-populist continuum. People who see a responsibility for the mass media to provide cultural and intellectual leadership fall at one extreme. At the other extreme are people who trust the general population to determine media content through marketplace dynamics. Certainly, there are economic incentives for the media to cater to mass tastes.

Most mass media in the United States are somewhere in the middle of the elitist-populist continuum. Fox Television offers some serious fare, not only hyped crime re-creations, and the New York *Times* has a sense of humor that shows itself in the wit of its columnists and in other ways.

media
convergence

Pull-Push Model

The communication revolution introduced by the web has required a new model to understand new ways in which the media work. One new model classifies some media as passive. These are **pull media,** which you, the consumer, steer. Pull media themselves are passive, there if you want them. Examples are the traditional media, such as radio and television, over which you have control to pull in a message. You can turn them on or off. You can pick up a newspaper, magazine or book and put it down. You can go to a movie or not.

Push media, by contrast, propel messages at you whether invited or not. A simple, low-tech example is a recorded voice in a grocery store aisle that encourages you to buy a certain brand of cornflakes as you pass by the cereals. Push media are taking sophisticated forms with the web and new technologies that are making the media more pervasive than ever. They are always on.

You can program some push media:

- A belt-loop beeper that updates the score of a football game you can't watch while you're doing something else.
- News and travel updates from Egypt that you request after booking airline tickets for a vacation to see the Pyramids.

Other push media intrude, gently or in your face, without your doing any programming:

- An automobile windshield display that flashes directions to nearby eateries.
- Advertising banners across your computer screen.

No model is perfect, which means that the pull-push media model uses extremes that rarely exist in reality. Most media messages are pull-push hybrids. A lot of push media, for example, doesn't intrude without a specific invitation, and they leave it to you to choose what to pull. If you don't want on-screen ads from your Internet service provider, you can switch providers.

pull media
Media in which the consumer decides whether to receive messages.

push media
Media that can propel messages uninvited at the consumer.

Economics of Mass Media

STUDY PREVIEW   With few exceptions the U.S. mass media are privately owned and must turn profits to stay in business. Except for books, sound recordings and movies, most media income is from advertising, with lesser amounts directly from media consumers. These economic realities are potent shapers of media content.

Economic Foundation

The mass media are expensive to set up and operate. The equipment and facilities require major investment. Meeting the payroll requires a bankroll. Print media must buy paper by the ton. Broadcasters have gigantic electricity bills to pump their messages through the ether.

To meet their expenses, the mass media sell their product in two ways. Either they derive their income from selling a product directly to mass audiences, as do the movie, record and book industries, or they derive their income from advertisers that place advertisements for mass audiences that the media provide, as do newspapers, magazines, radio and television. Newspapers and magazines are hybrids with both audience and advertising revenue streams. In short, the mass media operate in a capitalistic environment. With few exceptions they are in business to make money.

ADVERTISING REVENUE.   Advertisers pay the mass media for access to potential customers. From print media, advertisers buy space. From broadcasters they buy time.

Media Databank

Media Costs

Here is a sampler of rates for time and space in major U.S. media for one-time placements. Major advertisers pay less because they are given discounts as repeat customers.

CBS, Super Bowl XXXV	30-second spot	$2,500,000
Fox, Super Bowl XXXVI	30-second spot	1,900,000
CBS, "Survivor II" finale	30-second spot	1,000,000
NBC, "ER"	30-second spot	425,000
ABC, "Monday Night Football"	30-second spot	330,000
Fox, "X-Files"	30-second spot	238,000
Time	Full page	210,600
Wall Street Journal	Full page	148,000
New York *Times*	Sunday full page	99,000
Los Angeles *Times*	Sunday full page	52,900

Generally, the more potential customers a media company can deliver to advertisers, the more advertisers are charged for time or space. CBS had 130 million viewers for the 2001 Super Bowl, and it charged $2.5 million for 30-second commercials. A spot on a daytime program, with a fraction of the Super Bowl audience, typically goes for $85,000. *Time* magazine, claiming a 4.6 million circulation, charges $210,600 for a full-page advertisement. If *Time*'s circulation were to plummet, so would its advertising rates. Although there are exceptions, newspapers, magazines, television and radio support themselves with advertising revenues.

Book publishers once relied solely on readers for revenue, but that has changed somewhat. Today, book publishers charge for film rights whenever Hollywood turns a book into a movie or a television program. The result is that publishing houses now profit indirectly from the advertising revenue that television networks pull in from broadcasting movies.

Movies too have come to benefit from advertising. Until the 1950s movies relied entirely on box-office receipts for profits, but movie-makers now calculate what profits they can realize not only from movie-house traffic but also from recycling their movies through advertising-supported television and home videos. The home video aftermarket, in fact, now accounts for the lion's share of movie studio income. Today, movie-makers even pick up advertising directly by charging commercial companies to include their products in the scenes they shoot, although the revenue is relatively minor.

CIRCULATION REVENUE. While some advertising-supported mass media, such as network television, do not charge their audiences, others do. When income is derived from the audience, it's called **circulation** revenue. *Wall Street Journal* readers pay 75 cents a copy at the newsrack. *Rolling Stone* costs $3.95. Little if any of the newsrack charge or even subscription revenue ends up with the *Wall Street Journal* or *Rolling Stone*. Distribution is costly, and distributors all along the way take their cut. For some publications, however, subscription income makes the difference between profit and loss.

Direct audience payments have emerged in recent years in broadcasting. Cable and satellite subscribers pay a monthly fee. Audience support is the basis of sub-

circulation
Number of copies of a publication that circulate.

scription television such as commercial-free HBO. Noncommercial broadcasting, including the Public Broadcasting Service and National Public Radio, relies heavily on viewer and listener contributions. Record makers, movie-makers and book publishers depend on direct sales to the consumer.

Besides advertising and circulation revenue, some media units derive income from other sources. PBS, for example, has a thriving catalog mail-order business.

AUDIENCE DONATIONS. Audience donations are important to some media operations. Public radio and television stations, which carry no advertising, solicit their audiences for contributions. On-air fund drives, usually running as many as four weeks a year, raise as much as 30 percent of many stations' budgets. Why do listeners and viewers cough up $50 or more for public-station programming when so much free media content is available? During their fund drives, the stations stress their heavy emphasis on public affairs and highbrow cultural content, which is hard to find in advertising-supported media. The stations then state, quite frankly, that the continuance of the programming depends on volunteer contributions.

PRIVATE SUPPORT. The *Christian Science Monitor,* which maintains an expensive staff of foreign correspondents, has lost money for 30 years. Neither advertising nor subscription income is sufficient to meet expenses. In recent years the newspaper has been in the red $12 million to $16 million a year. The losses were made up, as always, by the Christian Science church, which sees part of its mission as providing high-quality news coverage of world affairs. Similarly, the Unification Church of the Reverend Sun Myung Moon underwrites the money-losing Washington *Times.*

Private support, largely from philanthropic organizations, helps to keep the Public Broadcasting Service and National Public Radio on the air. The Federal Communications Commission does not allow PBS, NPR or their affiliate stations to accept advertising.

GOVERNMENT SUBSIDIES. The idea of government support for the mass media might seem contrary to the democratic ideal of a press that is fiercely independent of government, if not adversarial. The fact, however, is that Congress has provided as much as $286 million a year in tax-generated dollars for a quasi-government agency, the Corporation for Public Broadcasting, to funnel to the nation's noncommercial television and radio system. Buffers are built into the structure to prevent governmental interference in programming. The buffers seem generally to have worked. Some states, including Minnesota, New Mexico and Wisconsin, provide state tax dollars for noncommercial broadcasting.

Some states require regulated industries, such as insurance companies, to buy space in the state's newspapers to publicize their financial reports. Although these reports, called *legal advertisements* or **legals,** are in tiny agate type, the same size as classified ads, the fees from them are important income for many publications. Some publications also have an indirect subsidy from school boards and other government units that are required by law to publish their minutes and sometimes budgets and other documents. These too are called legals.

GOVERNMENT ADVERTISING. The U.S. government pours tremendous amounts of money into the mass media through advertising. In 1998 the government was the 38th largest advertiser, spending $348 million. Government advertising includes the postal service and military recruiting.

Testimonials. Buena Vista Television, which produces the Keenan Ivory Wayans talk show, runs full-page advertisements in trade journals that local station executives read. Their goal is to convince stations to buy the program for local airing by claiming it will attract large audiences. With a large audience, stations can sell lucrative local advertising. In general, the larger the audience, the higher the ad rates a station can charge—a principle that applies also to radio, magazines, newspapers and the web.

legals
Government-required paid notices.

Government funding of the media also occurs at lower levels. Some states, for example, have large budgets for advertising to bring in tourists. Business magazines, such as *Forbes*, regularly contain multipage advertising sections from states that want companies to relocate.

AUXILIARY ENTERPRISES.   Many media companies have nonmedia enterprises that generate income that can relieve the profit pressure on their media operations. For years the Chicago *Tribune* made handsome profits selling newsprint from its Canadian paper factories. Such auxiliary enterprises can tide the media properties through lean times. In 1997 the Public Broadcasting System decided to exploit its brand name by stepping up the marketing of PBS products and services. These include T-shirts, tapes, toys and trinkets that are spin-offs from programs.

Economic Imperative

Economics figures into which messages make it to print or the airwaves. To realize their profit potential, the media that seek large audiences choose to deal with subjects of wide appeal and to present them in ways that attract great numbers of people. A subject that interests only small numbers of people does not make it into *Time* magazine. ABC, to take another example, drops programs that do not do well in the television ratings. This is a function of economics for those media that depend on advertising revenue to stay in business. The larger the audience, the more advertisers are willing to pay for time and space to pitch their goods and services.

Even media that seek narrow segments of the population need to reach as many people within their segments as possible to attract advertisers. A jazz radio station that attracts 90 percent of the jazz fans in a city will be more successful with advertisers than a competing jazz station that attracts only 10 percent.

The mass media's imperative to maximize income is no better demonstrated than by radio compresson technology introduced in 1999. Software, under the telling brand name Cash, allowed stations to squeeze 60 minutes of talk into 54 minutes to make more room for ads. The software cut out pauses and speeded delivery. At 1:10 compression, Rush Limbaugh sounded funny, but at 1:15 the change was hardly noticeable. Limbaugh objected to stations compressing his syndicated talk show by even a second, but the stations, lured by revenue from more ads, ignored him.

Media that do not depend on advertising also are geared to finding large audiences. For example, a novel that flops does not go into a second printing. Only successful movies generate sequels.

Upside and Downside

The drive to attract advertising can affect media messages in sinister ways. For example, the television station that overplays the ribbon-cutting ceremony at a new store is usually motivated more by a desire to please an advertiser than by a commitment to reporting news. The economic dependence of the mass media on advertising income gives considerable clout to advertisers, who may threaten to yank advertising out of a publication if a certain negative story appears. Such threats occur, though not frequently.

At a subtler level, lack of advertiser support can work against certain messages. During the 1950s, as racial injustice was emerging as an issue that would rip the

Alternative Media. With U.S. advertising spending at a record $233 billion in 2000, traditional media were filled up. Advertisers accelerated their search for alternative media. Car owners were paid to turn their vehicles into rolling billboards. One company, Hardwear International, introduced wearable video. The phenomenon was called "ad nauseum" by the trade journal *Advertising Age*.

nation apart a decade later, U.S. television avoided documentaries on the subject. No advertisers were interested.

The quest for audience also affects how messages are put together. The effect is relatively benign, although real, when a television preacher like Oral Roberts avoids mentioning that he is a Methodist so as not to lose listeners of other faiths. Leaving things unsaid can be serious. For years many publishers of high school science textbooks have danced gingerly around the subject of evolution rather than becoming embroiled in arguments with creationists and losing sales.

Media Demassification

STUDY PREVIEW   The idea that the mass audience is the largest number of people who can be assembled to hear mass messages is changing. Most media today seek narrow audience segments.

Technology and Demassification

Another contemporary economic phenomenon is **demassification.** The mass media are capable of reaching tremendous numbers of people, but most media today no longer try to reach the largest possible audience. They are demassifying, going after the narrower and narrower segments of the mass audience.

This demassification process, the result of technological breakthroughs and economic pressures, is changing the mass media dramatically. Radio demassified early, in the 1950s, replacing formats designed to reach the largest possible audiences with formats aimed at sectors of audience. Magazines followed in the 1960s and the 1970s, and today most of the 12,000 consumer magazines in the United States cater only to the special interests of carefully targeted groups of readers. Today, with dozens of television program services available via cable in most U.S. households, television also is going through demassification.

Effects of Demassification

The effects of demassification are only beginning to emerge. At first, advertisers welcomed demassification because they could target their pitches to groups of their

demassification
Media focus on narrower audience segments.

likeliest customers. The latest trend in demassification has advertisers producing their own media to carry their messages by mail to potential customers who, through computer sorting and other mechanisms, are more precisely targeted than magazines, newspapers, television and radio could ever do. The new **alternative media,** as they are called, include:

- Direct mail catalogs and flyers to selected addresses.
- Television commercials at the point of purchase, such as screens in grocery store shopping carts.
- Place-based media, such as magazines designed for distribution only in physicians' waiting rooms.
- Telemarketing, in which salespeople make their pitches by telephone to households determined by statistical profiles to be good potential customers.

If advertisers continue their shift to these and other alternative media, the revenue base of magazines, newspapers, radio and television will decline. Wholly new ways to structure the finances of these media will be necessary, probably with readers, listeners and viewers picking up the bill directly rather than indirectly by buying advertised products, which is the case today.

Media Conglomeration

alternative media
Emerging, narrowly focused advertising vehicles.

STUDY PREVIEW   Giant corporations with diverse interests have consolidated the U.S. mass media into relatively few hands. One result is that new talent and messengers have a harder time winning media attention.

Media Abroad

Thomson Conglomerate

The fact that the mass media are economic creatures can be illustrated no better than the story of Thomson newspapers. At its peak as a newspaper company, Canada-based Thomson owned 233 dailies and weeklies in the United States and Canada and 151 in Britain. It was a profitable business. In 1987, for every $1 that came in, 33.9 cents was profit. Imagine a return like that on your checking account! Then profits slipped—to 31.2 percent in 1988, 29.3 percent in 1989, 24.4 percent in 1990.

Thomson began looking elsewhere to make the returns it had come to expect and chose online publishing. In the early 1990s Thomson began unloading newspapers. By 1999 it was down to 50 dailies in the United States and eight in Canada. In that same period Thomson paid $3.4 billion for West Publishing of St. Paul, Minnesota, the leading publisher of law reference books, and its online Westlaw legal information service. Then Thomson bought Beta Systems, Computer Language Research, Creative Solu-

tions, digiTrack, Nelson Information and Technimetrics—all companies that generate and sell data. The revenue from these new enterprises was $4.8 billion in 1998 with profits of 26.6 percent. Profits at the remaining Thomson newspapers continued their drop and were running at 17.6 percent.

In 2000, Thomson began unloading the rest of its newspapers, with the lone exception being the flagship Toronto *Globe and Mail.*

Mass media companies, like other companies, go where the money is.

Media People

Roy Thomson

A barber's son, Roy Thomson quit school at 13. When he grew up, he became a traveling salesman in northern Ontario, hawking auto parts and washing machines. One day in 1932 somebody mentioned that a radio station was for sale. Things weren't going that well on the road, so Thomson scraped together a down payment. Years later, Thomson said his favorite radio music was "the sound of radio commercials at $10 a whack." Two years later, for $200 down, he bought the run-down Timmons, Ontario, *Weekly Press*. There, Thomson applied a two-part principle that would make him one of the richest people in the world: First, keep expenses minimal. Second, boost income by charging advertisers and subscribers as much as the market will bear. Eventually the paper went daily.

That began a buying binge. Before he died in 1976 at age 82, Roy

Thomson owned more than 200 newspapers in Canada and the United States. The Toronto *Globe & Mail* was the prestige flagship, but most Thomson newspapers were distinguished only as low-budget money machines. The adjective "cruddy" comes up often among media critics. Thomson, known for quips, once was asked to define news: "The stuff you separate the ads with."

Thomson was intrigued by his Scottish heritage, and even as his North American empire was expanding, he spread out to the British Isles. He bought mostly small dailies but also, in 1959, two of the England's leading newspapers: the *Sunday Times* of London and then the *Times* of London. Not long thereafter, Queen Elizabeth put him in the peerage, as Lord Thomson of Fleet. (For years, Fleet Street was the traditional home of London newspapers.)

Roy Thomson

When Lord Thomson died, he was worth almost $1 billion. His son Ken Thomson, of Toronto, still runs the company in the money machine style of his father. In 1981 he sold the London *Sunday Times* and *Times*. "Just a drag on profits," he said.

Ken Thomson was ranked the seventh richest person in the world in 1998 by *Forbes* magazine, his net worth estimated at $14.4 billion.

Media Ownership Consolidation

The trend toward **conglomeration** involves a process of mergers, acquisitions and buyouts that consolidates the ownership of the media into fewer and fewer companies. The deep pockets of a wealthy corporate parent can see a financially troubled media unit, such as a radio station, through a rough period, but there is a price. In time, the corporate parent wants a financial return on its investment, and pressure builds on the station to generate more and more profit. This would not be so bad if the people running the radio station loved radio and had a sense of public service, but the process of conglomeration often doesn't work out that way. Parent corporations tend to replace media people with career-climbing, bottom-line managers whose motivation is looking good to their supervisors in faraway cities who are under serious pressure to increase profits. In radio, for example, management experts, not radio people, end up running the station, and the quality of media content suffers.

A myopic profit orientation is not surprising, considering that the executives of parent corporations are responsible to their shareholders to return the most profit

conglomeration
Combining of companies into larger companies.

Ben Bagdikian
Critic of media consolidation.

possible from their diverse holdings. When a conglomerate's interests include enterprises as diverse as soccer teams, airlines, newspapers and timberland, as did the business empire of the late Robert Maxwell, it is easy to understand how the focus is more on the bottom line than on the product. The essence of this phenomenon was captured by *Esquire* magazine when it put this title on an article about the hotel magnate and financier who took over CBS in 1986 and, some say, hastened its decline: "Larry Tisch, Who Mistook His Network for a Spreadsheet."

Media Ownership Collaboration

Besides a consolidation of media ownership, the remaining giant companies have joint deals, some very complex. Even Ted Turner, who created CNN, and Rupert Murdoch, who created Fox, and who snipe publicly at each other regularly, are intertwined in deals. For example, AOL Time Warner, which owns CNN, carries Fox news on some of its cable systems. Murdoch's News Corporation, which owns Fox, carries Warner programming on its satellites. Until recently, 10 percent of Time Warner was owned by Tele-Communications Inc., a giant cable system operator, which had a joint venture with Fox/Liberty Sports, which is owned by News Corporation. Got all that? It gets more complicated. News Corporation has deals with Disney, whose properties include ABC; General Electric, whose properties include NBC; Viacom, whose properties include CBS; and manifold others. All the big players are in television and film production, Internet content, home video, interactive programs, cable, electronic games and sports teams. Most are also in books, music and records, television stations, newspapers, magazines, telephone and wireless communications. Disney, Time Warner and TCI own theme parks.

Sound like monopolies? The U.S. Justice Department thinks not. To use its trust-busting authority, the Justice Department needs to find collusion to fix prices. Media critic Ken Auletta, who studied the growing web of collaboration, concluded that fast-changing technology works against the restraints on competition that would make price-fixing likely. As the Justice Department sees it, people have more ways than ever before to receive media messages.

More serious than sinister economic impact, says Auletta, is the potential for self-serving control of content, particularly journalism: "Is NBC likely to pursue a major investigative series on its partner Microsoft? Is Fox News going to go after its partner TCI? Is a junior ABC news producer going to think twice before chewing on the leg of a Disney partner?" Writing in the *New Yorker,* Auletta noted that Steven Brill complained that Time Warner had tried three times to wield its clout as part-owner of his law publications to influence coverage. In one case, Brill said, there was an attempt to kill an article on Federal Trade Commission officials when the agency was reviewing the pending merger of Time Warner and Turner Broadcasting. Time Warner has denied Brill's allegation, but he has stood his ground. Whatever the truth of the Brill-Time Warner spat, corporate chain-of-command structures allow, if not encourage, meddling in media content.

Dubious Effects of Conglomeration

Critics such as **Ben Bagdikian** say that conglomeration affects the diversity of messages offered by the mass media. Speaking at the Madison Institute, Bagdikian portrayed conglomeration in bleak terms: "They are trying to buy control or market domination not just in one medium but in all the media. The aim is to control the entire process from an original manuscript or new series to its use in as many forms as possible. A magazine article owned by *the company* becomes a book owned by *the company*. That becomes a television program owned by *the company*, which then becomes a movie owned by *the company*. It is shown in theaters owned by *the company*, and the movie sound track is issued on a record label owned by *the company*, featuring the vocalist on the cover of one of *the company* magazines. It does not take an angel from heaven to tell us that *the company* will be less enthusiastic about outside ideas and production that it does not own, and more and more we will be dealing with closed circuits to control access to most of the public."

Bagdikian can point to the growing vertical integration among media corporations. In vertical integration a single company owns every step from production to distribution and then aftermarkets—and profits at every step of the way. Johnnie Roberts, writing in *Newsweek,* used the television show the "X-Files" as an example: Twentieth Century Fox Television, a subsidiary of Rupert Murdoch's News Corporation, produces 24 original episodes for each season. This costs $60 million. The Fox television network, also a subsidiary of Murdoch's News Corporation, sells national advertising time on the "X-Files." Sixteen stations owned and operated by Fox sell local advertising. This generates $139 million for Murdoch's News Corporation. Twentieth Century Fox Television, which owns the series, sells licenses to local stations that want to carry the "X-Files" in future seasons, recycling each episode usually three times. This generates $35 million for Murdoch's News Corporation. The Fox FX cable network carries the "X-Files." It is also licensed to television outlets in other countries. The program's omnipresence and hype build a market for "X-Files" merchandise. This generates $69 million for Murdoch's News Corporation.

The math: Over eight years, the series' projected eight-year life, that's a $1.5 billion return on a $60 million investment, not counting the 1999 movie spin-off.

Nobody begrudges a company making a profit. The difficulty comes when the recycling displaces creative new entries in the mass media marketplace. NBC executive Don Ohlmeyer concedes that a vertically integrated network is disinclined "in even considering projects in which they don't own a financial interest." Independent Hollywood producers, who once competed to produce network shows, are finding themselves out of the loop. The result, says Gary Goldberg, creator of "Spin City" on ABC: "You see this blandness and similarity to the shows. Consumers are the ones who get hurt."

One of the negative effects of conglomeration occurs when a parent company looks to its subsidiaries only to enrich conglomerate coffers as quickly as possible and by any means possible, regardless of the quality of products that are produced. This is especially a problem when a conglomerate's subsidiaries include, for example, widget factories, cherry orchards, funeral homes and, by the way, also some book

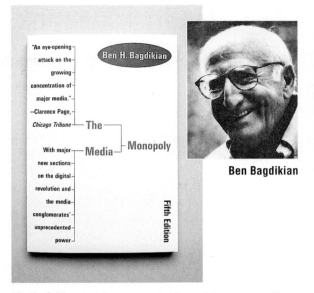

Media Critic. Ben Bagdikian, called "one of the most considerate voices in journalism today," says that huge media companies are ever more profit-obsessed. Their corporate strategies, he says, often sacrifice quality content and public service on the altar of increasing profits. Bagdikian has amassed distressing data on conglomeration in his book *The Media Monopoly.*

Media Databank

Biggest U.S. Media Companies

	Media Revenue		Media Revenue
AOL Time Warner	$36.7 billion	News Corporation	$5.0 billion
CBS-Viacom	10.7 billion	Gannett	4.9 billion
AT&T	9.9 billion	Cox	3.9 billion
Disney-ABC	7.5 billion	Advance	3.9 billion
GE-NBC	5.3 billion		

companies. The top management of such diverse conglomerates is inclined to take a cookie-cutter approach that deemphasizes or even ignores important traditions in book publishing, including a sense of social responsibility. Many of these conglomerates focus on profits alone. One result, according to many literary critics, has been a decline in quality.

QUALITY. Headquarters push subsidiaries to cut costs to increase profits, a trend that has devastated the quality of writing and editing. Fewer people do more work. At newspapers, for example, a reporter's story once went through several hands—editor, copy editor, headline writer, typesetter, proofreader. At every stage, the story could be improved. In today's streamlined newsrooms, proofreaders have been replaced by spell-check software, which not only introduces its own problems but also lacks the intelligence and judgment of a good proofer. The jobs of the reporter and the typesetter have been consolidated. In many newsrooms, so have the jobs of copy editors and headline writers.

Los Angeles *Times* reporter Tom Rosentiel, writing in the *Columbia Journalism Review,* tells how reporters, pressured to increase productivity, take shortcuts to generate more copy: "Newspapers and newsmagazine interviews today are increasingly conducted over the phone, with reporters assembling stories as much as reporting them, combining elements from electronic transcripts, data bases and television. A growing number of major events, reporters acknowledge, are covered without going to the scene. The stories . . . lack the advantage of serendipity or the authenticity of having been there."

In the book industry, media critic Jacob Weisberg has documented how several major publishers, including Simon and Schuster and Random House, have routinely eliminated important stages in the editing process to rush new titles to print and turn quicker profits. In a revealing article in the *New Republic,* Weisberg lists these results of these accelerated schedules:

- Factual errors, both major and minor, that in earlier times, he says, would have been caught by careful editing.
- Loose, flabby writing from deadline-pressured writers who once could rely on editors to tighten their work. Some books, Weisberg says, are running 100 pages longer than they should.

This issue of declining quality extends even to textbooks. In 1998 the Texas Board of Education found hundreds of errors, many of them glaring, in history books that were up for adoption. The errors echoed earlier findings, like these:

- The United States used the atomic bomb to end the Korean conflict.
- Robert Kennedy and Martin Luther King Jr. were assassinated while Richard Nixon was president.
- George Bush defeated Michael Dukakis in 1989.
- Sputnik was the first intercontinental ballistic missile, and it carried a nuclear warhead.
- The Wisconsin senator who was the 1950s namesake for McCarthyism was General Douglas MacArthur.

Shocked at such errors, the Texas board delayed certifying the books and told publishers to get their act together. The largest U.S. textbook publisher, Pearson Education, set up a blue-ribbon review board to identify errors and send e-mail corrections to adopters.

SAMENESS. You can fly from the East to the West Coast on the same day and read the same Associated Press stories word for word. Newspaper publishers learned long ago that sharing stories via the AP could reduce costs. The resulting economics came at the cost of less diversity in content.

Cultural sociologists fret about the sameness. In recorded music, for example, major record companies often encourage artists to imitate what is already popular. This result is that derivative music squeezes original artists and material out of the marketplace or at least makes it more difficult for these artists to find an audience. Sociologists think that the movement of culture in new directions is slowed by this process.

Barry Diller, who created popular television programs at ABC and later at Fox, says that the problem is the profit-driven trend to recycle existing material for a quick buck. In a speech to magazine executives, Diller pointed out the short-sightedness of recycling: "Taking a movie like *Jurassic Park* and turning it into a video game, that's repackaging. Taking a bestseller and putting it on tape, that's repackaging. Taking magazine articles and slapping them on-line, word for word, that's repackaging." He then likened repackaging to strip mining: "After you've extracted the riches from the surface, there's nothing left."

CORPORATE INSTABILITY. Conglomeration also has introduced instability. Profit-driven corporate parents are quick to sell subsidiaries that fall short of profit expectations even for a short term or just to raise cash. An alarming example of the cash problem unfolded in 1991 after media magnate **Robert Maxwell** died, apparently of suicide. Within days of his death it was discovered that Maxwell had been illegally shuffling vast amounts of money around his subsidiaries to cover loans he had taken out to expand his empire, which included Macmillan, the prestigious U.S. book-publishing company. Maxwell was not alone among conglomerate builders who found themselves in deep trouble after overextending themselves financially. The problem was not only in the instability wrought by their miscalculations and recklessness, but also in the products that their media subsidiaries produced. Michael Lennie, a San Diego textbook author attorney, put the problem this way: "The industry continues to grow more and more concentrated with large debt-ridden publishers too preoccupied with serving crippling debt to pay attention to the publishing of quality texts."

Robert Maxwell
Global media mogul who overexpanded.

AOL and Time Warner, Together. In a surprise announcement that shocked media people, Steve Case of America Online and Gerald Levin of Time Warner announced in 2000 that the companies would combine. Competitors, notably Disney, objected, but the government's approval process began moving. The combination would create a company with U.S. revenues of $31.9 billion a year—almost triple that of second-ranking CBS-Viacom and AT&T and quadruple that of Disney.

Positive Effects of Conglomeration

At the end of World War II, the mainline book-publishing business was dominated by family-run publishing houses, all relatively small by today's standards. Although there are still hundreds of small publishers in the United States today, consolidation has reduced the industry to six giants. Depending on whom you ask, the conglomeration has been a godsend or a disaster. Looking at the effects positively, the U.S. book industry is financially stronger:

- Parent corporations have infused cash into their new subsidiaries, financing expensive initiatives that were not financially possible before, including multimillion-dollar deals with authors.
- Because parent corporations often own newspapers, magazines and broadcast companies, book publishers have ready partners for repackaging books in additional media forms.
- Many of the new parent corporations own book companies abroad, which helps to open up global markets.

In today's business climate the lure of market dominance and profit, often on a global scale, keeps driving the concentration of media companies into fewer and fewer conglomerates.

Media Melding

STUDY PREVIEW   The different mass media are moving into digital transmission, which is eroding the differences between them. This technological melding is being accelerated by the continuing consolidation of companies that own the mass media.

AOL Time Warner Towers. Architectural scope historically has reflected society's values. Gigantic Medieval cathedrals that dwarfed everything else were a sign of the churches' centrality in people's lives and their power. In later times, schools and financial institutions were dominant. Newspaper buildings, like the New York *Times* building in Times Square, once were icons—a signal of the importance of the press. Today in U.S. society hardly anything compares to sports arenas. Due to be completed in 2004 in New York are the twin towers of the AOL Time Warner building overlooking Central Park. The 55-floor towers house the media giant's corporate headquarters. On the eighth floor, behind three-dimensional jutting windows, is the 98,000-square foot CNN broadcast facility with 24-foot ceilings. A showcase 11th floor stretches across the towers' base and includes screening rooms. A 150-foot "prow" showcases a sculpture. Atop each tower is a distinctive lantern.

Digitization

The eight primary mass media as we know them today are in a technological transition, a **melding** that is blurring the old distinctions that once clearly separated them. For example, newspapers are experimenting with electronic delivery via cable and telephone lines—"no paper" newspapers. Through personal computers thousands of people have access to data banks to choose the news coverage they want. This is called **digitization,** a process that compresses, stores and transmits data, including text, sound and video, in extremely compact and efficient ways. An example of the potential of digitization was **configurable video,** developed at the Massachusetts Institute of Technology Media Lab in the 1980s. The MIT configurable video systems integrated printed articles and video segments that a person could read and view in any sequence desired. The MIT system was an integration of traditional print and electronic media with a new twist: An individual, sitting at a screen, could control the editing by passing unwanted portions and focusing on what was most valuable.

Intracorporate Synergy

Some media melding has come about because competitors have recognized how partnerships could be mutually beneficial. When television became a media force in the 1950s, Hollywood lost millions of movie-goers and declared war on its new rival. For several years the movie industry even forbade television to play movies, and Hollywood developed distinctive technical and content approaches that television could

media convergence

melding
Conversion of all media to a common digital technology.

digitization
Efficient, compact storage and transmission of data.

configurable video
Integration of text, sound and video with the audience controlling the sequence of presentation.

not duplicate. The rivalry eased in time, and today Hollywood and the television industry are major partners. Hollywood produces a significant amount of programming for the television networks, and there are all kinds of joint ventures.

Media Future: Mass Media

Dynamics are at work that are changing the mass media as we know them. With digitization the media are converging into new forms. Old distinctions are fading. Is a book still a book if it's not on paper and bound but instead is available on an e-tablet? Too, it's not always easy to distinguish television from the web any more.

Digitization is furthering demassification because it's easier to identify segments of the mass audience and tailor messages to narrow interests. Some web news sites, for example, can be programmed to send coverage only on subjects you choose. What this means to the generalist is unclear. We do know, though, that it is increasingly possible to use the mass media to focus on your interests so narrowly that you are blind to other things happening in the world.

The long-term effect of concentration of media ownership is difficult to predict. Although technology has made it possible for a great diversity of media products to exist, the fact is that the major mass media products are controlled by fewer and fewer corporations. For most of us, relatively few corporations control the media to which we expose ourselves. The economic imperative of these companies—to increase profits—worries elitists. Their concern is that the traditional media commitment to enriching and bettering the society is being lost in the drive for profits.

Much of this is not a pretty picture. The upside is that if we as media consumers are aware of the dynamics at work, we can have a better understanding of why the media do what they do. That understanding can help us cope with the changes ahead.

chapter wrap-up

The mass media are the vehicles that carry messages to large audiences. These media—books, magazines, newspapers, records, movies, radio, television and the web—are so pervasive in modern life that many people do not even notice their influence. Because of that influence, however, we should take time to understand the mass media so that we can better assess whether they are affecting us for better or worse.

Questions for Review

1. How are the mass media pervasive in our everyday lives?
2. What are the three technologies on which the primary mass media are built?
3. Explain the models that scholars have devised to explain the mass media.
4. How do mass media organizations make money to stay in business?

5. Define demassification. Describe demassification that has occurred in radio, magazines and television.
6. Is conglomeration good for mass media consumers?
7. Where is technology taking the mass media?

Questions for Critical Thinking

1. Some people are confused by the terms *cool media* and *hot media* because, in their experience, radios

and television sets heat up and newspapers are always at room temperature. What is the other way of looking at hot and cool media?

2. The effectiveness of messages communicated through the mass media is shaped by the technical limitations of each medium. A limitation of radio is that it cannot accommodate pictures. Is it a technical limitation that the *Wall Street Journal* does not carry photographs, that the New York *Times* does not carry comics or that most radio news formats limit stories to 40 seconds? Can you provide examples of content limitations of certain media? What are the audience limitations that are inherent in all mass media?

3. For many years CBS television programs drew a generally older and more rural audience than the other networks. Did that make CBS a niche-seeking mass media unit? Did it make the CBS audience any less heterogeneous?

4. Which mass media perform the informing purpose best? The entertaining purpose? The persuading purpose? Which of these purposes does the advertising industry serve? Public relations?

5. Why do revolutionaries try to take over the mass media right away?

6. Which is more important to the U.S. mass media: profits or doing social good? What about the goals of supermarket tabloids like the *National Enquirer?*

7. Which mass media rely directly on consumer purchases for their economic survival? Advertising provides almost all the revenue for commercial radio and television stations, but indirectly consumer purchases are an important factor. In what way?

8. Are any types of mass media not dependent on advertising or consumer purchases?

Keeping Up to Date

Many mass media developments abroad are tracked in the monthly London-based *Censorship Index.*

Newsmagazines including *Time* and *Newsweek* cover major mass media issues more or less regularly, as do the New York *Times*, the *Wall Street Journal* and other major newspapers.

The monthly *Brill's Content*, launched in 1998, offers enterprise coverage of the news and information media, often with a critical edge.

Periodicals that track the mass media as business include *Business Week*, *Forbes* and *Fortune.*

The monthly *Inside*, which prefers the parenthetical affectation *[Inside]* as its title, was launched in 2000 to cover entertainment, media and technology. It's a partner to the inside.com media news site.

The Journal of Media Economics focuses on economic policy issues.

J. K. Rowling. *The success of her Harry Potter books surprised her. Rowling had expected a small following when the first book in the seven-volume series was introduced in 1997. Three years later, 35 million were in print in 35 languages—the most successful new book in history.*

2

Books

Joanne Rowling always liked telling stories. At age 5, maybe 6, she wrote her first book. The plot centered on a rabbit called Rabbit who came down with the measles and who was consoled by a giant bee. Her name: Miss Bee. All through school, Rowling regaled her school chums with stories.

After college she took a job in London, but her mind was elsewhere. On the boring train ride into the city every day, a story took form in her mind. At work she scribbled notes. At lunch she pulled her thoughts together on other pads.

Knowing that her obsession with the story was getting in the way of her work, Rowling quit. She left for a teaching job in Portugal. Returning to Britain a year later, she had half a suitcase of manuscript pages. A year later, in 1997, when Rowling was 28, the book, *Harry Potter and the Sorcerer's Stone,* was done.

Rowling hoped the book would find a loyal, albeit probably small, following. At 309 pages, the adventure story, about a boy wizard named Harry Potter, seemed a bit heavy for the Nintendo generation. She was wrong.

Word spread fast among kids. *Harry Potter* was a great story. Best of all, it was something their parents and teachers weren't telling them to read. It was their discovery, which gave it an allure somewhat like that of Nancy Drew and the Hardy Boys for earlier generations. Then adults too began reading *Harry Potter.*

J. K. Rowling wrote a sequel a year. By 2000, 35 million copies of her books were in print. The first printing of the fourth book, *Harry Potter and the Goblet of Fire,* was the largest in history—4.8 million. In 2001 worldwide sales of *Harry Potter* books passed $100 million.

At least one of the books was on the New York *Times* best-seller fiction list for 81 weeks straight by the time *Goblet of Fire* came out. It was squeezing other works off the list. The *Times* responded by creating a separate best-seller list for children's books.

The books have had detractors. Conservative religious leaders fretted that Harry was involved in magic, even witchery. Some schools banned the books. This gave the books a forbidden fruit attraction.

Although they are popular, are the Harry Potter books good literature? Will they have the enduring recognition of books by Robert Louis Stevenson? Or will they wear thin on a second reading, like Nancy Drew mysteries?

Rowling's fast-paced plots certainly are hard to put down. She has good guys and bad guys and also complex characters. The stories are scary, riveting even. Rowling's love of funny names adds charm—such as the evil Lord Voldemort (rhymes with "moldy wart").

How did Rowling come up with these names? "I was born in Chipping Sodbury General Hospital, which I think is appropriate for someone who collects funny names," she says. Harry Potter, it seems, was incubating in J. K. Rowling's mind from her earliest moments.

Books in the Culture

STUDY PREVIEW   Mass-produced books, first introduced in the mid-1400s, changed human history by accelerating the exchange of ideas and information among more people. Books have endured as a repository of culture. They are the primary vehicle by which new generations are educated to their society's values and by which they learn the lessons of the past.

Books in Human History

scribists
Monks who copied books manually.

Johannes Gutenberg
In mid-1400s, devised revolutionary printing process using metal letters.

movable metal type
Small blocks of type arranged into words, lines and pages.

The introduction of mass-produced books in the 15th century marked a turning point in human history. Before then, books were handwritten, usually by **scribist** monks who copied existing books onto blank sheets of paper letter by letter, one page at a time. These scribists could turn out only a few hand-lettered books in a lifetime of tedium.

In the mid-1400s **Johannes Gutenberg,** a tinkerer in what is now Germany, devised an innovation that made it possible to print pages using metal letters. Gutenberg's revolutionary contribution was in applying metallurgy to the printing process, which went back to ancient China. The idea for **movable metal type** occurred to

Media People

Johannes Gutenberg

Johannes Gutenberg was eccentric—a secretive tinkerer with a passion for beauty, detail and craftsmanship. By trade, he was a metallurgist, but he never made much money at it. Like most of his fellow 15th-century Rhinelanders (people from an area in present-day Germany), he pressed his own grapes for wine. As a businessman, he was not very successful, and he died penniless. Despite his unpromising combination of traits, quirks and habits—perhaps because of them—Johannes Gutenberg wrought the most significant change in history: the mass-produced written word. He invented movable metal type.

Despite the significance of his invention, there is much we do not know about Gutenberg. Even to friends, he seldom mentioned his experiments, and when he did, he referred to them mysteriously as his "secret art." When he ran out of money, Gutenberg quietly sought investors, luring them partly with the mystique he attached to his work. What we know about Gutenberg's "secret art" was recorded only because Gutenberg's main backer didn't realize the quick financial

First Mass-Produced Written Word. Johannes Gutenberg and his assistants could produce 50 to 60 imprints an hour with their modified wine press, but Gutenberg's real contribution was movable metal type, which expedited the putting together of pages and opened the age of mass communication.

return he expected on his investment and sued. The litigation left a record from which historians have pieced together the origins of modern printing.

The date when Johannes Gutenberg printed his first page with movable type is unknown, but historians usually settle on 1446. Gutenberg's printing process was widely copied—and quickly. By 1500, presses all over Western Europe had published almost 40,000 books.

Today, Gutenberg is remembered for the Bibles he printed with movable type. Two hundred **Gutenberg Bibles,** each a printing masterpiece,

were produced over several years. Gutenberg used the best paper. He concocted an especially black ink. The quality amazed everybody, and the Bibles sold quickly. Gutenberg could have printed hundreds more, perhaps thousands. With a couple of husky helpers, he and his modified wine press could have produced 50 to 60 imprints an hour. However, Johannes Gutenberg, who never had much business savvy, concentrated instead on quality. Forty-seven Gutenberg Bibles remain today, all collector's items. One sold in 1978 for $2.4 million.

Gutenberg in the mid-1430s. Instead of wood, which often cracked in the pressing process, he experimented with casting individual letters in a lead-based alloy. He built a frame the size of a book's page and then arranged the metal letters into words. Once a page was filled—with letters and words and sentences—he put the frame into a modified wine press, applied ink, laid paper and pressed. The process made it possible to produce dozens, even hundreds or thousands, of copies.

Gutenberg's impact cannot be overstated. The duplicative power of movable type put the written word into wide circulation and fueled quantum increases in literacy. One hundred years after Gutenberg, the state of communication in Europe had undergone a revolution. Elaborate postal systems were in place. Standardized maps

Gutenberg Bibles
Bibles printed by Gutenberg with movable type. Surviving Bibles are all collector's items.

Media Timeline

Development of Books

1440s	Johannes Gutenberg printed Bibles using movable type.
1638	Puritans established Cambridge Press.
1836	William Holmes McGuffey began influential reading textbooks.
1850s	A distinct American literature emerged in novels.

1895	Congress established the Government Printing Office.
1995	Amazon.com launched.
1998	E-book introduced.
2000	Stephen King issued a novella as a downloadable book.

produced by printing presses replaced hand-copied maps, with all their inaccuracies and idiosyncrasies. People began writing open letters to be distributed far and wide. Newspapers followed. The exchange of scientific discoveries was hastened through special publications. Johannes Gutenberg stands at a dividing point in the history of humankind. A scribist culture preceded him. The age of mass communication followed.

Books in National Development

Books were valued in the colonial period. In Massachusetts in 1638 the Puritans set up **Cambridge Press,** the first book producer in what is now the United States. Just as today, personal libraries were a symbol of the intelligentsia. Thomas Jefferson's personal library became the basis for the Library of Congress. **John Harvard** of Cambridge, Massachusetts, was widely known for his personal collection of 300 books, a large library for the time. When Harvard died in 1638, he bequeathed his books to Newtowne College, which was so grateful that it renamed itself for him. Today it is Harvard University.

William Holmes McGuffey's reading textbook series brought the United States out of frontier illiteracy. More than 122 million of McGuffey's readers were sold beginning in 1836, coinciding with the boom in public-supported education as an American credo.

In the mid-1800s, U.S. publishers brought out books that identified a distinctive new literary genre: the American novel. Still widely read are Nathaniel Hawthorne's *The Scarlet Letter* (1850), Herman Melville's *Moby Dick* (1851), Harriet Beecher Stowe's *Uncle Tom's Cabin* (1852) and Mark Twain's *Huckleberry Finn* (1884).

Today, most of the books that shape our culture are adapted to other media, which expands their influence. Magazine serialization put Ronald Reagan's memoirs in more hands than did the publisher of the book. More people saw Carl Sagan on television than have read his books. Stephen King's thrillers sell spectacularly, especially in paperback, but more people see the movie renditions. Books have a trickle-down effect through other media, their impact being felt even by people who cannot or do not read them. Although people are more in touch with other mass media day to day, books are the heart of creating U.S. culture and passing it on to new generations.

Cambridge Press
First publisher in the British American colonies.

John Harvard
Owned a major personal library.

William Holmes McGuffey
Wrote influential reading textbooks in the 1830s and 1840s.

Media People

William Holmes McGuffey

Just out of college, William Holmes McGuffey arrived at Miami University in Ohio on horseback in 1826 with a few books on moral philosophy and languages. At the university he tested his theories on education with neighborhood kids who gathered on his porch next to the campus. McGuffey confirmed that children learn better when sentences are accompanied by a picture. He also noted that reading out loud helps and that spelling is not very important in learning to read. McGuffey took notes on his observations and tested his ideas on other age groups. He also collected a mass of stories from a great variety of places.

In 1833 the Truman & Smith publishing company was scouting for someone to write a series of readers and found McGuffey. He culled his favorite stories for the new reader. Many were from the Bible, and most made a moral point. In 1836 the first of McGuffey's *Eclectic Readers* ap-

William Holmes McGuffey

McGuffey Readers. For a century, McGuffey's readers taught American children to read, contributing to quantum increases in literacy. The first book in the McGuffey series appeared in 1836.

peared. McGuffey still had lots of material that he had used with the children on his porch, and a second, a third and a fourth reader followed. Truman & Smith marketed the books vigorously, and they soon had a national following.

The company broke up, and the publishing and marketing of McGuffey's books changed hands several times. As the years went on, many editors had a hand in revisions,

and McGuffey had less and less direction regarding their content. McGuffey's brother Alexander completed the fifth and sixth readers in the series between 1843 and 1845 while McGuffey was busy with his teaching.

McGuffey's *Eclectic Readers* sold more than 122 million copies. A version was still being produced for school use in 1920. Today some are in print for home schooling.

Book Categories

STUDY PREVIEW When most people think about books, fiction and nonfiction aimed at general readers come to mind. These are called trade books, which are a major segment of the book industry. Also important are textbooks, which include not only schoolbooks but also reference books and even cookbooks. There are countless ways to further dissect books, but textbooks and trade books are the major categories.

Trade Books

The most visible part of the $24 billion a year that the U.S. book publishing industry produces is **trade books.** These are general interest titles, including fiction and nonfiction, that people usually think of when they think about books. Trade books can be incredible best-sellers. Since it was introduced in 1937, J. R. R. Tolkien's *The Hobbit* has sold almost 40 million copies. Margaret Mitchell's 1936 *Gone With the*

media online

McGuffey's Reader: The KISS Presentation and Analysis of McGuffey's Second Eclectic Reader. www2.pct.edu/courses/ evavra/ED498/R/McGuffey/M2/ Index.htm

trade books General interest titles, including fiction and nonfiction.

Media People

Alice Mayhew

Mention the 1974 book *All the President's Men,* about the Watergate scandal and the demise of Richard Nixon's presidency, and people still think reflexively of the Washington *Post* reporters who unearthed the scandal and then wrote the book: Bob Woodward and Carl Bernstein. The name Alice Mayhew doesn't come to mind, but as an editor at Simon & Schuster, Mayhew was the one who nurtured Woodward and Bernstein's manuscript into book form.

Considering the times, it's inconceivable that *All the President's Men* could have missed becoming a commercial success, but Mayhew's

editorial work established her as the premiere nonfiction book editor of our time. In fact, the book established Simon & Schuster clearly in the big time among U.S. publishers.

Since then, Mayhew has signed 18 to 20 serious nonfiction books a year, her goal being to shape them into best-sellers that become part of the national dialogue. These have included William Greider's 1987 book *Secrets of the Temple,* a 798-page work on the arcane subject of the Federal Reserve. She also handled *Undaunted Courage,* Steven Ambrose's detailed account of the 1803–1806 Lewis and Clark expedition, published in 1996.

Mayhew has been criticized for spending more time on marketing details than on actual editing. As a result, she's shy about being interviewed and photographed. Authors who work with her, however, say that she's a committed editor and ally—and that she is brave. Steven Ambrose tells the story of his choosing *Of Courage Undaunted* from a Thomas Jefferson quote for the title of his Lewis and Clark manuscript. Mayhew changed the title to *Undaunted Courage.* It had a firmer tone, she said. Ambrose told her, "Alice, you are the only woman in the whole world who would dare edit Thomas Jefferson."

---

media online

Association of American Publishers: Links to monthly list of campus paperback best-sellers.
www.publishers.org/home

BDD Online: Bantam Doubleday Dell.
www.bdd.com

Penguin USA: Publisher's site.
www.penguin.com

HarperCollins: Includes history of the venerable publishing house from the days when it published Mark Twain, the Brontë sisters, Thackery and Dickens through John Kennedy and Martin Luther King Jr.
www.harpercollins.com

textbooks
Educational, professional, reference titles.

Wind has passed 29 million. Most trade books, however, have shorter lives. To keep atop best-seller lists, Stephen King, Danielle Steel and other authors have to keep writing. Steel, known for her discipline at the keyboard, produces a new novel about every six months.

Although publishing trade books can be extremely profitable when a book takes off, trade books have always been a high-risk proposition. One estimate is that 60 percent of them lose money, 36 percent break even and 4 percent turn a good profit, and only a few in the latter category become best-sellers and make spectacular money.

Textbooks

Although the typical successful trade book best-seller can be a spectacular moneymaker for a few months, a successful **textbook** has a longer life with steady income. For example, Curtis MacDougall wrote a breakthrough textbook on journalism in 1932 that went through eight editions before he died in 1985. Then the publisher brought out a ninth edition, with Robert Reid bringing it up to date. This gave MacDougall's *Interpretative Reporting* a life span of more than 60 years. Although textbook publishers don't routinely announce profits by title, *Interpretative Reporting* undoubtedly has generated more income than many trade book best-sellers.

Textbooks, the biggest segment of the book market, include reference and professional books, college textbooks, and elementary and high school textbooks and learning materials.

Media People

Joy Hakim

The textbook industry has lost its way and is out of touch with kids, says history author Joy Hakim. "Most books today just state the facts. 'He was born here, he did this. . . .' " What makes Hakim different? She puts the facts into compelling stories. Her 11-volume, grade-school U.S. history textbook, *The History of US,* has sold 1 million copies.

Before Hakim began writing, she looked at a University of Minnesota study that compared kids' comprehension of journalistic writing and textbook writing. Researchers found that children's comprehension of journalism was 40 percent higher than their comprehension of textbooks. She then looked at books written for children 50 years ago. They were compelling, well-written and story-based. She

said, "Kids liked them. We knew our history and we somehow got away from that." She calls most textbooks a turnoff: "Have you ever stayed up late happily reading your textbook? We have a reading crisis in our land. The stuff we give them in schools isn't as good as television."

For *The History of US,* Hakim couldn't even find a textbook publisher. Finally, she convinced a scholarly publisher, Oxford University Press, to take it as a book for retail booksellers. Now it is approved for curriculums in five states and likely to be adopted elsewhere. Most of the first million sales, however, were directly to kids and their parents. Knowing that her book is reaching kids makes her grin. One letter from a grade-school pupil read, "I would rather read your books than play

Joy Hakim

Nintendo." One little girl told Hakim that Hakim's story "War, Terrible War" made her cry. "Why?" Hakim asked. The child answered, "Abraham Lincoln died."

When was the last time a textbook brought you to tears?

PROFESSIONAL AND REFERENCE BOOKS. Dictionaries, atlases and other reference works represent about 10 percent of textbook sales. Over the years the Christian bible and Noah Webster's dictionary have led reference book sales. Others also have had exceptional, long-term success that rivals trade books. Even after Benjamin Spock died in 1998, his *Baby and Child Care,* introduced in 1946, kept on selling. Total sales are past 50 million. Next: *The Better Homes and Gardens Cookbook.*

COLLEGE TEXTBOOKS. College textbooks sell in great numbers, mostly through the coercion of the syllabus. Although textbooks are written for students, publishers pitch them to the professors who order them for their students. Students, although the ultimate consumer, don't choose them, which may partly explain the hard feelings students have toward textbooks.

The resentment is usually directed at the college store, which many students are sure gouges them. The fact is that suspicions about bookstore gouging are misplaced. Markups typically are 20 to 30 percent—not out of line in retailing in general. From that markup, the store must meet payroll, rent and other expenses. Nor do publishers get rich. The industry's return on investment is not wickedly high, as investors will attest.

Contributing to the perception that textbooks are overpriced is that most students, until college, have had their schoolbooks provided free. Picking up the tab for the first time, except for $5 paperbacks, is a shock.

media online

Text and Academic Authors: Up-to-date news on the textbook industry. http://taa.winona.msus.edu/taa/

Allyn & Bacon: A textbook publisher that is developing web sites like this one to supplement its books. www.ablongman.com/vivian

EL-HI BOOKS.   Learning materials for elementary and high schools, known as the **el-hi** market, have unique marketing mechanisms. In most states, school districts are allowed to use state funds to buy books only from a state-approved list. This means that publishers gear books toward acceptance in populous states with powerful adoption boards. If the California adoption board is firm on multiculturalism, textbook publishers will take that approach to win California acceptance. Multiculturalism then becomes a theme in books for less influential states in the adoption process. If Texas, another key adoption state, insists that creationism be recognized, then so it will be in biology books for the whole nation.

Book Publishers

STUDY PREVIEW   Mergers and acquisitions have reduced the book industry to fewer and fewer companies, all with global interests. Even so, small publishing houses continue, many profitably, in niches.

Major Houses

Publishing houses think of themselves as widely recognized brand names: Simon & Schuster, Doubleday, HarperCollins, Penguin. To most people, though, a book is a book is a book no matter the publisher—though there are exceptions such as Harlequin, which is almost a household word for pulp romances. Scholars are exceptions. Their vocabularies are peppered with publishers' names, perhaps because of all the footnotes and bibliographies they have to wade through.

Major houses once had distinctive personalities that flowed from the literary bent of the people in charge. Scribner's, for example, was the nurturing home of Wolfe, Hemingway and Fitzgerald from the 1920s into the 1950s and very much bore the stamp of Charles Scribner and his famous editor Maxwell Perkins. Typical of the era, it was a male-dominated business, everybody wearing tweed coats and smoking pipes. Today the distinctive cultures have blurred as corporate pride has shifted more to the bottom line.

Book Industry Consolidation

As with other mass media industries, book publishing has undergone consolidation with companies merging with each other, acquiring one another, and buying lists from one another. Some imprints you still see are no longer stand-alone companies but part of international media conglomerates. Random House, a proud name in U.S. book publishing, is now part of the German company Bertelsmann. The company also owns the Bantam, Dell and Doubleday imprints, among other media subsidiaries, including RCA records and numerous magazines.

Harcourt was sold to Reed Elsevier of Europe and Thomson of Canada in 2001. Half of Simon & Schuster, once the world's largest book publisher, was sold to Pearson, a British conglomerate, in 1999. St. Martin's Press is now part of Holtzbrinck of Germany. HarperCollins is in the hands of Rupert Murdoch, whose flagship News Corp. has its headquarters in Australia.

The largest U.S.-owned book publisher, McGraw-Hill, had 1999 sales of $1.6 billion, only about two-thirds of Bertelsmann's. Globally, McGraw-Hill is also behind Pearson of Britain and Thomson of Canada. In short, fewer and fewer companies are dominating more and more of the world's book output.

el-hi
Elementary and high school book market.

Media Databank

Major Book Publishers

Measured by 1999 book and journal sales, these are the major international book publishing houses ranked by U.S. sales.

Pearson	Britain	$3.8 billion
Harcourt Brace	United States	2.1 billion
Random House	Germany	2.0 billion
McGraw-Hill	United States	1.7 billion
Thomson	Canada	1.6 billion

Government Printing Office

Not many people think of the federal government as a major player in book publishing. However, the **Government Printing Office** the U.S. government publisher, produces more titles than any commercial book publisher in the world.

The GPO, established in 1895 for the systematic distribution of U.S. government publications, has 27,000 titles in print, including a few best-sellers. A 108-page paperback called *Infant Care*, published first in 1914, has sold 14 million copies. *Your Federal Income Tax* is a perennial big seller as April 15 approaches.

When significant government documents are published, such as the Warren Commission report on the assassination of President John Kennedy, the Surgeon General's report on smoking or the Starr report on the Clinton-Lewinsky scandal, the GPO can rival commercial publishing houses in the number of sales.

Small Publishers

While conglomerates and major houses dominate the book industry, thousands of other publishers exist, mostly small. These houses have niches that the major houses, by and large, don't bother with. Some put out only a handful of books.

SMALL PRESSES. By some counts, there are 12,000 book-publishing companies in the United States. The catalogs of most contain only a few titles. Among these small presses are some important regional publishers that publish only low-volume books with a long life. Other small presses specialize in poetry and special subjects for limited audiences that wouldn't otherwise be served.

UNIVERSITY PRESSES. As part of their mission to advance and disseminate knowledge, universities have been in the publishing industry as far back as 1478. That's when Oxford University Press, the oldest English language book publisher, was founded. Ninety-nine university presses exist in the United States today, most of them founded to publish works that wouldn't be feasible for a commercial publisher. Their contribution has been notable. Harvard University Press, for example, brought out *The Double Helix* by James Watson, as well as poetry of Ezra Pound.

As university budgets have tightened, some university presses have disappeared. Others are under pressure to move into trade books to offset their losses and even turn a profit. Some have found profitable niches in regional histories, travelogues and cookbooks.

VANITY PRESSES. It's easy for an author to get a book published—if the author is willing to pay all expenses up front. Family histories and club cookbooks

Government Printing Office
The U.S. government publisher.

are a staple in this part of the book industry. So are many who's-who books and directories, which list names and then are sold to those whose names are in the books.

Some book publishers, called **vanity presses,** go further by soliciting manuscripts and letting the author infer that the company can make it a best-seller. These companies direct their advertising at unpublished authors and promise a free manuscript review. A custom-addressed form letter then goes back to the author, saying, quite accurately, no matter how good or how bad the manuscript, that the proposed book "is indicative of your talent." The letter also says the company would be pleased to publish the manuscript. Most vanity companies do little beyond printing, however. Their ability to promote and distribute a book is very limited, although an occasional best-seller emerges.

It can be argued that vanity publishers unscrupulously take advantage of unpublished authors who don't know how the book industry works. It can be argued too that a legitimate service is being provided. Ed Uhlan of Exposition Press, one of the largest vanity publishers, wrote an autobiographical book, *The Rogue of Publishers Row,* which details how slight the chance is that vanity press clients can make money. When he began including a free copy with the materials he sent inquiring authors, incredible as it seems, his business actually increased.

Book Production

At publishing houses, except for the smallest operations, the first hurdle for a manuscript is with an editor. Job titles vary, but *acquisitions editor* and *sponsoring editor* are common ones. The decision whether to add a book to the house's **list,** or catalog of titles, involves a committee of senior editors, perhaps even the president of the company for major projects. For textbooks, sample chapters are usually circulated among leading scholars. Their reaction is then folded into the decision-making process.

Publishing houses have editorial, art and marketing departments, although much of that work is hired out to freelancers that specialize in design, copyediting, typesetting, proofreading and packaging. Printing and binding also is contracted out.

Book Authors

STUDY PREVIEW   Authors come up with the ideas for many books, but publishers sometimes go looking for an author for a book to fill a hole in the market. The relationship of an author and a publisher is defined in contracts that specify royalties and other conditions and expectations for their partnership.

Authoring Process

No surefire formula exists for writing a successful book. Conventional wisdom at one point noted that books on Abraham Lincoln, on doctors and on dogs usually did well, leading one wag to suggest a book on Abraham Lincoln's doctor's dog.

SPECULATION.   Many books are written on speculation. The author has an idea, gets it on paper, then hunts for a publisher. That's how Robert Pirsig's *Zen and the Art of Motorcycle Maintenance* came to be. It's a classic case study.

Pirsig had not had an easy adulthood: mental breakdown, electro-shock treatment, itinerancy. He had grown up expecting more. A high point in his life was work-

vanity presses
Publishers that charge authors to publish their manuscripts.

list
A book company's catalog of titles.

ing out a relationship with his 11-year-old son. From his experiences emerged a gentle philosophy about life. An idea developed in Pirsig's mind for a book that wrapped it all together.

Finding a publisher was difficult. For more than six years, Pirsig sent out his proposal—121 times in all. Publishing houses doubted its commercial potential. It was a meandering, sometimes confusing manuscript that operated on many levels. At one level it was written around a motorcycle trip that Pirsig and his son had taken from Minnesota westward. At another level it was a highly cerebral exploration of values. Finally, the 122nd time that Pirsig mailed out the manuscript, it attracted the attention of James Landis, an editor at the William Morrow publishing house. The offbeat title was enticing, and Landis saw literary merit in the book. He decided to take a flier. Morrow published the book in 1974. Landis cautioned Pirsig against getting his hopes up. But *Zen and the Art of Motorcycle Maintenance* turned out to be the right book at the right time. Written in a soul-searching, soul-baring style, it touched readers emerging from the Haight-Ashbury flower child era. It became a best-seller. Not just a flash sensation, it had sales exceeding 100,000 a year for 20 years. It remains in print.

Every year, by one estimate, 30,000 manuscripts written on speculation arrive at the nation's trade publishing houses. Many do not receive even a cursory review. Nine out of 10 are rejected. Of the survivors, only a fraction make it to print.

PUBLISHER INITIATIVE.   While many authors seek publishers, as Pirsig did, it can also work the other way. When Warner Books saw profit potential in a sequel to Margaret Mitchell's enduring *Gone With the Wind*, it auditioned several leading authors. Alexandra Ripley was the choice. *Scarlett* resulted.

Barbara Tuchman's *Guns of August,* on the start of World War I, had a similar origin. A publisher, Macmillan, recognized a dearth of titles on the war and went looking for an author. Tuchman, an accomplished journalist, was an obvious choice. She liked the proposal.

Author-Publisher Relations

Under copyright law, authors are like other creators of intellectual property and almost always own what they write. A publisher's responsibility is to edit and polish the manuscript and then to manufacture, distribute and market the book.

ROYALTIES.   Authors usually give publishers the ownership of the book in exchange for these services. In a contractual arrangement, authors receive a percentage of their book's income, a **royalty.** The publisher takes the rest to cover expenses and, if a book does well, to make a profit.

In trade publishing, a typical royalty rate is 15 percent of the cover price, although publishers, seeking to trim expenses, have whittled at the standard in recent years. In textbooks the percentage is also 15 percent, but because the royalty is calculated from a wholesale, not retail price, it is actually more typically 11½ percent. Some authors have the negotiating clout for much greater royalties. Stephen King's is reportedly at 50 percent. Two textbook coauthors negotiated 21¾ percent for a promising cutting-edge work in the sciences.

Authors usually receive an **advance** of money from a publisher when they sign a contract. The idea of an advance is to tide an author over until royalties begin coming in. The advance then is deducted from the author's first royalty income. The Hollywood

royalty
Author's share of a book's income.

advance
Upfront money for an author to sign a contract with a publisher.

Media People

Maxwell Perkins

Maxwell Perkins epitomizes many people's image of a book editor. He wore tweeds, and he was genteel and quietly charming. When Thomas Wolfe delivered a huge, poorly organized manuscript in a battered trunk, Perkins, always patient, took the time to guide Wolfe in making it into a finely tuned novel worthy of Wolfe's greatness as an author. Perkins took the same care with Ernest Hemingway, F. Scott Fitzgerald and others. Time was less important than quality.

Perkins was a fixture at Charles Scribner's & Son, a respected New York publishing house. In fact, he dominated the place in those days when book publishing was a comfortable, clubby business.

Candid informality was his style. Charles Scribner Jr. once told of Perkins conducting a meeting for salesmen. "Now, here's a book by Robert Briffault," Perkins said. "I really don't know why we ever took that book." To doubters, Scribner explained, "I am not joking: That was the sales pitch for the book, informal to the point of being Pickwickian."

Maxwell Perkins

Maxwell Perkins died in 1947. Today he is still considered the foremost fiction editor of all time.

star system that has taken root in trade publishing, however, has changed the concept of advances. To sign big-name authors, publishers regularly offer authors far more advance money than is likely to be earned in royalties and never ask for the advance back. Some industry observers doubted, for example, that New York Senator Hillary Clinton's 2001 book, for which Simon & Shuster gave an $8 million advance, would ever **earn out,** as it's called when royalty income exceeds the advance.

Risk is involved in book publishing. For most books a publisher invests the same upfront money in editing, production and marketing whether the book sells well or bombs. Authors take a risk too because their advances are repayable, although advances are often forgiven if a book doesn't earn out. Why forgiven? Because publishers recognize their vulnerability to author claims in lawsuits that they marketed a book badly if it doesn't earn out.

AGENTS.   Most authors, except for textbooks, hire an **agent** to find an appropriate publisher and negotiate the contract. Typically, agents earn their keep with a 10 percent commission taken from the author's royalties. This arrangement encourages agents to negotiate the best terms possible for the author, at the same time knowing from experience when pushing too hard for certain terms can break a deal.

earn out
When royalty income to an author exceeds the advance.

agent
Person who represents an author in finding a publisher and in negotiating a contract.

Book Issues

STUDY PREVIEW   Mass marketing has changed the book industry fundamentally—not for the better, according to some. Meanwhile, the age-old issue of censorship won't go away.

Blockbusters

Nobody denies the importance of Harriet Beecher Stowe's *Uncle Tom's Cabin*. More Americans read it than any other book between 1852 and the Civil War. It stirred antislavery passions that, some say, led to the war. The book sold an unprecedented 100,000 copies a month the first three months it was out—the first blockbuster novel.

Publishers ever since have put the quest for blockbusters above all else, say book industry critics. The quest has snowballed, becoming so frenzied and also calculated that, according to the critics, the industry focuses myopically on creating blockbusters, which means slighting and even ignoring works of merit that might not be as profitable.

Although some critics overstate their case, there is no question that conglomeration has accelerated the blockbuster mania. Parent companies, under shareholder pressure to increase profits, incessantly seek a greater return from their book company subsidiaries. They put people in charge who will focus on that task. The bottom-line orientation fuels the concern among elitists that mediocre and even bad stuff ends up displacing good stuff in the marketplace.

In an important book, *The Death of Literature*, Alvin Kernan makes the case that the increasingly consumer-oriented book industry is stunting good literature. Worse, says Kernan, the lower level to which books are written, edited and marketed is undermining cultural standards by placing less of a premium on high literacy.

Indeed, major houses put growing emphasis on clever acquisitions, big-name authors and heavy promotion. Purists complain that blockbuster authors get multi-million-dollar advances before even writing a word because of the Hollywood-like star system that publishers have created to sell books through the author's name, not necessarily the quality of the book.

Publishing executives respond that producing books with limited popular appeal would put them out of business. Their argument: Without attention to profits, the industry would constrict—and where would cultural enhancement be then?

Mass Marketing

Evidence abounds that major houses have forsaken a balance on the elitist-populist continuum. The current classic example is the $600,000 that Warner Books

Media Databank

Blockbuster Authors

To anyone who thinks that all authors write in a garret under a bare bulb and have rent problems, consider Stephen King. The ongoing popularity of his horror books has enabled King to claim a 50 percent royalty rate. His 1999 gross income, estimated by *Forbes* magazine, put him behind only Tom Clancy among blockbuster authors.

Tom Clancy	$66 million
Stephen King	65 million
John Grisham	36 million
Dean Koontz	34 million
Michael Crichton	34 million

spent to promote *Scarlett,* Alexandra Ripley's 1991 sequel to *Gone With the Wind.* Litterateurs called the book mediocre at best, but Warner's orchestrated promotional campaign created a mass market for it. The book was the year's top seller despite dubious literary merit. Critics say that by channeling so many resources into the Ripley book, Warner either underpromoted or bypassed other works, including some of undoubtedly greater merit. We'll never know.

For sure, success has moved beyond the province of the literary-minded. More and more, the criteria that preoccupy publishing houses in choosing titles are these related questions:

- Will it sell?
- How can we make it sell?

Big retailers choose whether to stock a book on the basis of bulk discounts, publisher promotion budgets and big-name authors—not literary quality.

SELECTION CRITERIA. In deciding which books to sign, some publishing house editorial committees consider how photogenic the author will be in television interviews. An appearance on Oprah Winfrey's show can make all the difference. Toni Morrison's *Song of Solomon* languished for 19 years on the market before she appeared on *Oprah* in 1996. Related selection criteria:

- How would the author come across on radio?
- Would a three-week, 17-city sweep on local talk shows at the launch of a book add to sales?
- Does the manuscript lend itself to a screenplay?
- Would the movie have the potential for profitable soundtrack possibilities?
- Could the book be pitched so that a book club would choose it as a monthly selection?
- Could we price the book so that Wal-Mart would use a prominent point-of-purchase display?
- How enticing can we make the cover?
- How much would magazine serialization boost sales?

If any of these criteria speak to literary quality, it's only tangentially. Charles Scribner and Maxwell Perkins would cringe.

PROMOTION. Humorist Art Buchwald captured how book marketing can run amok. Noting how lascivious covers and hyped subtitles contribute to paperback sales, Buchwald once suggested that *Snow White and the Seven Dwarfs* be subtitled "The Story of a Ravishing Blonde Virgin Held Captive by Seven Deformed Men, All with Different Lusts."

Creating controversy sells. In a classic case, Stein & Day, the publisher of Elia Kazan's *The Arrangement,* found the book was being criticized as too explicit. In fact, the Mount Pleasant, Iowa, Library Board sent back its copy as too racy for its shelves. Stein & Day's president mailed a letter to the Mount Pleasant *News,* offering a free copy to everyone in the community, urging them to read the book and decide for themselves. Eight hundred people ordered their free copy, which generated a bundle of publicity. Sales soared nationally.

censorship
A ban on expression by authorities.

Book Censorship

Book burning has a long if hardly noble history. **Censorship,** the banning of expression by authorities, was no more tragic than in the 1500s when Spanish clergy, sure that theirs was a better way, destroyed the accumulated works of the Aztec people. In the vanguard was Father Juan de Zumárraga, who had introduced printing in the Americas. These clergy wiped out almost every record of the pre-Columbian civilization in the Americas. Book burnings of the take-no-enemies sort may be behind us in human development, but censorship is not.

In the United States a 1930 tariff law was used as an import restriction to intercept James Joyce's *Ulysses* at the docks because of four-letter words and explicit sexual references. When a judge said that the "unusual frankness" in Joyce's great work was protected by the U.S. Constitution's bar on government censorship, censors tried using postal regulations to keep objectionable material out of circulation. That tactic was thrown out by the courts after Grove Press objected that its U.S. edition of D. H. Lawrence's *Lady Chatterley's Lover,* introduced in 1959, was, in effect, being censored by being kept out of the mails.

Despite a litany of court decisions endorsing free expression, censorship remains a problem. As incredible as it seems, the tremendously popular series of Harry Potter books became targets for removal from school library shelves in 1999. Those who wanted the books suppressed saw too much of the occult in them.

The American Library Association, which has a proud record against censorship, tracks attempts to suppress books. The list of censored books perennially includes *The Chocolate War* by Robert Cormier, *Of Mice and Men* by John Steinbeck, *I Know Why the Caged Bird Sings* by Maya Angelou, *Catcher in the Rye* by J. D. Salinger, *The Song of Solomon* by Toni Morrison and *Huckleberry Finn* by Mark Twain.

Most complaints originate with social conservatives. In recent years, however, a growing number have come from liberals who want to be sensitive to people who might be offended. Such is the heart of complaints against Mark Twain, who included the word *nigger* in his late 19th-century dialogue in *Huckleberry Finn*. The critics called the word choice racist. But Twain's defenders note that the dialogue is typical of the period. More important, they argue, Twain, hardly a racist, was sympathetic to the plight of black people. The escaped slave Jim can be seen as the moral center of *Huckleberry Finn,* and Huck learns to rise above his own upbringing to help Jim, who has become his friend.

Evaluating Books

STUDY PREVIEW   A book's value can be measured by best-seller lists, though neither precisely nor qualitatively. Other measures include external recognition through awards and independent reviews.

Populist Measures

Book publishers that are obsessive about their bottom line measure success by the margins between sales revenue and costs: the profit margin. Rough gauges of this are **best-seller** lists that attempt to rank consumer purchases. Because tracking books through distribution channels with real-time precision is impossible, all the best-seller lists are less accurate than they seem. They're simply educated guesses.

The New York *Times* has the most-cited best-seller list. Despite the *Times*'s claims that it samples "3,050 bookstores plus wholesalers serving 38,000 other retailers," critics say the methodology is flawed. The critics say the *Times* favors independent bookstores over the chains and discount and airport outlets. That means that popular mystery, romance, science fiction and western books and paperbacks in

Campus Best-Seller List. The *Chronicle of Higher Education*, a weekly newspaper read mostly by college administrators and faculty, checks campus bookstores at selected universities for best-sellers among students. It bears some semblance to the New York *Times* weekly best-seller list, but there are differences that reflect issues and subjects with special attraction for people who frequent campus shops.

Best-Sellers. People in the book business track the list in the trade journal *Publishers Weekly*. The most quoted list, in the New York *Times,* ranks books by general categories. Critics say that the *Times* gives too much weight to highbrow independent book stores and that its list undervalues a lot of paperback fiction. The *Wall Street Journal* list uses an index feature to show the relative sales of books on its lists. *USA Today* also has a weekly list, but it is a hodgepodge of formats and genres that, say critics, makes it a list of oranges and apples.

media online

American Library Association: The voice of America's libraries.
www.ala.org

ISBN: Understanding the International Standard Book Numbering system.
www.isbn.spk-berlin.de

and an ISBN FAQ:
www.bowker.com/standards/home/isbn/us/isbnqa.html

general are woefully underreported. The *Times* disqualifies religious books from its list. Novelist Evan Maxwell faults the *Times* for a snobbish bias that undercounts books sold by independent distributors, rack jobbers, wholesalers and "beetle-browed teamsters who service smoke shops and newsstands."

Because many people use best-seller lists to guide their purchases, the lists are self-prophesying to some extent. In any event, they are attempts at measuring popularity, not necessarily quality.

Quality Measures

Qualitative measures are available for people who have a disdain for populist best-seller lists. Among respected prizes:

- **National Book Award.** For fiction, poetry and young people.
- **Nobel Prize.** For literature.
- **PEN/Faulkner Award.** For U.S. fiction.
- **Pulitzer Prize.** For fiction, nonfiction and poetry.
- **William Holmes McGuffey Award.** For textbooks.

A prestigious prize, such as a Pulitzer, can propel a book into best-seller status on the basis of merit. Yes, elitists are forced to admit, solid works can be best-sellers.

Another guide to quality for enduring titles is their appearance in numerous series of great works. Also, for contemporary works in a given field, many people follow book reviews in trade journals and specialized publications. Among general publications with great elitist followings for their book reviews are the New York *Times,* which puts out a weekly magazine on books, and the *Wall Street Journal.*

Some book clubs are a guide to quality. For many years Book-of-the-Month Club relied on a board of independent authorities to choose titles. A BOMC endorsement was important. Even so, being a matter of judgment, even of collective judgment, the BOMC imprimatur was not infallible. The club missed John Steinbeck's *Grapes of Wrath.* Alas, after becoming part of the Time Warner conglomerate, Book-of-the-Month Club scrapped the expert panel in 1994 and just offered books that publishers were pushing as likely best-sellers. Some book clubs that focus on niches, like history or a particular profession, still have strict selection standards.

Book Trends

STUDY PREVIEW   The book has a history of innovation. Modern paperbacks, introduced in the 1930s, have been credited with democratizing reading. For better or worse, retailing has shifted to market-driven models. Possibilities for the web are promising to upend the whole industry.

Paperback Books

The book industry is perceived wrongly as hidebound, even dowdy. Through history, books have been innovative in meeting the changing needs of the times. During the U.S. Civil War, thousands of troops in the field had idle time for reading, and several innovative publishers introduced low-cost books that soldiers could afford. They were coverless and lightweight, easy to pack in a knapsack when marching orders arrived.

The modern paperback was introduced in the United States by **Robert de Graff** in 1939. The nation was well into the Depression, and traditional books were beyond the means of many people. His **Pocket Books,** unabridged softcover titles that easily fit into a purse or pocket, cost only 25 cents. Within two months, sales reached 325,000 copies. Almost everybody could afford a quarter for a book. "The paperback democratized reading in America," wrote Kenneth Davis in his book *Two-Bit Culture: The Paperbacking of America.*

Book Retailing

Book retailing is undergoing rapid change. Traditionally, shops were owned by local merchants. In Boston, the first seat of intellectualism in the North American British colonies, booksellers were important people in the community who knew their customers individually. Shops carried distinctive inventories. That customer-driven model of book retailing, through **independent bookstores,** bookstores that are not part of a chain, worked for almost 250 years. Sales reps from publishers made individual calls on shop owners to chat about their wares, and the owners ordered what they knew their customers would want. Although independents still exist, they comprise fewer than one of five bookstores.

Robert de Graff
Originated Pocket paperbacks in the United States in 1939.

Pocket Books
First modern U.S. paperbacks.

independent bookstores
Bookstores that are not part of a chain.

Media Databank

Bookstore Chains

The largest bookstore chains in Canada and the United States, ranked by the number of stores:

Borders	1,195
Barnes & Noble	942
Chapters	326
Family Christian	290
Books-A-Million	180

BOOK CLUBS.   Some inroads against independents came with book clubs. The **Book-of-the-Month Club,** the oldest and largest, has shipped more than 500 million books since 1926. Originally, the club saw its market as small-town and rural people who lacked handy bookstores. The club offered packages of free books to entice people to join—on condition that they buy future books. The club used a **negative option** system: Members were sent descriptions of new titles 12 to 15 times a year. Unless they rejected a proposed offering, it was sent automatically. Typically, the club moves 200,000 copies of its featured selection.

Dozens of other book clubs followed, some specializing in narrow fields. Later, record clubs used a similar model.

Some kinds of books lend themselves to book clubs. More juvenile books are sold through clubs, led by Teen-Age Book Club, than through retail stores. The club promotes itself to teachers who encourage students to join. The club sells in 80 percent of U.S. elementary schools and 50 percent of the high schools.

DIRECT MAIL.   Several media companies, including Reader's Digest, Time, Meredith and American Heritage, sell books by mail. Promotional literature is sent to people on carefully selected mailing lists, and customers order what they want. Professional and academic publishing houses, whose products wouldn't find space on bookstore shelves, market primarily through the mail. These publishers buy mailing lists from professional organizations, which, loaded with good prospects for particular titles, usually ensure a profitable number of orders by return mail.

Book-of-the-Month Club
The oldest and largest book club.

negative option
Automatic book club shipments unless the subscriber declines in advance.

MALL STORES.   With the growth of mass merchandising and shopping malls in the 1970s, several bookstore chains emerged. Typified by B. Dalton and Waldenbooks, which together had 2,300 stores at their peak, these chains ordered books in huge lots from the publishers and stocked their stores coast to coast with identical inventories. Often, these chains bought books even before they were printed, basing their decisions on publishers' promises for promotional blitzes and big discounts for bulk purchases. When huge stocks arrived, the mall stores had to move them—sometimes going to extraordinary steps with displays and discounts to fulfill their own projections and sometimes without consideration for a book's literary qualities. Suddenly, bookselling became marketing-driven with flashy displays and other incentives prodding customers to buy— hardly the customer-driven way of doing business that litterateurs would prefer. Whatever their deficiencies, mall stores were in tune with the times. They sold a lot of books.

SUPERSTORES.   Marketing-driven book retailing entered a new dimension, literally, with stand-alone superbookstores in the 1990s. Barnes & Noble, Crown,

Media People

Jeff Bezos

When the government got out of the Internet business in 1994, **Jeff Bezos** foresaw a retailing revolution. He figured that anything that could be easily shipped could be sold on the web. He worked up a list of 20 products that might work. Books were on the list, but something seemed wrong. In all the history of direct-mail retailing, going back to Montgomery Ward in 1872, nobody had gone into books-by-mail in a comprehensive way. Why not? Was it because the catalog would need to be so massive that it would be too costly to ship?

Bezos, an engineer and computer scientist by training, knew next to nothing about the book trade. Hoping to pick up some insight, he dropped in at the American Booksellers' national convention and wandered booth to booth. There he learned that the nation had two major wholesalers: Ingram and Baker & Taylor. Both had master catalogs—on CD-ROMs.

That was one of those magic moments when everything comes together. Bezos, age 30, and his wife packed their Chevy Blazer and moved to Seattle, a haven of computer talent, to hire help and start the enterprise. Setting up his headquarters on sawhorses in the garage, Bezos began building a web site. Without fanfare the site, Amazon. com, went live in July 1995. Within a month there were customers in 45 states. Within a year the enterprise had drawn the attention of the *Wall Street Journal*. The article sent business rocketing.

It took a year or more for Barnes & Noble and other established booksellers to get sites operating. By then, Amazon.com was miles ahead. Sales reached $1 billion in 2000. Strange as it may seem, though, the company hadn't turned a profit. Bezos said that the best was yet to come. He kept building—more multiacre

Jeff Bezos. As Jeff Bezos saw it back in 1994, the web had great potential for e-commerce. But what to sell? Figuring that products that lent themselves to direct mail would also work well on the web, Bezos settled on books. He founded Amazon.com in the garage at his Seattle home, pioneering book retailing on the web. Sales in 2000 were $1 billion.

warehouses throughout the country, more webmasters, more packing clerks. Spending outpaced revenue by $350 million in 2000. No problem, said his investors. They had faith in his vision, which was putting Amazon.com into all kinds of new direct-mail lines: videos, pet products, bridal gifts, prescription drugs—even an online flea market.

Borders and Books-A-Million built 900 of the humongous stores, some bigger than grocery supermarkets and stocking 180,000 titles. The superstores do more than sell books. Part of their appeal has been to become community centers of sorts, with cafes, lectures, children's programs and poetry readings. The best news, though, was that their gigantic inventories meant that people could find just what they needed—an improvement over the mall stores, albeit a big blow to the remaining independents.

Superstores, however, may be in for their own comeuppance with the growth of electronic books.

WEB SHOPPING. A startup Seattle company, Amazon.com, created an online bookstore in 1995 with 1 million titles—far more than even the largest superstore. In 1997 Barnes & Noble entered the online business, and soon both stores were claiming more than 2.5 million titles. Those sites and other online bookstores are far more

media online

Bibliomania: Updated print texts in electronic and portable formats.
www.bibliomania.com

Classics at the Online Literature Library: Text of classics available over the web.
www.literature.org/authors/

Jeff Bezos (pronounced BAY-zos)
Founder of Amazon.com, the first web bookseller.

Bookshop Espresso. Trendy coffee cafes in book superstores fuel elitists' concerns that bookselling has wandered too far from its traditional focus as a cultivator of literary tastes. It's as though espresso dilutes intellectual stimulation. But in Boston, the cradle of colonial intellectualism, bookselling and coffee vending often were side-by-side enterprises in the same shop.

First E-Book. NuvoMedia introduced its Rocket eBook in 1998. Since then, e-books have become lighter, their screens are more readable, and their memory holds more material. Some have color screens.

media convergence

e-books
Portable electronic devices for on-screen reading of books downloaded from the web.

than ordering mechanisms. They carry personalized recommendations, book reviews, author biographies, chatrooms and other attractions. When competition was strongest, the online services offered steep discounts, sometimes 40 percent off retail, and made inroads into the book sales of traditional bookstores and superstores.

Electronic Books

Master storyteller Stephen King issued a novella in 2000 without ink or paper. The 16,000-word *Riding the Bullet* was available only on the web—at $2.50 a download. The book was not the first released on the web, but King was the most famous author until then to bypass book publishers completely.

The King book took advantage of new technology and formats that allow downloads to personal computers, including new specialized portables called **e-books.** The paperback-size Rocket eBook was the first on the market in 1998 at $499. Its price later dropped, and by 2001, a competitor had a model selling at less than $200. At first, few titles were available, but publishers, seeing a new market emerging, began to work out formats with e-book manufacturers and, given time, not only will Stephen King's work be available as downloads but even—hold your breath—textbooks.

Books and Media Melding

The melding of books with other media has been going on a long time. In fact, early printers didn't distinguish between media. They took whatever jobs they could to make a living: stationery, government forms, books, pamphlets, even newspapers. When a distinct U.S. book industry emerged in the 19th century as a nurturer of the culture's literary output, it seemed only natural that magazines were part of the mix. Some of the most important magazines in U.S. history, like *Scribner's* and *Harper's*, originated in the book companies whose names they bore.

SERIALIZATION. Although magazines departed into separate ownership, the book industry remains connected with other media. **Serialization,** publishing a book in segments in magazines or newspapers, represents a long-standing melding of media. Since 1936 it has been conventional wisdom that serializing a book in a magazine can boost book sales. There had been doubters, but that was settled when DeWitt Wallace, founder of the *Reader's Digest* magazine, won a bet of sorts with the Harper publishing house. Wallace had been turned down after offering $1,000 to serialize a Harper book. He responded by offering to pay $5,000—if book sales didn't increase. He didn't have to pay a cent. It was a win-win for *Reader's Digest* and for Harper's. Today, publishing houses routinely figure income from serialization into their budgets when planning a trade book.

Several theories exist as to why serialization boosts book sales. One is that people who read a condensation then want to read the whole book. Another theory, which assumes human vanity, is that readers of a condensed version want the real book on their shelves to point to with pride as they talk about having read the book, even though they might never have opened the book itself.

SUBSIDIARY RIGHTS. Serialization is one of many ways for publishers to generate additional revenue from what's called **subsidiary rights,** giving permission to make additional applications of the work. Other subsidiary rights are sold for softcover editions, book club editions, audio books, Braille editions and other outlets.

Subsidiary rights create additional revenue streams for book publishers, which, when done right, makes them profitable in themselves. But subsidiary rights also can generate new interest in the original work and spur more sales. When the 1999 movie *The Green Mile* was a hit, sales rebounded for the original Stephen King book on which it was based.

CROSSOVER PRODUCTS. Media mogul Sumner Redstone, no slouch at wringing new revenue by recycling products, added the Simon & Schuster book company to his Viacom conglomerate in 1994. His goal was to create a multiple media presence, with Simon & Schuster creating books from Viacom movie and television characters. Redstone envisioned a series of MTV books, Beavis & Butt-Head products and other Viacom merchandise. Even when he was strapped for cash and sold half of Simon & Schuster, a deal completed in 1999, he kept the half of the company that produces trade books to realize a profitable synergy between books and his other media activities.

Redstone is not alone as a multimedia entrepreneur seeking crossover opportunities by blurring the distinctions between media. He never saw himself as any more of a book publisher than a movie mogul or a television executive. With that kind of deep-pocket corporate support, further melding of media technologies, as with printed books and e-books, lies ahead.

E-Book Mainstream. Stephen King's 2000 thriller *Riding the Bullet* became the first contemporary work by a major author that could be downloaded from the web in many computer formats, including those of e-books. The publisher didn't even issue a print edition. Imagine reading Stephen King in the dark.

media online

Bookshelf: Specializing in history, science and technical books.
www.auldbooks.com

Rare Books Around the Net: Links to rare book resources.
www.bibliofind.com

Reference Books Online: Links to reference books online—dictionaries, thesauruses, encyclopedias, etiquette, etc.
www.bartleby.com/reference

Richard L. Pryll Jr. Lies:
http://interport.net/~rick/lies/lies.html

Books on Tape/CD: Rent or buy unabridged audio books.
www.booksontape.com

Gemstar eBook: One of the new electronic books now on the market.
www.ebook-gemstar.com

serialization
Publishing a book in segments in magazines or newspapers.

subsidiary rights
Rights to adapt book for additional markets.

Media Databank

Book-Based Movies

More movies are derived from books than many people realize. Recent examples:

Dream Story by Arthur Schnitzler	*Eyes Wide Shut* (1999)
The Green Mile by Stephen King	*The Green Mile* (1999)
American Hero by Larry Beinhart	*Wag the Dog* (1997)
Starship Troopers by Robert Heinlein	*Starship Troopers* (1997)
Forrest Gump by Winston Groom	*Forrest Gump* (1994)

chapter wrap-up

Book publishing is a high-risk business, especially for works geared toward general consumers. Most books do not make money, which means that publishing houses rely on best-sellers to offset the losses. Despite the risks, books can make enormous profits, which led many conglomerates to buy publishing houses in the 1980s. The new parent corporations pressed for more profitability. The result has been heightened competition for big-name authors and new attention to mass marketing. Multi-million-dollar advances to authors for popular, though not necessarily significant, works suggest that the book industry is backing away from its traditional role in furthering U.S. culture and public enlightenment.

Questions for Review

1. How did the mass-produced written word fundamentally change human history?
2. What are the main categories and subcategories of books?
3. Do small, specialized book publishers still have a place?
4. How do book concepts come to be?
5. How is the book industry changing? What are the implications?
6. How can the worthiness of a book be judged?
7. How is the web changing the book industry?

Questions for Critical Thinking

1. Trace the development of the book industry through the innovations of these people: Johannes Gutenberg, William Holmes McGuffey, and Robert de Graff.
2. What invention doomed the scribist culture that preceded the age of mass communication?
3. How do subsidiary rights multiply the profit potential of trade books?

4. Distinguish trade books and textbooks in terms of profit potential, duration on the market, distribution systems and the effect of mass-marketed paperbacks.
5. Subsidiary rights have become a major revenue source for book publishers. Discuss the kinds of subsidiary rights and their effect on the book industry.
6. For most people, book publishing brings McGraw-Hill, Simon & Schuster, HarperCollins and other major companies to mind. Describe how the following entities fit into the industry: Government Printing Office, Iowa State University Press and Exposition Press.
7. Is there a threat to high-quality literature from subsidiary rights? From mass marketing? From conglomeration? From the quest for blockbusters? From projection models?
8. What are ways in which the book industry can ensure its continued growth? How can the book industry protect itself from the need to retrench if growth stalls?
9. Where is the U.S. book industry heading with electronic publishing?

Keeping Up to Date

Publishers Weekly is the trade journal of the book industry.

The C-SPAN cable television network runs a continuing program, "Booknotes," which focuses on authors and new titles as well as book industry issues.

Book Research Quarterly, published by Rutgers University, is a scholarly journal.

www.ebooknet.com is a good site for keeping up to date on development in e-books.

Bob Petersen. *Automobile enthusiast Bob Petersen followed his passions and created* Hot Rod *maga-zine after World War II. Then came* Motor Trend, *and soon he had a bevy of special-topic enthusiast magazines that epitomized the new demassification trend in U.S. magazine publishing.*

3

Magazines

Just out of the military after World War II, and with a bit of experience in publicity, Bob Petersen, age 23, decided to pursue his passion: hot rods. He launched a magazine, titled *Hot Rod,* for a legion of veterans who were home again and pursuing their dreams, which often included high-tuning an automobile and racing too. Petersen wrote articles and shot photos for *Hot Rod.* He even hawked copies himself at dry-lake races, drag strips and auto shows.

Bob Petersen loved the rumble of big engines, the smell of peeling rubber and the chrome-bedecked cars of the time, and his love showed in *Hot Rod.* Journalistically, he tapped an undiscovered mass of enthusiasts who shared his passion. It wasn't all calculated, for nobody knew for sure how many people were so heavily into racing that they would buy the magazine, but Petersen was doing what he loved.

At the time, newsracks were dominated by big general interest magazines such as *Life, Look* and *Colliers.* Clearly, *Hot Rod* was a niche publication. But it took off. At 25 cents, 40,000 hot-rodders were buying the new magazine.

A year later Petersen launched another niche publication, *Motor Trend,* aimed more at consumers than at enthusiasts. Within a year *Motor Trend*'s circulation had passed 138,000, eclipsing *Hot Rod*'s. A slew of Petersen niche titles followed over the years. They focused not on broad issues, like the major, traditional magazines of the time, but on narrow topics. Consider these titles: *Guns and Ammo, Skin Diver, Stereophile, Motorcyclist* and *Dirt Rider.*

Petersen Publishing became a magazine powerhouse, defining much of what has happened in the magazine industry in the past half-century. Once, the leading magazines were geared for everyone in the mass audience, offering something for everybody. Now, almost all magazines are edited for narrow segments of the population. *Motor Trend,* with a circulation of 1.3 million, epitomizes the type of niche magazine that dominates the industry today.

The Petersen experience also tells us something else about the magazine industry. In 1998 Bob Petersen, in his 70s, retired and sold his magazines to EMAP Publications of London. It was a sign not only of conglomeration in the magazine industry, giving EMAP a total of 50 U.S. titles, but also of globalization. While Bob Petersen had a long, successful run at magazines, his passion for his subjects is what drove the company. The question now: Does EMAP have that kind of passion for hot rods?

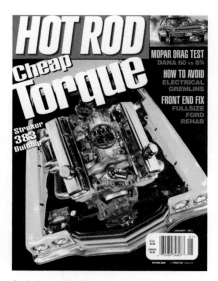

A niche enthusiasts' magazine.

Influence of Magazines

STUDY PREVIEW   Today, as through their whole history, the major magazines constitute a mass medium through which the distinctive U.S. culture is brought to a national audience. The periodicals pack great literature and ideas into formats that, unlike books, almost anybody can afford. Magazines are also a national unifier because they offer manufacturers a nationwide audience for their goods.

Contributing to Nationhood

The first successful magazines in the United States, in the 1820s, were much less expensive than books. People of ordinary means could afford them. Unlike newspapers, which were oriented to their cities of publication, early magazines created national audiences. This contributed to a sense of nationhood at a time when an American culture, distinctive from its European heritage, had not yet emerged. The American people had their magazines in common. The *Saturday Evening Post,* founded in 1821, carried fiction by Edgar Allan Poe, Nathaniel Hawthorne and Harriet Beecher Stowe to readers who could not afford books. Their short stories and serialized novels flowed from the American experience and helped Americans establish a national identity.

With the **Postal Act of 1879,** Congress recognized the role of magazines in creating a national culture and promoting literacy—in effect, binding the nation. The law allowed a discount on mailing rates for magazines, a penny a pound. Magazines were being subsidized, which reduced distribution costs and sparked dramatic circulation growth. New magazines cropped up as a result.

Saturday Evening Post
Early contributor to identifiable U.S. literature.

Postal Act of 1879
Discounted magazine mail rates.

National Advertising Medium

Advertisers used magazines through the 1800s to build national markets for their products, which was an important factor in transforming the United States from an agricultural and cottage industry economy into a modern economy. This too contributed to a sense of nationhood. The other mass media could not do that as effec-

Media Timeline

Magazines

1741 Andrew Bradford printed *American Magazine* and Benjamin Franklin printed *General Magazines*, the first magazines in the colonies.

1821 *Saturday Evening Post* was launched, ushering in the era of general interest magazines.

1828 Sara Josepha Hale began editing *Ladies' Magazine*, the first women's magazine.

1860s *Harper's Weekly* introduced visual news with Civil War illustrations.

1879 Congress gave discount postal rates to magazines.

1899 Gilbert Grosvenor introduced photographs in *National Geographic*.

1902 Ida Tarbell wrote a muckraking series on Standard Oil in *McClure's*.

1922 DeWitt and Lila Wallace founded *Reader's Digest*.

1923 Henry Luce and Briton Hadden founded *Time*, the first newsmagazine.

1924 Harold Ross founded the *New Yorker* and introduced the modern personality profile.

1936 Henry Luce founded *Life* and coined the term *photojournalism*.

1960s Oversize general magazines, including *Life*, folded as advertisers moved to network television.

1962 Hugh Hefner introduced the modern question-and-answer format in *Playboy*.

1996 Time Warner created the Pathfinder web site for its magazines.

tively. Few books carried advertisements, and newspapers, with few exceptions, delivered only local readership to advertisers.

Massive Magazine Audience

The American people have a tremendous appetite for magazines. According to magazine industry studies, almost 90 percent of U.S. adults read an average 10 issues a month. Although magazines are affordable for most people, the household income of the typical reader is 5 percent more than the national average. In general, the more education and higher income a person has, the greater the person's magazine consumption.

In short, magazines are a pervasive mass medium. Magazines are not only for the upper crust, however. Many magazines are edited for downscale audiences, which means that the medium's role in society is spread across almost the whole range of people. Even illiterate people can derive some pleasure and value from magazines, which by and large are visual and colorful.

The massiveness of the audience makes the magazine an exceptionally competitive medium. About 12,000 magazines vie for readers in the United States, ranging from general interest publications such as *Reader's Digest* to such specialized publications as *Chili Pepper*, for people interested in hot foods, and *Spur*, for racehorse aficionados. In recent years 500 to 600 new magazines have been launched annually, although only one in five survives into its third year. Even among major magazines, a huge following at the moment is no guarantee of survival. Of the 23 U.S. magazines with a circulation of more than 1 million in 1946, 10 no longer exist. Magazine publishing is a risky business.

Peterson Formula. Between 500 and 600 magazines a year are launched in the United States. Most fail for missing one of the ingredients for success identified by magazine scholar Theodore Peterson. First, a magazine must find an audience that no other magazine is serving or that is not being served well. Second, a magazine must adapt as conditions and readers' tastes change. Third, a magazine should reflect the personality of the person in charge.

Magazines as Media Innovators

STUDY PREVIEW   Magazines have led other media with significant innovations in journalism, advertising and circulation. These include investigative reporting, in-depth personality profiles, and photojournalism.

Investigative Reporting

Muckraking, usually called "investigative reporting" today, was honed by magazines as a journalistic approach in the first years of the 20th century. Magazines ran lengthy explorations of abusive institutions in the society. It was **Theodore Roosevelt,** the reform president, who coined the term *muckraking.* Roosevelt generally enjoyed investigative journalism, but one day in 1906, when the digging got too close to home, he likened it to the work of a character in a 17th-century novel who focused so much on raking muck that he missed the good news. The president meant the term derisively, but it came to be a badge of honor among journalists.

Muckraking established magazines as a powerful medium in shaping public policy. In 1902 **Ida Tarbell** wrote a 19-part series on the Standard Oil monopoly for *McClure's.* **Lincoln Steffens** detailed municipal corruption, and reforms followed. Other magazines picked up investigative thrusts. *Collier's* took on patent medicine frauds. *Cosmopolitan,* a leading muckraking journal of the period, tackled dishonesty in the U.S. Senate. Muckraking expanded to books with **Upton Sinclair**'s *The Jungle.* Sinclair shocked the nation by detailing filth in meat-packing plants. Federal inspection laws resulted. Later newspapers joined muckraking, but it was magazines that had led the way.

Personality Profiles

The in-depth **personality profile** was a magazine invention. In the 1920s **Harold Ross** of the *New Yorker* began pushing writers to a thoroughness that was new in journalism. They used multiple interviews with a range of sources—talking not only with the subject of the profile but also with just about everyone and anyone who could comment on the subject, including the subject's friends and enemies. Such depth required weeks, sometimes months, of journalistic digging. It's not uncommon now in newspapers, broadcasting or magazines, but before Harold Ross, it didn't exist.

Under **Hugh Hefner,** *Playboy* took the interview in new directions in 1962 with in-depth profiles developed from a highly structured question-and-answer format. This format became widely imitated.

Photojournalism

Magazines brought visuals to the mass media in a way books never had. *Harper's Weekly* sent artists to draw Civil War battles, leading the way to journalism that went beyond words.

The young editor of the *National Geographic,* Gilbert Grosvenor, drew a map proposing a route to the South Pole for an 1899 issue, putting the *Geographic* on the road to being a visually oriented magazine. For subsequent issues, Grosvenor borrowed government plates to reproduce photos, and he encouraged travelers to submit their photographs to the magazine. This was at a time when most magazines scorned photographs. However, Grosvenor was undeterred as an advocate for documentary photography, and membership in the National Geographic Society, a prerequisite for receiving the magazine, swelled. Eventually, the magazine assembled its own staff of photographers and gradually became a model for other publications that discovered they needed to play catch-up.

---

muckraking
Turn-of-century term for investigative reporting.

Theodore Roosevelt
Coined the term *muckraking.*

Ida Tarbell
Exposed Standard Oil.

McClure's
Turn-of-century muckraking magazine.

Lincoln Steffens
Exposed municipal corruption.

Upton Sinclair
Exposed the meat-packing industry.

personality profile
In-depth, balanced biographical article.

Harold Ross
Pioneered the personality profile.

Hugh Hefner
Adapted the personality profile to Q-and-A.

Harper's Weekly
Pioneered magazine visuals.

National Geographic
Introduced photography in magazines.

Media People

Margaret Bourke-White

The oversized *Life* magazine created by Henry Luce was the perfect forum for the work of Margaret Bourke-White. The giant pages, 13½ inches high and opening to 21-inch spreads, gave such impact to photos that they seemed to jump off the page at readers. Bourke-White was there at the beginning, shooting the immense Fort Peck Dam in Montana for *Life*'s first cover in 1936. Over her career, Bourke-White shot 284 assignments for *Life,* many of them enduring images from World War II. These included Holocaust victims in a Nazi concentration camp, great military movements, and the leaders of the time in both triumph and defeat. She was among the first great photojournalists.

Bourke-White's photojournalism went beyond the news and emotions of any given day to penetrate the core of great social problems. In collaboration with writer Erskine Caldwell, to whom she was later married, Bourke-White created a photo documentary on the tragic lives of sharecroppers in the American South. Later, in South Africa, she went underground to

photograph gold miners who were known only by numbers. Her haunting photos from the Midwest drought of the 1930s created indelible images in the minds of a generation. These were socially significant projects that moved people and changed public policy.

Margaret Bourke-White was fearless in her pursuit of photography.

Fearless Photojournalist. Margaret Bourke-White not only would take her camera anywhere, but also had a sense of stories that were worth telling photographically. She is remembered mostly for her work in *Life* magazine over 20 years beginning in the mid-1930s.

She took her camera, a weighty Speed Graphic, onto the ledges of skyscrapers to get the feel she wanted in her images. She shot the ravages of the war in Europe from airplanes. She lived her work, and was quoted once as saying, "When I die I want to die living."

She died in 1971 at age 67.

Aided by technological advances involving smaller, more portable cameras and faster film capable of recording images under extreme conditions, photographers working for the *Geographic* opened a whole new world of documentary coverage to their readers. Among *Geographic* accomplishments were:

- A photo of a bare-breasted Filipino woman field worker shocked some *Geographic* readers in 1903, but Grosvenor persisted against Victorian sensitivities to show the peoples of the world as they lived.
- The first photographs from Tibet, by Russian explorers, appeared in 1905 in an 11-page spread—extraordinary visual coverage for the time that confirmed photography's role in journalism.
- A 17-page, eight-foot foldout panorama of the Canadian Rockies in 1911 showed that photojournalism need not be limited by format.

National Geographic. The *Geographic* has remained in the vanguard of magazines photographically. For its 100th anniversary in 1988, the cover was the first hologram, a three-dimensional photograph, ever published in a mass-audience magazine. With a circulation of 8.7 million, the *Geographic* is not only among the oldest surviving U.S. magazines but also among the most read.

- The magazine's 100th anniversary cover in 1988 was the first hologram—a three-dimensional photograph—ever published in a mass-audience magazine. It was a significant production accomplishment.

Life magazine brought U.S. photojournalism to new importance in the 1930s. The oversize pages of the magazine gave new intensity to photographs, and the magazine, a weekly, demonstrated that newsworthy events could be covered consistently by camera. *Life* captured the spirit of the times photographically and demonstrated that the whole range of human experience could be recorded visually. Both real life and *Life* could be shocking. A 1938 *Life* spread on human birth was so shocking for the time that censors succeeded in banning the issue in 33 cities.

Consumer Magazines

STUDY PREVIEW   The most visible category of magazines is general-interest magazines, which are available on newsracks and by subscription. Called **consumer magazines,** these include publications like *Reader's Digest* that try to offer something for everybody, but mostly they are magazines edited for narrower audiences.

Circulation Leaders

consumer magazines
Sold on newsracks.

Reader's Digest
Largest circulation newsrack magazine.

Modern Maturity
Has the largest circulation but is limited to AARP members.

Reader's Digest is usually considered to have the largest circulation of any U.S. magazine, selling 12.6 million copies a month, not counting foreign editions. However, *Reader's Digest*'s lead in circulation is not technically correct because the circulation of the Sunday newspaper supplement *Parade* is triple that. Also, in recent years, with the graying of America, the magazine *Modern Maturity,* which is sent to members of the American Association of Retired Persons every two months, has reached a circulation of 20.4 million, considerably ahead of *Reader's Digest*.

Media Databank

Magazine Circulation

These are the circulation leaders among U.S. magazines. The figures do not include foreign editions, which add substantial circulation for some magazines. *Reader's Digest,* for example, publishes 40 editions in 18 languages for 12.2 million copies a month in addition to 12.6 million in the United States.

Monthlies	
Reader's Digest	12.6 million
National Geographic	8.5 million
Better Homes & Gardens	7.6 million
Family Circle	5.0 million
Good Housekeeping	4.5 million
Ladies' Home Journal	4.5 million
Woman's Day	4.3 million
McCall's	4.2 million
Playboy	3.2 million
AAA World	3.2 million
Prevention	3.0 million
American Legion	2.7 million
Redbook	2.3 million

Sunday Supplements	
Parade	37.2 million
USA Weekend	21.2 million

Weeklies	
TV Guide	11.1 million
Time	4.1 million
People	3.5 million
Sports Illustrated	3.3 million
Newsweek	3.1 million
The Cable Guide	3.0 million
National Enquirer	2.1 million

Biweeklies	
Rolling Stone	1.3 million

Bimonthlies	
Modern Maturity	20.4 million

The common notion that *Reader's Digest* is the largest magazine stems from its attempt to serve a true mass audience. Unlike *Modern Maturity,* the *Digest*'s easy-to-read articles cut across divisions of age, gender, occupation and geography. *Reader's Digest* is a mass magazine in the truest sense of the word. It tries in every issue to have something for everybody. The Sunday newspaper supplements are also edited for a truly mass audience.

Led by *Reader's Digest,* about 1,200 magazines are published in the United States for newsrack and subscription sales. A few, including newsmagazines, deal with subjects of general interest. Most, however, have a narrower focus, such as *Motor Trend,* which is geared toward automobile enthusiasts; *Forbes,* which appeals to business people and investors; and *Family Circle,* which targets homemakers.

One thing that consumer magazines have in common is a heavy reliance on advertising. Exceptions include *Consumer Reports,* which wants to be above any suspicion that advertisers influence its reporting; the nondenominational religious magazine *Guideposts;* and the feminist *Ms.*

Newsmagazines

Fresh out of Yale in 1923, classmates **Henry Luce** and Briton Hadden begged and borrowed $86,000 from friends and relatives and launched a new kind of magazine: *Time.* The magazine provided summaries of news by categories such as national affairs, sports and business. It took four years for *Time* to turn a profit, and some people doubted that the magazine would ever make money, noting that it merely rehashed what daily newspapers had already reported. Readers, however, came to like the handy compilation and the sprightly, often irreverent writing style that set *Time* apart.

Henry Luce
Founder of *Time* and later *Life.*

Time
First newsmagazine.

Media People

Walter Isaacson

Perhaps the most influential magazine editor of our time is Walter Isaacson at *Time*. He assumed the editorship in the early 1990s, when, it was feared, weekly newsmagazines had run their course. *Time* and the other newsmagazines seemed to be preempted by 24-hour news channels, a great number of new competitors and innovations on the web.

Isaacson reinvented *Time,* the largest of the U.S. newsmagazines, now with 4.2 million circulation. Rather than continuing as an omniscient compendium of the week's events, which had been *Time*'s thrust since 1923, Isaacson looked beyond the event-driven news of the day for issues and subjects that would engage people.

"What are people actually talking about? That's what drives this magazine," he says. "You have to make it very interesting and striking to get people engaged. If you start treating a magazine as some pulpit, you'll never connect."

Harvard-educated and a Rhodes scholar, Isaacson took no cheap sensationalistic shortcuts to grab readers. Rather, he emphasized themes that interested him, such as education and child-rearing.

Isaacson, who grew up in New Orleans, draws on his own past for a sense of what people are curious about. Isaacson's own 1997 cover article on Microsoft chief Bill Gates, whom he had known as a Harvard freshman, was based on days of relaxed interviewing in numerous settings. It was the landmark interview with Gates that clearly cemented Isaacson as a first-rate interviewer and writer.

Isaacson himself identifies about one cover issue a month on a subject that interests him. When women's soccer was taking off in the United States in 1999, his cover read: "What a Kick!" He made Latin singer Ricky Martin a cover story too, as did the other major newsmagazine, *Newsweek,* after a decent interval.

Isaacson didn't invent cover themes. Going back to the 1960s and occasionally before, *Time* had

Walter Isaacson

done exhaustive treatments of major issues that were not event-driven, such as the controversial "Is God Dead?" issue. But until Isaacson the thrust had been a recap of news in strictly defined departments such as International, Sports and Music. The compartmentalization of the week's events continues, but not as the main attraction.

A copycat, *Newsweek*, appeared in 1933. So did a third newsweekly, *U.S. News*, the forerunner to today's *U.S. News & World Report*. Despite the competition, *Time*, with 4.1 million copies weekly, has consistently led newsmagazine circulation.

While *Time, Newsweek* and *U.S. News & World Report* cover a broad range of subjects, specialized newsmagazines focus on narrower subjects. The largest category is those featuring celebrity news, including the gossipy sort. The supermarket tabloid **National Enquirer** focuses on the rich and famous, hyped-up medical research and sensational oddball news and is an incredible commercial success, with 2.1 million in circulation. Time-Life's *People* is at 3.5 million.

Newspaper Supplements

Sometimes overlooked as magazines are *Parade* and *USA Weekend,* the independently produced **Sunday supplements** that newspapers buy and stuff inside their weekend editions. They are designed for general family reading.

National Enquirer
Magazine or newspaper?

Parade
Largest magazine circulation.

USA Weekend
Second largest weekend newspaper supplement.

Sunday supplements
Free to buyers of Sunday newspapers.

Media People

DeWitt and Lila Wallace

DeWitt and Lila Wallace had an idea but hardly any money. The idea was a pocket-sized magazine that condensed informational, inspiring and entertaining nonfiction from other publications—a digest. With borrowed money the Wallaces brought out their first issue of *Reader's Digest* in 1922.

The rest, as they say, is history. In 1947 the *Digest* became the first magazine to exceed a circulation of 9 million. Except for the Sunday newspaper supplement *Parade*, *Reader's Digest* has been the nation's largest-circulation magazine most of the time since then. In 1999 *Reader's Digest*'s circulation was 12.6 million—not counting an additional 12.2 million overseas in 18 languages.

The magazine has remained true to the Wallaces' successful formula.

DeWitt and Lila Wallace, children of poor Presbyterian clergy, wanted "constructive articles," each with universal appeal. The thrust was upbeat but not Pollyanna. Digested as they were, the articles could be quickly read. America loved it. More than 90 percent of *Reader's Digest* circulation is by subscription, representing long-term reader commitment.

For its first 33 years, *Reader's Digest* was wholly reader supported. It carried no advertising. Rising postal rates forced a change in 1955. There was scoffing about whether advertisers would go for "postage-stamp-sized ads" in *Reader's Digest* with its diminutive pages, but the scoffers were wrong. The people who decide where to place advertisements never doubted that *Reader's Digest* was well read. To-

DeWitt and Lila Wallace.
Reader's Digest Founders

day, advertisers—except for cigarette manufacturers—pay more than $100,000 a page for a color advertisement. Consistent with the Wallaces' standards, cigarette advertisements are not accepted and never have been.

The weekend supplements have built-in advantages over other magazines. Readers neither subscribe nor buy them directly. The supplements need only convince a newspaper to carry them, and they have instant circulation. *Parade*'s circulation exceeds 37 million, which, technically speaking, makes it easily the largest magazine in the nation. *USA Weekend* exceeds 21 million.

Women's Magazines

The first U.S. magazine edited to interest only a portion of the mass audience, but otherwise to be of general interest, was *Ladies' Magazine*, which later became *Godey's Lady's Book*. **Sara Josepha Hale** helped start the magazine in 1828 to uplift and glorify womanhood. Its advice on fashions, morals, taste, sewing and cooking developed a following, which peaked with a circulation of 150,000 in 1860.

The *Godey's* tradition is maintained today in seven competing magazines known as the **Seven Sisters** because of their female following: *Better Homes & Gardens, Family Circle, Good Housekeeping, Ladies' Home Journal, McCall's, Redbook* and *Woman's Day.* While each sister can be distinguished from her siblings, there is a thematic connection: concern for home, family and high-quality living from a traditional woman's perspective.

An eighth sister is *Cosmopolitan*, although it may more aptly be called a distant cousin. Under Helen Gurley Brown and later Bonnie Fuller, *Cosmopolitan* has geared

Sara Josepha Hale
Founded first women's magazine.

Seven Sisters
Leading women's magazines.

Media People

Sara Josepha Hale

Sara Hale, widowed with five children, decided to write a novel to put the kids through college. *Northwood,* published in 1826, was one of the first books with America as its setting. The book attracted national attention, and all kinds of literary offers came Hale's way. She decided on the editorship of the new Boston-based *Ladies' Magazine.* Although some magazines of the time had women's sections, no previous magazine had wholly devoted itself to women's interests. Hale's innovations and sensitivities made the magazine and its successor a familiar sight in households throughout the nation for half a century. During her tenure Hale defined women's issues and in indirect ways contributed importantly to women's liberation.

As editor of *Ladies' Magazine,* Hale departed from the frothy romance fiction and fashion coverage in the women's sections of other magazines. Her focus was on improving women's role in society. She campaigned vigorously for educational opportunities for women. When Matthew Vassar was setting up a women's college, she persuaded him

Women's Magazine Pioneer. Sara Josepha Hale edited the first magazine designed for women, but just as important was the distinctive content. Whereas many magazines recycled articles from other magazines, mostly from England, Hale prided herself on original content. Her *Ladies' Magazine* enriched the nation's literary output with original work by Ralph Waldo Emerson, Nathaniel Hawthorne, Oliver Wendell Holmes, Washington Irving, Henry Wadsworth Longfellow, Edgar Allan Poe and Harriet Beecher Stowe.

to include women on the faculty—a novel idea for the time.

No fashion plate, Sara Hale encouraged women to dress comfortably yet attractively—no frills. For herself she preferred black for almost all occasions. When the owners of the magazine thought enthusiastic fashion coverage would boost circulation—and advertising— she went along, but in her own way. She pointed out how impractical and ridiculous the latest fashions were, and some she dismissed as trivial diversions.

Unlike other magazine editors of the time, she disdained reprinting articles from other publications. Hence, *Ladies' Magazine* created

opportunities for new writers, particularly women, and enriched the nation's literary output. One issue, in 1843, was produced entirely by women. In her heyday, from the mid-1830s through the 1840s, Hale attracted the best writers to her pages: Ralph Waldo Emerson, Nathaniel Hawthorne, Oliver Wendell Holmes, Washington Irving, Henry Wadsworth Longfellow, Edgar Allan Poe, Harriet Beecher Stowe.

Hale edited *Ladies' Magazine* from 1828 until 1837, when it was merged into the weaker *Godey's Lady's Book.* She moved to Philadelphia to become editor of the new magazine, which retained the *Godey* title. Circulation reached 150,000 in 1860.

---

itself to a subcategory of women readers: young, unmarried and working. It's the most successful in a large group of women's magazines seeking narrow groups. Among them are *Elle,* focusing on fashion; *Playgirl,* with its soft pornography; *Essence,* for black women; and *Seventeen,* for teenage girls.

Men's Magazines

Esquire
First classy men's magazine.

Founded in 1933, **Esquire** was the first classy men's magazine. It was as famous for its pinups as for its literary content, which over the years has included articles from Ernest Hemingway, Hunter S. Thompson and P. J. O'Rourke. Fashion has also been a cornerstone in the *Esquire* content mix.

Hugh Hefner learned about magazines as an *Esquire* staff member, and he applied those lessons when he created **Playboy** in 1953. With its lustier tone, *Playboy* quickly overtook *Esquire* in circulation. At its peak *Playboy* sold 7 million copies a month. The magazine emphasized female nudity but also carried journalistic and literary pieces whose merit attracted many readers. Readers who were embarrassed by their carnal curiosity could claim that they bought the magazine for its articles. Critics sniped, however, that *Playboy* published the worst stuff of the best writers.

Sociologists credit Hefner with capitalizing on the post-World War II sexual revolution in the United States and fanning it. By 2002, however, *Playboy* seemed tired. With its circulation down to 3.2 million, *Forbes* analyst Stephanie Fitch said *Playboy* was in death dance. Upstart *Maxim*, a rival, was at 2.5 million after only four years.

Not all men's magazines dwell on sex. The outdoor life is exalted in *Field & Stream*, whose circulation tops 2 million. Fix-it magazines, led by *Popular Science* and *Popular Mechanics*, have a steady following.

Intellectual Magazines

Several magazines with relatively small circulations have significant influence on public policy because they are forums for political, social and arts leaders and intellectuals to express themselves and share their views. The *Weekly Standard*, financed by media mogul Rupert Murdoch, known mostly for his Fox television enterprises, emerged as a policy agenda-setter under political-activist editor William Kristol in 2000. The *Standard* sold only 65,000 an issue, but it steered a lot of the Washington debate on how to execute foreign policy while the United States intensified its war on terrorism beginning in 2001.

Other highbrow journals include the *National Review*, founded by William Buckley, a leading conservative through the latter 20th century. Rich Lowry, who took over Buckley's mantle, calls the magazine's content "intellectual journalism." In an *American Journalism Review* interview, Lowry explained his magazine's role this way: "You make your argument and you change the feeling in the ether, that it will lead to a different action by the people who make policy." In the same article, a White House official acknowledged the intellectual magazines' influence: "It sets a kind of context, an atmosphere. You cannot connect the dots (on the precise impact), but people in the administration do pay attention. None of these decisions happens in a vacuum."

Washington reporters for major newspapers, magazines and the television networks track the intellectual magazines closely for trends, which compounds their influence. Much of the Sunday network television talk shows feature editors and writers from these journals.

Historically on the liberal side is the *Nation*. More iconoclastic is the *New Republic*. More widely read are the *Atlantic*, *Harper's* and the *New Yorker*, which sometimes are called **high-brow slicks**. None of these intellectual magazines has ever attracted sufficient advertising to meet its bills over the long term. Many are supported with infusions of philanthropic funding from time to time.

Nonnewsrack Magazines

STUDY PREVIEW Many organizations publish magazines for their members. Although these sponsored magazines, including *National Geographic*, *Modern Maturity* and *Smithsonian*, resemble consumer magazines, they generally are not available at newsracks. In fact, consumer magazines are far outnumbered by sponsored magazines and by trade journals.

Playboy
Widely imitated girlie/lifestyle men's magazine.

intellectual magazines
Small-circulation but influential journals, focusing mostly on political and social issues and the arts.

high-brow slicks
Magazines whose content is geared mostly at gadfly intellectuals, including literati.

Sponsored Magazines

The founders of the National Geographic Society decided in 1888 to put out a magazine to promote the society and build membership. The idea was to entice people to join by bundling a subscription with membership and then to use the dues to finance the society's research and expeditions. Within a few years the *National Geographic* had become a phenomenal success both in generating membership and as a profit center for the National Geographic Society. Today, more than 100 years old and with U.S. circulation at more than 9 million, the *Geographic* is the most widely recognized **sponsored magazine** in the nation. Other sponsored magazines include *Modern Maturity,* published by the American Association of Retired Persons for its members. Its circulation exceeds 20 million. Other major membership magazines include *Smithsonian,* by the Smithsonian Institute; *VFW,* by the Veterans of Foreign Wars; *American Legion;* and *Elks,* by the Elks lodge.

Many sponsored magazines carry advertising and are financially self-sufficient. In fact, the most successful sponsored magazines compete aggressively with consumer magazines for advertising. It is not unusual for an issue of *Smithsonian* to carry 100 pages of advertising.

While advertising has made some sponsored magazines into profit centers for their parent organizations, others come nowhere near breaking even. Typical is *Quill,* which the Society of Professional Journalists publishes as an organizational expense for the good of its membership. The society seeks advertising for *Quill,* but the magazine's relatively small readership has never attracted as much volume or the same types of advertising as the *National Geographic,* the *Smithsonian* or *Modern Maturity.*

Many sponsored magazines do not seek advertising. These include many university magazines, which are considered something that a university should publish as an institutional expense to disseminate information about research and scholarly activities and, not incidentally, to promote itself. Other sponsored magazines that typically do not carry advertising include publications for union members, in-house publications for employees, and company publications for customers. These publications do not have the public recognition of consumer magazines, but many are as slick and professional as consumer magazines. Altogether, they employ far more editors, photographers and writers than consumer magazines do.

Trade Journals

Every profession or trade has at least one magazine, or **trade journal,** for keeping abreast of what is happening in the field. In entertainment *Billboard* provides a solid journalistic coverage on a broad range of subjects in music: new recording releases, new acts, new technology and new merger deals. *Billboard* is essential reading for people in the music industry. About 4,000 trade journals cover a mind-boggling range of businesses and trades. Consider the diversity in these titles: *Rock and Dirt, Progressive Grocer, Plastics Technology, Hogs Today* and *Hardware Age.*

Like consumer magazines, the trades rely mostly on advertising for their income and profits. Some charge for subscriptions, but many are sent free to a carefully culled list of readers whom advertisers want to reach.

Many trade magazines are parts of companies that produce related publications, some with overlapping staffs. McGraw-Hill, the book publisher, produces more than 30 trade journals, including *Chemical Week* and *Modern Hospital.* Another trade

sponsored magazine
Generally nonnewsrack magazine, often member supported.

trade journal
Keeps members of profession, trade informed.

magazine company is Crain Communications, whose titles include *Advertising Age, AutoWeek, Electronic Media* and two dozen others.

Criticism of Trade Magazines

Many trade magazine companies, including McGraw-Hill and Crain, are recognized for honest, hard-hitting reporting of the industries they cover, but the trades have a mixed reputation. Some trade magazines are loaded with puffery exalting their advertisers and industries. For years, *Body Fashions,* formerly *Corset and Underwear Review,* unabashedly presented ads as news stories. As many trade journals do, it charged companies to run stories about them and covered only companies that were also advertisers. At some trades, the employees who solicit ads write news stories that echo the ads. These trades tend to be no more than boosters of the industries they pretend to cover. Kent MacDougall, writing in the *Wall Street Journal,* offered this especially egregious example: *America's Textile Reporter,* which promoted the textile industry from a management perspective, once dismissed the hazard of textile workers' contracting brown lung disease by inhaling cotton dust as "a thing brought up by venal doctors" at an international labor meeting in Africa, "where inferior races are bound to be afflicted by new diseases more superior people defeated years ago." At the time, in 1972, 100,000 U.S. textiles workers were afflicted with brown lung. Many trade magazines persist today in pandering to their trades, professions and industries, rather than approaching their subjects with journalistic truth-seeking and truth-telling.

Responsible trade journals are embarrassed by some of their brethren, many of which are upstarts put out by people with no journalistic experience or instincts. Because of this, and also because it takes relatively little capital to start a trade magazine, many bad trade magazines thrive. Several professional organizations, including the American Business Press and the Society of Business Press Editors, work to improve both their industry and its image. Even so, as former ABP President Charles Mill said, trades continue to be plagued "by fleabag outfits published in somebody's garage."

Newsletters

Even more focused than trade journals are subscription newsletters, a billion dollar industry. These newsletters are expensive, generally $600 to $1,000 a year, with some as much as $5,000. Why do people pay that much? Where else could Chamber of Commerce executives find the information that's in *Downtown Promotion Reporter?* And no other publication duplicates what's in *Food Chemical News, Beverage Digest* and *Inside Mortgage Finance.* John Farley, vice president of the largest newsletter company, Phillips Publishing, contends that newsletters are the purest form of journalism because they carry little or no advertising: "We're answerable to no one but our subscribers."

The first newsletter, launched in 1923, was a weekly update on government news for businesspeople called *Kiplinger Washington Newsletter.* It is still published. Today, more that 5,000 subscription newsletters are published in the United States. A few are daily, such as *Communication Daily,* which covers federal news on electronic media regulation. Not all are print products alone. *Subtext,* which tracks the book industry, puts out a Monday-morning e-mail update to keep subscribers abreast of developments between its biweekly mailed edition. Some newsletters now have subscription web sites.

Litigation Newsletters. Just out of college, Jon Hansen joined a newsletter company, Mealy Publications, and soon was reporting for two newsletters that follow lawsuits. One of them, *Emerging Drugs & Devices,* is published twice a month at 80 to 90 pages. It has 12 editors and reporters. Looking back at his early job hunting, Hansen, a Bucknell University history and English grad, is amused: "It is funny now. I look back at these law firm rejection letters, and they are from the same firms that call me now for information about various types of litigation."

Jon Hansen

Magazine Demassification

STUDY PREVIEW   Giant mass-audience magazines, led by *Life,* were major influences in their heyday, but television killed them off by offering larger audiences to advertisers. Today, the magazine industry thrives through demassification, the process of seeking audiences with narrow interests. Critics believe that demassification has changed the role of magazines in society for the worse.

Heyday of Mass Magazines

Magazines once were epitomized by *Life.* Henry Luce used the fortune he amassed from *Time* to launch *Life* in 1936. The magazine exceeded Luce's expectations. He had planned on an initial circulation of 250,000, but almost right away it was 500,000. *Life* was perfect for its time. At 10 cents a copy, *Life* was within the reach of almost everyone, even during the Great Depression. It had quality—fiction from the best authors of the day. It had daring—flamboyant photography that seemed to jump off its oversize pages. The term *photo essay* was a *Life* creation.

Imitators followed. *Look,* introduced in 1937, was a knockoff in the same oversize dimension as *Life.* The historic *Saturday Evening Post* and *Collier's* were revamped as oversize magazines.

Magazine Demassifica-tion. Advertisers favor magazines that are edited to specific audience interests that coincide with the advertisers' products. Fewer and fewer magazines geared to a general audience remain in business today.

Calvin and Hobbes by Bill Watterson

Assault from Television

The oversize mass-audience magazines do not exist today—at least not as they did in the old days. *Collier's,* bankrupt, published its final issue in 1956. Hemorrhaging money despite a circulation of 4 million, *Saturday Evening Post* ceased publication in 1969. In 1971 *Look* died. *Life* was not able to capitalize on the fact that it suddenly had less competition, and it went out of business the next year. It had lost $30 million over the previous three years. What had happened to the high-flying, oversize, mass-audience magazines? In a single word: television.

At its peak, *Life* had a circulation of 8.5 million, but in the 1950s the television networks had begun to deliver even bigger audiences to advertisers. The villain for the giant magazines was not merely television's audience size, but **CPM**—advertising jargon for cost per 1,000 readers, listeners or viewers (the M standing for the Roman numeral for 1,000). In 1970 a full-page advertisement in *Life* ran $65,000. For less money an advertiser could have one minute of network television and reach far more potential customers. CPM-conscious advertising agencies could not conscientiously recommend *Life*'s $7.75 CPM when the networks' CPM was $3.60, and advertisers shifted to television.

A Narrower Focus

With the demise of *Life*, doomsayers predicted that magazines were a dying breed of media. However, advertisers withdrew only from magazines with broad readerships. What they discovered was that although it was less expensive to use television to peddle universally used products such as detergents, grooming aids and packaged foods, television, geared at the time for mass audiences, was too expensive for products appealing to narrow groups. Today, relatively few magazines seek a truly mass audience. These include *Reader's Digest* and the Sunday magazine supplements.

Special-interest magazines, whose content focused on limited subjects and whose advertising rates were lower, fit the bill better than either television or the giant mass-audience magazines for reaching customers with special interests. For manufacturers of $7,000 stereo systems, for example, it made sense to advertise in a narrowly focused audiophile magazine such as *Stereo Review.* In the same way, neither mass-audience magazines nor television was a medium of choice for top-of-the-line racing skis, but ski magazines were ideal. For fancy cookware, *Food & Wine* made sense.

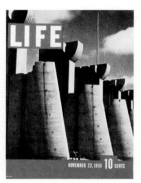

Life Defined America. Introduced in 1936, the giant general-interest magazine *Life* quickly found a huge following. The weekly's bold photojournalism emphasis, new at the time, appealed to a broad range of people. By the 1960s, however, *Life* was losing readers and advertisers to television. The parent company, Time Life, shut it down. The magazine was revived as a monthly in the 1980s but couldn't turn a profit and so was folded again. The brand name *Life* remained an asset, though, and Time Warner continued using it for occasional single-topic special editions.

CPM
Cost per thousand.

Among new magazines that emerged with the demassification in the 1960s were regional and city magazines, offering a geographically defined audience to advertisers. Some of these magazines, which usually bore the name of their city or region, including *New York*, *Texas Monthly* and *Washingtonian*, offered hard-hitting journalistic coverage of local issues. Many, though, focused on soft lifestyle subjects rather than antagonize powerful local interests and risk losing advertisers. Indeed, hypersensitivity to advertisers is a criticism of today's demassified magazines.

Critics of Demassification

Norman Cousins, once editor of the highbrow *Saturday Review,* criticized demassified magazines for betraying their traditional role of enriching the culture. Cousins said that specialization had diluted the intellectual role of magazines in the society. Advertisers, he said, were shaping magazines' journalistic content for their commercial purposes—in contrast to magazine editors independently deciding content with loftier purposes in mind.

Scholar Dennis Holder put this "unholy alliance" of advertisers and readers this way: "The readers see themselves as members of small, and in some sense, elite groups—joggers, for example, or cat lovers—and they want to be told that they are terribly neat people for being in those groups. Advertisers, of course, want to reinforce the so-called positive self-image too, because joggers who feel good about themselves tend to buy those ridiculous suits and cat lovers who believe lavishing affection on their felines is a sign of warmth and sincerity are the ones who purchase cute little cat sweaters, or are they cat's pajamas." Magazine editors and writers, Holder said, are caught in the symbiotic advertiser-reader alliance and have no choice but to go along.

Norman Cousins and Dennis Holder were right that most consumer magazines today tend to a frothy mix of light, upbeat features, with little that is thoughtful or hard-hitting. However, most readers want to know about other people, particularly celebrities, and about a great many trendy topics. And advertisers want to reach those readers, preferably by steering clear of any controversial magazine coverage that might hurt sales. So profitability for most magazines and their advertisers is locked into providing information their target audiences are interested in rather than serving an indefinable "public interest," which might sometimes be controversial. The emphasis on profits and demassification saddens a number of people who believe that magazines have a higher calling than a cash register. These critics would agree with Cousins, who warned that emphasizing the superficial just because it sells magazines is a betrayal of the social trust that magazine publishers once held. "The purpose of a magazine," he said, "is not to tell you how to fix a leaky faucet, but to tell you what the world is about."

There is no question that demassification works against giving readers any kind of global view. In demassified magazines for auto enthusiasts, as an example, road test articles typically wax as enthusiastically as the advertisements about new cars. These demassified magazines, edited to target selected audiences and thereby attract advertisers, make no pretense of broadening their readers' understanding of substantive issues by exploring diverse perspectives. The narrowing of magazine editorial content appears destined to continue, not only because it is profitable but also because new technologies, such as AOL Time Warner's geodemographic TargetSelect program, make it possible for magazine publishers to identify narrower and narrower segments of the mass audience and then to gear their publications to those narrower and narrower interests.

New Competition

An ominous sign for magazines is the cable television industry, which is eating into magazine advertising with an array of demassified channels, such as the ESPN sports channel, the Arts & Entertainment network and the Bloomberg financial news network. The demassified cable channels are picking up advertisers that once used magazines almost exclusively to reach narrow slices of the mass audience with a presumed interest in their products and services.

Another drain on magazine revenue is the growth of direct-mail advertising. Using sophisticated analysis of potential customer groups, advertisers can mail brochures, catalogs, fliers and other material, including video pitches, directly to potential customers at their homes or places of business. Every dollar that goes into direct-mail campaigns is a dollar that in an earlier period went into magazines and other traditional advertising media.

Web Magazines

Consumer and trade magazines adapted quickly to digital delivery in the late 1990s with web editions. Time Warner created a massive web site, Pathfinder, for *Time, Sports Illustrated, People* and its other magazines. With substantial original content, Pathfinder wasn't merely an online version of Time Warner magazines but a distinctive product. There were hopes that advertisers would flock to online magazine sites and make them profitable, but ad revenue only trickled in. In 1998

media online

ABC: The Audit Bureau of Circulations is responsible for certifying the circulations of over 3,000 magazines and newspapers around the world.
www.accessabc.com

Folio: The magazine for magazine management. Use the site's database to check out the Folio 500—the top-ranked 500 magazines—on their site.
www.mediacentral.com/Folio

Magazine Publishing: How a magazine is put together.
www.atompublishing.co.uk/issues/general/print.html

Zine. The giant software developer Microsoft moved into developing media content in the 1990s with, among other things, the online magazine *Slate.* To edit the magazine, Microsoft hired Michael Kinsley, known for his commentaries on CNN and his editorship of the political and cultural journal *New Republic.* Kinsley attracted a stable of prestigious, clever writers for the site.

Eustace Tilley. The *New Yorker* remembers its origins with an annual anniversary cover featuring Eustace Tilley, a character by Rea Irvin intended to capture the sophistication of the magazine on its first cover in 1925. The *New Yorker* remains an intelligent, witty and often irreverent weekly whose substantive coverage of political, social, cultural and other issues has maintained its respect among devoted readers.

highbrow slicks
Cerebral magazines, edited for the intelligentsia.

Pathfinder went to subscriptions to supplement the meager advertising revenues. An access code was issued to *Entertainment Weekly* subscribers for an extra $30 a year. For the *Money* site the fare was $30 to subscribers and $50 to everybody else. All in all, the Pathfinder exercise was not a success. Microsoft attempted to turn its esoteric, pop *Slate* from a free site to a subscription magazine, but lack of interest on the part of web surfers and competition from free sites forced Microsoft to make *Slate* free again. Time Warner also gave up on web subscriptions, dismantled Pathfinder and set up individual sites for its brand-name magazines. Meanwhile, the number of web sites offering magazine-type content continues to grow. The proliferation includes thousands of hand-crafted *zines*, as they're called, on the web.

Evaluating Magazines

STUDY PREVIEW Circulation and advertising revenue are measures of a magazine's populist success. More difficult is finding magazines that regularly fulfill their potential to examine significant issues and make an enduring contribution to a better society.

Populist Measures

Measures of commercials success in the magazine industry are easy to find. Circulation is one measure. *Parade, USA Weekend, Modern Maturity* and *Reader's Digest* all score well by that measure. Even more telling as a populist gauge of success is advertising revenue. Advertisers use all kinds of sophisticated research and analysis to determine where their ad dollars are most effectively spent. *People* draws more advertising revenue than any other magazine, $627 million a year—11.6 percent ahead of *Time,* the distant second.

Quality Measures

Critics say that commercial measures recognize magazines that pander to consumerism. Certainly, many magazines today work hard at being magnets for audience niches and for advertisers that seek access to those niches. *Better Homes & Gardens,* for example, offers a lot of predictable content on homemaking that a certain segment of consumers want, and advertisers are lined up to place ads in the magazines to reach those consumers. But is *BH&G* a magazine that makes people think? Or that offers insights into fundamentals issues of human existence? Or that contributes to a better world in a broad and enduring sense? Elitists would fault it on all those scores. *Better Homes & Gardens* may be immensely popular and make a lot of money, but, say elitists, it fails at realizing its potential to improve society.

What, then, are measures of excellence that would meet the standards of elitists?

Cerebral magazines with long records of commentary and analysis, often in the vanguard of thinking on enduring issues, include *Harper's* and *Atlantic.* Sometimes called **highbrow slicks,** these magazines steer an editorial course that's not beholden to narrow consumer niches or advertisers. The thrust is on social, economic, political and artistic and cultural issues, often analyzed at great length by leading authorities. It should be no surprise that Vannevar Bush's thoughts on possibilities for a worldwide web appeared in the *Atlantic* in 1945—almost 50 years ahead of Tim

Media Databank

Magazine Advertising Revenue

Circulation and advertising revenue are not always in sync. A weekly with less circulation than a monthly may carry more pages of advertising and generate more revenue. The weekly *People,* for example, carries far more advertising pages a year than the monthly *Reader's Digest.* Also, some magazines deliver an especially attractive audience segment to advertisers, like *Business Week, Forbes* and *Fortune,* all in the Top 10 for ad revenue but hardly in circulation.

People	$627 million
Time	562 million
Sports Illustrated	555 million
TV Guide	454 million
Better Homes & Gardens	410 million
Newsweek	400 million
Business Week	362 million
PC Magazine	314 million
Forbes	265 million
Fortune	254 million

Berners-Lee's invention of the web. The *New Yorker,* a weekly, prides itself on regularly breaking ground on significant issues in articles that run as long as the editors think is necessary, sometimes the length of a small book.

Outside of highbrow slicks, significant articles sprout occasionally in commercially oriented magazines. *Time* and *Newsweek* excerpt important new books from time to time. *Wired,* which focuses on future issues, gives cutting-edge thinkers all the space they need to explore their thoughts. Serious journalism appears occasionally in *Esquire, Outside* and other magazines amid all the advertiser-friendly pap but hardly as a staple.

The ideological magazines, like *New Republic, National Review* and *Nation,* frequently are cerebral, but partisanship often clouds their focus.

In short, it's hard to find magazines that consistently meet elitists' standards. The **National Magazine Awards,** granted by the American Society of Magazine Editors, recognize broad categories of excellence, but some awards, as for design, don't necessarily address the kind of measures elitists prefer. Awards for individual articles and authors are a starting point for a trip to the library to look up the piece, not a guide to which magazines are worth subscribing to because they deliver consistent excellence.

Media Future: Magazines

The future for magazines as a distinct mass medium is not clear. Hundreds of magazines have established web sites, where people can call up digital versions that physically bear no resemblance to the slick paper and stitching that we normally associate with magazines.

Too, the traditional content distinction between magazines and other media is vaporizing. Newspapers are offering more and more coverage of specialized issues and events that once were the province of magazines. This shift in newspaper content,

National Magazine Awards
Granted by the American Society of Magazine Editors.

which has been under way for at least 20 years, once prompted social commentator Norman Cousins to say, "The best magazine articles in the U.S. today are appearing not in magazines but in newspapers."

Conglomeration-driven convergence also is undermining magazines as a distinct medium. The joint projects of *Time* magazine and the CNN television network, now both owned by AOL Time Warner, are an example. *Newsweek* and the New York *Times* and other media brand names also have content-sharing arrangements with other media.

What can be said for sure is that many magazines are strong brand names—*Ladies' Home Journal, Esquire, Sports Illustrated, Rolling Stone.* Those names will survive. Whether the magazine itself makes it through the 21st century as a print media product is less certain. It may be that the coming technological transformation of magazines is being delayed by a swell in advertising generated by the roaring economy that began in the mid-1990s.

chapter wrap-up

The magazine industry once was defined by giant general interest magazines, epitomized by *Life,* that offered something for everybody. Advertisers soured on these oversized giants when television offered more potential customers per advertising dollar. Magazines shifted to more specialized packages. The focused approach worked. Magazines found advertisers who were seeking readers with narrow interests. Now, as other media—particularly television—are demassifying, magazines stand to lose advertisers, which poses new challenges.

Questions for Review

1. How have magazines contributed to U.S. culture?
2. How have magazines been innovative as a journalistic and as a visual medium?
3. How do sponsored magazines and trade journals differ from the consumer magazines available at newsracks?
4. Why are most magazines edited for the special interests of targeted audiences?
5. What is the status of demassification in the magazine industry?
6. Are magazines losing their influence as a shaper of the culture? Explain your answer.
7. Why do elitists criticize magazines that are edited for niches of consumers?

Questions for Critical Thinking

1. What characteristics do these magazine founders have in common: Sara Josepha Hale, Henry Luce, and DeWitt and Lila Wallace.
2. When U.S. magazines came into their own in the 1820s, they represented a mass medium that was distinct from the existing book and newspaper media. How were magazines different?
3. How was the U.S. identity that emerged in the 19th century fostered by magazines?
4. To some people, the word *muckraking* has a negative tone. Can you make the case that it should be regarded positively? Can you also argue the opposite?
5. Discuss the role of these innovators in contributing to magazines as a visual medium: Gilbert Grosvenor, Margaret Bourke-White and Henry Luce.

6. Can you name three consumer magazines in each of these categories: newsmagazines, the Seven Sisters, men's magazines?

7. The late Norman Cousins, a veteran social commentator and magazine editor, worried that trends in the magazine industry were undermining the historic role that magazines have had in enriching the culture. What is your response to Cousins's concerns?

8. Name three magazines of which elitists would approve and explain why.

Keeping Up to Date

Folio is a trade journal on magazine management. Among major newspapers that track magazine issues in a fairly consistent way are the New York *Times,* the *Wall Street Journal* and *USA Today.*

Wordless Society Ahead? No, says futurist George Gilder, not even the generation raised on MTV can communicate effectively without words. Visuals can enhance but not replace them, he says.

4

Newspapers

Do newspapers and other word-based print media have a future? Media seer George Gilder puts his money on word-based media over television, which relies on visuals to tell stories.

As Gilder sees it, people who see the communication of the future as primarily video have missed the fact that video works better than words for only an extremely narrow range of messages: "Video is most effective in conveying shocks and sensations and appealing to prurient interests of large miscellaneous audiences. Images easily excel in blasting through to the glandular substances of the human community; there's nothing like a body naked or bloody or both to arrest the eye." However, human communication goes far beyond shock scenes and sensual appeals, he says, noting that people communicate mostly through words.

The printed product you receive on your doorstep every morning may seem like a technological dinosaur from Johannes Gutenberg's time. The fact, however, is that newspapers are well into the digital age. Reporters dip into digitized data for source material and write stories on computers. Editors edit stories and lay out pages electronically. It is in final production that old technology reigns, with multimillion-dollar presses that consume tons and tons of newsprint and barrels and barrels of ink. In delivery too, with minimum-wage carriers entrusted to get the product to readers, newspapers lag.

That is changing. In the vanguard of changing to electronic production, rather than printing, and to electronic delivery, rather than "paperboys and the local newsstand," are newspapers ranging from modest circulation weeklies in the Dakotas to the lofty New York *Times*. Some online editions offer only word-for-word versions of what is in the print editions or just selected stories, but some newspapers are repackaging stories to take advantage of opportunities that electronic delivery offers. Still, true to their tradition, the online newspapers remain word-based. Visuals are a useful accoutrement but seldom the heart of the message.

Even as newspaper circulation withers, as it has in recent years, newspaper companies will survive. They are well positioned to dominate the future of news because, in almost every community, they have the largest, most sophisticated staffs for gathering and telling local news. That resource is unmatched by even the largest television or other news operations.

Importance of Newspapers

STUDY PREVIEW Newspapers are the primary mass medium from which people receive news. In most cities no other news source comes close to the local newspaper's range and depth of coverage. This contributes to the popularity and influence of newspapers.

Newspaper Industry Dimensions

The newspaper industry dwarfs other news media by almost every measure. More than one out of three people in the United States reads a newspaper every day, far more than tune in the network news on television in the evening. The data are staggering:

- About 1,570 daily newspapers put out 52.8 million copies a day, more on Sundays. Because each copy is passed along to an average of 2.2 people, daily newspapers reach 127 million people a day.
- Weekly newspapers put out 50 million copies. With their estimated pass-along circulation of four people a copy, these newspapers reach somewhere around 200 million people a week.

Perhaps because television has stolen the glitz and romance that newspapers once had, the significance of newspapers is easy to miss. But the newspaper industry is large by every measure. In an article marveling at an issue of a newspaper as "the daily creation," the Washington *Post*'s Richard Harwood, writing about his own newspaper, said: "Roughly 11,000 people are involved in the production and distribution each day, enough bodies to fill all the billets of an Army light infantry division." Although Harwood stretched to include even the delivery boys and girls in his startling number, his point is valid: In Washington and everywhere else, newspapers far outdistance other news media in the number of people who gather, edit and disseminate news.

Newspapers are the medium of choice for more advertising than competing media. For local advertising, daily newspapers attracted $38.9 billion in 1998. Over-air television stations and cable systems were a distant second at $14.6 billion. Nationwide, including network television's tremendous advertising revenue, newspapers still lead with $44.3 billion in advertising revenue compared to television's $39.2 billion.

Except for brief downturns in the overall economy and an occasional exceptional situation, daily newspapers have been consistently profitable enterprises through the 20th century. Less than double-digit returns on investment are uncommon. As a mass medium, the newspaper is not to be underrated.

Content Diversity and Depth

In most communities, newspapers cover more news at greater depth than competing media. A metropolitan daily such as the Washington *Post* typically may carry 300 items and much more on Sundays—more than any Washington television or radio station and at greater length. City magazines in Washington, for example, offer more depth on selected stories, but the magazines are published relatively infrequently and run relatively few articles. Nationally, no broadcast organization comes close to the number of stories or the depth of the two major national newspapers, the *Wall Street Journal* and *USA Today*.

Newspapers have a rich mix of content—news, advice, comics, opinion, puzzles and data. It's all there to tap into at will. Some people go right for the stock market tables, others to sports or a favorite columnist. Unlike radio and television, you don't have to wait for what you want.

People like newspapers. Some talk affectionately of curling up in bed on a leisurely Sunday morning with their paper. The news and features give people something in common to talk about. Newspapers are important in people's lives, and as a medium they adapt to changing lifestyles. The number of Sunday newspapers, for example, grew from 600 in the 1970s to almost 900 today, reflecting an increase in people's weekend leisure time for reading and shopping. Ads in Sunday papers are their guide for shopping excursions.

All this does not mean that the newspaper industry is not facing problems from competing media, new technology and ongoing lifestyle shifts. But to date, newspapers have reacted to change with surprising effectiveness. To offset television's inroads, newspapers have put new emphasis on being a visual medium and have shed their drab graphics for color and aesthetics. To accommodate the work schedule transition of Americans over recent decades from factory jobs starting at 7 a.m. to service jobs starting at 9 a.m., newspapers have emphasized morning editions, now that more people have a little extra time in the morning, and phased out afternoon editions, because more people are at work later in the day. Knowing that the days of ink-on-paper technology are limited, the newspaper industry is examining **electronic delivery** methods for the 21st century.

Some problems are truly daunting, such as the aversion of many young people to newspapers. Also, chain ownership has raised fundamental questions about how well newspapers can do their work and still meet the profit expectations of distant shareholders.

Newspaper Chain Ownership

STUDY PREVIEW   Through the 20th century, newspapers have been incredibly profitable, which, for better or worse, encouraged chain ownership. Today, chains own most U.S. newspapers.

Trend Toward Chains

Reasoning that he could multiply profits by owning multiple newspapers, **William Randolph Hearst** put together a chain of big-city newspapers in the late 1880s. Although Hearst's chain was not the first, his empire became the model in the public's mind for much that was both good and bad about **newspaper chains.** Like

electronic delivery
Sending news to readers' computer screens.

William Randolph Hearst
Chain owner who dictated contents of all his newspapers.

newspaper chain
Company that owns several newspapers.

Media Databank

Newspaper Chains

Here are the largest U.S. newspaper chains, ranked by circulation, with a sample of their major properties:

	Daily Circulation	Number of Dailies
Gannett	5.5 million	82
USA Today, Des Moines *Register,* Detroit *News*		
Knight-Ridder	3.6 million	27
Detroit *Free Press,* Miami *Herald*		
Newhouse	2.9 million	26
Cleveland *Plain Dealer,* Newark *Star Ledger*		
Tribune Company	5.2 million	30
Chicago *Tribune,* Los Angeles *Times,* Baltimore *Sun*		
Dow Jones	2.4 million	8
Wall Street Journal, Ottaway Newspapers		
New York Times	1.7 million	26
New York *Times,* Boston *Globe,* Florida dailies		

Gannett
A leading U.S. newspaper chain with 90 dailies.

other chains, Hearst also expanded into magazines, radio and television. The trend toward chain ownership continues, and today 160 chains own four of every five dailies in the United States. Chain ownership is also coming to dominate weeklies, which had long been a bastion of independent ownership.

Newspaper profitability skyrocketed in the 1970s and 1980s, which prompted chains to buy up locally owned newspapers, sometimes in bidding frenzies. Single-newspaper cities were especially attractive because no competing media could match a local newspaper's large audience. It was possible for new owners to push ad rates up rapidly, and local retailers, with no place else to put ads, had to go along. The profit potential was enhanced because production costs were falling dramatically with less labor-intensive back-shop procedures, computerized typesetting and other automation. Profits were dramatic. Eight newspaper companies tracked by *Forbes* magazine from 1983 to 1988 earned the equivalent of 23.9 percent interest on a bank account. Only soft drink companies did better.

Federal tax law also accelerated the shift from family-owned to chain-owned newspapers in two ways. Inheritance taxes made it easier for families that owned independent newspapers to sell the papers than to leave them to their heirs. Also, chains were very eager to acquire more newspapers because they could avoid paying tax on income from their existing properties if they reinvested it in new holdings.

The **Gannett** media conglomerate's growth typifies how newspapers became chains and then grew into cross-media conglomerates. In 1906 the chain consisted of six upstate New York newspapers. By 1982 Gannett had grown to more than 80 dailies, all profitable medium-size newspapers. Swimming in money, Gannett launched *USA Today.* Gannett not only absorbed *USA Today*'s tremendous start-up costs for several years but also had enough spare cash to outbid other companies for expensive metropolitan newspapers. In 1985 and 1986 Gannett paid $1.4 billion for the Detroit *News,* Des Moines *Register* and Louisville *Courier-Journal.* Along the way, Gannett acquired Combined Communications, which owned 20 broadcasting stations. Today Gannett owns 82 daily newspapers, 39 weeklies, 16 radio and eight television stations, the largest billboard company in the nation and the Louis Harris polling organization. It bought a Sunday newspaper magazine supplement, *This Week,* beefed it up and renamed it *USA Weekend.* No longer just a newspaper chain, Gannett has become a mass media conglomerate.

Assessing Chain Ownership

Is chain ownership good for newspapers? The question raised in Hearst's time was whether diverse points of view were as likely to get into print if ownership were concentrated in fewer and fewer hands. That concern has dissipated as chains have become oriented more to profits than to participating in public dialogue. Executives at the headquarters of most chains focus on management and leave coverage and editorials to local editors. While **local autonomy** is consistent with U.S. journalistic values, a corporate focus on profits raises a dark new question: Are chains so myopic about profits that they forget good journalism? The answer is that the emphasis varies among chains.

JOURNALISTIC EMPHASIS.   Some chains, such as **Knight-Ridder,** whose properties include the Miami *Herald,* the Philadelphia *Inquirer* and the Detroit *Free Press,* are known for a strong corporate commitment to high-quality journalism. In 1988 Knight-Ridder newspapers won six of the 14 Pulitzer Prizes, including one by the Charlotte *Observer* for revealing the misuse of funds by the PTL ministry that opened up the televangelism scandals.

BALANCED EMPHASIS.   Most chains are known for undistinguished though profitable newspapers. This is an apt description for Gannett, the largest U.S. chain, measured by circulation.

PROFIT EMPHASIS.   Several chains, including Donrey and American Publishing, have a pattern of cutting costs aggressively, reducing staffs and trimming news coverage. It is not uncommon for a new chain owner to fire veteran reporters and editors, in some cases almost halving the staff. To save newsprint, some chains cut back the number of pages. They hire inexperienced reporters right out of college, pay them poorly and encourage them to move on after a few months so they can be replaced by other eager but inexperienced, and cheap, new reporters. The result is a reporting staff that lacks the kind of local expertise that is necessary for good journalism. Only the shareholders benefit.

In general, the following realities of chain ownership work against strong local journalistic enterprise:

ABSENTEE OWNERSHIP.   Chain executives are under pressure to run profitable enterprises, which works against good, aggressive journalism that can strain a newsroom budget. Under **absentee ownership** the top chain executives do not live in the communities that are short-changed by decisions to emphasize low-cost news.

TRANSIENT MANAGEMENT.   The local managers of newspapers owned by chains tend to be career climbers who have no long-term stake in the community their

local autonomy
Independence from chain headquarters.

Knight-Ridder
Newspaper chain widely respected for journalism.

absentee ownership
Company headquarters in a faraway city.

newspaper serves. With **transient management** these people generally are not promoted from within a newspaper but are appointed by corporate headquarters. Generally they have short-term goals to look good to their corporate bosses so that they can be promoted to better-paying jobs with more responsibility at bigger newspapers in the chain.

WEAK ENTRY-LEVEL SALARIES. The focus of newspaper chains on enhancing profits to keep costs down has worked against strong salaries for journalists. By 2001 entry-level salaries typically were $17,000 to $19,000 at small chain-owned dailies. The result has been a brain drain. Many talented reporters and editors leave newspapers for more lucrative jobs in public relations and other fields.

HIGH NEWSROOM TURNOVER. Cost-conscious policies at many chain newspapers encourage newsroom employees to move on after a few pay raises so that they can be replaced by rookies at entry-level salaries. This turnover can denude a newsroom of people who are knowledgeable about the community the newspaper serves, thus eroding coverage.

Evaluating Newspapers

STUDY PREVIEW   Quantitative measures of a newspaper success include circulation and penetration. How to judge quality? Rankings and awards are indicators, although they are imperfect. You yourself can evaluate whether the newspaper gives adequate resources to coverage.

Circulation and Penetration

Once upon a time, measuring a newspaper's marketplace success against its competition was simple. The paper with the largest circulation won. Today, though, hardly any cities have competing dailies. Even so, numbers count. Is circulation growing? Declining? Because almost every newspaper reports its circulation to an auditing agency, you can track circulation year to year, even quarter to quarter.

Even more significant comparative data come from comparing **penetration.** Penetration is the percentage of people or households that get the paper. The ABC circulation auditing agency doesn't collect penetration data, but fairly reliable penetration is easy to calculate: Divide the population by the circulation. Seeking precise penetration data can get tricky. How you measure the circulation area, for example, can make a difference. There are other variables too. Even so, simple math can give you a good indicator of whether a newspaper's acceptance in the marketplace is improving.

Overall, penetration has slipped badly. In 1950, 356 copies of daily newspapers were printed for every 1,000 people in the United States. By 1995 the number was down to 234—a 34.2 percent drop. The numbers are even worse than they look because the decline has occurred while the nation's population has grown. Daily circulation, at 55.9 million today, has slipped 3 million since 1960—a period when the United States added 95 million people.

Quality Indicators

Being subjective, indicators of quality are problematic. *Time* magazine once did an often-quoted annual ranking. Now carefully considered rankings occasionally show up in *American Journalism Review* and other media critique journals. In these

transient management
High turnover among executives.

penetration
Percentage of persons or households that a newspaper reaches in its circulation area.

rankings, consider the fine print so you know the criteria that were used. Also, check for the qualities that impressed the evaluator.

Awards are an indicator too, though hardly perfect. The most prestigious award, the Pulitzer, is not the result of what most people assume—a thorough search for the best. The Pulitzer committee, like most awards groups, looks only at nominated work. Some newspapers, including the Los Angeles *Times,* have full-time employees who do nothing but assemble and submit glossy nomination materials.

With most journalistic contests accepting only self-nominated works, does bad work sometimes win? No, the quality of submissions is almost always high. Eager for bragging rights, most newspapers enter worthy pieces. But not all publications enter, so questions can be raised whether it's truly the best that's even considered.

Too, awards committees seldom do much legwork. Occasionally, as a result, there is an embarrassment. Everyone involved is still red-faced over the 1981 Pulitzer awarded to the Washington *Post*'s Janet Cooke. Afterward, it was learned that Cooke had fabricated her news story. The *Post* made her give the prize back. She left the newspaper and faded into journalistic obscurity.

Here are some quality indicators:

NEWS HOLE.   What percentage of the space in the newspaper goes to news? This is called the **news hole.** From a reader's perspective the bigger the news hole, the better. Discount postal rates are available only to newspapers that cap advertising at 70 percent. Many publications push the limit to maximize revenue, sometimes shorting readers on news coverage, commentary and other non-ad content.

CONTENT.   Because local coverage is more costly than stories from news agencies, a good measure of quality is whether a newspaper has extensive local coverage or loads up with wire stories. Is local coverage thorough? Is it accurate? Does the newspaper have its own state capitol reporter? Its own Washington bureau?

STAFF.   What kind of professionals report and edit the newspaper? Seasoned reporters who know the community well? Or beginners? Does the newspaper offer competitive salaries for the best talent? Salary scales generally are available on request at newspapers with collective-bargaining agreements.

MANAGEMENT.   Does top management have a permanent stake in the community? Or does leadership rotate in and out, with individuals focusing on making a name in order to move up in the corporate structure?

National Dailies

STUDY PREVIEW   Although the United States is a country of mostly local newspapers, three dailies are edited exclusively for a national audience. The *Wall Street Journal* is the most solidly established with most of its readership anchored in business and finance. The flashy *USA Today* has found a solid following. Prospects for the respected *Christian Science Monitor* are less certain.

Wall Street Journal

The *Wall Street Journal,* until recently the nation's largest newspaper, began humbly. **Charles Dow** and **Edward Jones** went into business in 1882. They roamed

news hole
Space in a publication after ads are inserted.

Wall Street Journal
Financially successful U.S. national daily.

Charles Dow
Wall Street Journal cofounder.

Edward Jones
Wall Street Journal cofounder.

Media Databank

Newsroom Salaries

Reporters, photographers and copy editors at 134 U.S. and Canadian newspapers are represented in contract negotiations by the **Newspaper Guild.** Reporters at the New York *Times* had the most lucrative Guild contract in 1999, almost $1,300 a week, $67,000 a year, with two years' experience. Many earn more for merit, in bonuses and for working odd hours.

    The lowest Guild salary for experienced reporters was $346 a week at the Battle Creek, Michigan, *Enquirer.*

    The Guild average was $711, almost $37,000 a year. The average for all newspapers, including more than 1,400 nonunion papers, is impossible to calculate because there's no reliable data-gathering mechanism.

	Salary per week
New York *Times*	$1,280 after two years
Boston *Globe*	1,090 after five years
Philadelphia *Inquirer* and *Daily News*	1,110 after five years
Chicago *Sun Times*	1,100 after five years
St. Louis *Post-Dispatch*	1,030 after five years
Minneapolis *Star Tribune*	1,020 after five years
Cleveland *Plain Dealer*	1,000 after four years
Honolulu *Advertiser* and *Star-Bulletin*	1,000 after five years
Pittsburgh *Post-Gazette*	990 after five years
St. Paul, Minn., *Pioneer Press*	980 after five years

Newspaper Guild
Collective bargaining agent at 134 U.S., Canadian newspapers.

Barney Kilgore
Created the modern *Wall Street Journal.*

the New York financial district for news and scribbled notes by hand, which they sent by courier to their clients. As more information-hungry investors signed up, the service was expanded into a newsletter. In 1889 the *Wall Street Journal* was founded. Advertisers eager to reach *Journal* readers bought space in the newspaper, which provided revenue to hire correspondents in Boston, Philadelphia and Washington. By 1900 circulation had reached 10,000, and it grew to 30,000 by 1940.

    The *Wall Street Journal* might have remained a relatively small albeit successful business paper had it not been for the legendary **Barney Kilgore,** who joined the newspaper's San Francisco bureau in 1929. Within two years Kilgore was the *Journal*'s

Drab but Read. The *Wall Street Journal,* the nation's largest daily, relies on its reputation for accurate and thorough reporting and good writing to attract readers. Every day the front page looks the same, with lengthy general interest stories beginning in Columns 1, 4 and 6. Barney Kilgore shaped the *Journal*'s distinctive look and approach to coverage after taking over as editor in the 1930s. Circulation today exceeds 1.8 million.

Barney Kilgore

news editor and in a position to shift the newspaper's journalistic direction. Kilgore's formula was threefold:

- Simplify the *Journal*'s business coverage into plain English without sacrificing thoroughness.
- Provide detailed coverage of government but without the jargon that plagued Washington reporting most of the time.
- Expand the definition of the *Journal*'s field of coverage from "business" to "everything that somehow relates to earning a living."

The last part of the formula, expanded coverage, was a risk. Critics told Kilgore that the newspaper's existing readers might switch to other financial papers if they thought the *Journal* was slighting business. Kilgore's vision, however, was not to reduce business coverage but to seek business angles in other fields and cover them too. It worked. Under Kilgore's leadership, *Journal* circulation reached 100,000 in 1947. When Kilgore died in 1967, a year after retiring as chairman of Dow Jones, publisher of the *Journal,* circulation had passed 1 million. Today, with circulation approaching 2 million, the *Journal* is the largest U.S. daily.

Although the *Journal* is edited for a general audience as well as for traditional business readers, it does not pander to a downscale audience. It carries no comics or horoscope columns, and its sports and entertainment coverage tends to focus on the front office and the box office. A mark of the *Journal* is its grayness. The only art on Page 1 is an occasional one-column etching. Inside, advertisements are lavish with photography, but line art dominates the news sections. In 1991 the *Journal* began accepting limited color in advertisements, but even so, the visual impression, a correct one, is that the *Journal* is a newspaper for readers to take seriously. Advertisers take the *Journal* seriously too, knowing its readers' average household income is $147,000 a year. No other newspaper comes close to delivering such a prosperous audience.

The *Journal* puts significant resources into reporting. It is not unusual for a reporter to be given six weeks for research on a major story. This digging gives the *Journal* big breaks on significant stories. In 1988, for example, the *Journal* reported, in a lengthy biographical piece on evangelist Pat Robertson, who was seeking the Republican presidential nomination, that one of his children was conceived out of wedlock. It was a revelation that affected the course of the campaign, especially in view of Robertson's moral posture on family issues. Although a serious newspaper, the *Journal* is neither stodgy nor prudish. Lengthy Page 1 pieces range from heavy-duty coverage of national politics to such diverse and unexpected stories as a black widow spider outbreak in Phoenix, archaeological research into human turds to understand lifestyles of lost civilizations, and how the admiral of landlocked Bolivia's navy keeps busy.

The *Wall Street Journal* has 500 editors and reporters, but not all are at the newspaper's Manhattan headquarters. The *Journal* has 37 foreign and 14 domestic bureaus, and its European and Asian editions have their own staffs.

The domestic U.S. editions are edited in New York, and page images are transmitted via orbiting satellite to 17 printing plants across the nation, so the paper is on the street and in the mail on the day of publication. Advertisers may pick and choose the editions in which they want their ads to appear.

The European and Asian editions are edited separately but lean heavily on the domestic U.S. edition for stories. The foreign editions are printed in Hong Kong, Japan, Malaysia, the Netherlands and Switzerland.

Graphics Innovator. Since its founding in 1981, *USA Today* has had a profound impact on many other newspapers. The most obvious influence has been to establish newspapers as a strong visual medium with color and graphics integrated with words. The newspaper's weather coverage and high story counts also have been widely imitated. *USA Today* is designed for travelers and as a "second buy" for people who have already read their hometown daily. Subscriptions are only a small part of *USA Today*'s circulation. Most sales are in distinctive TV-shaped newsracks and in airports, hotels and places where travelers pick it up for a fix on the news. Guaranteed in every issue are at least a few sentences of what's happening in news and sports from every state in the Union.

Copyright © 2000 USA Today.

Allen Neuharth

USA Today
Garnett national daily founded in 1981.

Allen Neuharth
Creator of *USA Today.*

The challenge for the *Journal* has been finding a balance between its original forte—covering business—and its expanding coverage of broader issues. It is a precarious balance. Numerous business publications, including *Business Week* and the Los Angeles-based *Investor's Daily,* vie for the same readers and advertisers with compacter packages, and numerous other national publications, including the newsmagazines, offer general coverage. So far, the *Journal* has succeeded with a gradual broadening of general coverage without losing its business readers.

USA Today

A strict format, snappy visuals and crisp writing give *USA Today* an air of confidence and the trappings of success, and the newspaper has its strengths. In less than a decade, circulation reached 1.6 million. By 2001 *USA Today* was at 2.2 million, passing the *Wall Street Journal.* Gannett executives exude sureness about long-term prospects. The optimism is underscored by the confident if not brash Page 1 motto: "The Nation's Newspaper."

USA Today has had a significant impact since its founding. Like the *Wall Street Journal, USA Today* seeks well-heeled readers, although in different ways. *USA Today* has relatively few subscribers, going instead after single-copy sales, mostly to business travelers who are on the road and want a quick fix on the news. Many of *USA Today*'s sales are at airport newsracks, where many buyers are corporate executives and middle-management travelers away from home. Gannett offers deep discounts to upscale hotels to buy the papers in bulk and slip them under guests' doors as a free morning courtesy. Stories strain to be lively and upbeat to make the experience of reading the paper a positive one. In contrast to the *Wall Street Journal,* almost all *USA Today* stories are short, which diverts little of a reader's time from pressing business. The brevity and crispness of *USA Today,* combined with the enticing graphics, have led some critics to liken the newspaper to fast food and dub it "McNewspaper"—not bad for you but not as nourishing as, say, the *Wall Street Journal.*

Despite its critics, *USA Today* has been true to founder **Allen Neuharth**'s original concept. Neuharth wanted to create a distinctive newspaper that would be positioned below the *Wall Street Journal* and the New York *Times,* both of which are available nationally, and yet provide a kind of coverage not available in the metropolitan dailies. Because many corporate travelers change jobs fairly often and make career moves from state to state, Neuharth decided to provide at least one news and one sports item every day from every state in the union. Not uncommon, for example, are items on Little League baseball championships in Idaho, if that happens to be the major sports event in Idaho on a particular day. Such tidbits from home are valuable to business travelers who have been on the road for days and cannot find such home-state items in local dailies or on television. Also for business people, the newspaper has a separate business section. This section lacks the depth of the *Wall Street Journal,* but readers can find several pages of stock data and stories, usually short, on breaking business news.

The introduction of *USA Today* came at a time when most newspapers were trying to distinguish themselves from television news with longer, exploratory and interpretive stories. While some major newspapers such as the New York *Times* and the Los Angeles *Times* were unswayed by *USA Today*'s snappy, quick-to-read format, many other newspapers moved to shorter, easily digested stories, infographics and more data lists. Color became standard. *USA Today* has influenced today's newspaper style and format.

Christian Science Monitor

Mary Baker Eddy, the influential founder of the Christian Science faith, was aghast at turn-of-the-century Boston newspapers. The Boston dailies, as in other major U.S. cities, were sensationalistic, overplaying crime and gore in hyperbolic battles to steal readers from each other. Entering the fray, Eddy introduced a newspaper with a different mission. Her **Christian Science Monitor,** founded in 1908, sought to deal with issues and problems on a high plane and to help the world come up with solutions.

Nobody, least of all Mary Baker Eddy, expected such an intellectually oriented newspaper to make money, at least not right away, so the church underwrote expenses when subscriptions, newsstand sales and advertising revenue fell short. The *Monitor* sought subscriptions nationwide and abroad, and it developed a following. Though edited in Boston, the *Monitor* was conceived as an international, not a local newspaper, and it became the first national daily newspaper in the United States.

The *Christian Science Monitor* tries to emphasize positive news, but it also deals with crime, disaster, war and other downbeat news, and it has won Pulitzer Prizes for covering them. The thrust, though, is interpretive, unlike the sensationalistic newspapers to which Mary Baker Eddy wanted an alternative. The *Monitor* does not cover events and issues to titillate its readers. Rather, as veteran *Monitor* editor Erwin Canham explained, the newspaper's mission is "to help give humankind the tools with which to work out its salvation." The *Monitor* is not preachy. In fact, only one plainly labeled religious article appears in each issue. The *Monitor* seeks to lead and influence by example.

A few seasoned foreign correspondents provide the backbone of the *Monitor*'s respected international coverage, and their stories are backed up with stories from reporters who work for other news organizations but who moonlight for the *Monitor.*

Mary Baker Eddy
Founded *Christian Science Monitor* in 1908.

Christian Science Monitor
Boston-based national U.S. newspaper.

Constructive Journalism. Since its 1908 founding, the *Christian Science Monitor* has emphasized solution-oriented journalism. The *Monitor,* based in Boston, began as an antidote to sensationalistic newspapers, emphasizing accurate and truthful coverage to help people address serious problems facing humankind.

Mary Baker Eddy

tabloid
Newspaper with half-size pages that are easy to hold. Not necessarily sensationalistic.

A staff in Washington anchors domestic coverage. The cultural coverage and editorials are widely read.

Circulation peaked at 239,000 in 1971, the year when the *Monitor* joined several leading newspapers, including the New York *Times,* in printing secret Pentagon documents over the objections of the Nixon administration. By then, the *Monitor* was being printed at plants near Boston, Chicago, Los Angeles and New York for same-day mail delivery to much of the nation, as well as at a plant near London for foreign distribution. Since the 1971 peak, however, circulation has deteriorated to less than 140,000. Failing to find a sufficient following among national advertisers, the *Monitor* has shrunk from a full-size newspaper to a thinner and thinner **tabloid.** A handicap in finding advertising revenue is the church's doctrine-based refusal to accept ads for alcoholic beverages, tobacco products and drugs.

It is unclear how much longer the church, whose membership has dwindled to 150,000 and whose overall income is estimated at only $85 million a year, can afford to carry out Mary Baker Eddy's goal for a strong Christian Science presence in the news media.

National Editions

The New York *Times* and the Los Angeles *Times* took to calling themselves national newspapers in the 1990s, but they really aren't. Both newspapers' national editions are mere add-ons to a core product edited for regional audiences in metropolitan New York and Los Angeles. For the national editions, editors replace local and regional coverage with Washington and foreign stories.

Even so, both the New York and Los Angeles *Times* have some characteristics of the three truly national dailies. For example, air delivery and satellite printing plants make the national editions available in many places the morning of publication. In some densely populated areas, home delivery is available.

These national editions are an attempt to capitalize on the strong reputations that the New York and Los Angeles *Times* have built over the years with their own Washington and foreign staffs. The newspapers hope to attract national advertisers—the same advertisers that have cottoned to the *Wall Street Journal, USA Today,* the newsmagazines and network television. Whether these national editions become profitable remains to be seen. The key to profitability is whether enough advertising can be found to cover distribution costs, which are high. The national editions themselves, as a repackaging of the existing core product, don't cost much to put out.

Media Timeline

Notable Dailies

1851 Henry Raymond founded the New York *Times.*

1889 Newsletter editors Charles Dow and Edward Jones founded the *Wall Street Journal.*

1908 Religious leader Mary Baker Eddy founded the *Christian Science Monitor.*

1919 Joseph Patterson and Robert McCormick founded the New York *Daily News.*

1955 Bohemian New York literati founded the *Village Voice.*

1967 Jim Michaels founded the Los Angeles–based *Advocate,* first gay newspaper.

1983 Gannett's Allen Neuharth founded *USA Today.*

Hometown Newspapers

STUDY PREVIEW   The United States has 1,570 daily newspapers, most oriented to covering hometown news and carrying local advertising. Big-city dailies are the most visible hometown newspapers, but medium-size and small dailies have made significant strides in quality in recent decades and have eroded the metro newspapers' outlying circulation.

Metropolitan Dailies

In every region of the United States there is a newspaper whose name is a household word. These are metropolitan dailies with extensive regional circulation. In New England, for example, the Boston *Globe* covers Boston but also prides itself on extensive coverage of Massachusetts state government, as well as coverage of neighboring states. The *Globe* has a Washington bureau, and it sends reporters abroad on special assignments.

When experts are asked to list the nation's best newspapers, the lists inevitably are led by the **New York** *Times.* Other newspapers with a continuing presence include the Baltimore *Sun,* Chicago *Tribune,* Dallas *Morning News,* Houston *Chronicle,* Los Angeles *Times,* Miami *Herald,* Minneapolis *Star Tribune,* Philadelphia *Inquirer,* St. Louis *Post Dispatch* and Washington *Post.*

Here are snapshots of three leading metro dailies:

NEW YORK *TIMES.*   Not a librarian anywhere would want to be without a subscription to the New York *Times,* which is one reason that the *Times* boasts at least one subscriber in every county in the country. Since its founding in 1851, the *Times* has had a reputation for fair and thorough coverage of foreign news. A large, widely respected staff covers Washington. It is a newspaper of record, printing the president's annual state of the union address and other important documents in their entirety. The *Times* is an important research source, in part because the *Times* puts out a monthly and annual index that lists every story. The editorials are among the most quoted.

The *Times* news sections added color photographs in 1998, but the presentation remains somber and stolid, fitting the seriousness with which the *Times* takes its coverage. Inside, though, dazzling, colorful graphics have become standard in recent

New York *Times*
Most respected U.S. hometown daily.

Old Gray Lady. True to the graphic spirit of the 19th century, when it rose in eminence, the New York *Times* is sometimes called the Old Gray Lady of American journalism. Even after color photos were added in 1997, the *Times* had a staid, somber visual personality. The coverage, writing and commentary, however, are anything but dull, and it is those things that have made the *Times'* reputation as the world's best newspaper. The paper is distinguished by international and Washington coverage, which is drawn mostly from its own staff reporters rather than the news services that most other newspapers rely on. Among Sunday features is the colorful, splashy *New York Times Magazine,* which runs lengthy examinations on serious issues. Also Sunday is a serious book review magazine. The New York *Times* crossword puzzle is one of the most popular in the world. The *Times* carries no comics or horoscopes, which contributes to the tone and mystique that set the newspaper apart.

years. The Sunday edition includes the glitzy New York *Times Magazine,* a serious book review magazine, and one of the world's most popular crossword puzzles. Unusual for a United States newspaper, especially one with a large Sunday edition, the *Times* carries no comics.

Washington *Post*
Established reputation covering Watergate.

WASHINGTON *POST.* The **Washington *Post*** cemented its reputation for investigative reporting by breaking revelation after revelation in the 1972 Watergate scandal, until finally Richard Nixon resigned the presidency in disgrace. The *Wall*

Media Databank

Best U.S. Newspapers

About 100 leading newspaper editors dispersed across the 50 states voted the New York *Times* the top newspaper in the nation in 1999. *Columbia Journalism Review* magazine, which sponsored the survey, asked editors to evaluate reporting, writing, editing, graphics, integrity, accuracy, fairness, vision, innovation, influence in the community and influence on the broader journalistic community. Of the three national papers, the *Wall Street Journal* was third, *USA Today* twelfth. The *Christian Science Monitor* did not show. Also, the survey was conducted before the Staples Arena scandal marred the Los Angeles *Times*.

1. New York *Times*
2. Washington *Post*
3. Wall Street *Journal*
4. Los Angeles *Times*
5. Dallas *Morning News*
6. (tie) Chicago *Tribune*
   Boston *Globe*
8. San Jose *Mercury News*
9. St. Petersburg *Times*
10. Baltimore *Sun*

Street Journal, New York *Times* and Los Angeles *Times,* all with large Washington staffs, compete aggressively with the *Post* for major federal stories, but the *Post* remains the most quoted newspaper for government coverage.

With the demise of the afternoon Washington *Daily News* and the *Star,* the *Post* was left the only local newspaper in the nation's capital, which upset critics who perceived a liberal bias in the *Post.* This prompted the Unification Church of the Reverend Sun Myung Moon to found the **Washington *Times*** as a rightist daily. The *Times* has only a fraction of the *Post*'s 840,000 circulation, but its scrappy coverage inserts local excitement into Washington journalism, as does its incessant sniping at the *Post* and *Post*-owned *Newsweek* magazine.

LOS ANGELES *TIMES.* The **Los Angeles *Times*** edged out the declining New York *Daily News* in 1990 as the nation's largest metropolitan daily when circulation reached 1.3 million. By many measures, the *Times* is huge. A typical Sunday edition makes quite a thump on the doorstep at four pounds and 444 pages.

The *Times* has 1,300 editors and reporters, some in 22 foreign bureaus and 13 U.S. bureaus. Fifty-seven reporters cover the federal government in Washington alone. To cover the 1991 war against Iraq, the *Times* dispatched 20 reporters and photographers to the Gulf region, compared with 12 for the New York *Times* and 10 for the Washington *Post,* the traditional leading U.S. metro dailies for foreign coverage.

The *Times*' reputation was built under Otis Chandler, who rode the wave of boom times beginning in the 1960s. Chandler put journalism first, building an extraordinary staff and expanding coverage. That heritage was undermined after he retired. In 1995 others in the Chandler family, seeking greater profits, hired a chief executive from outside the newspaper business. The *Times* began slipping on many fronts, capped by an ethics scandal in which the newspaper promoted the Staples sports arena in a secret deal in which it profited from Staples advertising. In 2000, the Tribune Company, owner of the Chicago *Tribune* and several other major papers, acquired the Los Angeles *Times,* replaced the top management and began restoring staff morale and the newspaper's old vigor.

Washington *Times*
Conservative newspaper.

Los Angeles *Times*
Largest-circulation U.S. hometown daily.

Hometown Dailies

With their aggressive reporting on national and regional issues, the metro dailies receive more attention than smaller dailies, but most Americans read **hometown dailies.** By and large, these locally oriented newspapers, most of them chain-owned, have been incredibly profitable while making significant journalistic progress since World War II.

Fifty years ago, people in small towns generally bought both a metropolitan daily and a local newspaper. Hometown dailies were thin, and coverage was hardly comprehensive. Editorial pages tended to offer only a single perspective. Readers had few alternative sources of information. Since then, these smaller dailies have hired better-prepared journalists, acquired new technology and strengthened their local advertising base.

Hometown dailies have grown larger and more comprehensive. The years between 1970 and 1980 were especially important for quantum increases in news coverage. A study of 10 hometown dailies, with circulations ranging from 60,000 to 542,000, found that the space available for news, called the news hole, more than doubled between 1964 and 1999. Many hometown dailies also gave much of their large news holes to bigger and more diverse opinion sections. Most editorial sections today are smorgasbords of perspectives.

Challenges for Daily Newspapers

STUDY PREVIEW   Daily newspapers remain incredibly profitable, despite declining circulation. Innovation and cost-cutting have contributed to their continuing financial success, but long-term prospects are far from rosy.

Daily Newspaper Finances

Except for the Depression of the 1930s, when good investments were hard to find, newspapers were among the most consistently profitable sectors of the U.S. economy throughout the 20th century. In 1998, the latest year for which data are available, operating profits were 20.7 percent for newspaper companies whose annual reports are publicly available.

How could daily newspapers still be making so much money? Their audience was declining, which would seem to indicate that they could command less for advertising space. That would mean, it would seem, that there would be less income from both circulation and advertising—a newspaper's primary revenue streams.

NEWSPRINT.   A newspaper's major raw material is newsprint, which accounts for about 20 percent of expenses on average. Because newsprint costs fluctuate wildly, they can dramatically affect profitability. When newsprint peaked in 1995, daily newspaper operating profits slipped to 14.5 percent—not shabby but still significantly off. Profits bounced back when newsprint dipped to a cyclical low of less than $500 a ton in 1999. Some analysts worried that low newsprint prices were temporarily masking the impact of circulation declines.

ECONOMY.   Like other industries, newspapers rode the economic boom of the late 1990s. Companies, mostly those specializing in digital consumer products,

Reader Configurable Newspaper. In October 2001 the New York *Times* took digital news delivery to a new level. The newspaper's new Electronic Edition was an exact page-by-page reproduction of the daily newspaper. Readers had far more options than with the original web edition. For example, tiny sports data boxes and stock prices could be magnified. Readers could jump instantly to stories continued on inside pages. Color was high-resolution. The edition had search tools to speed readers to topics and subjects that interested them. Unlike web editions, updates were not as posted on an ongoing basis. Instead, the electronic edition was exactly what people bought on the streets or had delivered to their doors.

hometown daily
Edited primarily for readers in a defined region.

Media Databank

Largest U.S. Newspaper Circulations

The Audit Bureau of Circulations, which tracks newspaper circulation, reported a spike after the September 11, 2001, terrorist attack. The increase reversed a steady erosion in newspaper circulation in the United States. The New York *Post* was up 22.2 percent, the growth fueled not only by news-hungry New Yorkers but a price cut from 50 to 25 cents a copy for the daily. Here are the nation's largest newspapers by circulation.

Newspaper	Daily	Sunday
USA Today	2.1 million	
Wall Street Journal	1.8 million	
New York *Times*	1.1 million	1.7 million
Los Angeles *Times*	944,000	1.4 million
Washington *Post*	760,000	1.1 million
New York *Daily News*	734,000	802,000
Chicago *Tribune*	621,000	1.0 million
Long Island *Newsday*	577,000	676,000
Houston *Chronicle*	552,000	745,000
New York *Post*	534,000	401,000

poured unprecedented amounts of money into consumer advertising in every medium available, including newspapers. In the 2001 economic downturn, in which weak sectors of the economy were shaken out, newspapers lost significant advertising. In short, the newspaper industry's fundamental strengths are sliding away.

Daily Newspaper Circulation

With losses in readership, newspaper publishers have a lot to worry about. And it's going to get worse. Young people aren't reading newspapers. A landmark 1965 Gallup study found that 67 percent of Americans under 35 had read a newspaper the day before—a much lower percentage than their parents. By 1990 the percentage was down to 30 percent. The trend has continued. Newspapers are failing to replace their aging readership.

Attempts to win a younger audience haven't worked. These have included *USA Today*'s color and glitz, originally aimed at younger readers. Also falling short have been many newspaper attempts to woo younger readers with beefed up music, movie and entertainment coverage.

By 2000 daily circulation was down to 52.8 million from a 62.8 million high in 1988. This was all the worse considering that the population had grown. As a financial analyst would say, **market penetration** has slipped.

Daily Newspaper Advertising

The heady days when newspapers could count on more advertising every year seem over. Projections into the early 21st century indicate that newspaper advertising will be lucky to hold its own. Television's growth is a factor, but other media, including ads distributed by mail, are eating into the historic dominance of the newspaper as an advertising medium. It is true the advertising revenues were still increasing in 2000, but the increases were bolstered by higher rates and a surge of ads from high-tech consumer advertisements. In other terms the situation was not so

market penetration
Sales per capita.

strong. While newspapers led all media with 27.7 percent of the total advertising pie in 1980, the slice was down to 22.0 percent by 1998. The situation varied from city to city, but overall newspaper advertising was flattening out.

Besides losses to television, daily newspaper advertising revenue has taken a hit from the **consolidation** of retailing into fewer albeit bigger companies. Local grocery, discount and department store mergers cut down on advertising revenue. Fewer competing retail chains meant fewer ads. This was a major loss because the grocery, discount and department stores were newspapers' largest source of income. The Los Angeles *Times* estimated that it lost $12 million in ad revenue because of mergers in one year alone.

A growing advertising practice, bypassing the traditional mass media and sending circulars and catalogs directly to potential customers, also is cutting into newspaper advertising income. This **direct mail** trend took off in the 1970s and accelerated into the 1990s. Today, direct mail advertising accounts for 19.7 percent of the money spent nationwide by advertisers. To win back advertisers that switched to direct mail, newspapers are willing to tuck preprinted advertising circulars, mostly from large retailers, inside the regular paper. In one sense, **preprints,** as they are called, represent lost revenue because in the days before direct mail those ads would have been placed in the regular pages of the newspaper at full ad rates. Newspaper preprint rates are discounted deeply to compete with postal rates.

Want ads, formally called **classified advertising,** continue to be highly profitable. At some newspapers, classifieds generate more than half of the revenue. The national average exceeds 40 percent. Television and radio have not found a way to offer a competing service, and not even free-distribution papers devoted to classified advertising have reversed the growth in daily newspaper classified revenue. The web, however, is well suited to classified advertising, and many sites, some operating as newspaper subsidiaries, have been set up.

Also, newspapers remain the dominant advertising medium for most major local advertisers: grocery stores, department stores, automobile dealerships and discount stores.

On the downside, daily newspapers have suffered major losses over the years in national advertising, mostly to magazines and network television. Despite the losses, newspapers have not given up on national advertising. Every newspaper has a broker, called a **national representative,** whose business is to line up national advertising for its client newspapers.

media
onvergence

consolidation
Retail mergers reduce number of major newspaper advertisers.

direct mail
Advertisements sent directly to consumers.

preprints
Separately printed ads inserted in a newspaper.

classified advertising
Want ads.

national representative
Newspaper's agency to solicit national advertisers.

Newspaper Web Sites

Today almost every daily newspaper in the United States has a web site. The people who run news organizations sense profits from the web at some future point, and they want to be on the ground floor. But how long will the wait be for these news sites to turn a profit? Hoag Levins, editor of mediainfo.com, published by the newspaper trade journal *Editor & Publisher,* expects that advertisers will flock to the web when penetration reaches 50 percent of a city's households. By 2000 more than 40 percent of U.S. homes had web access.

According to Levins, "A kind of critical mass can occur in metro areas when newspaper circulation drops to 50 percent of that area's households. Such declines can trigger a sudden, self-perpetuating downward spiral of cost-cutting, editorial quality decline, further readership loss and rapid erosion of advertiser confidence.

Niche Seeking. While many newspaper web sites offer the same wide range of coverage as the traditional print editions, many specialize in coverage for special audiences. Computer people worldwide, for example, tap into Mercury Center, a product of the daily San Jose *Mercury News* in California, for its concentration on nearby Silicon Valley. It's no surprise that the Milwaukee *Journal*'s news site offers concentrated coverage of the Green Bay Packers football team. The *Florida Today* site, out of Cocoa Beach, near Cape Canaveral and the Kennedy Space Center, has saturation coverage of the nation's space program.

"Any good reporter can see that the same dynamics are at work on the World Wide Web, only in the other direction—up. The web is now being accessed by over 20 percent of American households, a demographic that is steadily increasing. As this digital equivalent of 'circulation' increases to 50 percent of the households in any given community, it will achieve its own critical mass altering the communication and advertising realities of that community.

"Each year $66 billion is spent on advertising in local newspapers, magazines, shopper's guides, TV, cable, radio and other traditional outlets. And while the majority of local advertisers don't now consider the web a viable medium for effectively reaching their community, that will change. When household Internet access levels approach 50 percent, the web will suddenly provide those advertisers a 'door-to-door' electronic delivery system, for local neighborhoods comparable to that offered in printed newspapers."

That's not a pretty picture for the future of newspapers as an ink-on-paper product, but newspaper organizations with their own web sites are positioned for a transition in which their product—mostly news and information—is delivered by an alternative medium.

Innovations

To remain profitable even as sales decline, newspapers have tried innovations: Some work. Others seem to run their course.

SUNDAY EDITIONS.   Beginning in the 1970s, the number of high-profit Sunday editions nationwide grew dramatically. Lifestyles and shopping patterns had made Sunday a shopping day, and advertisers wanted to reach potential customers early in the morning. By 2000, however, there were signs that the Sunday edition phenomenon had peaked. In Boston, for example, the *Globe*'s Sunday circulation was down 2.4 percent, to 730,000.

To address the declines, some newspapers, in Boston and elsewhere, began to publish fat Saturday editions—in effect, an early Sunday edition. These editions, called **bulldog editions,** were intended to attract Saturday sales. The idea, too, was that the super-weekend Saturday edition would sit around the house longer and give advertisers an extra day of exposure for their ads, especially with Saturdays emerging as a major shopping day. To give the bulldog its own content and flavor, the *Globe* added 15 staff members. The strategy had worked earlier for *Newsday* on Long Island, New York, and for the Pittsburgh, Pennsylvania, *Post-Gazette* without substantially damaging circulation for the regular Sunday edition.

FRAGMENTATION.   Many metro dailies have long had **zoned editions,** each with news and ads for a particular neighborhood or outlying region. Now papers are looking not just at such geographic zoning but also at narrowing their overall focus.

The Miami *Herald,* the most extreme example, set up an entirely separate Spanish language newspaper—not just a spin-off zoned edition. The new paper, *El Nuevo Herald,* has a separate staff and is editorially on its own. The *Herald* decision came after repeated efforts, all unsuccessful, to build circulation in the city's Spanish-speaking sections.

The decision recognized fragmentation in the city and represented a departure from the traditional sociological view of newspapers as a vehicle for community building and social unification. This fragmentation is occurring elsewhere too. Among small dailies, the Garden City, Kansas, *Telegram* has its weekly tabloid *La Semana.* The Yuma, Arizona, *Sun* has the free weekly *Bajo el Sol.* Some observers see the new papers as a sad commentary on social fragmentation occurring throughout the country.

Cost-Cutting

To offset the impact of circulation declines and anticipating the advertising declines that seem sure to follow, many newspaper companies toyed with new cost-cutting approaches in the late 1990s.

PAPER COSTS.   Many dailies went to narrower pages to save paper costs. Narrower pages made papers easier for readers to hold, but there was a downside: less room for news.

NEWSROOM BUDGETS.   The tight-fisted Thomson media conglomeration, before it began selling off its newspapers in 1998, tried to reduce newsroom payrolls

bulldog edition
An early edition of a newspaper to catch extra sales, usually street sales.

zoned edition
An edition of a newspaper edited for a neighborhood or outlying area.

by establishing what it called "Thomson U." The idea was to send people, mostly high-school graduates, to a training program for a few weeks to become reporters and editors, rather than hiring more expensive college grads with academic preparation in journalism. At some Thomson papers the pay was $7 an hour.

At many newspapers, newsroom staffs were cut.

CLUSTERING.   Once newspaper chains bought available papers anywhere they could find them. No more. Today, chains try to acquire newspapers with adjoining circulations to cut costs. By the year 2000, more than 400 dailies—about a quarter of the total—were in what is called a **cluster.** Among its 26 papers the Newhouse chain, for example, has eight dailies across southern Michigan. The papers come off the same press, reducing the expense of having several multimillion-dollar presses at the individual newspapers. In some clusters, editors are not in the hometown but 30 or even 70 miles away. Clustering eliminates competition for advertisers that seek customers in several communities because cluster papers offer merchants a one-stop place to run all their ads.

Clusters have downsides. Critics say that out-of-town supervising editors lose touch with the communities that the papers serve. Also, editors face pressure to look for stories that can go in multiple papers, reducing news-gathering expenses—and also reducing the traditional local orientation, a historic hallmark of U.S. newspapers. Overall, fewer voices are present in the marketplace.

Proponents argue that clustering creates economies that can save newspapers that otherwise would go under.

Weekly Newspapers

STUDY PREVIEW   Many community weekly newspapers, especially in fast-growing suburbs, are thriving, while others, especially rural weeklies, have fallen on hard times. In all areas, free-distribution advertising sheets called *shoppers* have attracted strong followings.

Community Weeklies

Weekly newspapers are making strong circulation gains, especially in suburban communities, and some have moved into publishing twice a week. In all, almost 8,000 weekly newspapers are published in the United States, with circulation approaching 50 million. Weeklies are received in almost 60 percent of the nation's households, up almost one-third from 1970.

To the discomfort of metro dailies, many advertisers are following their customers to the suburban weeklies. Advertisers have found that they can buy space in weeklies for less and reach their likeliest customers. Ralph Ingersoll, whose weeklies give fits to the daily Long Island *Newsday* in New York, explained it this way in an interview with *Forbes:* "If you're an automobile dealer on Long Island, you can pay, say, $14,000 for a tabloid page in *Newsday,* most of which is wasted because the people that get it will never buy a car in your neck of the woods, or you can go into one of the weekender publications and pay a few hundred dollars and reach just the people likely to drive over to your shop."

Some weeklies, particularly those in upscale suburbs, offer sophisticated coverage of community issues. Others feature a homey mix of reports on social events such

clustering
Buying newspapers with adjoining circulations to cut operating costs.

media online

National Lesbian and Gay Journalists Association: NLGJA works from within the news industry to foster fair and accurate coverage of lesbian and gay issues and opposes newsroom bias against lesbians and gays and all other minorities.
www.nlgja.org

AfroAmeric@: News, culture, history and kid's links on a wonderful site.
www.afroam.org

National Association of Black Journalists: The National Association of Black Journalists is the largest media organization for people of color in the world.
www.nabj.org

National Association of Hispanic Journalists: The National Association of Hispanic Journalists (NAHJ) is dedicated to the recognition and professional advancement of Hispanics in the news industry. NAHJ created a national voice and unified vision for all Hispanic journalists.
www.nahj.org

as who visited whom for Sunday dinner. The success of these weeklies sometimes is called **telephone book journalism** because of the emphasis on names, the somewhat overdrawn theory being that people buy papers to see their names in print. Weeklies have in common that they cover their communities with a detail that metro dailies have neither staff nor space to match. There is no alternative to keeping up with local news.

Rural weeklies generally have fallen on rough times. Part of their problem is the diminishing significance of agriculture in the national economy and the continuing depopulation of rural America. In communities that remain retail centers, rural weeklies can maintain a strong advertising base. However, the Main Street of many small towns has declined as improved roads and the construction of major retail stores like Wal-Mart draw customers from 40 to 50 miles away. In earlier days those customers patronized hometown retailers, who placed significant advertising in hometown weeklies. Today many of these Main Street retailers, unable to compete with giant discount stores, are out of business.

Shoppers

Free-distribution papers that carry only advertisements have become increasingly important as vehicles for classified advertising. In recent years **shoppers** have attracted display advertising that earlier would have gone to regular newspapers. Almost all shoppers undercut daily newspapers on advertising rates. The number of shoppers has grown to about 1,500 nationwide, and they no longer are merely an ignorable competitor for daily newspapers for advertising.

By definition, shoppers are strictly advertising sheets, but beginning in the 1970s some shoppers added editorial content, usually material that came free over the transom, such as publicity items and occasional self-serving columns from legislators. Some shoppers have added staff members to compile calendars and provide a modicum of news coverage. Most of these papers, however, remain ad sheets with little that is journalistic. Their news-gathering efforts and expenses are minuscule compared with those of a daily newspaper.

Alternative and Minority Newspapers

STUDY PREVIEW   Most newspapers attempt broad coverage for a broad audience, but more specialized newspapers are important in the lives of many people. These include counterculture, gay, black and Spanish language newspapers, many of which are expanding and prospering today.

Counterculture Newspapers

A group of friends in the Greenwich Village neighborhood of New York, including novelist **Norman Mailer** and **Don Wolf,** decided to start a newspaper. Thus in 1955 was born the **Village Voice,** a free-wheeling weekly that became a prototype for a 1960s phenomenon called the **alternative press** and that has continued to thrive.

In its early days the *Village Voice* was a haven for bohemian writers of diverse competence who volunteered occasional pieces, some lengthy, many rambling. Many articles purported to be investigative examinations of hypocritical people and insti-

telephone book journalism
Listing readers' names.

shopper
An advertising paper without news.

Norman Mailer
Among the founders of *Village Voice.*

Don Wolf
Among the founders of *Village Voice.*

Village Voice
Model for contemporary alternative press.

alternative press
Generally antiestablishment publication for a young alienated audience.

tutions, but, as *Voice* veteran Nat Hentoff has noted, nobody ever bothered to check "noisome facts," let alone the "self-righteous author." The *Voice* seemed to scorn traditional, detached, neutral reporting. Despite its flaws, the amateurism gave the *Voice* a charm, and it picked up readership.

The *Voice* today is more polished and journalistically serious. The characteristics that made it distinctive in its early history, and that were picked up by other **counterculture newspapers,** include:

- Antiestablishment political coverage with a strong antimilitary slant.
- Cultural coverage that emphasizes contrarian music and art and exalts sex and drugs.
- Interpretive coverage focusing more on issues of special concern to alienated young people.
- Extensive entertainment coverage and listings of events.
- A conversational, sometimes crude style that includes four-letter words and gratuitous expletives for their shock value.
- Extensive personal ads for dating and sex liaisons.

By delivering a loyal readership that was hard to reach through mainstream media, many counterculture newspapers became fat with advertising. Today, about 100 alternative newspapers are published in the United States, and many are prospering. With a circulation of 172,000, the *Village Voice* is widely available in big-city newsracks and by mail throughout the country.

Gay Newspapers

Jim Michaels began publishing the nation's first gay newspaper, the Los Angeles-based *Advocate,* out of his living room in 1967. Today, 125 gay newspapers have a total circulation of more than 1 million. Most are free papers distributed at gay bars, nightclubs and businesses, and many are financially marginal. However, mainstream advertisers are beginning to take notice of the loyalty of gay readers to their newspapers. In 1990 the Columbia House Music Club tested a membership ad offering eight discs for $1 in 12 gay newspapers. The response rate was so high that the club began placing the ad in 70 gay papers within a year.

The success of the Columbia ad confirmed a 1988 study that found unexpected affluence among readers of eight major gay newspapers. Individual incomes averaged $36,800, which was three times the national average, and household incomes averaged $55,430, which was 2½ times the national average. The number of college graduates, 60 percent, and the number of people in professional and managerial jobs, 49 percent, were three times the national average. Other national advertisers followed Columbia into the gay press.

Black Newspapers

The ongoing integration of black and white people in U.S. society has eroded the role of black newspapers since World War II, but 172 black newspapers remain in publication. In all, the black newspapers have a circulation of 3.6 million, a ratio of about 1:10 to the nation's black population. At their peak after World War II, black newspapers included three nationally distributed dailies, from Baltimore, Chicago and Pittsburgh, whose combined circulation approached 600,000. The black dailies

counterculture newspapers
Challenge, defy mainstream values.

Jim Michaels
Founded the *Advocate.*

Advocate
First gay newspaper, 1967.

Frederick Douglass

Black Freedom Fighter. Antislavery orator Frederick Douglass, himself a former slave, created the *North Star* in 1857 to promote the abolitionist movement. The *North Star* was one of the most influential black newspapers, especially in dismantling the notion, prominent at the time, of natural racial inferiority. The newspaper was well written and edited, and within four years it became self-sustaining.

today, the Atlanta *Daily World*, **Chicago *Daily Defender*** and New York *Daily Challenge,* together have a circulation of 106,000, almost all local.

Black newspapers have been important in the U.S. civil rights movement, beginning in 1827 with John Russwurm and Samuel Cornish's *Freedom's Journal,* the first black newspaper. Frederick Douglass's **North Star,** founded in 1847, was a strident abolitionist sheet before the Civil War, and W. E. B. DuBois' *Crisis,* founded in 1910, was a militant voice for black advancement. Today, most black newspapers crusade for causes in the tradition of their early predecessors but focus on neighborhood social, church and sports events. The tone is moderate.

Prospects for black newspapers generally do not appear strong. Only 15 percent of the advertising placed in black media, including television, radio and magazines, goes to newspapers. Media scholar James Tinney found that middle-income blacks look to establishment newspapers rather than black newspapers for information, even while relying on other black institutions, such as the church and universities, for spiritual and intellectual stimulation.

Foreign-Language Newspapers

Through every wave of immigration, newspapers in foreign languages have sprouted to serve newcomers to the United States in their native tongue. In 1914 there were 140 foreign-language dailies published in the United States. About one-third were German, led by New York *Vorwarts* with a circulation of 175,000. The U.S. German-language press withered during World War I when its loyalty was challenged, but, like other foreign-language newspapers, it undoubtedly would have eventually disappeared anyway as the immigrants assimilated into the mainstream culture.

Today, the fast-growing Hispanic minority represents about 1 of every 15 Americans, and although most are bilingual, six daily newspapers and about 150 weeklies are published in Spanish. In general, these newspapers are thriving. The Knight-Ridder newspaper chain publishes *El Nuevo Herald* as a Spanish-language daily in Miami and sells 67,000 copies. In New York, the Gannett chain operates the 63,000-circulation daily *El Diario-La Prensa.* Most Spanish-language newspapers are owned by Hispanics, but the presence of the gigantic, profitable Knight-Ridder and Gannett chains bespeaks the commercial viability of these papers.

The profitability of Spanish-language newspapers is fueled partly by the desire of many national advertisers to tap into the large Hispanic market. The newspapers' penetration, however, is not especially high. In heavily Hispanic Los Angeles, *La Opinion* has a circulation of only 55,000 a day. In Miami the competing *El Herald*

Chicago *Daily Defender*
Daily black newspaper that continues with probing journalism.

Freedom's Journal
First black newspaper, founded 1827 by John Russwurm and Samuel Cornish.

North Star
Antislavery black newspaper founded 1847 by Frederick Douglass.

Crisis
Black newspaper founded 1910 by W. E. B. DuBois.

El Nuevo Herald
Leading Spanish-language daily, Miami.

News in Different Languages. Since 1996, like many dailies in areas with many Latinos, the San Jose, California, *Mercury News* has published a Spanish language edition. About a third of San Jose's population speaks Spanish, and *Nuevo Mundo* has a circulation of 59,000, compared to 290,000 for the English edition. A Vietnamese edition was launched in 1999 and has a circulation of 23,600. About 7 percent of San Jose's population is from Vietnam.

and *Diario Las Americas* together sell only 130,000 copies a day. In New York *El Diario-La Prensa* and *Noticias del Mundo* together have a circulation of less than 130,000 in a metropolitan area with 2.5 million Hispanic people.

Whether Spanish-language newspapers will disappear as did earlier foreign-language newspapers is uncertain. Although assimilation is occurring, many Hispanics are intent on maintaining their distinctive cultural identity and resist adopting English. Also, there is more sympathy for multiculturalism in the society than there was in the past. For the foreseeable future, Spanish-language newspapers will have a strong following among the continuing influx of people from Latin America and the Caribbean. With this immigration and a high fertility rate, the U.S. Hispanic population is growing about 4 percent a year.

Some analysts think that the Spanish-language media have peaked as Hispanics assimilate into the dominant U.S. culture. Frank Welzer, president of Sony's Latin music company, was quoted in a *Forbes* magazine analysis: "Hispanics watch as much English-language television as anyone else. It's only recent arrivals and the elderly who use Spanish media exclusively." Sigfredo Hernandez, a specialist in Hispanic marketing at Rider College in New Jersey, was quoted in the same article: "If you're trying to reach younger Hispanics, they've got to be addressed in English." Christopher Palmeri and Joshua Levine, who wrote the *Forbes* analysis, concluded: "Of course, there will always be a market for specialized advertising aimed at recent immigrants. Just recall the lively German, Italian and Yiddish language media of yore. But it is beginning to dawn on advertisers that the idea of a vast and unassimilated 'Hispanic market' is just a myth fostered by professional multiculturists and hucksters."

Multimedia Newsroom. Media companies are looking to combine forces to improve coverage and reduce expenses. In Tampa, Florida, the *Tribune,* television station WFLA and TBO.com are within the same walls and share news tips and staffs.

Media Future: Newspapers

The future of U.S. newspapers may be decided at Northwestern University, where in 1999 the newspaper industry established a think tank, the Readership Institute, to identify how circulation declines can be stemmed. The goal: Find ways to draw people back.

If the Readership Institute fails, it won't be for lack of trying. The scope of its fact-gathering is unprecedented. In its first two years the institute sent incredibly detailed questionnaires to 30,000 newspaper readers and nonreaders. More than 75,000 articles from 100 newspapers, plucked randomly, were analyzed for content, display and reader response. No question was too obtuse: Does feel-good participatory newsroom management somehow translate into sales—as opposed to militaristic newsrooms?

The Readership Institute's director, John Lavine, a veteran Wisconsin publisher who was involved heavily with journalism education, sees new understandings emerging for the studies—"a baseline," he calls it. Perhaps importantly, the institute has connections with both Northwestern's Medill School of Journalism and the Kellogg School of Management. For generations, many newspapers prided themselves on a firewall between the newsroom and the rest of the business—a division that is cracking, for better or worse, but which nonetheless remains part of newspaper culture.

A major Readership Institute focus is young adults. Unlike their parents, Baby Busters don't have strong newspaper habits. Only 20 percent of young adults, age 21 to 25, read a newspaper daily—compared to 60 percent only a quarter-century ago.

The Readership Institute began issuing its findings in 2002. There were no industry-transforming recommendations, but Lavine was looking to issue a series of findings over time that would make a difference.

c h a p t e r   w r a p - u p

Numerous, once-powerful newspapers have disappeared since the middle of the century, among them the Chicago *Daily News,* Los Angeles *Herald Examiner,* New York *Herald Tribune,* Philadelphia *Bulletin* and Washington *Star.* U.S. dailies, which numbered 1,745 in 1980, are down to 1,570. Other media, particularly television and its evening newscasts, have siphoned readers away from evening newspapers. Can newspapers survive? Even if people were to stop buying newspapers tomorrow, newspaper organizations would survive because they have an asset that competing media lack: the largest, most skilled newsroom staffs in their communities. The presses and the ink-on-newsprint medium for carrying the message may not have a long future, but newspapers' news-gathering capability will endure.

Questions for Review

1. Describe how newspapers are important in the lives of most Americans.
2. Explain the rise of newspaper chains. Have they been good for readers?
3. Why is the United States a nation mostly of provincial newspapers?
4. Many metropolitan daily newspapers have lost circulation, and some have shut down. Why?
5. What challenges to their dominance as a news and advertising medium do newspapers face?
6. Community newspapers, especially suburban weeklies, are booming. Why?
7. What kinds of newspapers aimed at narrow audience segments are prospering?

4. Can you explain why a greater percentage of U.S. newspapers are published for morning reading, not afternoon?
5. Identify advantages and disadvantages in the consolidation of U.S. newspapers, daily and weekly, into chains and cross-media conglomerates.
6. Can you identify how *USA Today* has changed U.S. newspapers by comparing an issue of your hometown paper today with an issue from the 1970s?
7. How have improvements in U.S. newspapers led to fewer households taking more than a single newspaper?
8. Considering the business orientation that makes newspaper chains so profitable, does it seem unusual that someone like Al Neuharth, whose background was in journalism rather than business, led Gannett through its incredible and profitable growth?

Questions for Critical Thinking

1. The United States is called a nation of provincial newspapers. Is the label correct? Do the *Wall Street Journal, USA Today* and *Christian Science Monitor* fit the provincial characterization?
2. How can you explain the declining number of U.S. newspapers and their losses in market penetration in view of the newspaper industry's profitability?
3. How have newspapers met challenges to their advertising revenue from radio, television, direct mail and shoppers?

Keeping Up to Date

Editor & Publisher is a weekly trade journal for the newspaper industry.

mediainfo.com. The trade journal *Editor & Publisher* launched this web site in 1997 to cover the emerging online news industry. www.mediainfo.com

Newspaper Research Journal is a quarterly dealing mostly with applied research.

Presstime is published monthly by the American Newspaper Publishers Association.

Shawn Fanning. His 1998 Napster music-downloading software gave millions of fans free access to more music than they could ever afford to buy. Record-makers, seeing profits slip away, launched lawsuits to curb what they considered piracy.

Recordings

In this chapter you will learn:

- Records compound the effect of music on human emotions.
- Five companies dominate the recording business.
- Sound recording began with mechanical, then electrical technology.
- Digital technology is used in record-making today.
- Rock 'n' roll is rooted in both black and white traditions.
- Artistic dynamics shape popular music.
- Commercial success and artistic success aren't necessarily the same.
- Home dubbing and piracy are major record industry problems.
- Moralists have long objected to lyrcs and performance styles.

Shawn Fanning grew up in a welfare family. Brothers and sisters were in and out of foster homes. His break came when an uncle brought Shawn to his Cape Cod computer game company and gave him a computer. Fascinated, the teenager found new direction. It didn't make him rich, though. When it came time for college, Fanning, with only $80, could afford to apply to only two colleges.

His freshman year at Northeastern in Boston was an academic disaster. Bored, he partied his time away. One day, his roommates complained that they couldn't find the music they wanted to download from the web, so Fanning decided to write a program to help. He obsessed over the project, writing code day and night until he had a system that would allow people to tap into each other's hard drives for MP3 downloads.

That was in 1998. The rest is history. Fanning dropped out of college, found a venture capitalist, moved to Silicon Valley and went into business. His program, called Napster after his childhood nickname, almost instantly attracted thousands of music fans who began trading millions of songs online. Napster did it all automatically, listing every song every participant had on a hard drive.

At age 19, to many, Shawn Fanning was a cyberhero.

He was also in trouble. The record industry watched sales tumble at campus-area record shops. Alarmed, the Recording Industry Association of America sued Fanning's company, charging that Napster enabled people to undermine the whole intellectual property legal apparatus that allowed music creators and owners to profit from their work. People, mostly college students, were acquiring music free, eliminating the economic incentive for composers and lyricists to create new works and for record companies to package and market them. Some artists were in a tizzy. Paul McCartney objected. Metallica and Dr. Dre sued.

Napster's popularity created campus problems. At some colleges, half the computer resources were being consumed by Napster traffic in the spring 1999 semester. Several colleges barred Napster, not only to clear the way for other web traffic but also because the colleges were being sued as accomplices.

Fanning responded that Napster was nothing more than an electronic way for people to swap records—an age-old practice. The court decisions went against Napster in 2001. Although the company's future was in doubt, Shawn Fanning's technology had prompted a fundamental rethinking of intellectual property rights. The issue was far from settled.

Stay tuned.

Recorded Music as a Social Force

STUDY PREVIEW   Music is a potent form of human expression that can mobilize hearts and minds. Think about the effects of hymns and anthems, martial music and love songs. For better or worse, these powerful effects are magnified by the technology of sound recording.

Rallying Power

Released in 1985, "We Are the World" right away was the fastest-selling record of the decade. Four million copies were sold within six weeks. Profits from the record, produced by big-name entertainers who volunteered, went to the USA for Africa project. The marketplace success paled, however, next to the social impact. The record's message of the oneness of humankind inspired one of the most massive outpourings of donations in history. Americans pumped $20 million into USA for Africa in the first six weeks the record was out. Within six months, $50 million in medical and financial support was en route to drought-stricken parts of Africa. "We Are the World," a single song, had directly saved lives.

The power of recorded music is not a recent phenomenon. In World War I, "Over There" and other records reflected an enthusiasm for U.S. involvement in the war. Composers who felt strongly about the Vietnam war wrote songs that put their views on vinyl. "The Ballad of the Green Berets" cast U.S. soldiers in a heroic vein, "An Okie from Muskogee" glorified blind patriotism, and there were dozens of antiwar songs.

Political speech writers know the political value of tapping into popular music. It was no accident in the 1992 primaries when George Bush paraphrased a Nitty Gritty Dirt Band song to a New Hampshire crowd: "If you want to see a rainbow, you've got to stand a little rain." In his 1988 State of the Union message, President Bush borrowed from Paul Simon's "The Boy in the Bubble" to make a point about the economy: "If this age of miracles and wonders has taught us anything, it's that if we can change the world, we can change America."

In short, music has tremendous effects on human beings, and the technology of sound recording amplifies these effects. The bugle boy was essential to Company B in earlier times, but today reveille is on tape to wake the troops. Mothers still sing Brahms' lullaby, but more babies probably are lulled to sleep by Brahms on CD. For romance, lovers today rely more on recorded music than their own vocal cords. The technology of sound recording gives composers, lyricists and performers far larger audiences than would ever be possible through live performances.

Leading and Reflecting Change

Besides explicit advocacy and its immediate, obvious effects, recorded music can have subtle impacts on the course of human events. **Elvis Presley,** "the white boy who sang colored," hardly realized in the mid-1950s that his music was helping to pave the way for U.S. racial integration. It was the black roots of much of Presley's music, as well as his suggestive gyrations, that made him such a controversial performer. Whatever the fuss, white teenagers liked the music, and it blazed a trail for many black singers who became popular beyond the black community. A major black influence entered mainstream U.S. culture. There was also a hillbilly element in early rock, bringing the concerns and issues of poor, rural whites—another oppressed, neglected minority—into the mainstream consciousness. Nashville ceased to be an American cultural ghetto.

While recorded music has the power to move people to war and peace, to love and to sleep, it also reflects changing human values. In 1991, as U.S. troops were massing at the Persian Gulf to reclaim Kuwait, U.S. record-makers issued music that reflected public enthusiasm for the war. Arista Records put Whitney Houston's Super Bowl version of "The Star Spangled Banner" on a single, which sold 750,000 audio copies in only eight days. It was the fastest-selling single in Arista's history. Boston Dawn's remake of the Shirelles' oldie "Soldier Boy," expressing a woman's love for her soldier overseas, included some rap lines from the soldier. It was very much a song of the times, and the record company, American Sound, had 25,000 backorders for the record almost as soon as it was released.

<aside>
m e **dia online**

Elvis Presley: He ain't nothin' but a hound dog. The official site.
www.elvis-presley.com
</aside>

Recording Industry

STUDY PREVIEW Although some recorded music is in-your-face, people take a lot of what the recording industry produces for granted. Even so, the industry is a $40 billion global enterprise with links to other mass media.

Industry Scope

When urban sophisticates in earlier eras wanted music, they arranged to attend a concert. If wealthy enough, they went to the parlor and sat at the piano. Rural folks had their music too—a fiddle on the front porch in the evening, a harmonica at the campfire. Music was a special event, something to be arranged. To those folks, life today would seem one big party—music everywhere all the time. Yes, we arrange for concerts and major musical events, but we also wake to music, shop to music, drive to music. Many of us work to music and study to music. In fact, the recording industry has products in so many parts of our lives that many people take most of them for granted.

The recording industry that brings music to mass audiences, both the flashy stuff and everything else, is gigantic. Global sales in 2000 were estimated at $40 billion

<aside>
Elvis Presley
Artist who melded black and white genres into rockabilly in the 1950s.
</aside>

Media People

David Geffen

Brooklyn-born **David Geffen,** whose mother was an immigrant from Russia and his father from Poland, built Geffen Records from scratch into the pre-eminent independent label. In 1990 he sold out to the MCA entertainment conglomerate for $710 million. The deal made him a billionaire—the first self-made billionaire in Hollywood history.

Geffen, born in 1943, learned the ropes in the mailroom at William Morris talent agency in Manhattan. Unlike most people at the strait-laced agency, Geffen went out scouting for talent in New York clubs and dives. Soon he had signed emerging megatalent, including the Youngbloods and the Association, both of which would score hits in the mid-1960s.

In 1970, living in Los Angeles, Geffen rented an old French château on Sunset Boulevard and created his own label: Asylum Records. He attracted promising talent, including Joni Mitchell, Linda Ronstadt and Tom Waits. Although Asylum issued only about 20 albums a year, Geffen made good money. As in New York, he worked the clubs in the evening searching for new talent. He found the Eagles by following a tip to a walkup apartment where the group jammed.

Records to Movies. David Geffen, after making a fortune in records—first at Asylum, then at Geffen Records—now is part of the Dreamworks movie studio, with partners Jerry Katzenberg and Steven Spielberg. Dreamworks, founded in 1994, became the first successful new major studio in Hollywood in almost 60 years.

Meanwhile, the Warner Communications conglomerate needed a record label. For $7 million, Geffen, at age 26, folded Asylum in with Warner's Nonesuch and Elektra labels. The hits kept coming with Carly Simon and Bob Dylan, among others.

What set Geffen apart? Biographer Stephen Singleton said: "Stimuli go straight into his pores, and then he turns it around as new entertainment products for consumers in the marketplace." About talent, Geffen was intuitive.

In 1975 Geffen saw an opportunity to realize a childhood dream of being in the movie business. He left Asylum to become vice chair of Warner Brothers Pictures. The highly structured Warner operation was a bad fit, however, and Geffen left a year later. After a diagnosis of cancer, he spent a few years collecting art and teaching at UCLA and Yale. But when the tumor turned out to be benign, he decided to go back to making records, creating Geffen Records in 1980. He dabbled in Broadway, too, including a 33 percent share of *Cats.* Geffen also put together movie deals, among them *Risky Business, Lost in America, Little Shop of Horrors* and *Beetlejuice.*

When Geffen sold Geffen Records to MCA in 1990, the proceeds made him the biggest individual taxpayer in the nation. But he wasn't about to retire. Next came Dreamworks, an $8 billion venture with director Steven Spielberg and ex-Disney executive Jeffrey Katzenberg. Dreamworks, founded in 1994, became the first major new Hollywood studio to succeed since 20th Century Fox was founded in 1935.

David Geffen
Recording, movie entrepreneur; first self-made billionaire in Hollywood.

with $15 billion in the United States alone. Those totals don't include the value of black-market music that the industry estimates at an additional third. Nor do the totals include symbiotic industries like fan magazines, music television and radio that, all together, claims revenues approaching $17 billion a year. Then there are concerts, performers' merchandise, sponsorships and a miscellany of other related enterprises.

Media Abroad

Global Market Downside

The U.S. record industry dominates the global music market. Of the $40 billion that people around the world pay for records every year, $32 billion is for U.S. products. That's 80 percent.

This global dominance has a downside. In 1999, as the Asian economies continued in economic depression, record sales plummeted. The problem severely dented revenue for the U.S. record-makers that had built substantial markets in Asia.

Exacerbating the situation was a dearth of super-sellers. Aside from the *Titanic* soundtrack, there were no megahits out of Nashville, California or anywhere else in 1999.

The stakes are big. David Geffen became the richest person in Hollywood by building Geffen Records from scratch, then sold it for three-quarters of a billion dollars. Thomas Middelhoff has invested a major part of the Bertelsmann media empire in the record industry. Edgar Bronfman has done the same with Seagram's Universal stake in Paramount, now part of Paris-based Vivendi. Time Warner and Sony are other big players.

The Big Five

The U.S. record industry is concentrated in five major companies with 84 percent of the market. Each of these majors is, in turn, part of a larger media conglomerate:

- **Paramount.** After late 1990s mergers, Paramount commanded 26.4 percent of U.S. record sales. Nobody else was larger. The parent company is Vivendi of France. Labels include Decca, Geffen, Kapp, MCA and UNI.
- **Warner.** Warner, a U.S. company owned by AOL Time Warner, commands 17.9 percent of the U.S. market. Labels include Atco, Atlantic, East West, Elektra, Giant, Interscope, Nonesuch, Reprise, Sire and Warner.
- **Sony.** This Japanese company bought Columbia Records from CBS in 1988. By 2000, Sony accounted for 16.3 percent of U.S. sales. Labels include Columbia, Epic and WTG.
- **BMG.** Bertelsmann Music Group, named for the German media conglomerate that owns the company, holds 16.1 percent of U.S. record sales. Labels include RCA and Artista.
- **EMI.** This London-based company, part of the Philips conglomerate in the Netherlands, holds 13.3 percent of the U.S. market. Labels include PolyGram, Motown, Mercury, Island, Deutsche Grammophon and ATM.

Indies

About 10 percent of the U.S. record market is held by independent companies. Although many indies are financially marginal, they are not to be written off. A Seattle indie, Sub Pop, did Nirvana's rough-edged first album *Bleach* in 1988. Some indies prosper in market niches. Windham Hill succeeded with high-tech jazz recordings in

Big Five
The five main companies in the U.S. recording industry.

Media People

Berry Gordy

With an $800 loan from his family, Berry Gordy Jr., a Detroit auto factory worker with a record store on the side, went into the recording business. That was in 1958. A few months later, in 1959, Motown Records was born. Successes piled on successes. By 1988, 30 years later, Motown was the largest black-owned business in the United States. The label's list, with "the Detroit Sound," as it was called, propelled many performers to huge success. Among them: Diana Ross, Smokey Robinson and Stevie Wonder.

Gordy wrote the early Motown music and found the performers. From a makeshift studio on West Grand, Gordy ran the recording sessions. Early on, he did just about everything. Gordy's knack was gliding performers into the style that became his signature. The music and lyrics captured urban life in Detroit, its pleasures and its disappointments, many of

them flowing from universal human experience. Young blacks throughout the country related to the Motown sound. So did white teenagers.

Then in 1988, after a nearly 30-year run, Gordy received an offer he couldn't refuse: $61 million from a major label, MCA, and an investors' group. The investment by MCA and its partners was profitable. Four years later, quintupling their money, they sold Motown to British-

Motown Sound. Berry Gordy, shown here with actress Della Reese, built Motown Records from scratch into dominance among independent labels, but even Motown was eventually absorbed into the majors. A predecessor to Paramount, now the world's largest record company, bought Motown in 1988. Today, five giant record companies, all part of global media conglomerates, sell almost 17 out of every 20 records sold in the United States.

based record giant Polygram for $300 million.

Not all had gone well under Polygram, however. Gradually, many of the label's acts had drifted elsewhere. Exceptions were Diana Ross, Stevie Wonder and the Temptations. New talent joined Motown, like Boyz II Men and Brian McKnight, but, by and large, the newcomers didn't develop the huge followings of the Gordy heyday.

Media Databank

Megadeals

Big-star megadeals have returned to fashion after almost ruining the U.S. record industry in 1979. The question, again, is whether the industry may be overextending itself financially. Recent deals surpass any of those of the 1970s. Many are multiyear packages, sometimes including more than records. Both Madonna and Michael Jackson's deals, for example, include movies. Here, according to industry insiders, are among the best deals of recent years:

Artist	Label	Deal
Prince	Warner	$108 million
Madonna	Warner	$75 million
Michael Jackson	Sony	$65 million
ZZ Top	BMG	$50 million
Aerosmith	Sony	$50 million
Janet Jackson	Virgin	$40 million

Media Timeline

Development of the Record Industry

1877 Thomas Edison introduced a recording-playback device, the Phonograph.

1887 Emile Berliner introduced technology to record discs simultaneously.

1920s Joseph Maxwell introduced electrical microphones and recording system.

1948 Peter Goldmark introduced long-play microgroove vinyl 33⅓-rpm records.

1950s Rock 'n' roll, a new musical genre, shook up the record industry.

1960 Stereo recordings and playback equipment were introduced.

1983 Digital recording on CDs was introduced.

1998 Streaming technology made downloading from the web possible.

the 1980s, as did 415 Records with its own brand of rock. A single hit can propel an independent label from a relatively obscure market niche into a major independent. For Rounder Records it was releases by George Thorogood and the Destroyers in the late 1970s. For Windham Hill it was a hit by pianist George Winston. IRS scored with the group R.E.M.

Sound-Recording Technology

STUDY PREVIEW The recording industry, as with all mass media, has been built on technological advances and breakthroughs, beginning with Thomas Edison's mechanical phonograph.

Thomas Edison's Phonograph

For years scientific journals had speculated on ways to reproduce sound, but not until 1877 did anyone build a machine that could do it. That was when U.S. inventor **Thomas Edison** applied for a patent for a talking machine. He used the trade name **Phonograph**, which was taken from Greek words meaning "to write sound."

The heart of Edison's invention was a cylinder wrapped in tin foil. The cylinder was rotated as a singer shouted into a large metal funnel. The funnel channeled the voice against a diaphragm, which fluttered to the vibrations. A stylus, which most people called a "needle," was connected to the diaphragm and cut a groove in the foil, the depth of the groove reflecting the vibrations. To listen to a recording, you put the cylinder on a player and set a needle in the groove that had been created in the recording process. Then you placed your ear to a megaphonelike horn and rotated the cylinder. The needle tracked the groove, and the vibrations created by the varying depths of the groove were fed through the horn. This process was called **acoustic recording.**

Edison's system contained a major impediment to commercial success: A recording could not be duplicated. In 1887 **Emile Berliner** introduced a breakthrough. Rather than recording on a cylinder covered with flimsy foil, as Edison did, Berliner used a sturdy metal disc. From the metal disc Berliner made a mold and then poured a thermoplastic material into the mold. When the material hardened, Berliner had a

media online
Thomas Edison: Learn more about the great inventor.
www.thomasedison.com

Thomas Edison
Built the first audio recorder-playback machine.

Phonograph
First recorder-playback machine.

acoustic recording
Vibration-sensitive recording technology.

Emile Berliner
His machine played discs that could be mass-produced.

Thomas Edison. Prolific U.S. inventor Thomas Edison devised a machine that took sound waves and etched them into grooves on a foil drum. When the drum was put on a replacing mechanism and rotated, you could hear the recorded sound. Edison's Phonograph, as he called it, was never a commercial success because his recordings could not be duplicated. It was a later inventor, Emile Berliner, who found a way to mass produce recorded music.

near-perfect copy of the original disc—and he could make hundreds of them. Berliner's system, called the Gramophone, led to mass production.

Electrical Recording

In the 1920s, the Columbia and Victor record companies introduced records based on an electrical system perfected by **Joseph Maxwell** of Bell Laboratories. Metal funnels were replaced by microphones, which had superior sensitivity. For listening, it was no longer a matter of putting an ear to a mechanical amplifying horn that had only a narrow frequency response. Instead, loudspeakers amplified the sound electromagnetically.

Joseph Maxwell
Introduced electrical recording in the 1920s.

Early Mechanical Recording. Band music was popular in the early days of sound recording. Brass sounds picked up well on the primitive mechanical recording equipment. In recording's early days, John Philip Sousa recorded hundreds of cylinders because the technology did not permit duplicating copies from masters. Each cylinder sold to a customer was an original. Some recording studios had up to 10 recording horns—which allowed 10 cylinders to be made at once. Still, recording was time-consuming.

Magnetic tape was developed in Germany and used to broadcast propaganda in World War II. In 1945 U.S. troops brought the German technology home with them. Ampex began building recording and playback machines. The 3M Company perfected tape. Recording companies shifted from discs to magnetic tape to record master discs. An advantage of tape was that bobbles could be edited out. Creative editing became possible.

While magnetic tape suggested the possibility of long-playing records, the industry continued to use brittle shellac discs that revolved 78 times a minute. One problem with the 10-inch **78-rpm** disc was that it could accommodate only three to four minutes of sound on a side.

Microgrooves and Stereo

One day **Peter Goldmark,** chief engineer at Columbia Records, was listening to a 78-rpm recording of Brahms' second piano concerto, Arturo Toscanini conducting. The concerto was divided onto six discs, 12 sides. Fed up with flipping discs, Goldmark got out his pencil and calculated whether a slower spin and narrower grooves could get the whole concerto on one disc. It was possible, although it would take both sides. At least the break could come between movements.

In 1948 Goldmark's long-playing record was introduced. Each side had 240 **microgrooves** per inch and contained up to 25 minutes of music. Offering several advantages, **LPs** soon replaced the 78-rpm record. Not only did each record have more music, but also the sound was better.

Until the late 1970s technical progress produced nothing as revolutionary as the microgroove, but the improvements, taken all together, made for dramatically better sound. Anyone who has grown up with Sting would hardly believe that record-buyers accepted the sound quality of Bill Haley records only 40 years earlier.

Stereo came in 1961. Multiple microphones recorded on separate tracks. Records played the sound back through two speakers, simulating the way people hear—through both left and right ears. Consumers went for the new quality. FM stereo radio was introduced about the same time.

Except for tapes, Edison's 1877 technology, refined by Maxwell half a century later, was at the heart of sound recording for 101 years. The technology was called **analog recording** because it converted the waves that were physically engraved in the grooves of the record into electrical pulses that coincided analogously with the waves in the grooves.

Digital Technology

STUDY PREVIEW Digital-based compact discs, introduced in 1983, gave music lovers crisper sound than ever before. The digital revolution moved up a notch when streaming was devised in the late 1990s so that music could be distributed on the web.

Compact Discs

Record-makers developed a technological revolution in 1978: the **digital recording.** No longer were continuous sound waves inscribed physically on a disc. Instead, sound waves were sampled at millisecond intervals, and each sample was logged in

magnetic tape
German invention that allowed sound editing.

78-rpm
Shellac records, rotated 78 times per minute, up to four minutes per side.

Peter Goldmark
Devised successful long-play records.

microgrooves
240 grooves per inch, 25 minutes per side at 33⅓-rpm.

LP
Long-play record, 33⅓-rpm, plastic, larger disc than 78s.

stereo
Left and right tracks.

analog recording
Sound waves physically engraved in the record.

digital recording
Recording and playback system using on-off binary code for sound.

computer language as an isolated on-off binary number. When discs were played back, the digits were translated back to the sound at the same millisecond intervals they were recorded. The intervals would be replayed so fast that the sound would seem continuous, just as the individual frames in a motion picture become a moving blur that is perceived by the eye as continuous motion.

By 1983 digital recordings were available to consumers in the form of **compact discs,** silvery 4.7-inch platters. The binary numbers were tiny pits on the disc that were read by a laser light in the latest version of the phonograph: the **CD** player. The player itself converted the numbers to sound.

Each disc could carry 70 minutes of uninterrupted sound, more than Peter Goldmark dared to dream. Consumers raved about the purity. Some critics argued, however, that there was a sterility in digital recording. The sound was too perfect, they said. Instead of reproducing performances, said the critics, compact discs produced a quality that was more perfect than a performance. Traditional audiophiles had sought to reproduce live music perfectly, not to create a perfection that could never be heard in a live performance.

Streaming

When the web burst into existence in the 1990s, everybody saw the potential, at least in theory, for the web to move sound and animation. One practical problem: **bandwidth.** The wires on which web messages moved were far short of the capacity, called bandwidth, to accommodate the massive digital files needed for re-creating sound and video. E-mail messages were tidy little packets that were easily handled. Web pages with illustrations and photos were fatter but manageable. But sound and animation? In 1997 it required 21.4 hours to move 18 minutes of animation.

Then came **compression** software that trimmed excess coding for digitized messages before transmission. With music, extreme sounds, generally beyond the range of human hearing, were dropped. In other ways too, the software trimmed the digital files. People still couldn't hear transmissions live, but if they waited a few minutes for a download to be completed, they could use the web for music and even video. **Streaming** technology went a step further, allowing earlier parts of a transmission to be seen or heard while later parts of the file were still being downloaded.

To be sure, quality suffered, but for many purposes the quality was good enough. With audio compression technology such as MPEG, Level 3, **MP3** for short, music fans could tap myriad sources for recorded music, many of them offering free access.

Recording technology had come a long way since Edison.

Evolution of Music

STUDY PREVIEW Evolving African-American folk music and hillbilly white music came together in the 1950s to create rock 'n' roll. This hybrid musical genre fueled the record industry and popular culture explosively. In the process of becoming big business, the authenticity of early rock was compromised.

American Folk Music

Most music historians trace contemporary popular music to roots in two distinctive types of American folk music, both of which emerged in the South.

---

compact disc
Digital record format; now dominant.

CD
Short for compact disc.

bandwidth
Capacity of a medium, such as a cable, to carry messages. The greater the bandwidth, the greater the capacity.

compression
Compacting audio and video messages to reduce transmission time over the web.

streaming
Allows a user to begin seeing or hearing a web message while parts of the message are still being transmitted.

MP3
Format in which digitized music is condensed for web transmission and smaller file size.

BLACK MUSIC.   Africans who were brought to the colonies as slaves used music to soothe their difficult lives. Much of the music reflected their oppression and hopeless poverty. Known as **black music,** it was distinctive in that it carried strains of slaves' African roots and at the same time reflected the black American experience. This music also included strong religious themes, expressing the slaves' indefatigable faith in a glorious afterlife. Flowing from the heart and the soul, this was folk music of the most authentic sort.

After the Civil War, black musicians found a white audience on riverboats and in saloons and pleasure palaces of various sorts. That introduced a commercial component into black music and fueled numerous variations, including jazz. Even with the growing white following, the creation of these latter-day forms of black music remained almost entirely with African-American musicians. White musicians who picked up on the growing popularity of black music drew heavily on black songwriters. Much of Benny Goodman's swing music, for example, came from black arranger Fletcher Henderson.

In the 1930s and 1940s a distinctive new form of black music, rhythm and blues, emerged. The people who enjoyed this music were all over the country, and these fans included both blacks and whites. Mainstream American music had come to include a firm African-American presence.

HILLBILLY MUSIC.   Another authentic American folk music form, **hillbilly music,** flowed from the lives of Appalachian and Southern whites. Early hillbilly music had a strong colonial heritage in English ballads and ditties, but over time hillbilly music evolved into a genre in its own right. Like black music, hillbilly fiddles and twangy lyrics reflected the poverty and hopelessness of rural folk, "hillbillies" as they called themselves. Also like black music, hillbilly music reflected the joys, frustrations and sorrows of love and family. However, hillbilly music failed to develop more than a regional following—that is, until the 1950s when a great confluence of the black and hillbilly traditions occurred. This distinctive new form of American music, called **rockabilly** early on, became rock 'n' roll.

Early Rock 'n' Roll

Music aficionados quibble about who invented the term *rock 'n' roll*. There is no doubt, though, that Memphis disc jockey **Sam Phillips** was a key figure. From his job at WREC, Phillips found an extra $75 a month to rent a 20-foot by 35-foot storefront, the paint peeling from the ceiling, to go into business recording, as he put it, "anything, anywhere, anytime." His first jobs, in 1949, were weddings and bar mitzvahs, but in 1951 Phillips put out his first record, "Gotta Let You Go" by blues singer Joe Hill Louis, who played his own guitar, harmonica and drums for accompaniment. In 1951 Phillips recorded B. B. King and then **Jackie Brenston's** "Rocket 88," which many musicologists call the first rock 'n' roll record. Phillips sold his early recordings, all by black musicians, mostly in the blues tradition, to other labels.

In 1952 Phillips began his own Sun Records label and a quest to broaden the appeal of the black music he loved to a wide audience. "If I could find a white man who had the Negro sound and the Negro feel, I could make a billion dollars," he said. In a group he recorded in 1954, the Starlight Wranglers, Sam Phillips found Elvis Presley.

black music
Folk genre from American black slave experience.

hillbilly music
Folk genre from rural Appalachian, Southern white experience.

rockabilly
Black-hillbilly hybrid that emerged in the 1950s.

Sam Phillips
Pioneered rockabilly, rock 'n' roll; discovered Elvis Presley.

Jackie Brenston
Recorded "Rocket 88," first rock 'n' roll record, in 1951.

A Premier Indie. Memphis music promoter Sam Phillips was the visionary who saw a mass audience for a hybrid of hillbilly music and black soul music. Looking for "a white boy who can sing colored," Phillips found Elvis Presley in a threesome that put out four singles, beginning with "That's All Right" in 1954, on Phillips' Sun label. Sun became a major indie.

Sam Phillips

Elvis Presley

Elvis' first Sun recording, "That's All Right," with Scotty Moore and Bill Black, found only moderate success on country radio stations, but Sam Phillips knew that he was onto something. It wasn't quite country or quite blues, but it was a sound that could move both white country fans and black blues fans. Elvis moved on to RCA, a major label. By 1956 he had two of the nation's best-selling records, the flip-side hits "Don't Be Cruel" and "Hound Dog," plus three others among the year's top 16. Meanwhile, Sam Phillips was recording Carl Perkins, Roy Orbison, Johnny Cash and Jerry Lee Lewis, adding to the distinctively American country-blues hybrid: wild, thrashing, sometimes reckless rock 'n' roll.

The new music found a following on radio stations that picked up on the music mix that Cleveland disc jockey Alan Freed had pioneered as early as 1951—occasional rhythm 'n' blues amid the mainstream Frank Sinatra and Peggy Lee. By 1955 Freed was in New York and clearly on a roll. Freed helped propel Bill Haley and the Comets' "Rock Around the Clock" to number one. Rock's future was cemented when "Rock Around the Clock" was the musical bed under the credits for the 1955 movie *Blackboard Jungle*. Young people flocked to the movie not only for its theme of teen disenchantment and rebellion but also for the music.

Changes in the Music Business

STUDY PREVIEW   The emergence of indies with rock 'n' roll in the 1950s changed the relationship of major record companies with performers. Artists gained new control of their work. Digital technology in the 1990s furthered this change, putting relatively low-cost production capabilities into the hands of artists.

Restructured Record Industry

In the late 1950s the relationship between indies and majors changed substantially. In effect, the indies became the talent research and development arm of the majors. When an indie's talent showed promise, the artist or group moved to a major label, or the indie entered a joint venture or distribution deal with a major.

Even so, the elitist-populist tension continued. Today, reviewers still pan the record industry's **Grammy Awards** for favoring derivative artists who may be as popular but whose artistic merits are second-rate. In 1991, Sinéad O'Connor, an especially talented and innovative artist, boycotted the Grammy ceremony. The awards, she said, were merely the record industry's hype to promote sales and had little to do with authentic artistry. Her point was underscored by reviewers who, in covering O'Connor's defection, noted that previous Grammy winners included such dubious talents as Debby Boone and the group Toto.

Profit can be made by imitating what's gone before and been successful. It is safer to be derivative than innovative. Critics note that conglomerate parent companies persistently pressure their record subsidiaries to increase profits, which, in effect, discourages artistic innovation and risk. This is not to say that there is no innovation, but there are financial lures and rewards for homogenization that supersede a sense of responsibility to foster artistic contributions.

Joe Smith, president of Capitol records, was unwittingly revealing about the profit-over-art orientation of the major record companies when he defended the televised Grammy awards by saying, "They get good ratings. This is not the International Red Cross."

Music Demassification

Although company-dictated homogenization is a factor in popular music, performers won't put up with corporate people choosing everything from their music to their wardrobe. The South Carolina quartet Hootie and the Blowfish, for example, started by making the rounds at college bars and frat houses in the late 1980s and, along the way, found the cash to produce the album *Kootchypop*. It was a distinctive work, hardly something manufactured by corporate marketing people, and Hootie gradually built a following. In fact, the group self-marketed an astounding 50,000 copies of *Kootchypop*, which headed them to the big time. Their 1994 album *Cracked Rear View*, on the major Atlantic label, sold 3 million the first year out, 2 million the next.

Technology has put sophisticated low-cost recording and mixing equipment within the means of a lot of **garage bands.** As little as $15,000 can buy 16-track recorders and 24-channel mixing boards, plus remodeling, to do what only a major studio could a few years ago. Back then, only big-name artists could afford their own studios. Now almost everyone can. Home recording studios in the United States now number more than 100,000. Since 1980 commercial studios have dwindled from 10,000 to 1,000. Dan Daley, an editor at the trade journal *Mix*, calls this the democratization of the recording industry, which has returned an independent attitude among artists that record companies have been forced to recognize.

The widespread availability of **mini-studios** is contributing to a **demassification** in recorded music that, in some respects, should please elitists. Music that flows from the soul and heart of the musicians, reflecting the life experiences of the artists without strong commercial imperatives, is being recorded. And some of this music

Grammy Awards
Annual record industry recognition for artists, technicians.

garage bands
Low budget, aspiring groups.

mini-studios
Use consumer-quality, not professional-quality, equipment.

demassification
Focusing of music at subgroups within the mass audience.

Stick Audio. Japanese manufacturers, the leaders in digital mobile devices, have introduced flash-memory cards, the size of a stick of chewing gum, that can scan the web, download music, and play it back on wristband and headband players. Sales were projected at $1.5 billion in 2000, $4.8 billion by 2004.

moves the culture in new directions. Early rap and hip-hop, for example, had authenticity. So did early Seattle grunge. Elitists note, though, that breakthroughs are always subsumed by derivative artists who try to pick up on a new sound that's become popular. The result, at worst, is a cultural setback and, at best, the cultural stagnation that comes from homogenization.

Streaming Adjustment

From the mainstream record industry's perspective, digital technology seemed to have gotten wildly out of control in the late 1990s. MP3 compression technology and streaming technology made it possible for fans to swap music on an unprecedented scale. Fans were exchanging free what they once had to buy through retail outlets and record clubs. Doomsayers forecasted the end of the industry or at least a devastating restructuring.

The record companies fueled the gloomy forecasts with frantic suits against Napster, MP3.com, Gnutella and other companies whose software made web swapping possible. Incredibly, one group, the heavy rockers Metallica, even went after its own fans. Metallica attorneys scoured the Napster site, found addresses of 330,000 people who had downloaded its music and demanded in court that Napster revoke their access.

In reality, record companies were far less desperate than it appeared. The lawsuits were designed to slow web inroads into sales while the companies created their own web marketing vehicles. The companies held several trump cards:

- Most major artists were contractually bound to major record-makers in long-term deals. With only a few exceptions, the popular talent wasn't leaving.
- The record companies had the marketing expertise and muscle—large budgets too—to create big hits. Odds were still against artists succeeding by going it alone on the web.

To the consternation of record-store chains and independent record shops, the record companies set up online sales channels. In 2000, Sony and Universal announced plans for a subscription service with single songs available for downloading, probably at 75 cents, easily within even a teenager's budget. Although subscription music wouldn't be free, the sites would have huge, easily navigated repertoires plus all kinds of other attractions: preview snippets, music news, gossip, trivia, games, concert tickets, artist merchandise.

Sheryl Crow. Recording performers are divided on the free downloading that streaming software makes possible. Sheryl Crow has called for controls, but she hesitates to use the word *pirates* to describe young fans who violate copyright law in downloading. "It happens to be at their fingertips," she says.

The major labels recognized the impossibility of wiping out illegal downloading but figured that aggressive court actions could minimize the threat. The majors were willing to leave free downloading to niche music and new performers seeking any exposure they could get.

Meanwhile, most business analysts project that the record industry will sustain the steady, though unspectacular, 3 to 6 percent growth rate of recent years.

Media Databank

Popular Recorded Music

Artist	Album	Sales
Michael Jackson	*Thriller*	25 million albums
The Eagles	*Greatest Hits, 1971–1975*	24 million albums
Pink Floyd	*The Wall*	22 million albums
Fleetwood Mac	*Rumours*	18 million albums
Billy Joel	*Greatest Hits,* Vols. 1–2	18 million albums
Led Zeppelin	*Led Zeppelin IV*	17 million albums
AC/DC	*Back to Black*	16 million albums
The Beatles	The White Album	16 million albums
Boston	*Boston*	16 million albums
Garth Brooks	*No Fences*	16 million albums
Whitney Houston	The *Bodyguard* soundtrack	16 million albums
Alanis Morissette	*Jagged Little Pill*	16 million albums

Marketing Records

STUDY PREVIEW   The success of the record industry is highly dependent on free air-play over radio and also music video outlets such as MTV. This dependence is no better illustrated than in the payola scandals that first surfaced in the 1950s.

Radio Airplay

Record companies ship new releases free to radio stations in hope of **airplay.** Few make it. Stations are inundated with more records than they can possibly audition. Also, most stations stick to a playlist of already popular music rather than risk losing

airplay
When a record receives free time on radio or a video channel.

Media Databank

Record Sales by Genre

Rock music has dominated record sales since the 1950s. These are 1998 data:

Rock	25.7 percent
Country	14.1 percent
Rhythm and blues	12.8 percent
Rap	10.0 percent
Pop	9.7 percent
Gospel	6.3 percent
Classical	3.3 percent
Jazz	1.9 percent
Soundtracks	1.7 percent

Media Abroad

MTV in Russia

The music video television service MTV added Russia in 1998 as the 86th country carrying variations of the home-bred U.S. core product. The inaugural show was a tape of a Moscow concert by the British race group Prodigy, followed by "Beavis & Butt-Head." About 15 million Rus-sians, in Moscow and St. Petersburg, could watch.

The MTV Russian launch could not have come at a worse time economically. The economy was collapsing, and advertising commitments dried up. Why advertise Levi's if people don't have any money? Pepsi kept a limited ad presence. MTV executive Bill Roedy said that MTV was confident that there would be a lucrative Russian audience over time. But he also said that plans to expand beyond Moscow and St. Petersburg were being shelved for a while.

listeners by playing untried records. To minimize the risk and yet offer some fresh sounds, most radio station music directors rely heavily on charts of what music is selling and being played elsewhere. The most-followed charts appear in the trade journal *Billboard*. There also are **tip sheets,** which leading disc jockeys and music directors put out as a sideline and sell by subscription.

Airplay is valuable because it is the way in which most people are first exposed to new releases that they might go out and buy. Also, airplay is efficient for record-makers because it is free except for the cost of shipping the sample records. Because an estimated 13 percent of record purchases are on impulse, promotional point-of-purchase displays also are important.

The relationship between the radio and record industries is a two-way street. Not only do radio stations need records, but record-makers need radio to air their products. Records that win airplay are almost assured success. This interdependence expanded to television in the 1980s when cable television services, such as MTV and VH-1, built their programming on video versions of popular music.

Payola

The relationship between the radio and record industries has had problems, notably **payola.** In 1958 the grapevine was full of stories about record companies' bribes to disc jockeys to play certain records. One audit found that $263,000 in "consulting fees" had been paid to radio announcers in 23 cities. The **Federal Trade Commission** filed unfair competition complaints against record companies. Radio station managers, ever conscious that their licenses from the Federal Communications Commission could be yanked for improprieties, began demanding signed statements from disc jockeys that they had not accepted payola. Dozens of disc jockeys in major markets quietly left town.

Payola scandals did not end with the 1950s. Competition for airplay has continued to tempt record promoters to "buy" airtime under the table. There were indictments again in the 1970s. And in 1988 two independent promoters were charged with paying $270,000 to program directors at nine widely imitated radio stations to place records on their playlists. One station executive was charged with receiving $100,000 over two years. Some payola bribery involved drugs.

Billboard
Weekly music trade journal.

tip sheets
Music newsletters.

payola
Bribes to radio people to promote new records.

Federal Trade Commission
U.S. government agency that ensures fairness in commerce.

Media People

Alan Freed

Alan Freed had always liked music. At Ohio State University, Freed played trombone in a jazz band called the Sultans of Swing. After an army stint during World War II, he landed an announcing job at a classical radio station in Pennsylvania. Later Freed went to Cleveland and became host for a late-night radio show. He played records by Frank Sinatra, Jo Stafford, Frankie Laine and other popular performers of the day.

That was before rock 'n' roll. In 1951 Cleveland record store owner Leo Mintz, who sponsored Freed's "Record Rendezvous" on WJW, decided one day to show Freed his shop. Neither the radio nor the record industry was ever the same again. Freed saw Mintz's shop full of white teenagers. They weren't listening to Frank Sinatra or Jo Stafford. They were dancing in the aisles to rhythm and blues—"Negro music," as it was called then. And they were buying it.

Freed went back to WJW and talked management into a new show, "Moon Dog House." With the new

Alan Freed. On his "Moon Dog House" radio show in Cleveland, Alan Freed laid the groundwork for rock 'n' roll in the early 1950s. By the time he reached New York, Freed was a major influence in the success of young, new performers.

show and a variety of promotions, Freed built a white audience for black music in Cleveland. Word spread. Soon Freed was syndicated on faraway stations with music that soon everyone was calling "rock 'n' roll." Within three years he was the top disc jockey in New York City. Rock 'n' roll was here to stay, and the U.S. record industry would be shaken to its roots.

Alan Freed embodied the best and the worst of the intertwined businesses of music, records and radio. He was an innovator at a pivotal point in music history. The rock 'n' roll that he played trans-

formed musical tastes almost overnight. Critics charged that his rock 'n' roll was corrupting a generation of teenagers, the same kind of controversy that still plagues the record business today.

For Freed, like many people in the music industry, life was in the fast lane. He became involved in shady deals with record-makers who were eager for him to play their music on the air, and he was prosecuted—some say persecuted—in the first of many payola scandals. Like many in the faddish record and music industry, Freed rose fast and died young—in 1965 at age 43.

Payola scandals illustrate the relationship that has taken shape between the record and radio industries. It is an interdependent relationship, but radio holds the upper hand. It is the record industry's need for airplay that precipitates the scandals.

Tracking Sales

A lot of the mystery about popularity lists for recorded music has disappeared. In 1991, amid growing concern that using lists based on calls to record shops wasn't working, Soundscan, Inc. launched a new system for *Billboard* magazine. Soundscan arranged with record shops to record sales by dragging CDs over a bar-code scanner. From the resulting data, Soundscan provided *Billboard* with information for its influential weekly lists.

media online

Alan Freed: The definitive online resource covering the life and work of the man who coined the phrase *rock 'n' roll* and helped to shape the future of popular music.
www.alanfreed.com

Alan Freed
Disc jockey who integrated black music, rock into playlists.

One problem with the earlier system, which involved calling up record shops and talking to whichever clerk answered, was that the clerks, who were usually young people, were more inclined to notice the pop stuff. As a result, country and middle-of-the-road music was slighted.

That the old system had problems was illustrated the first week of *Billboard*'s Soundscan lists. New, alternative music, such as that of Jesus Jones and Fishbone, plummeted. Jesus Jones dropped from fifth to 29th, Fishbone from 133rd to 182nd. Country singer Garth Brooks suddenly had two albums in the Top 30. The *Pretty Woman* soundtrack rose from 127th to 75th.

Evaluating Record Companies

STUDY PREVIEW Sales and profits are quantitative measures of a record company's success. How about its artistic success? Qualitative measures are harder to come by. Elitists give high marks to companies that have a commitment to music that breaks new ground artistically.

Commercial Success

The measure of success in the record-making business is the **gold record.** Once a single sells 1 million or an album sells 500,000 copies, the **Recording Industry Association of America** confers a gold-record award. A **platinum record** is awarded for 2 million singles sold or 1 million albums.

About half the records sold in the United States today are pop, a broad category that ranges from Barry Manilow's mellow sentimentalism to hard-edged rap. The rest are country, classical, jazz and the other musical genres.

Populist Measures

The easy measure of a record company's success is sales, reflected in market share. In 2001 Paramount led, but rankings can change overnight. A super-selling soundtrack such as *Titanic* or a runaway album like Michael Jackson's *Thriller* can mean a near-instant reshuffling.

Shareholders are interested more in bottom lines than in sales. This focus places a premium on cost controls. Lavish contracts that don't generate best-selling music hurt profits. Many conglomerates don't release profit figures for individual subsidiaries, but trade journals have inside sources on what's working and what's not. The promotion and firing of executives, all reported in the trade journals, are indicators of how things are going.

Quality Measures

Your evaluation of record companies will flow from your own values. For many rap fans and free-expression advocates, Gerald Levin assumed heroic dimensions at Time Warner for his eloquent defense of artistic liberties in a controversy over Ice T's *Cop Killer* album. Police groups and others calling for a ban were less impressed with Levin. Months later, Levin waffled on the issue and called for Warner artists to begin dialogue on standards. The fervid support of free-expressionists waned.

gold record
Award for sales of 500,000 albums, 1 million singles.

Recording Industry Association of America
Record industry trade organization.

platinum record
Award for sales of 1 million albums, 2 million singles.

A key qualitative measure of record companies is their support of new artistic directions. The majors once played it mostly safe, regurgitating already popular styles rather encouraging fresh material and new genres that could help define the human condition in new and telling ways. Elitists, who believe that the mass media should use their influence to advance culture, would be especially critical of toning down cutting-edge work to avoid confronting tough social issues and to sidestep controversy. This is less a problem than it was at one time, but a lot of safe pap is still issued.

A question worth asking: From a record company's products and rhetoric, what seems to be its commitment to the potential of the music to examine issues, both personal and social, to advance our understanding and our ability to live fulfilling lives?

Evaluating Music

While the popularity of records is measurable, quality is not. As with all art, beauty is in the eye of the beholder—and people have a great range of tastes. What is it, then, that elitists would identify as music that's important? Which music most improves our sense and understanding of our world, our existence, our relationships? These questions are difficult because many people are so emotionally tied up with their music that intelligent dialogue is impossible. Someone who is wound up in the incessant beat of rave might have little feel for the intricate elegance of a lullaby or the sophisticated interplay of a 132-piece orchestra's horn section performance of Jan Sibelius' "Symphony No. 2 in D, Opus 43."

Also, people change. Music that excites a 13-year-old who has just discovered pop on the radio might have no appeal to the same person 10 years later. Tastes change.

Developing a sense for excellence in recorded music, something transcending a visceral response, means joining the best dialogue. Finding music critics on your wavelength is an excellent starting point. Then stretch out to include other critics. Where to tap into the dialogue? Some genres receive continued and excellent comment in music magazines, including *Rolling Stone.* Major newspapers, notably the New York *Times* and *Wall Street Journal,* approach a wide range of recorded music seriously. Terry Gross' "Fresh Air" radio interview program from KHYY in Philadelphia, carried by many noncommercial stations, spends a lot of time on music.

Among yardsticks that elitists apply in evaluating music are:

- **Originality.** Nobody sees much artistic merit in imitative music. A toned-down cover version of a song, recorded merely to sell copies, clutters the marketplace with more of the same. This isn't to say that all remakes are artistic dead-ends. New renditions can be significant, fresh interpretations. But music that merely regurgitates doesn't score high on any kind of qualitative scale.
- **Commercial appeal.** Music that is recorded for commercial reasons, nothing more, cannot score well qualitatively. Many people derive pleasure from listening, but artistic significance is lacking.
- **Lyrics.** Lyrics are like poetry and can be scored in the same kinds of ways. In fact, some of our time's best poetry is from songwriters. There is also bad poetry out there.
- **Composition.** Like lyrics, the score and the arrangement are indicators of a recording's value.
- **Sophistication.** An appreciation of some music requires sophistication. Someone versed in Italian cultural history is likely to derive more from a fresh interpretation

Colin Powell on MTV. The music channel MTV strengthened its public affairs programming after the September 11th suicide jetliner attacks on New York and Washington. One special, "Be Heard," featured Secretary of State Colin Powell.

Nelly. The St. Louis rap lyricist-performer Nelly was named hiphop and rap Artist of the Year at the American Music Awards in 2002. Factors considered in recordings of all genres include originality in the music and lyrics.

Media People

Ricky Martin

In an age of globalized mass media, pop singer Ricky Martin is a record-maker's dream. Immersed since birth in Puerto Rico culture, Martin is at home with Español music that transcends many national boundaries. His experience with the Puerto Rico heartthrob group Menudo, beginning at age 12, gave him stage presence. Touring gave him a feel for audiences around the world. Playing Miguel Morez on the U.S. soap opera *General Hospital* added to his running start.

Whether Ricky Martin helped to create salsa's popularity as a music genre in the 1990s or whether he rode a salsa wave can be debated. The fact is that he was the genre's headline act. His first solo albums landed atop Latin charts, and his third album was followed by a triumphant tour of Mexico and South and Central America. His following was transnational. A fourth album included "La Copa de la Vida," which hit Number 1 in 22 countries. The song was the anthem for the 1998 World Cup in France. The album won Martin a Grammy.

Across-the-Board Musical Tastes. Although known for his salsa, Ricky Martin has a broad range of musical interests that he attributes to his mother. Fed up with the kids playing rock all day, she pulled them by their ears to a Celia Cruz concert. Now, says Martin, "I listen to everything. I'm like a sponge."

Is Martin lucky? He doesn't deny his good fortune but points out too that he has worked hard. He remembers being in choirs and school plays at age 6. Being with Menudo for five years was heady stuff for a teenager but also demanding. The same with his success in "Les Miserables" on Broadway, one show a day, seven days a week. As Ricky Martin will tell you, he has paid his dues.

He still is. Knowing the fickleness of media popularity and that music crazes come and go, Ricky Martin is building bridges to other genres. There is a British techno-acoustic strain in his ballad with Madonna. He has done a duet with Swedish songtress Mejo. His producers are a diverse bunch, including Emilo Estefan Jr., known for the Miami Sound, and Desmond Child, who has worked on Bon Jovi and Aerosmith albums. Martin also wants to continue building an intergenerational following, not just kids.

For a label like Sony, which has issued most of his work, one goal is to find products that can be marketed globally. Ricky Martin, right for the media's accelerating globalization in the 1990s, seems poised to remain so.

of Ottorino Respighi's Renaissance dance music than will someone who can't find Italy on a map. Some art, recorded music included, requires listeners to bring their special knowledge, intelligence and sensitivity to the table.

■ **Body of work.** The genius of a particular recording sometimes is best understood and appreciated in terms of its context. Does a song fit into a significant larger theme in Ricky Martin's latest album? Has Sinéad O'Connor moved into a new phase of her exploration of the human condition?

Heisting Music

STUDY PREVIEW   Record companies claim that home dubbing has eroded 20 percent of their sales—$1.5 billion a year worldwide. About the same is lost to pirates who are in the business of dubbing recorded music for the black market.

Home Dubbing

The lopsidedness of the relationship between the radio and record industries became obvious in another way in the 1970s. Instead of buying records and tapes at $9 each, people began sharing records and dubbing them onto relatively inexpensive blank tapes. Phonograph manufacturers offered machines that not only could dub tapes from records but also could record from the air at the flick of a toggle. Many FM stereo radio stations catered to home dubbers by announcing when they would play uninterrupted albums.

The economic effect of **home dubbing** on the record industry is hard to measure precisely, but the Recording Industry Association of America estimates that the industry loses $1.5 billion a year, one-fifth of its sales.

Although record-makers were unable to strike a deal with the radio industry to plug the home-dubbing revenue drain, progress was made on another front in 1991. The record-makers and their longtime foe on the home-dubbing issue, the manufacturers of home electronic equipment, agreed on a "taping tax." Anyone purchasing a blank tape pays a 1 percent fee that's passed on to songwriters, music publishers and others who lose royalty income from home dubbing. Congress approved the taping tax in 1992. The tax was later applied to blank CDs bought for dubbing.

Piracy

Criminal **piracy** involves dubbing records and videos and selling the dubs. An estimated 20 to 30 percent of the records and tapes sold are from shadowy pirate sources, mostly in Asia but also in other countries, including Saudi Arabia. These pirate operations have no A&R, royalty or promotion expenses. They dub CDs and

home dubbing
Recording music from a purchased record onto a blank tape or CD for personal use.

piracy
Manufacturing recorded music for sale without permission from record company, artists.

Recording Piracy. Seeking visibility for their occasional crackdowns, Thai officials steamroll seized pirated videotapes. Still, Bangkok is a major pirating center on the Pacific Rim. So is China, where Beijing vendors accost tourists for surreptitious street transactions. Illegal tapes often find their way into the black market ahead of their release through legal channels.

tapes produced by legitimate companies and sell them through black-market channels. Their costs are low, their profits are high.

These pirate operations are well financed and organized. It is not uncommon for a Bangkok pirate operation to have 100 "slave" tape-copying machines going simultaneously 24 hours a day and even to ship illegal copies before the official release by the U.S. distributor. Both the Recording Industry Association of America and the Motion Picture Association of America spend millions of dollars a year on formal trade complaints and private investigations in Bangkok and other piracy centers, but with limited success. Authorities in these places have other priorities, and antipiracy laws are weak. In an interview with *Fortune* magazine, Frank Knight, a Bangkok investigator who specializes in these cases, said, "Anybody who's been involved in past mischief, such as drug exports, finds this to be a highly lucrative crime that's easier and less punishable." Knight has tracked exports of illegal tapes to South Africa, to the Indian subcontinent, throughout the Asian Rim and to the United States. The RIAA estimates that $5 billion in music revenue is lost to pirates every year, and the MPAA estimates the loss to filmmakers at $4 billion a year.

Censorship and Recorded Music

STUDY PREVIEW A perennial problem for record-makers is pressure to sanitize lyrics to protect young listeners. Some would-be censors are at the reactionary and radical fringes of society. Others have received serious attention from congressional committees. By and large, the record industry has headed off government sanctions with voluntary labels on records.

Objectionable Music

Campaigns to ban records are nothing new. In the Roaring Twenties, some people saw jazz as morally loose. White racists of the 1950s called Bill Haley's rock "nigger music." War protest songs of the Vietnam period angered many Americans.

Government attempts to censor records have been rare, yet the **Federal Communications Commission** indirectly keeps some records off the market. The FCC can take a dim view of stations that air objectionable music, which guides broadcasters toward caution. Stations do not want to risk their licenses. Because the record industry is so dependent on airplay, hardly any music that might offend makes it to market.

The FCC has been explicit about obnoxious lyrics. In 1971 the commission said that stations have a responsibility to know "the content of the lyrics." Not to do so, said the commission, would raise "serious questions as to whether continued operation of the station is in the public interest." The issue at the time was music that glorified drugs.

Federal Communications Commission
U.S. government agency that licenses broadcast stations.

Parents Music Resource Center
Crusaded for labels on "objectionable" music.

Record Labeling

In the 1980s complaints about lyrics narrowed to drugs, sexual promiscuity and violence. A group led by Tipper Gore and wives of several other influential members of Congress, **Parents Music Resource Center,** claimed links between explicit rock music and teen suicide, teen pregnancy, abusive parents, broken homes and other social ills. The group objected to lyrics like Prince's "Sister," which extols incest; Mötley Crüe's "Live Wire," with its psychopathic enthusiasm for strangulation; Guns N' Roses' white racism; and rap artists' hate music.

The Parents Music Resource Center argued that consumer protection laws should be invoked to require that records with offensive lyrics be labeled as dangerous, like cigarette warning labels or the movie industry's rating system. After the group went to the FCC and the **National Association of Broadcasters,** record companies voluntarily began labeling potentially offensive records: "Explicit Lyrics—Parental Advisory." In some cases the companies printed lyrics on album covers as a warning.

In the preliminaries to the 1996 presidential campaign, Senate majority leader **Bob Dole,** a presidential hopeful, attacked record-makers in a bid to rally support. In his early posturing, Dole said, "We must hold Hollywood and the entire entertainment industry responsible for putting profit ahead of common decency." Another White House aspirant, **William Bennett,** focused on Time Warner, urging the media giant's bosses to remove objectionable lyrics. When Time Warner executives tried counterarguments, Bennett said, "Are you folks morally disabled?" Then House Speaker **Newt Gingrich** proposed boycotting radio stations that played "explicitly vicious" music.

The campaign found a new champion in Bob Dole's successor in the U.S. Senate in 1997. Newly elected Senator **Sam Brownback,** a Kansas Republican, announced a hearing called "An Examination of Violent Music on Youth Behavior and Well Being" and invited the news corps in. To the assembled reporters, as their tapes rolled, Brownback disgustingly recited lyrics from Marilyn Manson's "Irresponsible Hate Anthem." He then took testimony from music industry critics, including C. Delores Tucker. Robert Love, the managing editor of the music magazine *Rolling Stone,* lambasted Brownback for grandstanding but also found ironic humor in the senator's promise to keep the heat on music-makers: "That's good news for Marilyn Manson, since the only sure outcome of such government attention will be to send kids to the record store."

Lyrics and Young People

Despite countless studies, it is unclear whether mores are affected by lyrics. Two scholars from California State University at Fullerton found that most high school students are hazy on the meanings of their favorite songs. Asked to explain Bruce Springsteen's "Born in the U.S.A.," about the hopelessness of being born in a blue-collar environment, many teenagers were simplistically literal. "It's about the town Bruce Springsteen lives in," said one. Led Zeppelin's "Stairway to Heaven" has been criticized for glorifying drug or sexual rushes, but many teenagers in the study were incredibly literal, saying the song was about climbing steps into the sky. What does this mean? Professor Lorraine Prinsky of the Fullerton study concluded that teenagers use rock music as background noise. At most 3 percent, she said, are fully attentive to the lyrics.

Critics, however, see an insidious subliminal effect. Some songs repeat their simple and explicitly sexual messages over and over, as many as 15 to 30 times in one song. Said a spokesperson from the Parents Music Resource Center, "I can't believe it's not getting through. It's getting into the subconscious, even if they can't recite the lyrics."

National Association of Broadcasters
Radio, television trade organization.

Bob Dole
Sought 1996 political support by criticizing music, movies.

William Bennett
Attacked Time Warner as "morally disabled" for its music, movies.

Newt Gingrich
Congressional leader who proposed radio station boycott.

Sam Brownback
Kansas senator who held hearings to explore negative effect of violence in media on kids.

Media Future: Recordings

Now reduced to five major players, the record industry might not see further conglomeration on a grand scale. The majors can be expected, however, to gobble up indies that score big. Indies probably will proliferate with new technology that has dramatically cost the cut expense of studio equipment. It has become an easy business to get into.

As the majors join upstarts in distributing music on the web, the corner record store and even massive chain stores may become relics of the past. Web delivery is far more efficient than manufacturing, warehousing and shipping disks. Record companies probably will try a mixture of single sales and subscription sales on the web.

New artists undoubtedly will continue using the web to develop followings, but without big-budget support from recognized labels, theirs will still be an uphill struggle. The web will remain home for niche music and performers whose followers don't have enough fans to interest the Big Five or even indies.

The record industry will continue its battle against piracy, pressing especially hard on China through the World Trade Organization to enforce international copyright agreements. Crackdowns will never eradicate all piracy, however. It will be the same with bootleg music on the web. Record companies can discourage and reduce illegal activity but never eliminate it.

chapter wrap-up

For most of the 20th century, recorded music had been a banner that successive generations have used to identify themselves and their values: jazz, rock 'n' roll, bebop, disco, hip-hop, grunge. The record industry's continuing success depends on how well it can help each new generation set itself apart from mom and dad. The generational differences, however, are a two-edged issue for record-makers. Through most of the 20th century, record-makers had to deal with critics, generally older people and authorities, who believe that pop music is undermining traditional social values.

Questions for Review

1. Why is recorded music important?
2. Can you name the conglomerate owners of the major record companies?
3. Trace the technology of sound recording from Edison on.
4. What were the innovations of Thomas Edison, Emile Berliner, Joseph Maxwell and Peter Goldmark?
5. How is digital reproduction different?
6. What are the roots of U.S. popular music? How has it evolved?
7. What is the relationship of the record and radio industries?
8. How has the recording industry addressed losses through home dubbing and piracy?
9. How do would-be censors affect the record business?

Questions for Critical Thinking

1. In recent months, how has new recorded music shaped significant human events? Consider music that is inspiring human actions. This might be war music. It might be music that's flowing from a generation or subculture and giving it an identity. It might be a new love song that has become standard at weddings?
2. What has been the effect of global conglomeration in the record industry on the music you like?
3. Look into your crystal ball to assess how technological changes in the record business will play out in the future.
4. While rock 'n' roll has roots in hillbilly and black slave music, that music has even earlier roots. Trace the music to precolonial times. Also discuss what

additional streams of music have fed into modern popular music.

5. How has the relationship between artists and recording companies changed since World War II? Why has the change occurred?

6. How are measures of commercial and artistic success different in the recorded music business?

7. Why is airplay important to a recording becoming a commercial success? Explain the exceptions.

8. What do you see as a solution to the revenue drain created by MP3 technology on the record industry? If there is no solution, what will happen?

9. Discuss the effect of moralists and others who would like to change the content of some recorded music. How do these people go about trying to accomplish their goals? What common threads have there been to their criticism throughout the 20th century?

Keeping Up to Date

The weekly *Billboard* is the recording industry's leading trade journal.

Consumer magazines that track popular music and report on the record industry include *Rolling Stone* and *Spin*.

Entertainment Weekly has a regular section on music.

MISSING

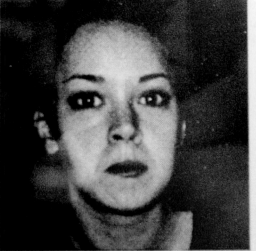

Heather Donahue
Age: 22   Height: 5'6"   Weight: 127lb
Eyes: hazel   Hair: brown

Joshua Leonard
Age: 23   Height: 5'10"   Weight: 152lb
Eyes: blue   Hair: blonde

Michael Williams
Age: 24   Height: 5'8"   Weight:
Eyes: brown   Hair: brown

Last seen camping in the Black Hills Forrest area, near Burkitsville.

PLEASE CALL FREDERICK COUNTY SHERIFF'S OFFICE WITH ANY INFORMATION YOU MAY HAVE!

(301)

***Promoting* Blair Witch.** *Nontraditional promotion for the movie* Blair Witch Project *included messages to stir curiosity among targeted young people. A lot of the messages were in unusual places, like a web site that included this authentic-appearing missing persons poster and a variety of official-looking investigation documents.*

6

Movies

Amorette Jones knew *The Blair Witch Project* was a long shot, but if, just if, she could reach an edgy youth audience, it might be a hit. She decided to build grass-roots curiosity through nontraditional avenues and fan the word-of-mouth about the movie.

It worked. *The Blair Witch Project* grossed $29 million its first weekend of wide release, outdoing the latest *Star Wars* in some movie houses. How did Amorette Jones work such magic on a cinemagraphically flawed movie with a thin story line?

Jones knew the nuances of the youth culture. She had been an executive with trendy Loud Records as well as at Universal and other studios. She signed on with Artisan Entertainment in 1997. Two years later, at age 33, as an Artisan marketing vice president, Jones found herself with the grainy, jittery *Blair Witch Project*, an offbeat first effort by directors Daniel Myrick and Eduardo Sanchez. They had made the movie for $35,000. At the Sundance Film Festival, which features works by new movie-makers, they sold it to Artisan for $1.1 million.

In May 1999 Jones began an intricate marketing campaign. She bought space on the Ain't It Cool News web site for a preview. Then she aired a teaser on MTV. That was followed by ads in college newspapers, then in *Rolling Stone* and alternative weeklies. The idea was not to make a splash but to fuel chatter about the movie.

Ads directed people to a web site for the film. The site suggested there had been a police cover-up in the disappearance of the three young filmmakers. Outtakes gave an eerie documentary feel. There were faked official documents. One day the site recorded 3 million hits.

Meanwhile, teams distributed missing-person flyers in places where young people congregated. A few screenings were conducted—just enough to whet the interest of people who didn't make one of them. The Sci-Fi Channel and Artisan together produced "The Curse of the Blair Witch." A "Blair Witch" comic book was issued. So was a book: *The Blair Witch Project—A Dossier.*

Only 15 percent of the prerelease marketing budget went to regular media, demonstrating how alternative marketing can be used to reach narrow segments of the mass audience. With the general release came a more traditional $25 million campaign for the movie—not much considering that worldwide revenues eventually reached $200 million.

What could Amorette Jones do for an encore? A *Blair* sequel followed.

Amorette Jones

media online
Blair Witch: Experience the legend online.
www.blairwitch.com

Importance of Movies

STUDY PREVIEW   The experience of watching a movie uninterrupted in a darkened auditorium has entranced people since the medium's earliest days. It is an all-encompassing experience, which has given movies a special power in shaping cultural values.

Overwhelming Experience

Movies have a hold on people, at least while they are watching one, that is more intense than any other medium. It is not unusual for a movie reviewer to recommend taking a handkerchief. Never will you hear such advice from a record reviewer and seldom from a book reviewer. Why do movies have such powerful effects? It is not movies themselves. With rare exceptions these evocative efforts occur only when movies are shown in a theater. The viewer sits in a darkened auditorium in front of a giant screen, with nothing to interrupt the experience. The rest of the world is excluded. Movies, of course, can be shown outdoors at drive-in theaters and on television, but the experience is strongest in the darkened cocoon of a movie-house.

People have been fascinated with movies almost from the invention of the technology that made it possible, even when the pictures were nothing more than wobbly, fuzzy images on a whitewashed wall. The medium seemed to possess magical powers. With the introduction of sound in the late 1920s and then color and a host of later technical enhancements, movies have kept people in awe. Going to the movies remains a thrill—an experience unmatched by other media.

Hollywood's Cultural Influence

When Clark Gable took off his shirt in the 1934 movie *It Happened One Night* and revealed that he was not wearing anything underneath, American men in great numbers decided that they too would go without undershirts. Nationwide, undershirt sales plummeted. Whether men prefer wearing underwear is trivial compared with some concerns about how Hollywood portrays U.S. life and its influence:

- Sociologist Norman Denzin says that the treatment of drinking in U.S. movies has contributed to a misleading bittersweet romanticism about alcoholism in the public consciousness.
- Scholars using content analysis have found that exponential increases in movie violence that far outpace violence in real life and contribute to perceptions that violence is a growing social problem in modern life.
- Political leaders express concern from time to time that movies corrupt the morals of young people and glamorize deviant behavior.
- Congressman Parnell Thomas once raised questions that Hollywood was advocating the violent overthrow of the government.

Movies are part of our everyday lives in more ways than we realize. Even the way we talk is loaded with movie metaphors. The *New Yorker* magazine noted this introducing an issue on Hollywood: "Our personal scenarios unspool in a sequence of flashbacks, voice-overs and cameos. We zoom in, cut to the chase, fade to black."

Because of the perceived influence of movies, some real, some not, it is important to know about the industry that creates them. This is especially true now that television entertainment programming has been largely subsumed by Hollywood and that the book, magazine and sound recording industries are closely tied into it.

Technical Heritage of Movies

STUDY PREVIEW   Motion picture technology is based on the same chemical process as photography. The medium developed in the 1880s and 1890s. By the 1930s movie houses everywhere were showing "talkies."

Adaptation from Photography

The technical heritage of motion pictures is photography. The 1727 discovery that light causes silver nitrate to darken was basic to the development of motion picture technology. So was a human phenomenon called **persistence of vision.** The human eye retains an image for a fraction of a second. If a series of photographs capture something in motion and if those photographs are flipped quickly, the human eye will perceive continuous motion.

All that was needed were the right kind of camera and film to capture about 16 images per second. Those appeared in 1888. **William Dickson** of Thomas Edison's laboratory developed a workable motion picture camera. Dickson and Edison used celluloid film perfected by **George Eastman,** who had just introduced his Kodak camera. By 1891 Edison had begun producing movies.

Edison movies were viewed by looking into a box. In France, the **Lumière brothers,** Auguste and Louis, brought projection to motion pictures. By running the film in front of a specially aimed powerful lightbulb, the Lumières projected movie images on a wall. In 1895 they opened an exhibition hall in Paris—the first movie house. Edison recognized the commercial advantage of projection and himself patented the Vitascope projector, which he put on the market in 1896.

persistence of vision
Fast-changing still photos create the illusion of movement.

William Dickson
Developed the first movie camera.

George Eastman
Devised celluloid film.

Lumière brothers
Opened the first movie exhibition hall.

Media Timeline

Movie Technology

1877 Eadweard Muybridge used sequential photographs to create the illusion of motion.

1888 William Dickson devised the motion picture camera.

1891 George Eastman devised flexible celluloid for motion pictures.

1922 Fox used sound in newsreels.

1927 Warner Brothers distributed the first talkie: *The Jazz Singer*.

1932 Disney issued the first full-color movie: *Flowers and Trees*.

1937 Disney issued the first animated feature: *Snow White*.

Adding Sound to Pictures

Dickson, at Edison's lab, came up with a sound system for movies in 1889. In the first successful commercial application, the Fox studio used sound in its 1922 Movietone newsreels. But it was four upstart movie-makers, the **Warner brothers,** Albert, Harry, Jack and Sam, who revolutionized movies with sound. In 1927 the Warners released *The Jazz Singer* starring Al Jolson. There was sound for only two segments, but it caught the public's fancy. By 1930, 9,000 movie houses around the country were equipped for sound.

Three Crises That Reshaped Hollywood

Warner brothers
Introduced sound.

The Jazz Singer
First feature sound picture.

STUDY PREVIEW In quick succession Hollywood took three body blows in the late 1940s. Right-wing political leaders sent some directors and screenwriters to jail in 1947 and intimidated movie-makers into creative cowardice. In 1948 the U.S. Supreme Court broke up the economic structure of the movie industry. Then television stole people from the box office.

Divided Hollywood. When some members of Congress set out in 1947 to unearth communist in-filtration in Hollywood, they heard what they wanted to hear from actor Robert Taylor. He testified that he had seen plenty of things "on the pink side" in Hollywood. Other Hollywood people saw through the congressional probe as a witch hunt and refused even to testify. Ten of them went to jail.

Media People

Robert Flaherty

Explorer **Robert Flaherty** took a camera to the Arctic in 1921 to record the life of an Eskimo family. The result was a new kind of movie: the documentary. While other movies of the time were theatrical productions with scripts, sets and actors, Flaherty tried something different: recording reality.

His 57-minute *Nanook of the North* was compelling on its own merits when it started on the movie-house circuit in 1922, but the film received an unexpected macabre boost a few days later when Nanook, the father of the Eskimo family, died of hunger on the ice. News stories of Nanook's death stirred public interest—and also attendance at the movie, which helped to establish the documentary as an important new film genre.

Flaherty's innovative approach took a new twist in the 1930s when propagandists saw reality-based movies as a tool to promote their causes. In Germany the Nazi government produced propaganda films, and other countries followed. Frank Capra directed the vigorous five-film series *Why We Fight* for the U.S. War Office in 1942.

After World War II there was a revival of documentaries in Flaherty's style—a neutral recording of natural history. Walt Disney produced a variety of such documentaries, in-

Nanook of the North. The documentary became a film genre with explorer Robert Flaherty's *Nanook of the North* in 1922. This film was an attempt to record reality— no actors, no props. The film was especially potent not only because it was a new approach and on a fascinating subject but also because, coincidentally, Nanook died of starvation on the ice about the time that it was released.

Robert Flaherty

cluding the popular *Living Desert* in the 1950s.

Today, documentaries are unusual in U.S. movie houses, with occasional exceptions such as movies built on rock concerts.

The CBS television network gained a reputation in the 1950s and 1960s for picking up on the documentary tradition with *Harvest of Shame,* about migrant workers, and *Hunger in America.* In the same period the National Geographic Society established a documentary unit, and French explorer Jacques Cousteau

went into the television documentary business.

Such full-length documentaries are mostly relegated to the Public Broadcasting Service and cable networks today. The major networks, meanwhile, shifted most documentaries away from full-length treatments. Typical is CBS's "60 Minutes," a twice-weekly one-hour program of three minidocumentaries. These new network projects combined reality programming and entertainment in slick packages that attracted larger audiences than traditional documentaries.

The Hollywood 10

Hollywood had a creative crisis in 1947 when Congressman Parnell Thomas, chair of the House Un-American Activities Subcommittee, began hearings on communists in Hollywood. Thomas summoned 47 screenwriters, directors and actors and demanded answers to accusations about leftist influences in Hollywood and the Screen Writers

Robert Flaherty
First documentary maker.

Media Abroad

Foreign-Language Films

In the 1950s when Hollywood was churning out lowbrow Doris Day movies, U.S. movie-goers who wanted an intellectual experience turned to foreign-language films. Every major city and a lot of smaller ones had at least one art house, featuring films from the likes of Sweden's Ingmar Bergman, Italy's Michelangelo Antonioni and Spain's Luis Buñuel. Some foreign fare also had sensual appeal, like the Brigitte Bardot and Gina Lollobrigida films, a kind of sensuality that Hollywood feared to try at the time.

By the 1960s almost 5 percent of the U.S. box-office revenue was from subtitled and dubbed imports. Some foreign-language films even made the mainstream circuit, among them Claude Lelouch's *A Man and a Woman* (France, 1966) and Constantin

Costa-Gavras' *Z* (France/Algeria, 1969). Federico Fellini's *La Dolce Vita* grossed more than $80 million in U.S. movie houses in 1961.

Today, foreign-language films are barely a blip in the U.S. movie exhibition industry. Rare is a foreign film that makes the circuit, including even award-winning movies from China's Wen Jiang, Greece's Theo Angelopoulos, Poland's Krzysztof Kielowski and France's Patrice Leconte. Foreign films have slipped to less than 1 percent of the U.S. box office.

What happened?

Hollywood, in the late 1960s, began treating sophisticated subjects, using many techniques that had been pioneered in Europe. U.S. movie-makers even trod close to sexual explicitness. This preempted

some of the appeal of the foreign films. Today it is unusual for even the most acclaimed works from abroad to show up on U.S. screens.

Another reason for the decline in foreign-language films on U.S. screens is that some of the best foreign directors today are pitching in on Hollywood projects, like Germany's Roland Emmerich (*Independence Day*), Hong Kong's John Woo (*Mission Impossible 2*) and Holland's Jan de Bont (*Twister*).

The fact remains, however, that U.S. moviegoers don't have access to most of the excellent work being produced in other languages and in other countries. Also, directors who produce films in other countries are missing out on access to the large U.S. audience. Nobody is better off for these developments.

Guild. Ten witnesses who refused to answer insulting accusations went to jail for contempt of Congress. It was one of the most highly visible manifestations of McCarthyism, a post-World War II overreaction to Soviet communism as a national threat.

The Thomas hearings had longer-lasting deleterious effects. Movie producers, afraid the smear would extend to them, declined to hire the **Hollywood 10**. Other careers were also ruined. One expert identified 11 directors, 36 actors, 106 writers and 61 others who suddenly were unwelcome in their old circles and could not find work.

Among the Hollywood 10 was screenwriter **Dalton Trumbo.** His powerful pacifist novel *Johnny Got His Gun* made Trumbo an obvious target for the jingoist Thomas committee. After Trumbo refused to answer committee questions, he was jailed. On his release, Trumbo could not find anybody who would accept his screenplays. He resorted to writing under the pseudonym Robert Rich. The best he could earn was $15,000 per script, one-fifth of his former rate. When his screenplay for *The Brave One* won an Academy Award in 1957, "Robert Rich" did not dare show up to accept it.

In a courageous act, **Kirk Douglas** hired Trumbo in 1959 to write *Spartacus.* Then Otto Preminger did the same with *Exodus.* Besides Trumbo, only screenwriter **Ring Lardner Jr.** rose from the 1947 ashes. In 1970, after two decades on the blacklist, Lardner won an Academy Award for *M*A*S*H.*

The personal tragedies resulting from the Thomas excesses were bad enough, but the broader ramification was a paucity of substantial treatments of major social and

Hollywood 10
Film industry people who were jailed for refusing to testify at congressional anti-Red hearings.

Dalton Trumbo
Blackballed screenwriter.

Kirk Douglas
Had the courage to hire Dalton Trumbo despite anti-Red pressure.

Ring Lardner Jr.
Blacklisted screenwriter who reemerged with *M*A*S*H.*

Media Timeline

The Movie Industry

1912 Carle Laemmle founded Universal, the first major Hollywood studio.

1916 Investors took a role in the art and creativity after the financial disaster of D. W. Griffith's *Intolerance.*

1919 Charlie Chaplin, Douglas Fairbanks, D. W. Griffith and Mary Pickford founded United Artists studio.

1923 Warner brothers founded the studio bearing their name.

1923 Walt Disney formed a studio.

1924 Metro-Goldwyn-Mayer founded.

1924 Columbia Pictures founded.

1929 RKO founded.

1948 Congressional hearings labeled leading Hollywood people as communist sympathizers.

1952 U.S. Supreme Court ruled that the First Amendment protects movies.

1950s Television eroded movie attendance.

political issues. Eventually, movie-makers rallied with sophisticated treatments of controversial subjects that, it can be argued, were more intense than they might otherwise have been. It was an anti-McCarthy backlash, which did not occur until the mid-1950s, when Hollywood began to reestablish movies as a serious medium.

Court Bans on Vertical Integration

The government has acted twice to break up the movie industry when it became so consolidated that there was no alternative to preventing abuses. **Adolph Zukor**'s Paramount became a major success as a producer and distributor of feature films in the 1920s, but Zukor wanted more. He began buying movie houses and eventually owned 1,400 of them. It was a classic case of **vertical integration,** a business practice in which a company controls its product all the way from inception to consumption. Not only was Paramount producing and distributing movies, but through its own movie houses Paramount was also exhibiting them. It was profitable. Soon other major Hollywood studios also expanded vertically.

Still not satisfied with his power and profits, Zukor introduced the practice of **blockbooking,** which required non-Paramount movie houses to book Paramount films in batches. Good movies could be rented only along with the clunkers. The practice was good for Zukor because it guaranteed him a market for the failures. Exhibitors, however, felt coerced, which fueled resentment against the big studios.

The U.S. Justice Department began litigation against vertical integration in 1938, using Paramount as a test case. Ten years later, in the 1948 **Paramount decision,** the U.S. Supreme Court told Paramount and four other major studios to divest. They had a choice of selling off either their production or distribution or exhibition interests. Most sold their theater chains.

The effect shook the whole economic structure on which Hollywood was based. No longer could the major studios guarantee an audience for their movies by booking them into their own theaters. What had come to be known as the **studio system** began to collapse. There was new risk in producing movies because movie houses decided what to show. Also, there was a hitherto missing competition among studios.

Adolph Zukor
Movie mogul whose Paramount epitomized vertical integration.

vertical integration
In the movies, controlling the whole creation-production-exhibition sequence.

blockbooking
Studio requirement that movie houses rent clunkers to get good movies.

Paramount decision
Required studios to loosen control on the whole creation-distribution-exhibition sequence.

studio system
The centralized studio-controlled movie industry that was disassembled by the Paramount decision.

Media Abroad

Movies of India

At 85 cents a seat, people jam Indian movie houses in such numbers that some exhibitors schedule five showings a day starting at 9 a.m. Better seats sell out days in advance in some cities. There is no question that movies are the country's strongest mass medium. Even though per capita income is only $1,360 a year, Indians find enough rupees to support an industry that cranks out 900 movies a year, three times more than U.S. movie-makers. Most are B-grade formula melodramas and action stories. Screen credits often include a director of fights. Despite their flaws, Indian movies are so popular that it is not unusual for a movie house in a Hindi-speaking area to be packed for a film in another Indian language that nobody understands. Movies are produced in 16 Indian languages.

The movie mania centers on stars. Incredible as it may seem, M. G. Ramachandran, who played folk warriors, and M. R. Radha, who played villains, got into a real-life gun duel one day. Both survived their wounds, but Ramachandran exploited the incident to bid for public office. He campaigned with posters that showed him bound in head bandages and was elected chief minister of his state. While in office, Ramachandran continued to make B-grade movies, always as the hero.

Billboards, fan clubs and scurrilous magazines fuel the obsession with stars. Scholars Erik Barnouw

Bollywood. The Indian movie industry, centered in Bombay and sometimes called Bollywood, pumps out an incredible 900 movies a year. Although India has some internationally recognized movie-makers, most Bollywood productions are formulaic action movies that critics derisively label curry-westerns.

and Subrahmanyam Krishna, in their book *Indian Film,* characterize the portrayals of stars as "mythological demigods who live on a highly physical and erotic plane, indulging in amours." With some magazines, compromising photos are a specialty.

A few Indian movie-makers have been recognized abroad for innovation and excellence, but they generally have an uphill battle against B-movies in attracting Indian audiences. Many internationally recog-

nized Indian films, such as those by Satyajit Ray, flop commercially at home.

In the late 1990s Indian movies developed a cult following in the United States. The major Indian movie export market, however, was in Hindi-speaking parts of the world. In Sri Lanka, for example, whose language Sinhalese is closely related to Hindi, the domestic movie industry is overshadowed by imported Indian movies.

Movie scholars say that the court-ordered divestiture, coming when it did, had a more damaging effect than the Justice Department and the courts foresaw. It was about this time that Parnell Thomas and his congressional committee were bashing producers, which undermined Hollywood's creative output. Now the whole way in which the industry operated was required to change overnight. Hollywood was coming apart.

Media People

Steven Spielberg

Although born in 1946, Steven Spielberg couldn't have made films like *Jaws*, *E.T.* and *Indiana Jones* if he weren't still a kid himself. At the dinner table with his seven children, Spielberg starts with a few lines from a story that has popped into his head, and then each kid adds a few lines. Where it will go, nobody knows, with everybody keeping the story moving.

Spielberg is chair of the Starbright Foundation, which has raised $40 million for hospitalized kids. He visits children's wards to coach kids on using Starbright-provided computers for e-mail and browsing.

Although Spielberg loves creating movies for kids, he has also taken on serious subjects. Some Spielberg movies deal with serious, even distressing, issues, such as genocide and slavery,

deftly making important points about the human condition. Among his movies geared not just for kids but for general audiences are these:

- *A.I.: Artificial Intelligence* (2001)
- *Saving Private Ryan* (1998): On the horrors of war.

Kid Stuff. Movie-maker Steven Spielberg is one of our time's most compelling storytellers. Since *Jaws* in 1975, he has directed movies involving history, science and fantasies, including many on issues that kids deal with, such as *E.T.* and *Jurassic Park*. Spielberg spends a lot of time in children's hospital wards, working with online links provided by the Starbright Foundation, which he heads.

- *Amistad* (1997): On slavery.
- *Schindler's List* (1991): On the Holocaust.
- *The Color Purple* (1985): On racial and sexual injustice.

Challenge from Television

Movie attendance in the United States peaked in 1946 at 90 million tickets a week. Every neighborhood had a movie house, and people went as families to see the latest shows, even those that were not very good. Movies, rivaled only by radio, had become the nation's dominant entertainment medium.

Then came television. Early television sets were expensive, and it was a major decision in many families whether to buy one. In many households there were family conferences around the kitchen table to decide whether to divert the weekly movie budget to buying a television. Movie attendance plummeted to 60 million a week by 1950 and then to 46 million by 1955. Today, only about 19 million people go to the movies in a typical week.

Not only had the movie industry been pummeled by Congress into creative timidity and then been broken up by the courts, but it had also lost the bulk of its audience. Doomsayers predicted an end to Hollywood.

Hollywood's Response to Television

STUDY PREVIEW Ironic as it seems, television has been the greatest force shaping the modern movie industry. When television began eroding movie attendance in the 1950s, movie-makers responded with technical innovations such as wraparound screens. There

***A Beautiful Mind* Producers.** Accepting Oscars for *A Beautiful Mind* are producers Ron Howard and Brian Grazer. Russell Crowe played the doomed genius John Nash.

also were major shifts in movie content, including treatments of social issues that early television would not touch.

Technical Innovation

When television began squeezing movies in the late 1940s, movie-makers scrambled for special effects to hold their audience. Color movies had been introduced in the 1930s. In the 1950s they came to be the standard—something that early television could not offer. Other technical responses included **CinemaScope** with an image 2½ times wider than it was high. CinemaScope seemed more realistic than the earlier squarish screen images. Gimmicky innovations included Smell-o-vision, a dubious, short-lived technique. Odors wafted through movie houses to enhance the audience's sensual involvement.

Content Innovation

Besides technical innovations, movie-makers attempted to regain their audiences with high-budget movies, with innovative themes and, finally, by abandoning their traditional mass audiences and appealing to subgroups within the mass audiences.

High-budget movies called **spectaculars** became popular in the 1950s. How could anybody, no matter how entranced by television, ignore the epic *Quo Vadis,* in which one scene included 5,500 extras? There were limits, however, to luring Americans from their television sets with publicity-generating big-budget epics. The lavish *Cleopatra* of 1963 cost $44 million, much of which 20th Century Fox lost. It just cost too much to make. Even so, movie-makers continued to risk occasional big-budget spectaculars. No television network in the 1960s would have put up $20 million to produce the profitable *Sound of Music.* Later, George Lucas' *Star Wars* movies were huge successes of the sort television could not contemplate.

CinemaScope
Horizontal screens.

spectaculars
Big-budget epic movies.

Television's capture of a broad mass audience was a mixed blessing. Television was in a content trap that had confined movies earlier. To avoid offending big sections of the mass audience, television stuck to safe subjects. Movie-makers, desperate to distinguish their products from television, began producing films on serious, disturbing social issues:

- *Blackboard Jungle* (1955): On disruptive classroom behavior, hardly a sufficiently nonthreatening subject for television.
- *Rebel Without a Cause* (1955): Starred James Dean as a rebellious teenager seeking identity.
- *Cat on a Hot Tin Roof* (1958): An adaptation of Tennessee Williams's play involving marital intimacy and implied homosexuality.

Meanwhile, television continued to be squeamish into the 1960s while Hollywood continued testing new waters. In 1967 a Sidney Poitier trilogy, *Guess Who's Coming to Dinner*, *To Sir with Love* and *In the Heat of the Night*, explored social inequity and injustice. In *The Wild Bunch* in 1969, director Sam Peckinpah brought new blood-spurting violence to the screen, in slow motion for additional impact. Similar effects in Arthur Penn's 1967 classic *Bonnie and Clyde* left audiences awed in sickened silence. Nevertheless, people kept coming back to movies that showed graphic violence. Sex was taboo on television but not at the movies. It was the theme in *Bob & Carol & Ted & Alice*, (1969) *Carnal Knowledge* (1971) and *I Am Curious, Yellow* (1969). Sex went about as far as it could with the hard-core *Deep Throat* of 1973, which was produced for porno houses but achieved crossover commercial success in regular movie houses.

Movies came to be made for a younger crowd. By 1985 regular movie-goers fell into a relatively narrow age group: from teenagers through college age. Fifty-nine percent of the tickets were purchased by people between the ages of 12 and 24. Even so, the industry did not produce exclusively for a young audience. Movie-makers recognized that the highest profits came from movies with a crossover audience. These were movies that attracted not only the regular box-office crowd but also infrequent movie-goers. Essential, however, was the youth audience. Without it a movie could not achieve extraordinary success. The immensely profitable *E.T.* was an example. It appealed to the youth audience, to parents who took their small children and to film aficionados who were fascinated by the special effects.

Melding of Movies and Television

STUDY PREVIEW   Hollywood's initial response to television was to fight the new medium, an effort that had mixed results. Next, Hollywood adopted the idea that if you can't beat them, join them. Today, most of the entertainment fare on television comes from Hollywood.

Reconciliation of Competing Industries

Despite Hollywood's best attempts to stem the erosion in attendance caused by television, box-office sales continued to dwindle. Today, an average of only 19 million tickets are sold a week, less than one-quarter of attendance at the 1946 box-office peak. Considering that the U.S. population has grown steadily during the period, the decline has been an even more severe indication of television's impact on movie attendance.

Edison's Kinetoscope.
Among the earliest mechanisms for watching movies was inventor Thomas Edison's kinetoscope. A person would look through a peephole as a strip of film was wound over a lightbulb. The effect was shaky. Later, Edison borrowed a technique from the Lumière brothers of Paris for the Vitascope system of projecting images on a wall.

Despite a near 50-year slide in box-office traffic, Hollywood has hardly lost its war with television. The movie industry today, a $4-billion-a-year component of the U.S. economy, is so intertwined with television that it is hard to distinguish them. Three-quarters of the movie industry's production today is for television.

There remains, however, an uneasy tension between the exhibitors who own movie houses and television. Theater traffic has not recovered, and while moviemakers and distributors are profiting from new distribution channels, especially home videos, these new outlets are hurting theater traffic.

First Runs and Aftermarkets

When movie-makers plan films today, they build budgets around anticipated revenues that go beyond first runs in movie houses. Unlike the old days, when movies either made it or didn't at the box office, today movie-makers earn more than 17 percent of their revenue from pay television services such as HBO after the movie has played itself out in movie houses. Another 8 percent comes from selling videotapes.

For most movies, foreign release is important. Movies are usually released in the United States and abroad simultaneously. Foreign distribution revenues can be significant. The box-office revenue from U.S. movies abroad, in fact, is significant in balance-of-trade figures with other nations. After-market revenue comes from pay-per-view television channels and the home video market.

Movie Exhibitors

STUDY PREVIEW　Most movie-goers today go to multiscreen theaters that show a wide range of movies. These multiplexes are a far cry from the first commercially successful exhibition vehicles: peep show machines that only one viewer at a time could watch. Intermediate exhibition vehicles ranged from humble neighborhood movie houses to downtown palaces.

Early Exhibition Facilities

In the early days, movie patrons peered into a box as they cranked a 50-foot loop over sprockets. These were called peep shows. When Thomas Edison's powerful incandescent lamp was introduced, peep show parlors added a room for projecting movies on a wall. Business thrived. Typical admission was a nickel. By 1908 just about every town had a nickelodeon, as these early exhibition places were called.

As television gained prominence in the 1950s, many movie houses fell into disrepair. One by one they were boarded up. Drive-in movies eased the loss. At their peak, there were 4,000 drive-ins, but that did not offset the 7,000 movie houses that had closed. Furthermore, **drive-ins** were hardly 365-day operations, especially in northern climates.

drive-ins
Outdoor screens viewable from automobiles.

multiscreen theaters
Several screens with central infrastructure.

Multiscreen Theaters

Since a nadir in 1971, when annual attendance dropped to 875 million, the exhibition business has evolved into new patterns. Exhibitors have copied the European practice of **multiscreen theaters,** and they have built them mostly in suburbs. The new multiscreen theaters, with as many as 28 screens, allow movie-goers to choose among

Media Timeline

Movie Exhibition

1895 Auguste and Louis Lumière opened a movie house in Paris.

1896 Koster and Bial's Music Hall was the site of the first public motion picture showing in United States.

1946 U.S. box office peaked at 90 million a week.

1970s Multiscreen movie houses became the norm.

several first-run movies at one location. A family can split up in the lobby—mom and dad to one screen, teenagers to another and the little kids to a G-rated flick. Stadium-style seating became the latest fashion.

Showing rooms are smaller today, averaging 340 seats compared with 750 in 1950. Most multiplexes have large and small showing rooms. An advantage for exhibitors is that they can shift popular films to their bigger rooms to accommodate large crowds and move other films to smaller rooms.

Multiplex theaters have lower overhead. There might be 12 projectors but only one projectionist, one ticket taker and one concession stand. The system has been profitable. Today there are more than 23,000 screens in the United States—more than double the number in 1970 and more than the total number of theaters when movies were the only game in town. In the 1990s ticket sales fluctuated from year to year, but the trend in attendance has been downward.

Inner-City Movie Houses

Movie-going is in a resurgence in inner-city neighborhoods. The trade journal *Target Market News* reported that box-office revenue from African Americans rose 49 percent between 1993 and 1997—more than double the industry's overall increase.

One reason for the increase was the construction of giant movie houses, some with 14 auditoriums, in black neighborhoods where no theaters had been built in decades. In Chicago, black-owned Inner City Entertainment opened its seventh South Side movie house in 1999 in a joint deal with the Cineplex Odeon chain. Alisa and Donzell Starks, the couple behind ICE, say that their theaters are among the Cineplex Odeon top 25 for ticket sales. In all, Cineplex has 1,600 theaters in the United States and Canada.

Other chains are also building in the 'hood. Sony Corporation and basketball star Magic Johnson, for example, have teamed up to build theaters in black neighborhoods in Atlanta, Houston and Los Angeles.

What makes these theaters economically successful? They target their audience. In Chicago, ICE goes with radio, a popular Chicago black medium, to promote movies. Alisa Starks arranged for a special screening of *Amistad*, a movie about black slaves fighting for their freedom. There was not a vacant seat.

Movies on black issues and themes are given longer runs than they are elsewhere—and receive continuing promotion. Promotion, in fact, is the key, says Alisa Starks. It was a packed house when Nike sponsored a panel in an ICE theater with black movie director Spike Lee and Chicago basketball characters. With the panel was a screening of Lee's *He Got Game*.

Even the concession fare has an ethnic attraction: popcorn shrimp and Louisiana hot links.

media online

Sony Pictures Entertainment: At home at Sony. www.spe.sony.com/pictures/ sonymovies/index.html.

Disney: Walt's world. www.disney.com

Paramount Pictures: This site is an entrance to Paramount movies now playing, as well as to home video releases. A link to Paramount's television production arm takes you to sites for more than 40 hours of network and syndicated programming the studio pumps out every week. www.paramount.com

Box-Office Income

Movie houses usually split box-office receipts with a movie's distributor. **Exhibitors** get an upfront payment, called the **nut,** to cover basic costs. After the nut, **distributors** take the lion's share of box-office revenue, often 90 percent for the first week. Deals vary, but eventually, it a movie runs long enough, the split ends up being 50:50. For movie houses, the concession stand is an important revenue source. Concessions are so profitable that exhibitors sometimes agree to give up their nut entirely for a blockbuster and rely on popcorn and Milk Duds to make money. Movie-house markups on confections are typically 60 percent, even more on popcorn.

The distributors that market and promote movies claim a share of movie revenue, taking part of the nut from exhibitors and charging booking fees plus expenses to the movie-makers. Distribution expenses can be significant. Advertising and marketing costs average $6 million per movie. Making multiple prints, 1,200 copies at $1,200 a piece, and shipping them around the country are expensive too. Distributors also take care of aftermarkets, including foreign exhibition, videocassette distributors and television—for a fee plus expenses.

With some movies not enough box-office income is generated for the producers to recoup their production expenses. These expenses can be staggering, about $51 million on average. However, when production budgets are kept low and the movie succeeds at the box office, the return to the producers can be phenomenal.

Movie Finances

STUDY PREVIEW   The financing of movies is based more on hardball assessments of their prospects for commercial success than on artistic merit. The money to produce movies comes from major movie studios, banks and investment groups. Studios sometimes draw on the resources of their corporate parents.

The Lesson of "Intolerance"

The great cinematic innovator **D. W. Griffith** was riding high after the success of his 1915 Civil War epic, *The Birth of a Nation.* Griffith poured the profits into a new venture, *Intolerance.* It was a complex movie that examined social injustice in ancient Babylon, Renaissance France, early 20th-century America and the Holy Land at the time of Christ. It was a critical success, a masterpiece, but film audiences had not developed the sophistication to follow a theme through disparate historical periods. At the box office it failed.

Intolerance cost $2 million to make, an unbelievable sum by 1916 standards. Griffith had used huge sets and hundreds of extras. He ended up broke. To make more movies, Griffith had to seek outside financing. The result, say movie historians, was a dilution in creativity. Financiers were unwilling to bankroll projects with dubious prospects at the box office. Whether creativity is sacrificed by the realities of capitalism remains a debated issue, but there is no doubt that movie-making is big business.

Financing Sources

Just as in D. W. Griffith's time, movies are expensive to make—about $51 million on average. Then there are the big-budget movies. Depending on how the ex-

exhibitors
Movie-house businesses.

nut
Upfront movie-house income from the distributor.

distributors
Companies that supply movies to theaters.

D. W. Griffith
Early producer known for innovations in *The Birth of a Nation* and loose spending in *Intolerance.*

Media People

Spike Lee

Spike Lee, a bright, clever young film director, was in deep trouble in 1992. He had persuaded Warner Brothers, the big Hollywood studio, to put up $20 million for a film biography of controversial black leader Malcolm X, one of his heroes. Lee insisted on expensive foreign shooting in Cairo and Soweto, and now, not only was the $20 million from Warner gone but so was $8 million from other investors. To finish the movie, Lee put up his own $3 million up-front salary to pay, he hoped, all the production bills.

The crisis was not the first for Lee, whose experience as a movie-maker illustrates several realities about the U.S. movie industry, not all of them flattering:

- Hollywood is the heart of the U.S. movie industry, and it is difficult, if not impossible, for feature film makers to succeed outside of the Hollywood establishment.
- Hollywood, with rare exceptions, favors movies that follow themes that already have proven successful rather than taking risks on innovative, controversial themes.

- Fortunes come and go in Hollywood, even studio fortunes. Although Warner is a major studio and often flush with money, it was on an austerity binge when Spike Lee came back for more money in 1992.
- The U.S. movie industry has been taken over by conglomerates, which, as in the case of Warner Brothers, at the time a subsidiary of Time Warner, was being pressured in 1992 to maximize profits to see the parent company through a difficult economic period.

To hear Spike Lee tell it, his problem also was symptomatic of racism

Public Enemy. Between movie projects, Spike Lee produces television commercials and videos, including music videos for the popular rap group Public Enemy. There have been many slow periods between movies for Lee, who finds Hollywood money hard to come by for his work, even though he is acclaimed as one of his generation's great moviemakers. Lee blames racism among those who control Hollywood purse strings.

in the movie industry. Addressing the Los Angeles Advertising Club during the *Malcolm X* crisis, Lee, who is black, was blunt: "I think there's a ceiling on how much money Hollywood's going to spend on black films or films with a black theme."

Although studio executives would deny Lee's charge, his perceptions were born of experience in making five movies, all critically acclaimed and all profitable but all filmed on shoestring budgets and with little or no studio promotion.

---

penses are tallied, the 1997 movie *Titanic* cost somewhere between $200 million and $240 million to make. Where does the money come from?

MAJOR STUDIOS.   Many movies are financed by **major studios** with profits from their earlier movies. Most movies, however, originate not with major studios but with **independent producers.** Although independent producers are autonomous in many respects, most of them rely on major studios for financing. The studios acquire the right to distribute the movies, usually a profitable enterprise involving rentals to movie houses and television networks, home video sales and merchandise licensing.

The majors have taken new interest in independently produced movies that show up at film festivals such as Robert Redford's Sundance Film Festival in Utah. Many

major studios
Include Warner Brothers, Paramount, Disney, MGM.

independent producer
Makes movies outside major studios but sometimes with major studio's cooperation.

Media Databank

Top-Earning Movies

These are the top-earning movies of all time, listed by U.S. and Canadian gross revenue. By some measures, *Jurassic Park* leads the list with global grosses exceeding $900 million.

Movie	Director	Domestic Gross	Year
Titanic	James Cameron	$600.8 million	1997
Star Wars	George Lucas	$460.9 million	1977
Star Wars: The Phantom Menace	George Lucas	$418.5 million	1999
E.T.: The Extra-Terrestrial	Steven Spielberg	$399.9 million	1982
Jurassic Park	Steven Spielberg	$357.1 million	1993
Forrest Gump	Robert Zemeckis	$329.7 million	1994
The Lion King	Roger Allers and Rob Minkoff	$312.9 million	1994
Independence Day	Roland Emmerick	$309.2 million	1996
Return of the Jedi	George Lucas	$309.1 million	1983
The Empire Strikes Back	George Lucas	$306.2 million	1980

of these are college projects and other first-tries by unknown producers that would otherwise never have much of an audience. Some can be acquired cheaply. *The Blair Witch Project,* for example, went for $35,000 in 1998 and within a year was a box-office smash with a prequel that screened in 2000.

For most independent projects in which a major studio invests money up front, the studios do more than write checks. To protect their investments, some involve themselves directly in film projects. They examine budgets and production schedules in considering a loan request. It's common for them to send representatives to shooting sites to guard against budget overruns.

Major studios that are part of conglomerates can draw on the resources of their corporate parents. In 1952 giant MCA acquired the ailing Universal studio and plowed its recording business profits into the studio. Universal turned profitable, and MCA became even stronger by having another profitable subsidiary. The Gulf + Western conglomerate later did the same with Paramount. Coca-Cola acquired Columbia in 1982 with a promise to help Columbia through the rough times that had beset the movie company.

In the 1980s several studios acquired new corporate parents, which made it easier to finance movies. The Japanese electronics giant Sony bought Columbia in 1989. At $3.4 billion, it was the biggest Japanese takeover of a U.S. corporation in history. The size of the deal was a sign of the new resources Columbia could tap to make movies. By the early 1990s three of the largest U.S. studios were owned by giant foreign companies with the ability to generate cash from other enterprises to strengthen their new U.S. movie subsidiaries.

INVESTOR GROUPS. Special investment groups sometimes are put together to fund movies for major studios. Among them is Silver Screen Partners, which provided millions of dollars in financing for Disney projects at a critical point in Disney's revival in the 1980s.

Less proven producers, or those whose track records are marred by budget overruns and loose production schedules, often seek financing from **risk investors,** which

risk investors
Put money into projects at interest rates commensurate with risk.

Disney Animation. Animator Walt Disney catapulted his success with Mickey Mouse (née Steamboat Willie) movie cartoons, introduced in 1928, into full-length features with *Snow White and the Seven Dwarfs* nine years later. *Snow White* was a high-risk endeavor, costing $1.5 million to put together, a lot at the time, with nobody knowing how much market there would be. The public loved it, leading to new animated Disney features, including such enduring favorites as *Pinocchio* and *Bambi.* Although Walt Disney died in 1966, the company's tradition in animation has lived on. The company also has expanded into a broad range of entertainment, including movies with mature themes from its Miramax subsidiary. In 1995 Disney turned a long relationship with ABC television into a full-fledged $19 billion merger that combined CapCities/ABC and Disney.

include venture capitalists, tax-shelter organizers and foreign distributors. Risk investors often take a bigger share of revenue in exchange for their bigger risk.

BANKS.   To meet front-end production expenses, studios go to banks for loans against their assets, which include their production facilities and warehouses of vintage films awaiting rerelease. By bankrolling movies early in Hollywood's history, California-based **Bank of America** grew into one of the nation's biggest banks.

Artistic versus Budget Issues

Movie-makers are expanding their supplemental incomes by charging other companies to use movie characters, themes and music for other purposes. This has raised questions about whether commercial imperatives have more priority than artistic considerations.

MERCHANDISE TIE-INS.   Fortunes can be made by licensing other companies to use characters and signature items from a movie. In one of the most successful **merchandise tie-ins,** 20th Century Fox and George Lucas licensed Ewok dolls, R2D2 posters and even *Star Wars* bed sheets and pillowcases. By 1985, seven years after the movie's release, tie-ins had racked up sales of $2 billion. The licensing fee typically is 10 percent of the retail price of the merchandise. *Batman* tie-ins rang up $500 million in sales in 1989, within six months of the movie's release, and Warner Brothers was earning 20 percent of the retail revenue on some products.

TOYS.   For the 1995 film *Batman Forever,* Warner Brothers let the Hasbro toy company dress the Riddler. Hasbro wanted tight pants, not the baggy ones in the script, so the Riddler action toy would look better. The result? The Riddler wore tight pants on screen. A recurrent report from *Pocahontas* animators is that their bosses

Bank of America
Became a giant institution by loaning money for movies.

merchandise tie-ins
Studio deals to profit from merchandise carrying movie names and logos.

Media People

Michael Eisner

When he was a kid, Michael Eisner wanted to be a doctor. It didn't work out. Today, as chief executive of the Walt Disney Company, Eisner is credited with the vision that put together a 1995 merger of Disney and CapCities/ABC into one of the world's largest media companies. It is a corporate marriage that financial observers agree makes sense. Disney's strength, producing media content, was merged with ABC's strength, its delivery system.

An early upshot of the merger was Disney taking over Saturday morning programming on the ABC television network. Even that was more than it seemed. The newly merged company began using "Disney" as a brand to sell advertisers integrated marketing packages. Advertisers not only bought time on children's programming on Saturday mornings, but also could get first dibs on Disney product promotions and licensing.

Where is Disney/ABC going? Speculation includes staging ABC-televised sports events at new arenas at Disney theme parks. Additional possibilities lie in the fact that the

Hollywood Leader. Media observers call Michael Eisner the most powerful person in Hollywood. Eisner, chief executive of Walt Disney Company, has presided over a string of successful but diverse movies, ranging in recent years from *The Lion King* to *Crimson Tide* and *Dead Presidents*. Even more significant, he engineered the 1995 Disney acquisition of CapCities/ABC, which gives Disney a new outlet for its creative output.

ESPN sports cable channel is part of the combined company.

Meanwhile, a string of successful Disney movies fuels the corporate coffers for new initiatives. *Pocahontas* and *Toy Story* were 1995 blockbusters. Even cutting-edge and niche 1995 movies from Disney subsidiaries, including *Dangerous Minds, Powder* and *While You Were Sleeping*, pulled in more than expected. The *Dangerous Minds* soundtrack, targeted at black Americans, swelled corporate coffers.

The key to Disney's success under Eisner has been building the Disney brand name; cross-promoting Disney initiatives, such as inscribing Disney's name on ABC television programming; extending product lines in additional directions; recycling Disney products, like reissuing classic animated Disney movies, such as *Cinderella*, on a schedule; repackaging existing products for new markets; and licensing the use of Disney logos to other companies for promotions, like the hamburger chains.

ordered them to have the raccoon Meeko braid the Indian maiden's hair so that Mattel could market Braided Beauty Pocahontas dolls.

Some movie-makers deny that the cart is ahead of the horse. Disney officials, for example, say that Mattel had no hand in the script for *Pocahontas:* The script comes first, the toys second. Even so, movie-makers have huge financial incentives to do whatever it takes to ensure success. Toy-makers pay licensing fees, typically 10 percent of a toy's retail price. Disney earned $16 million, the record, for the 1994 movie *The Lion King*. In 1995 *Batman Forever* paraphernalia generated $13 million, *Pocahontas* $10 million. Power Ranger gear, tied into both the movie and the television series, has totaled $300 million, of which an estimated $30 million went back to Fox—a significant revenue source requiring hardly any studio expense.

Is this kind of commercialism undermining the artistic autonomy that normally is associated with creative enterprises such as movie-making? This is the same elitist-populist issue that is at the heart of the ongoing debate about media content. At one extreme is the pristine elitist preference for creative forces to drive content oblivious to commercial considerations. At the other extreme is the laissez-faire populist belief that nothing is wrong with marketplace forces. Populists say that if a movie's box office suffers because toy-makers have had too much sway on script decisions, movie-makers will make future adjustments—and an appropriate balance will result eventually. Some elitists accept that argument but worry nonetheless about the commercial contamination that occurs in the meantime.

MUSIC.   Tie-ins are not new. Music, for example, was a revenue source for movie-makers even before talkies. Just about every early movie house had a piano player who kept one eye on the screen and hammered out supportive mood music, and sheet-music publishers bought the rights to print and sell the music to musicians who wanted to perform it on their own. This was no small enterprise. D. W. Griffith's *The Birth of a Nation* of 1915 had an accompanying score for a 70-piece symphony.

Today, music has assumed importance besides supporting the screen drama. It has become a movie-making profit center—just count the number of songs in the credits at the end of today's movies.

PRODUCT PLACEMENT.   Movie-makers also have begun building commercial products into story lines in a subtle form of advertising. It was no coincidence that Tom Cruise downed Pepsi in *Top Gun*. Some movie producers work brand names into their movies for a fee. When the alien E.T. was coaxed out of hiding with a handful of candy, it was with Reese's Pieces. The Hershey company, which makes Reese's, paid to have its candy used. Sales soared in the next few months. Producers had first offered the Mars company a chance for the candy to be M&Ms, but Mars executives were squeamish about their candy being associated with anything as ugly as E.T. They did not realize that movie-goers would fall in love with the little alien.

After *E.T.* the product placement business boomed. Miller beer paid to have 21 references in *Bull Durham*. The same movie also included seven references for Budweiser, four for Pepsi, three for Jim Beam and two for Oscar Meyer. A simple shot of a product in the foreground typically goes for $25,000 to $50,000. Some advertisers have paid $350,000 for multiple on-screen plugs.

Critics claim that **product placements** are sneaky. Some want them banned. Others say the word "advertisement" should be flashed on the screen when the products appear. Movie people, on the other hand, argue that using real products adds credibility. In the old days, directors assiduously avoided implicit endorsements. In a bar scene the players would drink from cans marked "beer"—no brand name. Today, says Marvin Cohen, whose agency matches advertisers and movies, "A can that says 'Beer' isn't going to make it anymore." The unanswered question is how much product-placement deals affect artistic decisions.

Movie Censorship

STUDY PREVIEW   The movie industry has devised a five-step rating system that alerts people to movies they might find objectionable. Despite problems inherent in any rating scheme, the NC-17, R, PG-13, P and G system has been more successful than earlier self-regulation attempts to quiet critics.

product placement
When a manufacturer pays for its products to be used as props.

Media Timeline

Movie Censorship

1896 Moralists outraged at *Dolorita in the Passion Dance.*

1907 Chicago ordinance banned objectionable movies.

1915 U.S. Supreme Court dismissed movies as "circuses" unworthy of First Amendment protection.

1922 Motion Picture Producers and Distributors of America tried to eliminate objectionable content to quiet critics.

1934 Hollywood established a mandatory production code to appease critics.

1934 Roman Catholic leaders created the Legion of Decency to deter people from seeing certain movies.

1952 U.S. Supreme Court ruled that the First Amendment protects movies in *The Miracle* case.

1960 Hollywood created a rating system to quiet critics.

2000 Federal Trade Commission accused Hollywood of marketing violent movies to kids. Congress demanded reform.

media online

Movie Ratings: A history of how the ratings evolved.
www.mpaa.org/movieratings/about/content.htm

Motion Picture Association of America: They rate the movies we all see.
www.mpaa.org/home.htm

Motion Picture Producers and Distributors of America
1922 Hollywood attempt to establish moral code for movies.

Will Hays
Led MPPDA.

Motion Picture Production Code
1930 Hollywood attempt to quiet critical moralists.

Daniel Lord
Priest who led a morality crusade against Hollywood.

Martin Quigley
Partner of Father Daniel Lord.

Legion of Decency
Church listing of acceptable movies.

Morality as an Issue

It was no wonder in Victorian 1896 that a movie called *Dolorita in the Passion Dance* caused an uproar. There were demands that it be banned—the first but hardly last such call against a movie. In 1907 Chicago passed a law restricting objectionable motion pictures. State legislators across the land were insisting that something be done. Worried movie-makers created the **Motion Picture Producers and Distributors of America** in 1922 to clean up movies. **Will Hays,** a prominent Republican who was an elder in his Presbyterian church, was put in charge. Despite his efforts, movies with titillating titles continued to be produced. A lot of people shuddered at titles such as *Sinners in Silk* and *Red Hot Romance.* Hollywood scandals were no help. Actor William Reid died from drugs. Fatty Arbuckle was tried for the drunken slaying of a young actress. When the Depression struck, many people linked the nation's economic failure with "moral bankruptcy." Movies were a target.

Under pressure, the movie industry adopted the **Motion Picture Production Code** in 1930, which codified the kind of thing that Will Hays had been doing. There was to be no naughty language, nothing sexually suggestive, and no bad guys going unpunished.

Church people led intensified efforts to clean up movies. The 1930 code was largely the product of Father **Daniel Lord,** a Roman Catholic priest, and **Martin Quigley,** a Catholic layperson. In 1934, after an apostolic delegate from the Vatican berated movies in an address to a New York church convention, U.S. bishops organized the **Legion of Decency,** which worked closely with the movie industry's code administrators.

The legion, which was endorsed by religious leaders of many faiths, moved on several fronts. Chapters sprouted in major cities. Some chapters boycotted theaters for six weeks if they showed condemned films. Members slapped stickers marked "We Demand Clean Movies" on car bumpers. Many theater owners responded, vowing to show only approved movies. Meanwhile, the industry itself added teeth to its own code. Any members of the Motion Picture Producers and Distributors of America who released movies without approval were fined $25,000.

Violence and Kids. Movie executives apologized for a "lapse in judgment" after the Federal Trade Commission reported in 2000 that studios were marketing violent fare to children. Sony acknowledged that its marketing planners had included kids as young as 9 in focus groups for R-rated movies. In Congressional hearings, movie companies were told to clean up their act or face government regulation. They said they would.

Movies and Changing Mores

In the late 1940s the influence of the policing agencies began to wane. The 1948 Paramount court decision was one factor. It took major studios out of the exhibition business. As a result, many movie houses could rent films from independent producers, many of which never subscribed to the code. A second factor was the movie *The Miracle*, which became a First Amendment issue in 1952. The movie was about a simple woman who was sure Saint Joseph had seduced her. Her baby, she believed, was Christ. Critics wanted the movie banned as sacrilege, but in the ***Miracle* case,** the Supreme Court sided with exhibitors on grounds of free expression. Film-makers became a bit more venturesome.

At the same time, with mores changing in the wake of World War II, the influence of the Legion of Decency was slipping. In 1953 the legion condemned *The Moon Is Blue,* which had failed to receive code approval for being a bit racy. Despite the legion's condemnation, the movie was a box-office smash. The legion contributed to its own undoing with a series of incomprehensible recommendations. It condemned significant movies such as Ingmar Bergman's *The Silence* and Michelangelo Antonioni's *Blowup* in 1966 while endorsing the likes of *Godzilla vs. the Thing.*

Current Movie Code

Movie-makers sensed the change in public attitudes in the 1950s but realized that audiences still wanted guidance they could trust on movies. Also, there remained some moralist critics. In 1968 several industry organizations established a new rating system. No movies were banned. Fines were out. Instead, a board representing movie producers, distributors, importers and exhibitors, the **Classification and Rating Administration Board,** placed movies in categories to help parents determine what movies their children should see. Here are the categories, as modified through the years:

media online

International Film Festivals: With reviews and awards, this is a Cannes-do site.
www.filmfestivals.com

Sundance Film Festival: America's answer to the international film festival.
www.sundance.org

International Movie Database: Possibly the most comprehensive film source of movie information on the Internet.
www.imdb.com

***Miracle* case**
U.S. Supreme Court ruled that the First Amendment protected movies from censorship.

Classification and Rating Administration Board
Rates movies on G, PG, PG-13, R, NC-17 scale.

- **G:** Suitable for general audiences and all ages.
- **PG:** Parental guidance suggested because some content may be considered unsuitable for preteens.
- **PG-13:** Parental guidance especially suggested for children younger than 13 because of partial nudity, swearing or violence.
- **R:** Restricted for anyone younger than 17 unless accompanied by an adult.
- **NC-17:** No children under age 17 should be admitted.

Whether the rating system is widely used by parents is questionable. One survey found that two out of three parents couldn't name a movie their teenagers had seen in recent weeks.

Evaluating Movies

STUDY PREVIEW: Populist measures of a movie's success are in box office, aftermarket and merchandise revenue. Critical success is harder to measure. Knowledgeable, sophisticated reviewers are helpful.

Media People

Jack Valenti

Since 1966 Jack Valenti has worked the halls of Congress, often with a movie star at his side, lobbying for the interests of Hollywood. His title is president of the Motion Picture Association of America. But more than anything, Valenti is the Washington lobbyist for Hollywood. He also is the most highly paid lobbyist in history—$1 million a year. His budget exceeds $60 million.

One of his biggest accomplishments was the 1968 forerunner of the current movie code. He put together the original G-through-X system, which quelled noises from Congress that federal regulation of the movie industry might be necessary to get rid of big-screen smut. Valenti argued that his system would give parents the information to make intelligent decisions on what their kids see. Also, he promised, movie

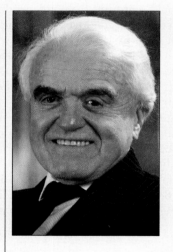

houses would book only movies that were related and not let the kids in to movies with mature ratings. Congress backed off.

You can bet the champagne flowed in Hollywood that day. What

Capitol Lobbyist. Jack Valenti is Hollywood's $1 million a year Washington lobbyist—and "worth every penny," say studio bosses.

Valenti's rating system did was replace the puritanical Hays Code, which was far more restrictive. The Hays Code, drafted in 1922, forbade casual sex, the words *damn* and *hell* and other four-letter words, and bad guys coming out ahead. The Hollywood studios had found the Hays Code onerous, claiming it favored a blandness that didn't attract as many people to the box office as they would like.

Writing about the Valenti movie code in *Forbes* magazine, Dyan Machan called Valenti clever: "Hollywood got what it wanted. The moralists got parental guidance ratings."

Box Office and Grosses

Weekends are when Hollywood studio executives bite their fingernails. The success or disappointment of their latest offerings are in the weekend box-office tabulations, the week-to-week tallies of how many customers the latest movies attracted. The numbers, gathered at the turnstile, are accurate in and of themselves. Too much can be inferred from them, though. A great new movie could be hurt if it was opening against strong rivals. Inversely, a weak movie may look better in a single weekend's books than it really should. Also, a single weekend's success is only part of the complex formula for a movie to break even financially. Many strong weeks might be needed to offset the costs of an expensive movie. A single good weekend could bring a low-budget movie into black ink right away.

An advance indicator of commercial success, though not entirely reliable, is the number of screens nationwide that a movie shows on. Movie houses choose movies according to what they anticipate will be their popularity. Although exhibitors are savvy about what will play well, they make occasional wrong calls.

The least reliable precursor of a movie's success is the predictable marketing hoopla accompanying a release. Actors and directors who make the talk-show rounds are enthusiastic. How could they be otherwise with their own careers in the balance? Trailers can be misleading. Some previews draw on scenes that don't even make the final cut.

The best check on a movie's popularity is the long-term box office record. The all-time leader easily is James Cameron's 1997 *Titanic*. Even with long-term, revenue-based data, look at the criteria on which a ranking is based. Some lists are true box office, the revenue from movie-house showings. Others include aftermarket revenue, like video rentals. Some include merchandise income. Some are domestic, some worldwide. Also, with ticket prices approaching $10 in many cities, currency inflation gives newer movies an edge over classics. Has *Titanic* really been more popular than 1939's *Gone With the Wind?*

Movie Criticism

Commercial success doesn't always equate with critical success, which is a subjective rating. Some critics applauded *Titanic*. The technical effects, for example, drew rave comments. The praise, however, wasn't universal. Some critics saw the story line as trite—a bodice-buster cliché that manipulated unsophisticated audiences.

How, then, can a serious media consumer go beyond the box office and the bottom line to assess movie? Many critics produce immensely helpful reviews and commentary that cut through hype and dazzle to bring a critical, cultivated eye to their reviews. The best reviewers know movies as a medium, including the techniques of the craft. They understand the commercial and artistic dynamics that go into a movie. They know the history of a movie's production, from its seminal moment in a book or whatever the conceptual source.

Where do you find such reviewers? The best sources over the years have included the *New Yorker* magazine and the New York *Times*. Even then, you need to come to know reviewers and their strengths and blind spots. In the end, it is you as a media consumer who makes a critical judgment. This comes from your own increasing sophistication, informed by the dialogue in which the best critics are engaging.

Media Abroad

Canada's Hollywood Problem

The Canadian feature film industry remained largely dormant until the 1960s, when Don Owen's *Nobody Waved Goodbye* and Gilles Groulx's *Le Chat dans le Sac* rejuvenated the industry. Both films were National Film Board productions in the documentary tradition and featured regional themes without the glamour of Hollywood movies.

By the late 1970s government incentives and tax breaks for producers investing in Canadian feature films created a glut of product—some good, some bad. The largest-grossing Canadian movie of all time, *Porky's,* was produced during this period.

How successful were government tax initiatives in stimulating the Canadian film industry? It is difficult to measure. Some years were better than others. However, the 1993 success of *Thirty-Two Short Films about Glenn Gould* and more recent films is evidence that Canadian movie-making has come a long way since *Porky's*.

Pay-television services such as TMN and Moviepix offer Canadians a chance to see Canadian movies that they might not otherwise see.

Media Future: Movies

The exhibition component of the movie industry is vulnerable. The 2000 summer season had no blockbusters. Two major movie-house chains went under. Others followed. Besieged by alternative ways for people to spend their time, including video rentals, exhibition has shrunk dramatically from the surefire business of the 1940s when attendance peaked.

The Hollywood part of the movie industry is secure. With feet in so many different media, the studios can survive the erosion at the box office. The major studios are all into records, video products, merchandise tie-ins and, with Disney and Fox, even news. Those other enterprises offset the vagaries of the movie business.

chapter wrap-up

Movies passed their 100th birthday in the 1980s as an entertainment medium with an especially strong following among young adults and teenagers. From the beginning, movies were a glamorous medium, but beneath the glitz were dramatic struggles between competing businesspeople whose success depended on catching the public's fancy. The most dramatic period came at midcentury. Fanatic anticommunists in Congress intimidated movie-makers into backing away from cutting-edge explorations of social and political issues, and then a government antitrust action forced the major studios to break up their operations. Meanwhile, television was siphoning people away from the box office. Movie attendance fell from 90 million to 16 million per week. It took a few years, but the movie industry regrouped. More than ever, political activism and social inquiry have become themes in American movies. Movie-makers met the threat from television by becoming a primary supplier of television programming.

Questions for Review

1. Why do movies as a mass medium have such a strong impact on people?
2. How does the technological basis of movies differ from the other primary mass media?
3. Why did movies begin fading in popularity in the late 1940s?
4. What was Hollywood's initial response to television?
5. What is the relationship between Hollywood and the television industry today?
6. How has the movie exhibition business changed over the years?
7. How do movie-makers raise cash for their expensive, high-risk projects?
8. How has Hollywood responded to criticism of movie content?

Questions for Critical Thinking

1. How would you describe the success of these innovations—Cinerama, CinemaScope, 3-D and Smell-o-vision—in the movie industry's competition against television?
2. Epic spectaculars marked one period of movie-making, social causes another, and sex and violence another. Have these genres had lasting effect?
3. Can you explain why films geared to baby boomers, sometimes called teen films, dominated Hollywood in the 1970s and well into the 1980s? Why are they less important now?

4. How did Eadweard Muybridge demonstrate persistence of vision, and how did that lead to early movie-making? Cite the contributions of William Dickson, George Eastman and the Lumière brothers.
5. Explain how these three developments forced a major change in Hollywood in the 1950s: the 1947 Thomas hearings, the 1948 Paramount court decision, and the advent of television.
6. Once the number of movie exhibitors in the nation was measured in terms of movie houses. Today it is measured by the number of screens. Why?
7. Explain how movie-makers finance their movies. What are the advantages and disadvantages of each method?
8. What has been the role of these institutions in shaping movie content: Motion Picture Producers and Distributors of America, Legion of Decency and Classification and Rating Administration Board?
9. Describe government censorship of movies in the United States.

Keeping Up to Date

People serious about movies as art will find *American Film* and *Film Comment* valuable sources of information.

Trade journals include *Variety* and *Hollywood Reporter*.

Among consumer magazines with significant movie coverage are *Premiere*, *Entertainment Weekly* and *Rolling Stone*.

The *Wall Street Journal*, *Business Week*, *Forbes* and *Fortune* track the movie industry.

Imus in the Morning. *Sometimes it's difficult to tell whether irreverent radio talk-show host Don Imus is running a spoof or interviewing real people. Despite his lack of orthodoxy, Imus lines up high-level guests who sometimes shed restraint and display another side of their personas. The Imus program is simulcast on the MSNBC television network and occasionally segments are live on NBC's "Today" show.*

7

Radio

**In this chapter
you will learn:**

- Radio reaches people every-where with opinion, news, entertainment and advertising.

- Radio signals move through the air by piggybacking on already existing electromagnetic waves.

- Most U.S. radio operates in the private sector of the economy and relies on advertising.

- Radio in the United States has an entertainment rather than an educational thrust.

- News is becoming less important in the programming mix of U.S. radio.

- National networks have been influential since the 1920s in shaping U.S. radio.

- U.S. radio is regulated by the federal government.

- New technology may trigger programming innovations.

Radio host **Don Imus** shed his **shock jock** roots to emerge as the hottest property in radio in the late 1990s. His often irreverent, abrupt manner and occasional tastelessness veil a bright mind and a good heart. By 2001 his morning program, which runs 4½ hours, five days a week, was carried by 100 stations nationwide to an estimated 10 million listeners—and not just the 18- to 35-year-old blue-collar male audience of the shock jocks. Evan Thomas, writing in *Newsweek,* said that Imus's appeal bridged both mass and class.

Imus produces wickedly funny on-air spoofs, but his guests are the heart of his show. People line up to be on "Imus in the Morning." Imus is picky. He likes bright politicians, like former Senator Bob Dole. He thought Republican Senator John McCain of Arizona should have been president.

Imus spurns most entertainers: "It's frightening how stupid they are." He calls shock jock Howard Stern "a pornographic little twit."

He has his favorite journalists. Andrea Mitchell checks in regularly by phone from Washington with Capitol tidbits. Usually Imus asks about "Crazy Al," his name for Mitchell's husband Alan Greenspan, the formal and powerful chair of the Federal Reserve. Imus calls Sam Donaldson "too tedious." He likes Maureen Dowd of the New York *Times.*

Intellectuals have a place on "Imus in the Morning." You might hear a Harvard theologian right after a rollicking rap spoof that decimates the president. Imus likes historian Doris Kearns Goodwin and Washington commentator and author Cokie Roberts. He interviews authors who he feels have something worth hearing.

153

Imus grew up poor in Arizona, getting his early sense of radio from listening to televangelists. When he made it to radio himself, one of his favorite characters was a dubious preacher whose offering plate was never big enough. Booze and dope sidetracked Imus' career in the late 1970s, but eventually, cured, he was back in New York at NBC. Today the show emanates from sports station WFAN. It's also carried live on the MSNBC cable television network, with studio cameras showing production details and everything else.

One of Imus' passions is a ranch that he and brother Fred have built for sick children in New Mexico. He has raised $50 million for the ranch and thrown in $1 million of his own. Imus spends a lot of time in New Mexico, especially with Fred, whose Auto Body Express in Santa Fe gets oodles of on-air plugs and does $10 million a year in business selling T-shirts and Western items.

Significance of Radio

STUDY PREVIEW   Radio is an important medium for opinion, news, entertainment and advertising. The portability of radio means that it is everywhere in our daily lives.

Radio as a Motivator

Radio can motivate people to action. When members of Congress were considering a 51 percent pay hike for themselves in 1988, radio talk show host **Jerry Williams** decided it was time for another Boston Tea Party. He stirred his Boston listeners to send thousands of tea bags to Congress as a not-so-subtle reminder of the 1773 colonial frustration over taxes that led to the Revolutionary War. Talk show hosts elsewhere joined the campaign. Congress, swamped with tea bags, scuttled the pay raise proposal.

Recording companies know the power of radio. Without radio stations playing new music, a new release is almost certainly doomed. Airplay spurs people to go out and buy a CD or cassette.

Advertisers value radio to reach buyers. Only newspapers, television and direct mail have a larger share of the advertising dollars spent nationwide, and radio's share is growing. From $7 billion in 1986, radio ad revenue soared almost 30 percent to beyond $15 billion in 1999.

Ubiquity of Radio

Don Imus
New York-based syndicated morning radio host.

shock jock
Announcer whose style includes vulgarities, taboos.

Jerry Williams
Influential Boston talk show host.

Radio is everywhere. The signals are carried on the electromagnetic spectrum to almost every nook and cranny. Hardly a place in the world is beyond the reach of radio.

There are 6.6 radio receivers on average in U.S. households. Nineteen of 20 automobiles come with radios. People wake up with clock radios, jog with headset radios, party with boomboxes and commute with car radios. People listen to sports events on the radio even if they're in the stadium. Thousands of people build their day around commentators like Paul Harvey. Millions rely on hourly newscasts to be up to date. People develop personal attachments to their favorite announcers and disc jockeys.

Statistics abound about radio's importance:

- **Arbitron,** a company that surveys radio listenership, says that teenagers and adults average 22 hours a week listening to radio.
- People in the United States own 520 million radio sets. Looked at another way, radios outnumber people 2:1.
- More people, many of them commuting in their cars, receive their morning news from radio than from any other medium.

Scope of the Radio Industry

More than 11,000 radio stations are on the air in the United States. Communities as small as a few hundred people have stations.

Although radio is significant as a $15 billion a year industry, its financial health is uneven. The big radio chains, one with 1,018 stations, do spectacularly. In 1999 Clear Channel, for example, had revenue of $3 billion, four times that of the year before. But many stations struggle, especially AM stations. In 1991, a particularly bad year, 153 stations signed off for the final time.

The potential for profit drives the price of some stations to astronomical levels. Here is a sampler of 1999 sales in relatively small markets:

- Kansas: Leavenworth: KKLO-AM—$1.3 million.
- New Hampshire: Concord: WNHI-FM, WRCI-FM and WJYY-FM—$3.6 million.
- Ohio: Bowling Green: WONW-AM and WZOM-FM—$4.3 million.

Technical Development

STUDY PREVIEW Human mastery of the electromagnetic spectrum, through which radio is possible, is only a century old. In 1895 an Italian physicist and inventor, Guglielmo Marconi, was the first to transmit a message through the air. Later came voice transmissions and better sound.

Electromagnetic Spectrum

Radio waves are part of the physical universe. They have existed forever, moving through the air and the ether. Like light waves, they are silent—a part of a continuing spectrum of energies: the **electromagnetic spectrum.** As early as 1873, physicists speculated that the electromagnetic spectrum existed, but it was an Italian nobleman, **Guglielmo Marconi,** who made practical application of the physicists' theories.

Young Marconi became obsessed with the possibilities of the electromagnetic spectrum and built equipment that could ring a bell by remote control—no strings, no wires; just turning an electromagnetic charge on and off. In 1895, when he was 21, Marconi used his wireless method to transmit codes for more than a mile on his father's Bologna estate. Marconi patented his invention in England, and his mother, a well-connected Irish woman, arranged British financing to set up the Marconi Wireless Telegraph Company. Soon oceangoing ships were equipped with Marconi radiotelegraphy equipment to communicate at sea, even when they were beyond the horizon—something never possible before. Marconi made a fortune.

m e d i a   o n l i n e

Arbitron: The company that collects radio listenership information.
www.arbitron.com

Electromagnetic Spectrum: The spectrum illustrated and explained.
http://imagine.gsfc.nasa.gov/docs/science/know_11/emspectrum.html

Arbitron
Radio listener survey company.

electromagnetic spectrum
Energy waves on which radio messages are piggybacked.

Guglielmo Marconi
Produced the first wireless transmission.

Who Invented Radio? Numerous theorists conceived of wireless transmission ahead of the Irish-Italian inventor Guglielmo Marconi. A dentist, Mahlon Loomis, detected signals between two mountains in Virginia in 1866 and won a patent for wireless telegraphy in 1872. Scottish mathematician James Maxwell and German physicist Heinrich Hertz did important theorizing. Who, then, invented radio? Marconi became interested in radio in 1894 and succeeded in a wireless transmission in 1895, and he aggressively exploited the potential of his experiments into a commercial success that tightly linked his name with the invention of radio in the public's mind. But admirers of a reclusive but brilliant Croatian-born American scientist, Nikola Tesla, have mounted a campaign for him to be recognized as the inventor of radio. Among their evidence is a 1943 U.S. Supreme Court decision recognizing that Tesla had transmitted on the electromagnetic spectrum before Marconi. The debate remains open, however, whether Tesla really conceived of the electromagnetic spectrum as a vehicle for transmitting messages. Tesla's focus at the time was wireless transmission of electricity.

Nikola Tesla

Transmitting Voices

Breakthroughs came quickly. In 1906 a message was sent across the Atlantic. In 1906 **Lee De Forest,** a promoter who fancied himself an inventor, created what he called the **audion tube** to make voice transmission possible. Some say he stole the underlying technology from Canadian inventor **Reginald Fessenden.** Whatever the truth of the matter, it was Fessenden who broadcast the first radio program, also in 1906. From Brant Rock, Massachusetts, where he had a laboratory, Fessenden played some recorded Christmas carols, shocking wireless operators on ships at sea. Instead of the dots and dashes of Morse code, suddenly there was music. De Forest, however, took

Lee De Forest
Inventor whose projects included the audion tube.

audion tube
Made voice transmission possible.

Reginald Fessenden
First radio program, 1906.

Bounce-Back Effect. When AM electromagnetic waves are transmitted, many of them follow the contour of the earth, which extends their range beyond the line-of-sight from the transmitter. Some AM waves go upward, and many of these are bounced back to earth by reflective layers in the ionosphere, which further extends a station's range. The bounce-back effect is weaker during the day, when the sun warms the ionosphere and reduces its reflective properties. FM transmissions have a shorter range than AM because the signals move in straight lines and tend not to adhere to the earth's contours. Also, upward-moving FM waves pass through the ionosphere rather than being reflected back.

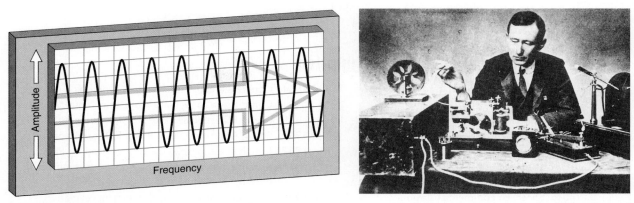

Unmodulated Wave. If you could see electromagnetic waves, they would look like the cross section of a ripple moving across a pond, except they would be steady and unending. Guglielmo Marconi figured out how to hitch a ride on these waves to send messages in 1895.

Guglielmo Marconi

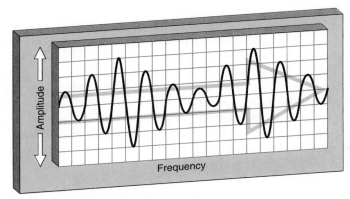

Amplitude-Modulated Wave. Lee De Forest discovered how to adjust the height of electromagnetic waves to coincide with the human voice and other sounds. De Forest's audion tube made voice transmission possible, including an Enrico Caruso concert in 1910.

Lee De Forest

Edwin Armstrong

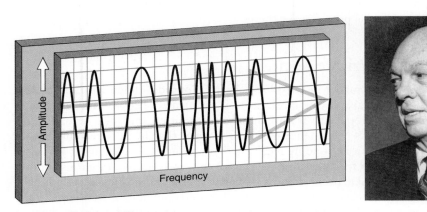

Frequency-Modulated Wave. FM radio transmissions squeeze and expand electromagnetic waves without changing their height. Edwin Armstrong introduced this form of broadcasting, which had superior clarity and fidelity, in the 1930s. Not even lightning interferes with transmission.

Media Timeline

Radio Technology and Regulation

1895 Guglielmo Marconi transmitted a message by radio.

1906 Lee De Forest created the audion tube that allowed voice transmission.

1912 **David Sarnoff** used radio to learn news of the *Titanic* disaster, putting radio in the public eye.

1920 Westinghouse puts KDKA, Pittsburgh, on air as the first licensed commercial station.

1927 Congress created the Federal Radio Communications Commission to regulate radio.

1934 Congress created the Federal Communications Commission to regulate radio, telephone, television. FCC replaced FRC.

1939 Edwin Armstrong put the first FM station on air.

1967 Congress established the Corporation for Public Broadcasting to create a national noncommercial system.

1996 Congress relaxed many government regulations on broadcasting, including ownership caps.

---

media online

David Sarnoff: The corporation that is the legacy of the broadcasting giant. Includes a history and an explanation of The Sarnoff Way.
www.sarnoff.com

Alan Freed: The definitive online resource covering the life and work of the man who coined the phrase *rock 'n' roll*.
www.alanfreed.com

the limelight with show-off broadcasts from the Eiffel Tower and other stunts. In 1910 De Forest clearly demonstrated radio's potential as an entertainment medium with a magnificent performance by the tenor Enrico Caruso from the New York Metropolitan Opera House.

Static-free transmission was developed by **Edwin Armstrong,** a Columbia University researcher. In 1939 Armstrong built an experimental station in New Jersey using a new system called **frequency modulation,** FM for short. FM's system, piggybacking sound on airwaves, was different from the older **amplitude modulation,** or AM method. In time, Armstrong developed FM stereo with two soundtracks, one for each ear, duplicating the sensation of hearing a performance live.

Characteristics of U.S. Radio

STUDY PREVIEW   The radio industry established itself early in the private, free enterprise sector of the economy. It chose entertainment rather than news, information and education, as its main programming thrust.

Radio in the Private Sector

David Sarnoff
His monitoring of the sinking of the *Titanic* familiarized people with radio; later NBC president.

Edwin Armstrong
Invented FM as an alternative transmission method.

frequency modulation
FM

amplitude modulation
AM

Frank Conrad
Pioneer whose work led to KDKA.

KDKA
First licensed commercial station.

A Westinghouse engineer in Pittsburgh, **Frank Conrad,** fiddled with radiotelegraphy in his home garage, playing music as he experimented. People with homemade receivers liked what they heard from Conrad's transmitter, and soon he had a following. When Conrad's Westinghouse bosses learned that he had become a local celebrity, they saw profit in building receivers that consumers could buy at $10 a set and take home to listen to. To encourage sales of the receivers, Westinghouse built a station to provide regular programming of news, sports and music—mostly music. That station, **KDKA,** became the nation's first licensed commercial station in 1920.

The licensing of KDKA by the government was important because it demonstrated the U.S. commitment to placing radio in the private sector. In Europe broadcasting was a government monopoly. KDKA's entertainment programming also sent

***Radio* Becomes a Household Word.** When the *Titanic* sank in 1912, newspapers relied on young radio operator David Sarnoff for information on what was happening in the mid-Atlantic. For 72 hours Sarnoff sat at his primitive receiver, which happened to be on exhibit in a department store, to pick up details from rescue ships. The newspaper coverage of the disaster made *radio* a household word, which paved the way for consumer acceptance over the next few years.

U.S. broadcasting in a certain direction. In many other countries, radio was used mostly for education and high culture, not mass entertainment.

Role of Advertising

Westinghouse never expected KDKA itself to make money, only to spur sales of $10 Westinghouse home receivers. The economic base of KDKA and the rest of American broadcasting changed in 1922 when **WEAF** in New York accepted $50 from a real estate developer for 10 minutes to pitch his new Long Island apartments. Then Gimbel's department store tried radio advertising. Within months, companies were clamoring for air time. The Lucky Strike Orchestra produced programs, as did the Taystee Loafers from the Taystee bread company, the A&P Gypsies, the Goodrich Silvertown Orchestra and the Interwoven Pair from the sock company.

In those first few years of the 1920s, U.S. radio took on these distinctive traits:

- Private rather than state ownership of the broadcast system.
- An entertainment thrust to programming that emphasized popular culture.
- An economic foundation based on selling time to advertisers that needed to reach a mass audience of consumers.

Noncommercial Radio

U.S. radio was already solidly established as a commercially supported medium when Congress established a regulatory agency in 1927, the **Federal Radio Commission.**

WEAF
New York station that carried the first commercial.

Federal Radio Commission
Original government regulatory agency for radio.

Media People

Greg Smith

When he was 3, Greg Smith was diagnosed with degenerative muscular dystrophy. By high school, as a wheelchair user, radio was a way for him to participate in sports as a play-by-play announcer on a suburban Chicago community radio station. At Arizona State University he was the sports director of the campus radio station, and after graduation, he pursued a career in radio sales. Frustrated by a lack of opportunities, he started a show that dealt with the very problems he faced as a person with a disability.

In 1992 Greg Smith resigned as research director and host of "Cardinal Talk" on KTAR-AM in Phoenix to launch a weekly show, "On a Roll: Talk Radio on Life and Disability." He quickly identified a corporate sponsorship market that has included Bank of America, Microsoft, General Motors and Invacare, a manufacturer of wheelchairs. By 1999 Smith's program was airing on 39 stations nationwide.

Greg Smith.
"Wheelchair dude with attitude."

The show has flavor. This is its opener: "And now, occupying the best parking place in syndicated radio, the wheelchair dude with attitude, the hip crip who gives ya tips: 'On a Roll' radio's host and founder Greg Smith!"

Topics focus on disability lifestyle issues, often with experts as Smith's guests. Among people whom he has interviewed on the air have been former Senator Bob Dole, television newscaster John Hockenberry and actor Christopher Reeve.

Smith, a father of three, has done the show from his home since 1997, using ISDN connections and computer production software for pre-produced elements. Every Sunday evening, he broadcasts from his wheelchair, his 65-pound body held upright by Velcro straps.

---

noncommercial stations
Stations licensed on the condition that they not carry commercials.

Public Broadcasting Act
Channels federal dollars to develop national noncommercial radio and television system.

National Public Radio
Network linking noncommercial stations.

Corporation for Public Broadcasting
Quasi-government agency to administer federal funds for noncommercial radio, television.

To ensure that radio's potential as an educational medium was not lost, the FRC reserved some licenses for **noncommercial stations.** These went mostly to stations operated by colleges and other institutions that would finance their operation without advertising. Today, about 10 percent of the nation's radio stations hold noncommercial licenses. Many of these are low-power stations that colleges operate as training facilities.

In 1967 Congress passed the **Public Broadcasting Act** to create a national noncommercial radio system. Every major city and most college towns have a public radio station, most of which carry specialized programs that do not have large enough audiences to attract advertisers. Classical music, news and documentaries are programming mainstays at most public stations.

Many noncommercial stations are affiliates of **National Public Radio,** a network that went on the air in 1970. NPR was created with support from the **Corporation for Public Broadcasting,** a quasi-governmental agency that channels federal funds into the national public radio system. Two NPR news programs, "Morning Edition" and

Media People

Terry Gross

"Fresh Air." Terry Gross' interview show has one of the nation's largest radio interview audiences.

In college Terry Gross majored in education, but teaching didn't work out. At a smidgen over five feet, Gross was shorter than most of her Buffalo, New York, eighth-graders. It was tough being an authority figure, she said. She quit after six weeks.

She moved through typing jobs, finally landing at Buffalo radio station WBFO. She loved it. Within three years Gross had moved to WHYY in Philadelphia to produce and host a daily three-hour interview show. Thus, in 1975, began one of radio's longest-running programs: "Fresh Air."

The show is still based at WHYY but is also carried by 330 National Public Radio network affiliates. Terry Gross typically has 2.9 million people listening to her cerebral interviewing on eclectic subjects

as diverse as avant-garde musical forms, breakthrough scholarship and the day's pressing political questions.

As an interviewer, Gross' probing is disarming. Even on tawdry subjects she casts her questions in terms of an intellectual interest that rarely fails to

penetrate her subjects. One exception was Monica Lewinsky after the White House sex scandal. Lewinsky walked out of the Gross' studio mid-interview. "Too intimate," Lewinsky said.

Over 25 years Gross has conducted 5,000 "Fresh Air" interviews.

"All Things Considered," have earned a loyal following. NPR offers about 50 hours of programming a week to affiliate stations.

Neither noncommercial stations nor their networks carry advertising, but supporting foundations and corporations are acknowledged on the air as underwriters. In recent years some of these acknowledgments have come to resemble advertising but without exhortations, which federal regulations prohibit.

Radio as Entertainment

STUDY PREVIEW   Radio stations today offer a wide range of formats, each geared to attract a narrow segment of the population. In earlier times, radio stations sought mass audiences with programs that had wide appeal. The programming was a culturally unifying influence on the nation. Today's more segmented programming came about when radio began losing the mass audience to television in the 1950s.

Early Mass Programming

In the early days, most stations were on the air at night with hotel teatime music. It was pleasant programming, offensive to no one. Sandwiched among the

Gordon McLendon.
McLendon was a programming genius who devised many niche formats, including all-news, Top 40 and beautiful music.

potted-palm music, as it was called, were occasional soloists, poets and public speakers. As broadcasting expanded into the daytime, stations used more recordings, which introduced a bit more variety. In the late 1920s, evening programming became more varied. Potted-palm music gave way to symphonies and big bands. Guy Lombardo, the Dorsey Brothers and Benny Goodman all found that radio helped to promote their record sales. In Nashville, WSM built a country music program on the Saturday night Southern tradition of picking, singing and gossiping with your neighbors on the front porch or the courthouse lawn. In 1928 the program was named the "Grand Ole Opry."

With more varied programs, radio attracted a true mass audience in the 1930s. Fred Waring and His Pennsylvanians demonstrated that variety shows could attract large audiences. Jack Benny, Milton Berle and Bob Hope did the same with comedy. Drama series were introduced—murder mysteries, soap operas, Westerns, thrillers. Quiz shows became part of the mix. In 1940 Texaco began sponsoring the Saturday matinees of the Metropolitan Opera from New York, which had been airing since 1931. The opera broadcasts remain the longest continuously sponsored program on radio.

The early radio programming, geared to attract large audiences, was a culturally unifying factor for the nation. Almost everyone had a common experience in the radio programs of the time.

Formats for Specific Audiences

Comedies, dramas and quiz shows moved to television beginning in the late 1940s and early 1950s, and so did the huge audience that radio had cultivated. The radio networks, losing advertisers to television, scaled back what they offered to stations. As the number of listeners dropped, local stations switched more to recorded music, which was far cheaper than producing programs.

Although most stations in the pretelevision period offered diversity, a few stations emphasized certain kinds of programming. Country music stations dotted the South. Some stations carried only religious programs. In the 1950s Cleveland announcer **Alan Freed** introduced rock 'n' roll, which became the fare at hundreds of stations and began wide-scale fragmentation in radio programming. Today, hardly any station tries to offer something for everyone, but everyone can find something on the radio to like. There is a format for everyone.

After Freed came the **Top 40** format, in which the day's top songs were repeated in rotation. The wizard of radio formatting, **Gordon McLendon,** perfected the format at **KLIF** in Dallas, Texas, by mixing fast-paced newscasts, disc jockey chatter, lively commercials and promotional jingles and hype with the music. It was catchy, almost hypnotizing—and widely imitated.

McLendon also designed so-called beautiful music as a format at **KABL,** San Francisco, in 1959; all-news at **XTRA,** Tijuana, Mexico, aimed at southern California, in 1961; and all-classified ads at **KADS,** Los Angeles, 1967. In all of his innovations, McLendon was firm about a strict structure. In Top 40, for example, there were no deviations from music in rotation, news every 20 minutes, naming the station by call letters twice between songs, upbeat jingles and no deadpan commercials. McLendon's classified-ad format bombed, but the others have survived.

The fastest-growing niche in radio programming is sports. Why? Because advertisers find that sports stations are good for reaching male potential customers, an

potted-palm music
Popular, inoffensive early radio programming.

Alan Freed
Pioneer rock 'n' roll disc jockey.

Top 40
Format that replays pop records.

Gordon McLendon
Program innovator; devised Top 40, all-news and beautiful-music formats.

KLIF
Top 40 innovator, Dallas.

KABL
Beautiful-music innovator, San Francisco.

XTRA
All-news innovator, Tijuana, Mexico.

KADS
All-ad innovator, Los Angeles.

elusive group that is outnumbered by women in many other media. By 2000 more than 600 all-sports stations were on the air.

Sports radio is a popular niche. One of the leading stations, WFAN in New York, brought in $50.3 million in ad revenue in 1997. The next New York station was a distant second at $7.9 million.

Meanwhile, networks have cropped up to provide programming to sports stations, including ESPN Radio and SportsZone, with 400-plus affiliates; One-on-One, with 300 affiliates; and Sports ByLine, with 250-plus affiliates.

Radio's fragmented programming has reduced its role as a culturally unifying factor. Almost everyone listens to radio, but listening to a hard-rock station gives a person hardly anything in common with people who listen to public-affairs-oriented stations or soul stations or beautiful-music stations. Today, the shared experience of radio does not extend beyond narrow segments of the population.

'80s Revival. In 2000 Michelle Engel switched to a pure-1980s format at KVMX-FM in Portland, Oregon, where she is program director. Immediately, the station shot from 16th to first in the ratings. The station, which had been mixing oldies and current pop, suddenly was widely imitated in the latest radio format fad.

Radio News

STUDY PREVIEW   Radio became a significant news source for many Americans during World War II. Today, a few large cities have at least one excellent all-news station, but in general radio has declined as a news medium. Listener call-in programs have become a popular format that has potential as a forum on public issues.

Pioneer Radio News

Radio news preceded radio stations. In November 1916, Lee De Forest arranged with a New York newspaper, the *American,* to broadcast election returns. Hundreds of people tuned in with home-built receivers to an experimental transmission to hear De Forest proclaim: "Charles Evans Hughes will be the next president of the United States." (Actually, Woodrow Wilson was reelected.) In November 1920, when KDKA in Pittsburgh became the nation's first licensed commercial station, it began by reporting returns in the Harding-Cox presidential race as they were being counted at the Pittsburgh *Post.* This time radio had the winner right.

Radio news came into its own in World War II, when the networks sent more correspondents abroad. Americans, eager for news from Europe, developed the habit of listening to the likes of **Edward R. Murrow** for first-person accounts of what was happening. Murrow's reporting compared with the best that newspapers were offering. Consider the potency of this 1940 Murrow report from London: "Today I went to buy a hat. My favorite shop had gone, blown to bits. The windows of my shoe store were blown out. I decided to have a haircut. The windows of the barbershop were gone, but the Italian barber was still doing business. 'Some day', he said, 'we smile again, but the food it doesn't taste so good since being bombed.' "

Edward R. Murrow
Eyewitness World War II accounts from London.

Media People

Edward R. Murrow

Not long out of college, Edward R. Murrow had a job arranging student exchanges for the Institute of International Education, including a summer seminar for American students and teachers in the Soviet Union. That was in 1932, and it seemed a good job—lots of travel, meeting interesting people, doing something worthwhile. In the early 1950s, though, the demagogic Red Scaremeisters tried to discredit Murrow as somehow being tied to the communist ideology on which the Soviet Union had been founded.

By that time Murrow had established his reputation as a broadcast journalist and was a CBS executive. Though personally offended at being branded a communist sympathizer, Murrow was even more outraged by the anticommunist hysteria that some members of Congress, notably Wisconsin Senator Joseph McCarthy, were stirring up. Many of his network colleagues had been blacklisted. A close friend committed suicide after

being falsely accused. In 1954, on his weekly CBS television program "See It Now," Murrow went after McCarthy, combining his narrative with film clips that exposed the senator's hypocrisy.

Many analysts say that was a pivotal moment in McCarthy's career. His innuendoes and lies, which had caused such great damage, were exposed to the public. Some say that the program, in bringing down one of most recognized members of the Senate, clearly demonstrated television's powerful potential for public affairs.

Murrow had begun with CBS as its representative in Europe, where he covered Adolf Hitler's arrival in Vienna in 1938 when Germany invaded Austria. Realizing that war was imminent in Europe, Murrow persuaded CBS to hire more staff to cover it. He devised the format for the "CBS World News Roundup," rotating from correspondent to correspondent around Europe for live

reports. During World War II he became known for his gripping broadcasts from London. Standing on rooftops with the sounds of sirens, antiaircraft guns and exploding German bombs in the background, he would describe what was happening around him. His reporting had poignancy, color and detail. Here is his description of an Allied air drop over Holland: "There they go. Do you hear them shout? I can see their chutes going down now. Everyone clear. They're dropping just beside a little windmill near a church, hanging there very gracefully. They seem to be completely relaxed like nothing so much as khaki dolls hanging beneath a green lamp shade."

One of Murrow's television signatures was an ever-present cigarette. His habit, however, didn't get in his way of his examining the dangers of smoking on "See It Now." Murrow developed cancer and died in 1965 at age 57.

McLendon's Influence

Local radio news improved after the war when reporters began using tape recorders to interview and to capture the sounds of the news. It was the innovation of tape that gave Gordon McLendon's KLIF newscasts the you-are-there quality that helped to propel the station to the top of the ratings in the 1950s. After XTRA in Tijuana turned profitable in the early 1960s, McLendon took over a Chicago station, renamed it WNUS and converted it to all-news. He used the same low-budget approach that had worked at XTRA—a skeletal announcing staff reading wire copy.

Taking notice, the Group W broadcasting chain began converting to all-news in 1965, but with strong local coverage by station reporters. CBS followed in 1967 with some of the stations it owned. Unlike McLendon, Group W and CBS went beyond spot news, investing in well-known commentators and including features. It worked. An estimated 35 percent of all New York listeners tuned in to either Group W's WINS or CBS's WCBS at least once a week. So successful were Group W and CBS that McLendon surrendered the all-news market in Chicago to CBS's WBBM and that in Los Angeles to Group W's KFWB in 1968.

All-news stations have prospered in a few major cities. New York, Los Angeles, Chicago and some other cities have sustained all-news stations with large reporting staffs that provide on-scene competitive coverage. Such news operations maintain the tradition of radio news at its best—instantaneous, informed and intelligent coverage of a sort that other media cannot match.

In many markets, however, some stations that call themselves all-news are all-news in name only and provide scant local coverage amid piped-in network newscasts, such as the 24-hour CNN audio network. So-called all-news stations in many markets actually run mostly listener call-in and lengthy interviews, and they originate less local coverage than some competitors that, although not all-news, have kept a stronger commitment to news.

Decline of Radio News

When the United States launched an air war against Iraq on January 16, 1991, ABC radio did not even try to cover what was happening. That whole evening, the network plugged its radio affiliates into the audio of the ABC television coverage being anchored by Peter Jennings. It was a telling moment, and a sad one, in the history of U.S. radio as a news medium. Instead of leading the way in originating coverage, ABC and other traditional radio networks gave a poor showing throughout the Persian Gulf war, mostly picking up audio from official briefings and sandwiching it inside brief scripts rewritten from the AP and other news services.

By the 1990s radio had become primarily an entertainment medium with low-cost programming based on playing records. Even the historic KDKA in Pittsburgh, which aired the first news reports as early as 1920, had by 1991 suspended local newscasts after 8 p.m. Many metropolitan stations had cut news to minimal local staffs, sometimes using just one or two people who anchored brief newscasts during commuting hours, and relied for global and national coverage on brief network summaries. Some stations don't even commit a person full-time to local news.

ON-SITE COVERAGE.   Nor do the commercial networks put much energy into gathering news for radio. Former congressional correspondent Edward Connors, writing in *Washington Journalism Review,* reported that radio network reporters in the nation's capital seldom go out after a story any more. Instead, they spend most of their time in studios, picking up audio feeds and watching coverage of scheduled events on the C-SPAN public affairs television network. ABC was down to four full-time radio reporters in Washington. CBS had only two. Every radio network except CBS subscribes to an audio-feed service that, for fees starting at $31,000 a year, provides raw coverage from which newscasters extract a few sentences to combine with boiled-down copy from the AP.

This remote coverage lacks the advantages of having a reporter at the scene. For example, when confirmation hearings for Supreme Court Justice David Souter were under way in 1990, newscasters in remote studios had no idea from their audio feeds that a demonstration had broken out in the back of the hearing room. They heard only the official exchange from microphones fixed to pick up senators' questions and Souter's responses. Incredible as it seems, only one radio reporter was at the hearing: Louise Schiavone of the AP. Schiavone scrambled with her recorder to the back of the room and had the only sound on a significant aspect of a major story.

Another disadvantage to remote coverage is that if reporters aren't present, they cannot ask questions to follow up on the official dialogue or to seek added perspective. David Oziel, UPI Radio news director, put it this way: "You are there to see expressions on people's faces and other human elements that can only be described by a reporter on the scene."

STEALTH NEWSCAST PROVIDERS.   Some stations that run news do little more than rewrite stories from the morning newspaper or import newscasts from news program providers that engage in the same kind of piracy. These rehash operations are popular with some budget-minded station owners because they are free. The largest provider, Metro Network, feeds newscasts to 490 stations, many in the same market. In return, stations agree to play a 10-second commercial after the newscast sign-off. Metro takes the revenue from the mini-ad. Everybody wins economically. But what about the listener?

Metro and its main competitor, the smaller Shadow Broadcast Services with 125 stations, are stealth news sources. They are never identified on the air. In fact, many stations go to great lengths to leave listeners with the false impression that the news comes from the station itself. Lead-ins tout the station's call letters.

Marc Fisher, radio columnist for the Washington *Post,* is critical of the stealth networks, which he describes as producing news with budgets so small that they can't even put a reporter out on the street. The staffs merely package material picked up from wherever it can be found for free. Writing in *American Journalism Review,* Fisher listed the coverage in a Metro newscast for a Washington, D.C., station: "Metro had six stories, three of them barely rewritten from the *Post* and three paraphrased from the suburban *Journal* newspapers."

Not only is coverage shallow, but it is also redundant. In Washington, 12 stations carry Metro newscasts and nine carry Shadow. But except for listeners who monitor a lot of stations, nobody knows that the news is not generated at the station they're tuned to.

NATIONAL PUBLIC RADIO.   Despite the decline of radio news, there are bright spots. One is National Public Radio, which has the largest radio network reporting staff in the nation's capital, with 12 people. NPR has many of the sources of the commercial networks—news services like AP and audio services—but it is different in the emphasis it places on staffing. The reporters also approach stories differently. Instead of keeping stories to 25 seconds, a recommended maximum at commercial networks, NPR allows reporters the airtime to tell their stories thoroughly and in depth.

Alone among the radio networks, NPR offers extended newscasts in the tradition of commercial networks in radio's heyday—"Morning Edition" and "All Things Considered." NPR's staff beyond Washington is limited, however, and the network leans heavily on the BBC for international coverage and on its noncommercial affiliates for coverage outside the Beltway. Occasionally, NPR sends reporters abroad and into the hinterlands of the United States, but with no advertising base, NPR has perennial budget problems that limit its full inheritance of the tradition of Edward R. Murrow and other radio news pioneers.

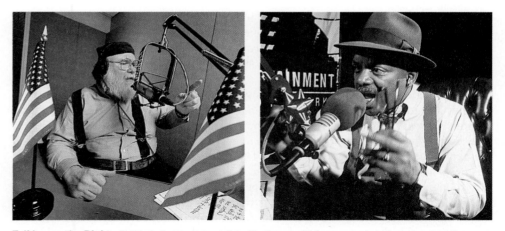

Talking on the Right. Political observers say talk radio shows, which are overwhelmingly conservative, were a key in the 1994 Republican takeover of Congress. In San Francisco, KSFO is an all-conservative format headlined by J. Paul Emerson. He holds back nothing. Pounding his fist on the broadcast studio console, he bellows that he "hates Japs." In Denver, Ken Hamblin, who calls himself the Black Avenger, holds forth with outspoken right-wing talk. Hamblin is syndicated on 63 stations around the nation. The effect of talkers, as they're known in the trade, cannot be overstated. A Los Angeles *Times*-funded poll found 44 percent of Americans pick up most of their political information from these shows.

Talk Radio

Talk formats that feature live listener telephone calls emerged as a major genre in U.S. radio in the 1980s. Many AM stations, unable to compete with FM's sound quality for music, realized that they were better suited to talk, which doesn't require high fidelity.

Call-in formats were greeted enthusiastically at first because of their potential as forums for discussion of the great public issues. Some stations, including WCCO in Minneapolis and WHO in Des Moines, were models whose long-running talk shows raised expectations. So did "Talk of the Nation" on National Public Radio. However, many talk shows went in other directions, focusing less on issues than on wacky, often vitriolic personalities. Much of the format degenerated into advice programs on hemorrhoids, psoriasis, face-lifts and psychoses. Sports trivia went over big. So did pet care. Talk shows gave an illusion of news but in reality were lowbrow entertainment.

Whatever the downside of **talkers,** as they're known in the trade, they have huge followings. **Rush Limbaugh** was syndicated to 660 stations at his peak, reaching an estimated 20 million people a week. Although down to 600 stations and 18.7 million listeners by 2000, Limbaugh remained a strong influence among his politically conservative audience.

A survey by the Times Mirror Center for the People and the Press found that 44 percent of Americans received most of their political information from talk radio. On AM radio, talk became the most common format in the 1990s.

TALK LISTENERSHIP. The influence of talkers can be overrated. A 1996 Media Studies Center survey of people who listen to political talk shows found that they are hardly representative of mainstream Americans.

talkers
Talk shows.

Rush Limbaugh
Most listened-to talk show host in the 1990s.

The political talk show audience is largely white, male, Republican and financially well off. It is much more politically engaged than the general population, but on the right-wing. Also, these people distrust the mainstream media, which they perceive as being biased to the left.

EFFECT ON NEWS.   Many stations with music-based formats used the advent of news and talk stations to reduce their news programming. In effect, many music stations were saying, "Let those guys do news and talk, and we'll do music." The rationale really was a profit-motivated guise to get out of news and public affairs, which are expensive. Playing records is cheap. The result was fewer stations offering serious news and public affairs programming.

To many people, talk formats leave a perception that there is more news and public affairs on radio than ever. The fact is that fewer stations offer news. Outside of major markets with all-news stations, stations that promote themselves as news-talk are really more talk than news, with much of the talk no more than thinly veiled entertainment that trivializes the format's potential.

Radio Networks

STUDY PREVIEW   Although the major networks—ABC, CBS, NBC and Mutual—have different roots, they all contributed to the shaping of the U.S. broadcasting industry. They were at the heart of radio in its heyday. Today, the networks are leaders in demographic programming.

Four Traditional Networks

WJZ
Participant in the first station linkup, New York.

National Broadcasting Company
First network; established by Radio Corporation of America.

American Telephone & Telegraph
Created network in 1926; later sold to NBC.

Edward Nobel
Financed the creation of ABC.

American Broadcasting Company
Created from one of NBC's two networks.

Columbia Broadcasting System
Primary early competitor to NBC.

NBC.   The Radio Corporation of America station in Newark, New Jersey, **WJZ,** and a station in Schenectady, New York, linked themselves by telegraph line and simultaneously carried the same broadcast of the 1923 World Series. It was the first network. More linkups with more stations followed. RCA recognized the commercial potential of networks and formed the **National Broadcasting Company** in 1926 as a service to local stations that eventually would link stations coast to coast.

Meanwhile, **American Telephone & Telegraph** developed a 27-station network that stretched as far west as Kansas City. However, in 1926, just as NBC was being formed, AT&T decided to get out of radio. AT&T was aware that the government was looking at restraint-of-trade issues and could break up the company. Also, the company wanted to concentrate on activities that promised more profit than it foresaw in radio. AT&T sold the network to NBC, which operated it as a separate enterprise.

ABC.   Although NBC operated the two networks independently, the Federal Communications Commission became increasingly doubtful about "chain broadcasting," as it was called. Under government pressure, NBC sold the old AT&T network in 1943 to **Edward Nobel,** who had made a fortune with Lifesavers candy. Nobel named his new corporation the **American Broadcasting Company,** and the ABC network was born with 168 stations.

CBS.   The new ABC network was in competition not only with the scaled-down NBC but also with the **Columbia Broadcasting System.** CBS had its roots in a 1927 experiment by **William Paley,** who was advertising manager for his father's Philadelphia cigar company. To see whether radio advertising could boost sales, young Paley placed advertisements on **United Independent Broadcasters,** a 16-station upstart network. Within six months sales skyrocketed from 400,000 to 1 million cigars a day. Impressed, Paley bought the network, called it CBS, and remained at the helm for almost 50 years.

MUTUAL.   When NBC and CBS signed up local affiliates, they guaranteed that no competing station would be given the network's programs, which put independent stations without popular network programs at a disadvantage. To compete, independents exchanged programs and sometimes linked up for one-shot coverage of events. In 1934 independent stations led by **WGN** in Chicago and **WOR** in New York created a new kind of network, the **Mutual Broadcasting System.** Any station could pick up Mutual programs no matter who else was airing them. Furthermore, in a departure from policy at NBC and CBS, Mutual stations were not required to carry programs they did not want. Many independent stations tapped into Mutual, and the network eventually claimed more affiliates than the other networks, though few stations carried all the material that Mutual made available.

Radio Networks Today

Today, inexpensive satellite relays have spawned a bevy of national and regional programming services, but these pale in comparison to the original Big Four networks in their heyday. In news, only four major players remain—and NBC exists in name only. NBC sold off its radio network in the 1980s to a Los Angeles company, Westwood One, which also bought the old Mutual operation. These are the major news networks:

ABC.   The original ABC is now split into demographic networks. Today they are called the Excel, Galaxy, Genesis, Platinum and Prime networks.

WESTWOOD.   Westwood has six networks, some with familiar names from the past: CNN-Plus, Country, Mutual, NBC, The Source and Young Adult.

INFINITY.   Infinity Broadcasting includes the former CBS network and a youth-oriented network called Spectrum.

AMERICAN URBAN.   This company uses its namesake for its network: American Urban Radio.

Affiliate-Network Relations

The early networks were attractive vehicles to advertisers seeking a national audience, which is how the networks made their money and how they still do. Networks base their fees for running commercials on the size of their huge multistation audiences. In general, the more **affiliate** stations and the larger the audience, the higher a network's revenue.

ABC, CBS and NBC each own stations called **o-and-o's,** short for *network owned and operated,* but most of a network's strength is in its affiliates. That is why networks

William Paley
Founded CBS.

United Independent Broadcasters
Predecessor to CBS.

WGN
Partner with WOR in establishing Mutual, Chicago.

WOR
Partner with WGN in establishing Mutual, New York.

Mutual Broadcasting System
Provided programming on nonexclusive basis.

affiliate
Station that subscribes to a network for programming.

o-and-o
Station owned and operated by a network; not to be confused with affiliate.

look to popular local stations to carry their programs and advertisements. Affiliate-network relationships are mutually advantageous. Local stations profit from network affiliations in two ways. Networks pay affiliates for running their national advertisements. These network payments average about 5 percent of the station's income. Also, strong network programs are audience builders. The larger a station's audience, generally, the more it can charge local advertisers to carry their messages.

A network and an affiliate define their relationship in a contract that is subject to periodic renegotiation and renewal. In radio's heyday, which ran into the early 1950s, network affiliations were so attractive and profitable to local stations that the networks could dictate terms. As television displaced radio as the preferred national entertainment medium, the networks relaxed exclusivity and other requirements. Today, local stations are in a stronger position in negotiating affiliation contracts and terms. There are also more possible affiliations because, with the economies possible through satellite hookup, so many networks have come into existence. About 40 percent of U.S. stations have a network affiliation.

Broadcast Regulation

STUDY PREVIEW Complex regulations govern U.S. broadcasting today. These regulations govern station engineering and ownership. Content is regulated in a limited way.

Trusteeship Rationale

Radio in the United States is regulated by the federal government, as is television—but not the print media. To understand why, you need to go back to the days after World War I when radio stations with powerful signals boomed their way onto the airwaves. There were not enough frequencies, and the airwaves became a deafening cacophony. A station finding itself drowned out might boost power to keep listeners, thereby drowning out weaker signals in a kind of king-of-the-mountain competition. An alternative was jumping to a less cluttered frequency and asking listeners to follow. It was chaos.

Failing to solve the problem among themselves, radio station owners finally called on the federal government for a solution. In 1927 Congress borrowed language from 19th-century railroad regulatory legislation and established the **Federal Radio Commission.** The commission was given broad licensing authority. The authorizing legislation, the Federal Radio Act, said that licenses would be for limited terms. The FRC could specify frequency, power and hours of operation.

The new commission's immediate problem was that 732 stations were on the air but the technology of the time allowed room for only 568. In the end, the commission allowed 649 stations to remain on the air with strict limits on transmission to prevent signal overlaps. Even so, some stations were silenced, solid evidence that government was in the business of broadcast regulation.

As might be expected in a nation with libertarian traditions, there was uneasiness about licensing a medium that not only purveyed information and ideas but was also a forum for artistic creativity. What about the First Amendment? As a practical matter, the broadcast spectrum had a real and absolute capacity. Someone had to be the arbiter of the airwaves, or a scarce resource would be rendered unusable. The **trusteeship concept** developed. It held that the airwaves are public property and should be subject to regulation for the public good, just as public roads are. The test

Federal Radio Commission
Assigned frequencies starting in 1927.

trusteeship concept
Government regulates broadcasting in public interest.

Media Databank

Radio Chains

For years the government restricted a radio company to owning no more than seven AM and seven FM stations, but the restrictions were gradually relaxed. Then the 1996 Telecommunications Act eliminated any cap, except that a single company could own no more than eight stations in a large market. Right away, radio chains began gobbling up stations and also other chains. The 1999 merger of Clear Channel and AMFM created an 838-station group. The FCC then relaxed the limit further. By 2000, Clear Channel owned 1,000-plus stations, including 10 in Los Angeles alone. These are the biggest radio chains:

Radio Chain	Stations
Clear Channel, San Antonio	1,018 stations
Cumulus Media, Atlanta	274 stations
Citadel, Las Vegas	207 stations
Infinity, New York	187 stations
Entercom, Cynwyd, Pennsylvania	98 stations
Cox Communications, Atlanta	83 stations
ABC, Dallas	52 stations
Saga, Grosse Pointe Farms, Michigan	51 stations
Hispanic Broadcasting, Dallas	46 stations

of who should be granted licenses, and who denied, would be service to the **"public interest, convenience and necessity,"** a phrase from the 1927 Federal Radio Act that remains a cornerstone of U.S. broadcasting.

With the Federal Communications Act of 1934, Congress replaced the FRC with the **Federal Communications Commission.** Television, under development at the time, was incorporated into the FCC's charge. Otherwise, the FCC largely continued the FRC's regulatory responsibility.

ENGINEERING REGULATIONS.   Over the years the FCC has used its regulatory authority to find room in the radio spectrum for more and more stations. Almost 4,800 AM stations are broadcasting today, compared with 649 when the FRC was set up, and there are more than 5,700 FM stations.

By limiting the power of station signals, the FCC squeezes many stations onto a single frequency. For example, WBAL in Baltimore, Maryland, and KAAY in Little Rock, Arkansas, both broadcast at 1090 on the dial, but restrictions on their signal strengths prevent overlapping. Dozens of stations, scattered around the nation, are sandwiched at some frequencies. At night, when the atmosphere extends the range of AM transmissions, many stations are required to reduce their power; go off the air; or transmit directionally, such as north-south, to avoid overlap. The FCC, with its licensing authority, insists that stations comply strictly with engineering restrictions to avoid the pre-1927 chaos.

OWNERSHIP REGULATIONS.   To encourage diverse programming and prevent big media chains from dominating radio, the FCC originally limited how many stations a single individual or company could own. By 1996, however, it was clear that the ownership regulations had failed. Programming, mostly recorded music, was redundant at stations across the land. So much for diversity. Also, the networks, though not chains in any formal sense, had become mighty purveyors of programming—much as the feared chain ownership had been expected to do back when the FCC was created.

"public interest, convenience and necessity"
Criteria for awarding broadcast licenses.

Federal Communications Commission
Replaced FRC; added mandate that included television, telephone.

Media People

John Brinkley

John Brinkley and his bride arrived in Milford, Kansas, population 200, in 1917 and rented the old drug store for $8 a month. Mrs. Brinkley sold patent medicines out front, while Brinkley talked to patients in a back room. One day an elderly gentleman called on "Dr. Brinkley" to do something about his failing manhood. As the story goes, the conversation turned to Brinkley's experience with goats in the medical office of the Swift meat-packing company, a job he had held for barely three weeks. Said Brinkley, "You wouldn't have any trouble if you had a pair of those buck glands in you." The operation was performed in the back room, and word spread. Soon the goat gland surgeon was charging $750 for the service, then $1,000, then $1,500. In 1918 Brinkley, whose only credentials were two mail-order medical degrees, opened the Brinkley Hospital. Five years later he set up a radio station, KFKB, to spread the word about his cures.

Six nights a week, Brinkley extolled the virtues of his hospital over the air. "Don't let your doctor two-dollar you to death," he said. "Come to Dr. Brinkley." If a trip to Milford was not possible, listeners were encouraged to send for Brinkley compounds. Soon the mail-order demand was so great that Brinkley reported he was buying goats from Arkansas by the boxcar. "Dr. Brinkley" became a household word. *Radio Digest* awarded Brinkley's KFKB (for Kansas First, Kansas Best) its Golden Microphone Award as the most popular radio station in the country. The station had received

Goat Gland Surgeon. Eager for publicity, John Brinkley obliges a photographer by placing a healing hand on a supposedly insane patient he is about to cure. Broadcasting such claims from his Kansas radio station, Brinkley developed a wide market for his potions. Because of his quackery, he lost the station in a significant First Amendment case.

356,827 votes in the magazine's write-in poll. Brinkley was a 1930 write-in candidate for governor. Harry Woodring won with 217,171 votes to Brinkley's 183,278, but Brinkley would have won had it not been for misspellings that disqualified thousands of write-in ballots.

Also in 1930 the KFKB broadcast license came up for renewal by the Federal Radio Commission, which had been set up to regulate broadcasting. The American Medical Association wanted the license revoked. The medical profession had been outraged by Brinkley but had not found a way to derail his thriving

quackery. In fact, Brinkley played to the hearts of thousands of Middle America's listeners when he attacked the AMA as "the meat-cutter's union." At the license hearing, Brinkley argued that the First Amendment guaranteed him freedom to speak his views on medicine, goat glands and anything else he wanted. He noted that Congress had specifically forbidden the FRC to censor. It would be a censorious affront to the First Amendment, he said, to take away KFKB's license for what the station put on the air. Despite Brinkley's arguments, the FRC denied renewal.

Brinkley challenged the denial in federal court, and the case became a landmark on the relationship between the First Amendment and American broadcasting. The appeals court sided with the FRC, declaring that broadcast licenses should be awarded for serving "the public interest, convenience and necessity." It was appropriate, said the court, for the commission to review a station's programming to decide on renewal. Brinkley appealed to the U.S. Supreme Court, which declined to hear the case. The goat gland surgeon was off the air, but not for long. In 1932 Dr. Brinkley, proving himself unsinkable, bought a powerful station in Villa Acuna, Mexico, just across the Rio Grande from Del Rio, Texas, to continue peddling his potions. By telephone linkup from his home in Milford, Brinkley continued to reach much of the United States until 1942, when the Mexican government nationalized foreign-owned property.

Congress revisited the ownership issue in 1996 and ordered the FCC to relax the restrictions. The FCC and the U.S. Justice Department followed through with a new cap on ownership: No company could own signals that reached a majority of the nation's population.

Unchanged is the FCC's insistence that licensees be of good character, follow sound business practices and operate within the letter and spirit of the law and FCC regulations. No nonsense is tolerated as shown by the notable case of WLBT-TV in Jackson, Mississippi, which made no attempt to bring blacks onto its staff even though Jackson was largely a black community. The station carried virtually no black-oriented programming and lost its license in a 1969 court order.

CONTENT REGULATIONS. The 1934 Federal Communications Act specifically forbids censorship, and the government has never had agents sitting at any radio station to keep things off the air. Yet the FCC has a powerful influence over what is broadcast because broadcasters are accountable for what they have aired when license renewal time comes up. Licenses are granted for eight years.

media online
BBC: Find out what the Brits are listening to on the radio.
www.bbc.co.uk/radio

The government has provided clues aplenty to broadcasters on what it, as trustee for the public, does not want on the air. Although FCC policy today has shifted somewhat, many broadcasters, not wanting to risk their licenses, still regard the lessons from these cases as indelible:

- **Unanswered personal attacks.** In 1962 a station in Pennsylvania aired an attack by a right-wing evangelist on author Fred Cook. Cook was called a liar, and it was implied that he championed communist causes. Cook asked for time to respond, but the station refused. The FCC sided with Cook, and eventually, so did the U.S. Supreme Court in a decision called *Red Lion* after the name of the company that owned the station.
- **Realistic, alarming spoofs.** The FCC fined a St. Louis station, KSHE, $25,000 in 1991 after disc jockey John Ulett broadcast a mock nuclear attack on the United States. The FCC was not amused.
- **Exclusive forum for licensee.** A Methodist preacher used his church-owned station, KGEF in Los Angeles, as an extension of the pulpit to attack Catholics, Jews, lawyers, judges, labor unions and other groups. The FRC denied renewal in 1930. On appeal, the courts said that a licensee has no unlimited right to spread hatred.
- **Dirty words.** WBAI-FM in New York, a noncommercial station, included a George Carlin comedy cut in a 1975 program examining social attitudes toward language. The Carlin monologue included "dirty words," which the FCC ruled indecent at times of day when children might be listening. The U.S. Supreme Court agreed.

A notable exception was shock jock **Howard Stern** whose New York-based syndicated program was full of ribaldry and offense. When Stern didn't respond to FCC complaints, the commission ratcheted up the fines to, finally, $1.3 million. Stern continued unabated, vowing that he wasn't going to have a government agency censor him. The owner of the flagship station, Infinity Broadcasting, said that it would stand behind Stern on principle. Also, it must be noted, Stern's large following made him a major revenue producer. In 1998 principle went out the window at Infinity. CBS bought all the Infinity stations, and as part of the deal, the Stern fines were paid straightaway.

Although stations are subject to discipline, the FCC provides only general guidance on what it does want aired. It encourages local origination of network

John Brinkley
Quack doctor who lost an appeal claiming that broadcast regulation was an infringement on free expression.

Howard Stern
Controversial New York radio host.

Media Abroad

Radio Martí

Twenty-six years after Fidel Castro took over Cuba and allied himself with the former Soviet Union, the U.S. government set up a radio station, **Radio Martí.** The station blanketed the Caribbean island, 90 miles off Key West, with news, commentary and entertainment. Outraged, Castro countered with a superpowered station of his own that drowned out some U.S. commercial stations, including one as far away as WHO in Des Moines, Iowa.

Radio Martí, founded in 1985 and funded at $20 million a year, broadcasts 24 hours a day. It has 165 employees, all Spanish-speaking. The signal goes out on shortwave from the government-operated U.S. Information Agency's **Voice of America** headquarters in Washington. Two Miami AM stations also carry Martí programming an hour a day.

In 1990 USIA added TV Martí, a $13 million a year, 80-staff operation that beams 2½ hours of programming a day at Cuba from a balloon antenna tethered above the Florida Straits.

programming, and it also encourages public affairs and community-oriented programming, but the FCC assiduously avoids dictating what goes on the air, even when under pressure to do so. Pressure shows up inevitably when a classical music station switches to another format. To classical music lovers who ask the FCC to intervene, the commission has said again and again that it considers formats a function of the marketplace. If a station cannot find enough listeners with one format to attract advertisers, then it should be free to try another.

Regulating Networks

The networks deliver programming to local stations, and local stations pass network programming on to listeners. Because networks themselves do not broadcast on the public airwaves, they have never been subject to FCC licensing as stations are. Even so, the government can put a lot of pressure on the networks. Consider:

- **Affiliate pressure.** As licensed entities, affiliate stations are answerable to the FCC, which means that network programming must conform to FCC standards. The networks have entire departments to review programs to ensure that they comply with acceptable guidelines.
- **Antitrust.** The size of the major networks leaves them vulnerable to **antitrust** action. It was after the FCC's rumblings that NBC was too powerful that the network sold one branch to candy manufacturer Edward Nobel in 1943 rather than risk an FCC recommendation to the Justice Department to dismantle the company.
- **Network licensees.** The networks themselves own radio and television stations, which are subject to licensing. The stations, all in major cities, are significant profit sources for the networks, which do not want to risk losing the FCC licenses to operate them.

Radio Martí
U.S. government radio targeted at Cuba.

Voice of America
U.S. government radio targeted at the former Soviet Union.

antitrust
Government action against monopolies.

Broadcast Deregulation

Ronald Reagan proclaimed that his presidency would "get government off the backs of business." In 1996, seven years after Reagan left office, it seemed that his deregulation dream had come true—at least in broadcasting. The government relaxed its age-old limits on how many radio stations a single company could own. Right away, radio companies began gobbling one another up in mergers that had some pundits predicting all of radio being in only a few corporate hands before long.

In one deal, the Clear Channel and AMFM chains merged. Together they had 957 stations. Although the new chain quickly sold some of the stations, it dominated several top markets. In Los Angeles alone, Clear Channel had 10 stations; in Houston it had 10; and in one relatively small market, Huntington, West Virginia and Ashland, Kentucky, it had 10. The company's 1999 revenue, estimated at $3.1 billion, was almost 20 percent of the U.S. industry's total.

Among the current federal limits are the following:

- No company can regularly have more than 50 percent of a market's audience share.
- No company may earn more than 50 percent of the radio advertising revenues in a market.
- No foreign ownership is allowed.

Quality on the Air

STUDY PREVIEW: With deregulation, radio programming has become more populist, formulaic and bland. Many stations are devoid of local identity. Even so, some stations set themselves apart with local and distinctive content.

Marketplace Values

Deregulation has let the marketplace drive radio programming, at least to the extent that the government has lessened its regulatory role. This is a populist's dream. Listeners reward stations they like by tuning in. The most popular stations, if they can translate listenership into advertising revenue, are also the greatest financial successes. The contest for popularity is unfettered by the old government requirement that news and public affairs be part of the programming mix. If the audience doesn't care about news, fine, there won't be any. At many stations there isn't.

Without the old government-enforced social responsibility in programming, stations are largely free to air whatever will fetch a target audience cost-efficiently. The audience is king, along with the bottom line.

Measuring Quality

Quality is in the beholder's eye—or ear. If wall-to-wall music is the measure of quality, then a lot of superb stations are on the air. Recorded music, though, is a low-overhead format that's so formulaic that stations have a hard time distinguishing themselves from each other. There are other measures.

The government originally licensed stations to designated communities partly to encourage local service. This didn't mean a mindless channeling of content manufactured in Hollywood, Nashville and New York to local communities. The idea was for radio to play the local community back to itself. How well do stations do this? By this standard, a station would get high marks for programming indigenous culture—performances by local musicians, coverage of local news, discussion of local issues, readings by local poets, play-by-plays of local athletic events. Radio can have a role in creating a distinctive local culture.

However, some stations are devoid of community content except for local weather forecasts and advertising. Some stations are conduits for programming services from far away, nothing more. Even the disc jockey is in a remote city, the music being transmitted to multiple stations simultaneously.

A station can be evaluated by the size and quality of its programming staff. How talented are on-air personalities? Is theirs mindless chatter? Or is it comedic genius? How many news reporters are on the street, on top of news? Or is news a rehash from the wires or piped in from networks? If the station runs public service announcements, are they geared to local causes?

Another defining measure of a station is its balance of advertising. Every 20-second ad is 20 seconds less of other content. It says something about a station to have a 1:3 ad ratio vis-à-vis a station with a 1:20.

Media Future: Radio

RISK-FREE BLAND PROGRAMMING. Like most mass media, radio in the United States is imitative. When major programming innovations occur, which is rare, the cloning begins. In the 1980s, when audiences glommed onto talk radio, for example, hundreds of stations copied the format. The coast-to-coast sameness of radio formats, and even the on-air voices and personalities, has been reinforced by the growth of chain ownership. Chain managers prefer tried-and-true routes to profits. They avoid the risks attendant on striking out in fresh directions.

National program services, which pipe programs to stations to relay to listeners, also contribute to the uniformity. In seeking large overall audiences in diverse parts of the country, these syndicates stick to safe, middle ground even within their format niches. The future promises much of the same unless something occurs that upends the whole industry.

The quality of radio transmissions made a quantum leap when Edwin Armstrong's FM finally took hold in the 1960s. When the economics make it possible—and don't hold your breath—we face another sound breakthrough: digital radio.

DIGITAL RADIO. In the late 1980s, when radio stations tore out their turntables and began playing CDs, many proclaimed a giant step forward in broadcasting. It was hollow hype. Although CDs have superior sound to old analog records, stations still transmitted in the same old analog way—and still do.

Technically, it is possible for stations to upgrade to digital transmission, picking up the long chain of binary 0s and 1s from CDs, with the transmission corresponding precisely to the binary encoding on the CD. The hitch is that the receivers most people own today—in their cars, at home, at work, wherever—cannot pick up digital signals. Digital receivers, really minicomputers, run $200 to $300, and few people are so dissatisfied with the current quality of radio sound that they will invest in expensive, duplicate equipment. Digital radio will come, but not tomorrow or even the day after.

WEB RADIO. Many radio stations and other companies have established music sites on the web. Theoretically, the quality of sound, being digital, should be excellent, but for the time being, the web's bandwidth limitations can't handle enough digital data for smooth delivery. Until bandwidth is expanded to accommodate real-time lis-

media
convergence

Media Abroad

Canadian National Identity

Since 1970 the Canadian Radio-Television Commission has required radio stations to play at least 30 percent Canadian content—"CanCon" for short. The policy is intended to strengthen the Canadian music industry and head off cultural inroads from the powerful U.S. media south of the border. Before imposition of these regulations, some experts estimate, stations played only 4 percent Canadian music.

What makes a song Canadian? In 1970 Stan Klees of *RPM* magazine developed the CanCon MAPL, as he called it, to help the radio industry define Canadian content. To be categorized as Canadian, a song must generally fulfill two of these four conditions:

- **M (music):** The music must be written by a Canadian citizen or landed immigrant.
- **A (artist):** The music or lyrics must be principally performed by a Canadian artist.
- **P (produced or performed):** The recording must have been produced or performed and broadcast live in Canada.
- **L (lyrics):** The lyrics must be written by a Canadian.

There are exceptions for early recordings that date to periods when little Canadian material was produced.

tening, streaming software is available that picks up web music and stores it for playback. Also, technology is finding ways to compress digital signals so that more and more data, including the binary 0 and 1 codes that underlie digital music, can be squeezed through the bottlenecks on the web pipelines.

Once technology catches up with the web's potential, probably when the Internet is upgraded entirely to fiber-optic cable, people might look to the web for radio-type services. On-demand programming is a possibility. Instead of waiting for your favorite song or the latest sports, you could call up what you want, and it would be played instantly for you—just for you when you want it. It is the telephone and cable television companies, which now are rewiring the nation and the world, that will offer this on-demand service.

NATIONAL RADIO. Two national radio operations, the first that the FCC ever licensed, went on the air in 2001. Both Sirius and XM beamed multiple programs from satellites, providing digital-quality sound, much of it commercial-free. The companies had a running start on building an audience by lining up automobile manufacturers to build receiving equipment into new vehicles—about 12 million a year. In the dealership, car buyers were asked to commit to $10 a month to pick up the signals. Both Sirius and XM offered 100 channels—pop, country and talk, sure, but also specialized programming like chamber music, Broadway hits, NPR, audio books and gardening tips.

For years, radio station owners, comfortable with their local niches, had argued against federal authorization of national stations. They feared losing listeners and advertisers. Their tone changed, however, when the FCC gave its go-ahead to Sirius and XM. The local station owners' new mantra, this time directed at advertisers, was that the national stations wouldn't have the local thrust that drew people to the radio.

Sirius Chief. David Margoles, head of the new Sirius national radio service, introduced in 2001, shows off the technology. Sirius, as well as competing XM, were likened to cable: You pay. For $10 a month, each service offered 100 channels, some ad-free. Most of the customers were new-car owners whose vehicles were equipped with special satellite digital receivers. The services were a dramatic departure from the U.S. radio system's traditional base of stations licensed to broadcast with relatively short-range signals from local communities.

To be sure, the national services also faced technical impediments. Building satellites, lofting them into orbit and maintaining them were far costlier than putting up terrestrial transmission towers. To start, Sirius had three satellites, XM two. Also, for Sirius and XM's satellite signals to reach inside tunnels, under bridges, around skyscrapers and through urban and geographical clutter, repeater transmitters needed to be installed. XM built 1,700 repeaters and Sirius 110 in densely populated areas. That may not have been enough. Doubters noted the companies would lose customers in droves if the signals couldn't reach places that terrestrial-based signals did. Time will tell.

c h a p t e r   w r a p - u p

The proliferation in radio programming can be expected to continue with stations narrowcasting into more and more specialized niches. Broadcast industry commentator Erik Zorn predicts hundreds of formats, some as narrow as Czech-language stations and full-time stations for the blind. With on-demand programming, listeners will be able to choose among literally hundreds of programs at any time—a far cry from pre-television days when mainstream radio was truly a mass medium and sought the whole audience with every program.

Questions for Review

1. Why is radio called a ubiquitous and influential medium?
2. How does radio move invisibly through the air on electromagnetic waves?
3. What are characteristics of the radio industry in the United States?
4. Why has U.S. radio historically had an entertainment rather than educational thrust?
5. What is the status of news in U.S. radio today?

6. Why did the government begin broadcast regulation in 1927? What has happened since?
7. What forces contribute to a sameness in U.S. radio programming? Will technology affect programming in the future?
8. How have the national networks shaped U.S. radio?

Questions for Critical Thinking

1. The telegraph was invented by Samuel Morse in 1844. Roughly 50 years later, Guglielmo Marconi introduced radio wireless telegraphy. What was the difference?
2. Lee De Forest was a technical and programming innovator. Explain the significance of his audion tube and his 1916 broadcast of election returns.
3. A new way of transmitting radio was developed by Edwin Armstrong in the 1930s, and by the 1980s it had left the nation's original AM broadcast system in economic peril. Discuss Armstrong's invention and how it has reshaped U.S. radio.
4. U.S. radio was shaped by the networks in the 1920s and 1930s and reshaped by the advent of television in the 1950s. Explain these influences, and be sure to cite radio's transition from literal *broadcasting* toward *narrowcasting*. What about the influence of Gordon McLendon? What of the future?

5. Explain the significance of KDKA of Pittsburgh, WEAF of New York, WOR of New York and WGN of Chicago.
6. How does demographic programming today differ from the potted-palm music of early radio? From newscasts of the 1930s when the networks set up their own reporting staffs? From newscasts of the late 1950s when AM stations improved local coverage?

Keeping Up to Date

The weekly trade journals *Broadcasting* and *Electronic Media* keep abreast of news and issues.

Other news coverage can be found in the *Wall Street Journal*, the New York *Times*, the Los Angeles *Times* and other major daily newspapers.

Scholarly articles can be found in the *Journal of Broadcasting*, *Electronic Media*, *Journal of Communication* and *Journalism Quarterly*.

On regulation, see the *Federal Communications Law Journal*.

Talkers magazine will keep you posted on talk shows.

R&R, a weekly trade journal published by Radio & Records, carries charts and playlists that not only reflect what's getting airtime but also shape what will be getting airtime.

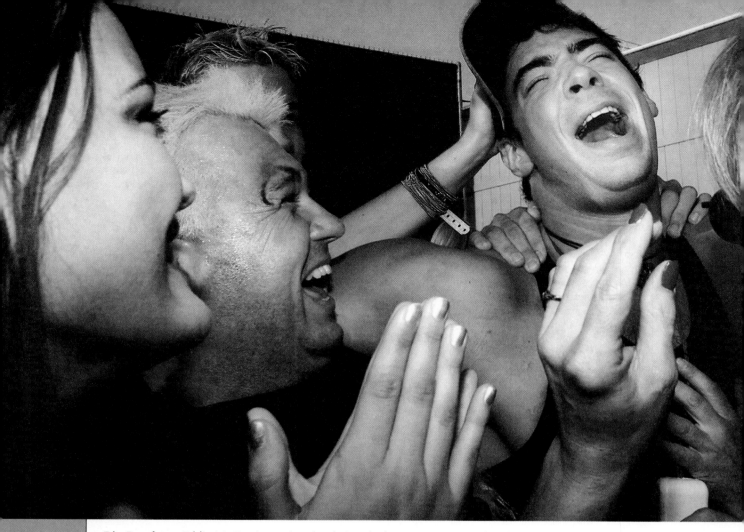

Big Brother. Eddie McGee is overjoyed at being the last person to exit the "Big Brother" house in one of a series of voyeur reality shows that made it big in U.S. television in 2000. Many of these shows were spawned from concepts honed by Dutch producer John de Mol. For "Big Brother," 28 cameras tracked volunteer contestants through the most minute details of their lives in unusual contrived situations. McGee won $500,000 for surviving the longest. In all, de Mol produced clones of the show for 20 countries.

8

Television

John de Mol and the creative crew at his Endemol television production company were dead-ending. They were under pressure from a Dutch broadcaster to create some new kind of show. Despite hours of brainstorming, nothing clicked. During a break, a buddy mentioned in passing that he had been reading about the Biosphere II experiment in Arizona. Volunteers had agreed to live in a self-sustaining ecosphere for months to test a number of things, including their psychological reaction to being isolated.

Voilà! Thus was born the concept for "The Golden Cage," a voyeuristic reality program. Dutch volunteers would live in isolation with 28 cameras following every detail of their lives for 100 days. The show, later rechristened "Big Brother," became the leader in a new genre of television globally in 2000. CBS ran an adaptation in the United States. Endemol produced clones for 20 other countries. De Mol was suddenly one of television's biggest international producers.

De Mol had broken into international television in 1979 when, as a struggling Dutch producer, he won the European broadcast rights to a John Denver concert in Amsterdam. In 1994 he founded Endemol. By 2000, when "Big Brother" debuted in the United States, de Mol was 45, and his Endemol was home to 400 television shows. More than 60 productions were quiz shows, which had elements of audience participation like the new voyeur reality genre.

Voyeur reality had been around for years. Television historians trace it to a 1971 PBS series, "An American Family," in which the audience eavesdropped on the most intimate details of a family in trouble. MTV did something similar with "Real World" beginning in 1992, taping the daily lives of a houseful of young adults.

CBS hit the ratings big time in 2000 with "Survivor," reviving the genre and sending every network scrambling to compete. Ready to go with an adaptation from the Dutch "Big Brother" was de Mol. In fact, he had a half dozen similar series ready for U.S. adaptation, including "The Hairdresser," with hidden cameras catching juicy dialogue in a salon. For "Chains of Love" he had five men chained to a woman for five days, she cutting one loose every day.

Trash? In 2000 it was the genre du jour, and Endemol, then six years old, was sold to a Spanish company, Telefonica, for $5 billion. If nothing else, John de Mol demonstrated the fast-changing tastes of television audiences. The new voyeur reality genre squeezed out dramas and sitcoms in prime time. He demonstrated how broadcasting remained a venue of quick fortunes but also a place that rewards imagination. His story was also a reminder of how fickle the mass audience can be: "ER" one season, "Who Wants to Be a Millionaire" the next, then "Big Brother" and "Survivor."

John de Mol

Impact of Television

STUDY PREVIEW   Television has strong influences on people, on the culture and on other media. In a remarkably short time, television has become the most popular U.S. medium for entertainment. Television has eroded newspapers' dominance for news.

Cultural Impact

Ninety-eight percent of U.S. households have at least one television set. On average, a set is on about seven hours a day in these households. There is no question that television has changed U.S. lifestyles, drawing people away from other diversions that once occupied their time. Churches, lodges and neighborhood taverns once were central in the lives of many people; today they are less so. For 26 million people "60 Minutes" is a Sunday night ritual that was not available two generations ago.

Television can move people. Revlon was an obscure cosmetics brand before it took on sponsorship of the "$64,000 Question" quiz show in the 1950s. Overnight, Revlon became a household word and an exceptionally successful product. In 1998 General Motors spent $778 million advertising its wares on the television networks; Proctor & Gamble, $670 million; Philip Morris, $412 million (for its non-cigarette products); and Johnson & Johnson, $368 million.

The role of television in riveting the nation's attention on serious matters was demonstrated in 1962, when President John Kennedy spoke into the camera and told the American people that the nation was in a nuclear showdown with the Soviet

Union. People rallied to the president's decision to blockade Cuba until the Soviet Union removed the ballistic missiles it was secretly installing. In 1963, when the President was assassinated, the nation spent days glued to the television—a national bonding in mass mourning.

Today, it is rare for a candidate for public office not to use television to solicit support. In fact, as presidential campaigns geared up for the year 2000, campaign managers looked for volunteers less to make door-to-door and other in-person contacts with voters than to help raise funds for television advertising. In state and many local races, too, television had emerged as the most cost-efficient and effective way to reach voters.

Fictional television characters can capture the imagination of the public. Perry Mason did wonders for the reputation of the law profession. Mary Tyler Moore's role as a television news writer showed that women could succeed in male-dominated industries. Roles played by Alan Alda were the counter-macho models for the bright, gentle man of the 1970s. In this same vein, however, Bart Simpson's bratty irreverence toward authority figures sent quivers through parents and teachers in the 1990s. Then came the alarm that Beavis and Butt-Head's fun with matches might lead kids all over the country to set everything in sight on fire.

Although television can be effective in creating short-term impressions, there also are long-term effects. A whole generation of children grew up with Teenage Mutant Ninja Turtles as part of their generational identity. Later came Pokémon. The long-term effects exist at both a superficial level, as with Teenage Mutant Ninja Turtles, and at a serious level. Social critic **Michael Novak** puts the effect of television in broad terms: "Television is a molder of the soul's geography. It builds up incrementally a psychic structure of expectations. It does so in much the same way that school lessons slowly, over the years, tutor the unformed mind and teach it how to think."

What are the lessons to which Novak refers? Scholars **Linda and Robert Lichter** and **Stanley Rothman,** who have surveyed the television creative community, make a case that the creators of television programs are social reformers who build their political ideas into their scripts. The Lichters and Rothman identify the television creative community as largely secular and politically liberal.

Scholars have different views on the potency of television's effect on the society, but they all agree that there is some degree of influence. Media scholar George Comstock, in his book *Television in America,* wrote, "Television has become an unavoidable and unremitting factor in shaping what we are and what we will become."

Mass Media Shake-Up

In a brash moment in 1981, television tycoon Ted Turner predicted the end of newspapers within 10 years. The year 1991 came and went, and as Turner had predicted, television was even more entrenched as a mass medium—but newspapers too were still in business. Turner had overstated the impact of television, but he was right that television would continue taking readers and advertisers from newspapers, just as it had from the other mass media.

Since its introduction in the early 1950s the presence of television has reshaped the other media. Consider the following areas of impact:

BOOKS. The discretionary time people spend on television today is time that once went to other activities, including reading for diversion and information. To stem the decline in reading, book publishers have responded with more extravagant

Michael Novak
Believes TV is broad shaper of issues.

Linda and Robert Lichter, Stanley Rothman
Scholars who claim TV is reformist.

promotions to draw attention to their products. A major consideration in evaluating fiction manuscripts at publishing houses is their potential as screenplays, many of which end up on television. Also, in deciding which manuscripts to accept, some publishers even consider how well an author will come across in television interviews when the book is published.

NEWSPAPERS.   Evening television newscasts and 24-hour news channels have been a major factor in the near disappearance of afternoon newspapers. Most have either ceased publication or switched to mornings. Also, hometown newspapers have lost almost all of their national advertisers, primarily to television. Most newspaper redesigns today, including Gannett's *USA Today*, attempt to be visually stimulating in ways that newspapers never were before television.

MAGAZINES.   Television took advertisers from the big mass circulation magazines such as *Life*, forcing magazine companies to shift to magazines that catered to smaller segments of the mass audience that television could not serve.

RECORDINGS.   The success of recorded music today hinges in many cases on the airplay that music videos receive on television.

MOVIES.   Just as magazines demassified after television took away many of their advertisers, Hollywood demassified after television stole the bulk of its audience. Today, savvy movie-makers plan their projects both for the big screen and for re-issuing, to be shown on television via the networks and for home video rental. These aftermarkets, in fact, have come to account for far more revenue to major Hollywood studios than the movies themselves.

RADIO.   Radio demassified with the arrival of television. The television networks first took radio's most successful programs and moved them to the screen. Having lost its traditional programming strengths, radio then lost both the mass audience and the advertisers it had built up since the 1920s. For survival individual radio stations shifted almost entirely to recorded music and geared the music to narrower and narrower audience segments.

Technology of Television

STUDY PREVIEW   Television is based on electronic technology. In the still-dominant analog technology, light-sensitive cameras scan a scene with incredibly fast sweeps across several hundred horizontally stacked lines. The resulting electronic blips are transmitted to receivers, which re-create the original image by sending electrons across horizontally stacked lines on a screen. Today a shift has begun from analog to digital technology.

Electronic Scanning

In the 1920s an Idaho farm boy, **Philo Farnsworth,** came up with the idea for using a vacuum tube to pick up moving images and then display them electronically on a screen. Farnsworth found financial backers to build a lab, and in 1927 the first live moving image was transmitted. At age 21 Philo Farnsworth had invented television. Farnsworth's tube, which he called the **image dissector,** was an incredible feat,

Philo Farnsworth
Invented technology that uses electrons to transmit moving images live.

image dissector
Farnsworth's television vacuum tube.

Philo Farnsworth

Philo Farnsworth was 11 when his family loaded three covered wagons to move to a farm near Rigby in eastern Idaho. Cresting a ridge, young Farnsworth, at the reins of one wagon, surveyed the homestead below and saw wires linking the buildings. "This place has electricity!" he exclaimed. Philo obsessed about the electricity, and soon he was an expert at fixing anything electrical that went wrong.

That day when the Farnsworths settled near Rigby, in 1919, was a pivotal moment in young Farnsworth's life that led to technology on which television is based.

The next pivotal moment came two years later when Philo Farnsworth was 13. He found an article saying that scientists were working on ways to add pictures to radio but they couldn't figure out how. He then went out to hitch the horses to a harvesting machine to bring in the potatoes. As he guided the horses back and forth across the field, up one row, down the next, he visualized how moving pictures could be captured live and transmitted to a faraway place. If the light that enables people to see could be converted to electrons and then transmitted one at a time but very fast as a beam, back and forth on a surface, then, perhaps, television could work.

The ideas simmered a few months and then, when he was 14, Farnsworth chalked a complicated diagram for "electronic television" on his chemistry teacher's blackboard. The teacher, Justin Tolman, was impressed. In fact, 15 years later Tolman would reconstruct those blackboard schematics so convincingly that Farnsworth would win a patent war with RCA and cloud RCA's claim

Farm Boy Invention. While harvesting an Idaho potato field in 1921, the 13-year-old Philo Farnsworth came up with the idea to transmit moving pictures live on a magnetically deflected electron beam. Crafting his own materials, including hand-blown tubes, Farnsworth completed his first image dissector while barely in his 20s. Later, RCA used the technology for its flamboyant public introduction of television.

that its Vladimir Zworykin invented television.

Farnsworth's native intelligence, earnestness and charm helped to win over the people around him. When he was 19, working in Salt Lake City, Farnsworth found a man with connections to San Francisco investors. With their backing, the third pivotal moment in Farnsworth's work, he set up a lab in Los Angeles, and later in San Francisco, and put his drawings and theories to work. In 1927, with hand-blown tubes and hand-soldered connections, Farnsworth had a gizmo he called the image dissector. It picked up the image of a glass slide and transmitted it. The Idaho farm boy had invented television.

When David Sarnoff, the patent-mongering vice president at RCA, hired Vladimir Zworykin in 1930 to develop television, he told Zworykin first thing to pay a visit to Farnsworth in California. Not knowing

that Zworykin was with RCA, Farnsworth gave him the run of the lab for three days. Not long thereafter, Sarnoff himself came by and saw television for the first time. He offered $100,000 for everything. The answer was no.

Three years later, RCA began touting a camera system based on something called an Iconoscope developed by its own Vladimir Zworykin. Indignant and feeling conned, Farnsworth challenged RCA's patent. It turned out that Zworykin's claim to being first, way back in 1923, was mushy. Farnsworth won the patent case. The RCA publicity machine, however, placed Zworykin in the public's mind as the father of the technology that begat television. To many people, rightly or wrongly, Farnsworth gets only honorable mention. The fact is that, in the end, RCA paid Farnsworth royalties to use his technology.

Media Timeline

Television

1927 Philo Farnsworth devised a tube that picked up moving images for transmission.	**1967** Congress authorized funds to create the Public Broadcasting System.
1939 RCA demonstrated television at the New York World's Fair.	**1975** Gerald Levin put HBO on satellite for cable systems.
1947 CBS began a newscast with Douglas Edwards, and NBC with John Cameron Swayze.	**1976** Ted Turner put WTBS, Atlanta, on satellite for cable systems.
1951 Edward R. Murrow and Fred Friendly began CBS documentaries.	**1986** Rupert Murdoch created the Fox network.
1951 "I Love Lucy" became a filmed and edited program, starting Hollywood in television production.	**1995** Time Warner created the WB network.
	1995 Viacom created the UPN network.
1952 FCC adopted a national standard for compatible black-and-white and color transmission.	**1998** Networks began occasional digital transmissions.

considering that some of the world's great corporate research labs, including RCA's, were trying to accomplish the same thing.

Not wanting to be upstaged, RCA claimed that its **Vladimir Zworykin** had invented a tube, the **iconoscope,** and deserved the credit for television. That would have meant, of course, that RCA would reap a fortune from patent rights. In a patent trial, however, it was learned that both Zworykin and his boss, RCA chief David Sarnoff, had visited Farnsworth's lab and had the opportunity to pirate his invention. Zworykin claimed that he had the idea for the iconoscope as early as 1923, but his evidence was not forthcoming. RCA ended up paying Farnsworth a license fee to use his technology.

In retrospect the technology seems simple. A camera picks up light reflected off a moving subject and converts the light to electrons. The electrons are zapped one at a time across stacked horizontal lines on a screen. The electrons follow each other back and forth so fast that they seem to show the movement picked up by the camera. As with the motion picture, the system freezes movement at fraction-of-second intervals and then replays it to create an illusion of movement—the **persistence of vision** phenomenon. There is a difference, however. Motion pictures use chemical-based photographic processes. Television uses electronics, not chemicals, and images recorded by the camera are transmitted instantly to a receiving tube.

Integrated Standardization

Westinghouse, RCA and General Electric pooled their television research in 1930, and Zworykin was put in charge to develop a national television system. By the time the United States entered World War II in 1941, 10 commercial stations had been licensed, and several companies were manufacturing home receivers. However, all these energies were diverted to the war effort.

Even after the war there were delays. The Federal Communications Commission, wanting to head off haphazard expansion that might create problems later, halted

m e d i a o n l i n e

Persistence of Vision:
Experiments that help in understanding persistence of vision.
www.exploratorium.edu/snacks/persistence_of_vision.html

Vladimir Zworykin
RCA engineer who claimed to have invented television.

iconoscope
Zworykin's television vacuum tube.

persistence of vision
Retina's capability to retain an image briefly, allowing brain to fill in gaps between successive images.

further station licensing in 1948. Not until 1952 did the FCC settle on a comprehensive licensing and frequency allocation system and lift the freeze. The freeze gave the FCC time to settle on a uniform system for the next step in television's evolution: color. RCA wanted a system that could transmit to both existing black-and-white and new color sets. CBS favored a system that had superior clarity, but people would have to buy new sets to pick it up, and even then they would not be able to receive black-and-white programs. Finally, in 1953, the FCC settled on the RCA system.

High-Definition Television

Just as the FCC was slow to approve a color television system, it also moved slowly on technology to improve on-screen picture quality. European television, with images created on 625 horizontal lines across the screen, was always sharper than the 525-line U.S. system. In the 1980s the Japanese introduced HDTV, short for high-definition television, with 1,124 lines. After exhaustive evaluations the FCC acted in 1997, not only to catch up but to leapfrog European and Japanese technology. The commission ordered a reshuffling of bandwidth and gave stations an additional channel to accommodate digital transmissions that can make super-sharp screen images possible. By the year 2006 all U.S. broadcasters are obligated to be transmitting in the new digital formats.

In the meantime, stations will phase in the new digital transmission equipment as consumers are weaned to new digital receivers. The ABC network took the lead, scheduling the 1998 Academy Awards for digital transmission. By 2001 the major networks all offered over-air affiliates some digital format programs.

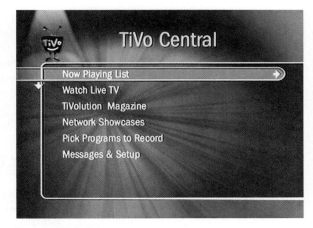

Personal Television. A hot consumer item beginning in 2000 was the PTV, short for "personal television," marketed under names such as TiVo and Replay TV. The devices store incoming programs digitally so people can playback programs in un-real time. Although designed as input devices, capable only of receiving programs, television networks and other content providers are uneasy that manufacturers might add output functions. That would enable people to use their PTVs like a PC to download programs from each other's devices. The result would be MP3-type legal issues about short-circuiting the usual suppliers of programming in a snub at copyright ownership.

Streaming

Broadcasters see the web as an additional delivery system, despite wobbly technology. The cables that make up the connections of the web lack the capacity to carry all the data that underlie video. A second-rate technique called **streaming** is used to move video on the web. In streaming, signals are broken up into packets for transmission and then accumulated in a viewer's computer for replay once it's downloaded. It's not live, and the video often has a jerky quality.

Even so, the networks and stations regard the web as a way to supplement their existing audience, especially for daytime newscasts that people can call up at work, where they may have computers but not television sets. The potential for streaming was demonstrated on December 16, 1998—the day that the U.S. House was voting to impeach President Clinton and that U.S. planes bombed Iraq. On that day, RealNetworks, a pioneer in television-over-the-web delivery, scored 1 million requests for video streams.

Considering the jerkiness of streaming and the delay in delivery, short segments, such as news accounts, work best. Said Forrester Research analyst Mark Hardie,

streaming
Downloading video and audio from the web in advance of playing.

"Online audiences have a couple minutes' worth of attention span. You're forcing them to sit for several minutes to watch poor quality video."

Also working against the web for television delivery any time soon is that many people have creaky, old computers that are maxing out their potential with simple word-processing. Just as serious, computers crash. As technology writer Walter Mossberg put it: "If you watch television on a PC, you're traded a very stable, inexpensive platform for a costly and erratic one. In effect, you've just brought into your family room the first television set that crashes."

Structure of U.S. Television

STUDY PREVIEW   The U.S. television system was built on both a local and a national foundation. As it did with radio, the FCC licensed local stations with the goal of a diversified system. At the same time networks gave the system a national character.

Dual National System

Congress and the Federal Communications Commission were generally satisfied with the U.S. radio system that had taken form by the 1930s, and they set up a similar structure for television. The FCC invited people who wanted to build stations in local communities to apply for a federal license. As a condition of their FCC license, station owners raised the money to build the technical facilities, to develop an economic base and to provide programming. These stations, which broadcast over the airwaves, the same as radio, became the core of a locally based national television system. It was the same regulated yet free-enterprise approach that had developed for radio. By contrast, governments in most other countries financed and built centralized national television systems.

Even though the FCC regulated a locally based television system, the U.S. system soon had a national flavor. NBC and CBS modeled television networks on their radio networks and provided programs to the new local television stations. Today, U.S. television still has a backbone in the networks. Of 1,160 full-power local over-air commercial stations, two-thirds are affiliates of one of the major networks: ABC, CBS, Fox or NBC. In every city it is the network-affiliated stations that have the most viewers.

Affiliate-Network Relations

A network affiliation is an asset to local stations. Programs offered by the networks are of a quality that an individual station cannot afford to produce. With high-quality network programs, stations attract larger audiences than they could on their own. Larger audiences mean that stations can charge higher rates for local advertisements in the six to eight minutes per hour the networks leave open for affiliates to fill. Stations also profit directly from affiliations. The networks share their advertising revenue with affiliates, paying each affiliate 30 percent of the local advertising rate for time that network-sold advertisements take. Typically, almost 10 percent of a station's income is from the network.

Affiliate-network relations are not entirely money-making bliss. The networks, whose advertising rates are based on the number of viewers they have, would prefer that all affiliates carry all their programs. Affiliates, however, sometimes have sufficient financial incentives to preempt network programming. Broadcasting a state bas-

Media Abroad

Japanese Television

Anyone who owns a television set in Japan can expect a knock on the door every couple of months. It is the collector from NHK, the Japan Broadcast Corporation, to pick up the $16 reception fee. This ritual occurs six times a year in 31 million doorways. The reception fee, required by law since 1950, produces $2.6 billion annually to support the NHK network.

NHK is a Japanese tradition. It went on the air in 1926, a single radio station, the first broadcast of which was the enthronement of Emperor Hirohito. Today, NHK operates three radio and two domestic television networks. It also runs Radio Japan, the national overseas shortwave service, which transmits 40 hours of programs a day in 21 languages.

The primary NHK television network, Channel One, offers mostly highbrow programming, which gives NHK its reputation as the good gray network. NHK airs about 600 hours a year of British and U.S. documentaries and dramas from the BBC and PBS. The network prides itself on its news.

Most Japanese viewers, however, spend most of their television time with stations served by four networks, all with headquarters in Tokyo: Fuji, NHK, NTV and Tokyo Broadcasting System. A few independent stations complete Japan's television system.

The commercial stations all offer similar fare: comedies, pop concerts and videos, quiz shows, sports and talk shows. In recent years news has gained importance in attracting viewers and advertisers, encroaching on one of NHK's traditional strengths.

ketball tournament can generate lots of local advertising. The networks also would prefer that affiliates confine their quest for advertising to their home areas, leaving national ads to the networks. Local stations, however, accept national advertising on their own, which they schedule inside and between programs, just as they do local advertising.

The networks have learned to pay more heed to affiliate relations in recent years. Unhappy affiliates have been known to leave one network for another. Television chains such as Group W or Gannett have a major bargaining chip with networks because, with a single stroke of a pen, they can change the affiliations of several stations. This happened in 1994 when Fox lured 12 stations away from the Big Three networks, eight of them from CBS alone.

Also, affiliates are organized to deal en masse with their networks. In 1982 the affiliates forced CBS and NBC to abandon plans to expand the evening network newscasts to 60 minutes. An hour-long newscast would have lost lucrative station slots for local advertising. One estimate is that the stations would have lost $260 million a year in advertising revenue, far more than network payments would have brought in.

Networks once required affiliates to carry most network programs, which guaranteed network advertisers a large audience. Most stations were not bothered by the requirement, which dated to network radio's early days, because they received a slice of the network advertising revenue. Even so, the requirement eventually was declared coercive by the FCC, which put an end to it. However, there remains pressure on affiliates to carry a high percentage of network programs. If a station does not, the network might transfer the affiliation to a competing station. At the same time the FCC decision increased the opportunities for affiliates to seek programming from nonnetwork sources, which increased pressure on networks to provide popular programs.

Campaign Advertising

Although government regulation establishes a level playing field and broadcasters all know the rules and how to profit from them, there is a price. In the spirit of public service, the government requires stations to carry political ads. In the 1998 election year more than $400 million was spent on television political advertising, a record for an off-year election. Almost all the advertising was on local over-air stations. Although $400 million is a lot of revenue, stations were not altogether pleased. Why? Federal requirements dictate that station's charge their lowest rates for candidate ads, so minute for minute, stations make less on campaign ads than on commercial ads.

Worse, from the perspective of station owners, the unprecedented 1998 volume of required candidate ads bumped commercial ads off the air. Stations have only so many minutes per hour for advertising. This meant not only lost revenue, because the political ads are less lucrative, but also that local television advertisers couldn't get on the air as much—if at all.

Stations worried that loyal advertisers had been alienated and might not come back after the election, especially if they had good experience in trying other media, particularly newspapers, free-distribution papers and radio.

Some advertisers thought that stations took advantage of the short supply of available time and the demand for time. Shelly Johnson, of an Indiana advertising agency, told the *Wall Street Journal* that a spot on the evening news cost $300 in February, before the campaign season, and $550 in October, before the election.

Delivery Systems

STUDY PREVIEW   Engineers, broadcast leaders and the Federal Communications Commission structured television delivery much like radio. The original over-air system is now supplemented with cable and satellite-direct delivery.

Over-Air Stations

The engineers and corporate leaders who conceived television really thought in terms of **radio with pictures.** That's not surprising. These people, from Vladimir Zworykin to David Sarnoff, were radio people. The television systems they built used towers, just like radio, to send signals via the electromagnetic spectrum to homes, just like radio. And as with radio, the FCC issued licenses to local station operators to encourage localism and diversity in programming.

The networks, primarily CBS and NBC, thwarted localism and diversity to a great extent by creating popular national programs for local stations. As with radio, this created a two-tier national television system. Stations were local and offered local programs, but the most popular shows came from the national networks. The networks really came into their own, with strong advertising revenue, when **coaxial cable** linked the East and West coasts in 1951. Pioneer broadcast newsman Edward R. Murrow opened his "See It Now" with live pictures from cameras on the Atlantic and Pacific oceans. People marveled.

radio with pictures
Simplistic definition of TV.

coaxial cable
Heavy-duty landline for video signals.

Media Databank

Broadcast Numbers

These are early 2001 rounded numbers.

Commercial FM stations	5,590	Local cable TV systems	11,600
Commercial AM stations	4,720	Commercial TV stations	1,310
Noncommercial FM stations	1,960	Noncommercial TV stations	370
Total	12,270	Total	13,280

Cable Systems

Two-thirds of U.S. households today receive television via wire. Beginning in the early 1950s, entrepreneurs in outlying towns with poor reception built towers to capture signals and then send them by wire to local viewers. In the 1980s major cities were wired. These cable systems carry programs from over-air stations in their area plus, since the late 1970s, a lot of exclusive programming picked up from satellites.

Cable companies tacked their wires on utility poles, but their coaxial cable was, in fact, much better than telephone wire because it had to carry much more sophisticated signals. Today, cable companies and phone companies are in a race to replace their wires with **optical fiber cable** to deliver more data and sharper pictures. Fiber optics can carry signals that can make on-screen delivery as sharp as a computer screen's visuals. In fact, cable and phone companies see their future in offering a vast array of telecomputer services.

Satellite-Direct

Stanley Hubbard owned a profitable over-air station in Minnesota, but he came to see that his KSTP was a dinosaur in an age of satellite communication. Why should people need to tune into his station, which picked up network signals from satellite, when they could tune in directly to the satellite? For more than a decade Hubbard poured millions of dollars into his vision for **direct-broadcast satellite delivery**—DBS for short. In 1994 Hubbard and a General Motors subsidiary, DirecTV, launched **Digital Satellite Service**. Since then, other satellite-direct services have begun operation to serve viewers not only in the United States but all over the world.

Northpoint

A Texas start-up company, **Northpoint,** has a television delivery technology awaiting FCC approval. If approved, Northpoint would be the fourth television delivery system—in addition to over-air stations, cable and satellite-direct. Northpoint would use relatively low-power, south-facing terrestrial transmitters that broadcast on the same frequencies as satellite-direct systems. Northpoint wouldn't interfere with the DBS signals because its signals would deflect off the backs and sides of satellite dishes, all of which are aimed southwest and upward where the satellites are in stationary orbit.

me**dia online**

EXN: Exploration Network, Discovery Channel's Canadian cousin.
http://exn.ca

Nova Online: Program schedules and transcripts of past "Nova" shows.
www.pbs.org/nova

Weather Channel: Sometimes you just have to know.
www.weather.com

Cable TV Networks: Links to more than a hundred cable TV networks.
www.teleport.com/~samc/cable9.html

Soaps: Miss today's soap drama? At Soap Links you can bring yourself up to date on the plot and check out player biographies and gossip.
http://members.aol.com/soaplinks/index.html

optical fiber cable
High-capacity glass filament for video signals.

Stanley Hubbard
Pioneer of direct broadcast transmission.

direct-broadcast satellite (DBS)
Transmission from orbit to receiver; no TV station or cable system intermediary.

Digital Satellite Service
Pioneer DBS company.

Northpoint
A company that uses DBS frequencies to broadcast television signals from terrestrial transmitters.

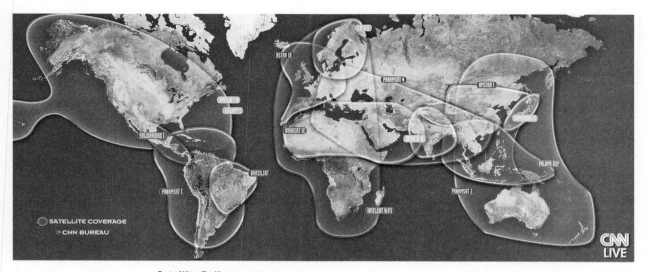

Satellite Delivery. With the notable exception of sparsely populated Siberia, CNN reaches most of Earth's landmasses with overlapping signals from 15 satellites. As this map of CNN coverage shows, you almost have to work at being beyond the reach of the "birds" on which the network buys signal-relay capacity. The satellites, in geosynchronous orbit, pick up signals that CNN aims upward, then the on-board equipment amplifies and relays the signals back to earth, feeding local cable systems, over-air stations, and hotels and other in-house distribution systems.

Northpoint would blanket urban areas with half-watt transmitters having a range of only eight miles or so. Subscribers' dishes would all face north—hence the company's name, Northpoint. Subscriptions would be competitive with DBS, about $20 a month for basic service. Northpoint would be a local service, like over-air stations and cable systems and unlike DBS services. The system could be a new competitor to over-air stations and cable systems for local advertising.

Interactive Television

Almost as soon as the web took root as a new mass medium, futurists saw television and the web melding into a single interactive medium. Their crystal ball had people watching television with hand-held keyboards that would let them simultaneously send and receive messages. The media hybrid was dubbed **interactive television.** Although technologically feasible, the concept took off slowly.

Microsoft acquired WebTV, an early interactive company, in 1997. Three years later it had only 1 million subscribers. There were impediments. For one thing, more than simply plugging in was required. For people receiving over-air or satellite television signals, a separate cable or telephone line needed to be installed for e-messaging and web downloading. Older cable systems couldn't handle two-way messages. Too, a full-fledged hybrid of cable television technology and still-temperamental web technology had practical problems.

In 2000 AOL Time Warner rolled out a relatively simple interactive service, AOLTV, in five cities to test whether it could capitalize on the huge subscriber bases of AOL, 23 million, and of Time Warner cable systems, 12.7 million. For an extra $15 to $25 a month, cable subscribers could get a set-top box that would allow them,

interactive television
A television-web hybrid that allows viewers to send and receive web messages on television sets.

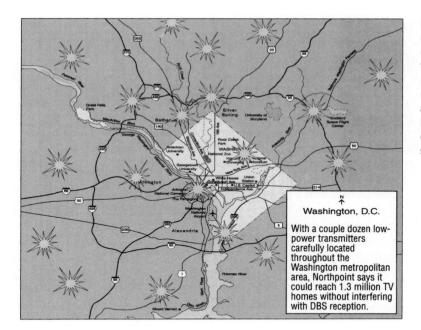

Northpoint. Using the District of Columbia as an example, backers say Northpoint could blanket the city with a dozen low-power transmitters aiming their signals southward. The system would use existing direct-satellite frequencies, eliminating the need to open up new frequencies. DBS signals are aimed northeastward from orbiting satellites, while Northpoint would aim the opposite direction. With opposite-facing dishes, neither DBS nor Northpoint subscribers would get competing signals.

with a hand-held keyboard, to squeeze the television picture and a web image onto the same screen. The possibilities:

- Send and receive e-mails during television commercials.
- Click to the web for more details on a television news story.
- Zap messages to friends that a great baseball game is tied in the ninth inning: "Better tune in."
- While you're watching "Ally McBeal," receive on-screen news flashes from web sources that you've programmed to keep you abreast on subjects you choose.
- Buy online an item that you see advertised on television even as the advertisement is playing.
- Go to a continually updated program directory on-screen rather than leafing through the pages of *TV Guide.*

Unlike the initial predictions for interactive television, AOLTV was not trying to turn television sets into personal computers with all the PC capabilities. The idea, rather, was to enhance television with limited interactive features.

Over-Air Networks

STUDY PREVIEW Three national networks, first NBC and CBS, then ABC, have dominated programming to local over-air stations since World War II. Today, newcomers Fox, Time Warner and Viacom are trying for a slice of the audience.

Traditional Networks

For 40 years television in the United States was dominated by three national networks: **ABC**, **CBS** and **NBC**. Their only early competitor, the Dumont network,

ABC
American Broadcasting Company. Built from ABC radio network. One of the Big Three over-air networks.

CBS
Columbia Broadcasting System. Built from CBS radio network under William Paley. One of the Big Three over-air networks.

NBC
National Broadcast Company. Built from NBC radio network under David Sarnoff. One of the Big Three over-air networks.

couldn't make it, began a slow withering in 1955 and died three years later. The **Big Three** networks built up local affiliates, about 200 each, to carry their programs in every major market and a lot of smaller ones.

NBC TELEVISION. The federal government licensed the first television stations in 1941, on the eve of U.S. entry into World War II. But when factories converted to war production, no more television sets were manufactured until after peace arrived in 1945. By 1948 the coaxial cables that were necessary to carry television signals had been laid to the Midwest, and NBC began feeding programs to affiliates. The coaxial linkup, with some stretches connected by **microwave relays,** connected the East and West coasts in 1951.

NBC innovations included two brainstorms by **Pat Weaver,** an ad executive recruited to the network as a vice president. In 1951 Weaver created a late-night comedy-variety talk show, precursor to the venerable "Tonight Show." Weaver also created an early morning entry, the still-viable "Today." With those shows, NBC owned the early morning and insomniac audiences for years. Weaver also authorized special one-shot programs, *spectaculars* as he called them, which preempted regular programs and drew regular viewers from other networks without losing NBC's regulars.

In 1985 **General Electric** bought NBC. During a three-year period, 1982–1985, all of the Big Three networks moved out of the hands of the broadcast executives, such as NBC's **David Sarnoff,** who grew up in the business and nurtured these giant influential entities. As it turned out, the Big Three's heyday was over with new competitive pressures from cable and other quarters. The new owners, with their focus on the bottom line and their cost-cutting instincts, fundamentally changed network television for a new era.

CBS TELEVISION. CBS was outmaneuvered by NBC in lining up affiliates after World War II but caught up. By 1953 CBS had edged out NBC in audience size by acquiring affiliates and creating popular programs.

The old CBS radio soap operas, transported to television in 1951, were a factor. So was a science fiction anthology, which paved the way for "The Twilight Zone." Also by 1953 the "I Love Lucy" sitcom series, which eventually included 140 episodes, was a major draw.

CBS established its legacy in television public affairs programming when **Edward R. Murrow,** famous for his live radio reporting from Europe, started "See It Now." Three years later, when Senator Joseph McCarthy was using his office to smear people as communists when they weren't, it was Murrow on "See It Now" who exposed the senator's dubious tactics. Many scholars credit Murrow with undoing McCarthy and easing the Red Scare that McCarthy was promoting.

The CBS television network was shepherded in its early years by **William Paley,** who had earlier created the CBS radio network. Paley retired in 1982, and Laurence Tisch, a hotel mogul, came into control of CBS. Today, Viacom owns the network.

ABC TELEVISION. ABC established its television network in 1948 but ran a poor third. Things began changing in 1953 when ABC merged with **United Paramount Theaters,** whose properties included several television stations. The new company went into fast production schedules of programs that were aimed at Hollywood-like mass audiences. Live programming, the hallmark of early network

---

Big Three
ABC, CBS, NBC.

microwave relays
Towers re-angle over-air signals to match the earth's curvature.

Pat Weaver
Created NBC's "Tonight Show," "Today."

General Electric
Current NBC owner.

David Sarnoff
Longtime NBC boss.

Edward R. Murrow
Reporter who criticized Joseph McCarthy.

William Paley
Longtime CBS boss.

United Paramount Theaters
Strengthened ABC in 1953 merger.

Media Abroad

British Broadcasting Corporation

Everybody has heard of the BBC, England's venerable public service radio and television system. Parliament created the British Broadcasting Corporation in 1927 as a government-funded entity that would have as much programming autonomy as possible. The idea was to avoid private ownership and to give the enterprise the prestige of being associated with the crown. The government appoints a 12-member board of governors, which runs BBC. Although the government has the authority to remove members of the board, it never has. BBC has developed largely independent of the politics of the moment, which has given it a credibility and stature that are recognized worldwide.

The Beeb, as BBC is affectionately known, is financed through a tax on new television sets equivalent to $160.

BBC is known for its global news coverage. It has 250 full-time correspondents, compared to CNN's 113. The Beeb's reputation for first-rate dramatic and entertainment programs is known among English-speaking people everywhere. The 1960s brought such enduring comedies as David Frost's "That Was The Week That Was" and later "Monty Python's Flying Circus." Sir Kenneth Clark's "Civilisation" debuted in 1969. Then came dramatic classics like "The Six Wives of Henry VIII," "War and Peace" and "I, Claudius."

The great issue today is whether the BBC should leave the government fold. Advocates of privatization argue that BBC could exploit its powerful brand name better if it were privatized. The privatization advocates say that BBC's government ties are keeping it from aggressively pursuing partnerships to make it a global competitor with companies like AOL Time Warner and Rupert Murdoch's News Corporation. But continuing to do business as always, they say, will leave the Beeb in everybody else's dust.

---

television, was not part of ABC's recipe. By 1969 more than 90 percent of the network's programs were on film, tightly edited and with no live gaffes. It worked. ABC's 1964 fall lineup made national network television a three-way race for the first time.

ABC's growth was pegged largely to two Disney programs: "Disneyland" in 1954 and "The Mickey Mouse Club" in 1955. Another audience builder was ABC's decision not to carry gavel-to-gavel coverage of the national political conventions. That brought criticism that ABC was abdicating its public responsibility, but by leaving the conventions mostly to CBS and NBC, ABC cleaned up in the ratings with entertainment alternatives. ABC picked up more steam in 1961 with its "Wide World of Sports," a weekend anthology with appeal that extended beyond sports fans. **Roone Arledge,** the network sports chief, created "Monday Night Football" in 1969. Network television was a three-way race again, but in 1975 ABC was leading by a hair.

CapCities Communications, a profitable Kansas City-based television station chain, bought ABC in 1985. The network's parent company operated as ABC/CapCities until Disney bought the operation in 1996. Today it is variously called ABC Disney or Disney ABC.

Other Networks

Although the Big Three networks have dominated U.S. television, there have been other players too.

Roone Arledge
Created ABC's "Monday Night Football."

CapCities Communications
Owner of ABC before it was purchased by Disney.

Murdoch-Diller Team.
Most people said a fourth
over-air television network
would never make it. Rupert
Murdoch proved the skeptics
wrong. Murdoch founded
Fox television in 1986, and
programming whiz Barry
Diller built programming one
night at a time, siphoning
viewers from ABC, CBS and
NBC.

Allen Dumont
Operated early fourth network.

Dumont network
Fourth network, operated
1950–1958.

Rupert Murdoch
Created Fox network.

Barry Diller
Created early successful Fox
programming.

Fox
Network launched in 1986.

DUMONT TELEVISION.   **Allen Dumont** sometimes ends up merely a footnote in television history, which is unfortunate. He was telecasting in New York as early as CBS, in 1939, and his station and NBC both aired the 1940 presidential election returns. After World War II Dumont was the right person in the right place. He had a company that manufactured the first television receivers, coinciding with the new public demand for them. Dumont, in fact, beat RCA to the market by several weeks. With his manufacturing profits, Dumont built stations in the District of Columbia and Pittsburgh. In 1950 he created the **Dumont network.**

At its peak the Dumont network transmitted 21 hours of prime-time shows to 160 affiliates, but it never rivaled ABC, CBS and NBC. The Big Three had a foundation of radio experience on which to build their television networks. Dumont didn't. Revenues, at best, were only a third those of the bigger networks. Dumont affiliates were mostly the poorest stations in their markets, with the smallest audiences. In 1955, when the investors were queuing up to buy television stations, Dumont sold his Pittsburgh station for $9.8 million—almost 10 times the value of its physical assets—and began deemphasizing the network, which went dark in 1958.

For many years nobody attempted a fourth network. The national television field was the exclusive domain of ABC, CBS and NBC from 1955 until 1986, when Fox came along.

FOX TELEVISION.   In the 1980s media baron **Rupert Murdoch** bought seven nonnetwork stations in major cities and also the 20th Century Fox movie studio. The stations gave Murdoch the nucleus for a fourth over-air television network, and 20th Century Fox gave him production facilities and a huge movie library. Murdoch recruited **Barry Diller,** whose track record included impressive programming successes at ABC, to head his proposed **Fox** network. In 1986 Fox went on the air, the signal going to Murdoch's stations and to affiliates among other independent stations nationwide. First there was a late-night talk show, then Sunday night shows and then Saturday night shows. Today Fox has at least two hours of prime-time programming every night. With 190 affiliates, Fox is close to the 200 of the other networks, although the Fox affiliates generally have smaller local followings.

Fox became profitable quickly. The plan was to build an audience one night at a time with relatively inexpensive programming. This included the crude, dysfunctional Bundys in "Married . . . With Children" and the cartoon series "The Simpsons." Those programs attracted mostly young people in their free-spending years, as did Fox's "Beverly Hills 90210" and "Melrose Place." That audience made the network hot with advertisers. Winning the bid for National Football League games in 1994 cemented Fox as a major competitor of ABC, CBS and NBC.

Controlling expenses was essential in the early Murdoch-Diller plan. To keep costs down, for example, Fox had no network news division in its start-up years. Programs such as "Cops" and "America's Most Wanted," built around live police footage and re-created crimes, were inexpensive to produce. A news department came in 1996 only as a spin-off after Murdoch launched an all-news cable network.

Late-Comers

Over-air television network competition intensified when the Warner Brothers and United Paramount networks signed on in 1995, both admittedly trying to ape Fox's appeal to a young audience.

WARNER BROTHERS.   Back in 1955 some people found the Warner Brothers cartoon "One Froggy Evening" funny. You judge for yourself. There was this frog that would break into song, usually "I'm Just Wild About Harry." His owner sensed a fast buck in this performing frog, but at every audition the frog would emit only a faint ribbit. Funny? Regardless, Time Warner chose Michigan J. Frog as the mascot for the new over-air television network it launched in 1995.

The **WB Television Network,** with $300 million in start-up funds from Time Warner, used much the same formula as Fox had a few years earlier. WB started with a limited schedule, two hours in prime time on Wednesdays, with the goal of building it up. The network aimed for a young adult audience, as had Fox.

Warner started with 43 affiliates, far short of roughly the 200 traditional networks, but Chicago superstation WGN, which is picked up by many cable systems, also carried WB programs. The company claimed that Michigan J. Frog was reaching 72 percent of the population.

UNITED PARAMOUNT.   A week after WB Television went on the air in 1995, **United Paramount Network** began beaming four hours of programming, on Mondays and Tuesdays, to stations that reached 79 percent of the country via 96 affiliates. Paramount predicted that it would match Fox's audience right away, primarily on the strength of yet another Star Trek series, "Voyager." The network didn't meet the initial expectations. Like Fox and WB, United Paramount played for a young audience.

Like Fox and WB, United Paramount was well financed. Paramount Communications was a subsidiary of the deep-pocketed Viacom media giant. By 2001, after Viacom acquired CBS, it was unclear how United Paramount would fit into Viacom's long-term plans.

Cable Television

STUDY PREVIEW   The cable television industry has grown from independent small-town community antenna systems into a well-heeled, consolidated industry. Today cable is a major threat to the traditional networks and their over-air affiliates.

Roots of Cable

Cable companies, which deliver pictures by wire, often on utility poles strung through alleys, have siphoned millions of viewers from television stations that deliver programming over the air. Cable and over-air broadcasters are now rivals, but it was not always so.

In the early 1950s the Big Three networks and their local affiliates reached only major cities. Television signals, like FM radio, do not follow the curvature of the earth, so communities 40 to 50 miles away were pretty much out of range. Rough terrain kept even nearer towns from receiving television. One by one, small-town entrepreneurs hoisted antennas on nearby hilltops to catch television signals from the nearest cities with over-air stations. These local cable television systems, called **CATV,** for community antenna television, ran a cable down into town and stretched wire on telephone poles to deliver pictures to houses from the hilltop antenna. Everybody was happy. Small-town America got big-city television, local entrepreneurs made money, and the networks and their stations gained viewers they couldn't otherwise reach.

WB Television Network
New network for over-air affiliates; started in 1995.

United Paramount Network
New network for over-air affiliates; started in 1995.

CATV
Short for community antenna television. An early name for cable systems.

Media Abroad

Globo Group of Brazil

Latin America's largest media power-house, Globo, began inauspiciously. Roberto Irineau Marinho rented three rooms at a Rio de Janeiro school in 1925 and cranked out the first edition of *O Globo*. He died a month later. The newspaper, though, did not. His son Roberto, only 21, took over and built the paper step by step into Rio's largest. In the 1940s he expanded into radio and comic books. Roberto Marinho moved into television in 1965, giving the company a broad media base. In Portuguese its name had become Organizações Globo.

Today the company also operates Brazil's largest cable television distribution system and it offers satellite television services. The Globo empire includes Brazil's major radio network. Then there are the magazines, of which it is the country's second largest producer. Of the $4.4 billion spent a year in advertising in Brazil, half goes into Globo enterprises.

Globo TV is known abroad mostly for its steamy *telenovelas*, which are translated into Spanish and exported throughout Latin America. Coming soon is an Internet portal in Spanish for Brazil's neighbors, many with struggling economies that have lagged in web development. The portal will be another outlet for content generated by Globo.

The company is operated by Robert Marinho's three sons. Their focus is attracting international capital to strengthen the company's dominance into the future. Telecom Italia, a mobile phone operator, is a partner in Internet initiatives. Microsoft of the United States is a partner in a broadband system being built to serve Brazilians at home.

With this larger, cable-enhanced audience, the networks and stations were able to hike advertising rates.

Gerald Levin and HBO

Television entered a new era in 1975 when **Gerald Levin** took over **HBO,** a Time-Life subsidiary. HBO had been offering movies and special events, such as championship boxing, to local cable systems, which sold the programs to subscribers willing to pay an extra fee. It was a **pay-per-view** service. Levin wanted to expand HBO to a pay-per-month service with 24-hour programming, mostly movies. If it worked, this would give local cable systems a premium channel from which to derive extra revenue.

For an expanded HBO to succeed, Levin needed to cut the tremendous expense of relaying HBO transmission across the country from microwave tower to microwave tower. Then it occurred to Levin: Why not bypass microwaving and instead send the HBO signal to an orbiting satellite, which could then send it back to earth in one relay to every local cable system in the country? Levin put up $7.5 million to use the Satcom 1 satellite. That allowed him to cut microwave costs while expanding programming and making HBO available to more of the country.

Turner Broadcasting System

The potential of HBO's satellite delivery was not lost on **Ted Turner,** who owned a nearly down-and-out, nonnetwork UHF station in Atlanta. Turner dubbed his WTBS a **superstation** and put it on satellite. Cable systems stumbled over themselves

Gerald Levin
Offered exclusive HBO programming to cable systems.

HBO
Short for Home Box Office. First cable programming via satellite.

pay-per-view
Cable companies charge subscribers for each program they watch.

Ted Turner
Cable pioneer with WTBS superstation, CNN and other program services to cable systems.

superstation
Over-air station available by satellite to local cable systems.

Media People

Gerald Levin

When Andrew Heiskell ran Time Inc., he liked to refer to Jerry Levin as his "resident genius." It was Levin who had taken Home Box Office, a pay-television service in Time's corporate backwaters, and persuaded Heiskell to rent a transponder on the Satcom I orbiting satellite. From Satcom, as Levin laid out his vision, the HBO signal could be amplified and retransmitted down to local cable systems.

Technologically, Levin's proposal was ambitious. Financially, it was risky. At the time, in 1975, cable offered no distinctive programming. Local systems merely picked up signals from relatively nearby over-air television stations and sent them by cable to people who couldn't get clear over-air reception with rooftop antennas.

There had been little thought since cable's beginnings a quarter century earlier to do anything more. Cable was a comfortable, if not sleepy, small-town business.

The early innovators who built the nation's hometown cable systems were either departed or sitting back collecting monthly fees from their subscribers. Back then the nation's cities were not wired. City people didn't need cable. They got clear reception with rabbit-ears that sat on top of their TV sets. Only outlying communities, at the fringes of the reach of over-air signals from the nearest city, needed cable.

Would Levin's proposal work? Would the nation's small-town cable operators invest in the 12-foot dish

and other equipment necessary to pick up the HBO signal from Satcom I? How many cable customers would pay extra for HBO programming, mostly movies that had already played the movie-house circuit months earlier? Would cable operators realize enough revenue to offset their capital outlay for reception equipment, to pay Time for HBO and to make some profit? Would Time have enough income to meet HBO expenses, including the substantial fee for Satcom time?

To all these questions, the answer was yes. In fact, Levin's conversion of HBO into the first satellite-interconnected cable programming network revolutionized the cable television industry.

Gerald Levin

Satellite Delivery. Gerald Levin, president of media titan Time Warner since 1992 and later a top executive at AOL Time Warner, made a name for himself by putting HBO on satellite to be transmitted to local cable systems in the 1970s. This revolutionized television by offering distinctive programming, besides that of over-air stations, for customers of local cable systems nationwide. The television industry has never been the same since. Although the cost of orbiting and maintaining complex communication satellites is steep, it is far cheaper than the old landline and microwave relay systems.

Media People

Ted Turner

With an inheritance, Ted Turner took over a floundering Atlanta television station that hardly anybody watched. Back then, in 1963, advertising revenue was thin, and it was not easy to make the rent for the decrepit building that housed the studios. Only 60 people were on the payroll. Fumigators sprayed for fleas weekly.

Young Turner threw himself energetically into making something of the inheritance. He did everything himself, even stocking the soda machine. More important, he recognized that the station was condemned to a shoestring future unless he could offer viewers more than old B movies and sitcom reruns. Desperate to diversify programming, Turner borrowed enough money to buy the cellar-dwelling Atlanta Braves and Atlanta Hawks teams in the mid-1970s. The purchases spread Turner's finances even thinner, but they gave his WTCG something distinctive to offer.

Turner then learned that HBO was planning to beam programs to an orbiting satellite for retransmission to local cable systems nationwide. He decided to do the same. Turner bought satellite time in 1976 and persuaded cable systems to make his "superstation" available alongside HBO. Overnight, Turner multiplied the audience for his old movies, sitcom reruns and Atlanta pro sports. For the first time, the station, now redubbed WTBS, began attracting national advertising.

Ted Turner stopped refilling the soda machine himself, but he still worked hard. He kept an old bathrobe at his office and slept on the couch when he worked late. His mind never stopped. He considered a second cable network—a 24-hour television news service. In 1980, again stretching his finances to the limit, Turner bought an old mansion, outfitted it with the latest electronic news-gathering and editing equipment, hired a couple dozen anchors and launched Cable News Network. A few months later, with CNN still deep in red ink, Turner learned that ABC and Westinghouse were setting up the Satellite News Channel, which would compete with CNN. To discourage cable systems from picking up the competitor, Turner decided over a weekend to establish a second news network himself, and "Headline News" was born. The gamble worked, and ABC and Westinghouse sold their news network to Turner, who promptly shut it down.

Almost overnight in 1991, a key part of Turner's vision came to fruition. CNN leaped to industry dominance with its 24-hour coverage of the Persian Gulf war. Government

Ted Turner

and industry leaders worldwide watched it for quicker and better information than they could obtain through their own sources. Not infrequently, other news organizations ended up quoting CNN because they couldn't match the network's no-holds-barred commitment to thoroughness and timeliness. Turner's audience swelled, as each day CNN earned greater and wider respect. Back when it went on the air, CNN had been laughed at as "Chicken Noodle News." No more.

Turner sold CNN and the whole bevy of his other networks to Time Warner in 1995, but he remained in charge of them all as a Time Warner vice president and later an AOL Time Warner executive.

to sign up. Turner was giving them an additional channel to entice people to hook up—even if they were already getting over-air stations without cable.

In 1980 Turner put together **CNN,** a 24-hour news service that enticed more people to subscribe to local cable services. Turner charged cable companies modestly for his services, a few pennies per month per local subscriber. He also worked at developing a stream of revenue from national advertisers.

CNN
Short for Cable News Network. First 24-hour TV news network.

Media Databank

Cable Operators

These are the U.S. cable industry's leading multisystem operators, called MSOs, with the number of their subscribers:

AT&T Broadband	16.4 million
AOL Time Warner	12.7 million
Charter	6.1 million
Cox	6.1 million
Comcast	5.7 million

Growth of Cable

media online

CNN: This is CNN.
www.cnn.com

Discovery Channel Online: The Discovery site offers clips from television shows.
www.discovery.com

HBO barely dented the over-air stations' viewership, reaching only 265,000 homes at the outset, but everyone recognized that HBO was leading the way toward a restructuring of the U.S. television industry. On Wall Street, cable became hot. Investors poured in dollars. This financed more cable network start-ups, construction of new cable systems and buyouts of existing cable systems.

NETWORK START-UPS. Ted Turner's operation became a money machine that financed a second news channel, CNN Headline News, and the TNT entertainment network. Soon there were other players: the ESPN sports network, a weather network, music video networks, home-shopping networks. While people once had a choice of ABC, CBS, NBC, PBS and perhaps an independent station or two, they now could choose among dozens of channels. The audience that was once the exclusive province of over-air networks and stations was fragmenting rapidly.

URBAN CABLE CONSTRUCTION. The original cable industry was made up of small-town operations to bring in distant signals. With the new satellite programs, however, companies with deep pockets smelled huge profits if they could wire major cities, which they did. Today, more than 90 percent of the U.S. population has access to cable, and 66.1 percent subscribes.

CABLE SYSTEM BUYOUTS. The prospects of huge profits led to a consolidation of the cable industry. TeleCommunications Inc. of Denver, usually called TCI, bought up small cable companies around the country and emerged a major player in U.S. mass media. Other companies, including Time Warner and Cox, built urban systems and bought up existing cable companies. The consolidation has continued; TCI itself was eventually absorbed and reborn as AT&T Broadband.

Advertising

Like the original CATV systems, the new cable companies made their money by charging subscribers a monthly fee to be hooked up. Soon, though, cable companies went after a second stream of revenue: advertisers. There was a model in the early satellite program services, such as Turner's WTBS and CNN, which had aggressively pursued advertisers from ABC, CBS and NBC. Local cable systems did it locally,

Media Databank

Cable Advertising

These are the leading cable networks ranked by advertising revenue:

ESPN	$ 1.0 billion
MTV	507.1 million
TNN	308.6 million
VH-1	118.5 million
BET	116.7 million

Desi Arnaz and Lucille Ball Introduced taping; led the television industry's move to Hollywood.

however, going after advertisers that over-air stations had regarded as exclusively theirs for 40 years.

The original cozy relationship between over-air broadcasters and those little CATV companies in small-town America was all over. The cable industry had become a giant.

Television Entertainment

STUDY PREVIEW Early national television networks patterned their programs on their successful radio experience, even adapting specific radio programs to the screen. Until "I Love Lucy" in 1951, programs were aired live. Today, most entertainment programming is taped and then polished by editing.

Early Programming

In the early days of television, the networks provided their affiliate stations with video versions of popular radio programs, mostly comedy and variety shows. Like radio, the programs originated in New York. With videotape still to be invented, almost everything was broadcast live. Early television drama had a live theatrical on-stage quality that has been lost with today's multiple taping of scenes and slick editing. Comedy shows like Milton Berle's and variety shows like Ed Sullivan's, also live, had a spontaneity that typified early television.

Desi Arnaz and Lucille Ball's "I Love Lucy" situation comedy, introduced in 1951, was significant not just because it was such a hit but because it was not transmitted live. Rather, multiple cameras filmed several takes. Film editors then chose the best shots, the best lines and the best facial expressions for the final production. Just as in movie production, sequences could be rearranged in the cutting room. Even comedic pacing and timing could be improved. Final responsibility for what went on the air shifted from actors to editors. Taping also made possible the libraries of programs that are reissued by syndicates for rerunning.

"I Love Lucy" also marked the start of television's shift to Hollywood. Because Arnaz and Ball, who were married to one another at the time, wanted to continue to live in California, they refused to commute to New York to produce the show. Thus, "Lucy" became television's first Los Angeles show. Gradually, most of television's entertainment production went west.

Entertainment programming has grown through phases. Cowboy programs became popular in the 1950s, later supplemented by quiz shows. The cowboy

Media Abroad

Edited-for-Asia Television

One of the first multinational media enterprises, *Reader's Digest,* learned early that foreign editions need special treatment. The *Digest,* for example, didn't run its Cold War anti-Soviet articles in its Finnish edition. In tiny Finland, prudence dictated not risking anything that might offend its giant, military-minded neighbor.

It's a lesson being relearned by latter-day entries in the media globalization business. The television pay service HBO, which runs movies uncensored in the United States, is not nearly so freewheeling in southeast Asia. The 1995 movie *Casino* required more than 300 snips. Sometimes it's just a word, sometimes a scene. The subtitle of the 1999 *Austin Powers* movie, "The Spy Who Shagged Me," was too much in prudish Singapore. No way could the television sitcom "Sex in the City" pass Singapore's standards. HBO had to fill 18 half-hours beamed to Singapore subscribers with something else.

Two classics by U.S. movie-maker Steven Spielberg haven't made it to Malaysian television. The cable distributor found naked slaves in *Amistad* unacceptable, and Spielberg refused to authorize cuts. A flash of nudity in Spielberg's *Schindler's List* also failed to pass Malaysian restrictions.

Ironically, considering its massive and open sex industry, Thailand is firmly prudish on television and movies. Cable companies are sensitive to nudity, violence and sex, but the f-word is OK. Go figure. The country-by-country variations are enough to drive global programmers crazy.

genre was replaced successively by doctor shows, spy shows and cop shows in the 1960s. Through the changes, sitcoms have remained popular, although they have changed with the times, from "Father Knows Best" in the 1950s through "All in the Family" in the 1970s to "Friends" in the 1990s. Revamped quiz shows like "Who Wants to Be a Millionaire" and voyeur-reality shows like "Big Brother" began a ride in 2000.

Daily Show. Host Jon Stewart of Comedy Central's "Daily Show" broadcast from the 2000 Republican and Democratic national conventions. The shows drew better than some mainstream coverage of the predictable and orchestrated conventions, particularly among college-age viewers.

Producing Entertainment Programs

Until 1995 the networks produced some entertainment programs but relied on independent companies for the majority of their shows. The independent companies create prototype episodes called **pilots** to entice the networks to buy the whole series, usually a season in advance. When a network buys a series, the show's producers work closely with network programming people on details.

In addition to buying programs from independent producers, networks buy motion pictures from Hollywood, some that have already been on the movie-house circuit and on pay television and others made expressly for the networks. Hollywood studios are among the largest producers of network entertainment programs.

Like the networks, stations buy independently produced entertainment programs. To do this, stations go to distributors, called **syndicators,** which package programs specifically for sale to individual stations, usually for one-time use. Syndicators also sell programs that previously appeared on the networks. Local stations, like the networks, also buy old movies from motion picture companies for one-time showing.

Changing Program Standards

Because the networks are responsible for the programs they feed their affiliates, the networks have **standards and practices** units that review every program for content acceptability and sometimes order changes. Although it is gatekeeping, not true censorship, standards and practices people sometimes are called "censors."

At all three major networks the censorship units once were cautious not to offend viewers, advertisers or the FCC. At one time censors regularly sent suggestive commercials back to agencies for revision, insisted that Rob and Laura Petrie of "The Dick Van Dyke Show" sleep in separate beds and even banned the Smothers Brothers' antiwar jabs at President Lyndon Johnson.

The standards and practices units have been downsized in recent years—in part because of greater audience and government acceptance of risqué language and forthright dramatizations. Today, sitcom couples no longer sleep in separate beds. Sex between unmarried adults, and even teens, is frequently in story lines.

New Ratings System

Congress insisted in 1996 that the television industry devise a ratings system to help people avoid objectionable programs. An age-based system was created, ranging from TV-Y for programs suitable for younger children to TV-M for mature audiences. In 1997 CBS settled on an M for Steven Bochco's "Brooklyn South"—the first prime-time show with an M. Acting on its own, CBS also flagged the series with additional alerts: L for language, S for sex, and V for violence.

V-Chip

While public concern over violence and rough language on television is difficult to measure, Congress decided in 1996 to do something about it. The Telecommunications Act of 1996 required a new kind of electronic chip in every television set—

pilot
Prototype show for a series.

syndicators
Independent program producers and distributors.

standards and practices
Network offices to review programs for suitability.

Jerry Falwell

Teletubbies. The British television characters Teletubbies delighted kids everywhere but not right-wing preacher Jerry Falwell. His *National Liberty Journal* saw a gay agenda in Tinky Winky, whose fuzzy-wuzziness was purple. Worse, a triangular antenna protruded from Tinky Winky's head. Purple, triangular, Gay Pride movement—get it? Most people didn't either. Amid a lot of ridicule, the Reverend Falwell eventually backed off. The flap demonstrated, however, how sensitive many people imagine the effect of television to be. Some people see subversive ploys to undermine public mores, especially those of young people.

except tiny economy sets with mini-screens. The V-chip, as it was called, was designed to permit parents to intercept objectionable programs their kids might watch when unattended. Broadcasters and cable companies were required to code objectionable programs beginning in February 1997 so that the V-chips could do their job. There were delays, however, in making the chip workable, and implementation was postponed.

When it finally is introduced, will the V-chip work? Moralists and parent groups that lobbied for the V-chip hailed the new law as a triumph, but rating programs is not an easy matter. Is it an act of violence when a boulder falls on Bugs Bunny's head, driving him halfway to China? Should a single act of violence render an entire episode unacceptable? How much skin is too much? These are imponderables that will remain in debate until after solutions are found to technical hitches with the V-chip and people try it out.

Television News

STUDY PREVIEW   The television networks began newscasts in 1947 with anchors reading stories into cameras, embellished only with occasional newsreel clips. Networks expanded their staffs and programming over the years. Documentaries, introduced in the 1950s, demonstrated that television could cover serious issues in depth.

Talking Heads and Newsreels

The networks began news programs in 1947, CBS with "**Douglas Edwards** and the News" and NBC with **John Cameron Swayze**'s "Camel News Caravan." The 15-minute evening programs rehashed AP and UP dispatches and ran film clips from movie newsreel companies. The networks eventually built up their own reporting staffs and abandoned the photogenic but predictable newsreel coverage of events like

Douglas Edwards
Pioneer anchor.

John Cameron Swayze
Pioneer anchor.

Television Exposure. The advent of 24/7 television news has added to the medium's role in political campaigns and governance. When interviewer Matt Lauer of NBC's "Today" talked with U.S. Senate candidate Hillary Clinton, snippets were replayed in countless other newscasts. The repetition compounded the impact of the interview.

beauty contests and ship launchings. With on-scene reporters, network news focused more on public issues. In 1963 the evening newscasts expanded to 30 minutes with NBC's **Chet Huntley-David Brinkley** team and CBS's **Walter Cronkite** in nightly competition for serious yet interesting accounts of what was happening. When Cronkite retired in 1981, surveys found him the most trusted man in the country—testimony to how important television news had become. Although news originally was an unprofitable network activity, sometimes referred to as a "glorious burden," it had become a profit center by the 1980s as news programs attracted larger audiences, which in turn attracted more advertisers.

Television's potential as a serious news medium was demonstrated in 1951 when producer **Fred W. Friendly** and reporter Edward R. Murrow created "See It Now," a weekly investigative program. Television gained new respect when Friendly and Murrow exposed the false, hysterical charges of Senator Joseph McCarthy about Communist infiltration of federal agencies.

Chet Huntley and David Brinkley
Headed first 30-minute network newscast.

Walter Cronkite
Best-known television news anchor, now retired.

Fred W. Friendly
Partner of Edward R. Murrow; showed power of TV news through "See It Now" and other programs.

magazine
Usually investigative news program with three to four unrelated segments.

Shift in Network News

Some say television news was at its best during the Murrow period. It is a fact that the Big Three networks have scaled down their global news-gathering systems since the mid-1980s. New, bottom-line-oriented owners and budget problems forced the changes. Newscasts have suffered most, losing a lot of original coverage from abroad.

Prime-time **magazine** programs, like "60 Minutes" and "20/20," once were a sideline of network news divisions. Today, those programs have become so popular with viewers that ABC, CBS and NBC news divisions have shifted resources to produce more of them. NBC's "Dateline," for example, airs four nights a week. The proliferation of magazine programs has further reduced the talent and budget for the newscasts that once were the main identity of the network's news. Critics point out that some network magazine projects are of the tabloid mold—flashy but not much substance. Edward R. Murrow set a higher standard.

Media Databank

Cable News Channels

Cable News Network once had 24/7 news all to itself. Now it shares the audience. Early 2000 data on the average number of viewers a day per hour:

CNN	365,000
CNBC	333,000
CNN Headline	169,000
MSNBC	161,000
Fox News	136,000

24-Hour Television News

When Ted Turner launched Cable News Network as an around-the-clock news services in 1980, critics belittled the shoestring operation as "Chicken Noodle News." Gradually, CNN built up its resources and an audience and advertiser base. CNN proved its mettle in the 1991 Persian Gulf War, routinely outdoing the Big Three networks in coverage from the Gulf and being wholly competitive from Washington and other world centers. Some ABC, CBS and NBC affiliates preempted their networks' war coverage to feed viewers CNN's reports. Newspapers around the world quoted the network. CNN viewership shot to 10 million U.S. households—almost one in 10. After the war the CNN audience slipped to 700,000 on many slow news days, sometimes lower, but there were dramatic spikes when major news broke. People had learned to count on CNN for breaking news. One CNN strength was international news built around staff coverage from 26 bureaus—more than any other network. In 1997 veteran CBS anchor Dan Rather seriously considered jumping to CNN. Although he stayed at CBS, he acknowledged CNN as a worthy competitor.

By the late 1990s, other players had joined the 24-hour news competition.

FOX NEWS. Fox hired a corps of respected Washington reporters, including Brit Hume from ABC, and launched the Fox News cable network. The Fox coverage was supplemented with feeds from local stations affiliated with the Fox over-air network, as well as with video reports from AP Television. Trendy sets and irreverent anchor banter, along with a Murdochian taste for the sensational, set Fox News apart. Slick presentation and an underdog's drive gave coverage an edge.

MSNBC. A Microsoft-NBC alliance evolved into the all-news MSNBC cable network. The network drew on NBC's resources, including widely recognized anchors like Tim Brokaw and Jane Pauley and also NBC's film archives going back to the 1950s. MSNBC had the depth to inspire viewer confidence.

The all-news networks overrode scheduled newscasts and news programs for live coverage of major events, always with expert analysis—a new dimension in television news.

Meanwhile, other all-news networks came on the air. A CNN spin-off, Headline News, offered quick summaries of news in 20-minute cycles. The Hubbard satellite-direct service operated a low-budget summary service out of St. Paul, Minnesota, emphasizing hometown news from local stations around the country. All-news services

Media People

Christine Craft

Kansas City television anchor **Christine Craft** was stunned. Her boss, the news director, had sat her down in his office and announced that he was taking her off the anchor desk. He flashed a consultant's report at her. "We've just gotten our research back," he said. "You are too old, too unattractive, and not sufficiently deferential to men." He went on, "When the people of Kansas City see your face, they turn the dial."

Christine Craft was incredulous. During her few months at KMBC, in 1981, the station had climbed to number one for the first time in three years. She was an experienced television journalist who had anchored in her hometown, at KEYT in Santa Barbara; reported in San Francisco, at KPIX; and anchored a sports show on the CBS network. At 36 she was hardly over the hill. What did her news director mean

that she was "not sufficiently deferential to men"? He explained that she had not played second fiddle to male co-anchors. "You don't hide your intelligence to make the guys look smarter. People don't like that you know the difference between the American and the National League."

Angry, Chris Craft sued. She charged that KMBC was demoting her on sexist grounds, claiming that male anchors were not held to the same standards in age, appearance or deference. Further, she said, the station had paid her unfairly, $38,500 compared with $75,000 for her male co-anchor. It was an important moment in U.S. television, triggering an overdue sensitivity to equal opportunity and treatment for women and men. Craft won her jury trial and even an appeal trial before a second jury. In further appeals, the Metromedia conglomerate,

Christine Craft

which owned KMBC, prevailed, but Craft had made her point on behalf of women broadcasters throughout the land.

Within two years Craft was back as an anchor and happy in Sacramento. Then she was named news director and managing editor, the first woman to hold the positions at a Sacramento television station.

Christine Craft
Fought for greater equity in on-air assignments.

emerged elsewhere too. The Canadian Broadcasting Corporation established the Newsworld International cable service. The British Broadcasting Corporation also went into the all-news business. CNN established foreign centers to serve regions abroad with distinctive news packages. Continental pride prompted a European consortium to create Euronews to counter CNN's inroads. In the United States, meanwhile, local cable companies in major markets—first New York, then Boston, then second-tier markets like Seattle and Tampa—went into the 24-hour news business.

One upshot on the proliferating news channels was further deterioration in Big Three news audiences. By 1998 the ABC, CBS and NBC evening newscasts commanded less than half of the television sets in the nation, contrasted to 95 percent 20 years earlier. Of course, other media choices also were fragmenting the old Big Three audiences. The all-news networks also lessened the pressure on other networks to provide breaking coverage of news, and the cleavage widened between entertainment networks and news networks rather than the hybrid Big Three model.

Local News

Local television news imitated network formats in the early days, but by the 1970s many innovations were occurring at the local level. Local reporting staffs grew, and some stations went beyond a headline service to enterprising and investigative reports. Many stations were quick to latch onto possibilities of satellite technology in the 1980s to do their own locally oriented coverage of faraway events. This reduced the dependence of stations on networks for national stories. Today, large stations send their own reporters and crews with uplink vans to transmit live reports back home via satellite. At the 2000 Democratic and Republican national conventions, for example, viewers could see local delegates being interviewed by local reporters who knew local issues, which was something the networks, always looking for broad, general stories, could not do. It was something not possible even a decade earlier.

Public Television

STUDY PREVIEW The quasi-governmental Corporation for Public Broadcasting funnels federal dollars into noncommercial television, including the PBS network. Despite attempts to buffer CPB from political meddling, President Nixon tried tampering with it in the 1970s, as did the new Republican-controlled House of Representatives in 1995.

Corporation for Public Broadcasting

Many school districts and universities set up noncommercial television stations in the 1960s in attempts to broaden their reach. The experiments had mixed results. Most programs were dull lectures, and the following was small. In some cities, meanwhile, citizen groups obtained licenses for noncommercial stations. By the late 1960s there were more than 300 of these stations. It was a grossly underdeveloped national resource.

In 1967 a blue-ribbon group, the **Carnegie Commission on Educational Television,** examined the situation and recommended the educational television concept be changed to **public television** to "serve the full needs of the American public." This put to rest the dowdy **educational television, ETV** for short, image of the early noncommercial stations.

Within months, Congress responded by creating the **Corporation for Public Broadcasting** to develop a national noncommercial broadcasting system for both television and radio. The goal was to offer high-quality programming distinct from that of the commercial networks, which, by their nature, pandered to mass markets.

In its early days CPB helped to build the **Public Broadcasting Service,** a network for noncommercial television stations, and also **National Public Radio.** Later CPB channeled more dollars to individual stations to buy programs from either PBS or other sources and thus made for more diversity.

Unlike commercial networks, PBS does not pay affiliates to carry its programs. Affiliates pay the network. Besides revenue from affiliates, PBS has income from corporations, foundations and viewers themselves—in addition to federal money from CPB.

Carnegie Commission on Educational Television
Recommended upgrading noncommercial broadcast system.

public televison
Post-Carnegie term for noncommercial TV.

educational television (ETV)
Early term for noncommerical TV.

Corporation for Public Broadcasting
Funnels federal money to public broadcast system.

Public Broadcasting Service
National TV network for noncommercial television stations.

National Public Radio
A national network for noncommercial radio stations.

Ken Burns

Jazz on PBS. Documentary producer Ken Burns drew more viewers to PBS with his 1990 Civil War series than had tuned in to any other program in the network's history. His 10-part, 10-hour series "Jazz," which tracks the history of the distinctive U.S. musical genre, was in the same spirit in 2001. Burns spent six years on the "Jazz" project.

Children's Television Workshop
Created "Sesame Street."

PBS does not produce programs. Rather, it acquires many programs from a handful of stations. These are mostly the production powerhouses KQED in San Francisco; WGBH, Boston; WNET, New York; WQED, Pittsburgh; and WTTW, Chicago. For diversity PBS also buys programs from independent producers.

PBS made its mark in 1970 with "Sesame Street," produced by the **Children's Television Workshop,** an independent producer. A drama that aired the same year, "The Andersonville Trial," won an Emmy. Other early fare included Julia Child on cooking, "Mister Rogers' Neighborhood," "Black Report" and the "MacNeil/Lehrer NewsHour." PBS also carried a lot of highbrow BBC programs, which led one wag to say that PBS stood for "Primarily British Shows." This was all distinctive programming that was not economically feasible for the commercial networks because, in general, the audiences were smaller than advertisers wanted.

As the years went on, cable began to encroach on what had been PBS' domain. The Discovery cable channel, for example, featured old documentaries and nature shows, and A&E began to show British productions. PBS lost a distinctive edge. Also many noncommercial stations blurred their own images when they began offering old movies and other programs that, said critics, were duplicating offerings of the commercial networks. Concerned that they would lose viewers to PBS, commercial broadcasters cried foul that a government-subsidized operation was intruding into their free-enterprise turf. PBS affiliates conceded that they were trying to expand their audience, but they also said that their movies were classics and were shown as cultural fare. That debate continues.

The greatest threat to PBS, however, has been from conservative ideologues who charge that the network is politically biased and liberal.

Pat Mitchell. People came to know Pat Mitchell in the 1980s as the first producer and host of a nationally syndicated talk show, the Emmy-winning "Woman to Woman." Later she was the CNN and Turner executive in charge of producing original nonfiction programming. In 2000 she became president of PBS. Her job: To develop programming to increase the noncommercial network's visibility. Prime-time ratings typically had been at 2.0 on a scale that had commercial network shows at 10.0 and higher.

Debate over Public Funding

A knotty problem when CPB was created was the possibility of government interference in programming. This was addressed in the 1967 Public Broadcasting Act, which specified that congressional funding go—no strings attached—to CPB in advance of programming decisions. The president appoints CPB's directors with the Senate's approval, but the law is specific that CPB is not a government agency. That provision was intended to prevent the corporation from becoming a political lackey.

Even so, there have been problems. In the early 1970s President **Richard Nixon** was upset over unflattering PBS documentaries. His telecommunications director, **Clay Whitehead,** went to broadcasters and proposed that public television emphasize local programs. The stated rationale was that the commercial networks offered enough national programming. Unstated was that locally originated programming was less likely to focus on national issues, reducing the administration's exposure to critical coverage.

In 1972 Nixon vetoed a two-year $154 million congressional funding package for CPB, saying that the corporation had too much power over local stations. Outraged, key CPB officials resigned. That gave the president an opportunity to appoint people who were more to his liking. The new CPB appointees wanted more cultural and local-origination programs and fewer documentaries. Coincidentally, just as a divisive battle was shaping up, the Watergate scandal erupted. The attention of the White House shifted to its own survival, not ideological games over public television.

Ideological opposition to PBS and also to NPR erupted again in the 1990s, cast more distinctly as liberalism versus conservatism. The Republican-controlled Congress began a phase-down of public funding. By 2000 PBS was down to 14 percent of its budget being from the federal government. Far more, $309 million, came from exploiting PBS as a brand name. Ever think about wanting a "Masterpiece Theatre" umbrella? Or a "Washington Week in Review" mug? PBS also stepped up its work to find corporate and philanthropic underwriters for programs.

To increase the PBS audience, a CNN programming veteran, Pat Mitchell, was brought in as president in 2000. One of her initiatives was further promoting the

Richard Nixon
U.S. president who vetoed CPB funding.

Clay Whitehead
Proposed bypassing CPB to localize noncommercial broadcasting during the Nixon administration.

"West Wing." The idealistic NBC series "West Wing," about a hypothetical but believable White House staff in continual turmoil, won a record-setting nine Emmy awards in 2000. Emmy winners are chosen by members of the Academy of Television Arts and Sciences. The method bridges some of the elitist-populist gap. Multiple-award winners generally all are popular and are held in high critical acclaim. Emmy winners for best dramatic series before "West Wing" included HBO's "Sopranos" and NBC's "ER."

brand name to build audience, not just to sell records, tapes and program-related paraphernalia but also to make it easier to attract underwriters. The original Carnegie Commission concept was that PBS was to be quality-driven, but fiscal realities have shifted the focus. Some would say the shift has been slight. Others would say it has been fundamental. Said Mitchell, "Whether or not we thrive will, in the end, depend on the content we provide."

Evaluating Television

STUDY PREVIEW   Ratings and People's Awards indicate the popularity of television programs. Measures of excellence are awards and professional recognition. The peer reviewing that goes into Emmy Awards recognizes success at several levels: commercial, artistic, technical.

Populist Measures

Every morning, television and advertising executives get the **Nielsen overnights,** tabulations on how many people watched network shows the night before. Although networks grumble at the Nielsens and attack its survey methods when ratings go south, all parties have agreed to use the numbers to adjust advertising rates. Millions of dollars ride on the Nielsens. A network that had promised 14 million viewers to an advertiser will have to reduce its bill for the commercials if fewer people tuned in. Ratings are used the same way for cable and lots of local programming. Nielsens are a reasonably reliable indicator of the popularity of programs.

Another populist measure, although methodologically loose, is **People's Awards,** as they're called. Viewers are asked to vote. While hardly as precise as Nielsens, the

Nielsen overnights
Quick television ratings on network programs the night before. Used to adjust advertising rates.

People's Awards
Based on viewer balloting.

People's Awards indicate longer-term popularity—not just for an episode but for a program over time.

Neither Nielsens nor People Awards, however, are measures of quality that would satisfy elitists, who say that media content should be judged by other standards—like artistic merit and contribution to understanding of significant public issues. Elitists are especially critical of People's Awards. As elitists see them, People's Awards are tainted not only as measure of mass popularity, but also by the sponsors' motivation to attract large television audiences to broadcasts of the awards ceremonies and to make money by selling advertising for the broadcasts.

Quality Measures

Some awards are measures of quality. Peabody Awards for news carry a lot of weight, as do DuPonts. The Academy of Television Arts and Sciences, sponsor of the **Emmy Awards,** offers peer review. Academy members, all television people, choose the annual winners. Industry politics can be a factor, but nobody challenges the quality of works, performances and contributions that win Emmys—even though some excellent candidates get sifted out for wrong reasons, like being on the outs with the industry mainstream at the moment.

In one sense, the Emmys represent both populist and elitist values. The television industry, by nature, is audience-responsive. As such, the Emmys are a measure of commercial success. At the same time, excellence is a value in Emmy considerations.

Emmy Awards
Selected by members of the Academy of Televisions Arts and Sciences to recognize excellence.

Media Future: Television

The pell-mell impact of the web on older mass media portends special importance for television. These two media share so many qualities. Both television and web messages are visual, in motion, auditory and live. Not to be overlooked is that both are received by appliances that are widely available. Television sets are in 98 percent of U.S. homes, and web-linked computers are in a majority and the number is growing. Television and the web are well into the processing of melding into a single medium.

Common delivery appliances, like WebTV, AOLTV and TiVo, have a foothold already. Cross-platform content is also here with streaming. Major media companies have simultaneous delivery. CNN and MSNBC, for example, have implanted their brands and content as firmly on the web as on television.

Will the web subsume television? Or will television subsume the web? It won't be a question of one disappearing into the other as much as an integration that wipes out the distinctions we see today between these media.

chapter wrap-up

U.S. television patterned itself after radio. From the beginning, television was a dual national system of locally owned commercial stations and national networks. Companies that were heavily involved in radio were also the television heavyweights. Even television's programming mimicked radio's. The Big Three networks—NBC, CBS and ABC—were the most powerful shapers of television, leading in entertainment programming and news. Gerald Levin and then Ted Turner led a restructuring when they realized that they could deliver programs to local cable companies via orbiting satellite. Levin's HBO and Turner's WTBS, both movie services, became unique features of cable companies in the 1970s. Now satellite technology is contributing to major changes.

Questions for Review

1. How does television influence people and society in the short term and the long term?
2. How is television technology different from movie technology?
3. How was radio the role model for early television programming?
4. How has television expanded beyond over-air delivery?
5. What is the relationship between the television networks and their local over-air affiliates?
6. What is the relationship between the cable and over-air television industries today?
7. Why did early television programs resemble their radio predecessors?
8. Why do critics say television news is in decline?
9. What is the connection between Congress and public television?

Questions for Critical Thinking

1. How did Philo Farnsworth's image dissector employ electronics to pick up moving images and relay them to faraway screens? Explain the difference between television and film technology.
2. What was the relationship between radio and early television programming? You might want to review Chapter 7 to explain the effect of television on radio.
3. Trace the development of television news from the newsreel days. Include the heyday of documentaries and explain what happened to them. What was the contribution of Fred W. Friendly and Edward R. Murrow? Explain expanded network newscasts and the importance of Walter Cronkite. What contribution has PBS made? Include magazine and talk show programs in your answer.
4. Outline the development of television networks. Besides the three major networks, include Allen Dumont's, Ted Turner's and Rupert Murdoch's

networks. Explain challenges faced today by the major networks, including how independent stations have become stronger, the innovation pioneered by Gerald Levin, the effect of FCC deregulation, expanded program production by syndicators and new technologies. How do you regard the observation of some critics that the Big Three networks will not exist in their present form a few years into the 21st century?

5. Historically, why have television stations sought affiliations with ABC, CBS and NBC? Discuss changes in network-affiliate relations. Is a network affiliation as attractive today as it was 20 years ago? Why or why not?
6. What happened to network Standards and Practices Departments in the late 1980s? Why?
7. How is the television industry funded? Remember that the financial base is different for the commercial networks, network-affiliated stations, independent stations, noncommercial networks and stations, superstations, cable networks, cable systems and subscriber services.
8. How does the career of Ted Turner epitomize the emergence of new program and delivery systems as a challenge to the traditional structure of television in the United States?

Keeping Up to Date

Broadcasting & Cable is a weekly broadcasting trade journal. Coverage of federal regulation, programming and ownership is consistently solid. Every issue includes a comprehensive table on prime-time Nielsens for the six over-air networks.

Electronic Media is a comprehensive broadcast industry trade journal.

Journal of Broadcasting and *Electronic Media* is a quarterly scholarly journal published by the Broadcast Education Association.

Television/Radio Age is a trade journal.

Videography is a trade journal focusing on production issues in corporate video and production.

Consumer magazines that deal extensively with television programming include *Entertainment* and *TV Guide.*

Newsmagazines that report television issues more or less regularly include *Newsweek* and *Time.*

Business Week, Forbes and *Fortune* track television as a business.

Major newspapers with strong television coverage include the Los Angeles *Times,* the New York *Times* and the *Wall Street Journal.*

Original Webmaster. *Tim Berners-Lee and his associates at a Swiss research facility created new Internet coding in 1989, dubbing it the World Wide Web. Today the coding is the heart of global computer communication.*

The Web

Single-handedly, **Tim Berners-Lee** invented the **World Wide Web.** Then, unlike many entrepreneurs who have used the web to amass quick fortunes, Berners-Lee devoted his life to refining the web as a medium of communication open to everyone free.

Berners-Lee, an Oxford engineer, came up with the web concept because he couldn't keep track of all his notes on various computers in various places. It was 1989. Working at **CERN,** a physics lab in the Swiss Alps, he proposed a system to facilitate scientific research by letting scientists' computers tap into each other. In a way, the software worked like the brain. In fact, Berners-Lee said that the idea was to keep "track of all the random associations one comes across in real life and brains are supposed to be so good at remembering, but sometimes mine wouldn't."

Working with three software engineers, Berners-Lee had a demonstration up and running within three months. As Berners-Lee traveled the globe to introduce the web at scientific conferences, the potential of what he had devised became clear. The web was a system that could connect all information with all other information.

The key was a relatively simple computer language known as **HTML,** short for **hyptertext markup language,** which, although it has evolved over the years, remains the core of the web. Berners-Lee also developed the addressing system that allows computers to find each other. Every web-connected computer has a unique address, a **universal resource locator (URL).** For it all to work, Berners-Lee also created a protocol that actually links computers: **HTTP,** short for **hypertext transfer protocol.**

In 1992 leading research organizations in the Netherlands, Germany and the United States committed to the web. As enthusiasm grew in the scientific research community, word spread to other quarters. In one eight-month period in 1993, web use multiplied 414 times. Soon "the web" was a household word.

As you would expect, Berners-Lee had offers galore from investors and computer companies to build new ways to derive profits from the web. He said no. Instead, he has chosen the academic life. At the Massachusetts Institute of Technology he works out of spartan facilities as head of the **W3 consortium,** which sets the protocol and coding standards that are helping the World Wide Web realize its potential.

It's hard to overrate Berners-Lee's accomplishment. The web is the information infrastructure that likely will, given time, eclipse other media. Some liken Berners-Lee to Johannes Gutenberg, who 400 years earlier had launched the age of mass communication with the movable type that made mass production of the written word possible.

World Wide Web

STUDY PREVIEW   The World Wide Web has emerged as the eighth major mass medium. Many newspaper and magazine companies are delivering colorful, often expanded editions electronically to people at computer screens. The web is more flexible than other media. Users can navigate paths among millions of on-screen messages.

New Mass Medium

From a dizzying array of new technologies, the World Wide Web emerged in the mid-1990s as a powerful new mass medium. What is the web? It is where ordinary people can go on their computer screens and, with a few clicks of a mouse button, find a vast array of information and entertainment that originates all over the world. Make no mistake, though: The web is not just singular on-screen pages. The genius of the web is that on-screen pages are linked to others. It is the people browsing the web, not editors and programmers, who choose which on-screen pages to go to, and which to pass by, and in what sequence. People don't need to go linearly from Newscast Story 1 to Newscast Story 2. By using all kinds of on-screen indexing and cross-referencing, they can switch instantly to what interests them. It's an almost seamless journey from a Disney promotion message for a new movie to a biography of the movie's leading lady in the *USA Today* archives to things as disparate as L. L. Bean's mail-order catalog and somebody's personal collection of family snapshots. In short, the web is an interface for computers that allows people anywhere to connect to any information anywhere else on the system.

Every major mass media company has put products on the web. Thousands of start-up companies are establishing themselves on the ground floor. The technology is so straightforward and access is so inexpensive that hundreds of thousands of individuals have set up their own web sites.

How significant is the web as a mass medium? Estimates are that the number of web users in the United States is approaching 100 million—six times the number

Tim Berners-Lee
Devised protocols, codes for the World Wide Web.

World Wide Web
System that allows global linking of information modules in user-determined sequences.

CERN
European particle physics research facility in Geneva, Switzerland.

Hypertext markup language (HTML)
Language that is the coding for messages on the web.

universal resource locator (URL)
The addresses assigned to a page on the web.

hypertext transfer protocol (HTTP)
The coding that allows web-linked computers to communicate with each other.

W3 consortium
Organizations that use the web work through the W3 consortium (World Wide Web, 3Ws, get it?) to update web coding.

News Online. Among the first major newspapers to go online with hypertext news was *USA Today*. By clicking the cursor on any of many hot spots, you can move to more detail or special sections. Hot spots on this web page include the headlines, the photograph, and the sections News, Money, Sports, Life, Tech and Weather. On each of those web pages are more options that link to hundreds of other web pages. Some links go to earlier editions. You can, for example, link to dozens of movie reviews that *USA Today* has carried over recent months.

in 1995, roughly 30 percent of the U.S. population. The percentage of web-knowledgeable people is mushrooming as personal computers become standard household equipment and as virtually every schoolchild becomes computer literate.

The significance of the web is measurable in other ways too. There are people who have given up reading the print edition of the *Wall Street Journal* and instead browse through one of the *Journal*'s constantly updated web editions. Hundreds of U.S. magazines and newspapers, 93 percent, had **web sites** by 2000, from the venerable but tech-savvy New York *Times* to local papers in the hinterlands.

The Web in Context

The terms *web* and *Internet* are often tossed around loosely, leading to lots of confusion. The fundamental network that carries messages is the Internet. It dates to a military communication system created in 1969. The early Internet carried mostly text.

The web is a structure of codes that permits the exchange not only of text but also of graphics, video and audio. Web codes are elegantly simple for users, who don't even need to know them to tap into the web's content. The underlying web codes are accepted universally, which makes it possible for anyone with a computer, a modem and a web connection to tap into anything introduced from anywhere on the global. The term *web* comes from the spidery links among millions of computers that tap into the system—a maze that not even a spider could visualize and that becomes more complex all the time.

web site
Where an institution establishes its web presence.

Media Abroad

British Diplomacy

The speed and efficiency of the Internet are illustrated by the actions of the British Foreign Office, which replaced its telegraph communication system in 1998. Telegrams between London and 221 outposts in the Empire had been the protocol since 1852, but the system was struggling under the weight of 2.3 million telegrams a year. It was taking 24 hours for a message to reach its destination. No wonder that British diplomats watched CNN. The telegraph system was so clogged that communication officers in embassies had to schedule a time to send telegrams, often hours ahead. To be sure, messages flagged "flash" had priority, but everything else was queued.

In 1998 the Foreign Service installed a $170 million Internet system that allows *e-grams,* as they're called, to be sent by a click of a mouse. The system has safeguards so that neither blunt diplomatic assessments nor delicate descriptions can be compromised.

For most practical purposes it is the web that's a mass medium, with messages posted for mass audiences. Other messages on the web, mostly e-mail, are more point-to-point communication than mass communication.

The prefix *cyber-* is affixed almost casually to anything involving communication via computer. *Cyberspace* is the intangible place where the communication occurs. *Cyberporn* is sexual naughtiness delivered on-screen. A *cyberpunk* is a kid obsessed with computer protocols and coding. The term *cyberspace* was introduced by science-fiction novelist **William Gibson** in his book *Neuromancer.* At that point, in 1984, he saw a kind of integration of computers and human beings. Paraphrasing a bit, here is Gibson's definition of *cyberspace:* "A consensual hallucination experienced daily by billions of people in every nation. A graphic representation of data

cyber-
Prefix for human connection via computers.

William Gibson
Sci-fi writer who coined the term *cyberspace.*

Media Timeline

Internet and Web

1945 Vannevar Bush proposed a memex machine for associative links among all human knowledge.

1947 AT&T developed the transistor.

1962 Ted Nelson introduced the term *hypertext.*

1969 U.S. Defense Department created the ARPAnet network linking military contractors and researchers.

1973 Mead Data Central opened Lexis, the first online full-text database.

1978 Mead Data Central went online with Nexis, the first online database with national news publications.

1979 CompuServe began service to consumers.

1983 The National Science Foundation linked researchers to supercomputers with Internet.

1989 Tim Berners-Lee devised coding that made the World Wide Web possible.

1993 Marc Andreessen created the Mosaic browser, followed by Netscape.

2000 Federal judge found Microsoft monopolistic, ordered its breakup.

	Today's Modem 56 kilobits per second	Future Modem, Upgraded Bandwith 4 megabits per second
Simple image 2 megabits	35.7 seconds	0.5 seconds
Short animation 72 megabits	21.5 minutes	18 seconds
Long animation 4.3 gigabits	21.4 hours	18 minutes

Improving Download Time. The more complex a graphical web message, the longer that downloading takes. Video takes forever, it seems, as you wait. Download times will improve as people acquire faster modems for their computers and as more capacity is built into the Internet, but real-time live video is a long way off. An interim solution is streaming, which downloads into your computer while you're doing other things. You can begin watching while the download is still in progress.

abstracted from the banks of every computer in the human system. Unthinkable complexity. Lines of light ranged in the nonspace of the mind. Clusters and constellations of data."

Bandwidth Limitations

The first newspaper and magazine forays onto the web were mostly text. Gradually, simple graphics and small photos joined the mix. Why not full-blown graphics, intense in color and detail? In a word: **bandwidth.** Bandwidth is the capacity available on a cable for transmission. There's only so much room. It's the same issue that prevents an unlimited number of television stations from being on the air—not enough channel room. On the Internet, text and simple graphics take up relatively little bandwidth. Fancy graphics take more, which means that they require more time to transmit. Superdetailed photos can take several minutes.

Music and video require lots of bandwidth, which raises the question: Will there ever be enough Internet space for real-time radio and television? How about full-length movies? With improvements in transmission technology, they're coming.

FIBER-OPTIC CABLE.   In the 1990s telephone and cable companies began replacing their cables with high-capacity lines made of **fiber-optic cable.** With fiber-optic cable, messages now are sent as pulses of light—theoretically at 186,000 miles an hour—rather than as much slower electrical pulses. The increases in capacity have been dramatic.

MULTIPLEXING.   With **multiplexing** technology a message is broken into bits for transmission through whatever cable pipelines have room at the moment. Then the bits are reassembled at the delivery point. So instead of a message getting clogged

bandwidth
Space available in a medium, such as cable or the electromagnetic spectrum, to carry messages.

fiber-optic cable
Glass strands capable of carrying data as light.

multiplexing
Technology to transmit numerous messages simultaneously.

Media Databank

Ranking Web Sites

Counting web visits is hazardous because different criteria are used as yardsticks. This is one attempt to count recent visits to news and entertainment sites.

		CNN.com	2.9 million
		Weather.com	2.9 million
		USAToday.com	2.5 million
		MSNBC.com	2.2 million
AOL.com	11.2 million	Pathfinder.com	2.2 million
MSN.com	6.3 million	ESPN.com	1.9 million
ZDNet.com	4.0 million	ABCNews.com	1.7 million

in a pipeline that's already crammed, the messages move in small bits called packets, each packet going through whatever pipeline has room. The message ends up at its destination faster.

COMPRESSION.   Technology has been devised that screens out nonessential parts of messages so that they need less bandwidth. This is especially important for graphics, video and audio, which are incredibly code-heavy. Coding for a blue sky in a photo, for example, need not be repeated for every dot of color. Even without redundant coding, the sky still appears blue. Audio too is loaded with redundant coding.

Some **compression** technology further streamlines a message by eliminating details that the human eye or ear will not miss. For example, compression drops sound that on a CD that would start dogs howling.

STREAMING.   When a message is massive with coding, such as audio and video, the message can be segmented with the segments stored in a receiving computer's hard drive for replay even before all segments of the message have been received. This is called **streaming.** Most audio and video today is transmitted this way, which means some downloading delay—often only seconds. The more complex the coding, the longer it takes.

The Internet

STUDY PREVIEW   The Internet is the wired infrastructure on which web messages move. It began as a military communication system, which expanded into a government-funded civilian research network. Today, the Internet is a user-financed system tying institutions of many sorts together into an "information superhighway."

The Information Highway

compression
Technology that makes a message more compact by deleting nonessential underlying code.

streaming
Technology that allows playback of a message to begin before all the components have arrived.

interstate highway system
Frequent analogy for the Internet.

Some historians say that the most important contribution of Dwight Eisenhower's presidency in the 1950s was the U.S. **interstate highway system.** It was a massive project, easily surpassing the scale of such previous human endeavors as the Panama Canal. Eisenhower's interstates bound the nation together in new ways and

Media Abroad

Cuba and the Web

Although Cuba had one of the Third World's most educated and tech-savvy populations, the country missed the first round of the web. Communist apparatchiks under Fidel Castro, wary that access to the web might undermine their authority, kept it out. As late as 1995, Cuba was not connected to the web. Even then, entrepreneurs had to beg the Ministry of Steel, Mechanics and Electronics for licenses to hook computers to the web.

The year 1995 was pivotal. Canadian entrepreneur Robert Sajo, a frequent visitor to Cuba, established Cubaweb.cu in Toronto—an offshore site. His timing was good. The year before, with subsidies evaporating from the former Soviet Union, the Castro regime told state enterprises they needed to find ways on their own to become profitable without government help. Knowing hotels were under pressure to generate new

business, Sajo talked one major chain into going on Cubaweb.cu. Another chain followed.

Then came a breakthrough. The government propaganda sheet for foreign distribution, *Granma,* joined Cubaweb.cu. Although *Granma* was a government agency, director Gabriel Molina Franchossi knew there was a loophole for pilot projects. That cut the red tape.

Sajo's Cubaweb.cu soon was scoring 6,000 hits a day—modest but a start.

Sajo's incremental progress might have gone unnoticed, had it not been for a 1996 international incident. The Cuban military shot down two planes flown by anti-Castro activists from the United States. The U.S.-based cable network CNN linked to the *Granma* site for the official Cuban side of the story. Immediately, Cubaweb.cu was scoring 60,000 hits a day.

Things quickly fell into place for Cubaweb.cu. Teledatos GET, the government tourist agency, applied to move Sajo's server to Cuba and make it official. The domestic Infomed network, a key player in Cuba's biotech industry, among the most advanced in the Third World, joined Cubaweb.cu to connect to the outside world. A new government agency for e-commerce was created.

In 1997 the government decreed that the island nation would be wired as fast as possible to fuel economic development. Still, much remains to be done. By 2001, in a nation of 11 million people, only 33,000 people had a web connection. Government permission still was needed. Only one person had that permission for a connection at home—Robert Sajo at his Havana home. By then, he had sold Cubaweb.cu to a fellow Canadian.

facilitated major economic growth by making commerce less expensive. Today, an **information superhighway** has been built—an electronic network that connects libraries, corporations, government agencies and individuals. This electronic superhighway is called the **Internet,** and it is the backbone of the World Wide Web.

The Internet had its origins in a 1969 U.S. Defense Department computer network called **ARPAnet,** which stands for Advanced Research Projects Agency Network. The Pentagon built the network for military contractors and universities doing military research to exchange information. In 1983 the **National Science Foundation,** whose mandate is to promote science, took over.

This new National Science Foundation network attracted more and more institutional users, many of which had their own internal networks. For example, most universities that joined the NSF network had intracampus computer networks. The NSF network, then, became a connector for thousands of other networks. As a backbone system that interconnects networks, **internet** was a name that fit.

The expense of operating the Internet is borne by the institutions and organizations that tie their computers into it. The institutions pay an average of $43,000 a year to hook in.

information superhighway
Loose term for Internet.

Internet
With a capital *I,* the backbone network for web communication.

ARPAnet
Military network that preceded Internet.

National Science Foundation
Developed current Internet to give scholars access to supercomputers.

internet
A network of computer networks.

Media People

Vint Cerf

Even as a kid, Vinton Cerf liked technical stuff. When he was 10, back in 1953, he built a volcano out of plaster of paris and potassium permanganate. Then he decorated the mountain with gelatin-coated glycerine capsules and waited for the gelatin to melt. The result: a thermite grenade that impressed and also scared his folks.

Today Cerf is called the Father of the Internet. Although he's uncomfortable with the title, the fact is that he was there. Cerf, "Vint" to his friends, and co-researcher Bob Kahn created the coding that allowed various computers to talk to each other over phone lines. In 1974 Cerf and Kahn, both at the University of California at Los Angeles, published an article explaining their intercomputer language protocols.

Kahn's interests shifted to other things, but Cerf kept working on details for linking the military's Advanced Research Projects Agency network to other networks in a way that would seem seamless to users.

Why does Cerf object to being called the Father of the Internet? "It's not right to think of the Internet as having only one father," he says. "It has at least two, and in reality thousands, because of the number of people who contributed to what it is today." Even so, it was Cerf who took the project to Stanford when he switched universities and shepherded it into maturity through 1982.

Father of the Internet

Later, in 1992, Cerf created the nonprofit Internet Society that coordinates Internet policy so that the system remains universally useful.

Online Services

The World Wide Web became operational in the 1990s, but commercial online services go back another 20 years. **Mead Data Central,** an Ohio company, offered **Lexis,** the first online full-text database, in 1973. Lexis carried state and federal statutes, court decisions and other legal documents. A lawyer could tap into Lexis for research and cut back on maintaining and updating the traditional expensive office law library. Because Lexis was delivered via telephone lines whose capacity precluded data-intensive graphics, there was nothing fancy about how Lexis looked—simple text on the computer screen. But it was just what lawyers and legal scholars needed, and they paid handsomely for the service.

Building on its Lexis success, Mead launched **Nexis** in 1978. Nexis was the first online database with national news organizations, including the New York *Times,* the Washington *Post,* the Associated Press and *U.S. News & World Report.* Nexis proved invaluable to researchers, who could search not only recent editions of participating newspapers and magazines but also back issues. Today, Nexis includes thousands of publications from around the world.

Lexis and Nexis remain full-text services, with massive amounts of unadorned, gray content. While they are still important to many people, especially as a research source, they have been eclipsed by flashy graphic-oriented services designed for mass audiences. Nexis comes nowhere near the glitz of America Online.

Commerce and the Web

STUDY PREVIEW   The web has emerged as a commercial medium. Some sites are built around products. Others, in a more traditional vein, are designed to attract an audience with content, such as news. The sites sell access to that audience to advertisers.

Advertising-Free Origins

Before the web, the Internet was a pristine, commerce-free medium. If somebody put out a message that had even a hint of filthy lucre, purists by the dozens, even hundreds, deluged the offender with harsh reminders that commerce was not allowed. By and large, this self-policing worked.

When the web was introduced as an advanced Internet protocol, its potential for commerce was clear almost right away. The World Wide Web Consortium, which sets standards for web protocols, created the dot-com suffix to identify sites that existed to do business. That decision transformed the web and our lives.

Web Commerce

Today, more than a decade after Tim Berners-Lee invented the web, hardly a major retailer is without a web presence.

POINT OF PURCHASE.   Web retailers display their wares on-screen, take orders and ship the products. The old **point-of-purchase** concept, catching consumers at the store with displays and posters, has taken on a whole new meaning. In the cyberworld the point of purchase is not the merchant's shop alone but the consumer's computer screen.

BUSINESS TO BUSINESS.   Another form of web commerce goes by the buzzword **B2B**, short for business-to-business commerce. Businesses that service other businesses have taken to the web to supplement their traditional means of reaching their customers.

ADVERTISING FORMS.   The web also carries advertising. At many sites the advertising is like a traditional ad that promotes a product or service and steers potential customers either to more information or to a place to make a purchase. These ads are akin to those in magazines, newspapers, radio and television. At these dot-coms, the noncommercial content is the attraction. You won't find usatoday.com touting that it has great ads. Rather, the dominant consumer product is news. Just as in the print editions of *USA Today,* the site sells advertisers on the access it provides them to an audience attracted by the news content.

Less traditional are dot-coms whose thrust is the product, like music sites that sell recordings. The site is one big advertisement, dolled up with factoids, games and

point-of-purchase
In-store advertising to catch buyers.

B2B
Short for business-to-business advertising. More focused than most consumer advertising.

Media Databank

Web Numbers

From a variety of sources, Tracy McNamara of the trade journal *Columbia Journalism Review* amassed these comparisons:

	1992	1999
Web advertising revenue	$1.9 billion	$4.6 billion
Web magazine advertising	$153.7 million	$687 million
News/information site advertising	$152 million	$368 million

trivia to keep customers at the site and prolong exposure to the product, thus increasing the probability of sales. These sites are like a jazzy catalog.

Web Advertising

Many retailing dot-coms were profitable early on, but the going was slow for media companies that looked to advertising to pay the freight for expensive content like news. Not until 1997 was any profit reported from a web site that was intending to be advertising supported. The first was the Channel 4000 site, operated by Minneapolis television station WCCO.

The lure of advertising revenue was at the heart of many business plans for news sites in the late 1990s. Venture capitalists poured billions of dollars into these sites. Building these sites into revenue producers took longer than expected. Some sites, like Microsoft's highbrow salon.com, stopped free access and began charging a subscription fee to supplement the disappointing advertising revenue stream. However, disappointing results caused salon.com to revert to free access. At some sites, investors pulled the plug. At the award-winning criminal justice site APB.com, investors decimated the staff in 2000 to stem the outflow of cash. Others quietly went out of business.

The 2000 shakeout may hasten the day when web sites become proven advertising-supported media units. No one doubts the potential. By 2000 almost 100 million people in the United States had web access—about half the adults. Twenty percent of the U.S. population was getting news from the web daily, compared to only 6 percent two years earlier.

With such encouraging numbers, why weren't web sites rolling in advertising dough? Despite the 2000 shakeout, there remained too many sites chasing too few advertising dollars. In time, demand was sure to catch up with supply, but the problem was here and now. A more serious problem was that web advertisers were never quite sure what they were buying. Measuring and categorizing the web audience were not easy.

Measuring the Web Audience

STUDY PREVIEW   The web's reach has grown to 20 percent of the North American population in 2000, fueling interest in cyberspace as an effective place for advertisers to reach consumers. A problem, however, is that nobody has solid data on how many people are surfing to web sites that carry ads.

Media Abroad

Ajeeb.com Egypt: Sakhr Software

To most people in the United States, the Arab world was faraway and mostly irrelevant until the terror attacks on the World Trade Center and the Pentagon. Suddenly the question was: "Why do they hate us so?" The suicide hijackings, all by Arabs, seemed so inexplicable. Americans and others in the West wanted to understand.

Within a month a Cairo-based software company, Sakhr, introduced a web portal that could almost instantly translate Arab web sites into English. Anyone who wanted to read the web site of Al-Jazeera, the dominant Arab television news channel, could go to Sakhr's portal, Ajeeb.com, for a free translation to English. Ajeeb chief executive Fahad Al-Sharekh called Sakhr software a breakthrough: "This is what's going to bridge the gap between the two civilizations."

Indeed, Ajeeb could send a web visitor straight to Al-Jazeera's Arabic web site to read news in English that never came through official U.S. government channels and to which Western reporters often didn't have access. Osama bin Laden videos, which the U.S. and British governments tried to keep off the air, were on Al-Jazeera. So were photos of slain Afghan villagers,

Arabic News in English. Software that translates Arabic into English makes the web site of the Al-Jazeera television news network readable to English speakers.

some plainly faked from propagandist sources, some real.

The Sahkr software underlying the Ajeeb portal had been long in the making. The company, in business since 1982, won praise in the mid-1980s for its digitized searchable Koran, the Muslim holy book. By 2001, Sahkr had pushed Arab-to-English translation so news text on the web could be translated as it was continuously updated. Sakhr used statistical probability calculations for the Ajeeb translations. Because Arabic and English don't share an alphabet and other lingual conventions, convoluted sentences and unpunctuated passages are not infrequent.

Ajeeb.com has human translators who monitor the most-visited pages to tweak the content into readable English. Their changes are fed into artificial intelligence computers, which means that automated translations will improve over time.

Sakhr has 50 people working full-time at Ajeeb to smooth the machine translations. On heavy news days another 100 translators are on call. U.S. users tap into Al-Jazeera and other Arabic sites through Sakhr's Ajeeb server in Boston.

Sakhr also has devised English-to-Arabic software, which gives Arab people access to CNN and other sites in English.

Inconsistent Data

The difficulty of measuring web audiences is illustrated by a numbers war that broke out in 1998 between news rivals cnn.com and msnbc.com.

The upstart MSNBC site, a spin-off of the Microsoft-NBC television network, claimed in news releases and advertisements that it had beaten CNN. A New York measurement firm, Media Metrix, had found that MSNBC had almost 4.3 million unique visitors a month with 7.4 percent reach. (Reach is the percentage of all web users who visit a site.) Somewhere in the dust, said Media Metrix, was CNN, with 3.4 million unique visitors and 6.9 percent reach.

Media Databank

Web Usage

Precise tracking measures on how many people use the web don't exist, but these estimates, on the low side for recent years, show the web's exponential growth:	1995	13.5 million	1998	62.0 million
	1996	29.0 million	1999	79.4 million
	1997	46.8 million	2000	98.1 million

CNN fired back that the comparison was unfair because it rated only CNN Interactive and not related sites: cnnfn.com, cnnsi.com and allpolitics.com. MSNBC, said CNN executives, covers finance, sports and politics all on one site. CNN's claim: We're Number One.

Numbers are tricky for other reasons too. Different survey companies use different methods to gather data. Furthermore, the companies haven't agreed on definitions. Some separate out workplace users, foreign users and others. Some don't. Consider the discrepancies from three companies who measured CNN in May 1998:

- **@Plan:** 11.8 million
- **RelevantKnowledge:** 5.6 million
- **Media Metrix:** 2.5 million

Advertisers, of course, want solid numbers on which to base decisions on placing their ads. To that end, the Internet Advertising Bureau and the Advertising Research Foundation are scrambling to come up with measurement guidelines that will compare apples with apples, not oranges.

Web's Advertising Reach

Despite upbeat Nielsen data about people who use the web, there remains a hitch in developing the web as a major advertising medium. Nobody has devised tools to measure traffic at a web site in meaningful ways. Such data are needed to establish advertising rates that will give advertisers confidence that they're spending their money wisely. For traditional media, advertisers look to standard measures like **cost per thousand (CPM)** to calculate the cost effectiveness of ads in competing media. Across-the-board comparisons aren't possible with the web, however—at least not yet. In some ways, buying space for cyber-ads is a crap shoot.

The most-cited measure of web audiences is the **hit.** Every time someone browsing the web clicks an on-screen icon or on-screen highlighted section, the computer server that offers the web page records a hit. Some companies that operate web sites tout hits as a measure of audience, but savvy advertisers know hits are a misleading indicator of audience size. The online edition of *Wired* magazine, HotWired, for example, records an average 100 hits from everybody who taps in. HotWired's 600,000 hits on a heavy day come from a mere 6,000 people.

Another measure of web usage is the **visit,** a count of the people who visit a site. But visits too are misleading. At *Playboy* magazine's web site, 200,000 visits are scored on a typical day, but that doesn't mean that *Playboy* cyber-ads are seen by 200,000 different people. Many of the same people visit again and again on a given day.

Some electronic publications charge advertisers by the day, others by the month, others by the hit. But because of the vagaries of audience measurements, there

cost per thousand (CPM)
Advertising measure of an ad's reach.

hit
Tallied every time someone goes to a web page.

visit
Tallied for every person who visits a web site.

is no standard pricing. Knowing that the web cannot mature as an advertising medium until advertisers can be given better audience data, electronic publications have asked several companies, including Nielsen, to devise tracking mechanisms. But no one expects data as accurate as press runs and broadcast ratings any time soon. In the meantime advertisers are making seat-of-the-pants assessments as to which web sites are hot.

Web Technology

STUDY PREVIEW   The 1947 invention of the transistor led to data digitization and compression. Without transistors the web would never have come into being. Nor would the other mass media be anything like we know them today. Another invention, Corning Glass' fiber-optic cable, makes it possible to transmit huge amounts of digitized data.

Transistors

Three researchers at AT&T's **Bell Labs** developed the **semiconductor** switch in 1947. **Walter Brattain, Jack Bardeen** and **William Shockley,** who would receive the 1956 Nobel Prize, took pieces of glasslike silicon (just sand, really) and devised a way to make them respond to a negative or positive electrical charge. These tiny units, first called **transistors,** now more commonly called semiconductors or chips, functioned very rapidly as on-off switches. The on-off technology, in which data are converted to on-off codes, is called **digitization** because data are reduced to a series of digits, 1 for on, 0 for off.

DIGITIZATION.   As might be expected, Bell researchers tried applying the junction transistor to telephone communication. Soon they found ways to convert the human voice to a series of coded pulses for transmission on telephone lines to a receiver that would change them into a simulation of the voice. These pulses were digital on-off signals that were recorded so fast at one end of the line and reconstructed so fast at the other that they sounded like the real thing. The rapid on-off signals worked like the persistence of vision phenomenon that creates the illusion of movement in motion pictures.

A milestone event occurred in 1962 when AT&T sent a message to Chicago from suburban Skokie using transistor technology—the first digital telephone call. Until that moment telephone communication was based on sound waves being converted to varying electrical currents for transmission. At the receiving end, the currents were changed back to sound waves. With digital transmission voices were instead converted to an incredibly fast-moving stream of discrete on-off digital pulses.

COMPRESSION.   Bell Labs also devised techniques to squeeze different calls onto the same line simultaneously, which increased the capacity of the nation's telephone network. With traditional telephone technology, dating to Alexander Graham Bell's 1876 invention of the telephone, only one message could be carried at a time on a telephone line. With digitization, however, a new process called **multiplexing** became possible. Tiny bits of one message could be interspersed with tiny bits of other messages for transmission and then sorted out at the other end.

AT&T introduced multiplex telephone services in 1965. People marveled that 51 calls could be carried at the same time on a copper wire with on-off digital switching technology. The capacity of the nation's telephone communication system was dramatically increased without laying even a single new mile of wire.

Bell Labs
AT&T facility where transistor invented.

semiconductor
Tiny sand-based transistor that responds to weak on-off charges.

Walter Brattain
Codeveloper of transistor.

Jack Bardeen
Codeveloper of transistor.

William Shockley
Codeveloper of transistor.

transistor
Semiconductor.

digitization
Converting on-off coding for storage and for transmission.

multiplexing
Compressing messages for simultaneous transmission on same line or radio wave.

Robert Noyce. A young researcher at Shockley Semiconductor Laboratory in 1953 recognized that a single semiconductor wasn't very useful by itself. Robert Noyce began thinking how to weave semiconductors together so they could perform tasks that required hundreds or even thousands of on-off functions a second. To do this, he built an integrated circuit, more commonly called a *microchip*—the key to further development of their new technology. In 1968 Noyce and fellow Shockley grad Gordon Moore founded Intel, which became the world's leading chip manufacturer.

miniaturization
Reducing the size of devices for data recording, storage, retrieval.

giant magneto-resistance (GMR)
Allows super-miniaturization.

Corning Glass
Company that developed fiber-optic cable.

junction transistor
Crystal with added impurities that switches on and off at tremendous speed and reliability.

Few people foresaw that digitization and compression would revolutionize human existence, let alone do it so quickly. The web wasn't even a glimmer in anyone's eye back then. Nonetheless, the building blocks for the web were being created.

MINIATURIZATION.   Radio and television were the first mass media beneficiaries of the transistor. In the 1940s broadcast equipment was built around electrical tubes, which looked somewhat like light bulbs. These tubes heated up and eventually burned out. In addition, they consumed massive amounts of electricity. Transistors, on the other hand, could perform the same functions with hardly any electricity and no heat. Important too, transistors were much, much smaller than tubes and much more reliable.

Consumers began benefiting directly from transistor **miniaturization** in the mid-1950s. Until then, even the smallest radios, called "table models," were hunky pieces of furniture. Then came a new product: hand-held, battery-powered transistor radios that people could carry anywhere. Those tiny radios, however, were merely glimpses at the mass communication revolution that transistors were ushering in.

Not only did the use of transistors dramatically reduce the size and weight of broadcast equipment, the size of computers shrank as well. In the 1940s early computers, based on tube technology, were so big that it took entire buildings to house them and large staffs of technicians to operate them. Today, the Marquardt Corporation estimates that all the information recorded in the past 10,000 years can be stored in a cube six feet by six feet by six feet. All 12 million books in the Library of Congress would take fewer than two cubic inches.

There seems no end to miniaturization. IBM has developed a computer drive that, using **giant magneto-resistance** (GMR) technology, crams an incredible 100 million digital characters on a thumbtack-size disk. IBM now expects to be producing GMR disks that can accommodate 2 billion characters on a thumbtack. That's equivalent to 2,000 novels.

EFFICIENCIES.   Transistor-based equipment costs less to manufacture and operates with incredible efficiency. The National Academy of Science estimates that it cost $130,000 to make 125 multiplications when the forerunners of today's computers were introduced in the 1940s. By 1970 the cost was a mere $4. Today, it can be done for pennies.

Fiber Optics

While AT&T was building on its off-on digital technology to improve telephone service in the 1960s, **Corning Glass** developed a cable that was capable of carrying light at incredible speeds—theoretically 186,000 miles per second. It was apparent immediately that this new fiber-optic cable, made out of silicon, could carry far more digitized multiplex messages than could copper. The messages were encoded as light pulses rather than as the traditional electrical pulses for transmission.

Media People

William Shockley

Physicist William Shockley felt cheated. He had developed the theory for the transistor, but two Bell Telephone Lab engineers, Jack Bardeen and Walter Brattain, had rigged up the first working transistor. And Shockley wasn't even there to see it happen. Bardeen and Brattain applied electric current to a crystal of germanium, and more power came out than went in.

That momentous event, in 1947, prompted Shockley to throw himself into coming up with further understanding of the phenomenon and figuring out where it might lead. Within a few weeks, Shockley devised the **junction transistor** that, given time, would transform almost every mechanical device that human beings use.

What was the junction transistor? It was a tiny, tiny sandwich of a crystal with impurities added. The crystal could go on and off at tremendous rates with unsurpassed reliability. Almost immediately, telephone engineers saw the potential for the device, which was dubbed the semiconductor, to replace bulky, hot vacuum tubes that were the heart of telephone systems at the time. Those tubes burned out quickly and had to be replaced often, which was expensive. Semiconductors, by contrast, were cool, reliable and long-lived.

In 1956 Shockley founded a research company in Palo Alto, California, and chose silicon instead of germanium for new semiconductors. Silicon, which fundamentally is sand, was cheap. This was the real

Transistor Inventors. The transistor, also called a semiconductor switch, can be likened to a tiny triple-decker sandwich. The sandwich, made of silicon, responds to slight variations in electrical current that allow incredibly fast processing of data that has been converted into on-off signals. In addition to speed, the transistor ushered in miniaturization of data-processing equipment and storage devices. Since 1947, when Bell Labs engineers devised the transistor, it has become possible to store thousands of pages of text on a device as small as a pinhead and to transmit them almost instantly to other devices, like your home computer. The 1956 Nobel Prize went to Bell Labs' Walter Brattain, Jack Bardeen and William Shockley for inventing the transistor.

birth of the semiconductor, and the Shockley Lab was the progenitor of virtually all the semiconductor companies that have come since. In one sense, by locating in Palo Alto, William Shockley created Silicon Valley, the fanciful appellation for the region south of San Francisco that has become the world center of semiconductor and computer research.

Sadly, Shockley didn't see the semiconductor as his greatest contribution. In the 1960s Shockley, who was white, began dabbling with dysgenics and concluded that white people were genetically more intelligent than black people. He even proposed voluntary sterilization for anyone whose IQ was less than 100. These ideas dominated the rest of his life, diminishing his contributions to technology in the minds of most people.

Global Fiber Optics. The Fiberoptic Link Around the Globe, "FLAG" for short, is the longest engineering project in human history—a 17,400-mile communication link of England and Japan. The blue lines are other undersea fiber-optic routes that are planned or in place. The world is being wired for faster World Wide Web communication.

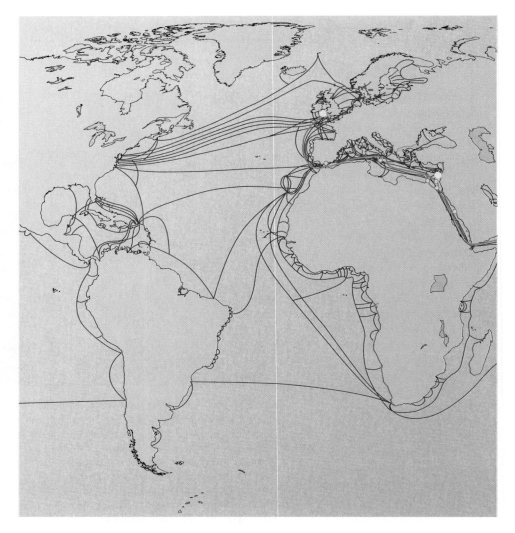

By the 1980s new equipment to convert data to light pulses for transmission was in place, and long-distance telephone companies were replacing their copper lines with fiber optics, as were local cable television systems. Today, with semiconductor switching combined with optical fiber cable, a single line can carry 60,000 telephone calls simultaneously. In addition to voice, the lines can carry all kinds of other messages that have been broken into digitized pulses. With fiber-optic cable the entire *Oxford English Dictionary* can be sent in just seconds. Such speed is what has made the web a mass medium that can deliver unprecedented quantities of information so quickly.

Nonlinear Communication

STUDY PREVIEW   Hypertext, a relatively recent concept for creating messages, is the heart of the web as a mass medium. With hypertext the people who receive messages can

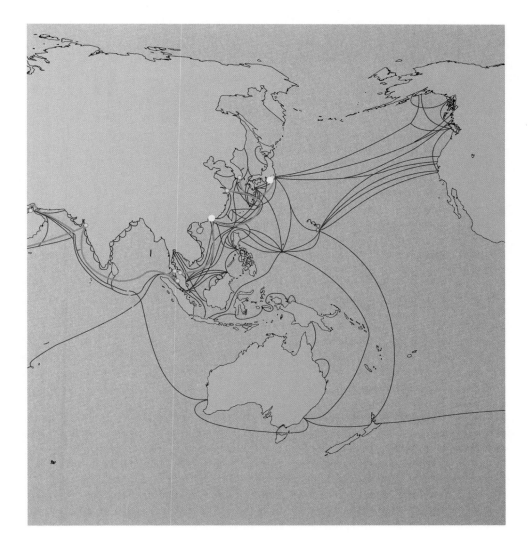

influence the sequence of the messages they receive. Once, it was only the communicators who had such power.

Vannevar Bush's Memex

Until recently, we were all accustomed to mass messages flowing from start to finish in the sequence that mass communicators figured would be most effective for most people. Many mass messages still flow linearly. Newscasts, as an example, start with the most important item first. A novel builds climactically to the final chapter. A television commercial catches your attention at the start and names the advertiser in the sign-off. This is **linear communication.**

Vannevar Bush, a leading thinker of his time, noted to *Atlantic* magazine readers in 1945 that knowledge had expanded exponentially in the 20th century, but the means for "threading through" the maze was "the same as used in the days of

linear communication
Messages in a specified start-to-end sequence.

Vannevar Bush
Proposed a machine for relational information retrieval.

Vannevar Bush. After World War II a leading intellectual, Vannevar Bush, proposed a machine that would hold all the information accumulated in human history. People using the machine could retrieve whatever they wanted in whatever sequence they wanted. The machine, which Bush called *memex,* was never built, but the concept is the heart of today's hypertext.

memex
Machine proposed by Vannevar Bush for nonlinear information access.

Ted Nelson
Coined the term *hypertext* for nonlinear communication.

hypertext
Method of interrelating messages so that users control their sequence.

square-rigged ships." Bush proposed a machine he called **memex** to mimic human thinking in organizing material. With his memex people could retrieve information through automated association with related information.

Alas, Bush's memex was never built, but a generation later, technologist **Ted Nelson,** who may have heard his grandfather read Bush's article aloud, picked up on the idea. In his 1962 book *Literary Machines,* Nelson coined the term **hypertext** for an alternate way for people to send and receive information. Nelson also used the term *nonsequential writing,* but it was *hypertext* that stuck.

With the web, people can proceed linearly or nonlinearly through material. Chapters 21 and 22 of this textbook exist only on the web. You can read them straight through from beginning to end. That would be linear. Or you can use your mouse to click highlighted words, called *hot spots,* and transport yourself beyond the textbook to related material, some designed as part of the chapter, like popup glossary definitions, and some existing elsewhere on the web and not even part of the textbook. This linking capability lets you roam the whole world nonlinearly to pursue what you regard as important. The web empowers you to choose your own course, going beyond what any individual author has to offer.

In primitive ways people have done a kind of hypertext learning for centuries. In the library a researcher may have two dozen books open and piled on a desk, with dozens more reference books handy on a shelf. Moving back and forth among the books, checking indexes and footnotes, and fetching additional volumes from the library stacks, the researcher is creating new meanings by combining information in new sequences. The computer has accelerated that process and opened up thousands of resources, all on-screen, for today's scholars.

Media People

Marc Andreessen

At his 240-student high school in New Lisbon, Wisconsin, Marc Andreessen didn't play sports or mingle a lot. He recalls those times as "introverted." Recovering from surgery, he spent his time reading up on computer programming. Back at school, he built a calculator on the library computer to do his math homework.

Later, at the University of Illinois, he honed his interest in computer languages. At his $6.85-an-hour campus job writing computer code, he decided that the web protocols devised by Tim Berners-Lee in Switzerland in 1989 needed a simple interface so that ordinary people could tap in. Marc Andreessen and fellow student Eric Bina spent three months, nights and weekends, writing a program they called Mosaic. It became the gateway for non-nerds to explore the web.

After Andreessen graduated, entrepreneur Jim Clark of Silicon Graphics heard about Mosaic

Mosaic Killer. At 21, Marc Andreessen and a geek buddy created Mosaic, which facilitated web access. Then they trumped themselves by creating Netscape.

and began some exploratory talks with Andreessen. At one point, as web folklore has it, Andreessen said, "We could always create a Mosaic killer—build a better product and build a business around it." Andreessen hired geek friends from Illinois, and Netscape was born. It was the pioneer browser for the masses. Andreessen and a bunch

of fellow 21-year-olds had democratized the web.

Netscape's revenues zoomed to $100 million in 1996. Meanwhile, Microsoft introduced the Explorer browser as a competitor, which hurt. But America Online, the giant content provider, bought Netscape in 1998 and folded it into AOL. Andreessen became a chief resident thinker at AOL, but he didn't cotton well to the New Jersey bureaucracy. By 1999 he was back in Silicon Valley, this time with the idea for a robotic site builder called Loudcloud, which quickly attracted multimillion-dollar bids for its emerging product line.

Hypertext

STUDY PREVIEW   Major news media are creating hypertext products that are revolutionizing how news is told. Whether hypertext will revolutionize other forms of storytelling, such as the novel, is unclear.

Pre-Hypertext Innovations

Although hypertext itself is not new, the shift from linear presentation in traditional media has been gradual. A preliminary stage was merely casting text in digital form for storage and transmission. This is what other early online services like Nexis did, providing linear full-text of news stories from cooperating newspapers. While a major step forward at the time, full-text is derisively called **shovelware** by hypertext enthusiasts because it is simply moved from a traditional medium to another

shovelware
Computer-delivered products without modification from the linear original.

Ananova. First you could read the news on-screen. Then, with the right software, you could hear it read. Now, PA New Media has introduced Ananova, a virtual, blue-haired anchor who reads the news to you, moving her lips and with expression. Ananova is available everywhere that wireless devices can pick her up.

Media Lab
Massachusetts Institute of Technology research facility.

Daily Me
Experimental computer newspaper with reader-determined content.

Personal Journal
Wall Street Journal computer newspaper with reader-determined content.

USA Today
Newspaper with one of the first nonlinear computer editions.

hyperfiction
Nonlinear novels, games, other fiction.

without much adaptation to the unique characteristics of the new medium. Shovelware falls short of the potential of the web.

The **Media Lab** at the Massachusetts Institute of Technology came up with the next refinement: the *Daily Me,* an experimental digital newspaper that provided subscribers information only on subjects they specified in advance. Take, for example, a car buff who follows baseball and who earns a living running a grocery store in Spokane, Washington. For this person a customized *Daily Me* would include news on the automobile industry, the American and National Leagues and the Spokane Indians farm club, livestock and produce market reports, news summaries from the Spokane area and neighboring British Columbia and Idaho and a brief summary of major national and world news.

MIT's *Daily Me* innovation took commercial form at the *Wall Street Journal,* which in 1995 launched the first customizable electronic newspaper. It was called *Personal Journal,* with the subtitle: "Published for a Circulation of One." *Personal Journal,* which cost $18 a month plus 50 cents per update, offered whatever combination a subscriber wanted of business and general coverage by category, market tables and selected quotes, sports and weather. Such customization, matching content to a user's interest, is now common.

Hypertext News

The potential of digital news was realized with the web. When **USA Today** established a web site, it offered a hypertext product—not shovelware. *USA Today* webmasters broke the newspaper's content into web page-size components, updated them 24 hours a day as events warranted, and linked every page with others. Every day, readers can choose among thousands of connections, in effect creating their own news package by moving around among the entire content of the newspaper. Hot spots include links to archived material from previous coverage that *USA Today*'s webmasters thought some readers would want to draw on for background.

All the major news products coming online today are state-of-the-art hypertext ventures. Some web sites offer users an opportunity to communicate immediately back to the creators of the products.

Hyperfiction

While digital technology is revolutionizing many aspects of human communication, it is unclear whether all literary forms will be fundamentally affected, but there have been experiments with hypertext fiction. For example, the computer games Myst and Riven put players in dreamlike landscapes where they wander through adventures in which they choose the course of events. Options, of course, are limited to those the authors put into the game, but the player has a feeling of creating the story rather than following an author's plot. Myst and Riven represent a new dimension in exploration as an experiential literary form.

Some futurists see interactivity overtaking traditional forms of human storytelling, and the term **hyperfiction** has been applied to a few dozen pioneer hypertext novels. One hyperfiction enthusiast, Trip Hawkins, who creates video games, laid out both sides in a New York *Times* interview: "Given the choice, do viewers really want to interact with their entertainment? Watching, say, *Jurassic Park,* wouldn't they prefer to have Steven Spielberg spin the tale of dinosaurs munching on their keepers in an island theme park?" For himself, however, Hawkins says, "I want to be on the island. I want to show that I could have done better than those idiots did. I could have gotten out of that situation."

Evaluating the Web

STUDY PREVIEW   The traditional gatekeeping process that filters media content for quality is less present on the web. Web users need to take special care in assessing the merit of what they find on the web.

Accuracy on the Web

The web has been called a democratized mass medium because so many people create web content. Almost anybody can put up a site. A downside of so much input from so many people is that the traditional media gatekeepers aren't necessarily present to ensure accuracy. To be sure, there are many reliable sites with traditional gatekeeping, but the web is also littered with junk.

Of course, unreliable information isn't exclusive to the web. But among older media, economic survival depends on finding and keeping an audience. Unreliable newspapers, for example, eventually lose the confidence of readers. People stop buying them, and they go out of business. The web has no such intrinsic economic imperative. A site can be put up and maintained with hardly any capital—in contrast to a newspaper, which requires tons of newsprint and barrels of ink, not to mention expensive presses, to keep coming out. Bad web sites can last forever.

To guard against bad information, web users should pay special heed to the old admonition: Consider the source. Is the organization or person behind a site reliable? If you have confidence in *USA Today* as a newspaper, you can have the same confidence in its web site. Another news site, no matter how glitzy and slick, may be nothing more than a lunatic working alone in a dank basement somewhere recasting the news with perverse twist and whole-cloth fiction.

In research reports, footnotes or endnotes need to be specific on web sources, including URL addresses. This allows people who read a report to go to the web source to make their own assessment—just as traditional footnotes allow a reader to go to the library and check a source.

Even with notations, a report that cites web sources can be problematic. Unlike a book, which is permanent once it's in print, web content can be in continuing flux. What's there today can be changed in a minute—or disappear entirely. To address this problem at least in part, notation systems specify that the date and time of the researcher's web visit be included.

In serious research, you can check whether an online journal is refereed. A mission statement will be on the site with a list of editors and their credentials and a statement on the journal's editorial process. Look to see whether articles are screened through a **peer review** process.

Strengths of Sites

Several organizations issue awards to excellent web sites. The most prestigious are the **Webby** awards, a term contrived from the nickname for the somewhat parallel

media online

Maryland Earthcast: The weather anywhere on the earth.
www.meto.umd.edu/~owen/EARTHCAST

Time Warner: Sites on the Time Warner media conglomerate Internet service includes daily news, sports and entertainment links.
www.pathfinder.com

Hypertext Places: George Rockwell of McMaster University compiled a searchable hypertext bibliography.
http://cheiron.mcmaster.ca/~htp

peer review
A screening mechanism in which scholarly material is reviewed by leaders in a discipline for its merits, generally with neither the author nor the reviewers knowing each other's identity.

Webby
A major award of excellence for web sites.

Flat-Screen iMac. Apple chief executive Steve Jobs unveils the latest Apple iMac, a machine striking in design but also a ready hub for multiple digital devices, including music players, cameras and handheld devices.

Emmy awards of television. Many web awards, though, are for design and graphics, not content, although there are many measures of a site's excellence.

CONTENT.   The heart of all mass media messages is the value of the content. For this, traditional measures of excellence in communication apply, such as accuracy, clarity, cohesion.

NAVIGABILITY.   Does the site have internal links so you can move easily from page to page and among various points on the site? Among the mass media, navigability is a quality unique to the web.

EXTERNAL LINKS.   Does the site connect to related sites on the web? The most distinctive feature of the web as a mass medium is interconnectivity with other sites on the global network. Good sites exploit this advantage.

INTUITIVE TO USE.   The best sites have navigational aids for moving around a site seamlessly and efficiently. These include road signs of many sorts, including clearly labeled links.

LOADING TIMES.   Well-designed sites take advantage of the web as a visual medium with images. At the same time, pages should load quickly so users don't have to wait and wait and wait for a page to write itself to their screens. This means the site needs a balance. Overdoing images, which require lots of bandwidth, works against rapid downloads. Absence of images makes for dull pages.

Media Melding

STUDY PREVIEW   Many mass media as we know them are converging into digitized formats. Complementing and hastening this technological melding is ownership conglomeration and joint ventures. Government deregulation is contributing to a freer business environment that encourages new ventures.

Technological Convergence

media convergence

    Johannes Gutenberg brought mass production to books, and the other primary print media, magazines and newspapers, followed. People never had a problem recognizing differences among books, magazines and newspapers. When sound recording and movies came along, they too were distinctive, and later so were radio and television. Today, the traditional primary media are in various stages of transition to digital form.

    The cable television systems and the Internet are consolidating with companies in the forefront, such as AT&T. This **technological convergence** is fueled by accelerated miniaturization of equipment and the ability to compress data into tiny digital bits for storage and transmission. And all the media companies, whether their products traditionally relied on print, electronic or photographic technology, are involved in the convergence.

    As the magazine *The Economist* noted, once-discrete media industries "are being whirled into an extraordinary whole." Writing in *Quill* magazine, *USA Today*'s Kevin Manay put it this way: "All the devices people use for commu-

technological convergence
Melding of print, electronic and photographic media into digitized form.

Carl Bernstein

Dot-Com Coverage. A dozen commercial web sites covered the 2000 national political conventions with video. America Online and Pseudo.com had skyboxes like the television networks. The web audience didn't rival television's, but the idea was to build dot-com brand names. Carl Bernstein, the Watergate reporter who is now an executive vice president of Voter.com, said interesting first-rate coverage would strengthen his dot-com's reputation into the future.

nicating and all the kinds of communication have started crashing together into one massive megamedia industry. The result is that telephone lines will soon carry TV shows. Cable TV will carry telephone calls. Desktop computers will be used to watch and edit movies. Cellular phone-computers the size of a notepad will dial into interactive magazines that combine text, sound and video to tell stories." This convergence is no better illustrated at a corporate level than the 2000 merger of AOL and Time Warner.

Transition Ahead

Nobody expects the printed newspaper to disappear overnight or for movie houses, video rental shops and over-air broadcasters to go out of business all at once. But all the big media companies have established stakes on the web, and in time, digitized messages delivered over the web will dominate.

Outside of the web itself, major media companies also are trying to establish a future for themselves in reaching audiences in new digital ways. Companies that identify voids in their ability to capitalize on new technology have created joint ventures to ensure they won't be left out. The NBC television network, for example, provides news on Microsoft's MSN online service. All of the regional Bell telephone companies have picked up partners to develop video delivery systems. Cable companies are gearing for telephonelike two-way interactive communication systems that will, for example, permit customers not only to receive messages but also to send them.

Government Deregulation

Until recent years a stumbling block to the melding of digital media was the U.S. government. Major components of today's melded media—the telephone, television

Media People

Bill Gates

Bill Gates was well into his courses at Harvard when his high school buddy Paul Allen drove across the country from Seattle to convince him to drop out. Gates did. The pair went to Albuquerque and set up shop to do computer stuff. Their company, Microsoft, today is the world's largest software producer, and it is moving rapidly into creating a dominant web presence. It also is becoming a major creator of media content. With the company's success, Gates became the world's richest person. By 2001, he was worth $80 billion. At one point, his assets were growing at $30 million a day.

In Albuquerque in 1976 Gates acquired the code that became the Microsoft Disk Operating System, usually abbreviated as MS-DOS and pronounced *m-s-doss*. Allen and Gates persuaded computer hardware manufacturers to bundle MS-DOS with their units, which pre-empted competitors. The bundling also gave Microsoft a growing and gigantic market for software application programs that operated only on MS-DOS. The company's word-processing program, Microsoft Word, for example, dominates globally. So do various Microsoft Windows operating systems that have updated MS-DOS.

With their initial success, Gates and Allen moved the company to their hometown, Seattle, where it remains. Allen bowed out after a debilitating disease was diagnosed (falsely, it turned out). Allen's departure left Gates in charge. Today, the company operates out of a 35-building campus in suburban Redmond.

Critics say that Microsoft products are neither the best nor the most innovative. These critics attribute the company's success to

Microsoft Chief

cutthroat competitive practices and marketing muscle, rather than product excellence. Detractors have built web sites that revile Gates as an unconscionable monopolist. Gates, who subscribes to Darwin's "survival of the fittest" theory, tried to explain away the criticism as envy.

But in 2000 a federal judge sided with the U.S. antitrust prosecutors and ordered that Microsoft be broken up. Gates vowed to challenge the decision.

media online

Bill Gates: *Time* magazine expands on Walter Isaacson's insightful January 13, 1997, cover story on Bill Gates, the computer whiz who runs Microsoft.
www.pathfinder.com/time/gates

OAK Software Repository: If you are looking for software, you'll find it here.
http://oak.oakland.edu

Ronald Reagan
President who pushed deregulation.

deregulation
Government policy to reduce regulation of business.

and computer industries—grew up separately, and government policy kept many of them from venturing into the others' staked-out territory of services. Telephone companies, for example, were limited to being common carriers. They couldn't create their own media messages, just deliver other people's. Cable companies were barred from building two-way communication into their systems.

In the 1970s government agencies began to ease restrictions on business. In 1984 President **Ronald Reagan** stepped up this **deregulation,** and more barriers came down. The pro-business Reagan administration also took no major actions against the stampede of media company mergers that created fewer and bigger media companies. George Bush, elected in 1988, and Bill Clinton, elected in 1992, continued Reagan's deregulation initiatives and also his soft stance on mergers. The Clinton position, however, was less ideological and more pragmatic. Clinton's thinking was based on the view that regulation and antitrust actions would hamstring U.S. media companies, and other enterprises too, in global competition.

In 1996 Congress approved a new telecommunications law that wiped out many of the barriers that heeded full-bore exploitation of the potential of new media. The law repealed a federal ban against telephone companies providing video program-

Media People

Neal Stephenson

New-Tech Novelist

Neal Stephenson emerged as an important new-tech novelist with his 1992 *Snow Crash*, which became the rage of Silicon Valley. The novel, a thriller that was originally intended as a Macintosh game, is set in a near-future when the United States has lost its leadership in everything but movies, software and high-speed pizza delivery. It's a bustling, not unfriendly "megaverse." Characteristic of Stephenson's work, *Snow Crash* has disparate story lines that come together and culminate quickly in the last few pages.

Critics applaud Stephenson's sense of language and culture, especially the interactions between groups of individuals and changing

technology. He also has demonstrated a good sense of what's technologically just ahead. His *Zodiac*, in 1988, was intended to be "day after tomorrow" fiction—a future that was very close. One of his characters writes computer games for 32-bit home computers, which soon became the norm in the marketplace.

Stephenson, born in 1959, has been hailed as a possible successor to William Gibson, author of *Neuromancer*, in the techno-thriller genre. Besides *Snow Crash*, Stephenson's works include *The Big U*, 1984; *Zodiac: The Eco-Thriller*, 1988; *Interface*, 1994; *The Diamond Age*, 1995, which was coauthored with his uncle under the

pseudonym Stephen Bury; *Cryptonomicon*, 1999; and *In the Beginning . . . Was the Command Line*, 1999, which discusses the past and future of personal computer operating systems.

ming. Just as significant, cable television systems were given a green light to offer two-way local telephone. The law, the **Telecommunications Act of 1996,** accelerated the competition that had been emerging between telephone and cable television companies to rewire communities for higher-quality, faster delivery of new audio and video services.

Public Policy and the Web

STUDY PREVIEW   The web is a content-neutral medium whose content is more directly user-driven than the traditional media. This makes the web hard to regulate, which has created new privacy issues. The ease with which messages can be created has resulted in problems for moralists concerned about indecent material. Authoritarian governments find censorship of the web difficult.

Universal Access

Although web use is growing dramatically, the fact is that not everybody has access. Those who can afford computers and access fees will benefit tremendously. What about everybody else? This is a profound public policy question, especially in a democracy that prides itself on ensuring equality for every citizen on basic matters like access to information.

Telecommunications Act of 1996
Repealed many limits on services that telephone and cable companies could offer.

universal access
Giving everyone the means to use the Web.

diffusion of innovation
Process through which news, ideas, values and information spread.

P3P
A web protocol that allows users to choose a level of privacy. Short for Platform for Privacy Preferences.

One line of reasoning is that the government should not guarantee **universal access.** This rationale draws on the interstate highway system as an analogy. The government builds the roads, but individuals provide the vehicles to drive around on the system.

The counterargument is that access to information will become so essential to everyone's well-being that we could end up with a stratified society of info-rich and info-poor people. Such a knowledge gap hardly is the democratic ideal.

Global Inequities

The exchange of information facilitated by the web boosted the United States into unprecedented prosperity going into the 21st century. One measure of efficiency, **diffusion of innovation,** improved dramatically. The time that innovations take to be widely used, which was once 10 years, dropped to one year. Giga Information Group projected that by 2002 businesses will be saving $1.3 trillion because of web commerce—an incredible 765 percent gain over five years.

A problem, though, is that much of the world isn't well plugged in. Even in Japan, a major industrial nation, only 17 percent of the population uses the web—in contrast, by some estimates, to almost 40 percent in North America. All of the Middle East and Africa have only 7.5 million web users in total.

In short, the United States stands to realize more of the economic advantages of the web than other countries, creating new international inequities. Aside from other oases such as Canada, Britain and Scandinavia, the rest of the world is falling further and further behind.

If maximum U.S. prosperity depends on free trade in a global economy, as many economists argue, then the rest of the world must be folded fully into the web.

Privacy and the Web

The genius of Tim Berners-Lee's original web concept was its openness. Information could be shared easily by anyone and everyone. Therein too was a problem. During the web's commercialization in the late 1990s, some companies tracked where people ventured on the web. The tracking was going on silently, hidden in the background, as people coursed their way around the web. Companies gathering information were selling it to other companies. There was fear that insurance companies, health-care providers, lenders and others had a new secret tool for profiling applicants.

Government agencies began hinting at controls. Late in 1999, Berners-Lee and the web protocol-authoring consortium he runs came up with a new architecture, **P3P,** short for Platform for Privacy Preferences, to address the problem. With P3P people could choose the level of privacy they wanted for their web activities. Microsoft, Netscape and other browser operators agreed to screen sites that were not P3P-compliant. In effect, P3P automatically bypassed web sites that didn't meet a level of privacy expectations specified by individual web users.

Yet to be determined is whether P3P, an attempt at web industry self-regulation, can effectively protect consumers from third parties sharing private information. If P3P fails, Congress and federal agencies might follow through with backup protections.

Cyberpornography

Authorities are trying to eradicate indecency from cyberspace, especially if children have access. How serious is the problem? No one is certain how much

Media Databank

Global Web Users

The disparity between computer-rich and computer-poor regions of the world is dramatic, as these data from the *Computer Industry Almanac* show. The numbers are the regular web users per 1,000 people.

North America	479.1
Western Europe	217.5
Eastern Europe	32.7
Asia-Pacific	16.6
South and Central America	21.1
Middle Asia and Africa	7.2

cyberpornography is out there. Vanderbilt University business professors Donna Hoffman and Thomas Novak estimate that only one-half of 1 percent of the files available on the Internet could be described as pornographic. How often kids visit those sites is impossible to measure. Some people would argue that even a single child's exposure to pornography is too much and justifies sanctions.

Policing the Internet, including web sites, presents unique challenges. The nature of the web is that it is unstructured and unregulated, and the available material is in ongoing flux. The anarchy of the web is its inherent virtue. The immensity of cyberspace is another problem for would-be regulators. The web system that Tim Berners-Lee and his associates devised has infinite capacity.

Among alternatives to protect children are desktop programs that have come on the market to identify objectionable Internet bulletin boards and web sites. **Surf-Watch,** for example, blocks access to such sites as soon as they are discovered. Bill Duvall of Los Altos, California, who created SurfWatch, hires college students to monitor cyberspace for sexual explicitness and updates SurfWatch regularly. He identifies five to 10 new smut sites a day.

Commercial online services keep close tabs on what goes on in their bulletin boards and chat rooms, and occasionally excise bawdy material. In addition, the industry is working on a ratings system, somewhat like Hollywood's movie ratings, to help parents to screen things they deem inappropriate for the kids. Since 1993, however, the commercial online services have been able to give their subscribers access to the unregulated Internet. Once out of an online service's gate, subscribers are beyond the protection of the service's in-house standards of acceptability.

Media Future: The Web

Futurists are scrambling—fruitlessly, it seems—to sort through technological breakthroughs to figure out where it's all going. Their vision extends only a few months ahead at best. Amid all the haze, two realities are clear. First, bandwidth improvements will expand capacity exponentially for the transmission and exchange of messages. Second, the web will untether itself from the landlines on which most messages move today. A wireless future will make the web a medium of ultimate portability. The possibilities that will come with further miniaturization of equipment and compression of messages are mind-boggling.

cyberpornography
Indecency delivered by computer.

SurfWatch
Software that intercepts indecent material.

The Eyeball as a Screen. A Seattle company, Microvision, is hoping to market a device that projects images directly onto the human eyeball. This VRD, short for "virtual retina display," is not much more cumbersome to wear than a pair of glasses, and it gives a sharper image than a 70-millimeter IMAX screen. With VRD, people would not need television or computer screens. Microvision says this device can be made for less than $100.

As the technological breakthroughs leapfrog over each other, we will see the traditional media shift increasingly to the web. Don't expect to wake up one morning, though, and find that the world is paperless and local television stations have vanished. Just as the horse and buggy and the automobile coexisted for 40 years, so will e-books and paper books. AOL-TV will still be television as we know it today, and many people will be satisfied with a living room set pretty much as now—although with bigger screens, sharper pictures and movie-house sound quality.

In short, media companies will need to use two redundant modes to maximize the audience. Already we see this with over-air radio stations that stream online, magazines and newspapers on paper and on the web, and recordings that are at the record store and also downloadable.

chapter wrap-up

The web utilizes the global Internet, so computers anywhere can exchange digitized data—including text, visuals and audio. Many media companies are investing heavily in cyberspace, and the expansion of high-capacity fiber-optic cable networks will increase capacity tremendously so that audio and moving visuals are on tap live on any computer screen connected to the Internet. Two-way communication via the web already is standard fare. With every passing day, more mass communication is occurring on the web.

Questions for Review

1. How can the web be defined as a new and distinctive mass medium?
2. How is the web related to the Internet?
3. What is the difficulty with the web as an advertising medium?
4. What is the effect of digitization and fiber-optic cable on mass communication?
5. What is the connection between the web and hypertext?
6. Will hypertext change the way that human beings create stories and receive them?
7. Why was digitizing a necessary prelude to the web?
8. Should public policy guarantee everyone, including children, total access to the web?

Questions for Critical Thinking

1. Will it ever be possible to condense all human knowledge into an area smaller than the 36-square-foot cube described by the Marquardt Corporation?
2. What makes books, magazines, newspapers, sound recordings, movies, radio and television different from one another? What will become of these distinctions in coming years?
3. Trace the development of the technology that has made the web possible.

4. What were the innovations that Tim Berners-Lee introduced that are revolutionizing mass communication?
5. How does hypertext depart from traditional human communication? And does hypertext have a future as a literary form?
6. What obstacles would you have in designing public policy to assure access for every citizen to the web?
7. Some people say there is no point in trying to regulate cybersmut. Do you agree? Disagree? Why?
8. Some mass media may be subsumed by the web. Pretend you are a futurist and create a timeline for this to happen.

Keeping Up to Date

Industry Standard is the main trade journal of e-commerce.

The magazine *Wired* offers hep coverage of cyberdevelopments, issues and people.

Trade journals *Editor & Publisher, Advertising Age* and *Broadcasting & Cable* have excellent ongoing coverage of their fields.

InfoWorld covers the gamut of cybernews.

Widely available news media that explore cyberissues include *Time, Newsweek,* the *Wall Street Journal* and the New York *Times.*

Don't overlook surfing the web for sites that track web developments.

Christiane Amanpour. *She hops from one world hot spot to another, reporting for both CNN and CBS.*

part two   Mass Messages

10

News

They all wanted her—ABC, CBS, NBC. The Cable News Network already had her, but her contract was expiring. **Christiane Amanpour,** having achieved worldwide acclaim as a war correspondent, was now the object of a bidding war. In the end, there were three winners: Amanpour herself, reportedly offered close to $2 million, making her the highest-paid foreign correspondent in the world; CNN, which would retain her as senior international correspondent; and CBS, which would feature her special reports on "60 Minutes."

Thirteen years had passed since the day in 1983 when Amanpour entered CNN's building in Atlanta to begin her entry-level job as an assistant to the international assignment desk. Ted Turner's news network was only three years old. Amanpour would grow with the company, becoming a reporter working out of CNN's bureaus in New York, Frankfurt and Paris.

But it was her work as a correspondent in the hot spots around the globe that caused the world to take notice. Wherever civil unrest and conflict broke out, wherever there arose political crises, turmoil, military actions, and all the human tragedies associated with such events, TV viewers could expect Amanpour to be there, showing and telling them what was happening. CNN's global audience expanded rapidly. Government leaders and ordinary citizens alike were tuning in to see on-the-spot coverage of breaking news. The vast changes in Central Europe, the breakup of the Soviet Union, the events in Sarajevo, Algeria, Haiti, Rwanda, Somalia, the Persian Gulf—all were covered in Amanpour's unique reporting style.

Colleagues in broadcast journalism praised her for her fearlessness. A sound technician who worked with her in a conflict area admired her instinctual ability to know exactly when to enter and exit perilous situations—"like a cat." A *TV Guide* writer remembers some American soldiers who asked her to pose for a picture with them. One of them quipped that being seen in a picture with Christiane Amanpour would prove they deserved their hazardous-duty pay.

Journalism Traditions

STUDY PREVIEW U.S. journalism has evolved through four distinctive eras: the colonial, partisan, penny press and yellow press periods. Each of these periods made distinctive contributions to contemporary news media practices.

Colonial Period

In the American **colonial period, Benjamin Harris** published the first newspaper, ***Publick Occurrences,*** in Boston in 1690. He was in hot water right away. Harris scandalized Puritan sensitivities by alleging that the king of France had dallied with his son's wife. In the colonies, just as in England, a newspaper needed royal consent. The governor had not consented, and Harris was put out of business after one issue.

Even so, Harris' daring was a precursor for emerging press defiance against authority. In 1733 **John Peter Zenger** started a paper in New York in competition with the existing Crown-supported newspaper. Zenger's New York *Journal* was backed by merchants and lawyers who disliked the royal governor. From the beginning, the newspaper antagonized the governor with items challenging his competence. Finally, the governor arrested Zenger. The trial made history. Zenger's attorney, **Andrew Hamilton,** argued that there should be no punishment for printing articles that are true. The argument was a dramatic departure from the legal practice of the day, which allowed royal governors to prosecute for articles that might undermine their authority regardless of whether the articles were true. Hamilton's argument prevailed, and Zenger, who had become a hero for standing up to the Crown, was freed. To the governor's chagrin, there was great public celebration in the streets of New York that night.

Zenger's success against the Crown foreshadowed the explosive colonial reaction after Parliament passed a stamp tax in 1765. The colonies did not have elected representatives in Parliament, so the cry was a defiant "No taxation without representation." The campaign, however, was less ideological than economic. It was led by colonial printers, who stood to lose from the new tax, which was levied on printed materials. Historian **Arthur Schlesinger** has called it the newspaper war on Britain. The newspapers won. The tax was withdrawn. Having seen their potential to force

---

Christiane Amanpour
Foreign correspondent known for CNN work from world hot spots.

colonial period
From the founding of the colonies to the American Revolution.

Benjamin Harris
Published *Publick Occurrences.*

Publick Occurrences
First colonial newspaper, Boston, 1690.

John Peter Zenger
Defied authorities in New York *Journal.*

Andrew Hamilton
Urged truth as defense for libel.

Arthur Schlesinger
Viewed newspapers as instigating Revolution.

Zenger Trial. Printer John Peter Zenger, in the dock, won his 1735 trial for criticizing New York's royal governor. The victory fed a colonial exuberance that culminated 46 years later in winning the revolution against British rule.

Media Timeline

Roots of Journalistic Practices

1735 Colonial jury exonerated John Peter Zenger of seditious libel.

1760s Colonial newspapers campaigned against stamp tax.

1833 Ben Day founded New York *Sun*, the first penny newspaper.

1840s James Gordon Bennett pioneered systematic news coverage.

1841 Horace Greeley established the editorial page.

1844 Samuel Morse devised the telegraph, hastening delivery of faraway news.

1880s Joseph Pulitzer and William Randolph Hearst's circulation war led to yellow press excesses.

1916 Presidential returns were broadcast on an experimental New York radio station.

1980 CNN introduced 24-hour television news.

1992 Albuquerque, New Mexico, *Tribune* launched an online edition.

the government's hand, newspapers then led the way in stirring other ill feelings against England and precipitating the American Revolution.

These traditions from the colonial period remain today:

- The news media, both print and broadcast, relish their independence from government censorship and control.
- The news media, especially newspapers and magazines, actively try to mold government policy and mobilize public sentiment. Today this is done primarily on the editorial page.
- Journalists are committed to seeking truth, which was articulated as a social value in Zenger's "truth defense."
- The public comes down in favor of independent news media when government becomes too heavy-handed, as demonstrated by Zenger's popularity.
- In a capitalistic system the news media are economic entities that sometimes react in their own self-interest when their profit-making ability is threatened.

Partisan Period

After the Revolution, newspapers divided along partisan lines. What is called the Federalist period in U.S. history is also referred to as the **partisan period** among newspaper historians. Intense partisanship characterized newspapers of the period, which spanned roughly 50 years to the 1830s.

Initially, the issue was over a constitution. Should the nation have a strong central government or remain a loose coalition of states? James Madison, Alexander Hamilton, Thomas Jefferson, John Jay and other leading thinkers exchanged ideas with articles and essays in newspapers. The *Federalist Papers,* a series of essays printed and reprinted in newspapers throughout the nation, were part of the debate. Typical of the extreme partisanship of the era were journalists who reveled in nasty barbs and rhetorical excesses. It was not unusual for an ideological opponent to be called a "dog," "traitor," "liar" or "cheat."

After the Constitution was drafted, partisanship intensified, finally culminating lopsidedly when the Federalist party both controlled the Congress and had the party leader, **John Adams,** in the presidency. In firm control and bent on silencing their detractors, the Federalists ramrodded a series of laws through Congress in 1798. One

media online

Newseum: The Interactive museum of news.
www.newseum.org

Archiving Early America: Source material from 18th-century America, all displayed digitally.
www.earlyamerica.com/earlyamerica

Tracing the Story of Journalism: A timeline of journalism in the United States.
www.writesite.org/html/tracing.html

Media History Project: Promoting the study of media history from petroglyphs to pixals.
www.mediahistory.com

partisan period
From the American Revolution at least to the 1830s.

Federalist Papers
Essays with diverse views on the form the new nation should take.

John Adams
Federalist president.

media online

Federalist Papers:
The original text of the Federalist Papers. View or download the entire plain text version of all of the Federalist Papers.
http://memory.loc.gov/const/fed/fedpapers.html

of the things the **Alien and Sedition Acts** prohibited was "false, scandalous, malicious" statements about government. Using these laws, the Federalists made 25 indictments, which culminated in 10 convictions. Among those indicted was **David Bowen,** a Revolutionary War veteran who felt strongly about free expression. He put up a sign in Dedham, Massachusetts: "No stamp tax. No sedition. No alien bills. No land tax. Downfall to tyrants of America. Peace and retirement to the president [the Federalist John Adams]. Long live the vice president [the Anti-Federalist **Thomas Jefferson**] and the minority [the Anti-Federalists]. May moral virtues be the basis of civil government." If only criticisms of recent presidents were so mild! But the Federalists were not of a tolerant mind. Bowen was fined $400 and sentenced to 18 months in prison.

Federalist excesses were at their most extreme when **Matthew Lyon,** a member of Congress, was jailed for a letter to a newspaper editor that accused President Adams of "ridiculous pomp, foolish adulation, selfish avarice." Lyon, an anti-Federalist, was sentenced to four months in jail and fined $1,000. Although he was tried in Rutland, Vermont, he was sent to a filthy jail 40 miles away. When editor Anthony Haswell printed an advertisement to raise money for Lyon's fine, he was jailed for abetting a criminal. The public was outraged at Federalist heavy-handedness. The $1,000 was quickly raised, and Lyon, while still in prison, was re-elected by a two-to-one margin. After his release from prison, Lyon's supporters followed his carriage for 12 miles as he began his way back to Philadelphia, the national capital. Public outrage showed itself in the election of 1800. Jefferson was elected president, and the Federalists were thumped out of office, never to rise again. The people had spoken.

Here are traditions from the partisan period that continue today:

- Government should keep its hands off the press. The First Amendment to the Constitution, which set a tone for this period, declared that "Congress shall make no law . . . abridging freedom . . . of the press."
- The news media are a forum for discussion and debate, as newspapers were in the *Federalist Papers* dialogue on what form the Constitution should take.
- The news media should comment vigorously on public issues.
- Government transgressions against the news media will ultimately be met by public rejection of those committing the excesses, which has happened periodically throughout U.S. history.

Penny Press Period

In 1833, when he was 22, the enterprising **Benjamin Day** started a newspaper that changed U.S. journalism: the **New York *Sun.*** At a penny a copy, the *Sun* was within reach of just about everybody. Other papers were expensive, an annual subscription costing as much as a full week's wages. Unlike other papers, which were distributed mostly by mail, the *Sun* was hawked every day on the streets. The *Sun*'s content was different too. It avoided the political and economic thrust of the traditional papers, concentrating instead on items of interest to common folk. The writing was simple, straightforward and easy to follow. For a motto for the *Sun,* Day came up with "It Shines for All," his pun fully intended.

Day's *Sun* was an immediate success. Naturally, it was quickly imitated, and the **penny press period** began. Partisan papers that characterized the partisan period continued, but the mainstream of American newspapers came to be in the mold of the *Sun.*

Alien and Sedition Acts
Discouraged criticism of government.

David Bowen
Punished for criticizing the majority party.

Thomas Jefferson
Anti-Federalist president.

Matthew Lyon
Member of Congress jailed for criticism of President Adams.

Benjamin Day
Published the New York *Sun.*

New York *Sun*
First penny newspaper, 1833.

penny press period
One-cent newspapers geared to mass audience and mass advertising.

Media People

Benjamin Day

Years later, reflecting on the instant success of his New York *Sun,* Benjamin Day shook his head in wonderment. He hadn't realized at the time that the *Sun* was such a milestone. Whether he was being falsely modest is something historians can debate. The fact is the *Sun,* which Day founded in 1833, discovered mass audiences on a scale never before envisioned and ushered in the era of modern mass media.

Ben Day, a printer, set up a shop in 1833, but business was slow. With time on his hands, he began a little people-oriented handbill with brief news items and, most important, an advertisement for his printing business. He printed 1,000 copies, which he sold for a penny apiece. The tiny paper, four pages of three columns of type, sold well, so Day decided to keep it going. In six months the *Sun,* the first of a new era of penny papers, had the highest circulation in New York. By 1836 circulation had zoomed to 20,000.

Fifty years later Day told an interviewer that the *Sun*'s success was "more by accident than by design." Even so, the *Sun* was the first newspaper that, at a penny a copy, was within the economic means of almost everyone. He filled the paper

Benjamin Day

Mass Media Pioneer. When Benjamin Day launched the New York *Sun* in 1833 and sold it for one cent a copy, he ushered in an era of cheap newspapers that common people could afford. Years later, his successors pushed circulation past 1 million a week. Today, mass media have many of the *Sun*'s pioneering characteristics. These include content of interest to a great many people, a financial base in advertising and easy access.

with the local police court news, which is the stuff that arouses universal interest. True to its masthead motto, "It Shines for All," the *Sun* was a paper for the masses.

At a penny a copy, Day knew he couldn't pay his bills, so he built the paper's economic foundation on advertising. This remains the financial basis of most mass media today—newspapers, magazines, television and radio. Just as today, advertisers subsidized the product to make it affordable to great multitudes of people.

Today it is technology that makes the media possible. The *Sun* was a pioneer in using the technology of its time: engine-driven presses. The *Sun*'s messages—the articles—were crafted to interest large, diverse audiences, as are mass messages today. Also like today, advertising drove the enterprise financially. The story of Day's *Sun* also demonstrates a reality, as true then as now, that the mass media must be businesses first and purveyors of information and entertainment second.

Merchants saw the unprecedented circulation of the **penny papers** as a way to reach great numbers of potential customers. Advertising revenue meant bigger papers, which attracted more readers, which attracted more advertisers. A snowballing momentum began that continues today with more and more advertising being carried

penny papers
Affordable by almost everyone.

by the mass media. A significant result was a shift in newspaper revenues from subscriptions to advertisers. Day, as a matter of fact, did not meet expenses by selling the *Sun* for a penny a copy. He counted on advertisers to pick up a good part of his production cost. In effect, advertisers subsidized readers, just as they do today.

Several social and economic factors, all resulting from the Industrial Revolution, made the penny press possible:

- **Industrialization.** With new steam-powered presses, hundreds of copies an hour could be printed. Earlier presses had been hand operated.
- **Urbanization.** Workers flocked to the cities to work in new factories, creating a great pool of potential newspaper readers within delivery range. Until the urbanization of the 1820s and 1830s, the U.S. population had been almost wholly agricultural and scattered across the countryside. Even the most populous cities had been relatively small.
- **Immigration.** Waves of immigrants arrived from impoverished parts of Europe. Most were eager to learn English and found that penny papers, with their simple style, were good tutors.
- **Literacy.** As immigrants learned English, they hungered for reading material within their economic means. Also, literacy in general was increasing, which contributed to the rise of mass-circulation newspapers and magazines.

A leading penny press editor was **James Gordon Bennett,** who, in the 1830s, organized the first newsroom and reporting staff. Earlier newspapers had been either sidelines of printers, who put whatever was handy into their papers, or projects of ideologues, whose writing was in an essay vein. Bennett hired reporters and sent them out on rounds to gather information for readers of his New York *Herald.*

Horace Greeley developed editorials as a distinctive journalistic form in his New York *Tribune,* which he founded in 1841. More than his competitors, Greeley used his newspaper to fight social ills that accompanied industrialization. Greeley's *Tribune* was a voice against poverty and slums, an advocate of labor unions and an opponent of slavery. It was a lively forum for discussions of ideas. Karl Marx, the communist philosopher, was a *Tribune* columnist for a while. So was Albert Brisbane, who advocated collective living. Firm in Greeley's concept of a newspaper was that it should be used for social good. He saw the *Tribune* as a voice for those who did not have a voice; a defender for those unable to articulate a defense; and a champion for the underdog, the deprived and the underprivileged.

In 1844, late in the penny press period, **Samuel Morse** invented the telegraph. Within months the nation was being wired. When the Civil War came in 1861, correspondents used the telegraph to get battle news to eager readers. It was called **lightning news,** delivered electrically and quickly. The Civil War also gave rise to a new convention in writing news, the **inverted pyramid.** Editors instructed their war correspondents to tell the most important information first in case telegraph lines failed— or were snipped by the enemy—as a story was being transmitted. That way, when a story was interrupted, editors would have at least a few usable sentences. The inverted pyramid, it turned out, was popular with readers because it allowed them to learn what was most important at a glance. They did not have to wade through a whole story if they were in a hurry. Also, the inverted pyramid helped editors to fit stories into the limited confines of a page—a story could be cut off at any paragraph and the most important parts remained intact. The inverted pyramid remains a standard expository form for telling event-based stories in newspapers, radio and television.

James Gordon Bennett
Organized the first methodical news coverage.

Horace Greeley
Pioneered editorials.

Samuel Morse
Invented the telegraph.

lightning news
Delivered by telegraph.

inverted pyramid
Most important information first.

Media People

Ida Wells-Barnett

Ida Wells bought a first-class ticket for a car at the front of the train, but when the conductor saw she was black, he told her to go to the rear. First-class, he said, was "set apart for white ladies and gentlemen." Wells, a small, sturdy woman, refused. The conductor, who was white, threw her off the train. Wells sued, citing various constitutional guarantees, and won before a Memphis jury. The Tennessee Supreme Court, however, said she was harassing the railroad and overturned the jury verdict.

The case, in 1885, was among the first involving racial equality in public transportation. The attention her case received made it clear to Wells, a 21-year-old schoolteacher, that the press could be a powerful vehicle to bring about change. She bought into a small weekly newspaper, the *Free Speech,* and began crusading for better schools for black children. The school board, embarrassed, fired her. So she went into journalism full time as editor of her newspaper.

In 1892 a mob lynched three black grocers whose store had been successful against white competitors. Wells pulled out all the stops in her coverage, reporting the details that led to the lynchings and denouncing the community for condoning what had

Dynamite in a Small Package. When she was 21, she sued a railroad for throwing her out of a whites-only car. Ida Wells learned the power of journalism. She went on to a distinguished career as a crusader for racial justice and, in particular, against the growing 1890s practice of lynching.

happened. It was thorough, courageous reporting, and it received wide attention. Soon Wells was writing for the New York *Age,* with her articles a fixture in almost all of the nation's 400 black newspapers. She continued her work on lynchings as mob vigilantism, amassing data that they were becoming more common. In 1892 she counted 2,565—triple the number 10 years earlier. She urged black readers to arm themselves for self-protection: "A Winchester rifle should have a place of honor in every home." Her office was attacked.

To continue her crusade, Wells went to England, beyond the mobs' reach, to rail against U.S. racial injustice, including lynchings of black men, on every forum she could find. Her book, *A Red Record,* contained

alarming statistics on U.S. lynchings. By now an internationally recognized figure, Wells felt relatively safe to return to the United States on the lecture circuit with the press sure to follow her every word. States began prosecutions for lynchings, and the number declined. Memphis had none for 25 years.

Wells eventually settled in Chicago, where she continued her journalistic crusade for racial justice and other reforms, including women's rights. In fearless pursuit of facts, she went alone to lynchings and riots. Her factual reports, published widely, provided indisputable evidence of injustice and persecution and built general sympathy for both law enforcement and for legislation to correct social wrongs.

Several New York newspaper publishers, concerned about the escalating expense of sending reporters to gather faraway news, got together in 1848 to share stories. By together sending one reporter, the newspapers cut costs dramatically. They called their cooperative venture the **Associated Press,** a predecessor of today's giant global news service. The AP introduced a new tone in news reporting. So that AP stories could be used by member newspapers of different political persuasions, reporters were told to write from a nonpartisan point of view. The result was a fact-oriented kind

Associated Press
Co-op to gather, distribute news.

Stunt Journalism. When newspaper owner Joseph Pulitzer sent reporter Nellie Bly on an around-the-world trip in 1890 to try to outdo the fictional Phileas Fogg's 80-day trip, stunt journalism was approaching its peak. Her feat took 72 days.

objective reporting
Telling news without bias.

yellow press period
Late 1800s; marked by sensationalism.

Joseph Pulitzer
Emphasized human interest in newspapers; later sensationalized.

Nellie Bly
Stunt reporter.

William Randolph Hearst
Built circulation with sensationalism.

of news writing often called **objective reporting.** It was widely imitated and is still the dominant reporting style for event-based news stories in all the news media.

There are traditions of today's news media, both print and electronic, that can be traced to the penny press period:

- Inverted pyramid story structures.
- Coverage and writing that appeals to a general audience, sometimes by trying to be entertaining or even sensationalistic. It's worth noting that the egalitarian thinking of Andrew Jackson's 1829–1837 presidency, which placed special value on the "common man," coincided with the start of the penny press and its appeal to a large audience of "everyday people."
- A strong orientation to covering events, including the aggressive ferreting out of news.
- A commitment to social improvement, which included a willingness to crusade against corruption.
- Being on top of unfolding events and providing information to readers quickly, something made possible by the telegraph but that also came to be valued in local reporting.
- A detached, neutral perspective in reporting events, a tradition fostered by the Associated Press.

Yellow Press Period

The quest to sell more copies led to excesses that are illustrated by the Pulitzer-Hearst circulation war in New York in the 1890s, in what came to be known as the **yellow press period.**

Joseph Pulitzer, a poor immigrant, made the St. Louis *Post-Dispatch* into a financial success. In 1883 Pulitzer decided to try a bigger city. He bought the New York *World* and applied his St. Louis formula. He emphasized human interest, crusaded for worthy causes, and ran lots of promotional hoopla. Pulitzer's *World* also featured solid journalism. His star reporter, **Nellie Bly,** epitomized the two faces of the Pulitzer formula for journalistic success. For one story Bly feigned mental illness, entered an insane asylum and emerged with scandalous tales about how patients were treated. It was enterprising journalism of great significance. Reforms resulted. Later, showing the less serious, show-biz side of Pulitzer's formula, Nellie Bly was sent out to circle the globe in 80 days, like Jules Verne's fictitious Phileas Fogg. Her journalism stunt took 72 days.

In San Francisco, Pulitzer had a young admirer, **William Randolph Hearst.** With his father's Nevada mining fortune and mimicking Pulitzer's New York formula, Hearst made the San Francisco *Examiner* a great success. In 1895 Hearst decided to go to New York and take on the master. He bought the New York *Journal* and vowed to "out-Pulitzer" Pulitzer. The inevitable resulted. To outdo each other, Pulitzer and Hearst launched crazier and crazier stunts. Not even the comic pages escaped the competitive frenzy. Pulitzer ran the *Yellow Kid,* and then Hearst hired the cartoonist away. Pulitzer hired a new one, and both papers ran the yellow character and plastered the city with yellow promotional posters. The circulation war was nicknamed "yellow journalism," and the term came to be a derisive reference to sensational excesses in news coverage.

The yellow excesses reached a feverish peak as Hearst and Pulitzer covered the growing tensions between Spain and the United States. Fueled by hyped atrocity stories, the tension eventually exploded in war. One story, perhaps apocryphal, epitomizes the no-holds-barred competition between Pulitzer and Hearst. Although Spain had consented to all demands by the United States, Hearst sent the artist **Frederic Remington** to Cuba to cover the situation. Remington cabled back: "Everything is quiet. There is no trouble here. There will be no war. Wish to return." Hearst replied: "Please remain. You furnish the pictures. I'll furnish the war."

Yellow journalism had its imitators in New York and elsewhere. It is important to note, however, that not all American journalism went the yellow route. **Adolph Ochs** bought the New York *Times* in 1896 and built it into a newspaper that avoided sideshows to report and comment seriously on important issues and events. The *Times*, still true to that approach, outlived the Pulitzer and Hearst newspapers in New York and today is the best newspaper in the world.

The yellow tradition, however, still lives. The New York *Daily News*, founded in 1919 and almost an immediate hit, ushered in a period that some historians characterize as **jazz journalism.** It was just Hearst and Pulitzer updated in tabloid form with an emphasis on photography. Today, newspapers like the commercially successful *National Enquirer* are in the yellow tradition. So are a handful of metropolitan dailies, including Rupert Murdoch's San Antonio, Texas, *Express-News.* It is

Yellow Journalism's Namesake. The Yellow Kid, a popular cartoon character in New York newspapers, was the namesake for the sensationalist "yellow journalism" of the 1880s and 1890s. Many newspapers of the period, especially in New York, hyperbolized and fabricated the news to attract readers. The tradition remains in isolated areas of modern journalism, such as the supermarket tabloids and trash documentary programs on television.

Joseph Pulitzer

William Randolph Hearst

Journalistic Sensationalism. Rival New York newspaper publishers Joseph Pulitzer and William Randolph Hearst tried to outdo each other daily with anti-Spanish atrocity stories from Cuba, many of them trumped up. Some historians say the public hysteria fueled by Pulitzer and Hearst helped to precipitate the Spanish-American War, especially after the U.S. battleship *Maine* exploded in Havana harbor. Both Pulitzer and Hearst claimed it was a Spanish attack on an American vessel, although a case can be made that the explosion was accidental.

Frederic Remington
Illustrator sent by Hearst to find atrocities in Cuba.

Adolph Ochs
Developed the New York *Times* as a serious newspaper.

jazz journalism
1920s, similar to yellow journalism.

obvious too in tabloid television interview programs like "Jerry Springer," which pander to the offbeat, tawdry and sensational.

While not as important in forming distinctive journalistic traditions as the earlier penny papers, yellow newspapers were significant in contributing to the growing feeling of nationhood in the United States, especially among the diverse immigrants who were arriving in massive numbers. Journalism historian Larry Lorenz put it this way: "The publishers reached out to the widest possible audience by trying to find a common denominator, and that turned out to be the human interest story. Similarities among groups were emphasized rather than differences. Readers, in their quest to be real Americans, seized on those common elements to pattern themselves after, and soon their distinctive characteristics and awareness of themselves as special groups began to fade."

Personal Values in News

STUDY PREVIEW Journalists make important decisions on which events, phenomena and issues are reported and which are not. The personal values journalists bring to their work and that therefore determine which stories are told, and also how they are told, generally coincide with mainstream American values.

Role of the Journalist

After years of wrestling to come up with a definition for *news*, NBC newscaster Chet Huntley threw up his hands and declared: "News is what I decide is news." Huntley was not being arrogant. Rather, he was pointing out that events that go unreported aren't news. Regardless of an event's intrinsic qualities, such as the prominence of the people involved and the event's consequence and drama, it becomes news only when it's reported. Huntley's point was that the journalist's judgment is indispensable in deciding what's news.

Huntley's conclusion underscores the high degree of autonomy that individual journalists have in shaping what is reported. Even a reporter hired fresh out of college by a small daily newspaper and assigned to city hall has a great deal of independence in deciding what to report and how to report it. Such trust is unheard of in most other fields, which dole out responsibility to newcomers in small bits over a lengthy period. Of course, rookie journalists are monitored by their newsroom supervisors, and editors give them assignments and review their stories, but it is the city hall reporter, no matter how green, who is the news organization's expert on city government.

The First Amendment guarantee of a free press also contributes to the independence and autonomy that characterize news work. Journalists know that they have a high level of constitutional protection in deciding what to report as news. While most reporters will agree on the newsworthiness of some events and issues, such as a catastrophic storm or a tax proposal, their judgments will result in stories that take different slants and angles. On events and issues whose newsworthiness is less obvious, reporters will differ even on whether to do a story.

Journalists' Personal Values

The journalistic ideal, an unbiased seeking of truth and an unvarnished telling of it, dictates that the work be done without partisanship. Yet as human beings, journalists have personal values that influence all that they do, including their work. Because the news judgment decisions that journalists make are so important to an informed citizenry, we need to know what makes these people tick. Are they left-wingers? Are they ideological zealots? Are they quirky and unpredictable? Are they conscientious?

A sociologist who studied stories in the American news media for 20 years, **Herbert Gans,** concluded that journalists have a typical American value system. Gans identified primary values, all in the American mainstream, that journalists use in making their news judgments:

ETHNOCENTRISM.   American journalists see things through American eyes, which colors news coverage. In the 1960s and 1970s, Gans notes, North Vietnam was consistently characterized as "the enemy." U.S. reporters took the view of the U.S. government and military, which was hardly detached or neutral. This **ethnocentrism** was clear at the end of the war, which U.S. media headlined as "the *fall* of South Vietnam." By other values, Gans said, the communist takeover of Saigon could be considered a *liberation.* In neutral terms, it was a *change in government.*

This ethnocentrism creates problems as the news media become global. During the Persian Gulf war in 1991, CNN discovered that the commonly used word *foreign,* which to U.S. audiences meant anything non-American, was confusing to CNN audiences in other countries. Eager to build a global audience, CNN boss Ted Turner banned the word *foreign* and told anchors and scriptwriters that they would be fined for uttering the word. *International* became the substitute word, as awkward as it sometimes sounded to American ears. The semantic change was cosmetic, however, for the CNN war coverage continued, inevitably, to be largely from the U.S. perspective, just as Gans found in his earlier studies. It is hard for all people, including journalists, to transcend their own skins.

COMMITMENT TO DEMOCRACY AND CAPITALISM.   Gans found that U.S. journalists favor democracy of the U.S. style. Coverage of other governmental forms dwells on corruption, conflict, protest and bureaucratic malfunction. The unstated idea of most U.S. journalists, said Gans, is that other societies do best when they follow the American ideal of serving the public interest.

Gans also found that U.S. journalists are committed to the capitalist economic system. When they report corruption and misbehavior in U.S. business, journalists treat them as aberrations. The underlying posture of the news coverage of the U.S. economy, Gans said, is "an optimistic faith" that businesspeople refrain from unreasonable profits and gross exploitation of workers or customers while competing to create increased prosperity for all. In covering controlled foreign economies, U.S. journalists emphasize the downside.

It may seem only natural to most Americans that democracy and capitalism should be core values of any reasonable human being. This sense itself is an ethnocentric value, which many people do not even think about but which nonetheless shapes how they conduct their lives. Knowing that U.S. journalists by and large share this value explains a lot about the news coverage they create.

SMALL-TOWN PASTORALISM.   Like most of their fellow citizens, U.S. journalists romanticize rural life. Given similar stories from metropolitan Portland and tiny Sweet Home, Oregon, editors usually opt for the small town.

Herbert Gans
Concluded that journalists have mainstream values.

ethnocentrism
Seeing things on the basis of personal experience, values.

Cities are covered as places with problems; rural life is celebrated. Suburbs are largely ignored. This small-town pastoralism, said Gans, helps to explain the success of Charles Kuralt's long-running "On the Road" series on CBS television.

INDIVIDUALISM TEMPERED BY MODERATION. Gans found that U.S. journalists love stories about rugged individuals who overcome adversity and defeat powerful forces. This is a value that contributes to a negative coverage of technology as something to be feared because it can stifle individuality. Gans again cited "On the Road," noting how Charles Kuralt found a following for his pastoral features on rugged individuals.

Journalists like to turn ordinary individuals into heroes, but there are limits. Rebels and deviates are portrayed as extremists who go beyond another value: moderation. To illustrate this propensity toward moderation, Gans noted that "the news treats atheists as extremists and uses the same approach, if more gingerly, with religious fanatics. People who consume conspicuously are criticized, but so are people such as hippies who turn their backs on consumer goods. The news is scornful both of the overly academic scholar and the oversimplifying popularizer; it is kind neither to high-brows nor to low-brows, to users of jargon or users of slang. College students who play when they should study receive disapproval, but so do 'grinds.' Lack of moderation is wrong, whether it involves excesses or abstention."

In politics, Gans says, both ideologues and politicians who lack ideology are treated with suspicion: "Political candidates who talk openly about issues may be described as dull; those who avoid issues entirely evoke doubts about their fitness for office."

SOCIAL ORDER. Journalists cover disorder—earthquakes, industrial catastrophes, protest marches, the disintegrating nuclear family, and transgressions of laws and mores. This coverage, noted Gans, is concerned not with glamorizing disorder but with finding ways to restore order. To critics who claim that the news media concentrate on disruption and the negative, Gans noted a study of television coverage of the 1967 race riots: Only 3 percent of the sequences covered the riots, and only 2 percent dealt with injuries and deaths. A full 34 percent of the coverage focused on restoring order. *Newsweek*'s coverage, according to the same study, devoted four times as many words to police and Army attempts to restore order as to describing the disturbances.

The journalistic commitment to social order also is evident in how heavily reporters rely on people in leadership roles as primary sources of information. These leaders, largely representing the Establishment and the status quo, are the people in the best position to maintain social order and to restore it if there's a disruption. This means government representatives often shape news media reports and thus their audiences' understanding of what is important, "true" or meaningful. No one receives more media attention than the president of the United States, who is seen, said Gans, "as the ultimate protector of order."

Journalistic Bias

Critics of the news media come in many colors. Conservatives are the most vocal, charging that the media slant news to favor liberal causes. Liberal critics see it in the opposite light. The most recurrent charge, however, is that the media are leftist, favoring Democrats over Republicans, liberals over conservatives, and change over the status quo.

The fact is that journalists generally fall near the political center. A landmark 1971 survey by **John Johnstone** found that 84.6 percent of journalists considered themselves middle-of-the-road or a little to the left or right. In 1983 **David Weaver** and **Cleveland Wilhoit** found 91.1 percent in those categories. At the same time, Gallup surveys put 90 percent of Americans at the center or a little left or right. The breakdown is as follows:

Political Leanings	Journalists 1971	Journalists 1983*	U.S. Adults 1982
Pretty far left	7.5	3.8	0.0
A little left	30.5	18.3	21.0
Middle of road	38.5	57.6	37.0
A little right	15.6	16.3	32.0
Pretty far right	3.4	1.6	0.0
No answer	4.5	2.5	10.0

*Percentages add up to 100.1 due to rounding.

The number of journalists who claimed to be a little leftist dropped considerably during the 12 years. Journalists had moved even more to the middle politically.

On party affiliation Weaver and Wilhoit found that journalists identified themselves as independents more than the general population:

Political Leanings	Journalists 1971	Journalists 1983*	U.S. Adults 1982
Democrat	33.5	38.5	45.0
Independent	32.5	39.1	30.0
Republican	25.7	18.8	25.0
Other	5.8	1.6	0.0
No answer	0.5	2.1	0.0

*Percentages add up to 100.1 due to rounding.

Despite such evidence, charges persist that journalists are biased. The charges are all the stranger considering that most U.S. news organizations pride themselves on a neutral presentation and go to extraordinary lengths to prove it. To avoid confusion between straight reporting and commentary, opinion pieces are set apart in clearly labeled editorial sections. Most journalists, even those with left or right leanings, have a zealous regard for detached, neutral reporting. Although they see their truth-seeking as unfettered by partisanship, they recognize that their news judgments often are made in confusing situations against deadline pressure, and they are usually the first, in self-flagellating postmortems, to criticize themselves when they fall short of the journalistic goals of accuracy, balance and fairness.

Considering the media's obsession with avoiding partisanship, how do the charges of bias retain any currency? First, critics who paint the media as leftist usually are forgetting that news, by its nature, is concerned with change. Everybody, journalists and media consumers alike, is more interested in a volcano that is blowing its top than in one that remains dormant. This interest in what is happening, as opposed to what is not happening, does not mean that anyone favors volcanic eruptions. However, the fact is that change almost always is more interesting than the status quo, although it is often more threatening and less comfortable. When journalists spend

John Johnstone
Found that most journalists see themselves as politically centrist.

David Weaver
Found that journalists' political positions shift with the population.

Cleveland Wilhoit
Collaborator with David Weaver.

time on a presidential candidate's ideas to eliminate farm subsidies, it is not that the journalists favor the change, just that the topic is more interesting than stories about government programs that are unchallenged. Because conservatives favor the status quo, it is natural that they would feel threatened by news coverage of change and proposals for change, no matter how disinterested and dispassionate the coverage, but this is hardly liberal bias.

The news media also are criticized because of an American journalistic tradition that is implicit in the U.S. Constitution: a belief that democracy requires the press to serve a watchdog function. Since the founding of the Republic, journalists have been expected to keep government honest and responsive to the electorate by reporting on its activities, especially on shortcomings. Unless the people have full reports on the government, they cannot intelligently discuss public issues, let alone vote intelligently on whether or not to keep their representatives. Sometimes, to the dismay of those in power, the news media are part of the U.S. system to facilitate change when it is needed.

In short, journalists' concern with change is not born of political bias. It is inherent in the nature of their work.

Variables Affecting News

STUDY PREVIEW   The variables that determine what is reported include things beyond a journalist's control, such as how much space or time is available to tell stories. Also, a story that might receive top billing on a slow news day might not even appear on a day when an overwhelming number of major stories are breaking.

News Hole

A variable affecting what ends up being reported as news is called the **news hole.** In newspapers the news hole is the space left after the advertising department has placed all the ads it has sold in the paper. The volume of advertising determines the number of total pages, and generally, the bigger the issue, the more room for news. Newspaper editors can squeeze fewer stories into a thin Monday issue than a fat Wednesday issue.

In broadcasting, the news hole tends to be more consistent. A 30-minute television newscast may have room for only 23 minutes of news, but the format doesn't vary. When the advertising department doesn't sell all the seven minutes available for advertising, it usually is public service announcements, promotional messages and program notes—not news—that pick up the slack. Even so, the news hole can vary in broadcasting. A 10-minute newscast can accommodate more stories than a 5-minute newscast, and, as with newspapers, it is the judgment of journalists that determines which events make it.

News Flow and News Staffing

Besides the news hole, the **flow** varies from day to day. A story that might be played prominently on a slow news day can be passed over entirely in the competition for space on a heavy news day.

On one of the heaviest news days of all time—June 4, 1989—death claimed Iran's Ayatollah Khomeini, a central figure in U.S. foreign policy; Chinese young people and

news hole
Space for news in a newspaper after ads are inserted; time in a newscast for news after ads.

flow
Significance of events worth covering varies from day to day.

Media Abroad

Foreign Press Corps

Leading U.S. news organizations scrambled to beef up their south Asia staffs in 2001 as the United States moved military forces into the region in the quest to demolish Osama bin Laden's al-Qaeda network. The number of U.S. reporters, photographers and video crews always increases during wars, but the trend in general has been a declining U.S. journalistic presence abroad.

Under pressure to increase profits, U.S. newspapers had steadily reduced their foreign bureaus for years. A 1998 survey by *American Journalism Review,* a media criticism magazine, found that U.S. newspapers had only 280 reporters in other countries—and this at a time when international commerce and globalization were changing the world profoundly.

According to the *AJR* data, these were the U.S. newspapers with the largest journalistic staffs abroad:

- *Wall Street Journal:* 90
- New York *Times:* 37
- Los Angeles *Times:* 27
- Washington *Post:* 25
- *Christian Science Monitor:* 11
- Chicago *Tribune:* 9
- *USA Today:* 6

- Boston *Globe:* 6
- Miami *Herald:* 5
- Long Island *Newsday:* 5

Peter Arnett, whose Vietnam war coverage for the Associated Press earned him a Pulitzer Prize, laments the decline in foreign correspondence. He blames readers themselves in part. In survey after survey, readers say they want more local news, and editors adjust their staffs to provide it. Arnett points out, however, that wanting more local news does not necessarily mean that readers want less foreign news.

the government were locked in a showdown in Tiananmen Square; the Polish people were voting to reject their one-party communist political system; and a revolt was under way in the Soviet republic of Uzbekistan. That was a heavy news day, and the flow of major nation-rattling events preempted many stories that otherwise would have been considered news.

Staffing affects news coverage, for example, whether reporters are in the right place at the right time. A newsworthy event in Nigeria will receive short shrift on U.S. television if the network correspondents for Africa are occupied with a natural disaster in next-door Cameroon. A radio station's city government coverage will slip when the city hall reporter is on vacation or if the station can't afford a regular reporter at city hall. When Iraq invaded Kuwait unexpectedly in August 1990, it so happened that almost all the U.S. and European reporters assigned to the Persian Gulf were on vacation or elsewhere on assignment. An exception was Caryle Murphy of the Washington *Post.* Like everyone else, Murphy hadn't expected the invasion, but she had decided to make a routine trip from her Cairo bureau for a firsthand look at Kuwaiti affairs. Only by happenstance did Murphy have what she called "a front-row seat for witnessing a small nation being crushed." Competing news organizations were devoid of eyewitness staff coverage until they scrambled to fly people into the region.

Perceptions About Audience

How a news organization perceives its audience affects news coverage. The *National Enquirer* lavishes attention on unproven cancer cures that the New York *Times* treats briefly if at all. The *Wall Street Journal* sees its purpose as news for

staffing
Available staff resources to cover news.

readers who have special interests in finance, the economy and business. Ted Turner's CNNfn was established to serve an audience more interested in quick market updates, brief analysis and trendy consumer news than the kind of depth offered by the *Journal.*

The perception that a news organization has of its audience is evident in a comparison of stories on different networks' newscasts. CNN may lead newscasts with a coup d'état in another country, while CNNfn leads with a new government economic forecast and MTV with the announcement of a rock group's tour.

Availability of Material

The availability of photographs and video also is a factor in what ends up being news. Television is often faulted for overplaying visually titillating stories, such as fires, and underplaying or ignoring more significant stories that are not photogenic. Newspapers and magazines also are partial to stories with strong accompanying visuals, as was shown in an especially poignant way in 1976 when a Boston woman and child sought refuge on their apartment's balcony when the building caught fire. Then the balcony collapsed, and the two fell. The woman died on impact; the child somehow survived. The tragedy was all the more dramatic because it occurred just as firefighters were about to rescue the pair. Most journalists would report such an event, but in this case the coverage was far more extensive than would normally be the case because Stanley Forman of the Boston *Herald-American* had photographed the woman and child plunging to the ground. On its own merits, the event probably would not have been reported beyond Boston, but with Forman's series of dramatic photographs, clicked in quick succession, the story was reported in visual media—newspapers, magazines and television—around the world. Forman won a Pulitzer Prize for the photos.

Radio news people revel in stories when sound is available, which influences what is reported and how. A barnyard interview with the leader of a farmers' organization, with cows snorting in the background, is likelier to make the air than the same leader saying virtually the same thing in the sterile confines of a legislative committee chamber.

Competition

One trigger of adrenaline for journalists is landing a scoop and, conversely, being scooped. Journalism is a competitive business, and the drive to outdo other news organizations keeps news publications and newscasts fresh with new material.

Competition has an unglamorous side. Although most journalists pride themselves on the autonomy they have in going about their work, they constantly monitor each other to identify events that they missed and need to catch up on to be competitive. This catch-up aspect of the news business contributes to similarities in coverage, which scholar Leon Sigal calls the **consensible nature of news.** It also is called "pack" and "herd" journalism.

In the final analysis news is the result of journalists scanning their environment and making decisions, first on whether to cover certain events and then on how to cover them. The decisions are made against a backdrop of countless variables, many of them changing during the reporting, writing and editing processes.

consensible nature of news News organization second-guesses competition in deciding coverage.

Influences on News

STUDY PREVIEW   The subtlety of most attempts outside the newsroom to control news coverage makes them difficult to count. Even one is too many. External influence undermines journalists as honest brokers of news and information. Troublesome sources of pressure are advertisers and even media executives and news sources themselves.

Advertiser Influence

Special interests sometimes try to squelch stories or insist on self-serving angles. Usually, these attempts are made quietly, even tacitly, among executives—country-club decision-making. Sometimes the pressure is exerted on media advertising people, who quietly exert influence on the newsroom.

When a Wyoming grocery store was concerned over a warning from a state agency that Bon Vivant vichyssoise was possibly tainted with botulism, the advertising manager at the Laramie *Boomerang,* the only newspaper in town, kept the story out of the paper. A Laramie radio station that aired the story lost the grocery store's advertising.

Pressure sometimes occurs after a story appears, sending clear signals never to do it again. In an egregious California case in 1994, the local car dealers' association yanked $1 million in advertising out of the San José *Mercury News* after the paper ran an in-depth consumer article on how to buy a car. The dealers didn't like the negotiation tips and other insider information that reporter Mark Schwanhausser included in the story. The *Mercury News* hasn't done that kind of story since. In an interview with *Columbia Journalism Review,* Schwanhausser talked about a chilling effect: "When you start guessing what people will react to, you can find all kinds of reasons not to write a story."

To their credit, most news organizations place allegiance to their audiences ahead of pleasing advertisers, as Terry Berger, president of an advertising agency representing the Brazilian airline Varig, found out from *Condé Nast's Traveler,* a travel magazine. After an article on air pollution in Rio de Janeiro, Berger wrote the magazine, "Is your editorial policy then to see how quickly you can alienate present and potential advertisers and at the same time convince your readers to stick closer to home? I really think that if you continue with this kind of editorial information, you are doing both your readers and your advertisers a disservice. For this kind of information, people read the New York *Times.* I therefore find it necessary to remove *Condé Nast's Traveler* from Varig's media schedule." Unintimidated, the magazine's editor, Harold Evans, did not recant. Not only did Evans print the letter, but he followed with this comment: "Mrs. Berger is, of course, entitled to use her judgment about where she advertises Brazil's national airline. I write not about that narrow commercial issue, but about her assertion that it is a disservice to readers and advertisers for us to print true but unattractive facts when they are relevant. This goes to the heart of the editorial policy of this magazine. . . . We rejoice in the enrichments of travel, but our aim is to give readers the fullest information, frankly and fairly, so they can make their own judgments."

Corporate Policy

No matter how committed journalists may be to truth-seeking and truth-telling, the people in charge have the final word on matters big and small. It is owners, publishers, general managers and their immediate lieutenants who are in charge. Their corporate responsibilities dictate that they are business executives before all else, even if once they were journalists. Executives sometimes make self-serving decisions on coverage that gall the journalists who work for them, but such is how chains of command work.

Lowell Bergman, former executive producer at "60 Minutes," recalls his days at CBS: "You could not do a story about a supplier or major advertiser. You could try to do it, but you were taking a lot of risks getting close to the limit." At both ABC and CBS, Bergman said, he was told that the networks would not initiate a critical story about the business practices and histories of National Football League team owners. The networks, of course, stood to derive handsome revenue from airing NFL games if they were awarded contracts for play-by-play coverage.

Admonitions not to go near certain stories are not in written policy, although they are real. ABC news people got an unusual overt reminder when Michael Eisner, chair of Disney, which owns ABC, said in an interview on the NPR program "Fresh Air," "I would prefer ABC not to cover Disney. I think it's inappropriate." Eisner went on to say that ABC News knew of his preference.

At the time ABC was working on a story about lax hiring screening at Disney World that allowed child molesters onto the payroll. The network decided against airing the story, which detailed an assault on a child at the Disney park.

In fairness, it must be said that media owners generally are sensitive to their truth-seeking and truth-telling journalistic responsibilities and assiduously avoid calling the shots on news coverage. Those who answer to a call other than journalistic soundness are within their court-recognized First Amendment rights, which allow media people to exercise their freedom responsibly as well as irresponsibly. Journalists who are bothered by wrongheaded news decisions have three choices: persuade wayward owners of the error of their ways, comply with directives, or quit and go work for a respectable journalistic organization.

Source Pressure

Journalists sometimes feel external pressure directly. At the courthouse valuable sources turn cold after a story appears that they don't like. A tearful husband begs an editor not to use his wife's name in a story that points to her as a bank embezzler. A bottle of Chivas Regal arrives at Christmas from a sports publicist who says she appreciates excellent coverage over the past year. Most journalists will tell you that their commitment to truth overrides external assaults on their autonomy. Even so, external pressures exist.

The relationship between journalists and publicists can be troublesome. In general, the relationship works well. Publicists want news coverage for their clients and provide information and help reporters to line up interviews. Some publicists, however, are more committed to advancing their clients' interests than to advancing truth, and they work to manipulate journalists into providing coverage that unduly glorifies their clients.

Staging events is a publicity tactic to gain news coverage that a cause would not otherwise attract. Some staged events are obvious hucksterism, such as Evel Knievel's ballyhooed motorcycle leaps across vast canyons in the 1970s and local flagpole-sitting stunts by celebrity disc jockeys. Covering such events is usually part of the softer side of news and, in the spirit of fun and games and diversion, is relatively harmless.

Of more serious concern are staged events about which publicists create a mirage of significance to suck journalists and the public into giving more attention than they deserve. For example, consider:

- The false impression created when hundreds of federal workers are released from work for an hour to see an incumbent's campaign speech outside a government office building.
- The contrived photo opportunity at which people, props and lighting are carefully, even meticulously, arranged to create an image on television.
- Stunts that bring attention to a new product and give it an undeserved boost in the marketplace.

Staged events distort a balanced journalistic portrayal of the world. Worse, they divert attention from truly significant events.

Gatekeeping in News

STUDY PREVIEW   The individual reporter has a lot of independence in determining what to report, but news work is a team effort. No individual acts entirely alone, and there are factors, such as gatekeeping, that affect what ends up on the printed page or over the air.

Gatekeepers' Responsibilities

News dispatches and photographs are subject to changes at many points in the communication chain. At these points, called gates, **gatekeepers** delete, trim, embellish and otherwise try to improve messages.

Just as a reporter exercises judgment in deciding what to report and how to report it, judgment also is at the heart of the gatekeeping process. Hardly any message, except live reporting, reaches its audience in its original form. Along the path from its originator to the eventual audience, a message is subject to all kinds of deletions, additions and changes of emphasis. With large news organizations this process may involve dozens of editors and other persons.

The gatekeeping process affects all news. A public relations practitioner who doesn't tell the whole story is a gatekeeper. A reporter who emphasizes one aspect of an event and neglects others is a gatekeeper. Even live, on-scene television coverage involves gatekeeping because it's a gatekeeper who decides where to point the camera, and that's a decision that affects the type of information that reaches viewers. The C-SPAN network's live, unedited coverage of Congress, for example, never shows members of Congress sleeping or reading newspapers during debate, even though such happens. C-SPAN has accepted rules of the House and Senate to focus only on who is speaking, even if to an empty chamber.

Gatekeeping can be a creative force. Trimming a news story can add potency. A news producer can enhance a reporter's field report with file footage. An editor can call a public relations person for additional detail to illuminate a point in a reporter's story. A newsmagazine's editor can consolidate related stories and add context that makes an important interpretive point.

gatekeeper
Person who decides whether to shorten, drop or change a story en route to the mass audience.

Media People

Matt Drudge

Seeing his 7-Eleven clerking as a dead end, Matt Drudge landed a job at a CBS gift shop in Los Angeles. It was still clerking, but the job somehow seemed nearer his first love: news. When his dad gave him a computer in 1994, Drudge got into chat rooms and posted tidbits about media gossip. Some information he had picked up from trash cans at CBS.

In 1996 he quit the gift shop to devote his time to the Drudge Report, as he called his news web site. Working out of his shabby North Hollywood apartment, Drudge read the trade press and worked the phone for stories. Among his regurgitation were scoops. The biggest came in January 1998: the Lewinsky sex scandal that led to the impeachment of President Bill Clinton.

Drudge, 30 at the time with barely any college, had brought together journalism and the web in a way nobody else had. Single-handedly, he gathered information, packaged it crudely and let 'er rip—no cautious gatekeeping. Readers ignored his sentence fragments, misspellings and syntax errors. They didn't seem to mind his amateurish all-caps, boldfacing and exclamation marks. In mid-1997, when he was probing for details about another

Maverick Journalism. The crudely formatted, gossipy Drudge Report, which broke the Monica Lewinsky scandal, draws as many as 3 million hits a day. It's a one-man operation.

Matt Drudge

Clinton sex scandal before the Lewinsky one blew up, Drudge said he scored 2,600 hits from White House web addresses in one 12-hour period. By 2001 he was typically scoring 3 million hits a day.

To be sure, Drudge's maverick journalism had critics, mostly mainstream journalists who deplored his rush to file, not always checking facts and sometimes getting it wrong. One Clinton aide, whom Drudge accused of spousal abuse, sued for $30 million.

Happy at his old IBM 486, operating alone, Drudge does journalism on his terms. He thrives on being

outside the journalistic fraternity and goes to pains even to look different. His trademark is a cocked-back hat, à la his hero, the 1920s gossip columnist Walter Winchell, whose yellowed clips Drudge read as a kid. And when he travels, he packs in duffel bags.

The Fox television network capitalized on Drudge's post-Lewinsky notoriety with a weekly news show. As the lights rose on the set, the voiceover announcer intoned, "He's the mod muckraker, Internet informer, citizen journalist. Everyone's dying to hear what he'll say next. You know his name. Now, here's Drudge."

Gatekeepers at Work

Most gatekeepers are invisible to the news audience, working behind the scenes and making crucial decisions in near anonymity on how the world will be portrayed in the evening newscast and the next morning's newspaper. Here, slightly updated, is how mass communication scholar Wilbur Schramm explained gatekeeping in 1960: "Suppose we follow a news item, let us say, from India to Indiana. The first gatekeeper is the person who sees an event happen. This person sees the event selectively, noticing some things, not others. The second gatekeeper is the reporter who talks to this 'news source.' Now, of course, we could complicate this picture by giving the reporter a number of news sources to talk to about the same event, but in any case the reporter has to decide which facts to pass along the chain, what to write, what shape and color and importance to give to the event. The reporter gives his message to an editor, who must decide how to edit the story, whether to cut or add or change. Then the message goes to a news service where someone must decide which of many hundreds of items will be picked up and telegraphed to other towns, and how important the story is, and therefore how much space it deserves.

"At a further link in the chain, this story will come to a United States news service and here again an editor must decide what is worth passing on to the American newspapers and broadcasting stations. The chain leads us on to a regional and perhaps a state news service bureau, where the same decisions must be made; always there is more news than can be sent on—which items, and how much of the items, shall be retained and retransmitted? And finally when the item comes to a local newspaper, an editor must go through the same process, deciding which items to print in the paper.

"Out of news stories gathered by tens of thousands of reporters around the world, only a few hundred will pass the gatekeepers along the chains and reach a local newspaper editor, who will be able to pass only a few dozen of those on to the newspaper reader."

Journalism Trends

STUDY PREVIEW   News has taken two divergent paths in content in recent years. Some news organizations have moved into sophisticated, interpretative and investigative reporting. Others have emphasized superficial, tantalizing news.

Exploratory Reporting

Norman Cousins acquired his reputation as a thinker when he edited the magazine *Saturday Review.* A premier journal under Cousins, the magazine tackled issues in depth and with intelligence. A few years later, Cousins said he couldn't find much of that kind of journalism in magazines anymore: "The best magazine articles in the U.S. today are appearing not in magazines but in newspapers." Cousins was taking note of a profound late-20th-century change in the concept of news: **exploratory reporting.** Newspapers and to a lesser extent television were tackling difficult issues that earlier were almost the exclusive provinces of magazines. Cousins especially admired the Los Angeles *Times,* which runs thoroughly researched, thoughtful pieces. It is not unusual for the Los Angeles *Times* to commit weeks, even months, of reporters' time to develop major stories, nor is that unusual at other major newspapers and some smaller ones.

Although U.S. newspapers have never been devoid of in-depth coverage, the thrust through most of their history has been to chronicle events: meetings, speeches, deaths, catastrophes. The emphasis began changing noticeably in the 1960s as it dawned on journalists that chronicling easily identifiable events was insufficient to capture larger, more significant issues and trends.

The failure of event-based reporting became clear when sections of Northern cities were burning in race riots in the late 1960s. Journalists had missed one of the

exploratory reporting
Proactive news-gathering.

Media People

Oriana Fallaci

Of necessity, **Oriana Fallaci** grew up fast. A teenager in Mussolini's Italy, she figured out early whose side she was on. She delivered grenades inside cabbage heads for the antifascist resistance. She had a keen sense of who were the good guys and who the bad. Later, as a journalist, she devised interview techniques to smoke them out. She is one of the foremost journalists of her time.

Both intelligent and hardworking, she learns a whole language to conduct interviews in her sources' native tongue. Sometimes she puts six months into preparing for one of her marathon interviews. She flouts danger. In fact, she was shot twice while covering stories in Mexico. She adapts to whatever the situation to get a story. Although not Muslim, she agreed to wear a Muslim veil, a chador, to interview Iranian leader Ayatollah Khomeini. As an interviewer, she keeps her sights on finding revealing truths about important people through cleverness, disquieting and unexpected questions, and persistence.

Those qualities show in Fallaci's famous interview with Ayatollah Khomeini in his Teheran quarters. In deference she wore the chador, which gave her an opportunity for a question that would so unsettle the ayatollah that she learned things no earlier interviewer had about his temper and his temperament. From her own account: "I was wearing the thing, all seven meters of it,

Oriana Fallaci

pins everywhere, perspiring, and I began to ask him about the chador as a symbol of women's role in Iran." The question penetrated to the core of Khomeini's value system. Off guard, he instantly turned nasty. In a revealing outburst he shouted, "If you don't like the chador, don't wear it, because the chador is for young, proper women!" Insulted, she ripped the veil off: "This is what I do with your stupid medieval rag!" Shocked, the ayatollah shot up and left, with Fallaci calling after him, "Where do you go? Do you go to make pee-pee?" Quick-witted Fallaci's pee-pee afterthought was calculated to elicit further personal revelations, but Khomeini didn't turn around.

Fallaci's detractors see her **caustic interview style** as grand theater. Others cringe at her willingness to insult sources, even to be

rude on issues as sensitive as customs that flow from deeply held religious beliefs. Whatever the criticism, her unconventional approach gives her readers fresh insights into her sources' characters.

Once an interview is under way, Fallaci won't take no for an answer. When Khomeini stomped out, she sat waiting for him to return. Again and again, aides asked her to leave. Finally, Khomeini's son came pleading for her to leave. On his fifth time back, he said Khomeini would see her the next day if she left. By that point, she recalled later, she too needed to pee-pee.

At the appointed hour the next day, Khomeini, faithful to his promise, arrived to continue the interview. And Fallaci, true to her goal, looked him in the eye: "Now Imam, let's start where we left off yesterday. We were talking about my being an indecent woman."

Carl Bernstein and Bob Woodward

Investigative Journalism. Dogged pursuit of meticulous fac- tual detail became a new wrinkle in 20th-century journalism after Washington *Post* reporters Carl Bernstein and Bob Woodward unearthed the Watergate scandal. For months they pursued tips that a break-in at the Democratic Party national headquarters in the Watergate hotel, office and apartment complex in Washington, D.C., had been authorized high in the Republican White House and that the White House then had tried to cover it up. In the end, for the first time in U.S. history, a president, Richard Nixon, resigned.

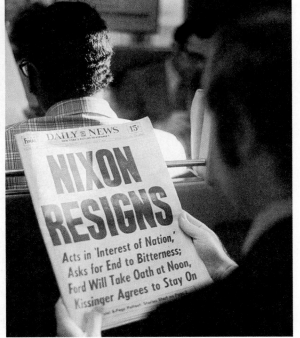

20th century's most significant changes: the northward migration of Southern blacks. Had journalists covered the migration and provided information on the festering social divisions that resulted, there might have been a chance to develop public poli- cies before frustration over racial injustices blew up, with heavy losses of life and property and great disruption.

The superficiality of mere chronicling was underscored in early coverage of the Vietnam war. By focusing on events, journalists missed asking significant questions about the flawed policies until it was too late.

Newspapers expanded significantly beyond a myopic focus on events in the 1970s for three reasons:

- Recognition that old ways of reporting news were not enough.
- Larger reporting staffs that permitted time-consuming enterprise reporting.
- Better-educated reporters and editors, many with graduate degrees.

Newspapers, profitable as never before, were able to hire larger staffs that permitted them to try more labor-intensive, exploratory kinds of journalism. Instead of merely responding to events, newspapers, particularly big ones, began digging for stories. Much of this **investigative journalism** was modeled on the Washington *Post*'s doggedness in covering Watergate, the White House-authorized break-in at Democratic National Headquarters during the 1972 presidential campaign. Twenty years earlier, the **Watergate** break-in scandal probably would not have gone beyond three paragraphs from the police beat. In 1972, however, the persistence of *Post* reporters **Carl Bernstein** and **Bob Woodward** posed so many questions about

Oriana Fallaci
Leading journalistic interviewer.

caustic interview style
Adversarial approach to subjects.

investigative journalism
Seeking stories that would not surface on their own and that subjects would prefer not be told.

Watergate
Reporting of the Nixon adminis- tration scandal.

Carl Bernstein
Washington *Post* reporter who dug up Watergate.

Bob Woodward
Bernstein's colleague in the Watergate revelations.

morality in the White House that eventually President Nixon resigned and 25 aides went to jail.

As late as 1960, many daily newspapers were still hiring reporters without college degrees. By 1970 that had changed, and many newspaper reporters were acquiring advanced degrees and developing specialties. Major newspapers hired reporters with law degrees for special work and encouraged promising reporters to go back to college for graduate work in science, business, medicine and the environment. The result was a new emphasis on proactive reporting in which journalists did not wait for events to happen but went out looking, even digging, for things worth telling.

Soft News

The success of the *National Enquirer,* whose circulation began to skyrocket in the 1960s, was not unnoticed, and when Time-Life, Inc. launched *People* magazine and the New York *Times* launched *Us* magazine, gossipy celebrity news gained a kind of respectability. In this period the newspaper industry began sophisticated research to identify what readers wanted, then fine-tuned the content mix that would improve market penetration. As a result, many dailies added "People" columns. The news services began receiving requests for more offbeat, gee-whiz items of the sensational sort. Newspapers had always run such material, but more is being printed today to appeal to a broader audience. Many newspapers today also carry more consumer-oriented stories, lifestyle tips and entertainment news. Television has shows like "Entertainment Tonight." This is called **soft news.**

Traditionalists decry the space that soft news takes in many newspapers today, but soft news generally has not displaced hard news. Rather, newspapers fit additional hard news, as well as soft news, into larger newspapers. The news hole, the space left after advertisements are put in a newspaper, increased from 19 pages on average in 1970 to 24 pages today.

Identifying Good Journalism

STUDY PREVIEW   Circulation, ratings, hits and other audience measures are indicators of popularity but not necessarily of quality journalism. News consumers are best guided by criteria such as accuracy, balance and fairness.

Audience Dimensions

For decades the sensationalizing *National Enquirer* has been the largest-circulation newspaper in the United States. On ABC radio Paul Harvey's entertaining presentation and oddball items drew the medium's largest news audiences. Audience size, of course, is one measure of success, but it's a measure that misses a qualitative question: Is a news product popular because it's good?

For 4 million people the *National Enquirer* is good. They keep buying it, every week. Among daily newspapers, the *Wall Street Journal* and *USA Today* are the national circulation leaders—but only with less than half of the *Enquirer*'s circulation. Are they not as good? Is the PBS "Newshour With Jim Lehrer" not as good as the "NBC Nightly News" with Tom Brokaw because its audience is smaller?

soft news
Geared to satisfying audience's information wants, not needs.

The quantitative measures of circulation, reach, penetration, visits and hits while useful to advertisers, aren't much help for individuals in choosing news sources that meet their needs.

Evaluative Criteria

Rather than following the pack, discerning people develop their own criteria for evaluating news sources. There are no cookie-cutter formulas. One size doesn't fit all. Among criteria to consider:

ACCURACY, BALANCE AND FAIRNESS. Deadline pressures, at the heart of news reporting, can work against accuracy—and balance and fairness take time. Some errors are forgivable, like those that occur in reporting an airliner hijacking, with all the attendant confusion. Unforgivable are doctored quotes, out-of-context data and slanted editing. The triad of accuracy, balance and fairness comprise a reasonable expectation for news media performance.

INTERPRETATION. Are journalists trying to help the audience make sense of what's happening? This interpretive aspect of journalism is tricky because a journalist's individual values are an underlying factor that, by their nature, aren't shared by everyone. The challenge for news consumers is to identify journalists whose judgment they trust to sort through information and present it in a meaningful context.

ORIGINAL CONTENT. News organizations package information from many sources. So much information is available from so many places that some newsrooms, especially in network radio, do nothing more than packaging. They hardly ever send a reporter out on the street, let alone to a war zone. A news organization deserves points for generating its own on-scene reporting. For example, when the Milosevic dictatorship ended in Yugoslavia in 2000, CNN kept two reporters in the country to track details. The network could have taken a less costly approach, drawing instead on news agency reports, pool video and government news releases. Going that route would have meant a dependence on sources whose reliability and motivation can be subpar.

Media Future: News

At its best, journalism is a truth-seeking and truth-telling media activity that's unfettered by anything except serving the public good. In reality, however, journalists don't operate in a pristine environment. Political and social pressures have always existed. Advertising has been a dynamic in the mix since the penny press period.

Today a great issue is whether journalism can insulate itself from the agendas of the giant corporations that own most journalistic enterprises when interests conflict. Classic cases: How does ABC cover Disney? How does NBC cover General Electric? A 2000 Pew Research Center survey found that almost one-third of journalists believe that their newsrooms ignore stories that might conflict with the financial interests of their owners or advertisers.

The issue of *editorial independence* is essential to truth-seeking, truth-telling and inspiring audience trust.

AOL Time Warner has devised a policy that might serve as an industry model. Norman Pearlstine, editor-in-chief of the company's magazines, has a mandate to "provide unbiased coverage of the myriad interests of advertisers and of Time Warner itself." The mandate has been signed by the parent company's board of directors and chief executive. Says Pearlstine, "If readers think there are stories that we're keeping from them or that there are stories that we're pulling our punches on, we're out of business. If you're going to have a magazine, it's clear to me that you have to have the highest level of editorial independence."

Is this a road that other media conglomerates will take with their news operations?

chapter wrap-up

Journalism is an art, not a science. Judgments, rather than formulas, determine which events and issues are reported and how—and no two journalists approach any story exactly the same way. This leaves the whole process of gathering and telling news subject to second-guessing and criticism. Journalists ask themselves all the time whether there are ways to do a better job. All journalists can do is try to find truth and to relate it accurately. Even then, the complexity of modern news-gathering—which involves many people, each with an opportunity to change or even kill a story—includes dozens of points at which inaccuracy and imprecision can creep into a story that started out well.

Questions for Review

1. What contemporary news practices are rooted in the colonial, partisan, penny press and yellow press periods of U.S. history?
2. What personal values do journalists bring to their work? Does this affect what is reported and how?
3. What variables beyond journalists' control affect news?
4. What pressures from outside the media affect news reporting?
5. What responsibilities do journalists have as gatekeepers?
6. Is there a contradiction between the two contemporary journalistic trends of exploratory reporting and soft news?

Questions for Critical Thinking

1. The 19-year-old son of the premier of a troubled Central American country in which the CIA has deep involvement died, perhaps of a drug overdose, aboard a Northwest Airlines plane en route from Tokyo to Singapore. On the plane was a young female country-western singer, his frequent companion in recent weeks. The plane was a Boeing 747 manufactured in Washington state. Northwest's corporate headquarters is in Minnesota. The death occurred at 4 a.m. Eastern time. Consider the six elements of news—proximity, prominence, timeliness, consequence, currency and drama—and discuss how this event might be reported on morning television newscasts in Miami, Minneapolis, Nashville, Seattle and the District of Columbia. How about in Managua? Singapore? Tokyo? Rome? Istanbul? Johannesburg? What if the victim were an ordinary college student? What if the death occurred a week ago?
2. Explain news judgment.
3. How do the news hole and news flow affect what is reported in the news media?
4. *Time* and *Newsweek* carry cover stories on the same subject one week. Does this indicate that executives of the magazine have conspired, or is it more likely to be caused by what Leon Sigal calls *the consensible nature of news*?
5. How does the nature of news provide ammunition to conservatives to criticize the news media as leftist promoters of change?

6. Discuss whether the U.S. news media reflect mainstream American values. Do you see evidence in your news media of an underlying belief that democracy, capitalism, rural small-town life, individualism and moderation are virtues?

7. Do you feel that the mass media revel in disorder? Consider Herbert Gans' view that the media cover disorder from the perspective of identifying ways to restore order.

8. If a college president calls a news conference and makes a major announcement, who are the gatekeepers who determine how the announcement is covered in the campus newspaper?

Keeping Up to Date

Among publications that keep current on journalistic issues are *Columbia Journalism Review, Quill, American Journalism Review,* and *Editor & Publisher.*

Bridging the gap between scholarly and professional work is *Newspaper Research Journal.*

Whenever inventor Dean Kamen allowed advanced peeks at his Segway HT transporter, the reception was enthusiastic. But peeks were carefully calculated, using proven publicity and promotion techniques to stir interest in the product.

11

Public Relations

In college Dean Kamen tinkered with a drug-infusion device that led to the first portable insulin pump. Then came the portable dialysis machine. Then heart stents. The most marveling Kamen invention was his six-wheel IBOT wheelchair that climbed stairs and could cruise through sand and gravel.

In no time Kamen became a multimillionaire and had 200 engineers working for him in a research plant alongside the Merrimack River in New Hampshire. In January 2001, when Kamen was 49, the question suddenly was what was going on there. A section of a forthcoming book about Kamen somehow had found its way onto a web magazine. The article talked about a still-in-development Kamen product, code-named IT, that would, the article claimed, transform human existence.

A media frenzy of speculation followed about what the Merrimack wonder machine might be. Hundreds of articles appeared, settling eventually on the fact that IT was a transportation device of some sort. Even the foul-mouth characters on "South Park" got in the act. With adroit timing, Kamen let some high-visibility people peek. Apple computer mastermind Steve Jobs was quoted, inaccurately he says, that cities would be rebuilt around the Kamen device. No matter where the misquote originated, Jobs was impressed, like everyone else who had an advance look.

Late in 2001, Kamen let *Time* magazine have an exclusive three-month advance look for a major story that he insisted be embargoed until December. Kamen admitted that the polished product hype might have been overdone: "It won't beam you to Mars or turn lead into gold," he told *Time*, then mocked himself: "So sue me."

What *Time* unveiled in great detail was a self-propelled, gyroscope-righted scooter that would carry the brand name Segway. The media leaks were a carefully plotted roll-out to pique public attention. When people saw their first Segway it would be, Kamen hoped, as momentous as when people of an earlier generation saw their first airplane. The difference with Segway was that the excitement was orchestrated through specialized public relations techniques that have become increasingly sophisticated.

Publicity campaigns are part of grand tradition of public relations going back to Edward Bernays, who called himself the Father of Public Relations. In the 1920s Bernays boasted how he could "engineer" public opinion. Today, publicity remains a core function of public relations, although, as you will learn in this chapter, public relations also involves much more.

In late 2001 Kamen began producing an $8,000 Segway model for industrial and commercial customers, including the U.S. Postal Service for mail delivery and Amazon.com for warehouse chores. With production at 40,000 a month he couldn't keep up with demand. Scarcity contributed to more curiosity and built up demand for the eventual $3,000 consumer model.

Dean Kamen

Meanwhile, the publicity machine rolled on. There were stories about Kamen's talks with the U.S. Army to adapt Segway for combat. Police purchasing agents received spiels on the efficiency of the two-wheel superscooters. Kamen invited more corporate and government leaders in for trials. Testimonials from the likes of Andy Grove of Intel and Jeff Bezos of Amazon.com, sincere and simultaneously giddy, made their way into print and onto the air.

Importance of Public Relations

STUDY PREVIEW   Public relations is a persuasive communication tool that people can use to motivate other people and institutions to help them achieve their goals.

Defining Public Relations

Edward Bernays, the public relations pioneer, lamented how loosely the term **public relations** is used. To illustrate his concern, Bernays told about a young woman who approached him for career advice. He asked her what she did for a living. "I'm in public relations," she said. He pressed her for details, and she explained that she handed out circulars in Harvard Square. Bernays was dismayed at how casually people regard the work of public relations. There are receptionists and secretaries who list public relations on their résumés. To some people, public relations is glad-handing, back-slapping and smiling prettily to make people feel good. Public relations, however, goes far beyond good interpersonal skills. A useful definition is that

public relations
A management tool to establish beneficial relationships.

276

Media Timeline

Evolution of Public Relations

1859 Charles Darwin advanced survival-of-the-fittest theory, which led to social Darwinism.

1880s Public became dissatisfied with unconscionable business practices justified with social Darwinism.

1906 Ivy Lee began the first public relations agency.

1917 George Creel headed a federal agency that generated support for World War I.

1927 Arthur Page became the first corporate public relations vice president.

1930s Paul Garrett created the term *enlightened self-interest* at General Motors.

1942 Elmer Davis headed a federal agency that generated support for World War II.

1965 Public Relations Society of America created the accreditation system.

1970s Herb Schmertz pioneered adversarial public relations at Mobil Oil.

1987 PRSA adopted an ethics code.

public relations is a management tool for leaders in business, government and other institutions to establish beneficial *relationships* with other institutions and groups. Four steps are necessary for public relations to accomplish its goals:

IDENTIFYING EXISTING RELATIONSHIPS. In modern society institutions have many relationships. A college, for example, has relationships with its students, its faculty, its staff, its alumni, its benefactors, the neighborhood, the community, the legislature, other colleges, accreditors of its programs, perhaps unions. The list could go on and on. Each of these constituencies is called a public—hence the term *public relations*.

EVALUATE THE RELATIONSHIPS. Through research, the public relations practitioner studies these relationships to determine how well they are working. This evaluation is an ongoing process. A college may have excellent relations with the legislature one year and win major appropriations, but after a scandal related to the president's budget the next year, legislators may be downright unfriendly.

DESIGN POLICIES TO IMPROVE THE RELATIONSHIPS. The job of public relations people is to recommend policies to top management to make these relationships work better, not only for the organization but also for the partners in each relationship. **Paul Garrett,** a pioneer in corporate relations, found that General Motors was not seen in friendly terms during the Great Depression, which put the giant auto maker at risk with many publics, including its own employees. GM, he advised, needed new policies to seem neighborly—rather than as a far-removed, impersonal, monolithic industrial giant.

IMPLEMENT THE POLICIES. Garrett used the term **enlightened self-interest** for his series of policies intended to downsize GM in the eyes of many of the company's publics. Garrett set up municipal programs in towns with GM plants and grants for schools and scholarships for employees' children. General Motors benefited from a revised image, and in the spirit of enlightened self-interest, so did GM employees, their children and their communities.

Public relations is not a mass medium itself, but PR often uses the media as tools to accomplish its goals. To announce GM's initiatives to change its image in the

Paul Garrett
Devised the notion of enlightened self-interest.

enlightened self-interest
Mutually beneficial public relations.

Media People

Paul Garrett

At one of the most precarious times in U.S. history, the Great Depression, Paul Garrett led public relations in new directions to win public support. Amid worries that people—many hungry, all distressed—would see huge corporations as scapegoats and perhaps upend capitalism, Garrett had an unprecedented challenge as General Motors' public relations chief. How precarious was the situation? Sit-down strikes were occurring at GM plants. Discontent was bubbling throughout the country.

Garrett, in the first generation of public relations people who had learned their craft from the government's Creel Committee in World War I, immediately sought to minimize the image of General Motors as some sort of monolithic giant that, being big and distant, was an especially easy target for hate.

To head off problems, Garrett introduced a public strategy called *en-lightened self-interest.* It was in GM's self-interest, he argued, to touch the lives of people in personal ways, such as with grants for local schools and scholarships for employees' children. General Motors, of course, nurtured publicity about these corporate good deeds.

Garrett summed it up this way: "The challenge that faces us is to shake off our lethargy and through public relations make the American plan of industry stick. For unless the contributions of the system are explained to consumers in terms of their own interest, the system itself will not stand against the storm of fallacies that rides the air."

Garrett also worked on GM's image at a macro level, aiming for consumers in general to think well of the company. A GM caravan, called the Parade of Progress, traveled from coast to coast in 1936 with a message that new technologies would facilitate progress and social change. In the same spirit, prominent radio announcer Lowell Thomas narrated a feature film, *Previews of Science,* that cast business, big business in particular, in heroic terms. In short, the genius of corporate science and initiative was creating a better tomorrow.

The National Association of Manufacturers caught Garrett's spirit. Garrett worked with the association to tie the public impression of big corporations into warm, albeit fuzzy, notions about Americanism. At a 1939 meeting, the association's public relations division, with Garrett on board, said that its job was to "link free enterprise in the public consciousness with free speech, free press and free religion as integral parts of democracy."

Public relations had become widely embraced as a way to channel the thinking of the country.

1930s, Paul Garrett issued news releases that he hoped newspapers, magazines and radio stations would pick up. The number of people in most of the publics with which public relations practitioners need to communicate is so large that it can be reached only through the mass media. The influence of public relations on the news media is extensive. Half of the news in many newspapers originates with formal statements or news releases from organizations that want something in the paper. It is the same with radio and television.

Public Relations in a Democracy

Misconceptions about public relations include the idea that it is a one-way street for institutions and individuals to communicate to the public. Actually, the good practice of public relations seeks two-way communication between and among all the people and institutions concerned with an issue.

A task force established by the **Public Relations Society of America** to explore the stature and role of the profession concluded that public relations has the potential to improve the functioning of democracy by encouraging the exchange of information and ideas on public issues. The task force made these points:

- Public relations is a means for the public to have its desires and interests felt by the institutions in our society. It interprets and speaks for the public to organizations that otherwise might be unresponsive, and it speaks for those organizations to the public.
- Public relations is a means to achieve mutual adjustments between institutions and groups, establishing smoother relationships that benefit the public.
- Public relations is a safety valve for freedom. By providing means of working out accommodations, it makes arbitrary action or coercion less likely.
- Public relations is an essential element in the communication system that enables individuals to be informed on many aspects of subjects that affect their lives.
- Public relations people can help to activate the social conscience of the organizations for which they work.

Origins of Public Relations

STUDY PREVIEW   Many big companies found themselves in disfavor in the late 1800s for ignoring the public good to make profits. Feeling misunderstood, some moguls of industry turned to Ivy Lee, the founder of modern public relations, for counsel on gaining public support.

media online

History of Public Relations: Interesting discussion of public relations activities from ancient Egypt to the late 1900s. www.snybuf.edu/~ronsmith/rdshistory.htm

Moguls in Trouble

Nobody would be tempted to think of **William Henry Vanderbilt** as being very good at public relations. In 1882 it was Vanderbilt, president of the New York Central Railroad, who said, "The public be damned," when asked about the effect of changing train schedules. Vanderbilt's utterance so infuriated people that it became a banner in the populist crusade against robber barons and tycoons in the late 1800s. Under populist pressure, state governments set up agencies to regulate railroads. Then the national government established the **Interstate Commerce Commission** to control freight and passenger rates. Government began insisting on safety standards. Labor unions formed in the industries with the worst working conditions, safety records and pay. Journalists added pressure with muckraking exposés on excesses in the railroad, coal and oil trusts; on meat-packing industry frauds; and on patent medicines.

The leaders of industry were slow to recognize the effect of populist objections on their practices. They were comfortable with **social Darwinism,** an adaptation of **Charles Darwin's** survival-of-the-fittest theory. In fact, they thought themselves forward-thinking in applying Darwin's theory to business and social issues. It had been only a few decades earlier, in 1859, that Darwin had laid out his biological theory in *On the Origin of Species by Means of Natural Selection.* To cushion the harshness of social Darwinism, many tycoons espoused paternalism toward those whose "fitness" had not brought them fortune and power. No matter how carefully put, paternalism seemed arrogant to the "less fit."

George Baer, a railroad president, epitomized both social Darwinism and paternalism in commenting on a labor strike: "The rights and interests of the laboring man will be protected and cared for not by labor agitators but by the Christian men to whom God in His infinite wisdom has given the control of the property interests of the country." Baer was quoted widely, further fueling sentiment against big business.

William Henry Vanderbilt
Embodied the bad corporate images of the 1880s, 1890s with "The public be damned."

Interstate Commerce Commission
First federal agency to rein in excessive business practices, 1890.

social Darwinism
Application of Darwin's survival-of-the-fittest theory to society.

Charles Darwin
Devised survival-of-the-fittest theory.

George Baer
Epitomized offensive corporate paternalism in the 1890s.

Ludlow Massacre. Colorado militiamen opened fire during a 1914 mine labor dispute and killed women and children. Overnight, John D. Rockefeller Jr. became the object of public hatred. It was a Rockefeller company that owned the mine, and even in New York, where Rockefeller lived, there were rallies asking for his head. Public relations pioneer Ivy Lee advised Rockefeller to tour the Ludlow area as soon as tempers cooled to show his sincere concern and to begin work on a labor contract to meet the concerns of miners. Rockefeller ended up a popular character in the Colorado mining camps.

Ivy Lee

Baer may have been sincere, but his position was read as a cover for excessive business practices by barons who assumed superiority to everyone else.

Meanwhile, social Darwinism came under attack as circuitous reasoning: Economic success accomplished by abusive practices could be used to justify further abusive practices, which would lead to further success. Social Darwinism was a dog-eat-dog outlook that hardly jibed with democratic ideals, especially not as described in the preamble to the U.S. Constitution, which sought to "promote the general welfare, and secure the blessings of liberty" for everyone—not for only the chosen "fittest." Into these tensions at the turn of the century came public relations pioneer Ivy Lee.

The Ideas of Ivy Lee

Coal mine operators, like the railroad magnates, were held in the public's contempt at the turn of the century. Obsessed with profits, caring little about public sentiment or even the well being of their employees, the mine operators were vulnerable in the new populist wave. Mine workers organized, and 150,000 in Pennsylvania went out on strike in 1902, shutting down the anthracite industry and disrupting coal-dependent industries, including the railroads. The mine operators snubbed reporters, which probably contributed to a pro-union slant in many news stories and worsened the operators' public image. Not until six months into the strike, when President Theodore Roosevelt threatened to take over the mines with Army troops, did the operators settle.

Shaken finally by Roosevelt's threat and recognizing Roosevelt's responsiveness to public opinion, the mine operators began reconsidering how they went about their business. In 1906, with another strike looming, one operator heard about **Ivy Lee,** a young publicist in New York who had new ideas about winning public support. He was hired. In a turnabout in press relations, Lee issued a news release that announced, "The anthracite coal operators, realizing the general public interest in conditions in the mining regions, have arranged to supply the press with all possible information." Then followed a series of releases with information attributed to the mine operators by name—the same people who earlier had preferred anonymity and refused all interview requests. There were no more secret strike strategy meetings. When operators planned a meeting, reporters covering the impending strike were informed. Although reporters were not admitted to the meetings, summaries of the proceedings were given to them immediately afterward. This relative openness eased long-standing hostility toward the operators, and a strike was averted.

Lee's success with the mine operators began a career that rewrote the rules on how corporations deal with their various publics. Among his accomplishments were:

CONVERTING INDUSTRY TOWARD OPENNESS. Railroads had notoriously secretive policies not only about their business practices but even about accidents as well. When the **Pennsylvania Railroad** sought Ivy Lee's counsel, he advised against suppressing news—especially on things that inevitably would leak out anyway. When a train jumped the rails near Gap, Pennsylvania, Lee arranged for a special car to take reporters to the scene and even take pictures. The Pennsylvania line was applauded in the press for the openness, and coverage of the railroad, which had been negative for years, began changing. A "bad press" continued plaguing other railroads that persisted in their secretive tradition.

TURNING NEGATIVE NEWS INTO POSITIVE NEWS. When the U.S. Senate proposed investigating International Harvester for monopolistic practices, Lee advised the giant farm implement manufacturer against reflexive obstructionism and silence. A statement went out announcing that the company, confident in its business practices, not only welcomed but also would facilitate an investigation. Then began a campaign that pointed out International Harvester's beneficence toward its employees. The campaign also emphasized other upbeat information about the company.

PUTTING CORPORATE EXECUTIVES ON DISPLAY. In 1914, when workers at a Colorado mine went on strike, company guards fired machine guns and killed several men. More battling followed, during which two women and 11 children were killed. It was called the **Ludlow Massacre,** and **John D. Rockefeller Jr.,** the chief mine owner, was pilloried for what had happened. Rockefeller was an easy target. Like his father, widely despised for the earlier Standard Oil monopolistic practices, John Jr. tried to keep himself out of the spotlight, but suddenly mobs were protesting at his mansion in New York and calling out, "Shoot him down like a dog." Rockefeller asked Ivy Lee what he should do. Lee began whipping up articles about Rockefeller's human side, his family and his generosity. Then, on Lee's advice, Rockefeller announced that he would visit Colorado to see conditions himself. He spent two weeks talking with miners at work and in their homes and meeting their families. It was a news story that reporters could not resist, and it unveiled Rockefeller as a human being, not a far-removed, callous captain of industry. A myth-shattering episode occurred one evening when Rockefeller, after a brief address to miners and their wives, suggested that the floor be cleared for a dance. Before it was all over, John D. Rockefeller Jr. had danced with almost every miner's wife, and the news stories about the evening did a great deal to mitigate antagonism and distrust toward Rockefeller. Back in New York, with Lee's

Ivy Lee
Laid out fundamentals of public relations.

Pennsylvania Railroad
Took Ivy Lee's advice, which favorably changed railroad's approach to public relations.

Ludlow Massacre
Colorado tragedy that Ivy Lee converted into a public relations victory.

John D. Rockefeller Jr.
Ivy client who had been the target of public hatred.

help, Rockefeller put together a proposal for a grievance procedure, which he asked the Colorado miners to approve. It was ratified overwhelmingly.

AVOIDING PUFFERY AND FLUFF.   Ivy Lee came on the scene at a time when many organizations were making extravagant claims about themselves and their products. Circus promoter **P. T. Barnum** made this kind of **puffery** a fine art in the late 1800s, and he had many imitators. It was an age of *puffed-up* advertising claims and fluffy rhetoric. Lee noted, however, that people soon saw through hyperbolic boasts and lost faith in those who made them. In launching his public relations agency in 1906, he vowed to be accurate in everything he said and to provide whatever verification anyone requested. This became part of the creed of good practice in public relations, and it remains so today.

Public Relations on a New Scale

The potential of public relations to rally support for a cause was demonstrated on a gigantic scale during World War I and again during World War II.

WORLD WAR I.   In 1917 President Woodrow Wilson, concerned about widespread antiwar sentiment, asked **George Creel** to head a new government agency whose job was to make the war popular. The Committee on Public Relations, better known as the Creel Committee, cranked out news releases, magazine pieces, posters, even movies. A list of 75,000 local speakers was put together to talk nationwide at school programs, church groups and civic organizations about making the world safe for democracy. More than 15,000 committee articles were printed. Never before had public relations been attempted on such a scale—and it worked. World War I became a popular cause even to the point of inspiring people to buy Liberty Bonds, putting up their own money to finance the war outside the usual taxation apparatus.

WORLD WAR II.   When World War II began, an agency akin to the Creel Committee was formed. Veteran journalist **Elmer Davis** was put in charge. The new Office of War Information was public relations on a bigger scale than ever before.

The Creel and Davis committees employed hundreds of people. Davis had 250 employees handling news releases alone. These staff members, mostly young, carried new lessons about public relations into the private sector after the war. These were the people who shaped corporate public relations as we know it today.

Lobbyist-Journalist Balance

The rationale for public relations is that everybody, including corporations, should have access to the best counsel available. The best public relations people serve their clients well and honorably, but exceptions abound. A statehouse reporter for the Detroit *News,* Jim Mitzelfeld, heard that lobbyists were planning a junket for members of the legislature. Camera in hand, Mitzelfeld showed up at the retreat at Gulf Shores, Alabama, and took pictures of a powerful lobbyist rubbing sunscreen on a legislator's shoulders. "The quintessential lube job," Mitzelfeld told the media watchdog magazine *American Journalism Review.*

Lobbying, as an ethical public relations function, is to offer advice to clients to advance their causes before policy-making bodies such as state legislatures. But lobbying can go too far, as at Gulf Shores. How many inappropriate attempts at influ-

P. T. Barnum
Known for exaggerated promotion.

puffery
Inflated claims.

George Creel
Demonstrated public relations works on a mammoth scale; World War I.

Elmer Davis
Led Office of War Information; World War II.

George Creel

War Popular. Contrary to myth, World War I did not begin as a popular cause with Americans. In fact, there were antidraft riots in many cities. This prompted President Woodrow Wilson to ask journalist George Creel to launch a major campaign to persuade Americans that the war was important to make the world safe for democracy. Within months, Americans were financing much of the war voluntarily by buying government bonds. This poster was only one aspect of Creel's work, which demonstrated that public relations principles could be applied on a massive scale.

ence occur? We'll never know, but indicators are that this is a growing phenomenon in the back halls and fairways of capital cities. Why? Not enough Jim Mitzelfelds are covering state government to catch "lube jobs." The number of statehouse reporters has fallen precipitously, while the number of lobbyists has grown dramatically.

How many lobbyists are there? Extrapolations from a 1990 Associated Press survey of registered state capital lobbyists would put the number at 120,000-plus today. The figure is probably low because loose enforcement of registration requirements misses lobbyists who never quite get around to registering. At the same time the amount that lobbyists spend is increasing exponentially. Charles Layton and Mary Walton, writing in *American Journalism*

Lobbying. Even in sparsely populated South Dakota, lobbyists are in great number when the Legislature is in session. Nationwide the number of lobbyists in state capitols was 120,000 in a 1990 attempt at a count.

Review, said that statehouse lobbying grew from $15 million nationwide in 1986 to $51 million in 1997.

Are journalists like Jim Mitzelfeld looking over the shoulders of lobbyists and legislators to keep things honest? Less and less. Under conglomerate pressure to cut costs, many newspapers have trimmed their statehouse staffs. At Mitzelfeld's Detroit *News,* the full-time staff in Lansing has dropped from six to four. The Detroit *Free Press* and the Lansing *State Journal* have cut full-time staff from three to two. Nationwide, 27 states have fewer reporters covering state government since the early 1990s. The Knight Ridder chain, as an example, cut statehouse coverage 16 percent at its papers.

An important checks-and-balances system is disappearing as the number of lobbyists increases and that of watchdog journalists declines.

Structure of Public Relations

STUDY PREVIEW   In developing sound policies, corporations and other institutions depend on public relations experts who are sensitive to the implications of policy on the public consciousness. This makes public relations a vital management function. Besides a role in policymaking, public relations people play key roles in carrying out institutional policy.

Policy Role of Public Relations

When giant AT&T needed somebody to take over public relations in 1927, the president of the company went to magazine editor **Arthur Page** and offered him a vice presidency. Before accepting, Page laid out several conditions. One was that he have a voice in AT&T policy. Page was hardly on an ego trip. He had seen too many corporations that regarded their public relations arm merely as an executor of policy. Page considered PR itself as a management function. To be effective as vice president for public relations, Page knew that he must contribute to the making of high-level corporate decisions as well as executing them.

Today, experts on public relations agree with Arthur Page's concept: When institutions are making policy, they need to consider the effects on their many publics. That can be done best when the person in charge of public relations, ideally at the vice presidential level, is intimately involved in decision-making. The public relations executive advises the rest of the institution's leaders on public perceptions and the effects that policy options might have on perceptions. Also, the public relations vice president is in a better position to implement the institution's policy for having been a part of developing it.

How Public Relations Is Organized

No two institutions are organized in precisely the same way. At General Motors 200 people work in public relations. In smaller organizations PR may be one of several hats worn by a single person. Except in the smallest operations, the public relations department usually has three functional areas of responsibility.

EXTERNAL RELATIONS.   **External public relations** involves communication with groups and people outside the organization, including customers, dealers,

Arthur Page
Established the role of public relations as a top management tool.

external public relations
Gearing messages to outside organizations, constituencies, individuals.

suppliers and community leaders. The external relations unit is usually responsible for encouraging employees to participate in civic activities. Other responsibilities include arranging promotional activities like exhibits, trade shows, conferences and tours.

Public relations people also lobby government agencies and legislators on behalf of their organization, keep the organization abreast of government regulations and legislation and coordinate relations with political candidates. This may include fundraising for candidates and coordinating political action committees.

In hospitals and nonprofit organizations a public relations function may include recruiting and scheduling volunteer workers.

INTERNAL RELATIONS. **Internal public relations** involves developing optimal relations with employees, managers, unions, shareholders and other internal groups. In-house newsletters, magazines and brochures are important media for communicating with organizations' internal audiences.

MEDIA RELATIONS. Communication with large groups of people outside an organization is practicable only through the mass media. An organization's coordinator of **media relations** responds to news media queries, arranges news conferences and issues news releases. These coordinators coach executives for news interviews and sometimes serve as their organization's spokesperson.

Public Relations Agencies

Even though many organizations have their own public relations staff, they may go to **public relations agencies** for help on specific projects or problems. In the United States today, hundreds of companies specialize in public relations counsel and related services. It is a big business. Income at global PR agencies like Burson-Marsteller runs about $200 million a year.

The biggest agencies offer a full range of services on a global scale. Hill & Knowlton has offices in Cleveland, its original home; Dallas; Frankfurt; Geneva; London; Los Angeles; New York, now its headquarters; Paris; Rome; Seattle; and Washington, D.C. The agency will take on projects anywhere in the world, either on its own or by working with local agencies.

Besides full-service agencies, there are specialized public relations companies, which focus on a narrow range of services. For example, clipping services cut out and provide newspaper and magazine articles and radio and television items of interest to clients. Among specialized agencies are those that focus exclusively on political campaigns. Others coach corporate executives for news interviews. Others coordinate trade shows.

Some agencies bill clients only for services rendered. Others charge clients just to be on call. Hill & Knowlton, for example, has a minimum $5,000-a-month retainer fee. Agency expenses for specific projects are billed in addition. Staff time usually is charged at an hourly rate that covers the agency's overhead and allows a profit margin. Other expenses are usually billed with a 15 to 17 percent markup.

Public Relations Services

STUDY PREVIEW Public relations deals with publicity and promotion, but it also involves less visible activities. These include lobbying, fund-raising and crisis management. Public relations is distinct from advertising.

---

media online

Public Relations Society of America:
www.prsa.org

Canadian Public Relations Society:
www.cprs.ca

---

internal public relations
Gearing messages to inside groups, constituencies, individuals.

media relations
Using mass media to convey messages.

public relations agencies
Companies that provide public relations services.

Media Databank

Major Public Relations Agencies

These are the largest U.S.-based public relations agencies. Because some agencies are part of larger companies that don't break out data on their subordinate units, some data here are estimates.

Company	Income Worldwide	Employees Worldwide
Burson-Marsteller	$204 million	2,100
Shandick	160 million	1,800
Hill & Knowlton	149 million	1,200
Edelman	80 million	800
Omnicon	66 million	1,000
Fleishman-Hillard	59 million	600
Ketchum	45 million	500
Rowland	44 million	500
Ogilvy Adams & Rinehart	36 million	300
Manning, Selvage & Lee	31 million	300

Activities Beyond Publicity

Full-service public relations agencies provide a wide range of services built on two of the cornerstones of the business: **publicity** and **promotion**. These agencies are ready to conduct media campaigns to rally support for a cause, create an image or turn a problem into an asset. Publicity and promotion, however, are only the most visible services offered by public relations agencies. Others include:

LOBBYING.   Every state capital has hundreds of public relations practitioners whose specialty is representing their clients to legislative bodies and government agencies. In North Dakota, hardly a populous state, more than 300 people are registered as lobbyists in the capital city of Bismarck.

Lobbying has been called a "growth industry." The number of registered lobbyists in Washington, D.C., has grown from 3,400 in 1976 to almost 10,000 today. In addition, there are an estimated 20,000 other people in the nation's capital who have slipped through registration requirements but who nonetheless ply the halls of government to plead their clients' interests.

In one sense, lobbyists are expediters. They know local traditions and customs, and they know who is in a position to affect policy. Lobbyists advise their clients, which include trade associations, corporations, public interest groups and regulated utilities and industries, on how to achieve their goals by working with legislators and government regulators. Many lobbyists call themselves "government relations specialists."

POLITICAL COMMUNICATION.   Every capital has political consultants whose work is mostly advising candidates for public office in **political communication**. Services include campaign management, survey research, publicity, media relations and image consulting. Political consultants also work on elections, referendums, recalls and other public policy issues.

IMAGE CONSULTING.   **Image consulting** has been a growing specialized branch of public relations since the first energy crisis in the 1970s. Oil companies, realizing

publicity
Brings public attention to something.

promotion
Promoting a cause, idea.

lobbying
Influencing public policy, usually legislation or regulations.

political communication
Advising candidates, groups on public policy issues, usually in elections.

image consulting
Coaching individuals for media contacts.

that their side of the story was not getting across, turned to image consultants to groom corporate spokespersons, often chief executives, to meet reporters one on one and go on talk shows. The groomers did a brisk business, and it paid off in countering the stories and rumors that were blaming the oil companies for skyrocketing fuel prices.

FINANCIAL PUBLIC RELATIONS. Financial public relations dates to the 1920s and 1930s, when the U.S. Securities and Exchange Commission cracked down on abuses in the financial industry. Regulations on promoting sales of securities are complex. It is the job of people in financial PR to know not only the principles of public relations but also the complex regulations governing the promotion of securities in corporate mergers, acquisitions, new issues and stock splits.

FUND-RAISING. Some public relations people specialize in fund-raising and membership drives. Many colleges, for example, have their own staffs to perform these functions. Others look to fund-raising firms to manage capital drives. Such an agency employs a variety of techniques, from mass mailings to telephone soliciting, and charges a percentage of the amount raised.

CONTINGENCY PLANNING. Many organizations rely on public relations people to design programs to address problems that can be expected to occur, known as **contingency planning.** Airlines, for example, need detailed plans for handling inevitable plane crashes—situations requiring quick, appropriate responses under tremendous pressure. When a crisis occurs, an organization can turn to public relations people for advice on dealing with it. Some agencies specialize in **crisis management,** which involves picking up the pieces either when a contingency plan fails or when there was no plan to deal with a crisis.

POLLING. Public-opinion sampling is essential in many public relations projects. Full-service agencies can either conduct surveys themselves or contract with companies that specialize in surveying.

EVENTS COORDINATION. Many public relations people are involved in coordinating a broad range of events, including product announcements, news conferences and convention planning. Some in-house public relations departments and agencies have their own artistic and audio-visual production talent to produce brochures, tapes and other promotional materials. Other agencies contract for these services.

Public Relations and Advertising

Both public relations and advertising involve persuasion through the mass media, but most of the similarities end there.

MANAGEMENT FUNCTION. Public relations people help to shape an organization's policy. This is a management activity, ideally with the organization's chief public relations person offering counsel to other key policy-makers at the vice-presidential level. **Advertising,** in contrast, is not a management function. The work of advertising is much narrower. It focuses on developing persuasive messages, mostly to sell products or services, after all the management decisions have been made.

contingency planning
Developing programs in advance of an unscheduled but anticipated event.

crisis management
Helping a client through an emergency.

advertising
Unlike public relations, advertising seeks to sell a product or service.

MEASURING SUCCESS.   Public relations "sells" points of view and images. These are intangibles and therefore are hard to measure. In advertising, success is measurable with tangibles, such as sales, that can be calculated from the bottom line.

CONTROL OF MESSAGES.   When an organization decides that it needs a persuasive campaign, there is a choice between public relations and advertising. One advantage of advertising is that the organization controls the message. By buying space or time in the mass media, an organization has the final say on the content of its advertising messages. In public relations, by contrast, an organization tries to influence the media to tell its story a certain way, but the message that actually goes out is up to the media. For example, a news reporter may lean heavily on a public relations person for information about an organization, but the reporter also may gather information from other sources. In the end, it is the reporter who writes the story. The upside of this is that the message, coming from a journalist, has a credibility with the mass audience that advertisements don't. Advertisements are patently self-serving. The downside of leaving it to the media to create the messages that reach the audience is surrendering control over the messages that go to the public.

Integrated Marketing

For many persuasive campaigns, organizations use both public relations and advertising. Increasingly, public relations and advertising people find themselves working together. This is especially true in corporations that have adopted **integrated marketing communication,** which attempts to coordinate advertising as a marketing tool with promotion and publicity of the sort that public relations experts can provide. Several major advertising agencies, aware of their clients' shift to integrated marketing, have acquired or established public relations subsidiaries to provide a wider range of services under their roof.

It is this overlap that has prompted some advertising agencies to move more into public relations. The WWP Group of London, a global advertising agency, has acquired both Hill & Knowlton, the third-largest public relations company in the United States, and the Ogilvy PR Group, the ninth largest. The Young & Rubicam advertising agency has three public relations subsidiaries: Burson-Marsteller, the largest; Cohn & Wolf, the 13th; and Creswell, Munsell, Fultz & Zirbel, the 50th. These are giant enterprises that reflect the conglomeration and globalization of both advertising and public relations.

To describe IMC, media critic James Ledbetter suggests thinking of the old Charlie the Tuna ads, in which a cartoon fish made you chuckle and identify with the product—and established a brand name. That's not good enough for IMC. "By contrast," Ledbetter says, "IMC encourages tuna buyers to think about all aspects of the product. If polls find that consumers are worried about dolphins caught in tuna nets, then you might stick a big 'Dolphin Safe' label on the tins and set up a web site featuring interviews with tuna fishermen." The new wave of IMC, according to one of its primary texts, is "respectful, not patronizing; dialogue-seeking, not monologuic; responsive, not formula-driven. It speaks to the highest point of common interest—not the lowest common denominator."

As advertising has shifted toward IMC, ad agencies have acquired or created public relations divisions or subsidiaries to provide a wide range of the services under one roof.

integrated marketing communication
Comprehensive program that links public relations, advertising.

James Burke

Product-Tampering Crisis. When cyanide-laced Tylenol capsules killed seven people in Chicago, the manufacturer, Johnson & Johnson, responded quickly. Company President James Burke immediately pulled the product off retailers' shelves and ordered company publicists to set up a press center to answer news media inquiries as fully as possible. Burke's action and candor helped restore the public's shaken confidence in Tylenol, and the product resumed its significant market share after the crisis ended. It turned out that it had been a crazy person outside Johnson & Johnson's production and distribution system who had contaminated the capsules rather than a manufacturing lapse.

Public relations and advertising crossovers are hardly new. One area of traditional overlap is **institutional advertising,** which involves producing ads to promote an image rather than a product. The fuzzy, feel-good ads of agricultural conglomerate Archer Daniels Midland, which pepper Sunday morning network television, are typical.

Media Relations

STUDY PREVIEW   Public relations people generally favor candor in working with the news media. Even so, some organizations opt to stonewall journalistic inquiries. An emerging school of thought in public relations is to challenge negative news coverage aggressively and publicly.

Open Media Relations

The common wisdom among public relations people today is to be open and candid with the mass media. It is a principle that dates to Ivy Lee, and case studies abound to confirm its effectiveness. A classic case study on this point is the Tylenol crisis.

Johnson & Johnson had spent many years and millions of dollars to inspire public confidence in its painkiller Tylenol. By 1982 the product was the leader in a crowded field of headache remedies with 36 percent of the market. Then disaster struck. Seven people in Chicago died after taking Tylenol capsules laced with cyanide. James Burke, president of Johnson & Johnson, and Lawrence Foster, vice president for public relations, moved quickly. Within hours, Johnson & Johnson:

- Halted the manufacture and distribution of Tylenol.
- Removed Tylenol products from retailers' shelves.
- Launched a massive advertising campaign requesting people to exchange Tylenol capsules for a safe replacement.

institutional advertising
Paid space and time to promote institution's image, position.

- Summoned 50 public relations employees from Johnson & Johnson and its subsidiary companies to staff a press center to answer media and consumer questions forthrightly.
- Ordered an internal company investigation of the Tylenol manufacturing and distribution process.
- Promised full cooperation with government investigators.
- Ordered the development of tamper-proof packaging for the reintroduction of Tylenol products after the contamination problem was resolved.

Investigators determined within days that an urban terrorist had poisoned the capsules. Although the news media exonerated Johnson & Johnson of negligence, the company nonetheless had a tremendous problem: how to restore public confidence in Tylenol. Many former Tylenol users were reluctant to take a chance, and the Tylenol share of the analgesic market dropped to 6 percent.

To address the problem, Johnson & Johnson called in the Burson-Marsteller public relations agency. Burson-Marsteller recommended a media campaign to capitalize on the high marks the news media had given the company for openness during the crisis. Mailgrams went out inviting journalists to a 30-city video teleconference to hear James Burke announce the reintroduction of the product. Six hundred reporters turned out, and Johnson & Johnson officials took their questions live.

To stir even wider attention, 7,500 **media kits** had been sent to newsrooms the day before the teleconference. The kits included a news release and a bevy of supporting materials: photographs, charts and background information.

The resulting news coverage was extensive. On average, newspapers carried 32 column inches of copy on the announcement. Network television and radio as well as local stations also afforded heavy coverage. Meanwhile, Johnson & Johnson executives, who had attended a workshop on how to make favorable television appearances, made themselves available as guests on the network morning shows and talk shows such as "Donahue" and "Nightline." At the same time Johnson & Johnson distributed 80 million free coupons to encourage people to buy Tylenol again.

The massive media-based public relations campaign worked. Within a year Tylenol had regained 80 percent of its former market share. Today, in an increasingly crowded analgesic field, Tylenol is again the market leader with annual sales of $670 million, compared with $520 million before the cyanide crisis.

Proactive Media Relations

Although public relations campaigns cannot control what the media say, public relations people can help to shape how news media report issues by taking the initiative. In the Tylenol crisis, for example, Johnson & Johnson reacted quickly and decisively and took control of disseminating information, which, coupled with full disclosure, headed off false rumors that could have caused further damage. This is a good example of **proactive media relations.**

media kit
A packet provided to news reporters to tell the story in an advantageous way.

proactive media relations
Taking initiative to release information.

PROACTIVE CRISIS RESPONSES. A principle in crisis management is to seize leadership on the story. This involves anticipating what journalists will want to know and providing it to them before they even have time to formulate their questions. Ivy Lee did this time and again, and Johnson & Johnson did it in 1982.

For successful crisis management, public relations people need strong ongoing relationships with an organization's top officials. Otherwise, when a crisis strikes, they likely will have difficulty rounding up the kind of breaking information they need to deal effectively with the news media. During the 1991 Persian Gulf war, Pentagon spokesperson **Pete Williams** received high marks as a public relations person for shaping news coverage of the conflict. Williams did this by tapping his close working relationships with Defense Secretary Dick Cheney and the Joint Chiefs of Staff for information favorable to the war effort. At regular news briefings, sometimes several a day, Williams provided so much grist for the journalistic mill that reporters were overwhelmed in putting it together for stories, which reduced the time available for them to go after stories on their own. The war was reported largely as the Pentagon wanted.

ONGOING MEDIA RELATIONSHIPS.   Good media relations cannot be forged in the fire of a crisis. Organizations that survive a crisis generally have a history of solid media relations. Their public relations staff people know reporters, editors and news directors on a first-name basis. They avoid hyping news releases on routine matters, and they work hard at earning the trust of journalists.

Many public relations people, in fact, are seasoned journalists themselves, and they understand how journalists go about their work. It is their journalistic background that made them attractive candidates for their PR jobs. Pete Williams, for example, was a television news reporter in Wyoming before making a midcareer shift to join Dick Cheney's staff in Washington when Cheney was first elected to Congress from Wyoming.

SOUND OPERATING PRINCIPLES.   An underlying strength that helped to see Johnson & Johnson through the Tylenol crisis was the company's credo. The credo was a written vow that Johnson & Johnson's first responsibility was to "those who use our products and services." The credo, which had been promoted in-house for years, said, "Every time a business hires, builds, sells or buys, it is acting *for the people* as well as *for itself,* and it must be prepared to accept full responsibility."

With such a sound operating principle, Johnson & Johnson's crisis response was, in some respects, almost reflexive. Going silent, for example, would have run counter to the principles that Johnson & Johnson people had accepted as part of their corporate culture for years.

Ambivalence in Media Relations

Despite the advantages of open media relations, there are companies that choose not to embrace that approach. The business magazine *Fortune* has listed these major corporations as notorious for not even returning phone calls from journalists:

- Amerada Hess, the huge crude oil and natural gas company.
- Winn-Dixie, the Southern supermarket chain.
- Texas Instruments, the semiconductor company.

Some corporations take a middle ground, currying media coverage selectively. This is an example of **ambivalent media relations.** Giant IBM, which receives 30,000 media queries a year, frets that news coverage would underscore its sheer size and invite federal antitrust scrutiny. IBM turns away questions on many issues, including the company's long-term planning. The corporation's PR chief, Seth McCormick, spurns Ivy Lee's maxim that corporate executives should be "on display." In an

Karen Hughes. A trusted aide to President George W. Bush applied public relations principles to an unprecedented global scale in 2001. Hughes headed a joint U.S. project called Coalition Information Centers, to build popular support in Muslim-dominated parts of the world for the U.S.-led war against terrorism. The organization booked guests on television and radio shows with strong Muslim audiences in north Africa and south Asia. This included the influential Al-Jazeera cable news network out of Qatar. The project recognized that public sympathy for terrorist leader Osama bin Laden, as well as deep-rooted antipathy toward the United States, could undermine the political and military coalition that the United States had assembled to battle terrorism.

media online
Advertorials: Examples of advertorials from the California Egg Commission. **www.eggcom.com/industry/ advertorials**

Pete Williams
Tilted news coverage by overwhelming the media with information during the Persian Gulf war.

ambivalent media relations
Mix of proactive, reactive and inactive media contacts.

Mobil Advertorial. Many public relations practitioners seek to avoid confrontation, but Herb Schmertz of Mobil bought space in newspapers and magazines beginning in the 1970s to lay out his company's positions on controversial issues and even to be confrontational. Schmertz tackled the news media when he felt Mobil had not received a fair shake in coverage. These position statements are called "advertorials" because they are in space purchased as advertising and their content is like an editorial.

Herb Schmertz

interview, McCormick told *Fortune:* "We control what is said about the company through the sparsity of heads for the outside world to talk to. We like it that way."

Procter & Gamble is another major U.S. company that generally is tight-lipped about how it conducts its business, with the notable exception of product promotions. Another notable exception was Procter & Gamble's full-scale public relations campaign in the 1980s to squelch persistent rumors that its corporate symbol—the moon and stars—had roots in Satanism.

Adversarial Public Relations

Public relations took on aggressive, even feisty tactics when Mobil Oil decided in the 1970s not to take media criticism lightly any more. **Herb Schmertz,** vice president for Mobil's public affairs, charted a new course by:

- Filing formal complaints with news organizations when coverage was unfair in the company's view.
- Taking Mobil's case directly to the general public with paid advertising, **advertorials,** as they are called, a splicing of the words "advertising" and "editorial," that explained the company's views.
- Sending corporate representatives on media tours to spread Mobil's side to as many constituencies as possible.

Schmertz's energetic counterattacks, an example of **adversarial public relations,** were a departure from conventional wisdom in public relations, which was to let criticism go unanswered or, at most, to complain privately to executives of news organizations that negative coverage is unwarranted. The conventional wisdom was that a public response would only bring more attention to the negative coverage.

In abandoning passivity, Mobil was adapting what sports fans call the Red Auerbach technique. Auerbach, the legendary coach of the Boston Celtics, was known for

Herb Schmertz
Pioneered advertorials.

advertorials
Paid advertisements that state an editorial position.

adversarial public relations
Attacking critics openly.

criticizing referees. He realized he would never get a ref to change a call, but he believed that refs would be less inclined to make questionable calls against the Celtics in the future if they knew that Auerbach would jump all over them. Mobil President Rawleigh Warner Jr. explained the new Mobil policy this way: "People know that if they take a swipe at us, we will fight back."

Schmertz employed the full range of PR tools in 1974 when ABC aired a television documentary that raised critical questions about the U.S. oil industry. Mobil objected first to ABC and then fired off a formal complaint to the National News Council, a volunteer media watchdog group. Mobil claimed 32 inaccuracies and instances of unfairness and requested that the council investigate. Mobil also issued an unusually lengthy news release, quoting from the documentary and offering point-by-point rebuttals.

Six Mobil executives were given a crash course on giving good interviews and sent out to meet the news media. In two years the executives and other Mobil representatives appeared on 365 television and 211 radio shows and talked with 80 newspaper reporters. Schmertz encouraged them to take the offensive. To counter the ABC impression that the oil industry still engaged in the bad practices of its past, Schmertz told executives to stress that such information was outdated. "Put the shoe on the other foot," he said, advising the Mobil executives to say the impression left by the ABC documentary was "comparable to Mobil's producing a documentary about today's television industry and pointing to a 1941 FCC decree requiring RCA to rid itself of one of its networks as evidence of a current conspiracy."

Advertorials were part of Mobil's initiatives. Under Schmertz, as much as $6 million a year went into newspaper and magazine ads explaining the company's position. Mobil also began producing its own television programs on energy issues and providing them free to stations. The programs had a journalistic tone, and many stations ran them as if they were actual documentaries rather than part of Mobil's media campaign.

The jury is still out on whether Schmertz's aggressive sparring is good policy. Most organizations continue to follow the traditional thinking that taking on the media only generates more attention on the original bad news. On the other hand, Schmertz's approach has been tried by some major corporations. Bechtel, Illinois Power and Kaiser Aluminum all have called for independent investigations of stories that reflected badly on them.

Another adversarial approach, though not recommended by most public relations people, is for an offended organization to sever relations with the source of unfavorable news—an **information boycott**. In 1954, in a spectacular pout, General Motors cut off contact with *Wall Street Journal* reporters and withdrew advertising from the newspaper. This approach carries great risks:

- By going silent, an organization loses avenues for conveying its message to mass audiences.
- An organization that yanks advertising to punish detractors is perceived negatively for coercively wielding its economic might.
- An organization that quits advertising in an effective advertising medium will lose sales.

A boycott differs from Schmertz's adversarial approach in an important respect. Schmertz responds to negative news by contributing to the exchange of information and ideas, which is positive in a democratic society. An information boycott, on the other hand, restricts the flow of information. Today, GM's policy has returned to the conventional wisdom of not arguing with anyone who buys paper by the ton and ink

information boycott
Severing ties with news media.

by the barrel—with the exception of its suit against NBC for faking the explosion of a GMC truck.

Professionalization

STUDY PREVIEW   Public relations has a tarnished image that stems from shortsighted promotion and whitewashing techniques of the late 1800s. Although some dubious practices continue, PR leaders are working to improve standards.

A Tarnished Image

Unsavory elements in the heritage of public relations remain a heavy burden. P. T. Barnum, whose name became synonymous with hype, attracted crowds to his stunts and shows in the late 1800s with extravagant promises. Sad to say, some promoters still use Barnum's tactics. The claims for snake oils and elixirs from Barnum's era live on in commercials for pain relievers and cold remedies. The early response of tycoons to muckraking attacks, before Ivy Lee came along, was **whitewashing**—covering up the abuses but not correcting them. It is no wonder that the term *PR* is sometimes used derisively. To say something is "all PR" means that it lacks substance. Of people whose apparent positive qualities are a mere façade, it may be said that they have "good PR."

Although journalists rely heavily on public relations people for information, many journalists look at PR practitioners with suspicion. Not uncommon among seasoned journalists are utterances such as "I've never met a PR person I couldn't distrust." Such cynicism flows partly from the journalists' self-image as unfettered truth-seekers whose only obligation is serving their audiences' needs. PR people, on the other hand, are seen as obligated to their employers, whose interests do not always dovetail with the public good. Behind their backs, PR people are called "flaks," a takeoff on the World War II slang for antiaircraft bursts intended to stop enemy bombers. PR **flakkers,** as journalists use the term, interfere with journalistic truth-seeking by putting forth slanted, self-serving information that is not necessarily the whole story.

The journalism-PR tension is exacerbated by a common newsroom view that PR people try to get free news hole space for their messages rather than buying airtime and column inches. This view might seem strange, considering that 50 to 90 percent of all news stories either originate with, or contain information supplied by, PR people. It is also strange considering that many PR people are former news reporters and editors. No matter how uncomfortable PR people and journalists are as bedfellows, they are bedfellows nonetheless.

Some public relations people have tried to leapfrog the negative baggage attached to the term *PR* by abandoning it. The U.S. military shucked *PR* and tried **public information,** but it found itself still dogged by the same distrust that surrounded "public relations." The military then tried *public affairs*, but that was no solution either. Many organizations have tried *communication* as a way around the problem. Common labels today include the military's current *public affairs* offices and businesses' *corporate communication* departments.

Standards and Certification

The Public Relations Society of America, which has grown to 12,000 members, has a different approach: improving the quality of public relations work, whatever

whitewashing
Covering up.

flakkers
Derisive word for public relations people.

public information
One alternative word for public relations; others are public affairs, corporate communication.

Media People

Edward Bernays

After graduation from college in 1912, Edward Bernays tried press agentry. He was good at it, landing free publicity for whoever would hire him. Soon his bosses included famous tenor Enrico Caruso and actor Otis Skinner. Bernays felt, however, that his success was tainted by the disdain in which press agents were held in general. He also saw far greater potential for affecting public opinion than his fellow press agents did. From Bernays' discomfort and vision was born the concept of modern public relations. His 1923 book *Crystallizing Public Opinion* outlined a new craft he called public relations.

Bernays saw good public relations as counsel to clients. He called the public relations practitioner a "special pleader." The concept was modeled partly on the long-established lawyer-client relationship in which the lawyer, or counselor, suggests courses of action. Because of his seminal role in defining what public relations is, Bernays sometimes is called the "Father of PR," although some people say the honor should be shared with Ivy Lee.

No matter, there is no question of Bernays' ongoing contributions. He

Edward Bernays. Integrity was important to public relations pioneer Edward Bernays. When he was asked by agents of fascist dictators Francisco Franco and Adolf Hitler to improve their images in the United States, he said no. "I wouldn't do for money what I wouldn't do without money," Bernays said.

taught the first course in public relations in 1923 at New York University. Bernays encouraged firm methodology in public relations, a notion that was captured in the title of a book he edited in 1955: *The Engineering of Consent.* He long advocated the professionalization of the field, which laid the groundwork for the accreditation of the sort the Public Relations Society of America has developed.

Throughout his career Bernays stressed that public relations people need a strong sense of responsibility. In one reflective essay, he wrote, "Public relations practiced as a profession is an art applied to a science in which the public interest and not pecuniary motivation is the primary consideration. The engineering of consent in this sense assumes a constructive social role. Regrettably, public relations, like other professions, can be abused and used for anti-social purposes. I have tried to make the profession socially responsible as well as economically viable."

Bernays became the Grand Old Man of public relations, still attending PRSA and other professional meetings past his 100th birthday. He died in 1993 at age 102.

the label. In 1951 the association adopted a code of professional standards. In a further professionalization step, the PRSA has established a certification process. Those who meet the criteria and pass exams are allowed to place **APR,** which stands for accredited public relations professional, after their names. The criteria are:

- Being recommended by an already accredited PRSA member.
- Five years of professional experience.
- Passing an eight-hour written examination on public relations principles, techniques, history and ethics.
- Passing an oral exam conducted by three professionals.

APR
Indicates PRSA accreditation.

International Association of Business Communicators
Professional public relations organization.

Public Relations Student Society of America
Student public relations organization.

The process is rigorous. Typically, a third of those who attempt the examination fail the first time. Once earned, certification needs to be renewed through continuing education, and the right to use "APR" can be taken away if a member violates the PRSA code. About 3,800 PRSA members hold APR certification.

The PRSA set of professional standards, intended to encourage a high level of practice, says a member shall:

- Deal fairly with clients or employees, past, present or potential; with fellow practitioners; and with the general public.
- Conduct his or her professional life in accord with the public interest.
- Adhere to truth and accuracy and to generally accepted standards of good taste.
- Not engage in any practice that tends to corrupt the integrity of channels of communication or the process of government.
- Not intentionally communicate false or misleading information.

The PRSA is not alone in encouraging the practice of public relations at a high level. The **International Association of Business Communicators**, with 125 chapters, also keeps dialogue going on professional issues with seminars and conferences. Some professional groups are highly specialized, like the Library Public Relations Council, the Bank Marketing Association and the Religious PR Council. The International Public Relations Association, with members in 60 countries, sponsors the World Congress of Public Relations every third year. The student arm of PRSA, the **Public Relations Student Society of America**, works through 145 campus chapters at improving standards.

chapter wrap-up

When Ivy Lee hung up a shingle in New York for a new publicity agency in 1906, he wanted to distance himself from the huckstering that marked most publicity at the time. To do that, Lee promised to deal only in legitimate news about the agency's clients and no fluff. He invited journalists to pursue more information about the agency's clients. He also vowed to be honest and accurate. Those principles remain the bulwark of good public relations practice today.

Questions for Review

1. What is public relations? How is public relations connected to the mass media?
2. Why did big business become interested in the techniques and principles of public relations beginning in the late 1800s?
3. How is public relations a management tool?
4. What is the range of activities in which public relations people are involved?
5. What kind of relationship do most people strive to have with the mass media?
6. Why does public relations have a bad image? What are public relations professionals doing about it?

Questions for Critical Thinking

1. When Ivy Lee accepted the Pennsylvania Railroad as a client in 1906, he saw the job as "interpreting the Pennsylvania Railroad to the public and interpreting the public to the Pennsylvania Railroad." Compare Lee's point with Arthur Page's view of public relations as a management function.
2. How are public relations practitioners trying to overcome the complaints from journalists that they are flakkers interfering with an unfettered pursuit of truth?
3. What was the contribution of the Committee on Public Information, usually called the Creel Committee, to public relations after World War I?

4. How do public relations agencies turn profits?
5. When does an institution with its own in-house public relations operation need to hire a PR agency?
6. Explain the concept of enlightened self-interest.
7. How did the confluence of the following three phenomena at the turn of the century contribute to the emergence of modern public relations?
   - The related concepts of social Darwinism, a social theory; laissez-faire, a government philosophy; and paternalism, a practice of business.
   - Muckraking, which attacked prevalent abuses of the public interest.
   - Advertising, which had grown since the 1830s as a way to reach great numbers of people.
8. Showman P. T. Barnum epitomized 19th-century press agentry with extravagant claims, such as promoting the midget Tom Thumb as a Civil War general. To attract crowds to a tour by an unknown European soprano, Jenny Lind, Barnum labeled her "the Swedish Nightingale." Would such promotional methods work today? Keep in mind that Barnum, explaining his methods, once said, "There's a sucker born every minute."

Keeping Up to Date

The trade journal *O'Dwyer's PR Services* tracks the industry on a monthly basis.

Other sources of ongoing information are *Public Relations Journal, Public Relations Quarterly* and *Public Relations Review.*

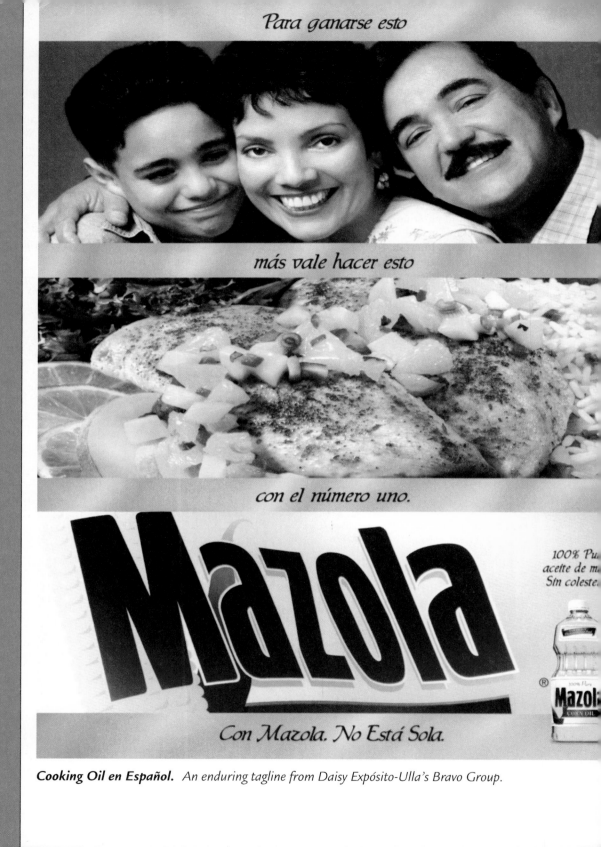

Para ganarse esto

más vale hacer esto

con el número uno.

Mazola

100% Pu
aceite de m
Sin coleste

Con Mazola. No Está Sola.

Cooking Oil en Español. *An enduring tagline from Daisy Expósito-Ulla's Bravo Group.*

12

Advertising

What could be more fitting than Daisy Expósito-Ulla heading the Bravo Group, the preeminent advertising agency aiming at the U.S. Hispanic market? She's Latina. When she was 11, her family fled Cuba for Spain, then moved to New York.

In college she began hanging around the studios where Dick Cavett, Merv Griffin and Johnny Carson taped their shows. She interned at the Public Broadcasting System. There, in 1981, she heard that Young and Rubicam, a premier advertising agency, was looking for someone to help pitch Chef Boyardee to Latinos. She had developed a liking for living in two cultures: her Hispanic roots and her adopted North America. Y&R seemed a good fit.

Expósito was on the ground floor of Y&R's Bravo Group, which evolved into a stand-alone unit. One after another, Bravo created winning campaigns. Bravo's Mazola tagline, "Con Mazola, No Esté Sola," became a catch phrase in Latino culture.

Daisy Expósito-Ulla became chief creative officer and president in 1990. In 2000, in a sign of recognition of her role in the industry, she was elected president of the Association of Hispanic Advertising Agencies.

Expósito-Ulla recognizes that U.S. Hispanics are in cultures as diverse as Miami and southern California. But, she says, a bond transcends the local flavors. She sees a growing sense of empowerment drawing the segments together.

How about assimilation? Not like the Germans, Poles and Italians, she answers. Earlier immigrants were cut off by an ocean, but a quick motor trip or a cheap airline ticket can take Latinos to the old country for a weekend.

Rather than assimilation, she sees acculturation, even a retro-acculturation, that bodes well for Hispanic advertising's future. As Expósito-Ulla explained it to *Advertising Age,* "Many second- or third-generation Hispanics may not speak Spanish perfectly. But they are very much Hispanic from a cultural standpoint: The food, the way they live, the customs—they're all there. They're very connected to their roots. As a result, we now have the process of retro-acculturation. You will find that many people who were told by their parents that they had to learn English to succeed are now parents themselves. And guess what? They're teaching their children Spanish. That doesn't mean you're less of an American. You can be both."

Daisy Expósito-Ulla

In this chapter you will see that insights into mass audiences, as Expósito-Ulla has into the U.S. Hispanic market, are what drives advertising that succeeds.

Importance of Advertising

STUDY PREVIEW   Advertising is vital in a consumer economy. Without it people would have a hard time even knowing what products and services are available. Advertising, in fact, is essential to a prosperous society. Advertising also is the financial basis of important contemporary mass media.

Consumer Economies

Advertising is a major component of modern economies. In the United States the best estimates are that advertisers spend about 2 percent of the gross domestic product to promote their wares. When the nation's production of goods and services is up, so is advertising spending. When production falters, as it did in the early 1990s, many manufacturers, distributors and retailers pull back their advertising expenditures.

The essential role of advertising in a modern consumer economy is obvious if you think about how people decide what to buy. If a shoe manufacturer were unable to tout the virtues of its footwear by advertising in the mass media, people would have a hard time learning about the product, let alone knowing whether it is what they want.

Advertising and Prosperity

Advertising's phenomenal continuing growth has been a product of a plentiful society. In a poor society with a shortage of goods, people line up for necessities like food and clothing. Advertising has no role and serves no purpose when survival is the question. With prosperity, however, people have not only discretionary income but also a choice of ways to spend it. Advertising is the vehicle that provides information and rationales to help them decide how to enjoy their prosperity.

Besides being a product of economic prosperity, advertising contributes to prosperity. By dangling desirable commodities and services before mass audiences, ad-

Media Abroad

Russia: Advertising Meltdown

The correlation of advertising and prosperity was confirmed when the Russian economy nose-dived in 1998. Multinational companies that had been establishing markets in Russia backed off. Russia suddenly wasn't an emerging consumer economy anymore. Out-of-control inflation left people with no discretionary income.

Said Michael Madel, regional president for the J. Walter Thompson ad agency, "A lot of shelves are empty or thinly stocked. If there's no product out there, it doesn't make sense to keep advertising."

Reporters Chris Rivituso and Laurel Wentz, writing in the trade journal *Advertising Age,* said that 1999 advertising spending would be off 50 percent—down from the already-deteriorating 1998 numbers. The Publicis agency cut its Russia staff from 40 to three. McCann Erickson went from 91 to 60. At the Leo Burnett agency, two major U.S. clients, Philip Morris and Procter & Gamble, suspended virtually all advertising.

vertising can inspire people to greater individual productivity so that they can have more income to buy the things that are advertised.

Advertising also can introduce efficiency into the economy by allowing comparison shopping without in-person inspections of all the alternatives. Efficiencies also can result when advertising alerts consumers to superior and less costly products and services, which displace outdated, outmoded and inefficient offerings.

Said Howard Morgens when he was president of Procter & Gamble, "Advertising is the most effective and efficient way to sell to the consumer. If we should ever find better methods of selling our type of products to the consumer, we'll leave advertising and turn to these other methods." Veteran advertising executive David Ogilvy made the point this way: "Advertising is still the cheapest form of selling. It would cost you $25,000 to have salesmen call on a thousand homes. A television commercial can do it for $4.69." McGraw-Hill, which publishes trade magazines, has offered research that a salesperson's typical call costs $178, a letter $6.63, and a phone call $6.35. For 17 cents, says McGraw-Hill, an advertiser can reach a prospect through advertising. Although advertising does not close a sale for all products, it introduces products and makes the salesperson's job easier and quicker.

Advertising and Democracy

Advertising first took off as a modern phenomenon in the United States, which has given rise to a theory that advertising and democracy are connected. This theory notes that Americans, early in their history as a democracy, were required by their political system to hold individual opinions. They looked for information so that they could evaluate their leaders and vote on public policy. This emphasis on individuality and reason paved the way for advertising: Just as Americans looked to the mass media for information on political matters, they also came to look to the media for information on buying decisions.

In authoritarian countries, by contrast, people tend to look to strong personal leaders, not reason, for ideas to embrace. This, according to the theory, diminishes the demand for information in these nondemocracies, including the kind of information provided by advertising.

Media Databank

Largest Advertisers

The top 100 U.S. advertisers pushed their spending to a record $83.9 billion in 2001, 7.6 percent more than the year before. The data, compiled by the trade journal *Advertising Age,* do not reflect spending declines resulting from the implosion of the dot-com industry in 2001. Dot-coms had been big advertising spenders, but not many were in the Top 100. These are the largest national advertisers:

General Motors	$3.9 billion
Phillip Morris	2.6 billion
Procter & Gamble	2.4 billion
Ford	2.3 billion
Pfizer	2.3 billion
Pepsi	2.1 billion
Daimler-Chrysler	2.0 billion
AOL Time Warner	1.8 billion
Disney	1.8 billion
Verizon	1.6 billion

Advertising has another important role in democratic societies in generating most of the operating revenue for newspapers, magazines, television and radio. Without advertising, many of the media on which people rely for information, for entertainment and for the exchange of ideas on public issues would not exist as we know them.

Origins of Advertising

STUDY PREVIEW   Advertising is the product of great forces that have shaped modern society, beginning with Gutenberg's movable type, which made mass-produced messages possible. Without the mass media there would be no vehicle to carry advertisements to mass audiences. Advertising also is a product of the democratic experience; of the Industrial Revolution and its spin-offs, including vast transportation networks and mass markets; and of continuing economic growth.

Stepchild of Technology

Advertising is not a mass medium, but it relies on media to carry its messages. **Johannes Gutenberg**'s movable type, which permitted mass production of the printed word, made mass-produced advertising possible. First came flyers, then advertisements as newspapers and magazines were introduced. In the 1800s, when technology created high-speed presses that could produce enough copies for larger audiences, advertisers used them to expand markets. With the introduction of radio, advertisers learned how to use electronic communication. Then came television.

Flyers were the first form of printed advertising. The British printer **William Caxton** issued the first printed advertisement in 1468 to promote one of his books. In America publisher **John Campbell** of the Boston *News-Letter* ran the first advertisement in 1704, a notice from somebody wanting to sell an estate on Long Island. Colonial newspapers listed cargo arriving from Europe and invited readers to come, look and buy.

Johannes Gutenberg
Progenitor of advertising media.

William Caxton
Printed the first advertisement.

John Campbell
Published the first ad in the British colonies.

Media Timeline

Development of Advertising

1468 William Caxton promoted a book with the first printed advertisement.

1704 Joseph Campbell included advertisements in the Boston *News-Letter*.

1833 Benjamin Day created the New York *Sun* as combination news and advertising vehicle.

1869 Wayland Ayer opened the first advertising agency, Philadelphia.

1890s Brand names emerged as an advertising technique.

1903 New York Legislature barred unauthorized commercial exploitation.

1910 Edward Bok of *Ladies' Home Journal* established a magazine advertising code.

1914 Congress created the Federal Trade Commission to combat unfair advertising.

1929 NBC established a code of acceptable advertising.

1942 Media industries created a predecessor to the Ad Council.

1950s Ernest Dichter pioneered motivational research.

1950s David Ogilvy devised brand imaging technique.

1950s Jack Trout devised positioning technique.

1957 James Vicary claimed success for subliminal advertising.

1960s Rosser Reeves devised unique selling proposition technique.

Industrial Revolution

The genius of **Benjamin Day**'s New York *Sun,* in 1833 the first penny newspaper, was that it recognized and exploited so many changes spawned by the Industrial Revolution. Steam-powered presses made large press runs possible. Factories drew great numbers of people to jobs within geographically small areas to which newspapers could be distributed quickly. The jobs also drew immigrants who were eager to learn—from newspapers as well as other sources—about their adopted country. Industrialization, coupled with the labor union movement, created unprecedented wealth, with laborers gaining a share of the new prosperity. A consumer economy was emerging, although it was primitive by today's standards.

A key to the success of Day's *Sun* was that, at a penny a copy, it was affordable for almost everyone. Of course, Day's production expenses exceeded a penny a copy. Just as the commercial media do today, Day looked to advertisers to pick up the slack. As Day wrote in his first issue, "The object of this paper is to lay before the public, at a price within the means of everyone, all the news of the day, and at the same time afford an advantageous medium for advertising." Day and imitator penny press publishers sought larger and larger circulations, knowing that merchants would see the value in buying space to reach so much purchasing power.

National advertising took root in the 1840s as railroads, another creation of the Industrial Revolution, spawned new networks for mass distribution of manufactured goods. National brands developed, and their producers looked to magazines, also delivered by rail, to promote sales. By 1869 the rail network linked the Atlantic and Pacific coasts.

Pioneer Agencies

By 1869 most merchants recognized the value of advertising, but they grumbled about the time it took away from their other work. In that grumbling, a young Philadelphia man sensed opportunity. **Wayland Ayer,** age 20, speculated that merchants,

Benjamin Day
His penny newspaper brought advertising to new level.

Wayland Ayer
Founded the first ad agency.

creative director
Key person in ad campaigns.

account executives
Agency reps to clients.

media buyers
Decide where to place ads.

and even national manufacturers, would welcome a service company to help them create advertisements and place them in publications. Ayer feared, however, that his idea might not be taken seriously by potential clients because of his youth and inexperience. So when Wayland Ayer opened a shop, he borrowed his father's name for the shingle. The father was never part of the business, but the agency's name, N. W. Ayer & Son, gave young Ayer access to potential clients, and the first advertising agency was born. The Ayer agency not only created ads but also offered the array of services that agencies still offer clients today:

- Counsel on selling products and services.
- Design services, that is, actually creating advertisements and campaigns.
- Expertise on placing advertisements in advantageous media.

Advertising Agencies

STUDY PREVIEW   Central in modern advertising are the agencies that create and place ads on behalf of their clients. These agencies are generally funded by the media in which they place ads. In effect, this makes agency services free to advertisers. Other compensation systems are also emerging.

Agency Structure

Full-service advertising agencies conduct market research for their clients, design and produce advertisements and choose the media in which the advertisement will run. The 500 leading U.S. agencies employ 120,000 people worldwide. In the United States they employ about 73,000. The responsibilities of people who work at advertising agencies fall into these broad categories:

CREATIVITY.   This category includes copywriters, graphics experts and layout people. These creative people generally report to **creative directors,** art directors and copy supervisors.

LIAISON.   Most of these people are **account executives,** who work with clients. Account executives are responsible for understanding clients' needs, communicating those needs to the creative staff and going back to clients with the creative staff's ideas.

BUYING.   Agency employees called **media buyers** determine the most effective media in which to place ads and then place them.

RESEARCH.   Agency research staffs generate information on target consumer groups, data that can guide the creative and media staffs.

Many agencies also employ technicians and producers who turn ideas into camera-ready proofs, color plates, videotape and film, audio cartridges and web-based ads, although a lot of production work is contracted to specialty companies. Besides full-service agencies, there are creative boutiques, which specialize in preparing messages; media buying houses, which recommend strategy on placing ads; and other narrowly focused agencies.

Recount Pizza. Knowing that people order lots of pizza during television football games, Pizza Hut's ad agency, BBDO, scrambled to capitalize on the huge audience following the recounts after the 2000 presidential election. To promote the new Insider pizza, the narrator suggested being part of history: "Someday you can tell your grandkids you were there when Florida decided the next President by voting for Bush—no Gore . . . no, no, Bush . . . no, Gore . . . Well, at least you can tell them you tried the Insider pizza."

Agency Compensation

Advertising agencies generally earn 15 percent of what their clients spend to buy space and time. An agency that can land a mega-account, like Procter & Gamble, which spends $2.6 billion a year, can realize $450 million in revenue. That isn't all gravy, however. Agencies have significant overhead, and the cost of producing a spectacular television ad can be astronomical. Also, it's worth noting, big advertisers like P&G spread their advertising among many agencies.

COMMISSIONS.   The 15 percent **commission system** is rooted in an old magazine and newspaper practice. Knowing that agencies were influential in deciding where advertisements were placed, publications offered them 15 percent discounts. A newspaper that listed $100 per column inch as its standard rate would charge agencies only $85. The agency, however, billed clients the full $100 and kept the 15 percent difference. To clients, it seemed as though agency services were free. There was nothing secret about the arrangement, and it remains standard practice for most national and some local advertising.

commission system
Agencies bill clients 15 percent more than media charge for time and space.

Media Databank

Advertising Agencies

The lineup of global advertising agencies changed so frequently in 2002 that you needed a scorecard to keep track. Mergers and acquisitions concentrated the industry into oligopolies. The largest of the superpowers, Interpublic, controlled $39.5 billion of worldwide advertising spending, about 15 percent of the total.

Holding Companies	Worldwide Billings
Interpublic	
Initiative Media	$21.5 billion
Universal McCann	17.2 billion
Others	865 million
Publicis	
Starcom MediaVest	16.5 billion
Optimedia	10.0 billion
Zenith	9.8 billion
WPP	
MindShare	18.4 billion
Mediaedge	16.7 billion
Omnicom	
OMD (DDB, BBDO, TBWA)	18.7 billion
PhD	2.8 billion

FEES. Although in place more than 100 years, the commission system has problems. For agencies, income fluctuates with changes in ad frequency. Also, advertisers suspect that agencies are self-serving when they recommend bigger campaigns. To address these problems, some agencies have gone to a **fee system.** Arrangements vary, but agencies usually bill clients for expenses as they are incurred, plus an agreed-upon percentage as profit.

PERFORMANCE. Procter & Gamble, which spends more on advertising than any other U.S. company in most years, has discussed a **performance system** to compensate agencies. The company would cover only an agency's costs plus a modest profit. If a campaign strikes a bonanza, then the agency shares in the treasure.

Advertiser's Role in Advertising

Most companies, although they hire agencies for advertising services, have their own advertising expertise among the in-house people who develop marketing strategies. These companies look to ad agencies to develop the advertising campaigns that will help them meet their marketing goals. For some companies the **advertising director** is the liaison between the company's marketing strategists and the ad agency's tacticians. Large companies with many products have in-house **brand managers** for this liaison. Although it is not the usual pattern, some companies have in-house advertising departments and rely hardly at all on agencies.

Placing Advertisements

STUDY PREVIEW   The placement of advertisements is a sophisticated business. Not only do different media have inherent advantages and disadvantages in reaching potential customers, but so do individual publications and broadcast outlets.

fee system
Agencies bill clients for expenses plus add-on percentage as profit.

performance system
Agency bills for expenses and modest profit but is rewarded extra for successful campaigns.

advertising director
Coordinates marketing and advertising.

brand manager
Coordinates marketing and advertising for a specific brand.

Media Plans

Agencies create **media plans** to ensure that advertisements reach the right target audience. Developing a media plan is no small task. Consider the number of media outlets available: 1,400 daily newspapers in the United States alone, 8,000 weeklies, 1,200 general-interest magazines, 10,000 radio stations and 1,000 television stations. Other possibilities include direct mail, banners on web sites, billboards, blimps, skywriting and even printing the company's name on pencils.

Media buyers use formulas, some very complex, to decide which media are best for reaching potential customers. Most of these formulas begin with a factor called **CPM,** short for cost per thousand. If airtime for a radio advertisement costs 7.2 cents per thousand listeners, it's probably a better deal than a magazine with a 7.3-cent CPM, assuming that both reach the same audience. CPM by itself is just a starting point in choosing media. Other variables that media buyers consider include whether a message lends itself to a particular medium. For example, radio wouldn't work for a product that lends itself to a visual pitch and sight gags.

Media buyers have numerous sources of data to help them decide where advertisements can be placed for the best results. The **Audit Bureau of Circulations,** created by the newspaper industry in 1914, provides reliable information based on independent audits of the circulation of most newspapers. Survey organizations like Nielsen and Arbitron conduct surveys on television and radio audiences. Standard Rate and Data Service publishes volumes of information on media audiences, circulations and advertising rates.

Media Choices

Here are the pluses and minuses of major media as advertising vehicles:

NEWSPAPERS.   The hot relationship that media theorist Marshall McLuhan described between newspapers and their readers attracts advertisers. Newspaper readers are predisposed to consider information in advertisements seriously. Studies show that people, when ready to buy, look more to newspapers than to other media. Because newspapers are tangible, readers can refer back to advertisements just by picking up the paper a second time, which is not possible with ephemeral media like television and radio. Coupons are possible in newspapers. Newspaper readers tend to be older, better educated and higher earning than television and radio audiences. Space for newspaper ads usually can be reserved as late as 48 hours ahead, and 11th-hour changes are possible.

However, newspapers are becoming less valuable for reaching young adults. To the consternation of newspaper publishers, there has been an alarming drop in readership among these people in recent years, and it appears that, unlike their parents, young adults are not picking up the newspaper habit as they mature.

Another drawback to newspapers is printing on newsprint, a relatively cheap paper that absorbs ink like a slow blotter. The result is that ads do not look as good as they do in slick magazines. Slick, stand-alone inserts offset the newsprint drawback somewhat, but many readers pull them out and discard them first thing when they open the paper.

MAGAZINES.   As another print medium, magazines have many of the advantages of newspapers plus longer **shelf life,** an advertising term for the amount of time

---

media plan
Lays out where ads are placed.

CPM
Cost per thousand; a tool to determine the cost effectiveness of different media.

Audit Bureau of Circulations
Verifies circulation claims.

shelf life
How long a periodical remains in use.

that an advertisement remains available to readers. Magazines remain in the home for weeks, sometimes months, which offers greater exposure to advertisements. People share magazines, which gives them high **pass-along circulation.** Magazines are more prestigious, with slick paper and splashier graphics. With precise color separations and enameled papers, magazine advertisements can be beautiful in ways that newspaper advertisements cannot. Magazines, specializing as they do, offer more narrowly defined audiences than do newspapers.

On the downside, magazines require reservations for advertising space up to three months in advance. Opportunities for last-minute changes are limited, often impossible.

RADIO.   Radio stations with narrow formats offer easily identified target audiences. Time can be bought on short notice, with changes possible almost until airtime. Comparatively inexpensive, radio lends itself to repeated play of advertisements to drive home a message introduced in more expensive media like television. Radio lends itself to jingles that can contribute to a lasting image.

However, radio offers no opportunity for a visual display, although the images that listeners create in their minds from audio suggestions can be more potent than those set out visually on television. Radio is a mobile medium that people carry with them. The extensive availability of radio is offset, however, by the fact that people tune in and out. Another negative is that many listeners are inattentive. Also, there is no shelf life.

TELEVISION.   As a moving and visual medium, television can offer unmatched impact, and the rapid growth of both network and local television advertising, far outpacing other media, indicates its effectiveness in reaching a diverse mass audience.

Drawbacks include the fact that production costs can be high. So are rates. The expense of television time has forced advertisers to go to shorter and shorter advertisements. A result is **ad clutter,** a phenomenon in which advertisements compete against each other and reduce the impact of all of them. Placing advertisements on television is a problem because demand outstrips the supply of slots, especially during prime hours. Slots for some hours are locked up months, even whole seasons, in advance. Because of the audience's diversity and size, targeting potential customers with any precision is difficult with television—with the exception of emerging narrowly focused cable services.

ONLINE SERVICES.   Like many other newspapers in the mid-1990s, the San José, California, *Mercury News* established a news web site on the Internet. Editors put news from the newspaper on the web site so that people with computers could pick up news online. Every time an electronic reader connected to Mercury Center, as the Mercury's web site was dubbed, it was recorded as a **hit.** In 1995 Mercury Center was receiving 325,000 hits a day, compared with the 270,000 circulation of the newsprint product. The potential of web sites as advertising vehicles has not been lost on newspapers or other organizations, including AT&T and Microsoft, which also have established news sites online.

One advantage of **online advertising** is that readers can click deeper and deeper levels of information about advertised products. A lot more information can be packed into a layered online message than within the space and time confines of a print or broadcast ad. High-resolution color is standard, and the technology is available for moving pictures and audio.

pass-along circulation
All the people who see a periodical.

ad clutter
So many competing ads that all lose impact.

hit
A recorded viewing of a web site.

online advertising
Provide messages to computers.

Media Abroad

Australia: Online Classified Advertising

Before dawn every morning you can go to the World Wide Web and read about hundreds of job openings all over Australia—and New Guinea too. In 1996 News Interactive of Sydney, part of the Murdoch media empire, put the classifieds ads from Murdoch's 12 Australian newspapers online at a site called News-Classifieds. More newspapers quickly joined. Within six months the site was getting 100,000 hits a day, growing about 10 percent a month.

Today, more than 100 newspapers, both dailies and weeklies, transmit their classified ads overnight to the NewsClassified's Sydney computer for consolidation into the world's largest classified section. Though geared to Australia, the site also includes ads from the Papau, New Guinea, *Post Courier,* which runs a lot of mining job ads that are of interest to Australians. The site was barebones classifieds ads, all words, to start. It has since added display employment ads. Also, job seekers can upload their

résumés directly to the site. Employers then e-mail back. The site carries the whole range of classified ads, not just jobs. Want a 1967 Holden sedan, low miles, not too rusty? Surf to News-Classifieds.

The idea of online classified ads has caught on elsewhere. In the United States the Gannett chain and others have moved rapidly into putting classified listings on the web to preempt competitors from staking early claims.

Advertisers are not abandoning traditional media, but they are experimenting with online possibilities. For mail-order products, orders can be placed over the Internet right from the ad. For some groups of potential customers, online advertising has major advantages. To reach college students, almost all of whom have computer access, online advertising makes sense.

The downside of web site advertising is that the Internet is accessible only to people with computers, modems and Internet accounts. Of course, the percentage of the computer-knowledgeable population is mushrooming and will continue to do so.

media online
Online Advertising:
What works best? A series of online columns.
www.clickz.com/column/oacr.html

Alternative Media

Through the 1990s the leading 100 U.S. advertisers hiked advertising outlays about 10 percent a year. Yet the national advertising dollars to the traditional media, magazines, newspapers, radio and television, hasn't been keeping pace. Where was the leakage? To follow fragmenting audiences, advertisers have moved into alternative media for reaching potential customers.

Every city has a business magazine, none of which by itself puts much of a dent into national magazine or local newspaper advertising, but they lure some dollars. The continuing growth in gay newspaper advertising, up almost 20 percent in 1996, was hardly missed by the giant media, but it contributed to a further division of the advertising pie. The Spanish-language television networks Univison and Telemundo, as well as local stations and Spanish radio, newspapers and magazines, brought in $1.2 billion in 1996. Direct-mail advertising sidesteps traditional media entirely, with advertisers making direct contact with potential customers. In the first quarter of 1997, advertisers paid $133 million for web advertising—six times a year earlier.

All told, alternative media have taken a chunk away from traditional major media.

Pitching Messages

STUDY PREVIEW   When the age of mass production and mass markets arrived, common wisdom in advertising favored aiming at the largest possible audience of potential customers. These are called lowest common denominator approaches, and such advertisements tend to be heavy-handed so that no one can possibly miss the point. Narrower pitches, aimed at segments of the mass audience, permit more deftness, subtlety and imagination.

Importance of Brands

A challenge for advertising people is the modern-day reality that mass-produced products intended for large markets are essentially alike: Toothpaste is toothpaste is toothpaste. When a product is virtually identical to the competition, how can one toothpaste maker move more tubes?

BRAND NAMES.   By trial and error, tactics were devised in the late 1800s to set similar products apart. One tactic, promoting a product as a **brand** name, aims to make a product a household word. When it is successful, a brand name becomes almost the generic identifier, like Coke for cola and Kleenex for facial tissue.

Techniques of successful brand name advertising came together in the 1890s for an English product, Pears' soap. A key element in the campaign was multimedia saturation. Advertisements for Pears' were everywhere—in newspapers and magazines and on posters, vacant walls, fences, buses and lampposts. Redundancy hammered home the brand name. "Good morning. Have you used Pears' today?" became a good-natured greeting among Britons that was still being repeated 50 years later. Each repetition reinforced the brand name.

BRAND IMAGE.   **David Ogilvy,** who headed the Ogilvy & Mather agency, developed the **brand image** in the 1950s. Ogilvy's advice: "Give your product a first-class ticket through life."

Ogilvy created shirt advertisements with the distinguished Baron Wrangell, who really was a European nobleman, wearing a black eye patch—and a Hathaway shirt. The classy image was reinforced with the accoutrements around Wrangell: exquisite models of sailing ships, antique weapons, silver dinnerware. To some seeing Wrangell's setting, the patch suggested all kinds of exotica. Perhaps he had lost an eye in a romantic duel or a sporting accident.

Explaining the importance of image, Ogilvy once said, "Take whiskey. Why do some people choose Jack Daniels, while others choose Grand Dad or Taylor? Have they tried all three and compared the taste? Don't make me laugh. The reality is that these three brands have different images which appeal to different kinds of people. It isn't the whiskey they choose, it's the image. The brand image is 90 percent of what the distiller has to sell. Give people a taste of Old Crow, and tell them it's Old Crow. Then give them another taste of Old Crow, but tell them it's Jack Daniels. Ask them which they prefer. They'll think the two drinks are quite different. They are tasting images."

brand
A nongeneric product name designed to set the product apart from the competition.

David Ogilvy
Championed brand imaging.

brand image
Spin put on a brand name.

Lowest Common Denominator

Early brand-name campaigns were geared to the largest possible audience, sometimes called an LCD, or **lowest common denominator,** approach. The term *LCD* is adapted from mathematics. To reach an audience that includes members with IQs of 100, the pitch cannot exceed their level of understanding, even if some people in the audience have IQs of 150. The opportunity for deft touches and even cleverness is limited by the fact they might be lost on some potential customers.

LCD advertising is best epitomized in contemporary advertising by USP, short for **unique selling proposition,** a term coined by **Rosser Reeves** of the giant Ted Bates agency in the 1960s. Reeves' prescription was simple: Create a benefit of the product, even if from thin air, and then tout the benefit authoritatively and repeatedly as if the competition doesn't have it. One early USP campaign boasted that Schlitz beer bottles were "washed with live steam." The claim sounded good—who would want to drink from dirty bottles? However, the fact was that every brewery used steam to clean reusable bottles before filling them again. Furthermore, what is "live steam"? Although the implication of a competitive edge was hollow, it was done dramatically and pounded home with emphasis, and it sold beer. Just as hollow as a competitive advantage was the USP claim for Colgate toothpaste: "Cleans Your Breath While It Cleans Your Teeth."

Perhaps to compensate for a lack of substance, many USP ads are heavy-handed. Hardly an American has not heard about fast-fast-fast relief from headache remedies or that heartburn relief is spelled R-O-L-A-I-D-S. USP can be unappealing, as is acknowledged even by the chairman of Warner-Lambert, which makes Rolaids, who once laughed that his company owed the American people an apology for insulting their intelligence over and over with Bates' USP slogans. Warner-Lambert was also laughing all the way to the bank over the USP-spurred success of Rolaids, Efferdent, Listermint and Bubblicious.

A unique selling proposition need be neither hollow nor insulting, however. Leo Burnett, founder of the agency bearing his name, refined the USP concept by insisting that the unique point be real. For Maytag, Burnett took the company's slight advantage in reliability and dramatized it with the lonely Maytag repairman.

Market Segments

Rather than pitching to the lowest common denominator, advertising executive **Jack Trout** developed the idea of **positioning.** Trout worked to establish product identities that appealed not to the whole audience but to a specific audience. The cowboy image for Marlboro cigarettes, for example, established a macho attraction beginning in 1958. Later, something similar was done with Virginia Slims, aimed at women.

Positioning helps to distinguish products from all the LCD clamor and noise. Advocates of positioning note that there are more and more advertisements and that they are becoming noisier and noisier. Ad clutter, as it is called, drowns out individual advertisements. With positioning, the appeal is focused and caters to audience segments, and it need not be done in such broad strokes.

Campaigns based on positioning have included:

- Johnson & Johnson's baby oil and baby shampoo, which were positioned as adult products by advertisements featuring athletes.

lowest common denominator
Messages for broadest audience possible.

unique selling proposition
Emphasizing a single feature.

Rosser Reeves
Devised unique selling proposition.

Jack Trout
Devised positioning.

positioning
Targeting ads for specific consumer groups.

■ Alka-Seltzer, once a hangover and headache remedy, which was positioned as an upscale product for stress relief among health-conscious, success-driven people.

Redundancy Techniques

Advertising people learned the importance of redundancy early on. To be effective, an advertising message must be repeated, perhaps thousands of times. Redundancy is expensive, however. To increase effectiveness at less cost, advertisers use several techniques:

■ **Barrages.** Scheduling advertisements in intensive bursts called **flights** or **waves.**
■ **Bunching.** Promoting a product in a limited period, such as running advertisements for school supplies in late August and September.
■ **Trailing.** Running condensed versions of advertisements after the original has been introduced, as automakers do when they introduce new models with multi-page magazine spreads, following with single-page placements.
■ **Multimedia trailing.** Using less expensive media to reinforce expensive advertisements. Relatively cheap drive-time radio in major markets is a favorite follow through to expensive television advertisements created for major events like the Super Bowl.

New Advertising Techniques

Inundated with advertisements, 6,000 a week on network television, double since 1983, many people tune out. Some do it literally with their remotes. Ad people are concerned that traditional modes are losing effectiveness. People are overwhelmed. Consider, for example, that a major grocery store carries 30,000 items, each with packaging that screams "buy me." More commercial messages are put there than a human being can handle. The problem is ad clutter. Advertisers are trying to address the clutter in numerous ways, including stealth ads, new-site ads and alternative media. Although not hidden or subliminal, stealth ads are subtle—even covert. You might not know you're being pitched unless you're attentive, really attentive.

barrages
Intensive repetition of ads.

flights
Intensive repetition of ads.

waves
Intensive repetition of ads.

bunching
Short-term ad campaign.

trailing
Shorter, smaller ads after campaign is introduced.

stealth ads
Advertisements, often subtle, in nontraditional, unexpected places.

STEALTH ADS.   **Stealth ads** fit so neatly into the landscape that the commercial pitch seems part of the story line. In 1996 the writers for four CBS television programs, including "Nanny" and "High Society," wrote Elizabeth Taylor into their scripts. And there she was, in over two hours of programming one winter night, wandering in and out of sets looking for a missing string of black pearls. Hardly coincidentally, her new line of perfume, Black Pearls, was being introduced at the time.

The gradual convergence of information and entertainment, called infotainment, has a new element: advertising. "Seinfeld" characters on NBC munched Junior Mints. The M&M/Mars candy company bought a role for Snickers in the Nintendo game *Biker Mice from Mars*. In 1997 Unilever's British brand Van den Bergh Foods introduced a video game that stars its Peperami snack sausage. In movies promotional plugs have become a big-budget item. The idea is to seamlessly work the presence of commercial products into a script without a cue—nothing like the hopelessly dated "And now a word from our sponsors."

Less subtle is the **infomercial,** a program-length television commercial dolled up to look like a newscast, a live-audience participation show or a chatty talk show. With the proliferation of 24-hour television service and of cable channels, airtime is so cheap at certain hours that advertisers of even offbeat products can afford it. Hardly anybody is fooled into thinking that infomercials are anything but advertisements, but some full-length media advertisements, like Liz Taylor wandering through CBS sitcoms, are cleverly disguised.

A print media variation is the **'zine**— a magazine published by a manufacturer to plug a single line of products with varying degrees of subtlety. 'Zine publishers, including such stalwarts as IBM and Sony, have even been so brazen as to sell these wall-to-wall advertising vehicles at newsstands. In 1996, if you bought a splashy new magazine called *Colors*, you paid $4.50 for it. Once inside, you probably would realize it was a thinly veiled ad for Benetton casual clothes. *Guess Journal* may look like a magazine, but guess who puts it out as a 'zine: The makers of the Guess fashion brand.

Stealth advertisements try "to morph into the very entertainment it sponsors," wrote Mary Kuntz, Joseph Weber and Heidi Dawley in *Business Week*. The goal, they said, is "to create messages so entertaining, so compelling—and maybe so disguised—that rapt audiences will swallow them whole, oblivious to the sales component."

NEW-SITE ADS. Ironically, solving the problem of ad clutter by going underground with stealth ads contributes to the clutter. Sooner or later, it would seem, people would also tire of advertising omnipresence. Snapple stickers adorn kiwis and mangoes at the grocery. Sports stadiums named for department stores or other companies, like the Target Center in Minneapolis and the Washington Redskins' FedEx Field, try to weave product names into everyday conversation and the news. Sports events galore bear the names of high-bidding sponsors. How omnipresent can advertising become? Consider the Bamboo lingerie company that stenciled messages on Manhattan sidewalks: "From here, it looks like you could use some new underwear."

Omnipresent Ads. Bamboo Lingerie's stenciled sidewalk messages may have been unsettling to some folks, but they sold underwear. Like many advertisers worried that their messages are lost in ad-crammed traditional media, Bamboo has struck out for nontraditional territory to be noticed. Regina Kelley, director of strategic planning for the Saatchi & Saatchi agency in New York said, "Any space you can take in visually, anything you can hear, in the future will be branded."

Research and Psychology

STUDY PREVIEW   Freudian ideas about the human subconscious influenced advertising in the 1950s, and research tried to tap hidden motivations that could be exploited to sell products and services. The extreme in appealing to the subconscious, called subliminal advertising, worried many people, but it was an approach whose effectiveness was never demonstrated.

infomercial
Program-length broadcast commercial.

'zine
Magazine whose entire content, articles and ads, pitches a single product or product line.

Motivational Research

Whatever naïveté Americans had about opinion-shaping was dispelled by the mid-20th century. Sinister possibilities were evident in the work of **Joseph Goebbels,** the Nazi minister of propaganda and public enlightenment. In the Pacific the Japanese beamed the infamous Tokyo Rose radio broadcasts to GIs to lower their morale. Then, during the Korean War, a macabre fascination developed with the so-called brainwashing techniques used on U.S. prisoners of war. In this same period the work of Austrian psychiatrist **Sigmund Freud,** which emphasized hidden motivations and repressed sexual impulses, was being popularized in countless books and articles.

No wonder, considering this intellectual context, advertising people in the 1950s looked to the social sciences to find new ways to woo customers. Among the advertising pioneers of this period was **Ernest Dichter,** who accepted Freud's claim that people act on motivations that they are not even aware of. Depth interviewing, Dichter felt, could reveal these motivations, which could then be exploited in advertising messages.

Dichter used his interviewing, called **motivational research,** for automotive clients. Rightly or wrongly, Dichter determined that the American male was loyal to his wife but fantasized about having a mistress. Men, he noted, usually were the decision makers in purchasing a car. Then, in what seemed a quantum leap, Dichter equated sedans, which were what most people drove, with wives. Sedans were familiar, reliable. Convertibles, impractical for many people and also beyond their reach financially, were equated with mistresses—romantic, daring, glamorous. With these conclusions in hand, Dichter devised advertisements for a new kind of sedan without a center door pillar. The hardtop, as it was called, gave a convertible effect when the windows were down. The advertisements, dripping with sexual innuendo, clearly reflected Dichter's thinking: "You'll find something new to love every time you drive it." Although they were not as solid as sedans and tended to leak air and water, hardtops were popular among automobile buyers for the next 25 years.

Dichter's motivational research led to numerous campaigns that exploited sexual images. For Ronson lighters the flame, in phallic form, was reproduced in extraordinary proportions. A campaign for Ajax cleanser, hardly a glamour product, had a white knight charging through the street, ignoring law and regulation with a great phallic lance. Whether consumers were motivated by sexual imagery is hard to establish. Even so, many campaigns based on motivational research worked.

Joseph Goebbels
Nazi propagandist.

Sigmund Freud
Examined hidden motivations.

Ernest Dichter
Pioneered motivational research.

motivational research
Seeks subconscious appeals that can be used in advertising.

Jim Vicary
Made dubious subliminal advertising claims.

subliminal advertising
Ads that cannot be consciously perceived.

Subliminal Advertising

The idea that advertising can be persuasive at subconscious levels was taken a step further by market researcher **Jim Vicary,** who coined the term **subliminal advertising.** Vicary claimed in 1957 that he had studied the effect of inserting messages like "Drink Coca-Cola" and "Eat popcorn" into movies. The messages, though flashed too fast to be recognized by the human eye, still registered in the brain and, said Vicary, prompted movie-goers to rush to the snack bar. In experiments at a New Jersey movie house, he said, Coke sales increased 18 percent and popcorn sales almost 60 percent. Vicary's report stirred great interest, and also alarm, but researchers who tried to replicate his study found no evidence to support his claim.

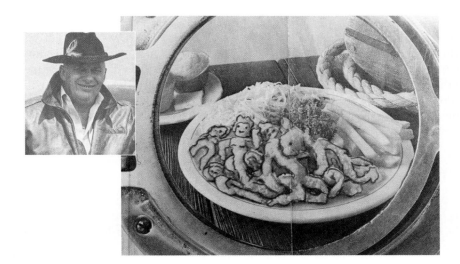

Sex in the Clams? Author Wilson Bryan Key is convinced that Madison Avenue hides sex in advertisements to attract attention and sell products. To demonstrate his point, he outlined the human figures that he saw in an orgy in a photograph of clam strips on a Howard Johnson restaurant placemat. Most advertising people dismiss his claims.

Despite doubts about Vicary's claims, psychologists have identified a phenomenon they call **subception,** in which certain behavior sometimes seems to be triggered by messages perceived subliminally. Whether the effect works outside laboratory experiments and whether the effect is strong enough to prod a consumer to go out and buy is uncertain. Nevertheless, there remains a widespread belief among the general population that subliminal advertising works, and fortunes are being made by people who peddle various devices and systems with extravagant claims that they can control human behavior. Among these are the "hidden" messages in stores' sound systems that say shoplifting is not nice.

This idea that advertising is loaded with hidden messages has been taken to extremes by **Wilson Bryan Key,** who spins out books alleging that plugs are hidden in all kinds of places for devil worship, homosexuality and a variety of libertine activities. He has accused the Nabisco people of baking the word "sex" into Ritz crackers. At Howard Johnson restaurants, he has charged, placemat pictures of plates heaped with clams portray orgies and bestiality. Though widely read, Key offers no evidence beyond his own observations and interpretations. In advertising circles, his views are dismissed as amusing but wacky. The view at Nabisco and Howard Johnson is less charitable.

In 1990 Key's views suffered a serious setback. He was a primary witness in a highly publicized Nevada trial on whether Judas Priest's heavy-metal album "Stained Class" had triggered the suicide of an 18-year-old youth and the attempted suicide of his 20-year-old friend. The families said that the pair had obsessed on a Judas Priest album that dealt with suicide and that one song was subliminally embedded with the words "Do it" over and over. The families' attorneys hired Key as an expert witness to help make their point. From Key's perspective the case did not go well. Millions of television viewers who followed the trial strained to make out the supposed words "Do it," but even when isolated from the rest of the music, they were almost impossible to make out. It turned out the sounds were neither lyrics nor even vocal but rather instrumental effects. Members of Judas Priest testified that they had not equated the sound to any words at all and had inserted it for artistic effect, hardly to encourage suicide. The jury sided with Judas Priest, and Key left

subception
Receiving subconscious messages that trigger behavior.

Wilson Bryan Key
Sees subliminal advertising widely used.

town with his wobbly ideas on subliminal messages having taken a serious blow under a jury's scrutiny.

David Ogilvy, founder of the Ogilvy & Mather agency, once made fun of claims like Key's, pointing out the absurdity of "millions of suggestible consumers getting up from their armchairs and rushing like zombies through the traffic on their way to buy the product at the nearest store." The danger of "Vote Bolshevik" being flashed during the "NBC Nightly News" is remote, and whether it would have any effect is dubious.

Advertising Regulation

STUDY PREVIEW　The "buyer beware" underpinning of much of 19th-century advertising has given way to "seller beware." Today, advertising is regulated on many fronts: by the media that carry advertisements, by the advertising industry itself and by government agencies.

Media Gatekeeping

A dramatic reversal in thinking about advertising has occurred in the 20th century. The earlier *caveat emptor* ("let the buyer beware") mindset tolerated extravagant claims. Anybody who believed that the same elixir could cure dandruff, halitosis and cancer deserved to be conned, or so went the thinking. Over the years, owing partly to the growing consumer movement, the thinking changed to *caveat venditor* ("let the seller beware"), placing the onus on the advertiser to avoid misleading claims and to demonstrate the truth of claims.

In advertising's early days newspapers and magazines skirted the ethics question posed by false advertisements by saying that their pages were open to all advertisers. Under growing pressure, publications sometimes criticized dubious advertisements editorially, but most did not ban them. **Edward Bok,** who made *Ladies' Home Journal* a runaway success in the 1890s, crusaded against dishonest advertising. In one exposé on Lydia E. Pinkham's remedies for "female maladies," Bok reported that Lydia, to whom women readers were invited in advertisements to write for advice, had been dead for 22 years. Yet the advertisements continued.

In 1929 NBC adopted a code of ethics to preclude false or exaggerated claims. Other networks followed. At the peak of the networks' concern about broadcast standards, it was estimated that half the commercials for products were turned away for violating network codes. Codes for broadcast advertising have come and gone over the years, all voluntary with stations that choose to subscribe.

The print media also have seen a variety of industry-wide codes, all voluntary. Most publications spurn misleading advertisements. Typical is the Minot *Daily News* in North Dakota, which refuses advertisements for "clairvoyance, fortune telling, magnetic healing, doubtful medicines and fake sales." Many college newspapers refuse advertisements from term-paper services. Some metropolitan papers turn away advertisements for pornographic movies.

A case can be made that the media do not go far enough in exercising their prerogative to ban dubious advertisements. Critics argue that on nettling questions, such as the morality of printing ads for carcinogenic tobacco products, with major revenue at stake, many newspapers and magazines sidestep a moral judgment, run

caveat emptor
Buyer beware.

caveat venditor
Seller beware.

Edward Bok
Set media standards for ads.

the advertisements, and reap the revenue. The critics note, for example, that most commercial broadcasters ran cigarette advertisements until the federal government intervened. The media, so goes the argument, are too devoted to profits to do all the regulating they should.

Industry Self-Regulation

The advertising industry itself has numerous organizations that try, through ethics codes and moral suasion, to eradicate falsity and deception. Besides the explicit purposes of these self-policing mechanisms, advertising people can cite their existence to argue that their industry is able to deal with misdeeds itself with a minimum of government regulation.

Advertising Globalization. Manufacturers on every continent are seeking markets elsewhere, which is generating accounts and revenues for advertising agencies with international operations. The Gap's new high-fashion outlet in Tokyo's ritzy Ginza district is among thousands of examples. Some of the greatest advertising agency expansion is in China, where by one count 50 foreign agencies are trying to carve a share out of a virtually untapped market of 1.2 billion people. The effect is tremendous. Steven Strasser, writing in *Newsweek,* said, "China cares about its athlete's foot problem. Johnson & Johnson's subsidiary made sure of that. When its recent J&J commercial revealed that a fungus caused the itch, sales of Daktarin fungicidal cream soared from Shanghai to Xian."

NATIONAL ADVERTISING REVIEW COUNCIL. The **National Advertising Review Council** investigates complaints from anybody. When it finds a problem, the council asks the offending advertiser to correct the situation. If that does not work, the council turns its file over to whichever government agency it thinks is appropriate.

Although it is a creation of advertising trade associations, the National Advertising Review Council has earned a reputation as a dispassionate attempt at self-regulation. Its 50 members include 10 people appointed from the public—with no connection to the advertising business. Of the complaints the council investigates, two-thirds typically are found to be deceptive advertising. About half of those advertisements are discontinued or modified under council pressure. The council has no legal authority, but its willingness to go to federal agencies or to state attorneys general, in effect recommending prosecution, is a powerful tool for honesty in advertising.

CODES. Typical of codes of advertising trade groups is that of the **American Association of Advertising Agencies,** which says member agencies are expected never to produce ads with:

- False, misleading statements or exaggerations, visual or verbal, including misleading price claims.
- Testimonials from unknowledgeable people.
- Unfair disparagement of competitive products.
- Distorted or insufficiently supported claims.
- Anything offending public decency.

Acceptance of the code is a kind of loose condition of membership—more a statement of the association's values than an enforcement tool.

National Advertising Review Council
Reviews complaints about ads.

American Association of Advertising Agencies
Advertising trade association.

Media Abroad

Vatican: Advertising Guidelines

The Pontifical Council for Social Communications, a Vatican unit of the Roman Catholic Church, issued its handbook *Ethics in Advertising* in 1997. The 37-page handbook, four years in the making, was aimed at helping people who create ads. It outlined abuses that are possible in advertising and also the potential for harm. It specifically admonished against shocking and exploitive ads. The council encouraged advertising people and everyone else who participates in the communication process "to eliminate its socially harmful aspects and observe high ethical standards in regard to truthfulness, human dignity and social responsibility." "Advertising," the report said, "has significant potential for good and sometimes it is realized."

How can advertising realize its potential for good? "The media of social communications have two options and only two. Either they help human persons to grow in their understanding and practice of what is true and good, or they are destructive forces in conflict with human well being. This is entirely true of advertising."

The council had harsh comments on brand advertising: "Often there are only negligible differences among similar products of different brands, and advertising may attempt to move people to act on the basis of irrational motives ('brand loyalty,' status, fashion, 'sex appeal,' etc.) instead of presenting differences in product quality and price as bases for rational choice."

The Vatican council said it's a cop-out for advertising people to excuse exploitive and debasing advertising by saying they merely mirror social values: "No doubt advertising, like the media of social communications in general, does act as a mirror. But, also, like media in general, it is a mirror that helps shape the reality it reflects, and sometimes it presents a distorted image of reality. Advertisers are selective about the values and attitudes to be fostered and encouraged, promoting some while ignoring others. This selectivity gives the lie to the notion that advertising does no more than reflect the surrounding culture."

The Vatican council commended advertising people for voluntary ethics codes but said they often are not enough. The codes, the report said, "are only as effective as the willingness of advertisers to comply strictly with them."

PUBLIC INTEREST ADVERTISING.   The advertising industry has set up an organization, the **Ad Council,** which creates advertisements free for worthy causes. Since the 1940s the council's existence has helped offset criticism that the advertising business is an unscrupulous manipulator.

The Ad Council has roots in World War II when the ad industry, major media organizations and advertisers created the War Advertising Council to create ads for the war effort. Advertisers funded the council, agencies created the advertisements gratis and media ran donated time and space for them. The first campaign, to recruit military nurses, stressed: "Nursing is a proud profession." Within weeks, 500,000 women applied for the Cadet Nurses Corps—almost eight times more than were needed. After the war the Ad Council was formed to continue *pro bono* work on behalf of socially significant national issues.

Because the ads are well done, the media are pleased to run them as a contribution to the public good. Magazines, newspapers and broadcasters donate about $800 million a year in time and space to the Ad Council's ads.

In a typical year 300 noncommercial organizations ask the Ad Council to take them on. The council chooses a dozen, which are turned over to agencies that rotate their services. The United Way has received continuing support from the council.

Ad Council
Ad industry group that creates free campaigns for worthy causes.

Other campaigns have included restoring the Statue of Liberty, combating illiteracy and improving U.S. productivity. Campaigns that have left an imprint on the public mind have included:

- Forest fire prevention with the character Smokey Bear.
- Environmental protection with the memorable "Don't be fuelish" slogan.
- Fund-raising for the United Negro College Fund, with the line "A mind is a terrible thing to waste."

Government Regulation

The federal government began regulating advertisements in 1914 when Congress created the **Federal Trade Commission.** The commission was charged with protecting honest companies that were being disadvantaged by competitors that made false claims. Today, nine federal agencies besides the FTC are involved heavily in regulating advertising. These include the Food and Drug Administration, the U.S. Postal Service, the Federal Communications Commission and the Securities and Exchange Commission. In addition, most states have laws against advertising fraud.

In its early days the Federal Trade Commission went about its work meekly, but fueled by the consumer movement in the 1960s, it became aggressive. Although the agency never had the authority to review advertisements ahead of their publication or airing, the FTC let it be known that it would crack down on violations of truth-in-packaging and truth-in-lending requirements. The FTC also began insisting on clarity so that even someone with low intelligence would not be confused. The FTC took particular aim at the overused word "free." To be advertised as "free," an offer had to be without conditions. The FTC moved further to protect the gullible. It was unacceptable, said the FTC, to leave the impression that actors in white coats speaking authoritatively about over-the-counter drugs and toothpastes were physicians or dentists. When Ocean Spray claimed that its cranberry juice offered "food energy," the FTC insisted that the language be changed to "calories." The FTC clamped down on a claim that Profile bread helped people lose weight, noting that the only difference from regular bread was thinner slices. The FTC pressed the Kroger grocery chain on its claim that it carried 150 everyday items cheaper than the competition, found that the claim was misleading and told Kroger to drop it.

Even with its crackdown, the FTC never ventured into regulating taste. Advertisements in poor taste were allowed, as long as they were not deceptive or unfair. **Puffery** was allowed, as long as there was no misstatement of fact. In borderline cases about what constituted puffery, an advertiser could always appeal to the courts.

Public Service. On a rotating basis, major U.S. advertising agencies donate their time and creativity to create public service messages on behalf of worthwhile causes. The Ad Council, which coordinates these efforts, produced ads on behalf of 35 clients in 2002. Magazines, newspapers, radio and television run these messages at no cost. One 2002 message, on behalf of the American Cancer Society, used a ballooned red patient comically to promote colon cancer detection and prevention.

Federal Trade Commission
Regulates advertising.

puffery
Legally permissible excesses in advertising.

The FTC has been less aggressive in regulating advertising since the Reagan administration, which deemphasized government regulation. Consumer activists, however, continue to complain to the FTC and other federal and state agencies and to bring pressure on the media not to run certain advertisements. Most of the concerns today are to protect impressionable children.

Today, some advertisers—especially the tobacco and liquor industries—face regulation of a different sort. To settle and head off civil lawsuits, tobacco companies have withdrawn advertising aimed at kids. There are fewer pictures of healthy, young people holding a cigarette or taking a puff. The liquor industry faces a different kind of government pressure. Historically, the industry has refrained from advertising hard liquor on television and radio, and many networks and stations had policies against it too. In the late 1990s, under increasing competitive pressure, the Canadian conglomerate Seagrams and some broadcasters broke ranks and began dabbling with television advertising. That prompted FCC rumbling on possibly banning such ads. Some congressional leaders also began talking tough. An FCC crackdown seemed unlikely, however, considering the general deregulation mood in government that left it to the marketplace to determine what's acceptable and what's not.

Problems and Issues

STUDY PREVIEW   People are exposed to such a blur of ads that advertisers worry that their messages are being lost in the clutter. Some advertising people see more creativity as the answer so that people will want to see and read ads, but there is evidence that creativity can work against an ad's effectiveness.

Advertising Clutter

Leo Bogart of the Newspaper Advertising Bureau noted that the number of advertising messages doubled through the 1960s and 1970s, and except for the recession at the start of the 1990s, the trend continues. This proliferation of advertising creates a problem: too many ads. The problem has been exacerbated by the shortening of ads from 60 seconds in the early days of television to today's widely used 15-second format.

At one time the National Association of Broadcasters had a code limiting the quantity of commercials. The Federal Communications Commission let station owners know that it supported the NAB code, but in 1981, as part of the Reagan administration's deregulation, the FCC backed away from any limitation. In 1983 a federal court threw out the NAB limitation as a monopolistic practice.

Ad clutter is less of an issue in the print media. Many people buy magazines and newspapers to look at ads as part of the comparative shopping process. Even so, some advertisers, concerned that their ads are overlooked in massive editions, such as a seven-pound metro Sunday newspaper or a 700-page bridal magazine, are looking to alternative means to reach potential customers in a less cluttered environment.

The clutter that marks much of commercial television and radio today may be alleviated as the media fragment further. Not only will demassification create more specialized outlets, such as narrowly focused cable television services, but there will be new media. The result will be advertising aimed at narrower audiences.

Media Abroad

Advertisement Cloning

Procter & Gamble, the Cincinnati-based global household product conglomerate, has taken aim at marketing costs to boost profits. The goal: to reduce marketing outflow to less than 20 percent of sales—a major cut from 1996's 24 percent.

How to do it?

One tactic is to reduce creative costs in advertising by cloning campaigns that succeed in one country and use them elsewhere. Eventually, this could also mean lower costs for producing advertisements.

In a trial of ad cloning, the "Demanding Experts" campaign for Tide detergent in the United States was exported to Mexico and Puerto Rico for P&G's Ariel brand.

Similarly, the company recycled its "Show and Smell" campaign for Gain detergent in the United States for its Daz brand in Britain.

Creative Excesses

Advertisers are reviewing whether creativity is as effective an approach as hard sell. **Harry McMahan** studied **Clio** Awards for creativity in advertising and discovered that 36 agencies that produced 81 winners of the prestigious awards for advertisements had either lost the winning account or gone out of business.

Predicts advertising commentator E. B. Weiss: "Extravagant license for creative people will be curtailed." The future may hold more heavy-handed pitches, perhaps with over-the-counter regimens not only promising fast-fast-fast relief but also spelling it out in all caps and boldface with exclamation marks: **F-A-S-T! F-A-S-T!! F-A-S-T!!!**

Advertising Effectiveness

Long-held assumptions about the effectiveness of advertising itself are being questioned. **Gerald Tellis,** a University of Iowa researcher, put together a sophisticated statistical model that found that people are relatively unmoved by television advertisements in making brand choices, especially on mundane everyday products like toilet paper and laundry detergents. Tellis' conclusions began with consumer purchasing studies in Eau Claire, Wisconsin. Not surprisingly, considering its self-interest, the advertising industry has challenged the Tellis' studies.

Meanwhile, other researchers have continued work on what makes effective advertising and which media work best. A 1995 study by **Yankelovich Partners** found that magazine ads entice only 13 percent of Americans to try new products; newspaper ads, 15 percent; and television ads, 25 percent. The study, with a statistically impressive sample of 1,000 consumers, shook the conventional wisdom that celebrity endorsements work. Only 3 percent of the respondents said that they would try a product based on a celebrity's testimonial. A Yankelovich official, Hal Quinley, explained the dismal report card on advertising's effectiveness on weak credibility. "Advertising has little confidence among consumers," he told the *Wall Street Journal*. "It rates below the federal government." A lot of people trust their friends, however. Six out of 10 would try a new product that was recommended by a friend or relative.

Harry McMahan
Dubious about ad creativity.

Clio
Award for advertising creativity.

Gerald Tellis
Dubious about TV ads.

Yankelovich Partners
Research group that issued a milestone 1995 study.

For advertisers the lesson from the Tellis and Yankelovich studies is not that advertising doesn't work but that throwing money into campaigns without careful study can be wasteful. For some products, some media are better than others. For new products, according to Yankelovich's findings, free samples are the best way to pique consumer interest. So are cents-off coupons. In short, though, advertising may be overrated. With countless variables affecting consumer decisions, advertisers cannot place total faith in advertising to move their products and services.

Media Future: Advertising

As an advertising medium, the web seems so exciting and new, but soon the web will be old hat. The future is interactivity with a hodgepodge of wireless devices through which messages can be highly individualized. Because these don't constitute a clearly defined medium, at least not yet, the vague term *new media* is applied to them. Despite the vagueness, nobody disputes the potential of these media as advertising platforms.

The wireless media encompass mobile phones, beepers, wireless laptop computers, and pocket and palm devices—and who knows what else is coming along? Each device has an identifying code, which can be read by the sender. Because the devices are used by individuals whose demographic characteristics can be identified, as well as buying patterns, messages can be narrowly focused. Most important, individuals can talk back. If an advertising message strikes a chord, the user can immediately tap into more information and even make a purchase. Hence the term *interactivity*.

The new Wireless Application Protocol, WAP for short, means the new devices all speak the same language. With this universal protocol, pitches can be directed at you no matter which device you're using at the moment.

How near is the future? Ovum, a British research company, projects that wireless advertising, only $4 million in the United States today, will reach $4.2 billion by 2005—a thousandfold increase over five years. Worldwide, says Ovum, the total will exceed $16 million.

Nobody's crystal ball predicts the disappearance of existing advertising platforms, but the new media are further dispersing the ways for advertisers to reach their customers.

chapter wrap-up

The role of advertising in U.S. mass media cannot be overstated. Without advertising, most media would go out of business. In fact, in the 1960s, when advertisers switched to television from the giant general-interest magazines such as *Life* and *Look,* those magazines went under. Today, the rapid expansion of cable networks is possible only because advertisers are buying time on the new networks to reach potential customers. In one sense, advertisers subsidize readers, viewers and listeners who pay only a fraction of the cost of producing publications and broadcasts. The bulk of the cost is paid by advertisers, who are willing to do so to make their pitches to potential customers who, coincidentally, are media consumers.

Besides underwriting the mass media, advertising is vital for a prosperous, growing consumer economy. It triggers demand for goods and services, and it enables people to make wise choices by providing information on competing products. The result is efficiency in the marketplace, which frees more capital for expansion. This all speaks to an intimate interrelationship involving advertising in a democratic and capitalistic society.

Today, as democracy and capitalism are reintroduced in Central and Eastern Europe, advertising can be expected to have an essential role in fostering new consumer economies. U.S., European and Japanese advertising agencies will be called on for their expertise to develop campaigns for goods and services that will make for better lives and stronger economies. This process will provide a greater revenue base for the mass media in these countries, which will result in better journalistic and entertainment content.

Questions for Review

1. Why is advertising essential in a capitalistic society?
2. Trace the development of advertising since the time of Johannes Gutenberg.
3. What is the role of advertising agencies?
4. Why do some advertisements appear in some media and not other media?
5. What are the major tactics used in advertising? Who devised each one?
6. How do advertising people use psychology and research to shape their messages?
7. What are the advantages and the problems of the globalization of the advertising industry?
8. Does advertising still follow the dictum "let the buyer beware"?
9. What are some problems and unanswered issues in advertising?

3. What were the contributions to advertising of Wayland Ayer, Rosser Reeves, Jack Trout, Ernest Dichter, Wilson Bryan Key and David Ogilvy?
4. What are the responsibilities of advertising account executives, copywriters, media buyers, researchers, brand managers, ad reps and brokers?
5. What are the advantages of the commission system for advertising agency revenue? Of the fee system? The disadvantages of both?
6. Describe these advertising tactics: brand name promotion, unique selling proposition, lowest common denominator approach, positioning and redundancy.
7. How is ad clutter a problem? What can be done about it?
8. How has the Ad Council improved the image of companies that advertise, agencies that create advertisements and media that carry advertisements? Give examples.

Questions for Critical Thinking

1. How does the development of modern advertising relate to Johannes Gutenberg's technological innovation? To the Industrial Revolution? To long-distance mass transportation? To mass marketing?
2. Why does advertising flourish more in democratic than in autocratic societies? In a capitalistic more than in a controlled economy? In a prosperous society?

Keeping Up to Date

Weekly trade journals are *Advertising Age* and *AdWeek*. Scholarly publications include *Journal of Marketing Research* and *Journal of Advertising*. The New York *Times* regularly reports on the industry.

The Journal of Consumer Psychology includes analysis, reviews, reports and other scholarship on the role of advertising in consumer psychology.

Andy Kohut. *He opted for public-opinion polling that's pristine from commercial underpinnings.*

chapter

13

Media Research

In this chapter you will learn:

- Surveys tell the mass media about their audiences.

- The size of mass media audiences is measured by monitoring press runs and sales and by surveying.

- Mass media organizations measure the reaction of people to make informed decisions on content.

- Audience analysis techniques include demographic, geodemographic and psychographic breakdowns.

- Mass media organizations are more interested in applied than theoretical research.

In college Andy Kohut learned polling from the experts. He first had a part-time job with the Gallup organization in Princeton, New Jersey. Polling fascinated Kohut more than his graduate studies, so he went full-time with Gallup and eventually worked his way up to president. What drew Kohut to Gallup? Kohut, who has a strong sense of civic responsibility, liked Gallup's continuing work on public opinion on the great issues.

Something bad, from Kohut's perspective, happened in 1988. Gallup was bought by a market research company whose interest was providing data to corporations to push their goods and services more efficiently. Social polling issues were sure to take a back seat.

Eventually, Kohut joined the Los Angeles *Times'* quasi-independent polling organization, the Times Mirror Research Center for People and the Press. Times Mirror had created the center to find how the public perceived the media, what interests people in the news, and the relationship among the people, press and politics. In many ways it was like the old Gallup. The Times Mirror studies provided scholars, as well as the media, with new baselines of understanding.

But like the old Gallup, it changed. Times Mirror, with a new bottom-line-focused management, let it be known in 1995 that Kohut's operation was on a cut list. Was there no place left for public policy polling? A philanthropic organization, Pew Charitable Trusts, was concerned about the loss of the Times Mirror polling unit and offered to take it over.

Today, Kohut's work generally is called the *Pew polls*. They are the most widely cited studies on U.S. public opinion. Robert Strauss, in a

Pew Research Center for the People & the Press
Survey Reports

Terror Coverage Boost News Media's Images
But Military Censorship Backed

Released: November 28, 2001

Questionnaire

PEW RESEARCH CENTER FOR THE PEOPLE AND THE PRESS
MID-NOVEMBER SURVEY
MEDIA ATTITUDES / YOUTH ENGAGEMENT / RELIGION AFTER 9/11
FINAL TOPLINE
NOVEMBER 13 - 19, 2001
N = 1,500

Q.1 Do you approve or disapprove of the way George W. Bush is handling his job as president?
[IF DK ENTER AS DK. IF DEPENDS PROBE ONCE WITH: Overall do you approve or disapprove
of the way George W. Bush is handling his job as president? [IF STILL DEPENDS ENTER AS DK]

	Approve	Disapprove	Don't Know
Mid-November, 2001	84	9	7=100
Early October, 2001	84	8	8=100
Late September, 2001	86	7	7=100
Mid-September, 2001	80	9	11=100
Early September, 2001	51	34	15=100
August, 2001	50	32	18=100
July, 2001	51	32	17=100
June, 2001	50	33	17=100
May, 2001	53	32	15=100
April, 2001	56	27	17=100
March, 2001	55	25	20=100
February, 2001	53	21	26=100

🔗 Done   ⦿ Internet

Pew Poll. The Pew Research Center's polls focus on public policy issues, as did this one on how people ranked President Bush before and after the September 11 terrorist attacks. This survey found his approval ratings soared from a middling 50 to 55 percent in the preceding months to 86 percent by the end of September.

biographical article, said that the Los Angeles *Times* cites Pew polls every five days on average and the Washington *Post* cites them every six days. Said James Beninger, when he was president of the American Association for Public Opinion: "It is reported in all of the places where people of influence seem to look, the New York *Times* and the like."

What separates Pew polls from others?

- **Impartiality.** Nobody can accuse Pew of being the hireling of special interests.
- **Distribution.** Pew findings are distributed free.
- **Independence.** Unlike news media–sponsored surveys, Kohut isn't driven by topicality and deadlines. The polls sometimes make news, but that's residual.
- **Social and political thrust.** Kohut and his staff don't need to weigh whether to do a lucrative marketing survey or an issues poll. Because their focus is on public issues alone, their focus is never diluted.

Public-Opinion Sampling

STUDY PREVIEW   Public-opinion polling is an important ancillary activity for the mass media. One polling technique, probability sampling, relies on statistical guidelines that can be incredibly accurate. Sad to say, less reliable survey techniques also are used, which sullies the reputation of serious sampling.

The Surveying Industry

Public-opinion surveying is approaching a $1 billion-a-year business whose clients include major corporations, political candidates and the mass media. Today, just as in 1935 when **George Gallup** founded it, the **Institute of American Public Opinion** cranks out regular surveys for clients. Major news organizations hire survey companies to tap public sentiment regularly on specific issues.

About 300 companies are in the survey business in the United States, most performing advertising and product-related opinion research for private clients. During election campaigns, political candidates become major clients. There are dozens of other survey companies that do confidential research for and about the media. Their findings are important because they determine what kind of advertising will run and where, what programs will be developed and broadcast and which ones will be canceled. Some television stations even use such research to choose anchors for major newscasts.

Probability Sampling

Although polling has become a high-profile business, many people do not understand how questions to a few hundred individuals can tell the mood of 250 million Americans. In the **probability sampling** method pioneered by George Gallup in the 1940s, four factors figure into accurate surveying:

SAMPLE SIZE.   To learn how Layne College students feel about abortion on demand, you start by asking one student. Because you can hardly generalize from one student to the whole student body of 2,000, you ask a second student. If both agree, you start developing a tentative sense of how Layne students feel, but because you cannot have much confidence in such a tiny sample, you ask a third student, and a fourth and a fifth. At some point between interviewing just one and all 2,000 Layne students, you can draw a reasonable conclusion.

How do you choose a **sample size?** Statisticians have found that **384** is a magic number for many surveys. Put simply, no matter how large the **population** being sampled, if every member has an equal opportunity to be polled, you need ask only 384 people to be 95 percent confident that you are within 5 percentage points of a precise reading. For a lot of surveys, that is close enough. Here is a breakdown, from Philip Meyer's *Precision Journalism*, a book for journalists on surveying, on necessary sample sizes for 95 percent confidence and being within 5 percentage points:

Population Size	Sample Size
Infinity	384
500,000	384
100,000	383
50,000	381
10,000	370
5,000	357
3,000	341
2,000	322
1,000	278

media online

Polls: The Gallup Poll people explain how they conduct polls.
www.gallup.com/poll/faq/faq000101.asp

About Polls: An online discussion on the different types of polls. Includes an article on when a poll is not a poll.
http://sociology.about.com/science/sociology/library/weekly/aa081900c.htm

DoubleClick: DoubleClick claims to be the industry leader at using technology, media and data expertise to create solutions that help advertisers and publishers unleash the power of the web for branding, selling products and building relationships with customers. The web site lets you create your own customized DoubleClick media kit.
www.doubleclick.net

A.C. Nielsen: Nielsen Media Research, the famous TV ratings company, is the leading provider of television information services in the United States and Canada.
www.nielsenmedia.com

Arbitron: The radio research people.
www.arbitron.com

George Gallup
Introduced probability sampling.

Institute of American Public Opinion
Gallup polling organization.

probability sampling
Everyone in population being surveyed has an equal chance to be sampled.

sample size
Number of people surveyed.

384
Number of people in a properly selected sample for results to provide 95 percent confidence that results have less than 5 percent margin error.

population
Group of people being studied.

At Layne, with a total enrollment of 2,000, the sample size would need to be 322 students.

SAMPLE SELECTION.   Essential in probability sampling is **sample selection,** the process of choosing whom to interview. A good sample gives every member of the population being sampled an equal chance to be interviewed. For example, if you want to know how Kansans intend to vote, you cannot merely go to a Wichita street corner and survey the first 384 people who pass by. You would need to check a list of the state's 675,000 registered voters and then divide by the magic number, 384:

$$\frac{675,000}{384} = 1,758$$

You would need to talk with every 1,758th person on the list. At Layne College 2,000 divided by 322 would mean an interval of 6.2. Every sixth person in the student body would need to be polled.

Besides the right sample size and proper interval selection, two other significant variables affect survey accuracy: margin of error and confidence level.

MARGIN OF ERROR.   For absolute precision every person in the population must be interviewed, but such precision is hardly ever needed, and the process would be prohibitively expensive and impracticable. Pollsters must therefore decide what is an acceptable **margin of error** for every survey they conduct. This is a complex matter, but in simple terms, you can have a fairly high level of confidence that a properly designed survey with 384 respondents can yield results within 5 percentage points, either way, of being correct. If the survey finds that two candidates for statewide office are running 51 to 49 percent, for example, the race is too close to call with a sample of 384. If the survey says that the candidates are running 56 to 44 percent, however, you can be reasonably confident who is ahead in the race because, even if the survey is 5 points off on the high side for the leader, the candidate at the very least has 51 percent support (56 percent minus a maximum 5 percentage points for possible error). At best, the trailing candidate has 49 percent (44 percent plus a maximum 5 percentage points for possible error).

Increasing the sample size will reduce the margin of error. Meyer gives this breakdown:

Population Size	Sample Size	Margin of Error
Infinity	384	5 percentage points
Infinity	600	4 percentage points
Infinity	1,067	3 percentage points
Infinity	2,401	2 percentage points
Infinity	9,605	1 percentage point

Professional polling organizations that sample U.S. voters typically use sample sizes between 1,500 and 3,000 to increase accuracy. Also, measuring subgroups within the population being sampled requires that each subgroup, such as men and women, Catholics and non-Catholics, or Northerners and Southerners, be represented by 384 properly selected people.

CONFIDENCE LEVEL.   With a sample of 384, pollsters can claim a relatively high 95 percent **confidence level,** that is, that they are within 5 percentage points of

sample selection
Process for drawing individuals to be interviewed.

margin of error
Percentage that a survey may be off mark.

confidence level
Degree of certainty that a survey is accurate.

being on the mark. For many surveys, this is sufficient statistical validity. If the confidence level needs to be higher, or if the margin of error needs to be decreased, the number of people surveyed will need to be increased. In short, the level of confidence and margin of error are inversely related. A larger sample can improve confidence, just as it also can reduce the margin of error.

m e d i a o n l i n e

Gallup: See results of current and past Gallup polls of public opinion.
www.gallup.com

Roper: Where thinking people go to learn what people are thinking.
www.ropercenter.uconn.edu

Yankelovich: More current opinion polls.
http://secure.yankelovich.com/solutions/public/studies.asp

Quota Sampling

Besides probability sampling, pollsters survey cross-sections of the whole population. This quota sampling technique gave Gallup his historic 1936 conclusions about the Roosevelt-Landon presidential race. With **quota sampling,** a pollster checking an election campaign interviews a sample of people that includes a quota of men and women that corresponds to the number of male and female registered voters. The sample might also include an appropriate quota of Democrats, Republicans and independents; of poor, middle-income and wealthy people; of Catholics, Jews and Protestants; of Southerners, Midwesterners and New Englanders; of the employed and unemployed; and other breakdowns significant to the pollster.

Both quota sampling and probability sampling are valid if done correctly, but Gallup abandoned quota sampling because he could not pinpoint public opinion more closely than 4 percentage points on average. With probability sampling, he regularly came within 2 percentage points.

Evaluating Surveys

Sidewalk interviews cannot be expected to reflect the views of the population. The people who respond to such polls are self-selected by virtue of being at a given place at a given time. Just as unreliable are call-in polls with 800 or 900 telephone numbers. These polls test the views only of people who are aware of the poll and who have sufficiently strong opinions to go to the trouble of calling in.

Journalists run the risk of being duped when special-interest groups suggest that news stories be written based on their privately conducted surveys. Some organizations selectively release self-serving conclusions.

To guard against being duped, the Associated Press insists on knowing methodology details before running poll stories. The AP tells reporters to ask:

- **How many people were interviewed and how were they selected?** Any survey of fewer than 384 people selected randomly from the population group has a greater margin for error than is usually tolerated.
- **When was the poll taken?** Opinions shift over time. During election campaigns, shifts can be quick, even overnight.
- **Who paid for the poll?** With privately commissioned polls, reporters should be skeptical, asking whether the results being released constitute everything learned in the survey. The timing of the release of political polls to be politically advantageous is not uncommon.
- **What was the sampling error?** Margins of error exist in all surveys unless everyone in the population is surveyed.
- **How was the poll conducted?** Whether a survey was conducted over the telephone or face to face in homes is important. Polls conducted on street corners or in shopping malls are not worth much statistically. Mail surveys

quota sampling
Demographics of the sample coincide with those of the whole population.

Media People

George Gallup

George Gallup was excited. His mother-in-law, Ola Babcock Miller, had decided to run for secretary of state. If elected, she would become not only Iowa's first Democrat but also the first woman to hold the statewide office. Gallup's excitement, however, went beyond the novelty of his mother-in-law's candidacy. The campaign gave him an opportunity to pull together his three primary intellectual interests: survey research, public opinion and politics. In that 1932 campaign George Gallup conducted the first serious poll in history for a political candidate. Gallup's surveying provided important barometers of public sentiment that helped Miller to gear her campaign to the issues that were most on voters' minds. She won and was reelected twice by large margins.

Four years after that first 1932 election campaign, Gallup tried his polling techniques in the presidential race and correctly predicted that Franklin Roosevelt would beat Alf Landon. Having called Roosevelt's victory accurately, his Gallup Poll organization had clients knocking at his door.

Gallup devoted himself to accuracy. Even though he predicted Roosevelt's 1936 victory, Gallup was bothered that his reliability was not better. His method, quota sampling, could not call a two-way race within 4 percentage points. With quota sampling, a representative percentage of women and men was surveyed, as was a representative percentage of Democrats and Republicans, Westerners and Easterners,

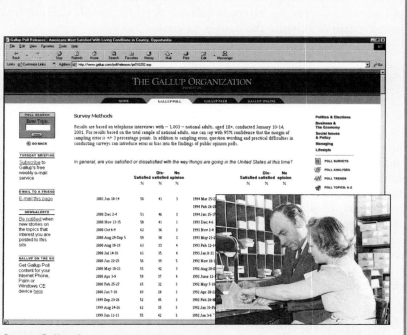

George Gallup Jr. Sorting data has become more sophisticated since George Gallup Jr. took over the polling organization from his father.

Christians and Jews and other constituencies.

In 1948 Gallup correctly concluded that Thomas Dewey was not a shoo-in for president. Nonetheless, his pre-election poll was 5.3 percentage points off. So he decided to switch to a tighter method, probability sampling, which theoretically gave everyone in the population being sampled an equal chance to be surveyed. With probability sampling, there was no need for quotas because, as Gallup explained in his folksy Midwestern way, it was like a cook making soup: "When a housewife wants to test the quality of the soup she is making, she tastes only a teaspoonful or two. She knows that if the soup is thoroughly stirred, one teaspoonful is enough to tell her

whether she has the right mixture of ingredients." With the new method, Gallup's **statistical extrapolation** narrowed his error rate to less than 2 percentage points.

Even with improvements pioneered by Gallup, public opinion surveying has detractors. Some critics say that polls influence undecided voters toward the front-runner—a bandwagon effect. Other critics say that polls make elected officials too responsive to the momentary whims of the electorate, discouraging courageous leadership. George Gallup, who died in 1984, tirelessly defended polling, arguing that good surveys give voice to the "inarticulate minority" that legislators otherwise might not hear. Gallup was convinced that public-opinion surveys help to make democracy work.

are flawed unless surveyors follow up on people who do not answer the original questionnaires.

- **How were questions worded and in what order were they asked?** Drafting questions is an art. Sloppily worded questions yield sloppy conclusions. Leading questions and loaded questions can skew results. So can question sequencing.

Polling organizations are serious when someone misuses their findings. In 1998 the Gallup organization publicly told the tobacco industry to stop saying that a 1954 Gallup poll found 90 percent of Americans were aware of a correlation between smoking and cancer. Not so, said Gallup. The question was "Have you heard or read anything recently that cigarette smoking may be a cause of cancer of the lung?" Ninety percent said that they were aware of a controversy, but, says Gallup, that doesn't necessarily mean those people believed there was smoking-cancer correlation. Gallup threatened to go to court to refute the flawed conclusion if a tobacco-maker used it again in any wrongful-death lawsuit. Lydia Saad of Gallup told the *Wall Street Journal* that her organization gives people lots of latitude in interpreting its surveys. But this, Saad added, "really crosses the line."

It is at great risk that a polling company's client misrepresents survey results. Most polling companies, concerned about protecting their reputations, include a clause in their contracts with clients that gives the pollster the right to approve the release of findings. The clause usually reads, "When misinterpretation appears, we shall publicly disclose what is required to correct it, notwithstanding our obligation for client confidentiality in all other respects."

Latter-Day Straw Polls

The ABC and CNN television networks and other news organizations dabble, some say irresponsibly, with phone-in polling on public issues. The vehicle was the **900 telephone number,** which listeners could dial at 50 cents a call to register yea or nay on a question. These **straw polls** are conducted on the web too. While they can be fun, statistically they are meaningless.

Just as dubious are the candid camera features, popular in weekly newspapers, in which a question is put to citizens on the street. The photos of half a dozen individuals and their comments are then published, often on the editorial page. These features are circulation builders for small publications whose financial success depends on how many local names and mug shots can be crammed into an issue, but it is only coincidental when the views expressed are representative of the population as a whole.

These **roving photographer** features are at their worst when people are not given time to formulate an intelligent response. The result too often is contributions to the public babble, not public understanding. The result is irresponsible pseudojournalism.

Measuring Audience Size

STUDY PREVIEW To attract advertisers, the mass media need to know the number and kinds of people they reach. This is done for the print media by audits and for the broadcast media by surveys. Although surveying is widely accepted for obtaining such data, some approaches are more reliable than others.

statistical extrapolation
Drawing conclusions from a segment of the whole.

900 telephone numbers
Used for call-in surveys; respondents select selves to participate and pay for the call.

straw poll
Respondents select themselves to be polled; unreliable indicator of public opinion.

roving photographer
Statistically unsound way to tap public opinion.

Media Timeline

Media Research

1914 Advertisers, publications created the Audit Bureau of Circulations to verify circulation claims.

1929 Archibald Crossley conducted the first listenership survey.

1932 George Gallup used quota sampling in an Iowa election.

1936 Gallup used quota sampling in a presidential election.

1940s A. C. Nielsen conducted a demographic listenership survey.

1948 Gallup used probability sampling in a presidential election.

1970s SRI introduced VALS psychographics.

1974 Jonathan Robbin introduced PRIZM geodemographics.

2000 Portable People Meters were introduced to track listenership for radio and television, including cable.

---

circulation
Number of readers of a publication.

Audit Bureau of Circulations
Checks newspaper, magazine circulation claims.

ratings
Measurements of broadcast audience size.

A. C. Nielsen Co.
Surveys television viewership.

demographics
Characteristics of groups within a population being sampled, including age, gender, affiliations.

Newspaper and Magazine Audits

The number of copies a newspaper or magazine puts out, called **circulation,** is fairly easy to calculate. It is simple arithmetic involving data like press runs, subscription sales and unsold copies returned from newsracks. Many publishers follow strict procedures, which are checked by independent audit organizations, like the **Audit Bureau of Circulations,** to assure advertisers that the system is honest and circulation claims comparable.

The Audit Bureau of Circulations was formed in 1914 to remove the temptation for publishers to inflate their claims to attract advertisers and hike ad rates. Inflated claims, contagious in some cities, were working to the disadvantage of honest publishers. Today, most newspapers and magazines belong to ABC, which means that they follow the bureau's standards for reporting circulation and are subject to the bureau's audits.

Broadcast Ratings

Radio and television audiences are harder to measure, but advertisers have no less need for counts to help them decide where to place ads and to know what is a fair price. To keep track of broadcast audiences, a whole **ratings** industry, now with about 200 companies, has developed. The **A. C. Nielsen Co.** tracks network television viewership.

Radio ratings began in 1929 when advertisers asked pollster Archibald Crossley to determine how many people were listening to network programs. Crossley checked a small sample of households and then extrapolated the data into national ratings, the same process that radio and television audience tracking companies still use, though there have been refinements.

In the 1940s Nielsen began telling advertisers which radio programs were especially popular among men, women and children. Nielsen also divided listenership into age brackets: 18 to 34, 35 to 49 and 50 plus. These were called **demographic** breakdowns. When Nielsen moved into television monitoring in 1950, it expanded

Broadcast**Watch**
COMPILED BY KENNETH RAY

FEB. 25–MAR. 3 *Broadcast network prime time ratings according to Nielsen Media Research*

Week 23

	abc	CBS	NBC	FOX	PAX TV	UPN	WB
Network	5.5/9	9.6/15	7.9/12	7.1/11	0.9/1	2.5/4	3.6/5

MONDAY

Time	abc (5.5/9)	CBS (9.6/15)	NBC (7.9/12)	FOX (7.1/11)	PAX (0.9/1)	UPN (2.5/4)	WB (3.6/5)
8:00	57. All New Bloopers 5.6/9	21. King/Queens 9.0/14; 23. Yes, Dear 8.9/13	31. Fear Factor 7.8/12	35. Boston Public 7.6/12	125. Miracle Pets 0.7/1	95. The Hughleys 2.3/4; 93. One on One 2.5/4	71. 7th Heaven 4.7/7
9:00	63. ABC Monday Night Movie—Practical Magic 5.4/9	4. Ev Lvs Raymnd 14.0/21; 12. Becker 11.2/17	39. Third Watch 7.1/11	44. Ally McBeal 6.6/10	118. Touched by an Angel 1.0/1	92. The Parkers 2.6/4; 90. Girlfriends 2.7/4	93. Angel 2.5/4
10:00		36. Family Law 7.3/12	23. Crossng Jordan 8.9/15		114. Diagnosis Murder 1.1/2		

TUESDAY

Time	abc (6.5/10)	CBS (10.0/16)	NBC (9.4/15)	FOX (5.7/9)	PAX (0.8/1)	UPN (2.3/4)	WB (3.7/6)
8:00	68. The Chair 5.0/8	14. JAG 10.9/17	20. Frasier 9.1/14; 15. Watchng Ellie* 10.8/16	49. That '70s Show 6.2/10; 57. That '70s Show 5.6/8	125. Mysterious Ways 0.7/1	84. Buffy the Vampire Slayer 3.1/5	80. Gilmore Girls 3.5/5
9:00	30. NYPD Blue 7.9/12	21. The Guardian 9.0/13	11. Frasier 11.4/17; 25. Scrubs 8.3/12	57. 24 5.6/8	125. Doc 0.7/1	107. Roswell 1.6/2	76. Smallville 3.9/6
10:00	46. Philly 6.5/11	18. Judging Amy 10.2/17	25. Dateline NBC 8.3/14		114. Diagnosis Murder 1.1/2		

WEDNESDAY

Time	abc (5.7/9)	CBS (12.3/19)	NBC (19.7/31)	FOX (5.4/8)	PAX (1.0/2)	UPN (2.4/4)	WB (2.2/3)
8:00	42. My Wife & Kids 6.8/11; 54. According to Jim 5.9/9	9. 44th Annual Grammy Awards 11.9/19	27. Ed 8.1/13	63. Fox Movie Special—Rush Hour 5.4/8	124. Candid Camera 0.8/1	85. Enterprise 3.0/5	96. Flix Wednesday—Dumb and Dumber 2.2/3
9:00	68. Drew Carey 5.0/7; 75. The Job 4.2/6		13. The West Wing 11.0/16		118. Touched by an Angel 1.0/2	106. Enterprise 1.7/3	
10:00	52. Downtown 6.1/10		7. Law & Order 12.3/20		111. Diagnosis Murder 1.2/2		

THURSDAY

Time	abc (3.7/5)	CBS (6.5/10)	NBC (14.4/22)	FOX (3.2/5)	PAX (1.0/1)	UPN (3.8/6)	WB (1.9/3)
8:00	88. Whose Line Is It 2.9/5; 77. Whose Line Is It 3.8/6	6. Survivor: Marquesas* 13.0/20	1. Friends 17.4/27; 4. Leap of Faith* 14.0/21	85. Family Guy 3.0/5; 83. Family Guy 3.2/5	121. It's a Miracle 0.9/1	77. WWF Smackdown! 3.8/6	103. Charmed 1.8/3
9:00	49. Who Wants to Be a Millionaire 6.2/9	2. CSI 17.1/26	8. Will & Grace 12.1/18; 17. Just Shoot Me 10.4/16	80. King of the Hill 3.5/5; 88. Futurama 2.9/4	121. Touched by an Angel 0.9/1		100. Charmed 1.9/3
10:00	42. Primetime Thursday 6.8/11	27. The Agency 8.1/13	3. ER 16.3/27		111. Diagnosis Murder 1.2/2		

FRIDAY

Time	abc (6.3/11)	CBS (5.3/9)	NBC (9.8/17)	FOX (3.3/6)	PAX (0.7/1)	UPN (1.6/3)	WB (2.1/4)
8:00	48. America's Funniest Home Videos 6.3/11	57. First Monday 5.6/10	19. Dateline NBC 9.4/17	82. 33rd NAACP Image Awards 3.3/6	129. Weakest Link 0.6/1		99. Sabrina/Witch 2.0/4; 103. Raising Dad 1.8/3
9:00	65. Best Commercials Never Seen 5.4/9	67. 51st Annual Miss USA Pageant 5.2/9			129. Encounters With the Unexplained 0.6/1	107. UPN Movie Friday—Batman Forever 1.6/3	90. Reba 2.7/5; 100. Maybe It's Me 1.9/3
10:00	39. 20/20 7.1/13		16. Law & Order: Special Victims Unit 10.7/19		118. Diagnosis Murder 1.0/2		

SATURDAY

Time	abc (3.7/7)	CBS (5.9/10)	NBC (6.4/11)	FOX (5.4/10)	PAX (0.8/1)	UPN	WB
8:00		56. Touched by an Angel 5.8/10		70. Cops 4.8/9; 66. Cops 5.3/9	121. Diagnosis Murder 0.9/2		
9:00	79. ABC Bond Picture Show—Diamonds Are Forver 3.7/7	71. The Agency 4.7/8	47. NBC Saturday Night Movies—U.S. Marshals 6.4/11	54. AMW: America Fights Back 5.9/10	125. PAX Big Event—Miracle of the Cards 0.7/1		
10:00		38. The District 7.2/13					

SUNDAY

Time	abc (7.2/11)	CBS (7.9/13)	NBC (5.2/8)	FOX (6.0/9)	PAX (1.2/2)	UPN	WB (1.8/3)
7:00	41. Wonderful World of Disney—Cinderella 7.0/11	10. 60 Minutes 11.6/19	85. NBA Basketball Game 2—Indiana vs. Sacramento 3.0/5	73. Futurama 4.5/8; 61. King of the Hill 5.5/9	111. Candid Camera 1.2/2		110. No Boundaries* 1.5/2
8:00		34. The Education of Max Bickford 7.7/12	74. Dateline NBC 4.3/7	31. The Simpsons 7.8/12; 36. Malcolm/Middl 7.3/11	107. Doc 1.6/2		103. Jamie Kennedy 1.8/3; 97. Jamie Kennedy 2.1/3
9:00	44. Alias 6.6/10		31. Law & Order: Criminal Intent 7.8/12	61. The X-Files 5.5/8	114. Ponderosa 1.1/2		97. Off Centre 2.1/3; 100. For Your Love 1.9/3
10:00	29. The Practice 8.0/13	52. CBS Sunday Movie—Crossed Over 6.1/10	49. Dateline NBC 6.2/10		114. Touched by an Angel 1.1/2		

	abc	CBS	NBC	FOX	PAX	UPN	WB
Week	5.8/9	9.1/15	8.9/14	5.2/8	0.9/2	2.5/4	2.5/4
S-T-D	6.5/11	8.1/13	9.2/15	6.2/10	0.9/1	2.8/4	2.5/4

KEY: RANKING/SHOW TITLE/PROGRAM RATING/SHARE
• TOP TEN SHOWS OF THE WEEK ARE NUMBERED IN RED
• TV UNIVERSE ESTIMATED AT 105.5 MILLION HOUSEHOLDS; ONE RATINGS POINT IS EQUAL TO 1,055,000 TV HOMES •
YELLOW TINT IS WINNER OF TIME SLOT • (NR)=NOT RANKED; RATING/SHARE ESTIMATED FOR PERIOD SHOWN
• *PREMIERE • PROGRAMS LESS THAN 15 MINUTES IN LENGTH NOT SHOWN • S-T-D = SEASON TO DATE
• SOURCES: NIELSEN MEDIA RESEARCH, CBS RESEARCH

Ratings and Shares. The trade journal *Broadcasting&Cable* reports the network Nielsens weekly. The numbers before each show indicates its place. NBC's *Friends,* at 9 p.m. Thursday, led this week. One measure of audience is the "rating," the percentage of television-equipped households viewing a program. *Friends* rating was 17.4 percent. Because 105.5 million U.S. households have television sets, each percentage point is valued at 1,055,000 households, which means 180,357 households were watching. A second audience measure is called "share," which is the percentage of all households with a television on. *Friends* had a 27 share, slightly outdistancing CBS' *CSI* at 26. The people in the other 47 percent of households that had a television on were watching something else.

interviews
Face-to-face, mail, telephone survey technique.

diaries
Sampling technique in which respondents keep their own records.

overnights
Next-morning reports on network viewership.

Portable People Meter
Monitor that tracks individual viewing habits.

audience data into more breakdowns. Today breakdowns include income, education, religion, occupation, neighborhood and even which products the viewers of certain programs use frequently.

While Archibald Crossley's early ratings were sponsored by advertisers, today networks and individual stations also commission ratings to be done. The television networks pass ratings data on to advertisers immediately. Local stations usually recast the raw data for brochures that display the data in ways that put the station in the most favorable light. These brochures are distributed by station sales representatives to advertisers. While advertisers receive ratings data from the stations and networks, major advertising agencies have contracts with Nielsen, Arbitron and other market research companies to gather audience data to meet their specifications.

Audience Measurement Techniques

The primary techniques, sometimes used in combination, for measuring broadcast audiences are:

INTERVIEWS. In his pioneer 1929 listenership polling, Archibald Crossley placed telephone calls to randomly selected households. Today, many polling companies use telephone **interviews** exclusively. Some companies conduct face-to-face interviews, which can elicit fuller information, although it is more expensive and time-consuming.

DIARIES. Many ratings companies give forms to selected households to record what stations were on at particular times. Some companies distribute **diaries** to every member of a household. Arbitron's diaries go to everybody over age 12 in selected households, which provide data on age and gender preferences for certain radio stations and programs. Participants mail these diaries back to Arbitron, which tabulates the results.

METERS. For television ratings, Nielsen uses meters. Older set-top meters monitor which channels are being watched. With some meters, household members click a button so that Nielsen can determine for whom programs have their appeal—men, women, children, oldsters. Some meters are programmed to see who is watching by sensing body mass. Meters transmit their data automatically to Nielsen's central computers. This allows Nielsen to generate next-day reports, called **overnights,** for the networks and advertisers.

Nielsen has 4,000 households wired with meters in the United States.

Television networks, unhappy with bad news about their declining audiences in recent years, have tried to discredit Nielsen. The networks toyed with creating an alternative ratings company, but the expense would have been overwhelming. Responding to the criticism, Nielsen installed more meters and tightened its methodology.

In 2000 Nielsen and Arbitron jointly tested portable meters for people to carry around. The pager-size **Portable People Meters,** weighing 2½ ounces, were set to pick up inaudible signals transmitted with programs. The goal: to track away-from-home audiences at sports bars, offices and airports. Tracking those "lost listeners" could affect ratings. ESPN estimates that 4 million people, without cable at home, watch sports on cable away from home in a typical week. The "walking

Walking Meter. The latest broadcast audience measuring device is a 2½-ounce gizmo for people to carry wherever they go. The portable meters track listening that is missed by household meters. The meters pick up an inaudible code embedded in the audio of television, radio and streamed programs. When people get home, they put the meters in a dock that transmits accumulated data to Nielsen and Arbitron computers for aggregation.

meters," as they are called, also track commuter radio habits for the first time. The **passive meters** don't require people to remember to turn them on, press buttons or make entries.

passive meter
Recognizes individuals by body mass to track viewing habits.

Broadcast Ratings Council
Accredits ratings companies.

Web Audience Measures

The leading web audience measuring company, Media Metrix, uses a two-track system to determine how many people view web sites. Media Metrix gathers data from 40,000 individual computers whose owners have agreed to be monitored. Some of these computers are programmed to track web usage and report data back by e-mail. In addition, Media Metrix has lined up other computer users to mail in a tracking disc periodically. In 1998 the Nielsen television ratings company set up a similar methodology. Other companies also are in the web ratings business.

How accurate are web ratings? Some major content providers, including CNN, ESPN and Time Warner, claim the ratings undercount their users. Such claims go beyond self-serving comments because, in fact, different rating companies come up with widely divergent ratings. The question is: Why can't the ratings companies get it right? The answer, in part, is that divergent data flow from divergent methodologies. Data need to be viewed in terms of the methodology that was used. Also, the infant web ratings business undoubtedly is hobbled by methodology flaws that have yet to be identified and corrected.

Criticism of Ratings

However sophisticated the ratings services have become, they have critics. Many fans question the accuracy of ratings when their favorite television program is cancelled because the network finds the ratings inadequate. Something is wrong, they say, when the viewing preferences of a few thousand households determine network programming for the entire nation. Though it seems incredible to someone unknowledgeable about statistical probability, the sample base of major ratings services like Nielsen generally is considered sufficient to extrapolate reliably on viewership in the 97 million U.S. households.

It was not always so. Doubts peaked in the 1940s and 1950s when it was learned that some ratings services lied about sample size and were less than scientific in choosing samples. A congressional investigation in 1963 prompted the networks to create the **Broadcast Ratings Council** to accredit ratings companies and audit their reports.

Ratings have problems, some inherent in differing methodologies and some attributable to human error and fudging:

DISCREPANCIES. When different ratings services come up with widely divergent findings in the same market, advertisers become suspicious. Minor discrepancies can be explained by different sampling methods, but significant discrepancies point to flawed methodology or execution. It was discrepancies of this sort that led to the creation of the Broadcast Ratings Council.

SLANTED RESULTS. Sales reps of some local stations, eager to demonstrate to advertisers that their stations have large audiences, extract only the favorable data

Fickle Audience. Television executives look to survey research to find ways to reach more viewers. In 2001 CNN was losing audience share to upstarts MSNBC and Fox News Channel. That prompted the network to cut back on newscasts and add more personality-driven talk and audience-involvement shows. Early in the programming shift, veteran anchor Bernie Shaw foresaw what was coming and announced his retirement.

Media Abroad

Global Television Ratings

Colgate-Palmolive, the global toiletries company, has a problem figuring out how much its ad dollars are buying in different countries because audience rating agencies in different countries have developed separate terminology. In Austria the word "housewife" means anyone, male or female, 18 or older, who maintains a house. The French, however, define "housewife" as a female shopper. Colgate isn't alone. All multinational advertisers end up comparing apples and oranges when they try to get a clear idea about how much to invest in different countries to reach comparable audiences of likely customers.

Several major advertising and television trade groups now are working up definitions to standardize television audience measurement terminologies. It's no small task. Should ratings include only live viewing or also VCR viewing? Should a 4-year-old count equally with an adult? How do you count viewers where one set serves a whole village that gathers and watches together? Should an impoverished minority-group member count as much as an affluent elite whose discretionary income glimmers in advertisers' eyes? And, yes, for the sake of Colgate-Palmolive, who is and who isn't a housewife?

Hashing out these questions, and also whether national and regional traditions and preferences will surrender to universal standards, are:

- Advertising Research Foundation, a United States organization.
- European Broadcasting Union.
- European Association of Advertising Agencies.
- Group of European Audience Researchers.
- World Federation of Advertisers.

The goal is to generate data that can be exchanged meaningfully across borders.

from survey results. It takes a sophisticated local advertiser to reconcile slanted and fudged claims.

SAMPLE SELECTION.   Some ratings services select their samples meticulously, giving every household in a market a statistically equal opportunity to be sampled. Some sample selections are seriously flawed: How reliable, for example, are the listenership claims of a rock 'n' roll station that puts a disc jockey's face on billboards all over town and then sends the disc jockey to a teenage dance palace to ask about listening preferences?

HYPING.   Ratings-hungry stations have learned how to build audiences during **sweeps** weeks in February, May and November when major local television ratings are done. Consider these examples of **hyping:**

- Radio give-aways often coincide with ratings periods.
- Many news departments promote sensationalistic series for the sweeps and then retreat to routine coverage when the ratings period is over. Just ahead of one 1988 Minneapolis sweeps, one station mailed out thousands of questionnaires, asking people to watch its programs and mail back the form. Accused of trickery to look good in the ratings, the station responded with a straight face that it merely was trying a new technique to strengthen viewership. The timing, it argued, was mere coincidence.
- Besides sweeps weeks, there are **black weeks** when no ratings are conducted. In these periods some stations run all kinds of odd and dull serve-the-public programs that they would never consider during a sweeps period.

sweeps
When broadcast ratings are conducted.

hyping
Intensive promotion to attract an audience during ratings periods.

black weeks
Periods when ratings are not conducted.

RESPONDENT ACCURACY.   Respondents don't always answer truthfully. People have an opportunity to tell interviewers or diaries that they watched "Masterpiece Theatre" on PBS instead of less classy fare. Shock radio and trash television may have more audience than the ratings show.

ZIPPING, ZAPPING AND FLUSHING.   Ratings services measure audiences for programs and for different times of day, but they do not measure whether commercials are watched. Advertisers are interested, of course, in whether the programs in which their ads are sandwiched are popular, but more important to them is whether people are watching the ads.

This vacuum in audience measurements was documented in the 1960s when somebody with a sense of humor correlated a major drop in Chicago water pressure with the Super Bowl halftime, in what became known as the **flush factor**. Football fans were getting off the couch by the thousands at halftime to go to the bathroom. Advertisers were missing many people because viewers were watching the program but not the ads.

This problem has been exacerbated with the advent of handheld television remote controls and systems like TiVo. Viewers can **zip** from station to station to avoid commercials, and when they record programs for later viewing, they can **zap** out the commercials.

Measuring Audience Reaction

STUDY PREVIEW   The television ratings business has moved beyond measuring audience size to measuring audience reaction. Researchers measure audience reaction with numerous methods, including focus groups, galvanic skin checks and prototypes.

Focus Groups

Television consulting companies measure audience reaction with **focus groups**. Typically, an interview crew goes to a shopping center, chooses a dozen individuals by gender and age, and offers them cookies, soft drinks and $25 each to sit down and watch a taped local newscast. A moderator then asks their reactions, sometimes with loaded and leading questions to open them up. It is a tricky research method that depends highly on the skill of the moderator. In one court case an anchor who had lost her job as a result of responses to a focus group complained that the moderator had contaminated the process with prejudicial assertions and questions:

- "This is your chance to get rid of the things you don't like to see on the news."
- "Come on, unload on those sons of bitches who make $100,000 a year."
- "This is your chance to do more than just yell at the TV. You can speak up and say I really hate that guy or I really like that broad."
- "Let's spend 30 seconds destroying this anchor. Is she a mutt? Be honest about this."

Even when conducted skillfully, focus groups have the disadvantage of reflecting the opinion of the loudest respondent.

Galvanic Skin Checks

Consulting companies hired by television stations run a great variety of studies to determine audience reaction. Local stations, which originate news programs and

flush factor
Viewers leave during commercials to go to refrigerator, bathroom, etc.

zipping
Viewers change television channels to avoid commercials.

zapping
Viewers record programs and eliminate commercial breaks.

focus groups
Small groups interviewed in loosely structured ways for opinion, reactions.

not much else, look to these consultants for advice on news sets, story selection, and even which anchors and reporters are most popular. Besides surveys, these consultants sometimes use **galvanic skin checks.** Wires are attached to individuals in a sample group of viewers to measure pulse and skin reactions, such as perspiration. Advocates of these tests claim that they reveal how much interest a newscast evokes and whether it is positive or negative.

These tests were first used to check audience reaction to advertisements, but today some stations look to them in deciding whether to remodel a studio. A dubious use, from a journalistic perspective, is using galvanic skin checks to determine what kinds of stories to cover and whether to find new anchors and reporters. The skin checks reward short, photogenic stories like fires and accidents rather than significant stories, which tend to be longer and don't lend themselves to flashy video. The checks also favor good-looking, smooth anchors and reporters, regardless of their journalistic competence. One wag was literally correct when he called this "a heart-throb approach to journalism."

Prototype Research

Before making major investments, media executives need as much information as they can obtain to determine how to enhance a project's chances for success or whether it has a chance at all. This is known as **prototype research.** The **American Research Institute** of Los Angeles specializes in showing previews of television programs and even promotional ads to sample audiences. It is a method originated by movie studios, which invite people to advance showings and watch their reaction to decide how to advertise a new film most effectively, how to time the film's release and even whether to re-edit the film.

When Gannett decided to establish a new newspaper, *USA Today,* it created prototypes, each designed differently, to test readers' reactions. Many new magazines are preceded by at least one trial issue to sample marketplace reaction and to show to potential advertisers.

In network television a prototype may even make it on the air in the form of a pilot. One or a few episodes are tested, usually in prime time with a lot of promotion, to see whether the audience goes for the program concept. Some made-for-television movies actually are test runs to determine whether a series might be spun off from the movie.

Audience Analysis

STUDY PREVIEW Traditional demographic polling methods divided people by gender, age and other easily identifiable population characteristics. Today, media people use sophisticated lifestyle breakdowns such as geodemographics and psychographics to match the content of their publications, broadcast programs and advertising to the audiences they seek.

Demographics

Early in the development of public-opinion surveying, pollsters learned that broad breakdowns had limited usefulness. Archibald Crossley's pioneering radio sur-

galvanic skin checks
Monitor pulse, skin responses to stimuli.

prototype research
Checks response to product still in development.

American Research Institute
Movie prototype research.

veys, for example, told the number of people who were listening to network programs, which was valuable to the networks and their advertisers, but Crossley's figures did not tell how many listeners were men or women, urban or rural, old or young. Such breakdowns of overall survey data, called demographics, were developed in the 1930s as Crossley, Gallup and other early pollsters refined their work.

Today, if demographic data indicate a political candidate is weak in the Midwest, campaign strategists can gear the candidate's message to Midwestern concerns. Through demographics, advertisers keen on reaching young women can identify magazines that will carry their ads to that audience. If advertisers seek an elderly audience, they can use demographic data to determine where to place their television ads.

While demographics remains valuable today, newer methods can break the population into categories that have even greater usefulness. These newer methods, which include cohort analysis, geodemography and psychographics, provide lifestyle breakdowns.

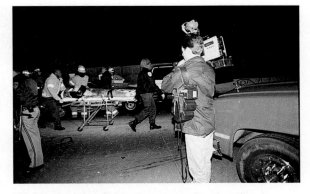

If It Bleeds, It Leads. Audience researchers have found newscast ratings go up for stations that consistently deliver graphic video. This has prompted many stations to favor fire stories, for example, even if the fire wasn't consequential, if graphic video is available. The ratings quest also prompts these stations to favor crimes and accidents over more substantive stories, like government budgets, that don't lend themselves to gripping graphics.

Cohort Analysis

Marketing people have developed **cohort analysis**, a specialized form of demographics, to identify generations and then design and produce products with generational appeal. Advertising people then gear media messages with the images, music, humor and other generational variables that appeal to the target cohort. The major cohorts are dubbed:

- **Generation X,** who came of age in the 1980s.
- **Baby Boomers,** who came of age in the late 1960s and 1970s.
- **Postwar Generation,** who came of age in the 1950s.
- **World War II Veterans,** who came of age in the 1940s.
- **Depression Survivors,** who came of age during the economic depression of the 1930s.

Cohort analysis has jarred traditional thinking that people, as they get older, simply adopt their parents' values. The new 50-plus generation, for example, grew up on Coke and Pepsi drinks and, to the dismay of coffee growers, may prefer to start the day with cola—not the coffee their parents drank.

The Chrysler automobile company was early to recognize that Baby Boomers aren't interested in buying Cadillac-type luxury cars even when they have amassed the money to afford them. In 1996 Chrysler scrapped plans for a new luxury car to compete with Cadillac and instead introduced the $35,000 open-top 1997 Plymouth Prowler that gave Baby Boomers a nostalgic feel for the hot rods of their youth. Chrysler also determined that graying Baby Boomers preferred upscale Jeeps to the luxo-barge cars that appealed to the Postwar Generation.

Advertising people who use cohort analysis know that Baby Boomers, although now in their 50s, are still turned on by pizzas and the Rolling Stones. In short, the

cohort analysis
Demographic tool to identify marketing targets by common characteristics.

Generation X
Today's 30-something generation.

Baby Boomers
Today's 40-something and 50-something generation.

Postwar Generation
Today's 60-something generation.

World War II Veterans
Today's 70-something and 80-something generation.

Depression Survivors
Today's 80-something and 90-something generation.

Cohort Analysis. When Oldsmobile realized in the 1980s that young buyers weren't maturing into clones of their parents, the company flaunted its cars with the advertising slogan "It's not your father's Oldsmobile." Unfortunately for Olds, the cars were not much different, and sales continued to skid. Today, marketing and advertising people are using cohort analysis to develop products, not just slogans, to appeal to different generations. Chrysler did this in the late 1990s, dropping plans for the LHX luxury car that might have appealed to people in their 50s a generation ago but not to today's aging Baby Boomers. For the new 50-something generation, Chrysler created the Plymouth Prowler hotrod, which stirred wonderful memories among affluent car buyers who grew up in the 1960s and 1970s.

habits of their youth stick with a generation as it gets older. What appealed to the 30-something a decade ago won't necessarily sail with today's 30-something set. David Bostwick, Chrysler's marketing research director, puts it this way: "Nobody wants to become their parents."

Geodemographics

While demographics, including cohort analysis, remain valuable today, new methods can break the population into categories that have even greater usefulness. These newer methods, which include geodemography, provide lifestyle breakdowns.

Computer whiz **Jonathan Robbin** provided the basis for more sophisticated breakdowns in 1974 when he began developing his **PRIZM** system for **geodemography.** From census data Robbin grouped every zip code by ethnicity, family life cycle, housing style, mobility and social rank. Then he identified 34 factors that statistically distinguished neighborhoods from each other. All this information was cranked through a computer programmed by Robbin to plug every zip code into 1 of 40 clusters. Here are the most frequent clusters created through PRIZM, which stands for Potential Rating Index for Zip Markets, with the labels Robbin put on them:

- **Blue-Chip Blues.** These are the wealthiest blue-collar suburbs. These Blue-Chip Blues, as Robbin calls them, comprise about 6 percent of U.S. households. About 13 percent of these people are college graduates.
- **Young Suburbia.** Child-rearing outlying suburbs, 5.3 percent of U.S. population; college grads, 24 percent.

Jonathan Robbin
Devised PRIZM geodemography system.

PRIZM
Identifies population characteristics by zip code.

geodemography
Demographic characteristics by geographic area.

- **Golden Ponds.** Rustic mountain, seashore or lakeside cottage communities, 5.2 percent; college grads, 13 percent.
- **Blue-Blood Estates.** Wealthiest neighborhoods; college grads, 51 percent.
- **Money and Brains.** Posh big-city enclaves of townhouses, condos and apartments; college grads, 46 percent.

Geodemographic breakdowns are used not only for magazine advertising but also for editorial content. At Time Warner magazines, geodemographic analysis permits issues to be edited for special audiences. *Time,* for example, has a 600,000 circulation edition for company owners, directors, board chairs, presidents, other titled officers and department heads. Among others are editions for physicians and college students.

Psychographics

A refined lifestyle breakdown introduced in the late 1970s, **psychographics,** divides the population into lifestyle segments. One leading psychographics approach, the Values and Life-Styles program, known as **VALS** for short, uses an 85-page survey that was used to identify broad categories of people:

- **Belongers.** Comprising about 38 percent of the U.S. population, these people are conformists who are satisfied with mainstream values and are reluctant to change brands once they're satisfied. Belongers are not very venturesome and fit the stereotype of Middle America. They tend to be churchgoers and television watchers.
- **Achievers.** Comprising about 20 percent of the population, these are prosperous people who fit into a broader category of inner-directed consumers. Achievers pride themselves on making their own decisions. They're an upscale audience to which a lot of advertising is directed. As a group, achievers aren't heavy television watchers.
- **Societally Conscious.** Comprising 11 percent of the population, these people are aware of social issues and tend to be politically active. The societally conscious also are upscale and inner directed, and they tend to prefer reading to watching television.
- **Emulators.** Comprising 10 percent of the population, these people aspire to a better life but, not quite understanding how to do it, go for the trappings of prosperity. Emulators are status seekers, prone to suggestions on what makes the good life.
- **Experientials.** Comprising 5 percent of the population, these people are venturesome, willing to try new things in an attempt to experience life fully. They are a promising upscale audience for many advertisers.
- **I-Am-Me's.** Comprising 3 percent of the population, these people work hard to set themselves apart and are susceptible to advertising pitches that offer ways to differentiate themselves, which gives them a kind of subculture conformity. SRI International, which developed the VALS technique, characterized I-Am-Me's as "a guitar-playing punk rocker who goes around in shades and sports an earring." Rebellious youth, angry and maladjusted, fit this category.
- **Survivors.** This is a small downscale category that includes pensioners who worry about making ends meet.

media online

VALS: Now that you've read all about VALS in the text-book, see where you fit in on the value and lifestyle hierarchy. You might be surprised after responding to this site's questionnaire.
http://future.sri.com/vals

psychographics
Breaking down a population by lifestyle characteristics.

VALS
Psychographic analysis by values, lifestyle, life stage.

INTEGRATED PEOPLE
These people have "put it all together," as the VALS theorists describe it. These people see many sides of an issue and are capable of assuming leadership if appropriate or a secondary role if that is appropriate.

OUTER-DIRECTED PEOPLE
These people are motivated by external things, like making money, keeping up with the neighbors and fitting in.
Achievers. These people are success-oriented, hard-working and materialistic.
Emulators. These people are status-seekers. Having the symbols of success is important to them.
Belongers. These people are conforming and tend to be conservative and conventional. They lean toward nostalgic sentimentalism with a puritanical streak.

NEED-DRIVEN PEOPLE
Basic human needs like food and shelter are central issues for need-driven people.
Sustainers. These people live from paycheck to paycheck. Although they engage in an occasional extravagance, they have little hope for improving their lot in life.
Survivors. These people worry about making ends meet. As a group, they are marked by poverty, low education, old age and limited access to upper mobility.

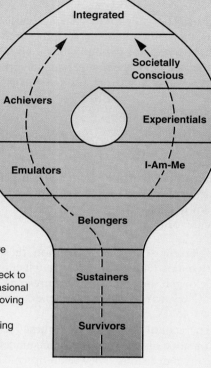

INNER-DIRECTED PEOPLE
These people are self-motivated in much that they do. They are oriented to personal growth.
Societally Conscious. These people feel obliged to improve the world and tend to be active on political and social issues.
Experientials. These people want new experiences and tend to be venturesome. They seek personal growth.
I-Am-Me's. These people work very hard at setting themselves apart. Sometimes they are obnoxious in trying to attract attention to how they are different.

VALS Hierarchy. Developmental psychologists have long told us that people change their values as they mature. Today, many advertisers rely on the Values and Life-Styles model, VALS for short, which was derived from developmental psychology, to identify potential consumers and to design effective messages. Relatively few advertising messages are aimed at survivors and sustainers, who have little discretionary income. However, belongers and people on the divergent outer-directed or inner-directed paths are lucrative advertising targets for many products and services.

- **Sustainers.** These people live from paycheck to paycheck. Although they indulge in an occasional extravagance, they have slight hope for improving their lot in life. Sustainers are a downscale category and aren't frequent advertising targets.
- **Integrateds.** Comprising only 2 percent of the population, integrateds are both creative and prosperous—willing to try different products and ways of doing things, and they have the wherewithal to do it.

Applying psychographics is not without hazard. The categories are in flux as society and lifestyles change. SRI researchers who chart growth in the percentage of I-Am-Me's, experientials and the societally conscious project that they total one-third of the population. Belongers are declining.

Another complication is that no person fits absolutely the mold of any one category. Even for individuals who fit one category better than another, there is no single mass medium to reach them. VALS research may show that achievers constitute the biggest market for antihistamines, but belongers also head to the medicine cabinet when they're congested.

Applied and Theoretical Research

STUDY PREVIEW   Media-sponsored research looks for ways to build audiences, to enhance profits and to program responsibly. In contrast, mass communication scholarship asks theoretical questions that can yield new understandings, regardless of whether there is a practical application.

Media-Sponsored Research

Studies sponsored by mass media companies seek information that can be put to use. This is called **applied research.** When broadcasters underwrite research on media violence, they want answers to help make programming decisions. Audience measures and analysis are applied research, which can be put to work to enhance profits.

Mass media research ranges from developing new technology to seeking historical lessons from previous practices. Here are some fields of applied media research:

TECHNOLOGICAL RESEARCH.   Mass media companies and their suppliers finance **technological research** to take economic advantage of new opportunities. Early television in the United States, for example, was spearheaded in the 1930s by RCA, which saw new opportunities for its NBC radio subsidiary.

POLICY ANALYSIS.   The media have intense interests in how changes in public policy will affect their business. The importance of good **policy analysis** was illustrated by the 1979 decision of the Federal Communications Commission to allow people to install backyard satellite dishes to pick up television signals. Analysts anticipated correctly that the television networks would go to satellites to send programs to their affiliates.

OPINION SURVEYS.   When anchor Dan Rather began wearing a sweater on the CBS Evening News, ratings improved. The network learned about the "sweater factor" from audience **opinion surveys.** Survey research helps media executives to make content decisions—whether to expand sports coverage, to hire a disc jockey away from the competition or to ax a dubious sitcom. Advertisers and public relations practitioners also look to public-opinion surveys.

Mass Communication Scholarship

In contrast to applied research, **theoretical research** looks for truths regardless of practical application. Scholars consider most theoretical research on a higher level than applied research, partly because the force that drives it is the seeking of truths for their own sake rather than for any economic goal.

Profit motivated as they are, media organizations are not especially enthusiastic about funding theoretical research. There usually is no apparent or short-term economic return from theoretical scholarship. For this reason most theoretical research occurs at major universities, whose institutional commitments include pushing back the frontiers of human knowledge, even if no economic reward is likely. Here are some of the kinds of studies and analyses that are the subject of theoretical research:

applied research
Usefulness, usually economic, is apparent.

technological research
To improve technology and find new technology.

policy analysis
Seeks implications of public policy, future effects.

opinion surveys
Seek audience reaction, views.

theoretical research
Goal to advance knowledge.

Media People

W. Joseph Campbell

For years school children learned that the Spanish-American War of 1898 was the fault of rival New York newspaper publishers William Randolph Hearst and Joseph Pulitzer. The story is that hyped stories about Spanish abuses in Cuba so enraged readers that the United States declared war on Spain. Historians have long tried to dampen the Newspaper War theory, pointing out that the evidence wasn't there. Even so, one particular story wouldn't die. The story is that famous illustrator Frederic Remington, whom Hearst had dispatched to Cuba, sent a telegram back that there was nothing worth illustrating. To that, Hearst cabled back: "You supply the pictures. I'll furnish the war." Or so went the story.

Although dubious, the story continued to be told because it so neatly and compactly captured Hearst's arrogance and power. But W. Joseph Campbell, in a significant piece of scholarship, the 2001 book *Yellow Journalism: Puncturing the Myths, Defining the Legends,* has made an exhaustive case that the exchange of Remington-Hearst cables never took place. Campbell makes these points:

- The story first appeared in a 1901 book by a popular journalist, James Creelman, whose book was noted for not letting the facts stand in the way of a good story.
- Creelman was on an extended reporting assignment in Europe at

Flamboyant Self-Promotion. William Randolph Hearst was his own best publicist. This 1897 front page announced the departure of star reporter Richard Harding Davis and premier illustrator Frederic Remington by special yacht to cover resistance against Spanish colonialism in Cuba.

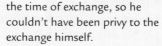

the time of exchange, so he couldn't have been privy to the exchange himself.
- Although Hearst was silent for years about the story, he flatly denied it in 1907.
- The cables have never been found in any files.
- At the time, *Journal* editorials were not urging U.S. military intervention in Cuba.
- Almost certainly, Spanish telegraph censors in Havana would have halted the cables.
- No evidence of the exchange has been found in Remington's papers.
- No evidence of the exchange has been found in the papers of Remington's partner for the *Journal* on the Cuba trip, celebrity reporter Richard Harding Davis.

It is true that Remington returned to New York after only a week, whereas he was supposed to spend a month in Cuba. But Campbell argues that Remington had gathered in a week all that he needed to illustrate the Cuban situation. Also, found in Richard Harding Davis' papers is a comment that he didn't like traveling as a twosome with Remington and asked him to leave early.

Perhaps Campbell's most compelling evidence that the cable exchange never took place is that the *Journal* prominently displayed Remington's Cuba illustrations rather than relegating his work to the trash basket, as Hearst could be expected to have done had Remington been defiant in coming home early.

EFFECTS STUDIES. The greatest ferment in mass communication scholarship has involved questions about effects. In the 1920s, as mass communication theory took form, scholars began exploring the effects of mass communication and of the mass media themselves on society and individuals. Conversely, scholars are also interested in how ongoing changes and adjustments in society influence the mass media and their content. The research is known as **effects studies.**

effects studies
Impact of media on society, of society on media.

PROCESS STUDIES.   A continuing interest among scholars is the mystery of how the process of mass communication works. Just as human beings have developed theories to explain other great mysteries, such as thunder being caused by unhappy gods thrashing about in the heavens, mass communication scholars have developed, in **process studies,** a great many explanations to help us understand mass communication.

GRATIFICATIONS STUDIES.   Beginning in the 1940s, studies about how and why individuals use the mass media attracted scholarly interest. These today are called **uses and gratifications studies.**

CONTENT ANALYSIS.   George Gerbner, a scholar of media violence, studied the 8 p.m. hour of network television for 19 years and found an average of 168 violent acts a week. Gerbner arrived at his disturbing statistic through **content analysis,** a research method involving the systematic counting of media content. Gerbner's tallying became a basic reference point for important further studies that correlated media-depicted violence with changes in incidents of violence in society at large.

It is also content analysis when a researcher tallies the column inches of sports in a newspaper to determine what percentage of available space goes to sports. While interesting for its own sake, such information can become a significant indicator of the changing role of sports in U.S. life.

process studies
To understand the mass communication process.

uses and gratifications studies
To explain why people choose their media outlets.

content analysis
Measuring media content to establish a database for analysis.

c h a p t e r   w r a p - u p

Theoretical research, which mostly is campus-based, and applied research, which the media eagerly fund, use many of the same tools. A unifying tool of these disparate research approaches is public-opinion sampling. It is used to track public opinion, which is essential in public relations work; to learn which television programs are the most watched, which is essential in programming and advertising decisions; and to determine the effects of media and how people use the media, which are scholarly endeavors.

Questions for Review

1. What do surveys tell the mass media about their audiences?
2. How is the size of mass media audiences measured?
3. How is the reaction of people to the mass media measured?
4. What are techniques of audience analysis?
5. Why are mass media organizations more interested in applied than theoretical research?

Questions for Critical Thinking

1. Street-corner polls are based on weak methodology. Explain how quota sampling and probability sampling are improvements.
2. What is the basis for arguments that public-opinion surveys subvert democracy? What is the counterargument?

3. The Audit Bureau of Circulations and television rating services like A. C. Nielsen and Arbitron are essential media services to advertisers. How are these services similar? How different?
4. How can local television and radio stations manipulate their ratings? Why can't the Broadcast Ratings Council do anything about it?
5. Explain how applied research and theoretical research differ.

Keeping Up to Date

Public Opinion Quarterly is a scholarly publication. *American Demographics* and *Public Opinion* have a lot of general-interest content for media observers.

Wilbur Schramm. *He defined mass communication as an academic discipline.*

14

Mass Communication

Some say Wilbur Schramm created mass communication as a hybrid academic discipline. There is no doubt Schramm's two influential anthologies shaped two generations of masscom scholars. His *Mass Communications,* compiled in 1949, combined seminal works in the social sciences with works by leading media practitioners and scholars. "It combined diversity of approach with unity of target," Schramm wrote in the introduction. That it did.

Enthusiastic word spread abroad, prompting requests from scholars for copies within a week of the book's release. Demand so outstripped supply that some used copies sold at triple the retail price. Schramm revised the trail-blazing book in 1959, again combining important work from anthropology, economics, political science, psychology and sociology with material from the growing field of mass communication studies.

In the meantime, in 1954, Schramm compiled another anthology, *The Process and Effect of Mass Communication.* Originally, *P&E,* as it was known, was intended as a research methods primer for U.S. information agency employees, but as Schramm pulled material together, it was clear the book had a larger appeal. *P&E* was a worthy successor to the *Mass Communications* anthology, but both remained in demand, and the University of Illinois Press kept reprinting them.

Thirty-one years after *P&E's* introduction, and with the second edition becoming outdated, the University of Illinois Press asked Schramm to do a third edition. His agenda full, Schramm declined but urged that someone do a revision. "The only obligation is to make a book that will be as good for the future as *P&E* was for its time," he said. Schramm was not being immodest. It was a fact, recognized everywhere, that *P&E* had become a mainstay in curricula of emerging mass communication departments throughout the country and abroad.

While Schramm's *Mass Communications* and *P&E* were major contributions, they were in a sense mere warm-ups. When Schramm died in 1987, his legacy included 30 books, 25 of them translated into other languages, and more than 120 research and scholarly papers and treatises. His personal papers, which his family holds, contain 18,722 pages.

The largest collection in his papers is 6,158 pages for his final book, *The Story of Human Communications: Cave Painting to Microchip,* which was in press when he died. The scope of the book, the whole spectrum through history, seemed an appropriate ultimate work for Wilbur Schramm, who was 80 when he died.

Types of Communication

STUDY PREVIEW The communication in which the mass media engage is only one form of **communication.** One way to begin understanding the process of mass communication is to differentiate it from other forms of communication.

Intrapersonal Communication

We engage in **intrapersonal communication** when we talk to ourselves to develop our thoughts and ideas. This intrapersonal communication precedes our speaking or acting.

Interpersonal Communication

When people talk to each other, they are engaging in **interpersonal communication.** In its simplest form, interpersonal communication is between two people physically located in the same place. It can occur, however, if they are physically separated but emotionally connected, like lovers on the telephone.

The difference between the prefixes *intra-* and *inter-* is the key difference between intrapersonal and interpersonal communication. Just as intrasquad athletic games are within a team, intrapersonal communication is within one's self. Just as intercollegiate games are between schools, interpersonal communication is between individuals.

Group Communication

There comes a point when the number of people involved reduces the intimacy of the communication process. That's when the situation becomes **group communication.** A club meeting is an example. So is a speech to an audience in an auditorium.

communication
Exchange of ideas, information.

intrapersonal communication
Talking to oneself.

interpersonal communication
Usually two people face to face.

group communication
More than two people; in person.

Media People

David Sarnoff

David Sarnoff had no childhood. In 1901, when he was 10, Sarnoff and his mother and two brothers arrived penniless in New York from Russia. Two days later he had a job as a delivery boy, then he added a newspaper route, then a newsstand. In spare moments he went to the library to read technical books. At 16 he landed a job with American Marconi, which sent him to an island station to exchange messages with ships at sea with the new technology of radio telegraphy. He earned $70 a month, of which $25 went to room and board at a nearby farm. He sent $40 back to his mother.

In 1912 Sarnoff was working at a Marconi demonstration in a New York department store when he picked up the first signals that the steamship *Titanic* had sunk. President Taft ordered every other radio telegraphy station off the air to reduce interference. For the whole world, young David Sarnoff was the only link to the rescue drama unfolding out in the North Atlantic. He stayed at his post 72 hours straight, then went to another site for better reception until the lists of living and dead were complete.

When he collapsed in bed sometime during the fourth day, Sarnoff, then 21, was a national hero, and *radio* had become a household word. Through Sarnoff the whole world suddenly recognized the importance of radio for point-to-point communication, which

David Sarnoff. His genius was seeing radio as mass communication.

was the business American Marconi was into. Sarnoff's most significant work, however, was yet to come.

In 1916 Sarnoff drafted a memo to his boss that demonstrated he grasped a potential for radio that everyone else at Marconi had missed. He proposed building "radio music boxes," to be sold as household appliances so people at home could listen to music, news, weather and sports. Sarnoff saw profit in manufacturing these home receivers and selling them for $75. His boss scoffed, but Sarnoff kept refining his proposal. By 1920 he won the ear of the people running RCA, which had succeeded American Marconi.

Sarnoff's proposal for radio music boxes demonstrated his genius. He grasped that radio could be more than a vehicle for telegraph-like point-to-point communication. He saw radio as a mass medium, which could send signals from a cen-

tral source to dozens, hundreds, thousands, indeed millions of people simultaneously. Sarnoff was not alone in conceptualizing radio as a mass medium. Lee De Forest, for example, had been broadcasting music, but as historian Erik Barnouw noted, "Sarnoff translated the idea into a business plan that began with the consumer." That business plan included a financial base for radio in advertising.

Under RCA auspices, Sarnoff went on to build NBC, the first radio network, and then NBC television. He also pioneered the business of mass producing music for mass audiences with RCA records. From humble origins, through hard work, insight and genius, Sarnoff came to preside for the rest of his life over one of the world's largest and most significant media empires: RCA. He died in 1971.

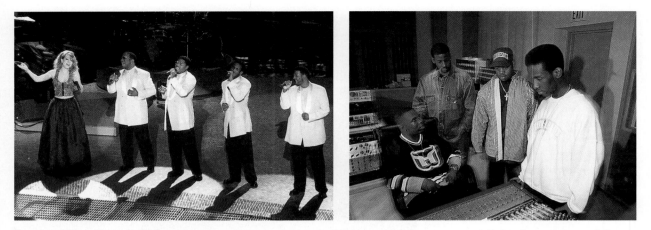

Group and Mass Communication. When Boyz II Men goes on stage, they are engaging in group communication. A spontaneous relationship with their audience is part of their performance—their communication. In the recording studio, Boyz II Men has to intuitively adjust their performance to an audience they cannot see. This lack of immediate feedback is a characteristic of mass communication that separates it from interpersonal and group communication.

Mass Communication

Capable of reaching thousands, even millions, of people is **mass communication,** which is accomplished through a mass medium like television or newspapers. Mass communication can be defined as the process of using a mass medium to send messages to large audiences for the purpose of informing, entertaining or persuading.

In many respects the process of mass communication and other communication forms is the same: Someone conceives a message, essentially an intrapersonal act. The message then is encoded into a common code, such as language. Then it's transmitted. Another person receives the message, decodes it and internalizes it. Internalizing a message is also an intrapersonal act.

In other respects, mass communication is distinctive. Crafting an effective message for thousands of people of diverse backgrounds and interests requires different skills than chatting with a friend across the table. Encoding the message is more complex because a device is always used—for example, a printing press, a camera or a recorder.

One aspect of mass communication that should not be a mystery is the spelling of the often-misused word *communication.* The word takes no "s" if you are using it to refer to a *process.* If you are referring to a communication as *a thing,* such as a letter, a movie, a telegram or a television program, rather than a process, the word is *communication* in singular form and *communications* in plural. When the term *mass communication* refers to a process, it is spelled without the "s."

Components of Mass Communication

mass communication
Many recipients; not face to face; a process.

STUDY PREVIEW   Mass communication is the process that mass communicators use to send their mass messages to mass audiences. They do this through the mass media. Think of these as the Five Ms: mass communicators, mass messages, mass media, mass communication and mass audience.

Mass Communicators

The heart of mass communication is the people who produce the messages that are carried in the mass media. These people include journalists, scriptwriters, lyricists, television anchors, radio disc jockeys, public relations practitioners and advertising copywriters. The list could go on and on.

Mass communicators are unlike other communicators because they cannot see their audience. David Letterman knows that hundreds of thousands of people are watching as he unveils his latest Top 10 list, but he can't see them or hear them chuckle and laugh. He receives no immediate feedback from his mass audience. This communicating with an unseen audience distinguishes mass communication from other forms of communication. Storytellers of yore told their stories face to face, and they could adjust their pacing and gestures and even their vocabulary to how they sensed they were being received. Mass communicators don't have that advantage, although a studio audience, as David Letterman has, is a loose substitute.

Mass Messages

A news item is a **mass message,** as are a movie, a novel, a recorded song and a billboard advertisement. The *message* is the most apparent part of our relationship to the mass media. It is for the messages that we pay attention to the media. We don't listen to the radio, for example, to marvel at the technology but to hear the music.

Mass Media

The **mass media** are the vehicles that carry messages. The primary mass media are books, magazines, newspapers, television, radio, sound recordings, movies and the web. Most theorists view media as neutral carriers of messages. The people who are experts at media include technicians who keep the presses running and who keep the television transmitters on the air. Media experts also are tinkerers and inventors who come up with technical improvements, such as compact discs, AM stereo radio and newspaper presses that can produce high-quality color.

Mass Communication

The process through which messages reach the audience via the mass media is called *mass communication*. This is a mysterious process about which we know far less than we should. Researchers and scholars have unraveled some of the mystery, but most of how it works remains a matter of wonderment. For example, why do people pay more attention to some messages than to others? How does one advertisement generate more sales than another? Is behavior, including violent behavior, triggered through the mass communication process? There is reason to believe that mass communication affects voting behavior, but how does this work? Which is most correct—to say that people can be controlled, manipulated or influenced by mass communication? Nobody has the answer.

mass communicators
Message crafters.

mass message
What is communicated.

mass media
Vehicles that carry messages.

Mass Audiences

The size and diversity of **mass audiences** add complexity to mass communication. Only indirectly do mass communicators learn whether their messages have been received. Mass communicators are never sure exactly of the size of audiences, let alone of the effect of their messages. Mass audiences are fickle. What attracts great attention one day may not the next. The challenge of trying to communicate to a mass audience is even more complex because people are tuning in and tuning out all the time, and when they are tuned in, it is with varying degrees of attentiveness.

Communication Models

STUDY PREVIEW   Scholars have devised models of the communication process in an attempt to understand how the process works. Like all models, these are simplifications and are imperfect. Even so, these models bring some illumination to the mysterious communication process.

Role of Communication Models

Hobbyists build models of ships, planes, automobiles and all kinds of other things. These models help them see whatever they are modeling in different ways. Industrial engineers and scientists do the same thing, learning lessons from models before they actually build something to full scale. Communication models are similar. By creating a facsimile of the process, we hope to better understand the process.

A reality about models is that they are never perfect. This reality is especially true when the subject being modeled is complex. An architect, for example, may have a model of what the building will look like to passersby, but there also will be models of the building's heating system, traffic patterns, and electrical, plumbing and ventilation systems. None of these models is complete or accurate in every detail, but all nonetheless are useful.

Communication models are like that. Different models illustrate different aspects of the process. The process itself is so complex that no single model can adequately cover it.

Basic Model

mass audiences
Recipients of mass messages.

Claude Shannon
Devised a basic communication model, with Warren Weaver.

Warren Weaver
Devised a basic communication model, with Claude Shannon.

basic communication model
Shows sender, encoding, transmission, decoding, receiver.

Two Bell telephone engineers, **Claude Shannon** and **Warren Weaver,** laid out a **basic communication model** in 1948. They were working on advanced switching systems. The model, fundamentally a simple diagram, gave them a reference point for their work. That model has become a standard baseline for describing the communication process. The Shannon-Weaver model identifies five fundamental steps in the communication process:

- The human stimulation that results in a thought.
- The encoding of the thought into a message.
- The transmission of the message.
- The decoding of the message by the recipient into a thought.
- The internalization of the message by the recipient.

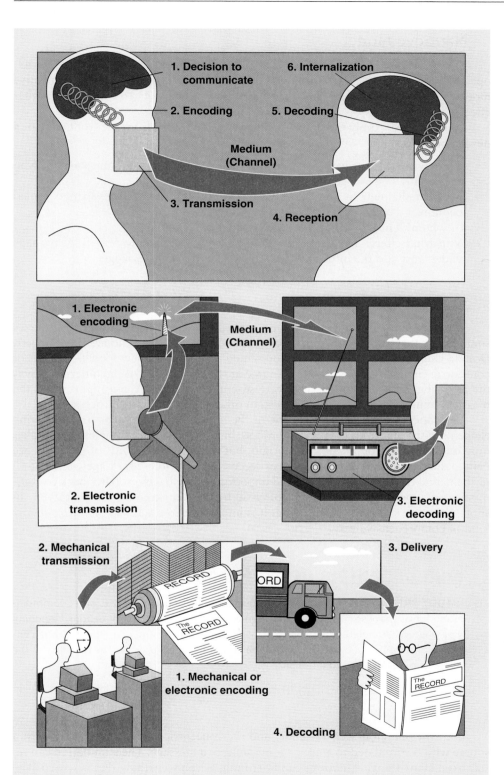

1. Decision to communicate
2. Encoding
3. Transmission
4. Reception
5. Decoding
6. Internalization
Medium (Channel)

1. Electronic encoding
2. Electronic transmission
3. Electronic decoding
Medium (Channel)

2. Mechanical transmission
1. Mechanical or electronic encoding
3. Delivery
4. Decoding
RECORD
The RECORD

Fundamentals of the Process. Claude Shannon and Warren Weaver reduced communication to fundamental elements in their classic model. Communication, they said, begins in the human mind. Messages are then encoded into language or gesture and transmitted. A recipient sees or hears the message and decodes from the language or other form in which it was transmitted and internalizes it. Those fundamental elements are also present in mass communication except that there is a double encoding and double decoding. In mass communication, not only does the communicator encode the message into language or another form to be communicated but also the message then is encoded technologically for transmission through a mass medium. In radio, for example, the words are encoded into electronic impulses. At the decoding site, a piece of machinery—a radio receiver, for example—decodes the impulses into words, which then are decoded again by the human recipient to internalize them. With print media, the two steps in decoding are not as obvious because the steps are so integrated. One is reading the words. The other is converting those representations into concepts.

Narrative Model

Yale professor **Harold Lasswell,** an early mass communication theorist, developed a useful yet simple model that was all words—no diagram. Lasswell's **narrative model** poses four questions: Who says what? In which channel? To whom? With what effect?

You can easily apply the model. Pick any bylined story from the front page of a newspaper.

- **Who says what?** The newspaper reporter tells a story, often quoting someone who is especially knowledgeable on the subject.
- **In which channel?** In this case the story is told through the newspaper, a mass medium.
- **To whom?** The story is told to a newspaper reader.
- **With what effect?** The reader decides to vote for Candidate A or B, or perhaps readers just add the information to their reservoir of knowledge.

Concentric Circle Model

The Shannon-Weaver model can be applied to all communication, but it misses some things that are unique to mass communication. In 1974 scholars Ray Hiebert, Donald Ungurait and **Thomas Bohn** presented an important new model—a series of concentric circles with the encoding source at the center. One of the outer rings was the receiving audience. In between were several elements that are important in the mass communication process but less so in other communication processes.

The **concentric circle model** is one of the most complete models for identifying elements in the mass communication process, but it misses many complexities. It takes only one message from its point of origin, but in reality thousands of messages are being issued simultaneously. Audiences receive many of these messages, but not all of them, and the messages are received imperfectly. Feedback resonates back to communicators unevenly, often muted, often ill-based. Gatekeeping too is uneven. In short, there are so many variables that it is impossible to track what happens in any kind of comprehensive way.

Harold Lasswell
Devised the narrative model.

narrative model
Describes process in words, not schematic.

Thomas Bohn
Devised the concentric circle model, with Ray Hiebert, Donald Ungurait.

concentric circle model
Useful radiating model of the mass communication process.

stimulation
Stirs someone to communicate.

Fundamentals in the Process

STUDY PREVIEW   Most models for mass communication as well as other communication forms share some fundamental elements. The elements are sequential, beginning with whatever stimulates a person to want to communicate and continuing through encoding and transmission. To complete the communication process, the recipient of the message must decode and internalize it.

Stimulation

Both the Shannon-Weaver model and the concentric circle model begin with a source who is stimulated to want to communicate a message. The **stimulation** can result from many things. Emotions can be stimuli, as can something that is sensed. The

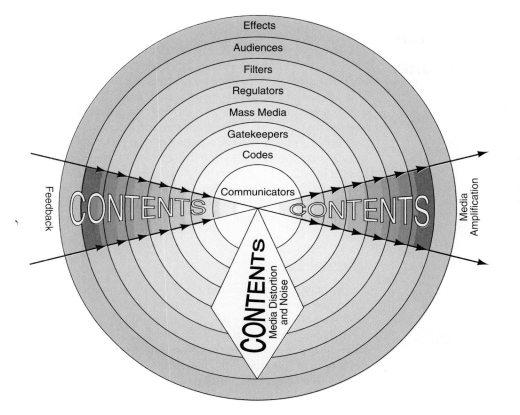

Effects
Audiences
Filters
Regulators
Mass Media
Gatekeepers
Codes
Communicators

Feedback

CONTENTS

CONTENTS

CONTENTS
Media Distortion and Noise

Media Amplification

Concentric Circle Model.
The scholars who designed the concentric circle model suggest thinking of it as a pebble being dropped in still water. The ripples emanating outward from the communicator go through many barriers before reaching the audience or having any effect. The model takes note of feedback, media amplification, noise and distortion introduced by the media.

stimulation can be as diverse as seeing a beautiful panorama, feeling a draft, or hearing a child cry.

Encoding

The second step is **encoding.** The source puts thoughts into symbols that can be understood by whomever is destined to receive the message. The symbols take many forms—for example, the written word, smoke signals or pictographs.

Transmission

The message is the representation of the thought. In interpersonal communication the message is almost always delivered face to face. In mass communication, however, the message is encoded so that it is suitable for the equipment being used for **transmission.** Shannon and Weaver, being telephone engineers, offered the example of the sound pressure of a voice being changed into proportional electrical current for transmission over telephone lines. In technical terms, telephone lines were channels for Shannon and Weaver's messages. On a more conceptual basis the telephone lines were the *media,* in the same way that the printed page or a broadcast signal is.

encoding
Putting something into symbols.

transmission
Sending a message.

Internalization. A consumer who has seen and heard ads for a product retrieves those messages from memory to weigh whether to make a purchase. Those retrieved messages are considered with packaging messages, which also are a form of mass communication.

Decoding

The receiver picks up signals sent by the transmitter. In interpersonal communication the receiver is a person who hears the message, sees it, or both. An angry message encoded as a fist banging a table is heard and perhaps felt. An insulting message encoded as a puff of cigar smoke in the face is smelled. In mass communication the first receiver of the message is not a person but the equipment that picks up and then reconstructs the message from the signal. This mechanical **decoding** is necessary so that the human receiver of the message can understand it. As Shannon and Weaver put it: "The receiver ordinarily performs the inverse operation that was done by the transmitter."

Internalization

In mass communication a second kind of decoding occurs with the person who receives the message from the receiving equipment. This is an intrapersonal act, **internalizing** the message. For this second kind of decoding to work, the receiver must understand the communication form chosen by the source in encoding. Someone who reads only English will not be able to decode a message in Greek. Someone whose sensitivities are limited to punk rock will not understand Handel's "Water Music." In other words, the source and the receiver must have enough in common for communication to occur. This common experience, which can be as simple as speaking the same tongue, is called **homophyly.** In mass communication the encoder must know the audience well enough to shape messages that can be decoded accurately and with the intended effect.

The audience and how it perceives a message are essential in the mass communication process. This is no better illustrated than in a front-page headline in the *National Examiner,* a sensationalizing weekly tabloid: "Cops Think Kato Did It!" Brian "Kato" Kaelin was a pal of O. J. Simpson and had been subjected to police interviewing off and on for months before the Simpson murder trial. Kaelin sued the *Examiner* over the headline. In court, the *Examiner* said the "it" in the headline didn't refer to the murders but to possible perjury. The *Examiner* argued that "it" was explained in a secondary head on Page 1: ". . . He Fears They Want Him for Perjury."

A three-judge federal appeals court sided with Kaelin, saying that *Examiner* readers were likely to infer that the police thought he was a murderer. This was despite the fact that the story made it clear that "it" was perjury, not murder, and also despite the secondary Page 1 head.

The judges noted that the headline came only a week after the widely reported Simpson acquittal and that, in the court's opinion, people who had followed the trial reasonably could have interpreted "it" to be murder. The decision allowed Kaelin to pursue his $15 million legal action against the *Examiner.*

decoding
Translating a symbolic message.

internalization
Making sense of a decoded message.

homophyly
A coding oneness that makes communication possible.

Gatekeeping. Despite favorable reviews as a gentle sitcom, "God, the Devil and Bob" worried some NBC affiliates. God, in the starring role, liked toaster pastries and occasionally sipped a light beer. Seven affiliates declined to carry the program—in Boise, Idaho; Pocatello, Idaho; Salt Lake City, Utah; Shreveport, Louisiana; South Bend, Indiana; Tupelo, Mississippi; and Twin Falls, Idaho.

For mass communicators the lesson is that strict, literal meanings are not always enough. Audience inferences, part of the intrapersonal decoding process, must also be considered.

Players in the Process

STUDY PREVIEW   Two great influences on the mass communication process are gatekeepers and regulators. Gatekeepers are media people who influence messages. Regulators are nonmedia people who do the same.

Gatekeepers

The most visible people in the mass communication process are the communicators. These are the Tom Brokaws, Danielle Steels and Rush Limbaughs. But mass communication is not a solo endeavor. Dozens, sometimes hundreds, of individuals are involved. A Stephen King thriller passes through several editors before being published. When it's adapted as a screenplay, substantial modifications are made by many other individuals, all expert in the medium of the movie. Later, when it is adapted for television, experts in television as a mass medium make further changes, and so might the network program standards office. Any media person who can stop or alter a message en route to the audience is a **gatekeeper.** Newscast producers are gatekeepers because they decide what is aired and what is not. They make decisions about what to emphasize and what to deemphasize. Magazine and newspaper editors do the same, sorting through hundreds of stories to choose the relatively few that will fit in their publications.

Gatekeepers have tremendous responsibility because they shape the messages that reach us. They even decide which messages don't reach us. When gatekeepers make a mistake, the communication process and also the message suffer.

gatekeepers
Media people who influence messages en route.

Regulators

Nonmedia people and institutions that try to influence mass-communicated messages before they reach the audience are **regulators.** The Federal Communications Commission is a government agency that serves as a regulator with its authority to fine a radio station for on-air indecency. The specter of FCC fines keeps most stations in line. Advertisers know the Federal Trade Commission and two dozen other federal regulatory agencies are looking over their shoulders. Local cable commissions throughout the country have a strong voice in what cable systems offer their subscribers.

Regulators in the mass communication process also include **pressure groups.** For several years the Parents Music Resource Center campaigned for controls on recorded music and videos, including album covers, that it found objectionable. The PMRC's plan for a rating system fell apart, but it was influential in persuading record-makers to place warning labels for parents on certain records. The Communications Office of the United Church of Christ prevailed in yanking the license of a racist television station, WLBT, in Jackson, Mississippi. Community groups that threaten media boycotts also are regulators.

Gatekeeper-Regulator Hybrids

Media trade and professional organizations influence media content. For many years the National Association of Broadcasters television programming standards influenced what many stations aired. An NAB maximum on the number of radio commercials per hour became an industry standard. Ethics codes from the Society of Professional Journalists and many other groups of media people have had wide influence.

Are organizations like the NAB and SPJ gatekeepers or regulators? Comprised of media people, they would seem to be gatekeepers, but because they do not operate on the front line of making content decisions directly, they have many characteristics of regulators. They are, in fact, **gatekeeper-regulator hybrids** that institutionalize peer pressure among media people to influence media content.

Impediments to Communication

STUDY PREVIEW   Some models emphasize things that interfere with a message being communicated. Feedback can influence a communicator to change a message. Noise is transmission interference. Filters are recipient factors that interfere with an easy or correct reception of the message.

Noise

If speakers slur their words, the effectiveness of their messages is jeopardized. Slurring and other impediments in the communication process before the message reaches the audience are called **noise.** In mass communication, which is based on complex mechanical and electronic equipment, the opportunities for noise interference are countless because so many things can go wrong. Noise occurs in three forms: channel noise, environmental noise and semantic noise.

regulators
Nonmedia people who influence messages.

pressure groups
Try to influence media messages, policies; include citizen groups, government agencies.

gatekeeper-regulator hybrids
Media trade, professional groups.

noise
Impedes communication before message reaches receiver.

The Lower case

"Some sort of post Supreme Court decision quote or reaction information should go in this slot right about here."

AL GORE
Reacts to Supreme Court decision

The Morning Call (Allentown, Pa.) 11/22/00

Copy editors find headline workshops irresistible

ACES September 2000

The importance of bondage between voter and government

The Fairfax (Va.) Journal 10/18/00

Last week for faulty art display

Central Florida Future 10/4/00

Egg plant must pay damages for fly problem

Star Tribune (Minneapolis, Minn.) 3/11/00

Need to breed spurs bird call from queen

The Des Moines Register 11/14/00

The two-headed management team is typical for Belo Interactive properties, the pair said.

The Press-Enterprise (Riverside, Calif.) 8/24/00

Faite R-P. Mack Jr., 56, a professor in the graduate education program at Grand Valley State University, said he has been frustrated by voters' take on Bush's debate performances.

"I'm mystified at how dumb Americans are in thinking Bush won those debates," said the Grand Rapids resident, who declined to give his age.

The Grand Rapids (Mich.) Press 10/17/00

Talks end in killing of black motorist

Lexington (Ky.) Herald-Leader 11/21/00

Young supports hitting coach

Pittsburgh Post Gazette 9/20/00

Drug firms urged to stop selling medicines

The Indiana (Pa.) Gazette 11/7/00

Steven Gartner, *one of the sexist U.S. bachelors*

The Seattle Times 9/28/00

Doughnut hole, nude dancing on council table

Redlands (Calif.) Daily Facts 4/3/00

Semantic Noise. In every issue, the *Columbia Journalism Review* delights in reproducing bad headlines and other newspaper gaffes as a reminder to journalists to be more careful. These gaffes are examples of semantic noise, in which ambiguous wording and other poor word choices interfere with clear communication.

SEMANTIC NOISE.   Mass communicators themselves can interfere with the success of their own messages by sloppiness. This is called **semantic noise.** Sloppy wording is an example. Slurring is also a semantic impediment to communication.

CHANNEL NOISE.   When you're listening to an AM radio station and static interrupts the transmission, you are experiencing **channel noise.** Other forms of channel noise include smudged ink on a magazine page and a faulty microphone on a television anchor's lapel.

ENVIRONMENTAL NOISE.   An intrusion that occurs at the reception site is **environmental noise.** This would include a doorbell interrupting someone's reading of an article. So would shouting kids who distract a viewer from the 6 o'clock news, which interferes with the decoding process.

---

semantic noise
Sloppy message-crafting.

channel noise
Interference during transmission.

environmental noise
Interference at reception site.

Mass communicators go to special lengths to guard against noise interfering with their messages. For example, in encoding, broadcast scriptwriters avoid "s" sounds as much as possible because they can hiss gratingly if listeners are not tuned precisely on the frequency. Because words can be unintentionally dropped in typesetting, many newspaper reporters write that a verdict was "innocent" rather than "not guilty." It would be a serious matter if noise resulted in the deletion of "not."

To keep noise at a minimum, technicians strive to keep their equipment in top-notch condition. Even so, things can go wrong. Also, mass communicators cannot control noise that affects individual members of their audience—such as the siren of a passing fire truck, a migraine headache or the distraction of a pot boiling over on the stove. Clear expression, whether sharp writing in a magazine or clear pronunciation on the radio, can minimize such interference, but most noise is beyond the communicator's control.

Repetition is the mass communicator's best antidote against noise. If the message does not get through the first time, it is repeated. Rare is an advertisement that plays only once. Radio newscasters repeat the same major news stories every hour, although they rehash the scripts so they will not bore people who heard the stories earlier.

Filters

Unwittingly, people who tune in to mass messages may themselves interfere with the success of the mass communication process. The causes of this interference are known as **filters.**

INFORMATIONAL FILTERS.   If someone doesn't understand the language or symbols a communicator uses, the communication process becomes flawed. It is a matter of an individual lacking information to decipher a message. This deficiency is called an **informational filter.** This filter can be partly the responsibility of the communicator, whose vocabulary may not be in tune with the audience's. More clearly, though, it is an audience deficiency.

PHYSICAL FILTERS.   When a receiver's mind is dimmed by fatigue, a **physical filter** is interfering with the mass communication process. A drunk whose focus fades in and out also suffers from a physical filter. Mass communicators have little control over physical filters.

PSYCHOLOGICAL FILTERS.   If a receiver is a zealous animal rights activist, **psychological filters** likely will affect the reception of news on medical research involving animals. Being on a different wavelength can be a factor. Imagine two women friends going to the movie *Fatal Attraction* together. One woman is married and monogamous; the other is involved with a married man. Having different ideas about and experiences with marital fidelity, which is at the heart of the movie, the women hear the same words and see the same images, but they see two "different" movies.

Results of Mass Communication

STUDY PREVIEW   Because mass communication reaches such large audiences, the process amplifies messages like a giant megaphone. Things that are mass communicated stand a better chance of becoming important than things that are not. Mass communication has its greatest influence when it moves people to action.

filters
Receiver factor that impedes communication.

informational filter
Receiver's knowledge limits impede deciphering symbols.

physical filter
Receiver's alertness impedes deciphering.

psychological filter
Receiver's state of mind impedes deciphering.

Media Amplification. After Super Bowl quarterback Boomer Esiason of the Cincinnati Bengals found out that his infant son Gunnar had cystic fibrosis, he vowed to make his fight to cure Gunnar a crusade, however quixotic it might turn out. The media picked up on Esiason's campaign, which not only has raised research funds but has shown that professional athletes, who seem so carefree and indestructible, have real problems just like the rest of us.

Amplification

The technology of the mass media gives mass communicators a megaphone. This is something other communicators don't have. A letter writer, for example, generally aims a message at one other person. A magazine writer, in contrast, has the printing press to reach thousands, if not millions, of readers. The printing press is a megaphone. Broadcasters have their transmission equipment. The equipment of the mass media allows mass communicators to **amplify** messages in ways that are not possible with interpersonal or even group communication.

Things that mass communicators choose to communicate have a status conferred on them. This is gatekeeping at work. Stories and views that don't survive the gatekeeping process have little chance of gaining widespread attention. Those that make it through the process have some inherent credibility just because they made it through so many hurdles.

Status conferral can work positively and negatively. For example, some scholars claim that the U.S. government overreacted in 1980 to the 444-day Iran hostage situation because media coverage kept fueling public reaction. In the same vein, Oliver North's name would not have become a household word had it not been for saturation media coverage of the Iran-Contra issue.

Status conferral is not limited to the news media. Ballads and music, amplified through the mass media, can capture the public's imagination and keep an issue alive and even enlarge it. In World War I catchy songs such as "Over There" helped to rally support for the cause. Fifty years later, "An Okie from Muskogee" lent legitimacy to the hawkish position on the war in Vietnam. Bob Dylan's 1975 song "Hurricane" reopened the investigation into the murder conviction of Rubin "Hurricane" Carter. Movies also have the power to move people and sustain issues. Sidney Poitier's movies of the 1960s, including *Guess Who's Coming to Dinner,* helped to keep racial integration on the American agenda. The 1988 movie *The Thin Blue Line* led to the exoneration of a death-row inmate.

amplification
Spreading message.

status conferral
Credence that a topic or issue receives because of media attention.

feedback
Recipient's response to the sender.

effect
Result of mass communication.

Feedback

Because mass communication is not the one-way street that the Shannon-Weaver model indicated, later theorists embellished the model by looping the process back on itself. The recipient of a message, after decoding, responds. The original recipient then becomes the sender, encoding a response and sending it via a medium back to the original sender, who becomes the new destination and decodes the response. This reverse process is called **feedback.**

In interpersonal communication you know if your listener does not understand. If you hear "Uhh?" or see a puzzled look, you restate your point. In mass communication, feedback is delayed. It might be a week after an article is published before a reader's letter arrives in the newsroom. Because feedback is delayed and because there usually is not very much of it, precise expression in mass communication is especially important. There is little chance to restate the point immediately if the television viewer does not understand. A mass communicator cannot hear the "Uhh?"

An inherent disadvantage of mass communication, when compared to interpersonal and group communication is delayed feedback. In interpersonal communication, feedback can be immediate: a quizzical arch of an eyebrow, a hand cupped around an ear to hear better, a fist in the face.

Technology has reduced delays in feedback, but feedback remains an impediment in mass communication that doesn't occur in face-to-face communication. Feedback left on a telephone answering machine, for example, will go unheard until somebody listens to the messages. E-mail can stack up. Faxes can go unread.

Despite feedback as a shortcoming in mass communication, there is an offsetting advantage: efficiency. Other forms of communication, including interpersonal and group, may have the advantage of on-the-spot feedback, but they cannot reach the massive audience of mass communication.

Effects

The whole point of communicating a message is to have an **effect.** A jokester wants to evoke at least a chuckle. A eulogist wants to inspire memories. A cheerleader wants to stir school spirit. The vast size of the mass communicator's audience compounds the potential for powerful effects. Because the potential effect is so great, we need to understand as much as possible about the process that leads to effects.

chapter wrap-up

Mass communication is a mysterious process. Many scholars have developed theories and models to help us understand some aspects of mass communication, but the process is so complex that we will never master it to the point of being able to predict reliably the outcome of the process. There are just too many variables. This does not mean, however, that the quest for understanding is pointless. The more we know about how mass communication works, the better mass communicators can use the process for good effects and the better media consumers can intelligently assess media messages before using them as a basis for action.

Questions for Review

1. Can you create a sentence that uses the Five Ms: mass communicators, mass messages, mass media, mass communication and mass audiences?
2. What good are mass communication and other models? What do models fail to do?
3. How does mass communication differ from other human communication?
4. How do gatekeepers and regulators influence media messages? How are they different from each other?
5. How do noise and filters impede mass communication?
6. Status conferral is one effect of mass media amplification. How does this work?

Questions for Critical Thinking

1. How is each of these types of communication—intrapersonal, interpersonal, group and mass—difficult to master?
2. All communication involves conceiving, encoding, transmitting, receiving and decoding, but some of these steps are more complicated for mass communication. In what way?

3. Different mass communication models offer different insights into the mass communication process. Describe the different perspectives of these models: Shannon-Weaver, concentric circle and narrative.
4. From your own experience, describe a message that went awry as it moved through the mass communication process. Did the problem involve gatekeepers? Regulators? Noise? Filters?
5. People in the physical sciences can predict with great accuracy how certain phenomena will work. Why will social scientists never be able to do this with the mass communication process?
6. From your own experience, describe how a lack of homophyly has damaged a mass communication attempt.

Keeping Up to Date

Scholarly discussion on the communication process can be found in *Communication Yearbook,* published since 1977, and *Mass Communication Review Yearbook,* published since 1986.

The *Journal of Communication* is a quarterly scholarly publication from Oxford University Press.

Orson Welles. Young Orson Welles scared the living daylights out of several million radio listeners with the 1938 radio drama "War of the Worlds." Most of the fright was short-lived, though. All but the most naive listeners quickly realized that Martians, marching toward the Hudson River to destroy Manhattan, really had not devastated the New Jersey militia.

15

Media
Effects

**In this chapter
you will learn:**

- Most media scholars today believe the effects of the mass media generally are cumulative over time.

- Individuals choose some mass media over others for the satisfactions they anticipate.

- Individuals have substantial control over mass media effects on them.

- Mass media have a significant role in helping children learn society's expectations of them.

- Scholars differ on whether media-depicted violence triggers aggressive behavior.

- The mass media set the agenda for what people are interested in and talk about.

- The mass media can work against citizen involvement in political processes.

The boy genius **Orson Welles** was on a roll. By 1938, at age 23, Welles' dramatic flair had landed him a network radio show, "Mercury Theater on the Air," at prime time on CBS on Sunday nights. The program featured adaptations of well-known literature. For their October 30 program, Welles and his colleagues decided on a scary 1898 British novel, H. G. Wells' *War of the Worlds.*

Orson Welles opened with the voice of a wizened chronicler from some future time, intoning an unsettling monologue. That was followed by an innocuous weather forecast, then hotel dance music. Then the music was interrupted by a news bulletin. An astronomer reported several explosions on Mars, propelling something at enormous velocity toward Earth. The bulletin over, listeners were transported back to the hotel orchestra. After applause the orchestra started up again, only to be interrupted: Seismologists had picked up an earthquake-like shock in New Jersey. Then it was one bulletin after another.

The story line accelerated. Giant Martians moved across the countryside spewing fatal gas. One at a time, reporters at remote sites vanished off the air. The Martians decimated the Army and were wading across the Hudson River. Amid sirens and other sounds of emergency, a reporter on a Manhattan rooftop described the monsters advancing through the streets. From his vantage, he described the Martians felling people by the thousands and moving in on him, the gas crossing Sixth Avenue, then Fifth Avenue, then 100 yards away, then 50 feet. Then silence.

To the surprise of Orson Welles and his crew, the drama triggered widespread mayhem. Neighbors gathered in streets all over the country, wet towels to their faces to slow the gas. In Newark, New Jersey, people, many undressed, fled their apartments. Said a New York woman, "I never hugged my radio so closely. . . . I held a crucifix in my hand and prayed while looking out my open window to get a faint whiff of gas so that I would know when to close my window and hermetically seal my room with waterproof cement or anything else I could get a hold of. My plan was to stay in the room and hope that I would not suffocate before the gas blew away."

Researchers estimate that one out of six people who heard the program, more than one million in all, suspended disbelief and braced for the worst.

The effects were especially amazing considering that:

- An announcer identified the program as fiction at four points.
- Almost 10 times as many people were tuned to a popular comedy show on another network.
- The program ran only one hour, an impossibly short time for the sequence that began with the blastoffs on Mars, included a major military battle in New Jersey, and ended with New York's destruction.

Unwittingly, Orson Welles and his Mercury Theater crew had created an evening of infamy and raised questions about media effects to new intensity. In this chapter, you will learn what scholars have found out about the effects of the mass media on individuals.

media online

War of the Worlds: Information and links to information regarding every version of *The War of the Worlds* ever released, including books, performances, music, movies, television shows, models and games.
www.war-of-the-worlds.org

Orson Welles
His radio drama casts doubt on powerful effects theory.

War of the Worlds
Novel that inspired a radio drama that became the test bed of the media's ability to instill panic.

powerful effects theory
Theory that media have immediate, direct influence.

Walter Lippmann
His *Public Opinion* assumed powerful media effects in 1920s.

Harold Lasswell
His mass communication model assumed powerful effects.

Effects Studies

STUDY PREVIEW   Early mass communication scholars assumed that the mass media were so powerful that ideas and even ballot-box instructions could be inserted as if by hypodermic needle into the body politic. Doubts arose in the 1940s about whether the media were really that powerful, and scholars began shaping their research questions on assumptions that media effects were more modest. Recent studies are asking about long-term, cumulative media effects.

Powerful Effects Theory

The first generation of mass communication scholars thought the mass media had a profound, direct effect on people. Their idea, called **powerful effects theory,** drew heavily on social commentator **Walter Lippmann**'s influential 1922 book *Public Opinion.* Lippmann argued that we see the world not as it really is but as "pictures in our heads." The "pictures" of things we have not experienced personally, he said, are shaped by the mass media. The powerful impact that Lippmann ascribed to the media was a precursor of the powerful effects theory that evolved among scholars over the next few years.

Yale psychologist **Harold Lasswell,** who studied World War II propaganda, embodied the effects theory in his famous model of mass communication: *Who, Says what, In which channel, To whom, With what effect.* At their extreme, powerful

Media Timeline

Understanding Mass Media Effects

1922 Walter Lippmann attributed powerful effects to the mass media.

1938 Hadley Cantril concluded that the "War of the Worlds" panic was drastically overstated.

1940s Mass communication scholars shifted from studying effects to uses and gratification.

1948 Paul Lazarsfeld challenged powerful effects theory in voter studies.

1967 George Gerbner launched his television violence index.

1970s Mass communication scholars shifted to cumulative effects theory.

1972 Maxwell McCombs and Don Shaw concluded that media create public agendas, not opinion.

effects theory devotees assumed that the media could inject information, ideas and even propaganda into the public. The theory was explained in terms of a hypodermic needle model or bullet model. Early powerful effects scholars would agree that newspaper coverage and endorsements of political candidates decided elections.

The early scholars did not see that the hypodermic metaphor was hopelessly simplistic. They assumed wrongly that individuals are passive and absorb uncritically and unconditionally whatever the media spew forth. The fact is that individuals read, hear and see the same things differently. Even if they did not, people are exposed to many, many media—hardly a single, monolithic voice. Also, there is a skepticism among media consumers that is manifested at its extreme in the saying "You can't believe a thing you read in the paper." People are not mindless, uncritical blotters.

Minimalist Effects Theory

Scholarly enthusiasm for the hypodermic needle model dwindled after two massive studies of voter behavior, one in Erie County, Ohio, in 1940 and the other in Elmira, New York, in 1948. The studies, led by sociologist **Paul Lazarsfeld** of Columbia University, were the first rigorous tests of media effects on an election. Lazarsfeld's researchers went back to 600 people several times to discover how they developed their campaign opinions. Rather than citing particular newspapers, magazines or radio stations, as had been expected, these people generally mentioned friends and acquaintances. The media had hardly any direct effect. Clearly, the hypodermic needle model was off base, and the powerful effects theory needed rethinking. From that rethinking emerged the **minimalist effects theory,** which included:

TWO-STEP FLOW MODEL. Minimalist scholars devised the **two-step flow** model to show that voters are motivated less by the mass media than by people they know personally and respect. These people, called **opinion leaders,** include many clergy, teachers and neighborhood merchants, although it is impossible to list categorically all those who are opinion leaders. Not all clergy, for example, are influential, and opinion leaders are not necessarily in an authority role. The minimalist scholars' point is that personal contact is more important than media contact. The two-step flow model, which replaced the hypodermic needle model, showed that

Paul Lazarsfeld
Found voters more influenced by other people than by mass media.

minimalist effects theory
Theory that media effects are mostly indirect.

two-step flow
Media effects on individuals are through opinion leaders.

opinion leaders
Influence friends, acquaintances.

whatever effect the media have on the majority of the population is through opinion leaders. Later, as mass communication research became more sophisticated, the two-step model was expanded into a **multistep flow** model to capture the complex web of social relationships that affects individuals.

STATUS CONFERRAL. Minimalist scholars acknowledge that the media create prominence for issues and people by giving them coverage. Conversely, neglect relegates issues and personalities to obscurity. Related to this **status conferral** phenomenon is **agenda-setting**. Professors **Maxwell McCombs** and **Don Shaw,** describing the agenda-setting phenomenon in 1972, said the media do not tell people *what to think* but tell them *what to think about*. This is a profound distinction. In covering a political campaign, explain McCombs and Shaw, the media choose which issues or topics to emphasize, thereby helping set the campaign's agenda. "This ability to affect cognitive change among individuals," say McCombs and Shaw, "is one of the most important aspects of the power of mass communication."

NARCOTICIZING DYSFUNCTION. Some minimalists claim that the media rarely energize people into action, such as getting them to go out to vote for a candidate. Rather, they say, the media lull people into passivity. This effect, called **narcoticizing dysfunction,** is supported by studies that find that many people are so overwhelmed by the volume of news and information available to them that they tend to withdraw from involvement in public issues. Narcoticizing dysfunction occurs also when people pick up a great deal of information from the media on a particular subject—poverty, for example—and believe that they are doing something about a problem when they are really only smugly well informed. Intellectual involvement becomes a substitute for active involvement.

Cumulative Effects Theory

In recent years some mass communication scholars have parted from the minimalists and resurrected the powerful effects theory, although with a twist that avoids the simplistic hypodermic needle model. German scholar **Elisabeth Noelle-Neumann,** a leader of this school, conceded that the media do not have powerful immediate effects but argues that effects over time are profound. Her **cumulative effects theory** notes that nobody can escape either the media, which are ubiquitous, or the media's messages, which are driven home with redundancy. To support her point, Noelle-Neumann cites multimedia advertising campaigns that hammer away with the same message over and over. There's no missing the point. Even in news reports there is a redundancy, with the media all focusing on the same events.

Noelle-Neumann's cumulative effects theory has troubling implications. She says that the media, despite surface appearances, work against diverse, robust public consideration of issues. Noelle-Neumann bases her observation on human psychology, which she says encourages people who feel they hold majority viewpoints to speak out confidently. Those views gain credibility in their claim to be dominant when they are carried by the media, whether they are really dominant or not. Meanwhile, says Noelle-Neumann, people who perceive that they are in a minority are inclined to speak out less, perhaps not at all. The result is that dominant views can snowball through the media and become consensus views without being sufficiently challenged.

multistep flow
Media effects on individuals come through complex interpersonal connections.

status conferral
Media attention enhances attention to people, subjects, issues.

agenda-setting
Media tell people what to think about, not what to think.

Maxwell McCombs and Don Shaw
Articulated agenda-setting theory.

narcoticizing dysfunction
People deceive themselves into believing they're involved when actually they're only informed.

Elisabeth Noelle-Neumann
Leading cumulative effects theorist.

cumulative effects theory
Theory that media influence is gradual over time.

To demonstrate her intriguing theory, Noelle-Neumann has devised the ominously labeled **spiral of silence** model, in which minority views are intimidated into silence and obscurity. Noelle-Neumann's model raises doubts about the libertarian concept that the media provide a marketplace in which conflicting ideas fight it out fairly, each receiving a full hearing.

Third-Person Effect

A remnant of now-discredited perceptions that the media have powerful and immediate influence is called **third-person effect.** In short, the theory holds that people overestimate the impact of media messages on other people. Scholar W. P. Davison, who came up with the concept in 1983, told a story about a community film board that censored some movies because they might harm people who watch them—even though the board members would deny that they themselves were harmed by watching them. The theory can be reduced to this notion: "It's the other guy who can't handle it, not me."

Davison's pioneering scholarship spawned many studies. Most of the conclusions can be boiled down to these:

- Fears about negative impact are often unwarranted.
- Blocking negative messages is often unwarranted.

Future Theories

Scholar Melvin DeFleur, who has chronicled developments in mass communication theory, is pessimistic about what's happening now in mass communication studies. DeFleur, of Boston University, says recent years have lacked milestones, seminal studies on mass communication, after a rich history of significant studies from the 1930s to the early 1980s. Writing in the scholarly journal *Mass Communication and Society* in 1998, DeFleur said, "When asked by my publisher to revise a book summarizing the existing milestones and adding new ones, I could not identify even one that fit the same criteria as the earlier investigations."

The Golden Age of masscom research, as DeFleur calls it, yielded "important concepts, generalizations and theories that are now part of the accumulated knowledge of how the U.S. media function and the kinds of influence that they have on individuals and society." Among those seminal projects:

- **Payne Fund Studies.** These studies, in the 1930s, established theoretical fundamentals on movies' effects on children.
- **"War of the Worlds" Study.** This 1940 study, by Hadley Cantril, questioned whether the mass media have a bullet effect on audiences. It helped to usher in more sophisticated ways of understanding mass communication.
- **Lazarsfeld Studies.** These studies, in 1940 and 1948, created a new understanding of how mass communication influences people.

Why is mass communication theory dead in the water? DeFleur says that one factor has been a brain drain from universities, where such research took place in earlier times. Corporations now offer much higher salaries than universities—sometimes double and triple—to attract people with doctoral degrees who can do research for their marketing and other corporate pursuits. Scholars are drawn to more practical

spiral of silence
Vocal majority intimidates others into silence.

third-person effect
One person overestimating the effect of media messages on other people.

and lucrative work that may help a detergent manufacturer to choose the right color for packaging the soap but fails to further our understanding of how the mass communication process works.

Uses and Gratifications Studies

STUDY PREVIEW   Beginning in the 1940s, many mass communication scholars shifted from studying the media to studying media audiences. These scholars assumed that individuals use the media to gratify needs. Their work, known as uses and gratifications studies, focused on how individuals use mass media—and why.

Challenges to Audience Passivity

As disillusionment with the powerful effects theory set in after the Lazarsfeld studies of the 1940s, scholars reevaluated many of their assumptions, including the idea that people are merely passive consumers of the mass media. From the reevaluation came research questions about why individuals tap into the mass media. This research, called **uses and gratifications** studies, explored how individuals choose certain media outlets. One vein of research said people seek certain media to gratify certain needs.

These scholars worked with social science theories about people being motivated to do certain things by human needs and wants, such as seeking water, food and shelter as necessities and wanting to be socially accepted and loved. These scholars identified dozens of reasons why people use the media, among them surveillance, socialization and diversion.

Surveillance Function

With their acute sense of smell and sound, deer scan their environment constantly for approaching danger. In modern human society, surveillance is provided for individuals by the mass media, which scan local and global environments for information that helps individuals make decisions to live better, even survive.

News coverage is the most evident form through which the mass media serve this **surveillance function.** From a weather report, people decide whether to wear a raincoat; from the Wall Street averages, whether to invest; from the news, whether the president will have their support. Although most people don't obsess about being on top of all that's happening in the world, there is a touch of the news junkie in everybody. All people need reliable information on their immediate environment. Are tornadoes expected? Is the bridge fixed? Are vegetable prices coming down? Most of us are curious about developments in politics, economics, science and other fields. The news media provide a surveillance function for their audiences, surveying the world for information that people want and need to know.

It is not only news that provides surveillance. From drama and literature people learn about great human issues that give them a better feel for the human condition. Popular music and entertainment, conveyed by the mass media, give people a feel for the emotional reactions of other human beings, many very far away, and for things going on in their world.

uses and gratifications
Theory that people choose media that meet their needs, interests.

surveillance function
Media provide information on what's going on.

Preparing for Y2K Crashes. Extensive media coverage of pending computer problems with the date conversion from 1999 to 2000 alerted everybody to prepare for a possible crisis. The coverage, which was in the news daily for months, prompted software changes and code writing to head off a disaster. Thanks to media surveillance, enough concern was generated at all levels in society to avert the crisis. Almost all computers rolled over seamlessly at midnight from 12311999 to 01012000.

Socialization Function

Except for recluses, people are always seeking information that helps them fit in with other people. This **socialization function,** a lifelong process, is greatly assisted by the mass media. Without paying attention to the media, for example, it is hard to participate in conversations about how the Yankees did last night, Tom Cruise's latest movie or the current Pentagon scandal. Jay Leno's monologues give late-night television watchers a common experience with their friends and associates the next day, as do the latest movie, the evening news and Sunday's football games.

Using the media can be a social activity, bringing people together. Gathering around the radio on Sunday night for the Mercury Theater in the 1930s was a family activity. Going to the movies with friends is a group activity.

The media also contribute to togetherness by creating commonality. Friends who subscribe to *Newsweek* have a shared experience in reading the weekly cover story, even though they do it separately. The magazine helps individuals maintain social relationships by giving them something in common. In this sense the media are important in creating community, even nationhood and perhaps, with global communication, a fellowship of humankind.

Less positive as a social function of the mass media is **parasocial interaction.** When a television anchor looks directly into the camera, as if talking with individual viewers, it is not a true social relationship that is being created. The communication is one-way without audience feedback. However, because many people enjoy the sense of interaction, no matter how false it is, many local stations encourage on-camera members of the news team to chat among themselves, which furthers the impression of an ongoing conversation with an extended peer group that includes the individual viewer.

This same false sense of reciprocal dialogue exists also among individuals and their favorite political columnists, lovelorn and other advice writers and humorists. Some people have the illusion that the celebrities David Letterman interviews on his program are their friends, and so are Jay Leno's and Larry King's. It is also illusory parasocial interaction when someone has the television set on for companionship.

socialized function
Media help people fit into society.

parasocial interaction
A false sense of participating in dialogue.

Diversion Function

Through the mass media, people can escape everyday drudgery, immersing themselves in a soap opera, a murder mystery or pop music. This is the **diversion function**. The result can be stimulation, relaxation or emotional release.

STIMULATION.   Everybody is bored occasionally. When our senses—sight, hearing, smell, taste and touch—lack sufficient external stimuli, a sensory vacuum results. Following the physicist's law that a vacuum must be filled, we seek new stimuli to correct our sensory deprivation. In modern society the mass media are almost always handy as boredom-offsetting stimulants. It's not only in boring situations that the mass media can be a stimulant. To accelerate the pace of an already lively party, for example, someone can put on quicker music and turn up the volume.

RELAXATION.   When someone's sensory abilities are overloaded, the media can be relaxing. Slower, softer music can sometimes help. Relaxation, in fact, can come through any change of pace. In some situations a high-tension movie or book can be as effective as a lullaby.

RELEASE.   People can use the mass media to blow off steam. Somehow a Friday night horror movie dissipates the frustration pent up all week. So can a good cry over a tear-jerking book.

Using the mass media as a stimulant, relaxant or release is quick, healthy escapism. Escapism, however, can go further, as when soap opera fans so enmesh themselves in the programs that they perceive themselves as characters in the story line. Carried too far, escapism becomes withdrawal. When people build on media portrayals to the point that their existence revolves on living out the lives of, say, Elvis Presley or Marilyn Monroe, the withdrawal from reality has become a serious psychological disorder.

Consistency Theory

Gratifications scholars learned that people generally are conservative in choosing media, looking for media that reinforce their personal views. Faced with messages consistent with their own views and ones that are radically different, people pay attention to the ones they're comfortable with and have slight recall of contrary views. These phenomena—selective exposure, selective perception, selective retention and selective recall—came to be called **consistency theory**.

Consistency theory does a lot to explain media habits. People read, watch and listen to media with messages that don't jar them. The theory raised serious questions about how well the media can meet the democratic ideal that they be a forum for the robust exchange of divergent ideas. The media can't fulfill their role as a forum if people hear only what they want to hear.

Individual Selectivity

STUDY PREVIEW   Individuals choose to expose themselves to media whose perspective and approach reinforce their personal interests and values. These choices, called

diversion function
Media entertain.

consistency theory
People choose media messages consistent with their individual views, values.

selective exposure, are consciously made. Similar selectivity phenomena are at work subconsciously in how individuals perceive and retain media content.

Selective Exposure

People make deliberate decisions in choosing media. For example, outdoors enthusiasts choose *Field & Stream* at the newsrack. Academics subscribe to the *Chronicle of Higher Education.* Young rock fans watch MTV. People expose themselves to media whose content relates to their interests. In this sense, individuals exercise control over the media's effects on them. Nobody forces these selections on anybody.

This process of choosing media, called **selective exposure,** continues once an individual is involved in a publication or a broadcast. A hunter who seldom fishes will gravitate to the hunting articles in *Field & Stream,* perhaps even skipping the fishing pieces entirely. On MTV a hard-rock aficionado will be attentive to wild music but will take a break when the video jock announces that a mellow piece will follow the commercial.

Selective Perception

The selectivity that occurs in actually reading, watching and listening is less conscious than in selective exposure. No matter how clear a message is, people see and hear egocentrically. This phenomenon, known as **selective perception** or **autistic perception,** was demonstrated in the 1950s by researcher Roy Carter, who found that physicians concerned about socialized medicine at the time would hear "social aspects of medicine" as "socialized medicine." Rural folks in North Carolina, anxious for news about farming, thought they heard the words "farm news" on the radio when the announcer said "foreign news."

Scholars Eugene Webb and Jerry Salancik explain it this way: "Exposure to information is hedonistic." People pick up what they want to pick up. Webb and Salancik state that nonsmokers who read an article about smoking focus subconsciously on passages that link smoking with cancer, being secure and content, even joyful, in the information that reinforces the wisdom of their decision not to smoke. In contrast, smokers are more attentive to passages that hedge the smoking-cancer link. In using the mass media for information, people tend to perceive what they want. As social commentator Walter Lippmann put it, "For the most part we do not first see and then define, we define first and then see." Sometimes the human mind distorts facts to square with predispositions and preconceptions.

Selective Retention and Recall

Experts say that the brain records forever everything to which it is exposed. The problem is recall. Although people remember many things that were extremely pleasurable or that coincided with their beliefs, they have a harder time calling up the memory's file on other things.

Selective retention happens to mothers when they tend to deemphasize or even forget the illnesses or disturbances of pregnancy and the pain of birth. This phenomenon works the opposite way when individuals encounter things that reinforce their beliefs.

selective exposure
People choose some media messages over others.

selective perception
People tend to hear what they want or expect to hear.

autistic perception
Synonym for *selective perception.*

selective retention
Subconsciously, people retain some events and messages, not others.

Selective Retention. The influence of the mass media is a function of both media and audience. The success of nostalgia magazines like *Memories,* which was introduced in 1989 and whose circulation soared to 650,000, is a result of the rose-colored lenses through which most people view the past. This is an example of selective retention at work.

Nostalgia also can affect recall. For example, many mothers grossly predate when an undesirable behavior like thumb sucking was abandoned. Mothers tend also to suggest precocity about the age at which Suzy or José first walked or cut the first tooth. In the same way people often use rose-colored lenses, not 20/20 vision, in recalling information and ideas from the media. This is known as **selective recall.**

In summary, individuals have a large degree of control over how the mass media affect them. Not only do individuals make conscious choices in exposing themselves to particular media, but also their beliefs and values subconsciously shape how their minds pick up and store information and ideas. The phenomena of selective exposure, selective perception and selective retention and recall are overlooked by people who portray the mass media as omnipotent and individuals as helpless and manipulated pawns.

The 1938 "War of the Worlds" scare demonstrates this point. The immediate response was to heap blame on the media, particularly Orson Welles and CBS, but panic-stricken listeners bore responsibility too. A Princeton University team led by psychologist **Hadley Cantril,** which studied the panic, noted that radio listeners brought to their radio sets predispositions and preconceptions that contributed to what happened. Among their subconscious baggage:

- A preconception, almost a reverence, about radio, especially CBS, as a reliable medium for major, breaking news.
- A predisposition to expect bad news, created by a decade of disastrous global economic developments and another war imminent in Europe.
- Selective perception, which caused them to miss announcements that the program was a dramatization. Although many listeners tuned in late and missed the initial announcement, others listened straight through the announcements without registering them.
- An awe about scientific discoveries, technological progress and new weapons, which contributed to gullibility.
- Memories from World War I about the horror of gas warfare.

selective recall
People recollect some events and messages for long term but not others.

Hadley Cantril
Concluded that there is less media effect than had been thought.

■ An inability to test the radio story with their own common sense. How, for example, could the Army mobilize for a battle against the Martians within 20 minutes of the invasion?

Socialization

STUDY PREVIEW   The mass media have a large role in initiating children into the society. This socialization process is essential to perpetuating cultural values, but some people worry that it can be negative if the media report and portray undesirable behavior and attitudes, such as violence and racism.

Media's Initiating Role

Nobody is born knowing how to fit into society. This is learned through a process that begins at home. Children imitate their parents and brothers and sisters. From listening and observing, children learn values. Some behavior is applauded, some is scolded. Gradually this culturization and **socialization** process expands to include friends, neighbors, school and at some point the mass media.

In earlier times the role of the mass media came late because books, magazines and newspapers required reading skills that were learned in school. The media were only a modest part of early childhood socialization. Today, however, television is omnipresent from the cradle. A young person turning 18 will have spent more time watching television than in any other activity except sleep. Television, which requires no special skills to use, has displaced much of the socializing influence that once came from parents. "Sesame Street" imparts more information on the value of nutrition than does Mom's admonition to eat spinach.

By definition, socialization is **prosocial.** Children learn that motherhood, baseball and apple pie are valued; that buddies frown on tattling; that honesty is virtuous; and that hard work is rewarded. The stability of a society is ensured through the transmission of such values to the next generation.

Role Models

The extent of media influence on individuals may never be sorted out with any precision, in part because every individual is a distinct person and because media exposure varies from person to person. Even so, some media influence is undeniable. Consider the effect of entertainment idols as they come across through the media. Many individuals, especially young people casting about for an identity all their own, groom themselves in conformity with the latest heartthrob. Consider the Mickey Mantle butch haircuts in the 1950s and then Elvis Presley ducktails, Beatle mopheads in the 1960s and punk spiking in the 1980s. Remember all the Spice Girls look-alikes in high school some years ago? This imitation, called **role modeling,** even includes speech mannerisms from whoever is hip at the moment—"Show me the money," "Hasta la vista, baby," and "I'm the king of the world." Let's not forget "yadda-yadda-yadda" from "Seinfeld."

No matter how quirky, fashion fads are not terribly consequential, but serious questions can be raised about whether role modeling extends to behavior. Many

media online

Media Effects: Links to articles on the effects of media presented by the Children, Youth and Family Consortium. www.cyfc.umn.edu/media/effects.html

Media Effects on Girls: One of a number of online statistics on the effects of media effects. This one brought by the National Institute of Media and the Family. www.mediafamily.org/research/fact/mediaeffect.shtml

socialization
Learning to fit into society.

prosocial
Socialization perpetuates positive values.

role modeling
Basis for imitative behavior.

Media People

Peggy Charren

After watching television with her two young daughters, Peggy Charren decided that something needed doing. "Children's television time was filled with cartoon adventures, often violent and rarely creative, in story or animation form," she said. "Youngsters were being told to want unhealthy food and expensive toys." Charren invited neighborhood moms to her living room to discuss the "wall-to-wall monster cartoons." Thus, in 1968, was born Action for Children's Television, which, with Charren in charge, became the most influential non-government entity shaping U.S. television for the next two decades.

The first target was "Romper Room," a Boston-produced show that was little more than a program-length commercial aimed at kids. The host shamelessly hawked "Romper Room's" own line of toys from sign-on to sign-off. ACT sponsored a university study of "Romper Room" and was ready to take the findings to the Federal Communications Commission when station WHDH, which produced the show, stopped the host-selling to get Charren off its back—ACT's first victory.

Action for Children's Television then requested meetings with the three big networks, but ABC and NBC said no. Insulted, Charren and her growing organization decided to

Children's Television. Peggy Charren, a homemaker and concerned mother, led a campaign in Washington for better kids' television, persuading the Federal Communications Commission, the Federal Trade Commission and Congress that reform was needed. After the Children's Television Act was passed in 1990, Charren disbanded her lobbying group, Action for Children's Television.

take their cause to the government. In 1970 ACT became the first public interest group to request a meeting with the FCC. The commission responded by creating a permanent group to oversee children's television issues. With the new government pressure, the National Association of Broadcasters, the major industry trade group, established new standards for children's television. The new guidelines barred host-selling and put a 12-minute per hour cap on commercials during children's television. The lesson for ACT was that government pressure works. "We found that when the regulators make noise, the industry takes action to keep the rules away," Charren said.

There were other battles, but the major victory for Charren and Action for Children's Television was the Chil-

dren's Television Act of 1990. The law established government expectations for children's programming across a wide range of issues, including advertising, content and quantity. In 1992, to the surprise of many people, Charren announced she was disbanding ACT. After 24 years, she said, ACT has met the objectives that she had set out to accomplish. With the Children's Television Act in effect, the need for ACT had passed. At that point, ACT had 10,000 members.

Through all her crusading for better children's programming, Charren never called for censorship. Her battle cry was choice. "Censorship meant fewer choices. We needed more choice, not less." She did, however, admit to pushing "to eliminate commercial abuses targeted to children."

people who produce media messages recognize a responsibility for role modeling. Whenever Batman and Robin leaped into their Batmobile in the campy 1960s television series, the camera always managed to show them fastening their seat belts. Many newspapers have a policy to mention in accident stories whether seat belts were in use. In the 1980s, as concern about AIDS mounted, movie-makers went out of their way to show condoms as a precaution in social situations. For example, in the movie

Broadcast News, the producer character slips a condom into her purse before leaving the house on the night of the awards dinner.

If role modeling can work for good purposes, such as promoting safety consciousness and disease prevention, it would seem that it could also have a negative effect. Some people linked the Columbine High School massacre in Littleton, Colorado, to a scene in the Leonardo DiCaprio movie, *The Basketball Diaries*. In one scene, a student in a black trench coat executes fellow classmates. An outbreak of shootings followed other 1990s films that glorified thug life, including *New Jack City, Juice,* and *Boyz N the Hood*.

Stereotyping

Close your eyes. Think "professor." What image forms in your mind? Before 1973 most people would have envisioned a harmless, absent-minded eccentric. Today, *The Nutty Professor* movie remake is a more likely image. Both the absent-minded and the later nutty professor images are known as stereotypes. Both flow from the mass media. Although neither is an accurate generalization about professors, both have long-term impact.

Stereotyping is a kind of shorthand that can facilitate communication. Putting a cowboy in a black hat allows a movie director to sidestep complex character explanation and move quickly into a story line, because movie-goers hold a generalization about cowboys in black hats: They are the bad guys—a stereotype. Newspaper editors pack lots of information into headlines by drawing on stereotypes held by the readers. Consider the extra meanings implicit in headlines that refer to the "Castro regime," a "Southern belle" or a "college jock." Stereotypes paint broad strokes that help create impact in media messages, but they are also a problem. A generalization, no matter how useful, is inaccurate. Not all Scots are tight-fisted, nor are all Wall Street brokers crooked, nor are all college jocks dumb—not even a majority.

By using stereotypes, the mass media perpetuate them. With benign stereotypes, there is no problem, but the media can perpetuate social injustice with stereotypes. In the late 1970s the U.S. Civil Rights Commission found that blacks on network television were portrayed disproportionately in immature, demeaning or comic roles. By using a stereotype, television was not only perpetuating false generalizations but also being racist. Worse, network thoughtlessness was robbing black people of strong role models.

Feminists have leveled objections that women are both underrepresented and misrepresented in the media. One study by sociologist Eve Simson found that most female television parts were decorative, played by pretty California women in their 20s. Worse were the occupations represented by women, said Simson. Most frequent were prostitutes, at 16 percent. Traditional female occupations—secretaries, nurses, flight attendants and receptionists—represented 17 percent. Career women tended to be man-haters or domestic failures. Said Simson, "With nearly every family, regardless of socioeconomic class, having at least one TV set and the average set being turned on 6.3 hours per day, TV has emerged as an important source for promulgating attitudes, values and customs. For some viewers it is the only major contact with outside 'reality,' including how to relate to women. Thus, not only is TV's sexism insulting, but it is also detrimental to the status of women."

Media critics like Simson call for the media to become activists to revise demeaning stereotypes. While often right-minded, such calls can interfere with accurate portrayals. In 2001 the American Italian Defense League sued HBO over "The

stereotyping
Using broad strokes to facilitate story-telling.

Sopranos," alleging that the award-winning television series implied that most Italian-Americans are mobsters.

Socialization via Eavesdropping

The mass media, especially television, have eroded the boundaries that people once respected between the generations, genders and other social institutions. Once adults whispered when they wanted to discuss certain subjects, like sex, when children were around. Today, children eavesdrop on all kinds of adult topics by seeing them depicted on television. Though meant as a joke, these lines ring true today to many squirming parents:

> **Father to a friend:**   My son and I had that father-and-son talk about the birds and the bees yesterday.
> **Friend:**   Did you learn anything?

Joshua Meyrowitz, a communication scholar at the University of New Hampshire, brought the new socialization effects of intergenerational eavesdropping to wide attention with his 1985 book, *No Sense of Place*. In effect, the old socially recognized institution of childhood, which long had been protected from "grown-up issues" like money, divorce and sex, was disappearing. From television sitcoms, kids today learn that adults fight and goof up and sometimes are just plain silly. These are things kids may always have been aware of in a vague sense, but now they have front row seats.

Television also cracked other protected societal institutions, such as the "man's world." Through television many women entered the man's world of the locker room, the fishing trip and the workplace beyond the home. Older mass media, including books, had dealt with a diversity of topics and allowed people in on the "secrets" of other groups, but the ubiquity of television and the ease of access to it accelerated the breakdown of traditional institutional barriers.

Media-Depicted Violence

STUDY PREVIEW   Some individuals mimic aggressive behavior they see in the media, but such incidents are exceptions. Some experts argue, in fact, that media-depicted violence actually reduces real-life aggressive behavior.

Learning About Violence

Joshua Meyrowitz
Noted that media have reduced generational, gender barriers.

observational learning
Theory that people learn behavior seeing it in real life, in depictions.

The mass media help to bring young people into society's mainstream by demonstrating dominant behaviors and norms. This prosocial process, called **observational learning,** turns dark, however, when children learn deviant behaviors from the media. In Manteca, California, two teenagers, one only 13, lay in wait for a friend's father in his own house and attacked him. They beat him with a fireplace poker, kicked him and stabbed him, and choked him to death with a dog chain. Then they poured salt in his wounds. Why the final act of violence, the salt in the wounds? The 13-year-old explained that he had seen it on television. While there is no question that people can learn about violent behavior from the media, a major issue of our time is whether the mass media are the cause of aberrant behavior.

Media Timeline

Mass Communication and Violence

200 b.c. Aristotle concluded that portrayals of violence have cathartic effect.

1961 Albert Bandura's Bobo doll studies suggested that media violence stirs aggressive behavior.

1963 Wilbur Schramm and associates discredited television as having much effect on most children.

1980s Numerous studies concluded that media violence by itself rarely triggers violence.

1984 Joshua Meyrowitz theorized that television was breaking down gender and generation gaps.

2000 Federal Trade Commission reported that violent fare was being advertised to children despite ratings that it was unsuitable, sparking political calls for restraint but not adding any new research to the core question of whether children are adversely affected.

Individuals on trial for criminal acts occasionally plead that "the media made me do it." That was the defense in a 1974 California case in which two young girls playing on a beach were raped with a beer bottle by four teenagers. The rapists told police they had picked up the idea from a television movie they had seen four days earlier. In the movie a young woman was raped with a broom handle, and in court, the youths' attorneys blamed the movie. The judge, as is typical in such cases, threw out media-projected violence as an unacceptable scapegoating defense and held the young perpetrators responsible.

Although the courts have never accepted transfer of responsibility as a legal defense, it is clear that violent behavior can be imitated from the media. Some experts, however, say that the negative effect of media-depicted violence is too often overstated and that media violence actually has a positive side.

Media Violence as Positive

People who downplay the effect of media portrayals of blood, guts and violence often refer to a **cathartic effect.** This theory, which dates to ancient Greece and the philosopher **Aristotle,** suggests that watching violence allows individuals vicariously to release pent-up everyday frustration that might otherwise explode dangerously. By seeing violence, so goes the theory, people let off steam. Most advocates of the cathartic effect claim that individuals who see violent activity are stimulated to fantasy violence, which drains off latent tendencies toward real-life violence.

In more recent times, scholar **Seymour Feshbach** has conducted studies that lend support to the cathartic effect theory. In one study, Feshbach lined up 625 junior high school boys at seven California boarding schools and showed half of them a steady diet of violent television programs for six weeks. The other half were shown non-violent fare. Every day during the study, teachers and supervisors reported on each boy's behavior in and out of class. Feshbach found no difference in **aggressive behavior** between the two groups. Further, there was a decline in aggression among boys watching violence. These boys were determined by personality tests to be more inclined toward aggressive behavior.

Opponents of the cathartic effect theory, who include both respected researchers as well as reflexive media bashers, were quick to point out flaws in Feshbach's

cathartic effect
People release violent inclinations by seeing them portrayed.

Aristotle
Defended portrayals of violence.

Seymour Feshbach
Found evidence for media violence as a release.

Media People

Sam Peckinpah

Nobody is neutral about Sam Peckin-pah. For all his Hollywood career, he had a reputation of being hard to work with. He was a drunk. Movie critic Pauline Kael, a friend of Peckin-pah, recalled his boozing at break-fast, straight up, nothing else. He reviled Hollywood producers. For four years they blacklisted him, but even then, they had to recognize his genius as a director and bring him back.

People split on the most evident part of Peckinpah's legacy: graphic violence. His 1969 Western master-piece, *The Wild Bunch*, with a grue-some slow-motion fury of death, drew heaps of criticism. He con-tinues to be blamed as the god-father of later Hollywood violence excesses—even today, though he died in 1984.

Friends remember Peckinpah as relishing the part of a bad boy. He worked at riling the producers who backed his movies financially, setting them up like straw men so that he could demonize them. A dismayed producer once wrote him, "I have no idea why you singled me out as an adversary." To which Peckinpah re-sponded, "My problem is, I do not suffer fools graciously and detest petty thievery and incompetence. Other than that, I find you charming, and on occasion, mildly entertaining."

About Peckinpah and producers, Kael said, "He needed their hatred

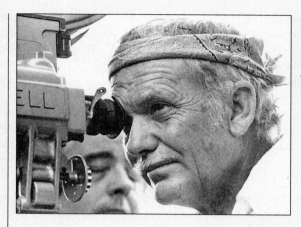

Movie Violence.
Director Sam Peckin-pah is remembered mostly for the graphic violence of his 1969 movie *The Wild Bunch*.

to stir up his own." His rage was his genius.

A theme in Peckinpah's movies is the rebel outlaw, a part he lived. Pri-vately, though, he was thoughtful and considerate even as a cocaine snorter and two-fisted boozer.

Peckinpah's early career was mostly as a writer and director for television Westerns, including "Gun-smoke" and "The Rifleman." He found in a 1965 television drama, "The Losers," that slow-motion vio-lence could be a poignant tool.

The themes in Peckinpah's major movies, beginning with *Ride the High Country* in 1962, included noble though flawed men who couldn't survive in a changing world. Mutual male respect, a camaraderie that didn't always come easily, was a staple that was morally more power-ful than adversarial forces—a point

that he made with tragic and violent punctuations. These themes were at the heart of *The Wild Bunch*. A band of Texas desperadoes allow them-selves to be slaughtered by a ruthless Mexican revolutionary rather than betray each other.

After making *The Wild Bunch*, Peckinpah was labeled "Bloody Sam." He hated it. The nickname missed the humanistic sensitivity in his work. It also missed his rage against how dehumanizing changes in the culture assault fundamental morality. An example were unlikely heroes, like the outlaws in *The Wild Bunch*.

Whatever Peckinpah's genius in filmic violence, countless directors— many less skilled, some plainly exploitive—have taken lessons from Peckinpah in racheting up ultraviolence.

research methods. Nonetheless, his conclusions carried a lot of influence because of the study's unprecedented massiveness—625 individuals. Also, the study was conducted in a real-life environment rather than in a laboratory, and there was a con-sistency in the findings.

Prodding Socially Positive Action

Besides the cathartic effects theory, an argument for portraying violence is that it prompts people to socially positive action. This happened after NBC aired "The Burning Bed," a television movie about an abused woman who could not take any more and set fire to her sleeping husband. The night the movie was shown, battered-spouse centers nationwide were overwhelmed with calls from women who had been putting off doing anything to extricate themselves from relationships with abusive mates.

On the negative side, one man set his estranged wife afire and explained that he was inspired by "The Burning Bed." Another man who beat his wife senseless gave the same explanation.

Media Violence as Negative

The preponderance of evidence is that media-depicted violence has the potential to cue real-life violence. However, the **aggressive stimulation** theory is often overstated. The fact is that few people act out media violence in their lives. For example, do you know anybody who saw a murder in a movie and went out afterward and murdered somebody?

We need to be careful in talking about aggressive stimulation. Note how scholar Wayne Danielson, who participated in the 1995–1997 National Television Violence Study, carefully qualified one of the study's conclusions: "Viewing violence on TV *tends* to increase violent behavior in viewers, more *in some situations* and less in others. For whatever reason, *when the circumstances are right,* we *tend* to imitate what we see others doing. Our inner resistance to engage in violent behavior *weakens.*"

The cable study concluded that children may be more susceptible than adults to media violence, but that too was far, far short of a universal causal statement.

Why, then, do many people believe that media violence begets real-life violence? Some early studies pointed to a causal link. These included the 1960 **Bobo doll studies** of **Albert Bandura,** who showed children a violent movie and then encouraged them to play with oversize, inflated dolls. Bandura concluded that kids who saw the film were more inclined to beat up the dolls than were other kids. Critics have challenged Bandura's methodology and said that he mistook childish playfulness for aggression. In short, Bandura and other aggressive stimulation scholars have failed to prove their theory to the full satisfaction of other scholars.

When pressed, people who hold the aggressive stimulation theory point to particular incidents they know about. A favorite is the claim by serial killer Ted Bundy that *Playboy* magazine led him to stalk and kill women. Was Bundy telling the truth? We will never know. He offered the scapegoat explanation on his way to the execution chamber, which suggests there may have been other motives. The Bundy case is anecdotal, and anecdotes cannot be extrapolated into general validity.

An alternative to aggressive stimulation theory is a theory that people whose feelings and general view of the world tend toward aggressiveness and violence gravitate to violence in movies, television and other media. This alternative theory holds that people who are violent are predisposed to violence, which is far short of saying the media made them do it. This leads us to the **catalytic theory,** which sees

Scapegoating. On the eve of his execution, serial killer Ted Bundy claimed his violence was sparked by girlie magazines. Whatever the truth of Bundy's claim, scholars are divided about whether media depictions precipitate violent behavior. At one extreme is the view that media violence is a safety valve for people inclined to violence. At the other extreme is the aggressive stimulation theory that media violence causes real-life violence. Most thinking, to paraphrase a pioneer 1961 study on television and children, is that certain depictions under certain conditions may prompt violence in certain persons.

aggressive stimulation
Theory that people are inspired to violence from media depictions.

Bobo doll studies
Kids seemed more violent after seeing violence in movies.

Albert Bandura
Found media violence stimulated aggression in children.

catalytic theory
Media violence is among factors that sometimes contribute to real-life violence.

media-depicted violence as having a contributing role in violent behavior, not as triggering it.

Catalytic Theory

Simplistic readings of both cathartic and aggressive stimulation effects research can yield extreme conclusions. A careful reading, however, points more to the media having a role in real-life violence but not necessarily triggering it and doing so only infrequently—and only if several nonmedia factors are also present. For example, evidence suggests that television and movie violence, even in cartoons, is arousing and can excite some children to violence, especially hyperactive and easily excitable children. These children, like unstable adults, become wrapped up psychologically with the portrayals and are stirred to the point of acting out. However, this happens only when a combination of other influences are also present. Among these other influences are:

- **Whether violence portrayed in the media is rewarded.** In 1984 David Phillips of the University of California at San Diego found that the murder rate increases after publicized prizefights, in which the victor is rewarded, and decreases after publicized murder trials and executions, in which, of course, violence is punished.
- **Whether media exposure is heavy.** Researcher Monroe Lefkowitz studied upstate New York third-graders who watched a lot of media-depicted violence. Ten years later, Lefkowitz found that these individuals were rated by their peers as violent. This suggests cumulative, long-term media effects.
- **Whether a violent person fits other profiles.** Studies have found correlations between aggressive behavior and many variables besides violence viewing. These include income, education, intelligence and parental child-rearing practices. This is not to say that any of these third variables cause violent behavior. The suggestion, rather, is that violence is far too complex to be explained by a single factor.

Most researchers note too that screen-triggered violence is increased if the aggression:

- Is realistic and exciting, like a chase or suspense sequence that sends adrenaline levels surging.
- Succeeds in righting a wrong, like helping an abused or ridiculed character get even.
- Includes situations or characters similar to those in the viewer's own experience.

All these things would prompt a scientist to call media violence a catalyst. Just as the presence of a certain element will allow other elements to react explosively but itself not be part of the explosion, the presence of media violence can be a factor in real-life violence but not a cause by itself. This catalytic theory was articulated by scholars **Wilbur Schramm,** Jack Lyle and Edwin Parker, who investigated the effects of television on children and came up with this statement in their 1961 book *Television in the Lives of Our Children,* which has become a classic on the effects of media-depicted violence on individuals: "For *some* children under *some* conditions, *some* television is harmful. For *other* children under the same conditions, or for the same children under *other* conditions, it may be beneficial. For *most* children, under

Wilbur Schramm
Concluded that television has minimal effects on children.

most conditions, *most* television is probably neither particularly harmful nor particularly beneficial."

Societally Debilitating Effects

Media-depicted violence scares far more people than it inspires to violence, and this, according to **George Gerbner,** a leading researcher on screen violence, leads some people to believe the world is more dangerous than it really is. Gerbner calculates that 1 in 10 television characters is involved in violence in any given week. In real life the chances are only about 1 in 100 per *year.* People who watch a lot of television, Gerbner found, see their own chances of being involved in violence nearer the distorted television level than their local crime statistics or even their own experience would suggest. It seems that television violence leads people to think they are in far greater real-life jeopardy than they really are.

The implications of Gerbner's findings go to the heart of a free and democratic society. With exaggerated fears about their safety, Gerbner says, people will demand greater police protection. They are also likelier, he says, to submit to established authority and even to accept police violence as a tradeoff for their own security.

Media Violence and Youth

Nobody would argue that Jerry Springer's television talk show is a model of good taste and restraint. In fact, the conventional wisdom is that such shows do harm. But do they? Two scholars at the University of Pennsylvania, Stacy Davis and Marie-Louise Mares, conducted a careful study with 292 high school students in North Carolina, some from a city and some from a rural area, and concluded from their data: "Although talk shows may offend some people, these data do not suggest that the youth of the U.S. is corrupted by watching them."

One issue was whether talk-show viewing desensitizes teenagers to tawdry behavior. The conventional wisdom, articulated by many politicians calling for television reform, is that teenagers are numbed by all the antisocial, deviant and treacherous figures on talk shows. Not so, said Davis and Mares: "Heavy talk-show viewers were no less likely than light viewers to believe that the victims of antisocial behavior had been wronged, to perceive that the victim had suffered, or to rate the antisocial behavior as immoral."

Do talk shows undercut society's values? According to Davis and Mares, "In fact, the world of talk shows may be quite conservative. Studio audiences reinforce traditional moral codes by booing guests who flout social norms, and cheering those who speak in favor of the show's theme. So, actually, it looks almost as though talk shows serve as cautionary tales, heightening teens' perceptions of how often certain behaviors occur and how serious social issues are."

Tolerance of Violence

An especially serious concern about media-depicted violence is that it has a numbing, callousing effect on people. This **desensitizing theory,** which is widely held, says not only that individuals are becoming hardened by media violence but also that society's tolerance for such antisocial behavior is increasing.

George Gerbner
Speculated that democracy is endangered by media violence.

desensitizing theory
Tolerance of real-life violence grows because of media-depicted violence.

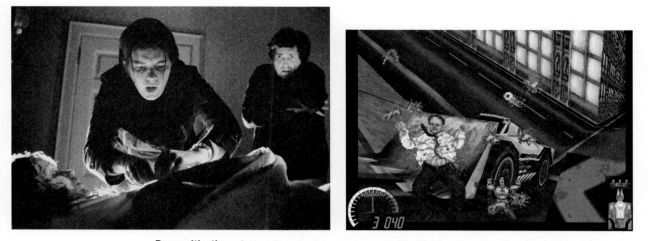

Desensitization. Critics of media violence say movies like *The Exorcist* desensitize people, especially teenagers, to the horrors of violence. That concern extends to video games. In one, Carmaggedon, kids are encouraged on the packaging blurb, "Don't slow down to avoid hitting that pedestrian crossing the street—aim, rev up and rack up those points." In one sequence in the Mortal Kombat video game, a crowd shouts encouragement for Kano to rip the heart out of Scorpion, his downed protagonist. Kano waves the dismembered heart to the crowd, which roars approvingly. Although scholars disagree about whether media violence begets real-life violence, most do agree that media violence leaves people more accepting of violence around them in their everyday lives.

Media critics say that the media are responsible for this desensitization, but many media people, particularly movie and television directors, respond that it is the desensitization that has forced them to make the violence in their shows even more graphic. They explain that they have run out of alternatives to get the point across when the story line requires that the audience be repulsed. Some movie critics, of course, find this explanation a little too convenient for gore-inclined movie-makers and television directors, but even directors not inclined to gratuitous violence feel their options for stirring the audience have become scarcer. The critics respond that this is a chicken-or-egg question and that the media are in no position to use the desensitization theory to excuse increasing violence in their products if they themselves contributed to the desensitization. And so the argument goes on about who is to blame.

Desensitization is apparent in news also. The absolute ban on showing the bodies of crime and accident victims in newspapers and on television newscasts, almost universal a few years ago, is becoming a thing of the past. No longer do newsroom practices forbid showing body bags or even bodies. During the 1991 Persian Gulf war, U.S. television had no reluctance about airing videos of allied troops picking up the bodies of hundreds of strafed Iraqi soldiers and hurling them, like sacks of flour, onto flatbed trucks for hauling to deep trenches, where the cameras recorded the heaped bodies being unceremoniously bulldozed over with sand.

In summary, we know far less about media violence than we need to. Various theories explain some phenomena, but the theories themselves do not dovetail. The desensitizing theory, for example, explains audience acceptance of more violence, but it hardly explains research findings that people who watch a lot of television actually

Media People

George Gerbner

George Gerbner worries a lot about media violence. And he's been doing this longer than just about anybody else. In 1967 Gerbner and colleagues at the University of Pennsylvania created a television violence index and began counting acts of violence. Today, more than three decades later, the numbers are startling. Gerbner calculates the typical American 18-year-old has seen 32,000 murders and 40,000 attempted murders at home on television.

In a dubious sense, there may be good news for those who fear the effects of media violence. Gerbner's index has found no significant change in the volume of violence since the mid-1970s. It may be maxed out.

Gerbner theorizes that the media violence has negative effects on society. It's what he calls "the mean-world syndrome." As he sees it, people exposed to so much violence come to perceive the world as a far more dangerous place than it really is. One of his concerns is that people become overly concerned for their own safety and, in time, may become willing to accept a police state to ensure their personal security. That, he says, has dire consequences for the free and open society that has been a valued hallmark of the American lifestyle.

It's a Mean World. Scholar George Gerbner, who has been tracking television violence since 1967, says a typical American child sees 32,000 on-screen murders before age 18. The result, he says, is many people see the world as much meaner than it really is.

Are there answers? Gerbner notes that the global conglomeration of mass media companies works against any kind of media self-policing. These companies are seeking worldwide outlets for their products, whether movies, television programs or music, and violence doesn't require any kind of costly translations. "Violence travels well," he says. Also, violence has low production costs.

Gerbner notes that violence is an easy fill for weak spots in a television story line. Also, in television, violence is an effective cliff-hanger before a commercial break.

While Gerbner's stats are unsettling, he has critics who say his numbers make the situation seem worse than it really is. The Gerbner index scores acts of violence without considering their context. That means when Bugs Bunny is bopped on the head, it counts the same as Rambo doing the same thing to a vile villain in a skull-crushing, blood-spurting scene. A poke in the eye on "The Three Stooges" also scores as a violent act.

Despite his critics, Gerbner has provided a baseline for measuring changes in the quantity of television violence. Virtually every scholar cites him in the ongoing struggle to figure out whether media violence is something that should worry us all.

have heightened anxiety about their personal safety. People fretting about their own safety are hardly desensitized.

Violence Studies

The mass media, especially television and movies that deal in fiction, depict a lot of violence. Studies have found as many as six violent acts per hour on prime-time

Vince McMahon. For football fans unable to go cold turkey after the Super Bowl, the creator of the World Wrestling Foundation had an answer. McMahon went into partnership with NBC to create the XFL pro-football league in 2001 with new rules and pizzazz that made the NFL seem stodgy. The premiere's audience exceeded expectations, although the games later fizzled in the ratings and were cancelled in May 2001.

network television. In and of itself, that may seem a lot, but a study at the University of California, Los Angeles, operating on the premise that the issue should not be how much violence is depicted but the context in which it occurs, came to a less startling conclusion: Slapstick comedic violence shouldn't be lumped with a graphic homicide in counting depictions of violence. Nor should a violent storm.

The UCLA research, called the Violence Assessment Monitoring Project, concluded in its first year that distressing human violence was much less prevalent than earlier studies counted. Of 121 prime-time episodes, only 10 had frequent violence and only eight had occasional violence. This was after comedic violence and nonhuman violence, such as hurricanes, were screened out. The next year, 1996, found violence in only five prime-time shows—half the number of the year before. Also, most of the shows didn't survive the season. In 1998 the number was down to two series.

The UCLA study added sophistication to counting acts of media-depicted violence but still didn't assess whether the violence affected people. In 1986 scholar William McQuire reviewed the literature on mediated violence and found that hardly any of the studies' evidence was statistically reliable. The exception was controlled laboratory studies, for which the statistics were more meaningful but didn't indicate much causality.

Media Agenda-Setting for Individuals

STUDY PREVIEW   Media coverage helps to define the things people think about and worry about. This is called agenda-setting. It occurs as the media create awareness of issues through their coverage, which lends importance to those issues. The media don't set agendas unilaterally but look to their audiences in deciding their priorities for coverage.

Media Selection of Issues

When the New York police wanted more subway patrols, their union public relations person, Morty Martz, asked officers to call him with every subway crime.

Martz passed the accounts, all of them, on to newspapers and television and radio stations. Martz could not have been more pleased with his media blitz. News coverage of subway crime, he later boasted, increased several thousand percent, although there had been no appreciable change in the crime rate itself. Suddenly, for no reason other than dramatically stepped-up coverage, people were alarmed. Their personal agendas of what to think about—and worry about—had changed. The sudden new concern, which made it easier for the union to argue for more subway patrols, was an example of media agenda-setting at work. Martz lured news media decision-makers into putting subway crime higher on their lists of issues to be covered, and individuals moved it up on their lists of personal concerns.

The agenda-setting phenomenon has been recognized for a long time. Sociologist **Robert Park,** writing in the 1920s, articulated the theory in rejecting the once-popular notion that the media tell people what to think. As Park saw it, the media create awareness of issues more than they create knowledge or attitudes. Agenda-setting occurs at several levels:

CREATING AWARENESS.   Only if individuals are aware of an issue can they be concerned about it. Concern about parents who kill their children becomes a major issue with media coverage of spectacular cases. In 1994 Susan Smith, a South Carolina woman, attracted wide attention with her horrific report that her sons, ages 3 and 1, had been kidnapped. The story darkened later when the woman confessed to driving the family car into the lake and drowning the boys herself. Over several days of intense media attention, the nation not only learned the morbid details of what happened but also became better informed about a wide range of parental, family and legal issues that the coverage brought to the fore.

ESTABLISHING PRIORITIES.   People trust the news media to sort through the events of the day and make order of them. Lead-off stories on a newscast or on Page One are expected to be the most significant. Not only does how a story is played affect people's agendas, but so do the time and space afforded it. Lavish graphics can propel an item higher.

PERPETUATING ISSUES.   Continuing coverage lends importance to an issue. A single story on a bribed senator might soon be forgotten, but day-after-day follow-ups can fuel ethics reforms. Conversely, if gatekeepers are diverted to other stories, a hot issue can cool overnight—out of sight, out of mind.

Intramedia Agenda-Setting

Agenda-setting also is a phenomenon that affects media people, who constantly monitor one another. Reporters and editors many times are concerned more with how their peers are handling a story than with what their audience wants. Sometimes the media harp on one topic, making it seem more important than it really is, until it becomes tedious.

The media's agenda-setting role extends beyond news. Over time, lifestyles and values portrayed in the media can influence not just what people think about but what they do. Hugh Hefner's *Playboy* magazine of the 1950s helped to usher in the sexual revolution. Advertising has created a redefinition of American values by whetting an appetite for possessions and glamorizing immediate gratification.

Robert Park
Argued that media create awareness.

Even so, individuals exercise a high degree of control in their personal agendas. For decades William Randolph Hearst campaigned with front-page editorials in all his newspapers against using animals in research, but animal rights did not become a pressing public issue. Even with the extensive media coverage of the Vietnam war, polls late in the 1960s found that many Americans still were unmoved. For the most part, these were people who chose to tune out the war coverage. The fact is that journalists and other creators of media messages cannot automatically impose their agendas on individuals. If people are not interested, an issue won't become part of their agendas. The individual values at work in the processes of selective exposure, perception and retention can thwart media leadership in agenda-setting.

Also, media agendas are not decided in a vacuum. Dependent as they are on having mass audiences, the media take cues for their coverage from their audiences. Penny press editors in the 1830s looked over the shoulders of newspaper readers on the street to see what stories attracted them and then shaped their coverage accordingly. Today, news organizations tap the public pulse through scientific sampling to deliver what people want. The mass media both exert leadership in agenda-setting and mirror the agendas of their audiences.

Media-Induced Anxiety and Apathy

STUDY PREVIEW   The pervasiveness of the mass media is not necessarily a good thing, according to some theorists who say a plethora of information and access to ideas and entertainment can induce information anxiety. Another theory is that the news media even encourage passivity by leaving an impression that their reporting is so complete that there's nothing left to know or do.

Information Anxiety

The New York *Times* had a landmark day on November 13, 1987. It published its largest edition ever: 12 pounds, 1,612 pages and 12 million words. How could anyone, even on a quiet Sunday, manage all that information? One of the problems in contemporary life is the sheer quantity of information technology allows us as a society to gather and disseminate. Even a relatively slender weekday edition of the New York *Times* contains more information than the average person in the 17th century was likely to come across in a lifetime, according to Richard Saul Wurman in his book *Information Anxiety.*

While educated people traditionally have thirsted for information, the quantity has become such that many people feel overwhelmed by what is called **information pollution.** We are awash in it and drowning, and the mass media are a factor in this. Consider college students at a major metropolitan campus:

- They pass newspaper vending machines and racks with a dozen different papers—dailies, weeklies, freebies—en route to class.
- On the radio, they have access to 40 stations.
- In their mailbox they find a solicitation for discount subscriptions to 240 magazines.
- They turn on their television during a study break and need to choose among 50 channels.

information pollution
Media deluge people with information and no sense of order, priority.

- At lunch they notice advertisements everywhere—on the placemat, on the milk carton, on table standups, on the butter pat, on the walls, on the radio coming over the public-address system, on the pen used to write a check.
- At the library and often in their dorm rooms they have almost instant online access through computer systems to more information than any human being could possibly deal with.

Compounding the quantity of information available is the accelerating rate at which it is available. Trend analyst John Naisbitt has made the point with this example: When President Lincoln was shot in 1865, people in London learned about it five days later. When President Reagan was shot in 1981, journalist Henry Fairlie, in his office one block away, heard about the assassination attempt from his London editor who had seen it on television and phoned Fairlie to get him to go to the scene. Databases and news organization's web sites to which almost every college student today has access are updated day by day, hour by hour, even second by second.

It is no wonder that conscientious people who want good and current data to form their judgments and opinions, even to go about their jobs, feel overwhelmed. Wurman, who has written exclusively on this frustration, describes information anxiety as the result of "the ever-widening gap between what we understand and what we think we should understand."

The solution is knowing how to locate relevant information and tune out the rest, but even this is increasingly difficult. Naisbitt reported in *Megatrends* that scientists planning an experiment are spending more time figuring out whether someone somewhere already has done the experiment than conducting the experiment itself.

On some matters, many people do not even try to sort through all the information that they have available. Their solution to information anxiety is to give up. Other people have a false sense of being on top of things, especially public issues, because so much information is available.

Media-Induced Passivity

One effect of the mass media is embodied in the stereotypical couch potato, whose greatest physical and mental exercise is heading to the refrigerator during commercials. Studies indicate that the typical American spends four to six hours a day with the mass media, mostly with television. The experience is primarily passive, and such **media-induced passivity** has been blamed, along with greater mobility and access to more leisure activities, for major changes in how people live their lives:

- **Worship services.** In 1955 Gallup found that 49 percent of Americans attended worship services weekly. Today, it is less than 40 percent.
- **Churches and lodges.** The role of church auxiliaries and lodges, such as the Masons, Odd Fellows and Knights of Pythias, once central in community social life with weekly activities, has diminished.
- **Neighborhood taverns.** Taverns at busy neighborhood corners and rural crossroads once were the center of political discussion in many areas, but this is less true today.
- **Participatory sports.** Despite the fitness and wellness craze, more people than ever are overweight and out of shape, which can be partly attributed to physical passivity induced by television and media-based homebound activities.

media-induced passivity
Media entice people away from social involvement.

Although these phenomena may be explained in part by people's increased use of the mass media and the attendant passivity, it would be a mistake not to recognize that social forces besides the media have contributed to them.

chapter wrap-up

The mass media influence us, but scholars are divided about how much. There is agreement that the media help to initiate children into society by portraying social and cultural values. This is a serious responsibility because portrayals of aberrant behavior, like violence, have effects, although we are not sure about their extent. This is not to say that individuals are unwitting pawns of the mass media. People choose what they read and what they tune in to, and they generally filter the information and images to conform with their preconceived notions and personal values.

In other respects too, the mass media are a stabilizing influence. The media try to fit into the lives of their audiences. An example is children's television programs on weekend mornings when kids are home from school but still on an early-rising schedule. The media not only react to audience lifestyles but also contribute to the patterns by which people live their lives, like going to bed after the late news. In short, the media have effects on individuals and on society, but it is a two-way street. Society is a shaper of media content, but individuals make the ultimate decisions about subscribing, listening and watching. The influence issue is a complex one that merits further research and thought.

Questions for Review

1. Why have most media scholars abandoned the powerful effects and minimalist effects theories for the cumulative theory?
2. What is the uses and gratifications approach to mass media studies?
3. Do individuals have any control over mass media effects on them?
4. What role do the mass media have in socializing children?
5. How do scholars differ on whether media-depicted violence triggers aggressive behavior?
6. What is meant when someone says, "The mass media don't tell people what to think as much as tell them what to think about"?
7. Does being informed by mass media necessarily improve citizen involvement in political processes?

Questions for Critical Thinking

1. Although generally discredited by scholars now, the powerful effects theory once had many adherents. How do you explain the lingering popularity of this thinking among many people?
2. Name at least three opinion leaders who influence you on issues that you do not follow closely in the media. On what issues are you yourself an opinion leader?
3. Give specific examples of each of the eight primary mass media contributing to the lifelong socialization process. For starters, consider a current non-fiction best-selling book.
4. Explain how selective exposure, selective perception and selective retention would work in the case of a devout Christian conservative to whom George W. Bush spoke at Bob Jones University, a conservative Baptist college, during the 2000 presidential primaries. Compare how these same people recorded other candidates' campaign speeches in their minds that same day.
5. Discuss the human needs that the mass media help to satisfy in terms of the news and entertainment media.
6. Among the functions that the mass media serve for individuals are diversion and escape. Is this healthy?
7. Explain the prosocial potential of the mass media in culturization and socialization. What about the media as an antisocial force in observational learning?
8. Cite at least three contemporary role models who you can argue are positive. Explain how they might

also be viewed as negative. Cite three role models who you can argue are negative.

9. What stereotype comes to your mind with the term *Uncle Remus*? Is your image of Uncle Remus one that would be held universally? Why or why not?

10. How can serious scholars of mass communication hold such diverse ideas as the cathartic, aggressive stimulation and catalytic theories? Which camp is right?

Keeping Up to Date

The interdisciplinary scholarly journal *Media Psychology*, a quarterly, focuses on theory-based research on media uses, processes and effects.

Marshall McLuhan. The controversial Canadian theorist blamed Gutenberg for social alienation, but not all was lost. He also foresaw a transforming global village.

16

Mass Media and Society

- The mass media seek to reach large audiences rather than to extend cultural sensitivity.

- The mass media contribute to stability in the society by providing common rituals.

- People communicate with generations into the future and with faraway people through the mass media.

- Scholar Marshall McLuhan foresaw television easing the alienation of human beings from their true nature.

- Societies that dominate economically and politically export their values elsewhere for better or worse.

Canadian communication theorist **Marshall McLuhan** didn't invent the term *global village,* but he certainly cemented the notion in public dialogue. In numerous books and the scholarly journal *Explorations,* which he founded in 1954, McLuhan talked about the world shrinking, at least metaphorically. In a wired world, he said, television could present live information from anywhere to everyone. The result, as he saw it, could change human existence profoundly, reversing a trend that went back to the mass-produced printed word in the 1400s.

As McLuhan saw it, Gutenberg's invention had a dark side. Reading, a skill necessary to partake of print media, is hardly a natural act. It requires so much concentration and focus that it squeezes out other sensory perceptions that a human being would normally sense and respond to. Reading requires you to block out the world around you. For example, if you are really into a book, you might miss a knock on the door.

Television would reverse this perversion of human nature, McLuhan said. With a wired world, people would respond spontaneously—or, as he saw it, naturally. Receiving the message would no longer be an isolated, insulated act. This global village, like pre-Gutenberg villages, could help human beings to return to a pristine form of existence, their senses in tune with their surroundings and their responses governed more by instinct than contrivances like reading, which, he said, had alienated human beings from their true nature.

McLuhan, whose works include theoretical best-sellers in the 1960s, was confusing in some of his writing, using concepts and terms in different ways over a long career of thinking about mass communication. Even so, his contributions to our understanding remain bulwarks in many advanced mass communication curriculums even two decades after his death.

Mass Media Role in Culture

STUDY PREVIEW   The mass media are inextricably linked with culture because it is through the media that creative people have their strongest sway. Although the media have the potential to disseminate the best creative work of the human mind and soul, some critics say the media are obsessive about trendy, often silly subjects. These critics find serious fault with the media's concern for pop culture, claiming it squeezes out things of significance.

Elitist versus Populist Values

The mass media can enrich society by disseminating the best of human creativity, including great literature, music and art. The media also carry a lot of lesser things that reflect the culture and, for better or worse, contribute to it. Over time, a continuum has been devised that covers this vast range of artistic production. At one extreme is artistic material that requires sophisticated and cultivated tastes to appreciate it. This is called **high art.** At the other extreme is **low art,** which requires little sophistication to enjoy.

One strain of traditional media criticism has been that the media underplay great works and concentrate on low art. This **elitist** view argues that the mass media do society a disservice by pandering to low tastes. To describe low art, elitists sometimes use the German word *kitsch,* which translates roughly as "garish" or "trashy." The word captures their disdain. In contrast, the **populist** view is that there is nothing unbecoming in the mass media's catering to mass tastes in a democratic, capitalistic society.

In a widely cited 1960 essay, "Masscult and Midcult," social commentator **Dwight Macdonald** made a virulent case that all popular art is kitsch. The mass media, which depend on finding large audiences for their economic base, can hardly ever come out at the higher reaches of Macdonald's spectrum.

This kind of elitist analysis was given a larger framework in 1976 when sociologist **Herbert Gans** categorized cultural work along socioeconomic and intellectual lines. Gans said that classical music, as an example, appealed by and large to people of academic and professional accomplishments and higher incomes. These were **high-culture audiences,** which enjoyed complexities and subtleties in their art and entertainment. Next came **middle-culture audiences,** which were less abstract in their interests and liked Norman Rockwell and prime-time television. **Low-culture audiences** were factory and service workers whose interests were more basic; whose educational accomplishments, incomes and social status were lower; and whose media tastes leaned toward kung fu movies, comic books and supermarket tabloids.

Gans was applying his contemporary observations to flesh out the distinctions that had been taking form in art criticism for centuries—the distinctions between high art and low art.

HIGHBROW.   The high art favored by elitists generally can be identified by its technical and thematic complexity and originality. High art is often highly individu-

---

Marshall McLuhan
Blamed human alienation on mass-produced written word.

high art
Requires sophisticated taste to be appreciated.

low art
Can be appreciated by almost everybody.

elitism
Mass media should gear to sophisticated audiences.

kitsch
Pejorative word for trendy, trashy, low art.

populism
Mass media should seek largest possible audiences.

Dwight Macdonald
Said all pop art is kitsch.

Herbert Gans
Said social, economic and intellectual levels of audience coincide.

high-, middle- and low-culture audiences
Continuum identified by Herbert Gans.

Media Timeline

Mass Communication and Culture

1960s Marshall McLuhan theorized that television could end human alienation caused by print media.

1960s Dwight Macdonald equated pop art and kitsch.

1965 Susan Sontag saw pop art as emotive high art.

1969 Herbert Schiller articulated cultural imperialism concerns.

1976 Herbert Gans related cultural sensitivity to social and economic status.

---

alistic because the creator, whether a novelist or a television producer, has explored issues in fresh ways, often with new and different methods. Even when it's a collaborative effort, a piece of high art is distinctive. High art requires a sophisticated audience to appreciate it fully. Often it has enduring value, surviving time's test as to its significance and worth.

The sophistication that permits an opera aficionado to appreciate the intricacies of a composer's score, the poetry of the lyricist and the excellence of the performance sometimes is called **highbrow.** The label has grim origins in the idea that a person must have great intelligence to have refined tastes, and a high brow is necessary to accommodate such a big brain. Generally, the term is used by people who disdain those who have not developed the sophistication to enjoy, for example, the abstractions of a Fellini film, a Matisse sculpture or a Picasso painting. Highbrows generally are people who, as Gans noted, are interested in issues by which society is defining itself and look to literature and drama for stories on conflicts inherent in the human condition and between the individual and society.

MIDDLEBROW.   **Middlebrow** tastes recognize some artistic merit but without a high level of sophistication. There is more interest in action than abstractions—in Captain Kirk aboard the starship Enterprise, for example, than in the childhood struggles of Ingmar Bergman that shaped his films. In socioeconomic terms, middlebrow appeals to people who take comfort in media portrayals that support their status quo orientation and values.

LOWBROW.   Someone once made this often-repeated distinction: Highbrows talk about ideas, middlebrows talk about things, and **lowbrows** talk about people. Judging from the circulation success of the *National Enquirer* and other supermarket tabloids, there must be a lot of lowbrows in contemporary America. Hardly any sophistication is needed to recognize the machismo of Rambo, the villainy of Darth Vader, the heroism of Superman or the sexiness of Catherine Zeta-Jones.

The Case Against Pop Art

Pop art is of the moment, including things like mood rings, hula-hoops and hip-hop garb—and trendy media fare. Even elitists may have fun with pop, but they traditionally have drawn the line at anyone who mistakes it as having serious artistic merit. Pop art is low art that has immense although generally short-lived popularity.

highbrow, middlebrow and lowbrow
Levels of media content sophistication that coincide with audience tastes.

Media People

The Lichters and Stanley Rothman

It was love over the statistics. **Linda and Robert Lichter** met while working on a massive study of major media decision-makers and married. Later, they formed the **Center for Media and Public Affairs** in Washington, which today is a leading research organization on the mass media and social change. One of the most troubling findings of the Lichters and coresearcher **Stanley Rothman** is that the major U.S. media are out of touch with the American people. This conclusion comes out of massive studies of the people who run the entertainment media.

The Lichter-Rothman studies say that television executives and key creative people are overwhelmingly liberal on the great social issues of our time. More significantly, the studies have found that the programming these people produce reflects their political and social agenda. For example:

- Television scripts favor feminist positions in 71 percent of the shows, far more than public-opinion surveys find among the general population.
- Three percent of television murders are committed by blacks, compared with half in real life.
- Two out of three people are portrayed in positive occupations on television, but only one out of three businesspeople is depicted in a positive role.

Stanley Rothman

These examples, according to the Lichters and Rothman, indicate a bias toward feminism and minority people and against businesspeople. The Lichter-Rothman work documents a dramatic turnaround in television entertainment fare. Two generations ago, leading programs, ranging from sitcoms like "Leave It to Beaver" to dramatic programs like "Wagon Train," extolled traditional values. In the 1970s came programs like "Mork and Mindy" and "All in the Family" that questioned some values. Today, network schedules make plenty of room for programs like "The Simpsons" and "Ally McBeal" that examine nontraditional views and exhibit a dramatically different social orientation than, say, "Leave It to Beaver."

It is hazardous, of course, to paint too broad a picture of contemporary television, where a sitcom such as "The King of Queens" is much in the 1950s mode, but the Lichters and Rothman,

Linda and Robert Lichter

by analyzing 620 shows over a 30-year period, argue persuasively that there has been a dramatic shift. They characterize the shift this way: "Television's America may once have looked like Los Angeles' Orange County writ large—Waspish, businesslike, religious, patriotic and middle class. Today it better resembles San Francisco's Marin County—trendy, self-expressive, culturally diverse and cosmopolitan."

Elitists see pop art as contrived and artificial. In their view, the people who create **popular art** are masters at identifying what will succeed in the marketplace and then providing it. Pop art, according to this view, succeeds by conning people into liking it. When Nehru jackets were the fashion rage in the late 1960s, it was not be-

Gearing News to the Audience. The level of intellectual interest necessary to enjoy high-end news coverage, like that in the New York *Times,* is much more sophisticated than that needed to enjoy low-end tabloids.

cause they were superior in comfort, utility or aesthetics, but because promoters sensed that profits could be made in touting them via the mass media as new and cashing in on easily manipulated mass tastes. It was the same with pet rocks, Tickle-Me Elmo and countless other faddy products.

The mass media, according to the critics, are obsessed with pop art. This is partly because the media are the carriers of the promotional campaigns that create popular followings but also because competition within the media creates pressure to be first, to be ahead, to be on top of things. The result, say elitists, is that junk takes precedence over quality.

Much is to be said for this criticism of pop art. The promotion by CBS of the screwball 1960s sitcom "Beverly Hillbillies," as an example, created an eager audience that otherwise might have been reading Steinbeck's critically respected *Grapes of Wrath.* An elitist might chortle, even laugh, at the unbelievable antics and travails of the Beverly Hillbillies, who had their own charm and attractiveness, but an elitist would be concerned all the while that low art was displacing high art in the marketplace and that the society was the poorer for it.

Pop Art Revisionism

Pop art has always had a few champions among intellectuals, although the voices of **pop art revisionism** were usually drowned out in the din of elitist pooh-poohing. In 1965, however, essayist **Susan Sontag** wrote an influential piece, "One Culture and the New Sensibility," which prompted many elitists to take a fresh look at pop art.

POP ART AS EVOCATIVE.   Sontag made the case that pop art could raise serious issues, just as high art could. She wrote: "The feeling given off by a Rauschenberg painting might be like that of a song by the Supremes." Sontag soon was being called the high priestess of pop intellectualism. More significantly, the Supremes were

m e dia online

Center for Public and Media Affairs: The web site's Media Monitor includes a political newswatch, economic studies, media factoids, TV studies, late night comedy counts, and more.
www.cmpa.com

Linda and Robert Lichter
Their research indicates a liberal agenda in entertainment programming; colleagues of Stanley Rothman.

Center for Media and Public Affairs
Media research organization.

Stanley Rothman
His research indicates a liberal agenda in entertainment programming; colleague of the Lichters.

popular art
Art that tries to succeed in the marketplace.

pop art revisionism
Pop art has inherent value.

Susan Sontag
Saw cultural, social value in pop art.

being taken more seriously, as were a great number of Sontag's avant-garde and obscure pop artist friends.

media online

Pop Art: Index of pop artists.
www.fi.muni.cz/~toms/PopArt/contents.html

POPULARIZATION OF HIGH ART.   Sontag's argument noted that the mass appeal of pop artists meant that they could convey high art to the masses. A pop pianist like Liberace might have omitted the trills and other intricacies in performing a sonata, but he nonetheless gave a mass audience an access to Mozart that otherwise would never have occurred. Sontag saw a valuable service being performed by artists who both understood high art and could "translate" it for unsophisticated audiences, a process known as **popularization.**

As Sontag saw it, the mass media were at the fulcrum in a process that brings diverse kinds of cultural products and audiences together in exciting, enriching ways. The result of popularization, Sontag said, was an elevation of the cultural sensitivity of the whole society.

POP ART AS A SOCIETAL UNIFIER.   In effect, Sontag encouraged people not to look at art on the traditional divisive, class-conscious, elitist-populist continuum. Artistic value, she said, could be found almost anywhere. The word "camp" gained circulation among 1960s elitists who were influenced by Sontag. These highbrows began finding a perversely sophisticated appeal in pop art as diverse as Andy Warhol's banal soup cans and ABC's outrageous "Batman." The mass media, through which most people experienced Warhol and all people experienced "Batman," became recognized more broadly than ever as a societal unifier.

The Sontag-inspired revisionist look at pop art coincides with the view of many mass media historians that the media have helped bind the society rather than divide it. In the 1840s, these historians note, books and magazines with national distribution provided Americans of diverse backgrounds and regions with common reference points. Radio did the same even more effectively in the 1940s. Later, so did network television. In short, the mass media are purveyors of cultural production that contributes to social cohesion, whether it be high art or low art.

HIGH ART AS POPULAR.   While kitsch may be prominent in media programming, it hardly elbows out all substantive content. In 1991, for example, Ken Burns' public television documentary "The Civil War" outdrew low art prime-time programs on ABC, CBS and NBC five nights in a row. It was a glaring example that high art can appeal to people across almost the whole range of socioeconomic levels and is not necessarily driven out by low art. Burns' documentary was hardly a lone example. Another, also from 1991, was Franco Zeffirelli's movie *Hamlet,* starring pop movie star Mel Gibson, which was marketed to a mass audience yet could hardly be dismissed by elitists as kitsch. In radio, public broadcasting stations, marked by highbrow programming, have become major players for ratings in some cities.

Social Stability

STUDY PREVIEW   The mass media create rituals around which people structure their lives. This is one of many ways in which the media contribute to social stability. The media foster socialization throughout adulthood, contributing to social cohesion by affirming beliefs and values and helping reconcile inconsistent values and discrepancies between private behavior and public morality.

popularization
Adjust media content to appeal to broader audience.

Media-Induced Ritual

Northwest Airlines pilots, flying their Stratocruisers over the Dakotas in the 1950s, could tell when the late-night news ended on WCCO, the powerful Minneapolis radio station. They could see lights at ranches and towns all across the Dakotas going off as people, having heard the news, went to bed. The 10 o'clock WCCO news had become embedded as a ritual. Today, for people on the East and West coasts, where most television stations run their late news at 11 p.m., the commonest time to go to bed is 11:30, after the news. In the Midwest, where late newscasts are at 10 o'clock, people tend to go to bed an hour earlier and also to rise an hour earlier. Like other rituals that mark a society, media-induced rituals contribute order and structure to the lives of individuals.

The effect of media-induced rituals extends even further. Collectively, the lifestyles of individuals have a broad social effect. Consider just these two effects of evening newspapers, an 1878 media innovation:

EVENING NEWS. E. W. Scripps changed people's habits with his evening newspapers, first in Cleveland in 1878, then elsewhere. Soon, evening papers outnumbered morning papers. The new habit, however, was not so much for evening newspapers as for evening news, as newspaper publishers discovered a hundred years later when television siphoned readers away with evening newscasts. The evening ritual persists, even though the medium is changing as evening papers go out of business or retreat to mornings.

COMPETITIVE SHOPPING. In the era before refrigeration and packaged food, household shopping was a daily necessity. When evening newspapers appeared, housewives, who were the primary shoppers of the period, adjusted their routines to read the paper the evening before their morning trips to the market. The new ritual allowed time for more methodical bargain hunting, which sharpened retail competition.

Besides shaping routines, ritual contributes to the mass media's influence as a shaper of culture. At 8:15 a.m. every Sunday, half the television sets in Japan are tuned to "Serial Novel," a tear-jerking series that began in the 1950s. Because so many people watch, it is a common experience that is one element in the identification of contemporary Japanese society. A ritual that marked U.S. society for years was "Dallas," on Friday at 9 p.m. Eastern time, 8 p.m. Central time. Then came "Survivor" on CBS in 2000. Other rituals are going to Saturday movie matinees, reading a book at bedtime and watching Monday night football.

Media and the Status Quo

In their quest for profits through large audiences, the mass media need to tap into their audience's common knowledge and widely felt feelings. Writers for network sitcoms avoid obscure, arcane language. Heroes and villains reflect current morals. Catering this way to a mass audience, the media reinforce existing cultural beliefs and values. People take comfort in learning through the media that they fit into their community and society, which furthers social cohesion. This is socialization continued beyond the formative years. It also is socialization in reverse, with the media taking cues from the society and playing them back.

Sherry Turkle. Some people create new personalities for themselves when they're online in Internet chat rooms. This has given rise to computer sociology as a specialized academic field. Sherry Turkle, a professor at the Massachusetts Institute of Technology, is in the vanguard exploring the Internet's influence on behavior. Some people, Turkle has discovered, like the anonymity of the Net to play with personas they wouldn't dare experiment with in face-to-face, real-life situations. Some individuals like their new Net personality so much they integrate it into other aspects of their lives.

The media's role in social cohesion has a negative side. Critics say that the media pander to the lowest common denominator by dealing only with things that fit the status quo easily. The result, the critics note, is a thwarting of artistic exploration beyond the mainstream. Critics are especially disparaging of predictable, wooden characters in movies and television and of predictability in the subjects chosen for the news.

A related negative aspect of the media's role as a contributor to social cohesion is that dominant values too often go unchallenged, which means that some wrong values and practices persist. Dudley Clendinen, a newspaper editor who grew up in the South, faults journalists for, in effect, defending racism by not covering it: "The news columns of Southern papers weren't very curious or deep or original in the late 1940s and 1950s. They followed sports and politics actively enough, but the whole rational thrust of Southern culture from the time of John C. Calhoun on had been self-defensive and maintaining. It had to be, to justify the unjustifiable in a society dedicated first to slavery and then to segregation and subservience. Tradition was everything, and the news pages were simply not in the habit of examining the traditions of the South."

Media and Cognitive Dissonance

The media are not always complacent. Beginning in the late 1950s, after the period to which Clendinen was referring, media attention turned to racial segregation. News coverage, literary comment and dramatic and comedy portrayals began to point up flaws in the status quo. Consider the effect, through the mass media, of these individuals on American racism:

- **John Howard Griffin.** In 1959 Griffin, a white journalist, dyed his skin black for a six-week odyssey through the South. His book *Black Like Me* was an inside look at being black in America. It had special credibility for the white majority because Griffin was white.
- **George Wallace.** The mass audience saw the issue of segregation personified in news coverage of Governor George Wallace physically blocking black students from attending the University of Alabama. The indelible impression was that segregation could be defended only by a clenched fist and not by reason.
- **Martin Luther King Jr.** News photographers captured the courage and conviction of Martin Luther King Jr. and other civil rights activists, black and white, taking great risks through civil disobedience to object to racist public policies.
- **Archie Bunker.** Archie Bunker, a television sitcom character, made a laughingstock of bigots.

To some people, the media coverage and portrayals seemed to exacerbate racial tensions. In the longer run, however, media attention contributed to a new consensus through a phenomenon that psychologists call **cognitive dissonance.** Imagine white racists as they saw George Wallace giving way to federal troops under orders from the White House. The situation pitted against each other two values held by individual racists: segregation as a value and an ordered society as symbolized by the presidency. Suddenly aware that their personal values were in terrible disharmony, or dissonance, many of these racists avoided the issue. Instead of continuing to express racism among family and friends, many tended to be silent. They may have been as racist as ever, but they were quiet or watched their words carefully. Gradually, their untenable view is fading into social unacceptability. This is not to say that racism does

cognitive dissonance
Occurs when people realize their values are inconsistent.

Cognitive Dissonance. Many white Americans from racist backgrounds found themselves challenging their own values when the federal government adopted proactive civil rights policies in the 1950s and 1960s. This dissonance escalated as these people followed news coverage of the long-overdue demands of blacks for fair treatment, as in this 1963 march. Some white racists resolved the discrepancy by abandoning racism. Many others simply retreated from discussion on the issue.

not persist. It does and continues to manifest itself in American life, though, in many ways, in forms much muted since the media focused on the experiment of John Howard Griffin, the clenched fist of George Wallace and the crusade of Martin Luther King Jr.

When the media go beyond pap and the predictable, they are examining the cutting-edge issues by which the society defines its values. Newsmagazines, newspapers and television, using new printing, photography and video technology in the late 1960s, put war graphically into U.S. living rooms, pointing up all kinds of discrepancies between Pentagon claims and the Vietnam reality. The glamorized, heroic

If you forget to bring along a designated driver, remember, you can always rent one.

TAXI

MADD
Mothers Against Drunk Driving

Public Service. Major agencies produce public service advertisements on a rotating basis for the Ad Council. These magazines and newspaper ads, as well as television and radio public-service announcements, are distributed free. The media run them at no cost. The Council chooses about a dozen organizations a year to benefit from the in-house creative genius at the agencies that produce the ads *pro bono*.

Agenda-Setting. Media attention to certain events spotlights issues by which the society defines its values. In 1998, when a gay University of Wyoming student, Matthew Shepard, was lynched by rednecks outside of town, gay rights moved higher on the national agenda. Coverage of the gruesome death was an example of the media agenda-setting.

Matthew Shepard

view of war, which had persisted through history, was countered by media depictions of the blood and death. Unable to resolve the discrepancies, some people withdrew into silence. Others reassessed their views and then, with changed positions or more confident in their original positions, they engaged in a dialogue from which a consensus emerged. And the United States, the mightiest power in history, began a militarily humiliating withdrawal. It was democracy at work, slowly and painfully, but at work.

Agenda-Setting and Status Conferral

Media attention lends a legitimacy to events, individuals and issues that does not extend to things that go uncovered. This conferring of status occurs through the media's role as agenda-setters. It puts everybody on the same wavelength, or at least a similar one, which contributes to social cohesion by focusing our collective attention on issues we can address together. Otherwise, each of us could be going in separate directions, which would make collective action difficult if not impossible.

Examples abound of how media attention spotlights certain issues. An especially poignant case occurred in 1998 when a gay University of Wyoming student, Matthew Shepard, was savagely beaten, tied to a fence outside of town and left to die. It was tragic gay-bashing, and coverage of the event moved gay rights higher on the national agenda. Coverage of the gruesome death was an example of the media agenda-setting and of status conferral.

Media and Morality

A small-town wag once noted that people read the local newspaper not to find out what is going on, which everybody already knows, but to find out who got caught. The observation was profound. The mass media, by reporting deviant behavior, help to enforce society's moral order. When someone is arrested for burglary and sentenced, it reaffirms for everybody that human beings have property rights.

Beyond police blotter news, the mass media are agents for reconciling discrepancies between **private actions** and **public morality**. Individually, people tolerate minor infractions of public morality, such as taking pencils home from work. Some people even let life-threatening behavior such as child abuse go unreported. When the deviant behavior is publicly exposed, however, toleration ceases, and social processes come into action that reconcile the deviance with public morality. The reconciling process maintains public norms and values. Consider Douglas Ginsburg. In the 1970s Ginsburg, a young law professor, smoked marijuana at a few parties. It was a misdemeanor, but Ginsburg's friends tolerated it, and not a word was said publicly. In 1988, however, when President Reagan nominated Ginsburg to the U.S. Supreme Court, reporter Nina Totenberg of National Public Radio reported Ginsburg's transgressions. Exposed, he withdrew his name. There was no choice. His private action, publicly exposed, could not be tolerated, and his withdrawal maintained public norms and values, without which a society cannot exist.

This same phenomenon occurred in the 1980s when homelessness became a national issue. For years homeless people in every major city had slept in doorways and alleys and, during winter, on steam vents. The homeless were seen but invisible. When social policies and economic factors in the 1980s sent the numbers skyrocketing, homelessness became a media issue that could not be ignored, and the society had to do something. Under the glare of media attention, people brought their private behavior, which had been to overlook the problem, into conformity with the tenet of public morality that says we are all our brothers' keepers. Across the nation, reform policies to relieve homelessness began moving through legislative channels.

Cultural Transmission

STUDY PREVIEW   The mass media transmit cultural values through history. Past generations talk to us through mass media, mostly books, just as we, often not realizing it, talk to future generations. The media also diffuse values and ideas contemporaneously.

Historical Transmission

Human beings have a compulsion to leave the wisdom they have accumulated for future generations. There is a compulsion, too, to learn from the past. In olden times, people gathered around fires and in temples to hear storytellers. It was a ritual through which people learned the values that governed their community. This is a form of **historical transmission**.

Five thousand years ago, the oral tradition was augmented when Middle Eastern traders devised an alphabet to keep track of inventories, transactions and rates of exchange. When paper was invented, clay tablets gave way to scrolls and eventually books, which became the primary vehicle for storytelling. Religious values were passed on in holy books. Military chronicles laid out the lessons of war. Literature provided lessons by exploring the nooks and crannies of the human condition.

Books remain the primary repository of our culture. For several centuries it has been between hard covers, in black ink on paper, that the experiences, lessons and wisdom of our forebears have been recorded for posterity. Other mass media today

private actions versus public morality
Dichotomy that exposes discrepancies between behavior and values.

historical transmission
Communication of cultural values to later generations.

Values Transmission. Mass media attention to the violent behavior and lyrics of rapper Eminem has many people worried that his values may be embraced by a new generation. The concern is triggered by the demonstrable effect of other offbeat media subjects, like the relatively trivial imitation of attire and hairstyles, and also the media's less easily documented diffusion of "innovations" that leads eventually to fundamental social change.

contemporary transmission
Communication of cultural values to different cultures.

diffusion of innovations
Process through which news, ideas, values, information spread.

share in the preservation and transmission of our culture over time. Consider these archives:

- Museum of Broadcasting in New York, with 1,200 hours of television documentaries; great performances, productions, debuts and series; and a sample of top-rated shows.
- Library for Communication and Graphic Arts at Ohio State University, whose collection includes editorial cartoons.
- Vanderbilt Television News Archive in Nashville, Tennessee, with 7,000 hours of network nightly news programs and special coverage such as political conventions and space shots.

Contemporary Transmission

The mass media also transmit values among contemporary communities and societies, sometimes causing changes that otherwise would not occur. This is known as **contemporary transmission.** Anthropologists have documented that mass communication can change society. When Edmund Carpenter introduced movies in an isolated New Guinea village, the men adjusted their clothing toward the Western style and even remodeled their houses. This phenomenon, which scholars call **diffusion of innovations,** occurs when ideas move through the mass media. Consider the following:

- **American Revolution.** Colonists up and down the Atlantic seaboard took cues on what to think and how to act from newspaper reports on radical activities, mostly in Boston, in the decade before the Declaration of Independence. These included inflammatory articles against the 1765 Stamp Act and accounts of the Boston Tea Party in 1773.
- **Music, fashion and pop culture.** In modern-day pop culture, the cues come through the media, mostly from New York, Hollywood and Nashville.
- **Third World innovation.** The United Nations creates instructional films and radio programs to promote agricultural reform in less developed parts of the world. Overpopulated areas have been targets of birth control campaigns.
- **Democracy in China.** As China opened itself to Western tourists, commerce and mass media in the 1980s, the people glimpsed Western democracy and prosperity, which precipitated pressure on the Communist government to westernize and resulted in the 1989 Tiananmen Square confrontation. A similar phenomenon was a factor in the glasnost relaxations in the Soviet Union in the late 1980s.
- **Demise of Main Street.** Small-town businesses are boarding up throughout the United States as rural people see advertisements from regional shopping malls, which are farther away but offer greater variety and lower prices than Main Street.

Scholars note that the mass media can be given too much credit for the diffusion of innovations. Diffusion almost always needs reinforcement through interpersonal communication. Also, the diffusion is hardly ever a one-shot hypodermic injection but a process that requires redundancy in messages over an extended period. The 1989

Responding to *Kursk* Tragedy. Russians demonstrated their dissatisfaction with their government's bungling when the submarine *Kursk* sank off Murmansk, losing all hands. Huge bulletin boards posted with newspapers kept people up to date. At work too was a mass communication process—diffusion of innovation—that Western-style demonstrations against government policy are acceptable, an unthinkable option in earlier periods.

outburst for democracy in China did not happen because one Chinese person read Thomas Paine one afternoon, nor do rural people suddenly abandon their local Main Street for a Wal-Mart 40 miles away. The diffusion of innovations typically involves three initial steps in which the mass media can be pivotal:

- **Awareness.** Individuals and groups learn about alternatives, new options and possibilities.
- **Interest.** Once aware, people need to have their interest further whetted.
- **Evaluation.** By considering the experience of other people, as relayed by the mass media, individuals evaluate whether they wish to adopt an innovation.

The adoption process has two additional steps in which the media play a small role: the trial stage, in which an innovation is given a try, and the final stage, in which the innovation is either adopted or rejected.

Mass Media and Fundamental Change

STUDY PREVIEW   The detribalization theory says the written word changed tribal communities by deemphasizing interpersonal communication. Written communication engaged the mind, not the senses, and according to the theory, a lonely, cerebral-based culture resulted. Now, as sense-intensive television displaces written communication, retribalization is creating a global village.

Human Alienation

An intriguing, contrarian assessment of the media's effects on human society was laid out by Canadian theorist Marshall McLuhan in the 1960s. McLuhan argued that the print media had **alienated** human beings from their natural state. In pre-mass

alienation
Dissatisfaction with individual and cultural deviations from basic nature.

detribalization
The removal of humankind from natural, tribal state.

retribalization
Restoring humankind to natural, tribal state.

global village
Instantaneous connection of every human being.

media times, McLuhan said, people acquired their awareness about their world through their own observation and experience and through their fellow human beings, whom they saw face to face and with whom they communicated orally. As McLuhan saw it, this was a pristine communal existence—rich in that it involved all the senses—sight, sound, smell, taste and touch. This communal, tribal state was eroded by the written word, which involved the insular, meditative act of reading. The printing press, he said, compounded this alienation from humankind's tribal roots. The written word, by engaging the mind, not the senses, begat **detribalization,** and the printing press accelerated it.

According to McLuhan, the printed word even changed human thought processes. In their tribal state, he said, human beings responded spontaneously to everything that was happening around them. The written word, in contrast, required people to concentrate on an author's relatively narrow, contrived set of data that led from Point A to Point B to Point C. Following the linear serial order of the written word was a lonely, cerebral activity, unlike participatory tribal communication, which had an undirected, helter-skelter spontaneity.

Television and the Global Village

McLuhan saw television bringing back tribalization. While books, magazines and newspapers engaged the mind, television engaged the senses. In fact, the television screen could be so loaded with data that it could approximate the high level of sensual stimuli that people found in their environments back in the tribal period of human existence. **Retribalization,** he said, was at hand because of the new, intensely sensual communication that television could facilitate. Because television could far exceed the reach of any previous interpersonal communication, McLuhan called the new tribal village a **global village.**

With retribalization, McLuhan said, people will abandon the print media's linear intrusions on human nature. Was McLuhan right? His disciples claim that certain earmarks of written communication—complex story lines, logical progression and causality—are less important to today's young people, who grew up with sense-intensive television. They point to the music videos of the 1980s, which excited the senses but made no linear sense. Many teachers say that children are having a harder time finding significance in the totality of a lesson. Instead, children fasten on to details.

As fascinating as McLuhan was, he left himself vulnerable to critics who point out that, in a true nonlinear spirit, he was selective with evidence and never put his ideas to rigorous scholarly examination. McLuhan died in 1980. Today, the jury remains divided, agreeing only that he was a provocative thinker.

chapter wrap-up

The media contribute both to social stability and to change. A lot of media content gives comfort to audiences by reinforcing existing social values. At the same time, media attention to nonmainstream ideas, in both news and fiction forms, requires people to reassess their values and, over time, contributes to social change.

Questions for Review

1. Why are mass media more interested in reaching large audiences than in contributing to cultural sensitivity?
2. How do the mass media contribute to stability in the society?
3. What are historical and cultural transmission?
4. How did scholar Marshall McLuhan foresee that television would ease the human alienation that he said was created by the mass-produced written word?

Questions for Critical Thinking

1. Why do the mass media find little room for great works that could elevate the cultural sensitivity of the society?
2. Explain essayist Susan Sontag's point that the mass media bring culturally significant works to mass audiences through the popularization process.
3. Give examples of how people shape their everyday lives around rituals created by the mass media. Also, give examples of how the mass media respond to social rituals in deciding what to present and how and when to present it.
4. Why would a radical social reformer object to most mass media content?

5. How has cognitive dissonance created through the mass media worked against racial separatism in American society since the 1950s?
6. How do the mass media help to determine the issues that society sees as important?
7. How do the media contribute to social order and cohesion by reporting private acts that deviate from public morality? You might want to consider the case of President Bill Clinton and Monica Lewinsky.
8. Give examples of the mass media allowing cultural values to be communicated through history to future societies. Also, give examples of contemporary cultural transmission.
9. Explain scholar Marshall McLuhan's theory that the mass-produced written word has contributed to an alienation of human beings from their true nature. How did McLuhan think television could reverse this alienation?

Keeping Up to Date

Recommended are *Journal of Popular Culture, Journal of American Culture* and *Journal of International Popular Culture*, all scholarly publications.

Murdoch Everywhere. In 2000 media mogul Rupert Murdoch consolidated his content delivery and satellite delivery system under a new banner: Sky Global. It was the largest distribution platform in the world—an outlet for Murdoch products from 20th Century Fox, News Corporation and other media enterprises.

17

Global Mass Media

Dozens of media companies have worked for years to expand their business overseas, a quest that's accelerating. But nobody has it figured out quite like Australian-born media mogul **Rupert Murdoch.**

In 2000 Murdoch created a new subsidiary, **Sky Global Networks**—the first comprehensive global content generation and delivery system. Sky Global, a new subsidiary of Murdoch's umbrella News Corporation, consolidates all of his delivery systems around the world plus a miscellany of related enterprises. The system includes the satellites of his StarTV, which provides television programming to most of Asia; of B-Sky-B, which does the same for Britain; and of his Latin American services. Murdoch, frank about the new Sky Global subsidiary, called it "the largest distribution platform in the world."

It's not just that Murdoch's Sky Global controls the orbiting platforms to distribute media content to the four corners of the globe but also that it will carry content from other Murdoch enterprises. These include 20th Century Fox, the movie studio; the Fox television network and its production arms; and all the Fox cable channels. In addition, Murdoch has been buying his way into and out of online services, newspapers magazines and all kinds of other content creators.

New Sky Global Logo

media online

Reader's Digest is now published in more than 20 countries. From the U.S. web site you can access foreign web versions. Here are some of them:

United States:
www.readersdigest.com

Argentina:
www.rdargentina.com/Frames/frame.htm

Czech Republic:
www.vyber.cz

Italy:
www.selezionerd.it/index.html

Sweden:
www.readersdigest.se/docs/se/seindex.htm

Global Conglomeration

STUDY PREVIEW   Media titan Rupert Murdoch has created the first global content creation and delivery system under a single corporate umbrella, but he's not alone in putting together a global media empire. Many media companies have international operations, though none as comprehensive. Still developing are the ways in which global media companies adapt to the web.

Multinational Companies

The mass media have had international sales for centuries, going back to early book printers. Until the 20th century, however, media companies designed little specifically for export.

FOREIGN BRANCHES.   A new awareness of potential markets abroad came in the 1930s, typified by the *Reader's Digest*'s first foray overseas. The magazine, born in the United States in 1922, had obvious international potential. In 1938 owners De-Witt and Lila Wallace established a British edition. It was largely the same as the U.S. edition, but British editors replaced some articles. Today, the magazine is published in 18 languages. Some editions are extensively edited for distinct audiences.

In the same spirit, U.S. movie producers began eyeing foreign markets in the 1930s and added subtitles or dubbed dialogue.

ACQUISITIONS.   Another model for international media companies, again not as comprehensive as Murdoch's, emerged in the 1980s. Media companies began buying up foreign media companies. Bertelsmann of Germany bought its way into many foreign markets. Acquisitions included the RCA and Arista record labels in the United States, then 14 women's magazines owned by the New York *Times,* then the venerable U.S. book company Random House. Other Bertelsmann properties in the United States include Bantam, Dell and Doubleday books. Bertelsmann has 200 operating units with 44,000 employees in 25 countries.

MERGERS.   Some media companies have found synergies in merging. A merger of Hachette of France and Filapacchi of Italy created cross-fertilization opportunities that generated more profits from existing products. The new company also exported concepts, such as the French fashion magazine *Elle* being adapted for additional markets, including the United States.

ALLIANCES.   Unlike Murdoch and his Sky Global Networks, in which he controls distribution, most media companies rely on other companies for foreign distribution of their content. Viacom, for example, sells its television programs to existing networks and stations in other countries. Several magazine publishers have agreements with native companies to produce and distribute foreign editions.

Web and Globalization

Rupert Murdoch's orbiting birds give him direct delivery to consumers. StarTV and B-Sky-B satellites beam signals directly to consumers, bypassing traditional distributors such as over-air local television stations. In the same sense, the web

Rupert Murdoch
Australian-born owner of the global company News Corporation.

Sky Global Networks
Comprehensive media content generation and delivery system developed by News Corporation.

Hometown News Everywhere. A Dutch company, PEPC, is installing kiosks in hotels worldwide to print out guests' hometown newspapers. Meanwhile, Xerox is introducing a system for newspapers to produce special editions for faraway electronic delivery. Editions range from 24 to 60 pages, each 11 × 17 inches, bound with a clear glue. The system uses Xerox document delivery technology.

bypasses traditional delivery media. These new technologies open the way for more companies to seek global audiences directly at relatively low cost. E-books, for example, don't require expensive presses to produce. Nor do they need massive warehouses or require expensive shipping. Producers of radio and television programs can use streaming instead of having to negotiate complex deals with networks or individual stations for distribution. In short, the web can eliminate middlemen.

Easy access to the web opens opportunities for upstarts to reach global audiences. Whether new companies can establish web followings that compete with the majors, which also have created presences on the web, isn't clear. With the massiveness of their repertoires, the major players certainly have a leg up.

The question for media critics, concerned about conglomeration on a global scale, is whether the web will level the playing field to give little guys a chance. The resulting diversity would ease concerns about the media becoming concentrated in only a few hands. If the majors continue to dominate the creation of content, as well as delivery, the critics of conglomeration will have added cause for alarm.

Effects of Globalization

STUDY PREVIEW   Foreign ownership worries some media critics. At stake, as these critics see it, is control of the direction of cultural advancement—something they believe should not be farmed out. Other experts say that global media companies are neutral as to content and have no ideological preferences except making money.

Cultural Subversiveness

Experts disagree about the effect of globalization. Some critics, including respected media critic Ben Bagdikian, fret that "anonymous superpowers" such as Bertelsmann are a potential threat to U.S. cultural autonomy and the free flow of information and ideas. In his book *The Media Monopoly,* Bagdikian said, "The highest levels of world finance have become intertwined with the highest levels of mass media ownership, with the result of tighter control over the systems on which most of the public depends for its news and information."

Other observers, such as Toni Heinzl and Robert Stevenson at the University of North Carolina, note that many global media companies, including Bertelsmann, have learned to let their local operating companies adapt to local cultures: "Following a global strategy, it is the company's policy to respect the national characteristics and cultural traditions in each of the more than two dozen countries in which it operates. It is impossible to detect even hints of German culture from the product lineup of Bertelsmann's companies abroad. Targeting specific preference of a national public or audience, the company has custom-tailored its products for each country: French culture in France, Spanish culture in Spain, American culture in the United States, and so on." The target is growth. In 1999, Bertelsmann increased the percentage of its profits from the United States to 37 percent from 20 percent.

Corporate Ideology

By and large, the agenda of media conglomerates is profits and nothing more. They do not promote ideology. U.S. movie-goers did not see Japanese overtones in Columbia movies or CBS records after the Sony takeover or in MCA products after the Matsushita takeover. At the same time, it cannot be ignored that Bertelsmann tried to transplant its successful German geographic magazine *Geo* in the United States in 1979, only to give it up two years and $50 million later when it realized that *National Geographic*'s following was unshakable. In the same vein, Murdoch imported British tabloid editors to reshape some of the U.S. newspapers he bought. What can be said with certainty about media globalization is that it is occurring and that observers are divided about its consequences.

Cultural Intrusion

STUDY PREVIEW Some experts claim that the export of U.S. and other Western popular culture is latter-day imperialism motivated by profit and without concern for its effect on other societies. The theory is that Third World countries are pawns of Western-based global media companies. Other experts see charges of cultural imperialism as overblown and hysterical.

Latter-Day Imperialism

The great concern about media globalization has been about the flow of values not among developed countries but to developing countries. Critics use the term **cultural imperialism** for this dark side of international communication. Their view is that the media are like the 19th-century European colonial powers, exporting Western values, often uninvited, to other cultures. At stake, these critics say, is the cultural sovereignty of non-Western nations. These critics note that the international communication media have their headquarters in the United States and in the former European colonial powers. The communication flow, they claim, is one way, from the powerful nations to the weak ones. The result, as they see it, is that Western values are imposed in an impossible-to-resist way. A Third World television station, for example, can buy a recycled American television program for far less than it costs to produce an indigenous program.

cultural imperialism
One culture's dominance of another.

Transglobal Transplant. Indian movie star Amitabh Bachchan welcomes participants to the television quiz show "Kaun Banega Crorepati," Hindi for "Who Wants to Be a Millionaire," in Bombay. The Indian version of the successful British show drew the highest viewership in Indian television, with millions of viewers glued to their television sets from Mondays to Thursdays after its 2000 launch. A U.S. variation, with Regis Philbin, was also a prime-time leader.

Scholar **Herbert Schiller,** who wrote *Mass Communications and American Empire,* argued that the one-way communication flow is especially insidious because the Western productions, especially movies and television, are so slick that they easily outdraw locally produced programs. As a result, says Schiller, the Western-controlled international mass media preempt native culture, a situation he sees as robbery, just like the earlier colonial tapping of natural resources to enrich the home countries.

India is a fascinating recent example of cultural intrusion, if not cultural imperialism. Until 1991 this nation had only one television network, which ran programs that originated in India almost exclusively. Then came StarTV, global media mogul Rupert Murdoch's satellite service from Hong Kong, which carried lots of U.S.-originated programming. Writing in *Media Studies Journal,* India media critic Shailaja Bajpai offered these observations:

- Many Indians were dressing like the Americans they saw on "Baywatch."
- While Indian boys once wanted to grow up to be great cricket players, they now wanted to shoot baskets like Michael Jordan.

Other anecdotal evidence of U.S. culture rubbing off elsewhere is in South Africa. According to Sebiletso Mokone-Matabane, an executive with the Independent Broadcasting authority there, robbers were shouting "freeze," a word that had no roots in Afrikaans or the indigenous languages, when they stormed into a bank. The robbers had been watching too much U.S. television.

Non-Downward Media Exchange

In some ways, cultural imperialism is in the eyes of the beholder. Some Latin American countries, for example, scream "cultural imperialism" at the United States but don't object when Mexico exports soap operas to the rest of Latin America, as do Brazil and Argentina. Although they are exercising a form of cultural imperialism, nobody puts the label on them. Media observer Larry Lorenz, who has studied this phenomenon, explains it this way: "What is occurring is simply internationalism brought on by the ever more sophisticated media of mass communication."

The cultural imperialism theory has other doubters among scholars. The doubters note that the theory is a simplistic application of the now-discredited hypodermic needle model of mass communication. Media messages do not have immediate direct effects.

Herbert Schiller
Saw Western cultures subsuming others.

Media People

Herbert Schiller

Nobody could provoke a debate quite like Herbert Schiller, whether among his college students or in the whole society. As Schiller saw it, corporations in the United States were coming to dominate cultural life abroad. He amassed his evidence in a 1969 book, *Mass Communications and American Empire.* The book sensitized readers to the implications of exporting movies, music and other U.S. media products. It also put leading media companies on notice that Mickey Mouse in Borneo, no matter how endearing, had untoward implications for the indigenous culture. U.S. corporate greed, Schiller said, was undermining native cultures in developing countries. It was an insidious destruction of heritage because U.S.

media products were so well produced, so slick, that it was hard for people elsewhere to resist them.

Some scholars argued that Schiller had overstated his case. Media leaders, most of whom hadn't considered the cultural implications of exporting their products, responded with a defensiveness that masked their vulnerability. Theirs was a populist argument that people wanted their products and that the products weren't being forced on anybody. They also missed Schiller's point.

The debate still rages even after Schiller's death in 2000 at age 80. In one sense, he has had the last word. His last book, *Living in the Number One Country: Reflections from a Critic of*

Herbert Schiller

American Empire, was published posthumously in May 2000, four months after he died.

Also overstated are charges that news from Europe and the United States dominates coverage in other parts of the world. One study found that 60 to 75 percent of the foreign news in the Third World is about other Third World countries, mostly those nearby. While the giant Western news services—AP, Agence France-Presse and Reuters—are the main purveyors of foreign news, the coverage that reaches Third World audiences is extremely parochial.

Emerging Global Media

Concern about Western cultural imperialism is slowly changing as two related things occur. First, the number of international media players, many in neither Europe nor the United States, is increasing. Second, rather than merely recycling domestic products abroad, United States-based media companies are creating new, local-oriented content in the countries where they do business.

Prime-time U.S. television soap operas "Dallas" and "Dynasty" once were on prime-time fare throughout the world, either with subtitles or dubbed awkwardly into local languages. Today, local media people who have mastered Western production techniques are producing local media content. Their programs go over big, attracting viewers and advertisers better than imported programs. Allan Ng, a Far East investment analyst, has seen the change at the giant Hong Kong satellite television service TVB. To *Business Week* reporter Joyce Barnathan, Ng said, "TVB dares not show 'Dynasty' until 11 at night."

Media Abroad

Americanizing the World

British traders introduced opium in China in the 1600s. The habit spread, and soon the British had a profitable trade importing opium to Chinese ports and exporting silver to pay for it. Resentful at British profits from the death and misery they had introduced, the Chinese government acted in 1839 against any further opium importation. In response, the British bombarded Canton, and the Opium War ensued.

Today, a similar struggle, dubbed the Second Opium War, is under way.

Yielding to U.S. trade pressure, Japan, South Korea and Taiwan lifted bans on foreign tobacco in 1987, and the Marlboro man instantly became a familiar poster figure. Propelled by huge advertising budgets and American-style promotion, U.S. tobacco sales increased 24-fold almost overnight in Taiwan to 5.1 billion cigarettes a year.

Is this cultural imperialism at its worst? Massachusetts Congressman Chet Atkins called it "the ultimate ugly Americanism." Noting that the U.S. government had mounted an exten-

sive domestic campaign against smoking, Atkins said, "We are sending a message through our trade negotiators that Asian lungs are more expendable than American lungs." In Taiwan a leading antismoking activist, David Yen, said, "We want American friendship, machinery and food—but not your drugs."

Meanwhile, the Marlboro man, taller in the saddle than ever, rides on. Smoking in Japan, South Korea and Taiwan continues to grow to record levels.

Indigenous local programming not only is taking hold in other countries, especially those with a developing middle class, but also many of these emerging media are exporting their material. Throughout Latin America, for example, people watch soap operas produced by TV Globo in Brazil and Televisa in Mexico. The Belgian broadcast company RTL, which once spent most of its programming dollars on imports like "Dallas" and "Dynasty," now produces most of its own shows. The French TF-1 and Italian Rai Uno television services have cut back substantially on U.S. programs. The turnaround in Europe has been fueled not only by audience preferences for local material but also by a European Union policy that half of each nation's broadcast programming must originate within the union.

There is also new competition, much of it well financed. In Europe the television service Canal One has teamed up with Bertelsmann of Germany to create a formidable competitor for the whole European audience. TVB in Hong Kong has its eye on dominating media fare to China, Southeast Asia and the Subcontinent. What once were easy pickings for U.S. media companies are now tough markets.

To compete, U.S. media companies are investing in other countries to develop local programming. MTV and ESPN both have built advanced production studios in Singapore. In 1995 Viacom relaunched its MTV service to Asia with local hosts. In Europe, U.S. companies are forming local partnerships. NBC, for example, which bought the European Super Channel cable network in 1993, has added business news from the *Financial Times*, a London newspaper. NBC has teamed up with TV Azteca in Mexico to tap into local programming and marketing savvy. Time Warner's HBO is in partnership with Omnivision, a Venezuelan cable company, for the HBO Olé pay-television service in Latin America.

While many countries are developing significant local media powerhouses, some countries are decades away from having their own media production facilities, financing and know-how. Their complaint today is not about cultural imperialism solely from the United States but also from Bonn, Caracas, Hong Kong, London, Mexico City, Paris and Sao Paulo.

Insidious Western Influence

Although more media content is being originated in home countries, some critics say don't be fooled. Shailaja Bajpai, editor of an Indian television magazine, says that Indian TV producers clone U.S. television: "The American talk show has inspired Indian imitations. Never have so many Indians revealed so much about their private lives to such a wide audience. Every day a new show is planned. If nothing else, American television has loosened tongues (to say nothing of our morals). Subjects long taboo are receiving a good airing." Those Indian programs may be produced in India, but the concept is hardly Indian.

Transnational Cultural Enrichment

Some scholars see transnational cultural flow in more benign terms than Herbert Schiller and his fellow cultural imperialism theorists. George Steiner has noted that European and American culture have been enriched, not corrupted, by the continuing presence of Greek mythology over 2,000 years.

In a homey way, sociologist Michael Tracey makes a similar point: "I was born in a working-class neighborhood called Oldham in the north of England. Before the First World War, Oldham produced most of the world's spun cotton. It is a place of mills and chimneys, and I was born and raised in one of the areas of housing—called St. Mary's—built to serve those mills. I recently heard a record by a local group of folk singers called the Oldham Tinkers, and one track was about Charlie Chaplin. This song was apparently very popular with local children in the years immediately after the First World War. Was that evidence of the cultural influences of Hollywood, a primeval moment of the imperialism of one culture, the subjugation of another? It seems almost boorish to think of it that way. Was the little man not a deep well of pleasure through laughter, a pleasure that was simply universal in appeal? Was it not Chaplin's real genius to strike some common chord, uniting the whole of humanity? Is that not, in fact, the real genius of American popular culture, to bind together, better than anything, common humanity?"

Global Media Models

STUDY PREVIEW   Models help us visualize different media systems. Models have different levels of sophistication, such as going from a bipolar model for political systems to a more complex continuum to an even more complex compass. Besides political systems, models can demonstrate media cultural environments, developmental state, and other characterizing criteria.

bipolar model
Portrays extremes as opposites, as libertarian and authoritarian political systems.

Bipolar Model

To compare media systems, some scholars use a **bipolar model** with two extremes: authoritarianism at one end and libertarianism at the other. The model

MAP OF PRESS FREEDOM 2000

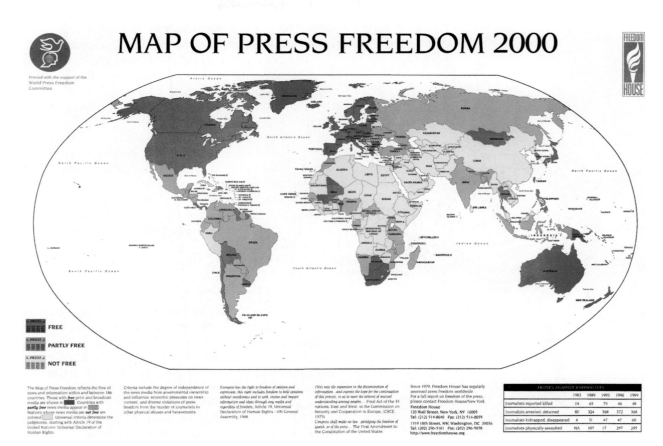

Printed with the support of the
World Press Freedom
Committee

FREE

PARTLY FREE

NOT FREE

The Map of Press Freedom reflects the flow of news and information within and between 186 countries. Those with *free* print and broadcast media are shown in ▆. Countries with *partly free* news media appear in ▆. Nations whose news media are *not free* are colored ▆. Universal criteria determine the judgments, starting with Article 19 of the United Nations' Universal Declaration of Human Rights.

Criteria include the degree of independence of the news media from governmental ownership and influence, economic pressures on news content, and diverse violations of press freedom from the murder of journalists to other physical abuses and harassments.

Everyone has the right to freedom of opinion and expression; this right includes freedom to hold opinions without interference and to seek, receive and impart information and ideas through any media and regardless of frontiers. Article 19, Universal Declaration of Human Rights - UN General Assembly, 1948

[We] note the expansion in the dissemination of information...and express the hope for the continuation of this process, so as to meet the interest of mutual understanding among peoples... Final Act of the 35 nations, East and West, in the Commission on Security and Cooperation in Europe, (CSCE, 1975)

Congress shall make no law...abridging the freedom of speech, or of the press... The First Amendment to the Constitution of the United States

Since 1979, Freedom House has regularly assessed press freedom worldwide. For a full report on freedom of the press, please contact Freedom House/New York.
Freedom House
120 Wall Street, New York, NY 10005
Tel: (212) 514-8040 Fax: (212) 514-8055
1319 18th Street, NW, Washington, DC 20036
Tel: (202) 296-5101 Fax: (202) 296-5078
http://www.freedomhouse.org

ABUSES AGAINST JOURNALISTS	1983	1989	1993	1996	1999
Journalists reported killed	14	63	74	46	48
Journalists arrested, detained	80	324	368	372	368
Journalists kidnapped, disappeared	4	31	47	47	60
Journalists physically assaulted	NA	107	17	297	295

Press Freedom. The Freedom House, which tracks press freedom worldwide, reports relatively few countries where news and information flow freely within and across their borders. Massive sections of Africa and Asia, plus Cuba and scattered small European countries, do not have free flows and exchanges. In making its determinations, Freedom House considered media independence from government ownership and economic pressure.

demonstrates opposites in an extreme way. Just as east is opposite from west, so is freedom from control. Bipolar models are useful beginning points to separate political systems.

Continuum Model

More sophisticated than a simple bipolar model is a variation called the **continuum model.** The basics of the continuum political system model are bipolar, with the extremes being authoritarianism and libertarianism, but there is an added element of sophistication. The media system of each country is placed not at an extreme but at points along the line. The United States would be near the libertarian end, although not quite at the extreme because, indeed, the U.S. media operate within limitations, such as laws of treason, libel and intellectual property law, and broadcast regulation. Britain, with more restrictive libel laws than the United States, would still be in libertarian territory on the continuum but not as near the extreme. On the other end

continuum model
A scale with authoritarianism at one end, libertarianism at the other, and media systems at varying points in between.

would be tinhorn dictatorships and other repressive countries with tight controls on the mass media.

The continuum model recognizes the uniqueness of media systems in different countries. By assessing variables, scholars can plant individual countries on the continuum, which facilitates grouping countries for comparison.

Sometimes the continuum model is represented in maps. One of the most useful for a quick sense of the status of libertarianism is updated regularly by **Freedom House,** a New York organization that tracks media freedom worldwide. Freedom House categorizes media systems as free, partly free and not free and color-codes them on a map of the planet. Other continuum models offer more categories.

Compass Model

In his book *The Imperative of Freedom,* scholar **John Merrill** looped the libertarian-authoritarian continuum around so that its ends meet themselves. On the loop Merrill marked the four major philosophical underpinnings as compass points that define the major media systems and their underlying political systems.

Among Merrill's points with the **compass model** is that a social responsibility system might not be just a variation on libertarianism but actually authoritarian. Merrill's compass addresses the troubling question about the Hutchins Commission recommendation for a socially responsible media: Who ensures responsibil-

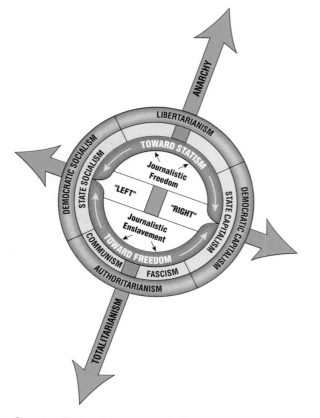

Compass Model. Scholar John Merrill rethought the libertarian-authoritarian continuum and folded in the four theories model to develop this compass model. The result: a graphic representation that a responsible press, if responsibility is by government mandate, is frighteningly close to traditional authoritarianism.

Media Abroad

Malaysia

Malaysian courts don't take kindly to criticism or anything close. Canadian journalist Murray Hiebert, a reporter for the Hong Kong–based *Far Eastern Economic Review,* was sentenced to six weeks in jail for a 1997 article. The article, a straightforward account of a rash of multimillion-dollar lawsuits in Malaysia, was built around a case filed by the wife of a high judge who sued her son's school for dropping

him from the debate squad. The judge hearing Hiebert's case on appeal said that the article "strikes at the very core of the due administration of justice." In other words, any allusion that the courts perceived as slighting was punishable.

Malaysia has strict laws to control the mass media, but they are rarely invoked against the country's own media. Generally, there is little need.

Most newspapers are owned by the Straits Group, which the dominant political party controls.

It is the occasional less-than-flattering stories in foreign media that irk the government. That's what happened to Murray Hiebert, who was writing for the *Far Eastern Economic Review,* which is owned by U.S.-based Dow Jones, publisher of the *Wall Street Journal.*

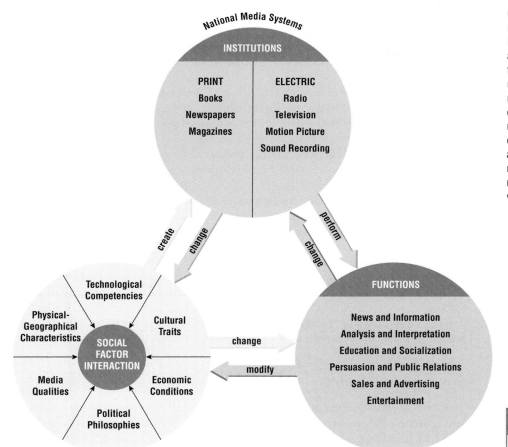

National Media Systems

INSTITUTIONS

PRINT
Books
Newspapers
Magazines

ELECTRIC
Radio
Television
Motion Picture
Sound Recording

create
change
perform
change

Technological
Competencies

Physical-
Geographical
Characteristics

Cultural
Traits

**SOCIAL
FACTOR
INTERACTION**

Media
Qualities

Economic
Conditions

Political
Philosophies

change

modify

FUNCTIONS

News and Information
Analysis and Interpretation
Education and Socialization
Persuasion and Public Relations
Sales and Advertising
Entertainment

Change Model. A 1974 model developed by scholars Ray Hiebert, Donald Ungurait and Thomas Bohn expanded the four theories model to recognize other factors in media systems, including economic conditions, technological competence and even geography. The model also attempts to show how media systems and performance are affected by many variables.

m e d i a   o n l i n e
Freedom House: Review Freedom House's annual survey of freedom country scores, 1972-1973 to 1999-2000.
www.freedomhouse.org

Freedom House
A private agency that tracks media freedom worldwide.

John Merrill
Introduced the compass model, which showed that social responsibility and authoritarianism could be bedmates.

compass model
A looped model that juxtaposes traditional authoritarian and social responsibility models.

change model
Shows the effect of mass media on numerous social variables and the effect of those variables on the media.

ity? If it's government, then we have introduced shades of authoritarianism. If not government, then who?

Change Model

The effects of culture and geography on media systems is taken into account in the **change model,** which shows the interaction of many variables on media and systems and performance. One of the best of these models, introduced in 1974 by scholars Ray Hiebert, Don Ungurait and Tom Bohn, asks for an assessment of a country's political philosophy, as had Siebert, Peterson and Schramm with their four theories model, but the Hiebert, Ungurait and Bohn model goes much further by taking into account other variables:

■ **Economics.** In impoverished parts of the world, such as Chad, few people can afford access to the mass media. There is no advertising. This lack of an economic base means a weak media system that is generally subservient to political leadership. A wealthy elite, of course, may have access to all kinds of media, often from other countries, which helps to maintain its advantage and privilege.

- **Culture.** A country's mass media reflect cultural values. The media of Iran, run by religious fundamentalists, are far different from the media of India, a democracy that accommodates a diversity of religions. Social norms, mores and values vary from country to country, all with an effect on the mass media. So do language and traditions.
- **Technology.** Outdated equipment can undermine the service that media provide. For print media, poor roads can limit distribution. In much of the Third World, presses are hand-me-downs from more developed countries, not only outdated but also prone to breakdowns.
- **Climate.** In tropical climates, where trees used for pulp to make paper can't grow, the print media have extraordinary production expenses for importing paper. Mexico is an example.
- **Geography.** Broadcasters in a mountainous country like Nepal have a hard time getting signals to people living in narrow valleys shielded by steep terrain. This is a factor in the economics of broadcasting and also a station's influence.
- **Literacy.** If people can't read, the print media are handicapped. In Cameroon, for example, compulsory education goes only to age 12. Even then, one third of Cameroon's children don't attend school. The literacy rate is only 63 percent.
- **Media.** A country's media infrastructure can be an indicator of other realities. If the primary mass medium is radio, for example, it may be an indicator that low literacy has stunted growth of the print media. A country wired well for the web has a basis for sophisticated delivery of messages of all sorts.

Subsystem Model

The mass media have grown in complexity, especially in economically advanced countries. Some scholars are making a case that it doesn't make sense any more to evaluate media in the traditional broad terms of major media, like television, magazines and newspapers. Instead, they advocate classifying media by subsystems to understand what's happening. The following are among the elements in a **subsystem model:**

- **Commercial media.** These are the profit-seeking media that have traditionally been the focus of comparative studies.
- **Government media.** Controlled by the government. May coexist with commercial media.
- **Public media.** Financed by citizens and government money to further the public good, like PBS and NPR in the United States.
- **Organizational media.** Aimed at serving nongovernment bodies, such as professional groups, tribes, religions and corporations.
- **Individualized media.** Media customized to an individual's needs and interests, as is possible through the web.
- **Political media.** Used by political parties.

The subsystem model recognizes the folly in describing a nation's mass media system in broad, singular terms. The divisions that the advocates of the subsystem model favor are well suited to today's media fragmentation and decentralization.

The subsystem model also distinguishes between the motivation that media owners have for their products, the range of content they offer, the audience they seek, the results that occur, and how their audiences provide feedback.

subsystem model
Examines media in terms of originator and intended audience.

Media Abroad

Voice of America

The Voice of America, a government-sponsored radio news service to other peoples, entered another crisis over its mission as the United States went global with its war on terrorism after the 2001 terrorist attacks in New York and Washington. The issue: Should VOA be a news service or a government propagandist tool?

The issue boiled over when VOA aired an interview with Taliban leader Mullah Muhammad Omar. At the time the United States was trying to oust the Afghan leader. Critics resurrected a colorful but exaggerated snipe by Senator Jesse Helms, a Republican from North Carolina, that the VOA would have given "equal time for Hitler."

The issue now is a 1976 law that defines the VOA's mission. The law

assigns VOA to provide "accurate, objective and comprehensive" news. That would seem to include an interview with Mullah Muhammad Omar of the Taliban or, in Senator's Helms' example, even Hitler. The law also assigns the VOA with providing a clear, effective presentation of U.S. policies. In 2001, with Mullah Muhammad Omar was a declared enemy cast by President Bush as a protector of the epitome of evil, Osama bin Laden.

Traditionally VOA executives have seen room both for news in the neutral, detached style of commercial U.S. news organizations and for editorials. A typical hour of VOA programming has 57 minutes of news and two to three minutes of editorials. Editorials are clearly identified as such and are approved by the U.S.

State Department. News goes through no such gatekeeping.

VOA was created in World War II. It broadcasts several hours a day in 53 languages on AM, FM and short-wave radio. It also operates voanews.com. Programming is aimed at 90 million people outside the United States. VOA employs 60 journalists in Washington and others in bureaus in Chicago, Los Angeles, Miami, New York and abroad.

In 2001, with heightened U.S. attention on south Asia, VOA broadcasts aimed at Afghanistan and Pakistan were expanded by one hour a day in both major Afghan tongues, Pashtu and Dari.

Global Media Players

STUDY PREVIEW   The first media companies to extend their operations abroad significantly were news agencies such as the Associated Press, Reuters and United Press International. Today, companies that produce all kinds of media messages, not just news, are engaged in finding global markets.

News Agencies

Hundreds of agencies cover news around the world and sell their accounts to subscribing media organizations. Most of these are national and regional services. The primary global players are Associated Press, Reuters, Agence France-Presse, Interfax, Worldwide Television News and, to a lesser extent, United Press International.

ASSOCIATED PRESS.   The **Associated Press** is the largest news-gathering organization in the world. There are 8,500 subscribers in 112 countries. About 1,400 U.S. daily newspapers and 6,000 television, radio and cable system subscribers carry AP news. In addition, about 1,000 radio stations carry newscasts from AP Network News, which is the largest single radio network in the United States. In the United States, the AP has more than 3,000 employees.

Associated Press
U.S.-based global news service; largest newsgathering organization in the world.

The AP is a nonprofit cooperative organization owned by daily newspapers. Each newspaper is obligated to furnish its local stories to the AP for distribution to other AP member newspapers and clients. Each member newspaper owns a share of the company based on its circulation and numerous other factors. Periodically the expenses are tallied, and member newspapers are billed for their share. Policies are set by member newspapers, which meet regularly.

In addition, the AP owns profit-making subsidiaries that offset some costs. Subsidiaries include Press Association, which sells news scripts to television and radio stations; Wide World, which sells pictures from the immense archive that AP has built over the years; APTV, which was established in 1994 to provide global video news coverage to television networks; AP Network, a newscast and actuality service for radio stations; and ARI, which services weeklies, including many college newspapers.

The AP, based in New York, has 93 foreign bureaus in 72 countries. The APTV subsidiary has 130 employees plus 400 stringers and freelance camera operators worldwide, in addition to backup from the rest of AP's journalistic and technical staff. Domestically, the AP operates 142 bureaus in state capitals and major cities. The domestic bureaus provide comprehensive regional and state coverage.

REUTERS.　**Reuters** serves 6,500 media organizations worldwide, including 290 in the United States. Altogether, counting subscribers to its financial and business news services, Reuters has 27,000 subscribers worldwide. The service is offered in 11 languages. There are 120 bureaus in 80 countries. U.S. video clients include CNN and NBC.

AGENCE FRANCE-PRESSE.　Paris-based **Agence France-Presse** was founded by Charles Havas in 1835. Using carrier pigeons, Havas supplied Paris newspapers by noon with news that had happened that same morning in London and Brussels.

Today AFP is the third largest global agency. AFP has 2,000 people in 150 bureaus worldwide, including 850 full-time journalists. Text, photo, audio and video services are transmitted in Arabic, English, French, German, Spanish and Portuguese to 500 newspapers, 350 radio and 200 television clients and to 99 national news agencies that pass AFB stories on to more media outlets. AFP has more than 50 U.S. media clients.

INTERFAX.　This Moscow-based news agency was founded as Tass in 1925. Today, reconstituted and renamed **Interfax,** the agency supplies reports in Russian, English, German, Spanish and Arabic. At its peak, the agency claimed 5,500 media and nonmedia subscribers, but the disintegration of communism and the shriveling of Russian influence has meant inevitable declines.

UNITED PRESS INTERNATIONAL.　Newspaper magnate E. W. Scripps, who founded one successful afternoon paper after another beginning in the 1880s, was frustrated that he couldn't run Associated Press stories. Older morning newspapers had exclusive AP franchises. In 1907, Scripps countered by founding United Press. The service became a formidable competitor but never caught up with AP, even after a 1958 merger with William Randolph Hearst's International News Service.

A perennial money loser, **United Press International** eventually was sold by Scripps' successors. It passed through a series of owners. All of them scaled back to cut losses. Nothing worked. Today UPI has a few bureaus in only a few key cities. UPI has given up U.S. regional coverage.

The latest owner, News World, operated by Unification Church, took over in 2000. There were assurances that the Reverend Sun Myung Moon, head of the

Reuters
British-based global news agency.

Agence France-Presse
Paris-based global news agency.

Interfax
Russian news agency.

United Press International
Faded major news agency.

Media Databank

Supplemental News Agencies

While the Associated Press is the dominant U.S.-based news agency, four others have a significant number of domestic clients and some abroad. In general, these **supplemental agencies,** as they're called, offer background and analysis. With breaking news, they attempt to offer distinctive angles from the minute-by-minute updates of the Associated Press.

- **Los Angeles Times-Washington Post News Service.** Draws on reporting of both newspapers for 650 clients.
- **New York Times News Service.** Draws on *Times* reporting for 600 clients.

- **Knight Ridder/Tribune Information Service.** Draws on Knight Ridder and Tribune Company resources, including the Chicago *Tribune* and *Newsday,* for 600 newspaper clients and others.
- **Scripps-Howard News Service.** Draws from Scripps-Howard resources, particularly the Washington bureau, for 400 clients.

  Numerous other supplemental agencies include Gannett News Service, the Christian Science Monitor News Service, BPI Entertainment News Wire and Religion News Service.

church, would not interfere with content. Among doubters was Helen Thomas, UPI's most visible reporter as a 39-year veteran on the White House beat. She quit. Other parts of the Unification Church media empire, including the Washington *Times*, have a conservative thrust that is consistent with Reverend Moon's politics.

Video News Services

The major news networks—ABC, CBS, CNN and NBC—prefer to cover foreign stories with their own crews, but they also subscribe to global video services for stories and pictures that they miss. The largest news video suppliers are, not surprisngly, the world's two largest news services: New York-based Associated Press and London-based Reuters.

APTV, a subsidiary of the Associated Press, cemented its leadership by buying Worldwide Television News, WTN for short, in 1998. WTN's owners, including the ABC television network, cashed in for $44 million. The deal left only London-based Reuters as a major AP competitor in the business of providing video feeds for television.

The video news business grew rapidly in the 1990s for several reasons:

NETWORK CUTBACKS. Beginning in the early 1980s corporate bosses at ABC, CBS and NBC slashed their news divisions' budgets. The cuts forced news executives to make painful decisions. At each network, foreign staffing took the hardest hits. At CBS, the cuts were wrenching. Since 1938, when it launched "World News Roundup" radio newscasts with staff reporters in Europe, CBS had prided itself on distinctive foreign coverage.

Critics lamented the decline of the networks' foreign coverage, but others said the foreign staffs were bloated and reductions were overdue. Also, relatively few foreign stories made it on the air. Newscast producers recognized that Americans are not international minded and, all others things being equal, favor domestic over foreign stories.

Today, ABC, CBS and NBC operate only a handful of foreign bureaus. From those bureaus, reporters fly to hot spots. Always short-staffed, these bureaus miss stories,

media online

LA Times-Washington Post News Service: www.newsservice.com

New York Times News Service: http://nytsyn.com/newsservice

Scripps-Howard News Service: www.scripps.com/ corporateoverview/businesses/ newspaper/shns.shtml

supplemental agencies Agencies that provide backup, depth coverage.

so producers in New York pick up material from APTV and Reuters. Unlike the other U.S. networks, CNN has expanded its foreign bureaus, but even CNN's foreign staff cannot feed producers enough stories to satisfy the 24-hour news network's voracious appetite. So CNN too leans heavily on the video news services.

GOVERNMENT DEREGULATION.   Several European nations have deregulated broadcasting, and entrepreneurs have launched networks and stations. Stephen Claypole, an old Reuters hand who joined the new APTV in 1994, estimates the market for international news will grow 50 percent by early in the new century.

INDEPENDENT STATIONS.   Years ago, network-affiliated stations learned that news is a good lead-in to build audiences for other programming. Today, many independent stations have established newscasts that draw on the video news stories for faraway coverage. Affiliates of the Fox network, which didn't offer network news its first few years of existence, were among subscribers to the video news services to provide at least some distant coverage.

NEW TECHNOLOGIES.   The video that APTV and Reuters shoot is digital, which means it can be adapted easily to other media. Reuters, for example, can provide its subscribing newspapers and magazines with stills from its television service. The market will expand as newspapers and magazines shift to digital delivery that includes moving images.

media convergence

Syndicates

After Union recruiters swept through Baraboo, Wisconsin, and signed up the local boys for the Civil War, **Ansell Kellogg** lacked the staff to get out his four-page Baraboo *Republic,* so he took to borrowing the inside pages of another newspaper. The practice not only saw Kellogg through a staffing crisis, but also sparked an idea to save costs by supplying inside pages at a fee to other short-handed publishers. By 1865 Kellogg was in Chicago providing ready-to-print material for newspapers nationwide. In journalism history, Kellogg is remembered as the father of the newspaper **syndicate.**

In the 1880s **S. S. McClure** had a thriving syndicate, putting out 50,000 words a week in timeless features on fashion, homemaking, manners and literature. McClure and other syndicators charged subscribing newspapers a fraction of what each would have to pay to generate such material with its own staff. Features, poetry, opinion and serialized stories by the period's great literary figures, including Jack London, Rudyard Kipling, George Bernard Shaw, Robert Louis Stevenson and Mark Twain, became standard fare in many newspapers through syndication.

Today syndicates seek international audiences, spreading expenses among more subscribers and building new revenue. Some syndicate material doesn't travel easily, like sophisticated humor columns and comic strips that flow from a particular culture. It's hard to imagine that "Family Circle" or "Beetle Bailey" would go over in South Asia, for example. But other syndicated material, like "Dear Abby" and medical advice columns, is easily adapted to many overseas audiences.

Global Media Companies

National origins of companies in the media business are blurring. In 2000 the French media giant Vivendi bought Seagram's of Canada, thus acquiring the Universal-MCA movie and music empire in the United States. Sony of Japan owned

Ansell Kellogg
Founded the first syndicate.

syndicates
Provide low-cost, high-quality content to many news outlets.

S. S. McClure
Expanded syndicate concept.

a share of United States-based AOL Time Warner. Bertelsmann of Germany was everywhere, it seemed, and looking to expand through internal growth and mergers and acquisitions.

U.S.-BASED COMPANIES. Four U.S. media rivals have established themselves as major players in other countries.

- **AOL Time Warner.** AOL Time Warner, which operates in 70-plus countries, is among the world's largest media companies—a position strengthened by the 2000 merger of America Online and Time Warner. Worldwide, the company is valued at $183 billion. In Latin America the company has adapted its HBO pay-television service and calls it HBO Olé. It's the most widely distributed cable network in Latin America. Elsewhere, the company has alliances with Itochu and Toshiba.
- **Disney-ABC.** Disney became one of the world's largest media company in 1995 when it acquired Cap Cities/ABC. The new company has annual revenues estimated at more than $19 billion. The consolidation included major assets in movies, television, newspapers and cable. Since 1995 the company has sold off some major properties, including several metro newspapers and also magazines to narrow its focus.
- **Viacom.** Viacom's MTV has been an entree into foreign markets. The music-video network reaches 240 million households in 63 countries, which is a model for Viacom to expand its VH-1 music and Nickelodeon satellite networks into other countries. There is a lot more that Viacom can market abroad. It holds 50,000 hours of television shows that it first sold to U.S. networks and now is recycling abroad.
- **News Corporation.** Australian-born Rupert Murdoch owns News Corporation, the interests of which go far beyond his 20th Century Fox movie studio, the Fox television network and U.S. newspapers and magazines. In Asia his satellite television service, Star TV, beams signals to China, India, Taiwan and Southeast Asia. Through Star TV, two-thirds of the world's population, 3 billion people, have access to programming that Murdoch's company creates or buys from other sources, including MTV, ESPN and Bart Simpson. Murdoch owns half of Sky Broadcasting, which sends signals from satellite to all of Europe. He also owns newspapers in Australia, Britain and the United States.

NON-U.S. COMPANIES. Once U.S. media companies held the commanding lead for overseas markets, but home-grown companies are pumping out more content all the time. Some of these companies have become global players themselves.

- **Bertelsmann.** The German company Bertelsmann established itself globally as a book and magazine company. It has 200 subsidiaries in 25 countries, many of them operating under the name they had when Bertelsmann acquired them. In the United States these include Random House, Bantam, Dell and Doubleday books. The company's U.S. interests include RCA records.
- **Hachette Filipacchi.** The French-Italian company Hachette Filipacchi publishes 74 magazines in 10 countries. This includes the 4.5 million circulation *Woman's Day*, which Hachette acquired when it bought the CBS magazine empire in 1988. Another Hachette magazine in the United States is the fashion magazine *Elle*.
- **Televisa.** Throughout Latin America, people watch soap operas, called *telenovelas*. Most of these originate from Televisa, a Mexican media giant.
- **TVB.** Hong Kong-based TVB has started an Asian television-satellite service. This company has plenty to put on the satellite. Its production runs about 6,000 hours a year in both Cantonese and Mandarin.

media online

AOL Time Warner: The world's first fully integrated media and communications company.
www.aoltimewarner.com

Newscorp: News Corporation is the world's leading publisher of English-language newspapers, with operations in the United Kingdom, Australia, New Zealand, Fiji, Papua New Guinea and the United States.
www.newscorp.com

Viacom:
www.viacom.com

Media Abroad

Qatar: Al-Jazeera

The emir of the tiny Persian Gulf country of Qatar was fascinated with CNN's growing global reach in the mid-1990s. But for the Arab world, CNN's English-language presentation may as well have been Greek. In 1996, Shiek Hamad bin Khalif al-Thani decided to fill the niche. He launched Al-Jazeera, an Arabic-language all-news service beamed by satellite to the Arab world from north Africa to south Asia.

Al-Jazeera was a bold move. In a region infamous for biased news and dull propaganda on state-owned channels, Al-Jazeera offered comparatively independent coverage. It was a bid for a pan-Arab audience that transcended national boundaries. Soon, by most estimates, Al-Jazeera was the region's second most-watched television network, trailing only the entertainment network LBC Sat from Lebanon.

Al-Jazeera was not welcomed by governments that had enjoyed strict control of the media within their borders. The kingdoms of Jordan, Kuwait and Saudi Arabia blocked Al-Jazeera signals, but the censorship spawned a blackmarket in videotapes of Al-Jazeera programs. The censorious governments resigned themselves to coexistence with the upstart news source. From its base in Qatar and with the sheik's deep pockets, Al-Jazeera remains an autonomous source of news for Arabs of diverse political and religious creeds.

Al-Jazeera content is lively with no-holds-barred political talk shows.

Arab Newsroom. Al Jazeera is a 24/7 satellite-delivered news service in Arabic founded in Qatar in 1996.

Perhaps the strongest testimony to the network's record of independence is that major-league rivals eventually sought air time to espouse their causes. Global terrorist Osama bin Laden, for example, released his tapes from Afghan hiding places to Al-Jazeera. In the United States, the undersecretary of state for public diplomacy, Charlotte Beers, acknowledged that the U.S. government had considered buying airtime on Al-Jazeera to get its message to the Arab world after the September 11, 2001, attacks on New York and Washington.

Despite its journalistic success, Al-Jazeera was far from profitable for Shiek bin Khalifi al-Thani and fellow investors. Many Arab companies shun the network rather than risk angering the governments. In Qatar itself, only the Doha Bank buys time on the network. Also, Al-Jazeera's advertising policy recognizes certain political realities: No advertising is accepted from Israel because of the risk of an Arab backlash.

The biggest advertisers are non-Arab auto manufacturers General Motors, Mitsubishi and Nissan. Procter and Gamble put a lot of money into pushing Head & Shoulders shampoo. Even so, Al-Jazeera ad revenue was estimated at a mere $15 million in 2001, less than a sixth of LBC Sat from Lebanon.

media online

Bertelsmann:
www.bertelsmann.com

Hachette Filipacchi:
www.hfnm.com

Televisa:
www.esmas.com/televisa

TVB:
www.tvb.com

TV Globo:
http://redeglobo.globo.com/
globointernacional

■ **TV Globo.** A Brazilian media company, TV Globo, true to its name, has developed a global audience. Its telenovelas air in all the Spanish-speaking and Portuguese-speaking countries and beyond, including China.

Media Pressure Points

STUDY PREVIEW   The struggle between a free media and a controlled, suppressed or badgered media plays and replays around the world. Case studies include Russia, where old ways die hard, and Colombia, where drug lords have strong sway.

Media People

Jineth Bedoya Lima

After Jineth Bedoya Lima wrote about executions during a Bogota prison riot, she got word that a paramilitary leader inside the prison wanted to give her his side. "Come alone," she was told. Like all Colombian journalists, Bedoya, 25 at the time, was aware of the dangers of reporting news, especially on subjects sensitive to warring factions. Her editor and a photographer went with her.

As they waited outside the prison, the photographer left to buy sodas, then the editor followed him. When they came back, Bedoya was gone. Guards at the prison gate said they had seen nothing.

Many hours later, a taxi driver found Bedoya at a roadside garbage dump. She said that two men had

Jineth Bedoya Lima. She was kidnapped and raped while pursuing a story.

grabbed her and forced a drugged cloth over her face. She regained consciousness in a nearby house, where her captors taped her mouth, blindfolded her, and bound her hands and feet. They then drove her three hours to another city. They said they were going to kill her, as well as several

other journalists they named. Then they beat and raped her and threw her off at the dump.

Her story, typical of violence against media people in Colombia, was disseminated widely by the Committee to Protect Journalists. It's a cautionary tale. Bedoya, who believed that she was being trailed months later, was assigned two government bodyguards. Even so, she feels at risk. Why does she still do it? Frank Smyth of CPJ, writing in *Quill* magazine, quoted her: "I love my work, and I want to keep doing it. The worst thing that could happen has already happened."

Russia

Optimists expected the dust of the imploding Soviet empire in 1989 would yield a robust, prosperous free society. In Russia, however, despite occasional signs of new media independence, old ways die hard.

The **NTV** network, part of the country's largest media chain, gained respect as an independent voice for its critical reports on Kremlin policies in the early **perestroika** period. Then in 2000, NTV owner Vladimir Gusinsky was arrested after months of harassment by the Kremlin. Gusinsky was dumped in one of Moscow's filthiest jails. It all smacked of authoritarianism. Embarrassed at the worldwide media attention on the heavy-handedness, the president of Russia, Vladimir Putin, distanced himself from the arrest and called it excessive. Still, it was Putin's administration that had gone after Gusinsky.

Meanwhile, NTV's coverage of the latest Russian military campaign against Chechnya separatists was toned down. From 1994 to 1996 the network had gained respect for fearless frontline reporting on stalled Russian tactics. Video showed frightened teenage Russian troops in over their heads against grizzled Chechens. When Russian troops destroyed Grozny, the coverage was not pretty and hardly heroic. As Russian public pressure shifted against the war, the Kremlin opted to act in old ways. NTV was told its broadcast license was in jeopardy.

The Kremlin underscored its seriousness in 2000 when a Radio Free Europe correspondent from the first Chechnyan war, Andrei Babitsky, tried again to roam independently for balanced coverage. Suddenly Babitsky's reports stopped. He had been arrested by Russian forces, badly beaten up and jailed for 40 days—a chilling effect that showed in all coverage, including NTV's.

NTV
Privately owned Russian television network.

perestroika
Russian policy to restructuring institutions in the spirit of candor and openness.

It's not just government that has failed in the transition to a free mass media. In 1996 the president of Gusinsky's NTV managed the re-election campaign of President Boris Yeltsin. The infrastructure for independent media wasn't in place. At lower levels, too, many career media people, rewarded for years as loyal Leninists, found themselves suddenly in a strange transitional environment and couldn't deal with it. In many cities local media were beholden to town mayors for office space, equipment and supplies—just as in the old days.

Organized crime and corruption also work against a free media. According to the Committee to Protect Journalists, 34 journalists died doing their work in Russia in the 1990s, mostly in war zones but some murdered elsewhere. Hundreds have reported being attacked.

Colombia

High drama is popular on Colombia radio stations, but it is hardly theatrical. In Colombia thousands of people, both wealthy and ordinary, are kidnap captives. Families go on the air to express love and support in the hope that their kidnapped kin are listening. It makes for powerful radio. Tragically, it's real.

Drug lords and petty criminals alike have found kidnapping lucrative in a country where anarchy is close to an everyday reality. The mass media are hardly immune. In the 1990s, according to the U.S.-based Committee to Protect Journalists, 31 journalists were killed because of their work. Sixteen others have died in incidents that may or may not be related to their work. In a typical year, six to 10 journalists are kidnapped in a country whose population is less than that of the U.S. Pacific Coast states.

A political satirist, Jamie Garzón, was gunned to death in 1999 after a television show. *El Espectador,* a leading newspaper, has armed guards at every entrance and around the perimeter, as do most media operations. Many reporters are assigned bodyguards, usually two, both armed. Two *El Espectador* reporters have fled the country under threat. The editor of another daily, *El Tiempo,* fled in 2000 after supporting a peace movement.

Beset with corruption fueled by the powerful cocaine industry, the government has no handle on assaults against the media. Although hypersensitive to negative coverage, the drug industry is not the only threat to the Colombian media. The Committee to Protect Journalists, Human Rights Watch, Amnesty International and other watchdogs blame renegade paramilitary units and guerrillas, some of whom are ideologically inspired. Also, the Colombian military itself and some government agencies have been implicated.

Media Future: Global Mass Media

For better or worse, globalization of the mass media can be expected to accelerate. Technology is improving all the time to support the delivery of mass messages globally, and companies are finding new ways to score profits from audiences in other countries.

The prospect of there someday being only a few major media companies in the world is worrying. Governments have been a traditional check on unbridled business growth and monopolies, but most governments in countries with major media production centers have been reluctant to slow the expansion of home-based companies for fear that their industries will lose a competitive edge. In countries whose own media are being subsumed by imported products, governments are stymied about what to do. It's almost impossible to prohibit people from picking up satellite signals, though China has tried with limited success to regulate direct-from-satellite reception. The fact is that imported media products are popular in the Third World. Stopping the flow is not a realistic option.

Some developing countries have objected through the United Nations about news coverage that they claim is slanted to favor the major powers. These calls, however, have been overstated if not hysterical. Hard data do not support claims that indigenous media are the pawns of the media of former colonial powers. The fact is that local media outlets, in developing countries as elsewhere, tend to be parochial in their news coverage. The foreign items that they pick up from global news agencies are, by and large, detached and neutral—hardly propagandist.

The technology that facilitates easy access to the web may diversify the sources of media sources around the world, but still upstarts are disadvantaged Davids against multinational Goliaths like AOL Time Warner, News Corporation, Bertelsmann and Vivendi.

chapter wrap-up

Models to help explain the world's great variety of mass media systems are important in this fast-changing era of globalization. The most useful model focuses on change—how economics, culture, technology and other factors influence media infrastructures and content in an interactive way. Models alone, however, are insufficient to explain media policy in a global context. Economic imperatives are at the heart of understanding why mass media companies behave as they do. The implications are important in explaining media effects on different cultures, both positive and negative.

Questions for Review

1. How does Sky Global represent a fundamental restructuring in the control of mass communication?
2. What kind of ideology are global media companies interested in exporting?
3. Assess the negative connotation of Herbert Schiller's term *cultural imperialism*.
4. How does the continuum model bypass the bipolar model in sophistication?
5. How have global news agencies affected nations they cover for the rest of the world?
6. Where are the major global media companies based?
7. What problems beset media people in countries without independent media.

Questions for Critical Thinking

1. Describe the globalization of the mass media in terms of content generation and distribution.
2. What impediments face global media companies in authoritarian countries with controlled economies?
3. Assess the view that *cultural imperialism* is a loaded term that misses an enriching aspect of transnational communication.
4. Use the subsystems model to explain the mass media in a particular developing nation.

5. Some Third World leaders argue that news agencies like AP and Reuters are lackeys of government policy in their home nations. Can these arguments be sustained?
6. Global media companies have subsidiary operations. List and organize these subsidiaries by their location, then analyze the implications.
7. What trends can you ascertain about media-government relations worldwide?

Keeping Up to Date

Index on Censorship. Published in London. Provides monthly country-by-country status reports.

Scholarly journals that carry articles on foreign media systems, international communication and media responsibility include the *International Communication Bulletin*, *Journal of Broadcasting and Electronic Media*, *Journal of Communication*, and *Journal and Mass Communication Quarterly*.

Professional journals that carry articles on foreign media systems and on media responsibility include *Columbia Journalism Review*, *Quill*, and *American Journalism Review*.

Ongoing discussions on media responsibility also appear in the *Journal of Mass Media Ethics*.

Dean of White House Correspondents. Helen Thomas joined the White House press corps in 1961 and covered every president from then on. In 1995, on her 75th birthday, President Clinton threw Thomas a surprise party.

18

Mass Media and Governance

Helen Thomas grew up in Detroit, one of nine children of Syrian immigrants. Her father couldn't read or write English. Helen and her brothers and sisters read the newspapers to him. By high school she had decided to be a journalist. After graduating from her hometown Wayne University, she headed to Washington. That was in 1942, and prospects for women in the male-dominated capital press corps were not as bleak as usual because World War II was sucking almost every able-bodied male, including journalists, into the military. Helen Thomas landed a job as a copy girl with the Washington *Daily News* for $17.50 a week. After a couple other jobs, she joined the old United Press news agency. Somehow she survived the pink slips that most women journalists received when men began returning to their old jobs from the war.

In 1961 Helen Thomas switched to the White House. Within a few years she found herself the senior reporter, which meant, by tradition, that she and the Associated Press reporter alternated asking the first question of the president at news conferences. Also, as senior reporter, it fell to her to close news conferences after an agreed-upon 30 minutes by saying, "Thank you, Mr. President."

During her tenure Helen Thomas consistently improved the status of women in journalism and the respect they deserved. She joined the Women's National Press Club, which had been formed in 1908 because the National Press Club refused to admit women even to cover newsworthy speeches. Thomas became president of the women's club in 1960 and kept pressure on its male counterpart to admit women. Finally, in 1971, the National Press Club admitted women.

Things have changed dramatically since then in Washington journalism. Thomas herself was elected president of the National Press Club in 1975, and she broke gender barriers at the Overseas Press Club, the White House Correspondents Association and the Gridiron Club.

In 2000 UPI was sold to News World Communications, a company operated by the conservative Reverend Sung Myung Moon of the Unification Church. Helen Thomas quit. World Communications executives spent several days trying to talk her into staying. They said the Reverend Moon was only a financial backer and wouldn't dictate coverage. Thomas, age 79, was her typically firm self: She wouldn't work for the new owner.

Media Role in Governance

STUDY PREVIEW The news media are sometimes called the fourth estate or the fourth branch of government. These terms identify the independent role of the media in reporting on the government. The media are a kind of watchdog on behalf of the citizens.

Fourth Estate

Medieval English and French society were highly structured into classes of people called *estates*. The first estate was the clergy. The second was the nobility. The third was the common people. After Gutenberg the mass-produced written word began emerging as a player in the power structure, but it couldn't be pigeonholed as part of one or another of the three estates. In time the press came to be called the **fourth estate.** Where the term came from isn't clear, but **Edmund Burke,** a member of the British Parliament, used it in the mid-1700s. Pointing to the reporters' gallery, Burke said, "There sat a Fourth Estate more important by far than them all." The term remains for all journalistic activity today. The news media report on the other estates, ideally with roots in none and a commitment only to truth.

The fourth-estate concept underwent an adaptation when the United States was created. The Constitution of the new republic, drafted in 1787, set up a balanced form of government with three branches: the legislative, the executive and the judicial. The republic's founders implied a role for the press in the new governance structure when they declared in the Constitution's First Amendment that the government should not interfere with the press. The press, however, was not part of the structure. This led to the press informally being called the **fourth branch** of government. Its job was to monitor the other branches as an external check on behalf of the people. This is the **watchdog role** of the press. As one wag put it, the founders saw the role of the press as keeping tabs on the rascals in power to keep them honest.

Government-Media Relations

Although the First Amendment says that the government shouldn't place restrictions of the press, the reality is that exceptions have evolved.

BROADCAST REGULATION. In the early days of commercial radio, stations drowned one another out. Unable to work out mutually agreeable transmission rules

fourth estate
The press as a player in medieval power structures, in addition to the clerical, noble and common estates.

Edmund Burke
British member of Parliament who is sometimes credited with coining the term *fourth estate.*

fourth branch
The press as an informally structured check on the legislative, executive and judicial branches of government.

watchdog role
Concept of the press as a skeptical and critical monitor of government.

to help the new medium realize its potential, station owners went to the government for help. Congress obliged by creating the Federal Radio Commission in 1927. The commission's job was to limit the number of stations and their transmitting power to avoid signal overlaps. This the commission did by requiring stations to have a government-issued license that specified technical limitations. Because more stations were broadcasting than could be licensed, the commission issued and denied licenses on the basis of each applicant's potential to operate in the public interest. Over time, this criterion led to numerous requirements for broadcasters, in radio and later television, in their coverage of public issues.

Because of the limited number of available channels, Congress tried to ensure an evenhandedness in political content through the **equal time rule.** If a station allows one candidate to advertise, it must allow competing candidates to do so under the same conditions, including time of day and rates. The equal time requirement is in the law that established the Federal Radio Commission and also the 1934 law that established its successor, the Federal Communications Commission. The rule has since been expanded to require stations to carry a response from the opposition party immediately after broadcasts that can be construed as political, like the president's state of the union address.

From 1949 to 1987 the Federal Communications Commission also required stations to air all sides of public issues. The requirement, called the **fairness doctrine,** was abandoned in the belief that a growing number of stations, made possible by improved technology, meant the public could find plenty of diverse views. Also, the FCC figured the public's disdain for unfairness would undermine the ability of lopsided stations to keep an audience. The commission, in effect, acknowledged the marketplace could be an effective force for fairness—without further need for a government requirement.

Abandonment of the fairness doctrine was part of the general movement to ease government regulation on business. This shift has eased the First Amendment difficulties inherent in the federal regulation of broadcasting. Even so, the FCC remains firm against imbalanced political broadcasting. In 1975, for example, the commission refused to renew the licenses of stations owned by **Don Burden** after learning that he was using them on behalf of political friends. At KISN in Vancouver, Washington, Burden had instructed the news staff to run only favorable stories on one U.S. Senate candidate and negative stories on the other. At WIFE in Indianapolis he ordered "frequent, favorable mention" of one U.S. senator. The FCC declared it would not put up with "attempts to use broadcast facilities to subvert the political process." Although the Burden case is a quarter-century old, the FCC has sent no signals that it has modified its position on blatant slanting.

PRINT REGULATION.   The U.S. Supreme Court gave legitimacy to government regulation of broadcasting, despite the First Amendment issue, in its 1975 **Tornillo opinion.** Pat Tornillo, a candidate for the Florida Legislature, sued the Miami *Herald* for refusing to print his response to an editorial urging voters to the other candidate. The issue was whether the FCC's fairness doctrine could apply to the print media—and the Supreme Court said no. As the Court sees it, the First Amendment applies more directly to print than broadcast media.

This does not mean, however, that the First Amendment always protects print media from government interference. The Union Army shut down dissident newspapers in Chicago and Ohio during the Civil War. Those incidents were never challenged in the courts, but the U.S. Supreme Court has consistently said it could envision

equal time rule
Government requirement for stations to offer competing political candidates the same time and the same rate for advertising.

fairness doctrine
Former government requirement that stations air all sides of public issues.

Don Burden
Radio station owner who lost licenses for favoring some political candidates over others.

Tornillo opinion
The U.S. Supreme Court upheld First Amendment protection for the print media even if they are imbalanced and unfair.

circumstances in which government censorship would be justified. Even so, the court has laid so many prerequisites for government interference that censorship seems an extremely remote possibility.

media online

Internet Regulation: Issue overview from *Issues and Controversies on File.* www.facts.com/cd/i00043.htm

Election Results: Complete results of U.S. presidential elections from 1789 to 2000. http://gi.grolier.com/presidents/results/restable.html

Federal Election Commission: The duties of the FEC, which is an independent regulatory agency, are to disclose campaign finance information, to enforce the provisions of the law such as the limits and prohibitions on contributions and to oversee the public of presidential elections. www.fec.gov

INTERNET REGULATION.   The Internet and all its permutations, including chat rooms and web sites, are almost entirely unregulated in terms of political content. The massive quantities of material, its constant flux and the fact that the Internet is an international network make government regulation virtually impossible. Even Congress' attempts to ban Internet indecency in 1996 and again in 1999 fell apart under judicial review. The only inhibition on Internet political content is not through government restriction but through civil suits between individuals on issues like libel and invasion of privacy.

Media as Information Sources

STUDY PREVIEW   Most news media influence is through opinion leaders. Newspapers and magazines are especially important to these opinion leaders. For the public, television is the preferred source of national political news. For politically engaged people, talk radio and online media are also significant sources.

Direct versus Indirect

Many people once saw a direct link between press reports and individual decision-making. Today we know the linkage between the media and individuals generally is less direct. **Paul Lazarsfeld**'s pioneering studies on voter behavior in 1940 and 1948 found most people rely on personal acquaintances for information about politics and governance. Lazarsfeld called this a **two-step flow** process, with **opinion leaders** relying heavily on the news media for information and ideas, and other people relying on the opinion leaders. In reality, this is hardly a clinically neat process. The influence of opinion leaders varies significantly from issue to issue and even day to day, and people who normally don't use the media much may do so at some points and then rely less on opinion leaders. As Lazarsfeld came to recognize the complexity of the process, he renamed it **multistep flow**.

In short, news coverage and media commentary have influence on the public, but usually it is through the intermediaries whom Lazarsfeld called opinion leaders. Lazarsfeld's observation is underscored every time network television reporters talk on-camera with political leaders and refer to the public in the third person as "they," as if *they* aren't even watching. Implicit in the third person is the reporters' and political leaders' understanding that their audience is made up more of opinion leaders than the body politic.

Paul Lazarsfeld
Sociologist who concluded that media influence on voters generally is indirect.

two-step flow
Media effect on individuals is through opinion leaders.

opinion leaders
Media-savvy individuals who influence friends and acquaintances.

multistep flow
Political information moves from the media to individuals though complex, ever-changing interpersonal connections.

Citizen Preferences

Which media do people use most for political news? Opinion leaders lean heavily on newspapers and magazines, which generally are more comprehensive and thorough than broadcast sources. Not surprisingly, scholar Doris Graber found that better-educated people favor newspapers. Even so, there is no denying that television has supplanted newspapers as the primary source for national news for most people.

Media Databank

Sources of Election News

Most voters got most of their news about the 2000 presidential campaigns from television, according to a survey by TechnoMetrica Market Intelligence. The survey, commissioned by the newspaper trade journal *Editor & Publisher,* said cable television was the number one source early in the campaign but over-air network television moved ahead later. Newspapers were third. Likely voters were asked, "Where have you been getting most of your news about the presidential election campaign?" These were the results the week before the election:

Network television	28.6 percent
Cable television	23.5 percent
Newspapers	18.3 percent
Local television	12.1 percent
Radio	7.5 percent
Web	5.4 percent
Magazines	1.7 percent

A TechnoMetrica survey found that people relied more on television than newspapers by a 2:1 margin in the 2000 presidential campaign. For national coverage the television networks present news attractively and concisely.

For local and state political news, however, television isn't as respected. Newspapers, political scientist William Mayer found, are the primary source for most people on local political campaigns. In many communities, local television coverage is superficial and radio coverage almost nonexistent. In state-level gubernatorial and senatorial races, television is favored 5:3 as a primary information source, according to Mayer's 1992 studies—roughly half as much as at the national level.

Media preference studies generally ask people to rank their preference, which can lead to a false conclusion that the second-ranked preference isn't relied on at all. While people may use television most, this hardly means that they don't read newspapers at all. The daily press turns out more than 60 million copies a day nationwide. Also, newspapers and magazines, especially those with veteran political reporters and commentaries, are looked to by broadcast assignment editors for ideas on stories to pursue. Daniel Patrick Moynihan, the former New York senator, once noted that the New York *Times* is the standard by which other media decide what's worth covering.

Specialized Media

Sometimes overlooked in considering the influence of media political coverage are the specialized sources.

POLITICAL JOURNALS. Intellectual magazines, such as the *Nation* and the *New Republic,* have small circulations, but their audiences have a higher proportion of opinion leaders than many larger publications. This gives them great potency when you consider Lazarsfeld's trickle-down multistep flow.

The specialization that the mass media have undergone through demassification, with individual media units seeking narrow audience segments, has spawned new forums devoted to political news and exchanges.

Media People

Brian Lamb

Brian Lamb, a quiet, contemplative man, had knocked around news in Washington for 22 years. He had seen government as a UPI radio reporter. He had practiced public relations on the Hill and at the White House. In the 1970s, as satellite-relayed television came into being and as cable was growing, Brian Lamb saw something no one else did: possibilities for television that dealt exclusively with public affairs.

In Lamb's mind, this would be a television network using relatively cheap satellite time to cover sessions of Congress live and beam them down to cable systems. The network wouldn't try expensive production. It would just have somebody with a camera at places where news was occurring and turn it on. Why would anybody want to carry such **talking head** programs? Lamb told cable industry leaders that it would give them prestige with public-minded viewers. The cable people saw it as a low-cost way to blunt elitists' criticism that they weren't offering anything much worth watching. They agreed to offer the new network free

to every subscriber and to give Lamb a few pennies a month for each of those subscribers.

In 1978 **C-SPAN,** short for Cable-Satellite Public Affairs Network, began a 24-hour service that showed the U.S. House of Representatives live when it was in session and filled the rest of the time with interviews and discussions on public affairs. With its headquarters only a couple of blocks from the Capitol, C-SPAN has become a regular stopping point for major players on the issues of the day. Viewers call in and exchange their thoughts with the nation's movers and shakers. C-SPAN calls itself **"America's town hall."**

When budget allows, C-SPAN sends crews out into the country with lightweight video equipment. They use no complicated production techniques. They just turn the camera on and record America's pulse beat. These forays beyond the Beltway, according to media commentator Jeff Greenfield, are C-SPAN at its best: "The real pearls come when C-SPAN picks up its camera and winds up at a coffee klatch in Iowa, or a lobster

C-SPAN Architect

dinner in New Hampshire, when a presidential hopeful is speaking. Or when it covers a conversation between a political strategist and a group of reporters and editors over coffee and doughnuts. Or when it shows up at the hundreds of seminars in Washington on media coverage of politics."

The C-SPAN audience is not huge. Perhaps 10 million people tune in at least once a month. But the audience is an important one—educated, bright, concerned.

Brian Lamb
Created C-SPAN.

talking heads
Negative term for dialogue-based television shows.

C-SPAN
Cable network for public and cultural affairs; covers Congress live.

America's town hall
Fanciful term for C-SPAN.

DEMASSIFIED TELEVISION. The C-SPAN television network never claimed a large audience, but its emphasis on Washington has made it a source that many opinion leaders tap into. The proliferation of all-news networks, including CNN, MSNBC and Fox News Channel, all with around-the-clock coverage from Washington, has added to the diversity of sources for national political and government news. So has the growth of specialized programs on over-air networks, such as the nightly "Newshour with Jim Lehrer" on PBS and the Sunday discussion programs on the other networks.

TALK RADIO. Demassification reached massive audiences with the advent of **talk radio** in the 1980s. **Rush Limbaugh,** the most popular **talker** host, went on the air in 1988 and built an audience of 20 million a week over a network of 600-plus stations. The topic: politics. With seven of the nine leading talk shows, the slant is conservative. Some studies found these shows appeal mostly to "angry white males," and those were, in fact, the voters who turned out the Democratic Congress in 1994.

The influence of talkers may have peaked. By the 1996 election, when Bill Clinton won a second term by a large margin, the talkers, led by the Clinton-bashing Limbaugh, were unable to deliver a critical mass of voters. In the 2000 elections, talkers still had their followers, but with the razor-thin Bush-Gore presidential race and the Senate and House almost evenly split, it seemed that the talkers were past their prime. Diminished or not, the talkers remained a source of information and ideas for a politically engaged audience.

WEB. The web is a significant source of political information. Every candidate for dog catcher, it seems, has a web site come election time. Online magazines, like the **'zine** *Slate*, are digital versions of the traditional political journals. In fact, Michael Kinsley left the editorship of the *New Republic* in Washington to edit *Slate* out of Seattle. The finances of 'zines are uncertain. Not even Microsoft-backed *Slate* has been profitable, but neither have most of the traditional intellectual magazines.

An immeasurable quantity of political dialogue occurs on the Internet. **Chat rooms** devoted to candidates, issues, causes and politics in general come and go regularly, some with only a handful of followers, others with thousands. There are also Usenet newsgroups, e-mail lists, and web-based discussion boards devoted to political discussion.

Media Effects on Governance

STUDY PREVIEW Media coverage shapes what we think about as well as how to think about it. This means the media are a powerful linkage between the government and how people view their government. A negative aspect is the trend of the media to pander to transitory public interest in less substantive subjects, like scandals, gaffes and negative events.

Agenda-Setting

A lot of people think the news media are powerful, affecting the course of events in godlike ways. It's true that the media are powerful, but scholars, going back to sociologist Paul Lazarsfeld in the 1940s and even Robert Park in the 1920s, have concluded that it's not in a direct tell-them-how-to-vote-and-they-will kind of way. Media scholars Maxwell McCombs and Don Shaw cast media effects succinctly when they said the media don't tell people *what to think* but rather *what to think about*. This has come to be called **agenda-setting**.

CIVIL RIGHTS. The civil rights of American blacks were horribly ignored for the century following the Civil War. Then came news coverage of a growing reform movement in the 1960s. That coverage, of marches and demonstrations by Martin Luther King Jr. and others, including film footage of the way police treated peaceful black demonstrators, got the public thinking about racial injustice. In 1964 Congress passed the Civil Rights Act, which explicitly forbade discrimination in hotels and eateries, government aid and employment practices. Without media coverage the public agenda would not have included civil rights at a high enough level to have precipitated change as early as 1964.

media online

American Spectator: A conservative thought magazine that gained a reputation for Clinton-bashing in the 1990s. www.amspec.org

New Republic: A magazine of commentary and essays on political and cultural issues. www.thenewrepublic.com

Slate: The Microsoft-sponsored thought magazine edited by Michael Kinsley, formerly editor of the *New Republic*. www.slate.com

Drudge Report: www.drudgereport.com

Columbia Journalism Review: News about news. Includes great report on who owns what in the media. www.cjr.org

American Journalism Review: http://ajr.newslink.org

Brill's Content: Great magazine that reviews the media. www.brillscontent.com

talk radio
Stations or programs based on discussion, some with listener participation.

Rush Limbaugh
Conservative radio personality with the largest talk-show following.

talkers
Informal term for talk radio.

'zine
Informal term for an online magazine.

chat room
An Internet site, usually for an assigned topic, at which people may sign in, read other people's messages and contribute their own.

agenda-setting
The process through which issues bubble up into public attention through mass media selection on what to cover.

CNN Effect. Fund-raisers for famines in Ethiopia, Rwanda and Somalia all have found a correlation between television coverage and donations. When coverage fades, so do donations. This phenomenon has been labeled the CNN effect.

WATERGATE. Had the Washington *Post* not doggedly followed up on a break-in at the Democratic Party's national headquarters in 1972, the public would never have learned that people around the Republican president, Richard Nixon, were behind it. The *Post* set the national agenda.

WHITE HOUSE SEX SCANDALS. Nobody would have spent much time pondering whether President Bill Clinton engaged in sexual indiscretions if David Brock, writing in the *American Spectator* in 1993, had not reported allegations by Paula Jones. Nor would the issue have reached a feverish level of public attention without Matt Drudge's 1997 report in his online *Drudge Report* about Monica Lewinsky.

By and large, news coverage does not call for people to take positions, but based on what they learn from coverage, people do take positions. It's a catalytic effect. The coverage doesn't cause change directly but serves rather as a catalyst.

CNN Effect

Television is especially potent as an agenda-setter. For years nobody outside Ethiopia cared much about a devastating famine. Not even after four articles in the New York *Times* was there much response. The Washington *Post* ran three articles, and the Associated Press distributed 228 stories—still hardly any response. The next year, however, disturbing videos aired by BBC captured public attention and triggered a massive relief effort. In recent years many scholars looking at the agenda-setting effect of television vis-à-vis other media have focused on CNN, whose extensive coverage lends itself to study. As a result, the power of television to put faraway issues in the minds of domestic audiences has been labeled the **CNN effect**.

CNN effect
The ability of television, through emotion-raising video, to elevate distant issues on the domestic public agenda.

Priming

Media coverage not only creates public awareness but can also trigger dramatic shifts in opinion. An example was the fate of George Bush. In 1991 his approval ratings were at record highs. In 1992 the people thumped him out of office. What had happened? During the Persian Gulf war in 1991, the media put almost everything else on the back burner to cover the war. The president's role in the coverage was as commander-in-chief. Primed by the coverage, the public gave Bush exceptionally favorable ratings. When the war ended, media coverage shifted to the economy, which was ailing, and the president was hardly portrayed heroically. His ratings plummeted, and in 1992 he lost a re-election bid.

In 1991 the media coverage created an environment that primed the public to see the president positively, and in 1992 the environment changed. It was a classic example of **priming,** the process in which the media affect the standard that people use to evaluate political figures and issues. This is hardly to say that the media manipulate the environments in which people see political figures and issues. No one, for example, would argue that the Persian Gulf war should not have been covered. However, the fact is that it was through the media that people were aware of the war and concluded the president was doing a great job.

Media Obsessions

Although critics argue that the media are politically biased, studies don't support this. Reporters perceive themselves as middle-of-the-road politically, and by and large they work to suppress personal biases. Even so, reporters gravitate toward certain kinds of stories to the neglect of others—and this flavors coverage.

PRESIDENTIAL COVERAGE.   News reporters and editors have long recognized that people like stories about people, so any time an issue can be personified, the better. In Washington coverage this has meant focusing on the president to treat issues. A study of the "CBS Evening News" found 60 percent of the opening stories featured the president. Even in nonelection years the media have a near-myopic fix on the White House. This displaces coverage of other important governmental institutions, like Congress, the courts, and state and local government.

CONFLICT.   Journalists learn two things about conflict early in their careers. First, their audiences like conflict. Second, conflict often illustrates the great issues by which society is defining and redefining its values. Take, for example, capital punishment, abortion or the draft. People get excited about these issues because of the fundamental values involved.

Part of journalists' predilection toward conflict is that conflict involves change—whether to do something differently. All news involves change, and conflict almost always is a signal to the kind of change that's most worth reporting. Conflict is generally a useful indicator of newsworthiness.

SCANDALS.   Journalists know too that their audiences like scandal stories—a fact that trivializes political coverage. Talking about coverage of Bill Clinton early in his presidency, political scientists Morris Fiorina and Paul Peterson said, "The public was bombarded with stories about Whitewater, Vince Foster's suicide, $200 haircuts, parties with Sharon Stone, the White House travel office, Hillary Clinton's investments, and numerous other matters that readers will not remember. The reason you do not remember is that, however important these matters were to the individuals involved, they were not important for the overall operation of government. Hence, they have been forgotten."

No matter how transitory their news value, scandal and gaffe stories build audiences, which explains their increase. Robert Lichter and Daniel Amundson, analysts who

priming
Process in which the media affect the standard that people use to evaluate political figures and issues.

Media People

James Carville and Mary Matalin

He sent her fresh flowers and his special food creations. He charmed her office staff and made everybody laugh. And although he was in his 40s, everybody referred to him as her "boyfriend." The two had so much in common—especially their immersion in politics and their work as political consultants.

Mary Matalin was a Republican, and not just any Republican, however. At the time, she was chief of staff of the Republican National Committee, working out of its Washington, D.C., headquarters. And James Carville, the man she was dating, was not just any Democrat but a close Clinton adviser.

Despite their political differences, Carville and Matalin began dating in 1991. A week later, Matalin was appointed political director of the campaign to re-elect President George Bush. The battle was on.

Like her Democratic boyfriend, Matalin used the media to her candidate's advantage. "When in doubt, spin," she explained at one point in their book. The 1992 presidential campaign was taking place at a time when terms such as "candidate packaging," "image building," "stonewalling," "spin doctors," "handlers," "leaks," "crisis resolution" and "damage control strategy" were becoming part of the common parlance.

Perhaps no concept sums up modern political strategizing so much as the notion of *spin*—an intentional slant to the way informa-

Political Odd Couple. Ideologically opposite, they don't talk politics across the kitchen table.

tion is presented so that the public will interpret and respond to events in ways favorable to the candidate or political party. The term comes from a baseball pitcher's ability to spin a ball so that its trajectory is not what the opposing team expects.

Carville and Matalin were unabashedly masters of spin. Each of them tried to keep one step ahead of what the media would say about the candidates they served. That meant helping their candidates present an image and message that would appeal to voters. It was Carville who insisted that the Clinton campaign stay on the dollar issues that concerned the American people and who coined the phrase "It's the economy, stupid."

However, this was not a competition between two hired political strategists, each out to better the other. Both Matalin and Carville were ideologically committed to their respective parties. Although Matalin had come from a family

of Democrats and for a time had even embraced the hippie culture, she had undergone a complete turnabout after writing a paper on political conservatism for a college course. Carville had grown up in a segregated Southern culture and found his thinking changing when, as a schoolboy, he read *To Kill a Mockingbird*. He had also observed that it was the intervention of federal agents who made sure school integration was carried out, which helped to convince him of the federal government's power to do good.

In the end, Bill Clinton won the election, the romance between Carville and Matalin survived the campaign, and they later were married and became parents. Carville continued his work as a political consultant and presidential adviser. Matalin found avenues for sharing her political views as a television commentator and radio talk show host.

monitor Washington news coverage, found policy stories outnumbered scandal stories 13:1 in 1972 but only 3:1 in 1992. During that same period, news media have been become savvy at catering to audience interests and less interested in covering issues of significance. This also has led to more negative news. Lichter and Amundson found that negative stories from Congress outnumbered positive stories 3:1 in 1972 but 9:1 in 1992.

HORSE RACES. In reporting political campaigns, the news media obsess on reporting the polls. Critics say this treating of campaigns as **horse races** results in substantive issues being underplayed. Even when issues are the focus, as when a candidate announces a major policy position, reporters connect the issue to its potential impact in the polls.

BREVITY. People who design media packages, such as a newspaper or newscast, have devised presentation formats that favor shorter stories. This trend has been driven in part by broadcasting's severe time constraints. Network anchors, most notably Dan Rather, have complained for years that they have to condense the world's news into 23 minutes on their evening newscasts. The result: short, often superficial treatments. The short-story format shifted to many newspapers and magazines, beginning with the launch of *USA Today* in 1981. *USA Today* obtained extremely high story counts, covering a great many events by running short stories—many only a half-dozen sentences. The effect on political coverage has been profound.

The **sound bites** in campaign stories, the actual voice of a candidate in a broadcast news story, dropped from 47 seconds in 1968 to 10 seconds in 1988 and have remained short. Issues that require lengthy explorations, say critics, get passed up. Candidates, eager for airtime, have learned to offer quippy, catchy, clever capsules that are likely to be picked up rather than articulating thoughtful persuasive statements. The same dynamic is available in *USA Today*-style brevity.

Some people defend brevity, saying it's the only way to reach people whose increasingly busy lives don't leave them much time to track politics and government. In one generalization, brevity's defenders note, the short attention span of the MTV generation can't handle much more than 10-second sound bites. Sanford Ungar, the communication dean at American University, applauds the news media for devising writing and reporting styles that boil down complex issues so they can be readily understood by great masses of people. Ungar: "If *USA Today* encourages people not to think deeply, or not to go into more detail about what's happening, then it will be a disservice. But if *USA Today* teaches people how to be concise and get the main points across sometimes, they're doing nothing worse than what television is doing, and doing it at least as well."

While many news organizations have moved to briefer and trendier government and political coverage, it's unfair to paint too broad a stroke. The New York *Times*, the Washington *Post* and the Los Angeles *Times* do not scrimp on coverage, and even *USA Today* runs four lengthy articles in every issue, occasionally on government and politics. The television networks, which have been rapped the most for sound-bite coverage, also offer in-depth treatments outside of newscasts—such as the Sunday morning programs.

Candidates have also discovered alternatives to being condensed and packaged. In 2000 both George W. Bush and Al Gore made appearances on Oprah Winfrey's, Jay Leno's and David Letterman's shows and even "Saturday Night Live."

horse race
An election campaign treated by reporters like a game—who's ahead, who's falling back, who's coming up the rail.

sound bite
The actual voice of someone in the news, sandwiched in a correspondent's report.

Presidents and the Media. Franklin Roosevelt was not popular with most newspaper and magazine publishers. Editorials opposed his election in 1932, and whatever sparse support there was for his ideas to end the Great Depression was fading. Two months after taking office, Roosevelt decided to try radio to communicate directly to the people, bypassing the traditional reporting and editing process that didn't always work in his favor. In his first national radio address, Roosevelt explained the steps he had taken to meet the nation's financial emergency. It worked. The president came across well on radio, and people were fascinated to hear their leader live and direct. Roosevelt's "fireside chats" became a fixture of his administration, which despite editorial negativism would continue 13 years—longer than any in U.S. history. John Kennedy used television as Roosevelt had used radio, and every political leader since, for better or worse, has recognized the value of the mass media as a vehicle for governance.

Government Manipulation of Media

STUDY PREVIEW   Many political leaders are preoccupied with media coverage because they know the power it can have. Over the years they have developed mechanisms to influence coverage to their advantage.

Influencing Coverage

Many political leaders stay up nights figuring out ways to influence media coverage. James Fallows, in his book *Breaking the News*, quoted a Clinton White House official: "When I was there, absolutely nothing was more important than figuring out what the news was going to be. . . . There is no such thing as a substantive discussion that is not shaped or dominated by how it is going to play in the press."

The game of trying to outsmart the news media is nothing new. Theodore Roosevelt, at the turn of the 20th century, chose Sundays to issue many announcements. Roosevelt recognized that editors producing Monday newspapers usually had a dearth of news because weekends, with government and business shut down, didn't generate much worth telling. Roosevelt's Sunday announcements, therefore, received more prominent play in Monday editions. With typical bullishness Roosevelt claimed he had "discovered Mondays." Compared to how sophisticated government leaders have become at manipulating press coverage today, Roosevelt was a piker.

Trial Balloons and Leaks

To check weather conditions, meteorologists send up balloons. To get an advance peek at public reaction, political leaders also float **trial balloons.** When Richard Nixon was considering shutting down radio and television stations at night to conserve electricity during the 1973 energy crisis, the idea was floated to the press by a subordinate. The reaction was so swift and so negative that the idea was shelved. Had there not been a negative reaction or if reaction had been positive, then the president himself would have unveiled the plan as his own.

Trial balloons are not the only way in which the media can be used. Partisans and dissidents use **leaks** to bring attention to their opponents and people they don't much like. In leaking, someone passes information to reporters on condition that he or she not be identified as the source. While reporters are leery of many leakers, some information is so significant and from such reliable sources that it's hard to pass up.

The quantity of off-the-record leaks became so great in the 1960s—and it hasn't abated since—that Alfred Friendly, managing editor of the Washington *Post,* put labels on how reporters should handle information from sources.

ON THE RECORD.   Anything said may be used and attributed by name to the source. This is what journalists prefer. News conferences, of course, are on the record, and so are most interviews. For example: "Flanders Domingo, a deputy assistant secretary of the Navy, said. . . ."

OFF THE RECORD.   This information is not to be passed on, even in conversation. Information is offered off the record for many reasons. Sometimes a source wants to help a reporter better understand a confusing or potentially harmful situation. Or it may be intended to head off a damaging error that a source thinks a reporter might make if not informed.

ON BACKGROUND.   What's said may be used in print or on the air, but the source cannot be identified. For example: "A source close to the Secretary of Defense said. . . ."

ON DEEP BACKGROUND.   The source's information may be used but with no attribution whatsoever—not even a hint as to the source. As a result, the information must stand on the reporter's reputation alone. "The 7th Fleet is standing by to sail into the South China Sea." Period.

It's essential that reporters understand how their sources intend information to be used. It is also important for sources to have some control over what they tell reporters. Even so, reporter-source relationships lend themselves to abuse by manipulative government officials. Worse, the structures of these relationships allow officials to throttle what's told to the people. As political scientists Karen O'Connor and Larry Sabato said, "Every public official knows that journalists are pledged to protect the confidentiality of sources, and therefore the rules can be used to an official's own benefit—but, say, giving reporters derogatory information to print about a source without having to be identified with the source." This manipulation is a regrettable, though unavoidable, part of the news-gathering process.

trial balloon
A deliberate leak of a potential policy, usually from a diversionary source, to test public response.

leak
A deliberate disclosure of confidential or classified information by someone who wants to advance the public interest, embarrass a bureaucratic rival or supervisor, or disclose incompetence or skullduggery.

Stonewalling

When Richard Nixon was under fire for ordering a cover-up of the Watergate break-in, he went months without a news conference. His aides plotted his movements to avoid even informal, shouted questions from reporters. He hunkered down in the White House in a classic example of **stonewalling.** Experts in the branch of public relations called political communications generally advise against stonewalling because people infer guilt or something to hide. Nonetheless, it is one way to deal with difficult media questions.

A variation on stonewalling is the **news blackout.** When U.S. troops invaded Grenada, the Pentagon barred the press. Reporters who hired runabout boats to get to the island were intercepted by a U.S. naval blockade. While heavy-handed, such limitations on media coverage do, for a limited time, give the government the opportunity to report what's happening from its self-serving perspective.

Overwhelming Information

During the Persian Gulf buildup in 1990 and the war itself, the Pentagon tried a new approach in media relations. Pete Williams, the Pentagon's chief spokesperson, provided so much information, including video, sound bites and data, that reporters were overwhelmed. The result was that reporters spent so much time sorting through material, all of it worthy, that they didn't have time to compose difficult questions or pursue fresh story angles of their own. The result: War coverage was almost entirely favorable to the Bush administration.

Status of the Watchdog

STUDY PREVIEW   The quality of news coverage of the political and governing process varies. The presidency, for example, is covered much better than federal agencies. Also, reporters are sometimes late in dealing with fundamental changes such as being bypassed by candidates who talk directly to the people on talk shows—with no reporter as intermediary.

Campaign Coverage

News coverage of the 1988 Bush-Dukakis presidential campaigns disappointed even media people. A forum of correspondents gave the coverage a C-minus report card. Lessons learned, postmortems were better for the 1992 and 1996 campaigns. Initial analysis of the 2000 coverage was favorable, albeit the election night gaffe when the television networks called Florida prematurely for Al Gore and then for George W. Bush, contributing to the ensuing confusion over who was the actual winner.

- **Issues.** Reporters need to push for details on positions and ask tough questions on major issues, not accept generalities. They need to bounce one candidate's position off other candidates, creating a forum of intelligent discussion from which voters can make informed choices.
- **Agenda.** Reporters need to assume some role in setting a campaign agenda. When reporters allow candidates to control the agenda of coverage, they become mere conduits for self-serving news releases and images from candidates. **Pseudo-events** with candidates, like visits to photogenic flag factories, lack substance. So

---

stonewall
To refuse to answer questions, sometimes refusing even to meet with reporters.

news blackout
When a person or institution decides to issue no statements despite public interest and also declines news media questions.

pseudo-event
A staged event to attract media attention, usually lacking substance.

photo op
Short for *photo opportunity.* A staged event, usually photogenic, to attract media attention.

Convention Coverage. The chair of the Federal Communications Commission, Bill Kennard, accused the NBC and Fox television networks of ignoring their public service responsibilities for cutting back coverage of the 2000 national political conventions. NBC ran baseball, and Fox ran its usual prime-time programming. Kennard said: "Once a network begins to counter-program against the debates, others will be under increasing financial pressure not to cover the debates." Kennard called on broadcasters to focus "the nation's collective electorate on arguably the most important political decision most Americans make."

Bill Kennard

do staged **photo ops.** Reporters need to guard against letting such easy-to-cover events squeeze out substantive coverage.

- **Interpretation.** Campaigns are drawn out and complicated, and reporters need to keep trying to pull together what's happened for the audience. Day-to-day spot news isn't enough. There also need to be explanation, interpretation and analysis to help voters see the big picture.

- **Inside coverage.** Reporters need to cover the machinery of the campaigns—who's running things and how. This is especially important with the growing role of campaign consultants. Who are these people? What history do they bring to a campaign? What agenda?

- **Advertising.** In 1988 analytical reporting on campaign spots was weak. For example, background and analysis came late on the Bush campaign's Willie Horton ad, which appealed to white racism. By 1992 the media had improved their reporting on campaign advertising.

- **Polling.** Poll results are easy to report but tricky and inconsistent because of variations in methodology and even questions. News operations should report on competing polls, not just their own. In tracking polls, asking the same questions over time for consistency is essential. To their discredit, several news organizations, including CNN, changed gears two weeks before the 1992 election by changing its sample from registered voters to likely voters, creating an apples-and-oranges situation that muddied attempts to compare new data with earlier data.

- **Instant feedback.** Television newsrooms have supplemented their coverage and commentary with e-mail instant feedback from viewers. Select messages are flashed on-screen within minutes. In some programs a reporter is assigned to analyze incoming messages and identify trends. While all this makes for "good television," the comments are statistically dubious as indicators of overall public opinion. Too much can be read into them.

- **Depth.** With candidates going directly to voters in debates and talk-show appearances, reporters need to offer something more than what voters can see and hear for themselves. Analysis and depth add a fresh dimension that is not redundant to what the audience already knows.

Florida Recount. The close 2000 presidential election spurred recount after recount, with Americans riveted to the mass media for every unfolding detail. It turned out to be a national civics lesson in election law and judicial prerogatives. The election commissioner in Palm Beach County, Florida, was among the first officials to make a call by ordering a partial recount, then an entire recount, the yet another recount.

Body Watch
White House term for media tracking of the president 24 hours a day, seven days a week.

news secretary
Responsible for media relations. In this age of broadcasting, the term *press secretary* is outdated.

news briefing
When an assistant makes announcements to reporters and, usually, fields questions.

news conference
When a person in charge, like the president, makes announcements to reporters and, usually, fields questions.

regional reporter
A reporter assigned by a hometown newsroom to look for regional news in Washington that the news agencies wouldn't cover.

On most of these criteria, coverage improved dramatically in 1992. In a Media Studies Center poll, 12 leading correspondents gave coverage a B-minus report card—a vast improvement from 1988's C-minus.

Federal Coverage

Coverage of the national government ranges from near-saturation, in covering the president, to dismal at the agencies.

WHITE HOUSE. White House reporters call it the **Body Watch,** always keeping tabs on the president. When the president leaves the White House on the Marine One helicopter, reporters are there to see the takeoff. Someone at the other end is there to witness the arrival. At Camp David, the presidential retreat in Maryland's Catoctin Mountains, reporters have a duck blind from which to wait and watch for the helicopters from Washington. Helen Thomas, who began covering the White House in 1961, once followed President Kennedy to a men-only golf club. Because she couldn't get in, Thomas hid in the bushes.

Befitting the most powerful person on the planet, the media watch and monitor the president more closely than anyone else on earth. When the president goes on a long trip, reporters are aboard Air Force One. If there aren't enough press seats, a second plane follows.

In the White House is an elaborate press suite, equipped with all the power outlets and ports needed for today's journalistic equipment. The president's staff establishes rules of coverage and accredits reporters who are allowed in. An incredible 1,700 reporters have White House credentials. In the Reagan years reporters were free to wander down a hall to the office of the president's **news secretary.** The Clinton administration ended those roaming privileges for a while but later relented.

Usually, White House reporters are briefed twice a day. With cameras taping and sometimes the all-news networks broadcasting live, the president's news secretary makes an announcement and fields questions in what is called a **news briefing.** When the president does this, it's called a **news conference.** Practice has varied, but recent presidents have held news conferences as often as twice a week, though generally less.

Reporters ask tough questions, and presidents don't relish the grilling. Even so, the news conference has emerged as the only institution for the people to hold the president accountable, short of impeachment and the next election. Reporters see themselves as surrogates for the citizenry, asking questions that a well-informed citizen would ask. What is said at a news conference is actually a two-way street. As Harry Truman told reporters after leaving the presidency, "For eight years, you and I have been helping each other. I have been trying to keep you informed of the news from the point of view of the presidency. You, more than you realize, have been giving me a great deal of what the people of this country are thinking."

CONGRESS. On Capitol Hill the primary reporting focuses on the Senate and House leadership that controls the law-making process through an elaborate committee system. Reporters cover hearings and listen to testimony on major issues, but they also lean on news releases issued by committees, caucuses and members of Congress. They spend a lot of their time interviewing aides and others, sometimes for a scoop, sometimes just to be up to speed on emerging issues that will break as major news.

A second tier of reporters covers the Hill for regional stories that the news agencies and television networks pass over but that have hometown importance. A **regional reporter** for the Seattle *Times,* for example, would leave national stories

Media Databank

Federal Agency Coverage

John Herbers and James McCartney compiled data on how many newspapers and agencies covered federal agencies regularly in 1999. These figures were extracted from their report in an *American Journalism Review* series on the state of U.S. newspapers.

Agency	Today	Formerly
State Department	15	25
Defense Department	15	15
Treasury Department	13	13
Justice Department	11	11
Internal Revenue Service	6	6
Federal Communications Commission	6	6
Food and Drug Administration	6	6
Federal Aviation Administration	5	9
Agriculture Department	4	9
Social Security Administration	4	4
Environmental Protection Agency	3	3
Labor Department	3	10
Nuclear Regulatory Commission	3	5
Veterans' Affairs	2	5
Interior Department	0	4
Totals	**96**	**131**

from Congress to the news agencies that serve the *Times* and concentrate instead on stories of local interest—like maritime, timber and aerospace issues in the case of Seattle.

AGENCIES. While the White House remains thoroughly covered, and Congress too, though to a lesser extent, federal agencies are increasingly neglected. The U.S. Department of the Interior is an example. It controls 500 million acres of public land and administers the national parks, the U.S. Bureau of Indian Affairs and the U.S. Fish and Wildlife Service. Its policies and regulations affect key issues such as water rights, mining and logging. Because the Department of the Interior has great effects on Western states, it was no surprise, several years back, that several Western newspapers, including the Denver *Post*, had reporters posted at the agency, as did the New York *Times* and the Washington *Post*. Today, none do.

When breaking news occurs in a noncovered agency, news bureaus send a reporter over for a story. But the expertise that comes from knowing regular sources day to day is missing. So is the kind of background on agency personalities and policies without which enterprise stories are not possible.

Some of the staffing attrition is due to the introduction of thematic beats, as opposed to building beats. Some editors have opted for health beats that span many agencies, for example, rather than a beat at the Department of Health and Human Services. Even so, fewer reporters are covering the beats that generate regular coverage of your government at work.

Some slack is being picked up by the growing **trade journal** and **newsletter** industry. At the Federal Communications Commission, for example, major agencies and newspapers have only six reporters, but the trade journal *Broadcasting & Cable* keeps its readers up to date. Hundreds of such journals and newsletters come out of

trade journal
A magazine edited for people in a specific profession or trade.

newsletter
A simple-format informational bulletin covering a narrowly defined field.

Washington for specialized audiences. But because these journals are so focused, typical citizens have less news about federal agencies.

COURTS.　When ABC, CBS and NBC were the major television networks, each had a full-time reporter assigned to the U.S. Supreme Court. In 1997 ABC was last to have a full-time reporter at the Court, Tim O'Brien, and then he was reassigned. Today, only 27 reporters have Supreme Court credentials to use the Court's media facilities. Only 11 news organizations cover the Court as a regular beat.

After conducting a major study on beat coverage of federal agencies, John Herbers and James McCartney, writing in *American Journalism Review*, said, "Citizens were best connected to Washington by their local newspapers through the news dispatches, analyses and columns of their paper's staff in the capital, with numerous regional papers competing with their larger and more influential counterparts for leaks and exclusive information. In the process, they were able to follow and judge, at least to some extent, the policies and actions of the national government. Not anymore."

State and Local Coverage

A massive study by Charles Layton and David Allan, published in *American Journalism Review*, found a distressing drop in reporters covering state government. Only two newspapers had double-digit staffs in their state capital cities: the Los Angeles *Times*, with 14, and the Newark, New Jersey, *Star-Ledger*, with 10. Chain newspapers had cut statehouse staffs. Gannett, as an example, had only 62 statehouse reporters for its 89 newspapers in 1998. In the mid-1980s Michigan newspapers had 25 full-time reporters in Lansing, but by 1998 it had merely 12. Furthermore, the reporters are less experienced overall. At the Indiana Capitol in Indianapolis, as an example, Lesley Stedman of the Fort Wayne *Journal Gazette* was a senior reporter after two years at age 26.

There are exceptions but not many. The Sacramento press corps has 44 full-time reporters, including 14 from the Los Angeles *Times*, 12 from the Sacramento *Bee* and 10 from the news services.

Not only are newspapers running less news on state government, but with fewer reporters scrambling to cover day-to-day events, there is less investigative and interpretive reporting.

The decline in state government coverage is all the more serious for two reasons:

- **New Federalism.** Gradually, since the early 1990s, Congress has shifted many programs from federal to state responsibility, in a trend known as the **New Federalism**. More dollars are collected and spent by state government than ever before on education, prisons, welfare and other priorities. The U.S. Bureau of Labor Statistics lists state government as the nation's eighth largest growth industry, spending $854 billion a year, which breaks down to more than $2,000 a person. Yet fewer reporters are tracking what's happening, which means that citizens have less information to form opinions and make judgments on how their government is working.
- **Lobbying.** Private interests have increased **lobbying** dramatically. A 1990 survey by the Associated Press found 42,500 lobbyists registered in the 50 states, an increase of 20 percent in four years. Although no one has repeated the AP study, there is no reason to believe that the number of lobbyists hasn't continued to grow. Two thousand lobbyists are registered in California. In New York, lobbyist spending rose from $15 million in 1986 to $51 million in 1997. The growing lobbyist corps outnumbers reporters 150:1 in Georgia's capital, a ratio not untypical of other states.

New Federalism
The shift in funding and administration of programs from the federal to state government.

lobbying
Trying to persuade legislators and regulators to a position.

Media Databank

State Capitol Coverage

Newspapers have the largest staff and strongest coverage of state government, but it's declining. Data compiled by Charles Layton and David Allan found a national decline in newspaper reporters at state capitols. Here is a sampler of their 1998 data on Florida on the number of full-time reporters assigned to state government, with a note on how staffing has changed since 1990:

Tampa *Tribune*	5	Down
St. Petersburg *Times*	4	Up
Miami *Herald*	3	Down
New York *Times*—Florida papers	3	Up
Fort Lauderdale *Sun-Sentinel*	2	Down
Palm Beach *Post*	2	Unchanged
Orlando *Sentinel*	2	Down

Jacksonville Florida *Times Union*	2	Down
Gannett Florida papers	2	Down
Tallahassee *Democrat*	2	Down
Bradenton *Herald*	1	Unchanged
Freedom Florida papers	1	Unchanged
Wall Street Journal	1	Up
Dayton Beach *News-Journal*	0	Unchanged

The good news: Eight of the 14 newspapers bolsters staffing during legislative sessions, and some bring on part-timers and interns. Check on your state in the article: Charles Layton and Mary Walton, "Missing the Story at the Statehouse," *American Journalism Review* (July/August 1998), pages 42-63.

Their job: to create, promote and influence legislation to adjust public policy to their own benefit. Never was there a greater need for media watchdogs.

Media-Government Issues

STUDY PREVIEW   Serious questions of trust are at stake as media owners become more business oriented. Other issues: Can news be trusted if reporters pick up outside income from special interests? Does political advertising pander to emotional and superficial instincts? Should television be required to give candidates free airtime? Should we look to the Internet to make government instantly responsive to public will?

Political Favors

Public confidence in media coverage suffers whenever doubts arise about whether the media are truly the public's watchdogs on government. Such doubts have grown as media control has been concentrated in fewer hands through conglomeration and with the concomitant growth in media leaders being business people first and media people second. Rupert Murdoch, whose media empire includes the Fox television network, lost tremendous credibility when it was discovered he had offered House Speaker Newt Gingrich $4.5 million for a yet-unwritten manuscript to be published by Murdoch's HarperCollins book subsidiary. At the time Murdoch was facing a federal challenge to his ownership of Fox. Book industry experts said there was no way Gingrich's book could earn $4.5 million—and, in fact, it flopped. When the deal was exposed, Murdoch and Gingrich both backpedaled and proclaimed Murdoch's problems on the Hill and the book deal were unfortunate coincidences.

Whatever the truth of the Murdoch-Gingrich deal, the interplay of media and government raises questions about whether the media are more responsive to their financial interest or to the public interest. Murdoch once yanked BBC off his Star-TV

What Might Beijing Say? HarperCollins editors were eager to sign Britain's last governor of Hong Kong, Chris Patten, to write his memoirs. Then their bosses realized the book might include unfriendly thoughts about the Chinese government in Beijing. They alerted their top boss, media mogul Rupert Murdoch, who said publishing the book would be a mistake. Why? Because Murdoch needed the continued good will of Beijing for numerous media projects—including his Star-TV satellite service to Asia. When word leaked out that Murdoch was killing a significant book rather than risk his relationship with the repressive Chinese government, many leading authors threatened to boycott HarperCollins. Meanwhile, Patten had no problem finding another publisher to bring out the book.

Herbert Alexander
His studies have concluded that media advertising is only one of many variables in political campaigns.

Thomas Patterson and Robert McClure
Effect of political advertising on voters is critical only in close campaigns.

satellite service to China after Chinese government leaders objected to BBC coverage. At the time Murdoch had numerous business initiatives needing Chinese governmental approval. In a similar incident, in 1998, Murdoch canceled a publication of a forthcoming book from HarperCollins because of passages that were critical of China's human rights record. Murdoch's action became known only because the author, the respected former British governor of Hong Kong, went public with his objections.

It's impossible to know how many media decisions are driven by business rather than public interests because the participants don't advertise them as such. Such decisions become public only through roundabout ways, and while the participants are embarrassed, it doesn't seem they derive any lessons and change their ways—at least not in the case of Rupert Murdoch.

Campaign Advertising

The mass media have become essential tools not only for national political leaders. Even candidates for state and many local offices have media advisers. Critics note that this techno-politics has serious downsides. In the age of television, photogenic candidates have an unfair built-in advantage. According to the critics, good looks rather than good ideas sway the electorate. Perhaps more serious, in some critics' view, is that slick presentation is more important than substance when it comes to 15-second TV spots.

Can candidates buy their way to office with advertising? While a candidate who vastly outspends another would seem to have an advantage, well-heeled campaigns can fail. In the most expensive U.S. Senate campaign in history, in New Jersey in 2000, Jon Corzine spent $60 million. He won. But in 1994 Michael Huffington spent $18 million on a California campaign for the U.S. Senate, the most ever to date, and lost to Diane Feinstein, who spent only $9 million.

In presidential campaigns too, no correlation has been established between winning and media spending. **Herbert Alexander,** a University of Southern California political scientist who tracks campaign spending, noted that George Bush outspent Bill Clinton $43 million to $32 million in 1992 and lost. Ross Perot also outspent Clinton, buying almost $40 million in media time and space. In 1988, however, Bush outspent Michael Dukakis $32 million to $24 million and won. The data point to campaign advertising being only one of many variables in elections.

The fact remains, however, that a political campaign has a cost of admission. Candidates need media exposure, and a campaign without advertising would almost certainly be doomed.

It would be a mistake to conclude that political advertising has no effect. A major 1976 study by **Thomas Patterson** and **Robert McClure** concluded that 7 percent of the people in a 2,700-person sample were influenced by ads on whether to vote for Richard Nixon or George McGovern for president. While that was a small percentage, many campaigns are decided by even slimmer margins. The lesson from the Patterson-McClure study is that political advertising can make a critical difference.

Free Airtime

Television advertising accounts for most of candidates' campaign budgets, which has put growing pressure on candidates to raise funds to buy the time. This pressure has resulted in campaign finance irregularities that end up haunting candidates later. Many political observers, for example, questioned whether Al Gore's year 2000 presidential hopes could survive the Buddhist Temple fund-raising scandal back during the 1996 Clinton-Dole campaign. Not surprisingly, Gore became an advocate of requiring television stations to give free airtime to candidates.

One proposal, from the Center for Governmental Studies in Los Angeles, would require stations to give two hours to candidates in the 60 days before an election. To allay station objections to losing revenue, the center proposed tax credits to offset station costs. Broadcasters still objected on numerous grounds. Shelby Scott, of the American Federation of Television and Radio Artists, said, "I don't want any more 30-second spots. I don't think they inform the electorate." Other television people noted that political ads, which are sold at cheap rates, would displace more lucrative commercial ads. Broadcasters also noted a coerciveness in being required to give free airtime to political candidates, noting that stations are beholden to the federal government for their licenses to remain in business.

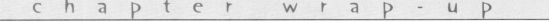

chapter wrap-up

No one denies that the news media are influential in U.S. governance and politics, but the influence generally is indirect through media-savvy opinion leaders. Even so, the media are powerful players in public life because they shape the public's agenda by reporting some issues and ignoring or downplaying others. The media also frame issues and prime how people see the issues.

Questions for Review

1. What does the term *fourth estate* mean?
2. How do the news media influence people on political issues?
3. How do media agenda-setting and priming work?
4. How do government leaders manipulate media coverage?
5. How good are the news media as a watchdog?

Questions for Critical Thinking

1. Who are opinion leaders in your life? How do they influence your views?
2. What personal values would influence you as a news reporter who sets public agendas and frames issues and primes how people see them?
3. What perils face a reporter who accepts information off the record from one source and later receives the same information on deep background from another source?
4. Considering the dynamics in government-media relations, what are the prospects for plans to require television to give free airtime to political candidates?
5. If you were managing a television network's news coverage of a presidential campaign, what instructions would you give your reporters?

Keeping Up to Date

Professional journals that carry articles on media coverage of political issues and governance include *Columbia Journalism Review, Quill, American Journalism Review,* and *Brill's Content.*

Ongoing discussion on media responsibility also appears in the *Journal of Mass Media Ethics.*

John Perry Barlow. *He doubts the traditional notion that creativity is dependent on the financial incentive created by copyright law. New technology, Barlow says, is rendering copyright concepts archaic—a fascinating but contentious view.*

19

Mass Media Law

- The heart of U.S. mass media law is the First Amendment's guarantee of free expression.

- The government may only rarely prohibit expression.

- Anyone who is falsely slandered by the mass media may sue for libel.

- The mass media generally may not intrude on someone's solitude.

- The news media may cover the courts and government however they see fit.

- Obscenity is not protected by the First Amendment, but pornography is.

- Most censorship battles today are fought at the local level.

- Copyright law protects intellectual property from being stolen from its owners.

As John Perry Barlow envisions the future, giant media companies will shrivel. The web makes it possible for people to acquire mass messages, like pop music, directly from artists. Such direct transactions between artists and consumers undermine the profitable role that media companies have been playing in the dissemination of messages.

To make his point, Barlow, cofounder of the Electronic Frontier Foundation, points to Napster file-sharing technology that burst onto the scene in 1999. Until the courts stopped the practice in 2001, music fans used Napster to bypass media companies and traditional record-sales channels to acquire music directly from artists. Record companies were cut out. What's happened with records, Barlow says, inevitably will happen with other kinds of mass messages.

No wonder media executives were watching closely when the record industry went to court to shut Napster down. The issue was copyright law, which guarantees that people who create intellectual property, like music, hold the right to benefit financially from their work. According to conventional wisdom, the financial incentive inspires creative people to keep producing and thus enrich society.

Until the web, creative people almost always turned over the ownership of their work to media companies because those companies owned the only means to disseminate messages to mass audiences. In exchange, media companies give a percentage of their revenue to the creative people.

In court against Napster, the record companies argued that composers, lyricists and performers were in danger of losing their share of the revenue generated by the record companies. Without that financial incentive, according

David Boies. His intellectual fierceness showed in the lengthy case against Microsoft. Representing Microsoft's competitors, Boies prevailed in 2000 in federal appellate court. That same year Boies had a setback representing Al Gore for the Florida presidential vote recount. Then in 2001, Boies had another setback in the Napster intellectual property case that might have upended the business model on which all mass media companies are dependent. A federal panel ruled that Napster, the brainchild of Shawn Fanning, standing behind Boies, could be sued for trafficking in copyrighted music.

to these anti-Napster forces, creativity would suffer, perhaps dry up.

To that, Barlow said balderdash. He argues that creative people hardly need copyright protection to do their thing. Rhetorically, he asks, how about Shakespeare? Da Vinci? Homer? His point is that creativity is inherent in human nature and occurs independently of financial incentives. Further, Barlow says, technology makes it possible for the first time in modern history for creative people to reach mass audiences on their own. In short, as he sees it, the underlying premise for copyright is an archaic relic from earlier times. Equally archaic, he says, is the need for creative people to rely on media companies to disseminate their creative work and, in return, take a lion's share of the revenue. In short, Napster and similar technologies undermine the entire financial foundation on which media companies have been built.

In this chapter you will explore copyright to help you assess the merits of Barlow's argument, as well as that of the media companies. You also will learn about other aspects of mass media law.

The U.S. Constitution

STUDY PREVIEW   The First Amendment to the U.S. Constitution bars the government from limiting freedom of expression, including expression in the mass media, or so it seems. However, for the first 134 years of the amendment's existence, it appeared that the states could ignore the federal Constitution and put their own restrictions on free expression because it did not apply to them.

First Amendment

First Amendment
Bars government from limiting free expression.

James Madison
Author of the First Amendment.

The legal foundation for free expression in the United States is the **First Amendment** to the Constitution. The amendment, penned by **James Madison,** boiled down the eloquence of Benjamin Franklin, Thomas Jefferson and earlier libertarian thinkers during the American colonial experience to a mere 45 words: "Congress shall make no law respecting an establishment of religion, or prohibiting the free exercise thereof;

or abridging the freedom of speech, or of the press; or of the right of the people peaceably to assemble, and to petition the Government for a redress of grievances."

The amendment, which became part of the Constitution in 1791, seemed a definitive statement that set the United States apart from all other nations at the time in guaranteeing that the government wouldn't interfere with free expression. It turned out, however, that the First Amendment did not settle all the questions that could be raised about free expression. This chapter looks at many of these unsettled issues and attempts to clarify them.

Scope of the First Amendment

The First Amendment explicitly prohibited only Congress from limiting free expression, but there was never a serious legal question that it applied also to the executive branch of the national government. There was a question, however, about whether the First Amendment prohibited the states from squelching free expression.

From the early days of the republic, many states had laws that limited free expression, and nobody seemed to mind much. In fact, all the way through the 1800s the First Amendment seemed largely ignored. Not until 1925, when the U.S. Supreme Court considered the case of **Benjamin Gitlow,** was the First Amendment applied to the states. In that case Gitlow, a small-time New York agitator, rankled authorities by publishing his "Left Wing Manifesto" and distributing a Socialist paper. He was arrested and convicted of violating a state law that forbade advocating "criminal anarchy." Gitlow appealed that the First Amendment to the U.S. Constitution should override any state law that contravenes it, and the U.S. Supreme Court agreed. Gitlow, by the way, lost his appeal on other grounds. Even so, his case was a significant clarification of the scope of the First Amendment.

Prior Restraint

STUDY PREVIEW When the government heads off an utterance before it is made, the government is engaging in prior restraint. Since the 1930s the U.S. Supreme Court has consistently found that prior restraint violates the First Amendment. At the same time the Court says there may be circumstances, though rare, in which the public good would justify such censorship.

Public Nuisances

The U.S. Supreme Court was still finding its voice on First Amendment issues when a Minnesota case came to its attention. The Minnesota Legislature had created a "public nuisance" law that allowed authorities to shut down "obnoxious" newspapers. The Legislature's rationale was that government has the right to remove things that work against the common good: Just as a community can remove obnoxious weeds, so can it remove obnoxious "rags." In 1927 in Minneapolis, authorities used the law to padlock the *Saturday Press,* a feisty scandal sheet owned by **Jay Near** and **Howard Guilford.**

Most people would agree that the *Saturday Press* was obnoxious, especially its racist hate-mongering. Other people, however, including publisher **Robert McCormick** of the Chicago *Tribune* and the fledgling **American Civil Liberties Union,**

media online

Napster: The big news in copyright is about Napster's battles with the music companies. Follow the news on Napster's web site.
www.napster.com

Copyright Myths: Ten myths about copyright explained.
www.templetons.com/brad/copymyths.html

The Copyright Web Site:
This site endeavors to provide real-world, practical and relevant copyright information of interest to infonauts, netsurfers, webmasters, content providers, musicians, appropriationists, activists, infringers, outlaws and law-abiding citizens.
www.benedict.com

Benjamin Gitlow
His appeal resulted in a ban on state laws that restrict free expression.

Jay Near
His appeal resulted in a strong ruling against government prior restraint on expression.

Howard Guilford
Colleague of Jay Near in producing the *Saturday Press.*

Robert McCormick
Chicago *Tribune* publisher who supported *Near* v. *Minnesota* appeal.

American Civil Liberties Union
Backed *Near* v. *Minnesota.*

NEW YORK, SUNDAY, JUNE 13, 1971   75¢ beyond 50-mile zone from New York City, except Long Island. Higher in air delivery cities.   BQLI   50 CENTS

Vietnam Archive: Pentagon Study Traces 3 Decades of Growing U. S. Involvement

By NEIL SHEEHAN

A massive study of how the United States went to war in Indochina, conducted by the Pentagon three years ago, demonstrates that four administrations progressively developed a sense of commitment to a non-Communist Vietnam, a readiness to fight the North to protect the South, and an ultimate frustration with this effort—to a much greater extent than their public statements acknowledged at the time.

The 3,000-page analysis, to which 4,000 pages of official documents are appended, was commissioned by Secretary of Defense Robert S. McNamara and covers the American involvement in Southeast Asia from World War II to mid-1968—the start of the peace talks in Paris after President Lyndon B. Johnson had set a limit on further military commitments and revealed his intention to retire. Most of the study and many of the appended documents have been obtained by The New York Times and will be described and presented in a series of articles beginning today.

Three pages of documentary material from the Pentagon study begin on Page 35.

Though far from a complete history, even at 2.5 million words, the study forms a great archive of government decision-making on Indochina over three decades. The study led its 30 to 40 authors and researchers to many broad conclusions and specific findings, including the following:

¶That the Truman Administration's decision to give military aid to France in her colonial war against the Communist-led Vietminh "directly involved" the United States in Vietnam and "set" the course of American policy.

¶That the Eisenhower Administration's decision to rescue a fledgling South Vietnam from a Communist takeover and attempt to undermine the new Communist regime of North Vietnam gave the Administration a "direct role in the ultimate breakdown of the Geneva settlement" for Indochina in 1954.

¶That the Kennedy Administration, though ultimately spared from major escalation decisions by the death of its leader, transformed a policy of "limited-risk gamble," which it inherited, into a "broad commitment" that left President Johnson with a choice between more war and withdrawal.

¶That the Johnson Administration, though the President was reluctant and hesitant to take the final decisions, intensified the covert warfare against North Vietnam and began planning in the spring of 1964 to wage overt war, a full year before it publicly revealed the depth of its involvement and its fear of defeat.

¶That this campaign of growing clandestine military pressure through 1964 and the expanding program of bombing North Vietnam in 1965 were begun despite the judgment of the Government's intelligence community that the measures would not cause Hanoi to cease its support of the Vietcong insurgency in the South, and that the bombing was **Continued on Page 38, Col. 1**

U.S. URGES INDIANS AND PAKISTANIS TO USE RESTRAINT

Calls for 'Peaceful Political Accommodation' to End Crisis in East Pakistan

FIRST   PUBLIC   APPEAL

Statement Is Said to Reflect Fear of Warfare if Flow of Refugees Continues

By TAD SZULC
Special to The New York Times

WASHINGTON, June 12—The United States appealed today to India and Pakistan to exercise restraint and urged the Pakistanis to restore normal conditions in East Pakistan through "peaceful political accommodation."

It was the first public statement by the United States on the situation in the subcontinent

NIXON CRITICIZED | Vast Review of War Took a Year

Daniel Ellsberg

Neil Sheehan

Pentagon Papers Story. In 1971, when the New York *Times* began running a detailed series on the blundering U.S. policy on Vietnam over a quarter of a century, the federal government ordered the newspaper to stop. Because the series was based on secret documents, taken illegally from the Pentagon by researcher Daniel Ellsberg, the government claimed that national security would be jeopardized by the appearance of additional installments. The *Times* appealed, and the U.S. Supreme Court concluded that freedom of the press outweighed the government's concern.

saw another issue. In their thinking, the First Amendment protected all expression from government interference, no matter how obnoxious. They also were bothered that government, in this case the county prosecutor, was the determiner of what was obnoxious.

Three and one-half years after the *Saturday Press* was silenced, the U.S. Supreme Court, in a 5-to-4 decision, threw out the Minnesota law. The Court ruled that **prior restraint,** prohibiting expression before it is made, was disallowed under the U.S. Constitution. Said Chief Justice **Charles Evans Hughes,** "The fact that the liberty of the press may be abused by miscreant purveyors of scandal does not make any less the immunity of the press from previous restraint in dealing with official misconduct."

The decision was a landmark limitation on governmental censorship, although the Court noted, as it always does in such cases, that protection for the press "is not absolutely unlimited." The Court has always noted that it can conceive of circumstances, such as a national emergency, when prior restraint might be justified.

National Security

The U.S. Supreme Court, which is the ultimate interpreter on constitutional questions, has been consistent that government has a censorship right when national security is at stake. This position was underscored in the **Pentagon Papers** case. A government contract researcher, **Daniel Ellsberg,** spent several years with a team preparing an internal Pentagon study on U.S. policy in Vietnam. In 1971, at the height of the war, Ellsberg

prior restraint
Prohibiting expression in advance.

Charles Evans Hughes
Chief justice who wrote the decision in *Near* v. *Minnesota.*

Pentagon Papers
Case in which government attempted prior restraint against New York *Times.*

Daniel Ellsberg
Leaked Pentagon documents on Vietnam war to New York *Times.*

Jay Near

Jay Near and Howard Guilford, who started a scandal sheet in Minneapolis in 1927, did not have far to look for stories on corruption. Prohibition was in effect, and Minneapolis, because of geography, was a key U.S. distribution point for bootleg Canadian whiskey going south to Chicago, St. Louis and other cities. A former county prosecutor was knee-deep in the illicit whiskey trade. Mose Barnett, the leading local gangster, never needed an appointment with the police chief. He could walk into the chief's office any time. The mayor was on the take. A standard joke was that city hall had been moved to McCormick's Cafe, notorious for its payoff activity. Gambling, prostitution and booze palaces flourished in blatant violation of the law. Mobsters extorted protection payments from local merchants. Contract murder went for $500, on slow days $200.

Hearing about the kind of newspaper that Near and Guilford had in mind, the crooked police chief, aware of his own vulnerability, told his men to yank every copy off the newsstands as soon as they appeared. The *Saturday Press* thus became the first U.S. newspaper banned even before a single issue had been published.

The confrontation between the corrupt Minneapolis establishment and the Near-Guilford scandal-mongering team worsened. One afternoon a few days after the first issue was published, gunmen pulled up beside Guilford's car at an intersection and fired four bullets at him, one into his abdomen. Not even that silenced the *Saturday Press*. While Guilford lay critically wounded in the hospital, Near stepped up their crusade, pointing out that mob kingpin Mose Barnett had threatened Guilford before the attack. Near also

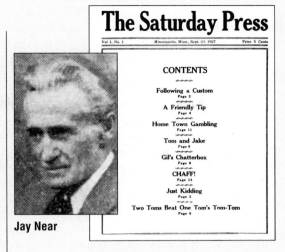

Jay Near

The Saturday Press

Vol 1, No. 1   Minneapolis, Minn., Sept. 21, 1927   Price 5 Cents

CONTENTS

Following a Custom
Page 2

A Friendly Tip
Page 4

Home Town Gambling
Page 11

Tom and Jake
Page 8

Gil's Chatterbox
Page 9

CHAFF!
Page 13

Just Kidding
Page 3

Two Toms Beat One Tom's Tom-Tom
Page 6

1927 Scandal Sheet. Page One of Jay Near and Howard Guilford's inaugural issue looked bland enough, but inside were stories that infuriated officials. The officials eventually declared the *Saturday Press* a public nuisance and shut it down to head off further incriminating coverage of local corruption. In the landmark court case that resulted, *Near* v. *Minnesota*, the U.S. Supreme Court ruled that such prior restraint was unconstitutional.

went after Barnett for ordering thugs to terrorize an immigrant launderer who had bought his own dry cleaning equipment rather than send his customers' laundry to a mob-controlled plant. Near's other targets included the mayor, the police chief, the head of the law enforcement league, the grand jury and the county prosecutor.

Two months after the first issue of the *Saturday Press*, Floyd Olson, the prosecutor, was fed up, and he went to court and obtained an order to ban Near and Guilford from producing any more issues. Olson based his case on a 1925 Minnesota gag law that declared that "a malicious, scandalous and defamatory newspaper" could be banned as a public nuisance.

Despite their crusading for good causes, Near and Guilford's brand of journalism was hard to like. Both were bigots who peppered their writing with references to "niggers," "yids," "bohunks" and "spades." Could they get away with saying such things in print?

The U.S. Supreme Court said "yes" in a landmark decision known as *Near* v. *Minnesota*. The court said that no government at any level has the right to suppress a publication because of what it might say in its next issue. Except in highly exceptional circumstances, such as life-and-death issues in wartime, legal action against a publication can come only after something has been published.

After the ruling, Near resumed the *Saturday Press* and Guilford rejoined the enterprise. The paper floundered commercially, however, and Guilford quit. In 1934 Guilford announced his candidacy for mayor and promised to campaign against the underworld. Before campaigning got started, gangsters crowded Guilford's car to the curb and fired a shotgun into his head.

Two years later, Near, age 62, died of natural causes. The local obituary didn't even mention *Near* v. *Minnesota*, despite its being one of the most important court decisions in U.S. media history.

media online

Pentagon Papers:
"The Day the Presses Stopped" is the Washington *Post* version of the Pentagon Papers case.
http://washingtonpost.com/
wp-srv/style/longterm/books/
chap1/daythepr.htm

decided that the public should have an inside look at Pentagon decision-making. He secretly photocopied the whole 47-volume study, even though it was stamped "top secret," and handed it over to New York *Times* reporter Neil Sheehan. After several weeks the *Times* began a front-page series drawn from the Pentagon Papers. Saying that the study could hurt national security, but also knowing that it could embarrass the government, the Nixon administration ordered the *Times* to stop the series.

The *Times* objected that the government was attempting prior restraint but agreed to suspend the series while it appealed the government order. Meanwhile, the Washington *Post* somehow obtained a second copy of the Pentagon Papers and began its own series, to which the government also objected. Before the U.S. Supreme Court, the government argument that national security was at stake proved weak, and the *Times* and the *Post* resumed their series. So did dozens of other newspapers, and the Pentagon Papers eventually were published in their entirety and sold at bookstores throughout the land.

Despite the journalistic victory in the Pentagon Papers case, the Court said that it could conceive of circumstances in which the national security could override the First Amendment guarantees against prior restraint. In earlier cases, justices had said that the government would be on solid ground in restraining reports on troop movements and other military activities in wartime if the reports constituted "a clear and present danger."

Military Operations

At times the United States has employed battlefield censorship, requiring correspondents to submit their copy for review before transmission. This practice was discarded by the time of the Vietnam war, but it appeared in a variant form in 1983 when the Reagan administration ordered troops to the Caribbean island of Grenada. The Pentagon, which controlled all transportation to the battle area, refused to take reporters along. A few print reporters rented yachts and airplanes and made it through a naval barricade, but photographers and television crews, their equipment giving away their identity as journalists, were turned back.

Journalists objected strenuously to the Grenada news blackout. As a result, the Pentagon agreed to include a few **pool reporters** in future military actions. These reporters' stories then would be made available to other news organizations. The pool system was used in the 1989 invasion of Panama, but the military manipulated the arrangement. Reporters were confined to a windowless briefing room at a U.S. Army post and given history lessons on U.S.-Panama relations, not current information on what was happening. Overall, the pool arrangement suited the military, not the media.

Most journalists were skeptical of the military's argument that it needed to control reporters to keep information on its activities from the enemy. Journalists said the true motive was to prevent honest and truthful reporting that might undermine public support at home for the military intervention. This skepticism proved well founded in 1991 when the Pentagon went to extraordinary lengths to shape field reporting from the Persian Gulf war. These were the main Pentagon tactics, none involving explicit censorship but being nonetheless effective in shaping news coverage:

pool reporters
News media-selected reporters who share stories, photos with others.

- The military arranged reporter pools for some coverage, which facilitated showing reporters what the military wanted seen.
- The military placed vast areas off limits to reporters with a variety of explanations, including sensitivity to the policies of host nations such as Saudi Arabia.

Media Timeline

Landmarks in Media Law

1791 States ratified the First Amendment, the free expression section of U.S. Constitution.

1901 Iowa Supreme Court ruled performers must accept criticism of performances.

1919 Justice Oliver Wendell Holmes coined the "fire!" in a crowded theater example for prior restraint.

1927 Congress created an agency to regulate radio.

1930 Court overruled the import ban on *Ulysses.*

1931 U.S. Supreme Court banned prior restraint in *Near* v. *Minnesota.*

1952 U.S. Supreme Court accorded First Amendment protection to movies.

1964 U.S. Supreme Court ruled that public figures can sue for libel only if the media were reckless.

1966 U.S. Supreme Court ruled that courts, not media, are responsible for ensuring fair trials.

1966 Congress passed the Freedom of Information Act.

1968 U.S. Supreme Court ruled local community standards determine obscenity.

1971 U.S. Supreme Court banned prior restraint in *New York Times* v. *United States* national security case.

1972 U.S. Supreme Court ruled journalists can be compelled to name confidential sources.

1980s Reagan administration's deregulation of business, including mass media, began.

- Pentagon public relations people overwhelmed reporters with carefully structured news briefings and news conferences with top brass and provided so much data, including spectacular video, that reporters had scant time left for pursuing alternative perspectives.

"Fire!" in a Crowded Theater

Prior restraint has been justified in situations other than national security. Supreme Court Justice **Oliver Wendell Holmes** wrote in a 1919 case, "The most stringent protection of free speech would not protect a man in falsely shouting 'fire' in a theater and causing panic." In other words, the government would be justified in stopping the man. The problem, however, is for government agents to draw the line between speech that must be banned and letting go all the rest. To help, Holmes developed what he called the **clear and present danger** test. Using this test, the courts place a heavy burden on the government to demonstrate that the expression would have caused so serious an effect that prior restraint was justified. Yes or no, was there a clear and present danger?

It is a judgment call whether an anticipated negative effect warrants suppression, but the Court has rendered decisions that give some sense of when prior restraint is justified. In one case the Supreme Court upheld the conviction of Philadelphia Socialist **Charles Schenck,** who published 15,000 leaflets during World War I that described that war as a Wall Street scheme and that encouraged young men to defy their draft orders. Although Schenck's case did not involve prior restraint, the Court's line of reasoning included a guideline on when restraint may be permissible. The Court declined to say that Schenck's leaflets constituted a clear and present danger, but it ruled that they were unacceptable in a time of war. This was called the **bad tendency test,** which could be applied in times of domestic unrest and riot.

Oliver Wendell Holmes
Justice who wrote "Fire!" in crowded theater justification for prior restraint.

clear and present danger test
A long-lived justification for government prior restraint.

Charles Schenck
His appeal resulted in the first articulation of clear and present danger.

bad tendency test
An early justification for government prior restraint.

Media Abroad

Press Law in Britain

When a professional soccer player in Aberdeen, Scotland, was charged with indecent exposure, the Scottish *Daily Record* ran his picture the next morning. Under British law it was a mistake. The British mass media are prohibited from publishing anything that might prejudice a criminal defendant's right to trial by an impartial jury. For running the picture, the court held the *Record* in contempt of court and said somebody should go to jail, but because the supervising editor was at home sick when the decision was made, there was only a $21,000 fine against the paper and a $1,400 fine against the assistant editor.

Such government action against the mass media would be unthinkable in the United States, but it demonstrates how another country with many of the same traditions has developed a vastly different approach to media law. Consider the following aspects of British restrictions on news reporting:

- Crimes may be reported, but the names of suspected persons, even when they have been charged, may be used only if the police request or authorize the use of the name.
- If the government learns that a story defaming the royal family is in the works, it may enjoin the publication or broadcast organization from going ahead.
- The government may seek an injunction to stop stories it suspects will damage national security—even before they are published or aired.

The bad tendency and the clear and present danger tests are closely related, but there is a distinction. It is harder for the government to make a convincing case that an article or utterance represents a clear and present danger than it is to argue that there is merely a bad tendency. Over the years since the Schenck case, the courts generally have insisted that the government be held to the stiffer clear and present danger test, and the bad tendency rationale is hardly ever considered in prior-restraint cases anymore. Today, the right to free expression has very few exceptions.

Slander and Mass Media

STUDY PREVIEW   When the mass media carry disparaging descriptions and comments, they risk being sued for libel. The media have a strong defense if the libel was accurate. If not, there can be big trouble. Libel is a serious matter. Not only are reputations at stake when defamation occurs but also losing a suit can be so costly that it can put a publication or broadcast organization out of business.

Concept of Libel Law

If someone punched you in the face for no good reason, knocking out several teeth, breaking your nose and causing permanent disfigurement, most courts would rule that your attacker should pay your medical bills. If your disfigurement or psychological upset causes you to lose your job, to be ridiculed or shunned by friends and family or perhaps to retreat from social interaction, the court would probably order your attacker to pay additional amounts. Like fists, words can cause damage. If someone writes false, damaging things about you, you can sue for **libel**. Freedom of speech and the press is not a license to say absolutely anything about anybody.

libel
A written defamation.

Media People

Oprah Winfrey

The crowd outside the federal courthouse in Amarillo, Texas, waited expectantly for the jury's verdict. When the doors opened, a confident and beaming Oprah Winfrey walked out, thrusting her fists upward and outward to signal a triumphant "Yes!" The country's number one talk show host had just won an important legal victory.

"Free speech not only lives, it rocks!" Winfrey told the cheering well-wishers that February morning in 1998. She vowed never again to take free speech for granted. And she would not stop speaking out. "I come from a people who struggled and died to use their voice in this country, and I refuse to be muzzled," she said.

For nearly six weeks, she had sat as a defendant in a lawsuit over a segment on mad cow disease on her nationally syndicated television show. When cattle prices plummeted shortly after the program aired, a group of cattle ranchers blamed Winfrey for their financial losses and sued.

Winfrey told the court that her programs are designed to "inform, enlighten, uplift and entertain" through a discussion format. For a feature on food safety, it seemed appropriate to discuss mad cow disease, which had taken several lives in Britain.

The major factor in the suit was a Texas law that holds a person liable for falsely disparaging perishable agricultural products.

Product Disparagement. Agricultural lobbyists succeeded in several states in the 1990s with laws against product disparagement. In a showdown on the viability of these laws, Texas cattle ranchers sued talk-show host Oprah Winfrey for telling her audience she would never eat another burger because some cattle are fed ground-up bovine renderings. In the so-called Oprah Crash that followed, cattle prices plummeted. The jury found for Winfrey, a setback for the product-disparagement strain of libel law.

While proponents of such laws say that they are necessary to protect farmers' and ranchers' livelihoods, opponents say that they stifle free speech by intimidating, squelching debates and impeding investigations that help to ensure food safety. Winfrey's attorney said that whereas he once thought veggie libel laws silly, he now considers them scary.

The Winfrey trial was expected to test the constitutionality of such laws. It did not. Rather, the judge ruled that the suit did not fit the perishable agricultural products disparagement law (cattle, as live cattle, are not perishable products). Instead, the suit had to proceed under conventional business defamation law in which plaintiffs must prove malice and the deliberate spreading of falsehoods about a plaintiff's business. The jury could not be convinced that this had occurred.

During the trial Winfrey voiced her firm belief in the First Amendment. At one point she remarked that just as the cattle ranchers didn't like some of her comments, she hasn't liked many of the things people have said about her. "But this is America," she said. "People are allowed to say things about you that you don't like."

If a libeling statement is false, the utterer may be liable for millions of dollars in damages. This is serious for the mass media. When the *Saturday Evening Post* reported that Alabama football coach Bear Bryant and Georgia athletic director Wally Butts had fixed a game, Butts sued. The magazine lost the case, and it was ordered to pay $6 million in damages. Although the amount was eventually reduced, the judgment contributed to the demise of the magazine. When a former Miss Wyoming felt embarrassed by a fictional article in *Penthouse* magazine, she was awarded $26.5 million even though she was not even named in the article. The verdict was set aside on appeal, but there was concern for a time about the magazine's well-being. A $9.2 million judgment against the Alton, Illinois, *Telegraph* forced the newspaper to file for bankruptcy protection.

The largest jury award to date, in 1997 against the *Wall Street Journal,* was almost twice the earnings that year of the *Journal*'s parent company, Dow Jones Inc. The award was reduced substantially on appeal, but the fact remains that awards have grown dramatically in recent years and can hurt a media company seriously.

Sullivan Case

Elected officials have a hard time winning libel suits today. Noting that democracy is best served by robust, unbridled discussion of public issues and that public officials are inseparable from public policy, the U.S. Supreme Court has ruled that public figures can win libel suits only in extreme circumstances. The Court has also said that people who foist themselves into the limelight forfeit some of the protection available to other citizens.

The key court decision in developing current U.S. libel standards originated in an advertisement carried by the New York *Times* in 1960. A civil rights coalition, the Committee to Defend Martin Luther King and the Struggle for Freedom in the South, escalated its antisegregationist cause by placing a full-page advertisement in the *Times*. The advertisement accused public officials in the South of violence and illegal tactics against the civil rights struggle. Although the advertisement was by and large truthful, it was marred by minor factual errors. Police Commissioner L. B. Sullivan of Montgomery, Alabama, filed a libel action saying that the errors damaged him, and he won $500,000 in an Alabama trial. On appeal to the U.S. Supreme Court, the case, *New York Times* v. *Sullivan,* became a landmark in libel law. The Supreme Court said that the importance of "free debate" in a democratic society generally was more important than factual errors that might upset and damage public officials. To win a libel suit, the Court said, public officials needed to prove that damaging statements were uttered or printed with the knowledge that they were false. The question in the *Sullivan* case became whether the *Times* was guilty of "**reckless disregard** of the truth." The Supreme Court said it was not, and the newspaper won.

Questions lingered after the *Sullivan* decision about exactly who was and who was not a public official. The courts struggled for definition, and the Supreme Court eventually changed the term to *public figure*. In later years, as the Court refined its view on issues raised in the *Sullivan* case through several decisions, it remained consistent in giving the mass media a lot of room for error, even damaging error, in discussing government officials, political candidates and publicity hounds.

- **Government officials.** All elected government officials and appointed officials with high-level policy responsibilities are public figures as far as their performance in office is concerned. A member of a state governor's cabinet fits this category. A cafeteria worker in the state capitol does not.
- **Political candidates.** Anyone seeking public office is subject to intense public review, during which the courts are willing to excuse false statements as part of robust, wide-open discussion.

New York Times* v. *Sullivan
Libel case that largely barred public figures from the right to sue for libel.

reckless disregard
Supreme Court language for a situation in which public figures may sue for libel.

■ **Publicity hounds.** Court decisions have gone both ways, but generally people who seek publicity or intentionally draw attention to themselves must prove "reckless disregard of the truth" if they sue for libel.

How far can the media go in making disparaging comments? It was all right, said a Vermont court, when the Barre *Times Argus* ran an editorial that said a political candidate was "a horse's ass, a jerk, an idiot and a paranoid." The court said open discussion on public issues excused even such insulting, abusive and unpleasant verbiage. Courts have generally been more tolerant of excessive language in opinion pieces, such as the Barre editorial, than in fact-based articles.

Fair Comment and Criticism

People flocked to see the **Cherry Sisters'** act. Effie, Addie, Jessie, Lizzie and Ella toured the country with a song and dance act that drew big crowds. They were just awful. They could neither sing nor dance, but people turned out because the sisters were so funny. Sad to say, the Cherry Sisters took themselves seriously. In 1901, desperate for respect, they decided to sue the next newspaper reviewer who gave them a bad notice. That reviewer, it turned out, was Billy Hamilton, who included a lot of equine metaphors in his piece for the Des Moines *Leader:* "Effie is an old jade of 50 summers, Jessie a frisky filly of 40, and Addie, the flower of the family, a capering monstrosity of 35. Their long skinny arms, equipped with talons at the extremities, swung mechanically, and anon waved frantically at the suffering audience. The mouths of their rancid features opened like caverns, and sounds like the wailings of damned souls issued therefrom. They pranced around the stage with a motion that suggested a cross between the *danse du ventre* and the fox trot—strange creatures with painted faces and hideous mien. Effie is spavined, Addie is stringhalt, and Jessie, the only one who showed her stockings, has legs with calves as classic in their outlines as the curves of a broom handle."

Cherry Sisters
Complainants in a case that barred performers from suing critics.

Fair Comment and Criticism. Upset with what an Iowa reviewer wrote about their show, the Cherry Sisters sued. The important 1901 court decision that resulted said that journalists, critics and anybody else can say whatever they want about a public performance. The rationale was that someone who puts on a performance for public acceptance has to take a risk also of public rejection.

The outcome of the suit was another setback for the Cherrys. They lost in a case that established that actors or others who perform for the public must be willing to accept both positive and negative comments about their performance. This right of **fair comment and criticism,** however, does not make it open season on performers in aspects of their lives that do not relate to public performance. The *National Enquirer* could not defend itself when entertainer Carol Burnett sued for a story that described her as obnoxiously drunk at a restaurant. Not only was the description false (Carol Burnett abstains from alcohol), but Burnett was in no public or performing role at the restaurant. This distinction between an individual's public and private life also has been recognized in cases involving public officials and candidates.

Trespass, Fraud and Libel

An emerging legal tactic against the news media for disparaging coverage is not libel but trespass and other laws. In 1998 the Utah Restaurant Association sued television station KTVX for a report on roaches in restaurant kitchens and unsanitary food handling and storage. Wesley Sine, attorney for the restaurants, did not sue for libel. Sine argued instead that it was illegal to go into a private area, like a kitchen, without permission.

Such end-runs around libel law worry media people. The defenses that usually work in libel cases are hard to apply if the media are sued over disparaging reports on grounds other than libel. This was a factor in a case involving the Food Lion supermarket chain that resulted in a $5.5 million jury verdict against ABC television. Food Lion was riled over a 1992 report on rats and spoilage in store backrooms as well as unfair labor practices. In its suit Food Lion never challenged ABC's accuracy. Rather, Food Lion said, among other things, that ABC had committed fraud by sending undercover reporters to get on the Food Lion payroll to investigate the backrooms. On appeal, the damages against ABC were reduced almost to zero—a moral victory, but it took seven years and lots of expensive lawyers.

Privacy Law

STUDY PREVIEW   The idea that people have a right to limit intrusions on their privacy has been taking form in U.S. law through much of this century. In general, permission is not required in news coverage, although the courts have been consistent in saying that there are limits on how far news reporters can go with their cameras and in writing about personal information.

Intruding on Solitude

fair comment and criticism
Doctrine that permits criticism of performers, performances.

privacy law
Recognizes a right to be left alone.

Dorothy Barber
Successfully sued when photos of her in the hospital were published.

Using **privacy law,** the courts have recognized a person's right to solitude and have punished overzealous news reporters who tap telephone lines, plant hidden microphones, use telephoto lenses and break into homes and offices for stories. In general, reporters are free to pursue stories in public places and, when invited, in private places. Sometimes the courts have had to draw the line between public and private places. Here are some examples:

- **A hospital room. Dorothy Barber** entered a Kansas City hospital with a metabolic disorder. No matter how much she ate, she lost weight. One day, two news-

Media Abroad

Mailing-List Privacy

Magazines and mail-order companies in the United States reap residual income by selling lists of their customers, including addresses, phone numbers and other data. In Europe, however, privacy laws strictly forbid transferring such information. With the coming globalization of customer databases, the European Community is pressuring the United States to make its laws conform to the European restrictions.

At the heart of the European law is a provision that data can be collected only for specific, explicit and legitimate purposes and then may not be passed on for any reason inconsistent with the original purpose.

Also, data that are kept for reuse must be kept up to date and purged when the original purpose no longer exists.

paper reporters, one with a camera, paid Barber a visit for a story and took a picture without permission. United Press International distributed the photograph, showing Dorothy Barber in her hospital bed, and *Time* magazine ran the picture. The caption read: "The starving glutton." Barber sued *Time* and won. The court said that reporters have a right to pursue people in public places, but the right of privacy protects a person in bed for treatment and recuperation.

- **Inside a private business.** A Seattle television photographer wanted to videotape a pharmacist charged with Medicaid fraud, but the man would not cooperate. The photographer then set himself on the sidewalk outside the pharmacy and filmed the pharmacist through a front window. The pharmacist sued, charging the television station with photographic eavesdropping, but the court dismissed the suit, ruling that the photographer recorded only what any passerby was free to see. The outcome would have been different had the photographer gone into the shop, a private place, and taped the same scene without permission.

- **Expectation of privacy.** Some intrusion cases have hinged on whether the person being reported on had "a reasonable expectation of privacy." Someone lounging nude at a fenced-in backyard pool would have a strong case against a photographer who climbed a steep, seldom-scaled cliff with a telephoto lens for a picture. A similar case can be made against hidden cameras and microphones.

Harassment

By being in a public place, a person surrenders most privacy protections, but this does not mean that journalists have a right to hound people mercilessly. **Ron Galella,** a freelance celebrity photographer, learned this lesson—or should have—in two lawsuits filed by **Jacqueline Kennedy Onassis.** Galella stalked the former First Lady, darting and jumping and grunting at her to catch off-guard facial expressions that would make interesting photographs that he could sell to magazines and photo archives. Mrs. Onassis became Galella's specialty, but he also was building a photo file on the Kennedy children. Galella broke Mrs. Onassis' patience in 1973 when he frightened a horse ridden by young John Kennedy and the horse bolted. John Kennedy escaped serious injury, but Mrs. Onassis asked her Secret Service protection detail to intervene to prevent Galella from endangering her children. Not long thereafter, the

Ron Galella
Celebrity photographer.

Jacqueline Kennedy Onassis
Successfully barred a photographer from hounding her children, herself.

media online

News Media and the Law: Legal scholar Michael Sherer's articles from *News Photographer* magazine with a focus on photojournalism issues are online through this site.

www.nppa.org/services/reports/legacy

guards and Galella got into a tussle. Galella filed a $1.3 million suit, claiming that he had been roughed up and that the guards were interfering with his right to earn a livelihood. He also claimed that his First Amendment rights were being violated. Mrs. Onassis responded with a $1.5 million suit, asking for an injunction to halt Galella.

A federal judge acknowledged that Galella could photograph whomever he wanted in public places and write stories about them but that the First Amendment could not justify incessant pursuits that "went far beyond the reasonable bounds of news gathering." The judge said that harassment was impermissible, and he ordered Galella to stay 300 feet from the Onassis and Kennedy homes and the schools of the Kennedy children, 225 feet from the children in public places, and 150 feet from Mrs. Onassis.

Nine years later, Mrs. Onassis returned to court to object to Galella's overzealous journalistic techniques. He was found in contempt of court for violating the 1973 order on 12 separate occasions. The Onassis-Galella issue was a further recognition that a **right to be left alone** exists among other constitutional rights, including the right of a free press.

Journalism Law

STUDY PREVIEW   The Constitution gives journalists great liberty in covering trials, seeking access to information held by the government and even in withholding confidential information from the government.

Court Coverage

News media have great liberty under the First Amendment to cover events as they see fit. Such was the case with **Sam Sheppard,** a Cleveland osteopath who was convicted of murder amid a media circus. Even when he was acquitted after 12 years in prison, it was too late for him. He was unable to reestablish his medical practice. He died, a ruined man, a few years later.

A free press does not come without cost, and some people, like Sheppard, end up paying dearly. It is from such cases, however, that we learn the implications of the First Amendment and how to sidestep some of the problems it creates. When the U.S. Supreme Court ordered a new trial for Sheppard in 1966, it declared that it is the responsibility of the courts to assure citizens a fair trial regardless of media irresponsibility. The justices were specific about what the judge presiding at Sheppard's trial could have done. Among options:

- Seat only jurors who have not formed prejudicial conclusions.
- Move the trial to another city not so contaminated by news coverage.
- Delay the trial until publicity has subsided.
- Put jurors under 24-hour supervision so they will not have access to newspapers and newscasts during the trial.
- Insist that reporters respect appropriate courtroom decorum.
- Order attorneys, litigants and witnesses not to talk with reporters.
- Issue gag orders against the media but only in "extraordinary circumstances."

In other cases the U.S. Supreme Court has allowed actions against the media to preclude unfavorable, prejudicial coverage of hearings, but those involve unusual

right to be left alone
Principle underlying most privacy cases and law.

Sam Sheppard Case
Plaintiff in a case in which judges were told that they, not the news media, are responsible for a fair trial.

circumstances. In the main, the news media have First Amendment-guaranteed access to the courts and the freedom to cover court stories regardless of whether the courts are pleased with the coverage. The same applies to news coverage of government in general.

Sunshine Laws

Implicit in any democracy is that public policy is developed in open sessions where the people can follow their elected and appointed leaders as they discuss issues. Every state has an open meeting law that specifically declares that legislative units, including state boards and commissions, city councils, school boards and county governing bodies, be open to the public, including journalists. The idea is for public policy to be created and executed in the bright sunshine, not in the secrecy of back rooms. For this reason laws such as open meeting laws are often called **sunshine laws.**

Open meeting laws vary. Some insist that almost every session be open. Others are not nearly as strict with the state legislatures that created them as they are with city, county and school units and with state executive agencies. Some of these laws proclaim the virtues of openness but lack teeth to enforce openness. In contrast, some states specify heavy fines and jail terms for public officials who shut the doors. Here are provisions of strong open meeting laws:

- Legislative units are required to meet at regular times and places and to announce their agendas ahead of time.
- Citizens can insist on quick judicial review if a meeting is closed.
- Closed sessions are allowed for only a few reasons, which are specifically identified, such as discussion on sensitive personnel matters, collective bargaining strategy and security arrangements.
- Any vote in a closed session must be announced immediately afterward.
- Decisions made at a closed meeting are nullified if the meeting is later declared to have been closed illegally.
- Penalties are specified for any official who illegally authorizes a closed meeting.

Besides open meeting laws, the federal and state governments have open record laws to ensure public access to government documents. These laws are important to journalists in tracking policy decisions and actions that they could not cover personally. Journalists especially value documents because, unlike human sources, documents do not change their stories.

The federal **Freedom of Information Act** was passed in 1966, specifying how people could request documents. Since 1974 federal agencies have been required to list all their documents to help people identify what documents they are seeking and help the agencies locate them quickly. Despite penalties for noncompliance, some agencies sometimes drag their feet and stretch the FOI Act's provisions to keep sensitive documents off-limits. Even so, the law was a landmark of legislative commitment to governmental openness that allowed only a few exceptions. Among those exceptions are:

- Documents classified to protect national security.
- Trade secrets and internal corporate information obtained on a confidential basis by the government.
- Preliminary drafts of agency documents and working papers.

sunshine laws
Require government meetings, documents be open.

Freedom of Information Act
Requires many federal documents to be available to public.

Media Abroad

Jamaica: Document Access

Jamaican institutions were patterned after the British model when the Caribbean island won independence in 1962. Consistent with democratic principles, citizens have access to government documents, albeit with a few exceptions.

A proposed revision of the national law on access to documents would require two kinds of private organizations to make their documents available to inquiring citizens, and, of course, to the news media:

- Companies that perform critical public services
- Companies that hold an economic monopoly

If approved, the new provisions would put Jamaica in the forefront of legally guaranteed public access. Some provisions of the proposal, however, are less open. Closed would be records that the government deems could damage the country's economy. Off limits too would be records that the government believes could be defamatory. Records older than seven years could be closed too.

- Medical and personnel files for which confidentiality is necessary to protect individual privacy.
- Police files that, if disclosed, might jeopardize an investigation by tipping off guilty people or, worse, falsely incriminating innocent people.

Confidential Sources

One unresolved conflict between government and the news media involves confidential sources. There are important stories, although not many, that would never be written if reporters were required to divulge their sources. In 1969, at a time of racial unrest in the United States, **Earl Caldwell** of the New York *Times* spent 14 months cultivating sources within the Black Panthers organization and produced a series of insightful stories on black activism. A federal grand jury in San Francisco, where Caldwell was assigned, was investigating bombings and other violence blamed on the Black Panthers, and Caldwell's stories caught the jury's attention, especially quotations attributed to unnamed Black Panther leaders, such as "We advocate the direct overthrow of the government by ways of force and violence." The grand jury asked to see Caldwell's notebooks, tapes and anything else that could help its investigation. Caldwell defied the subpoena, saying his appearance before the grand jury would interfere with his relationship with his sources. Furthermore, he had promised these sources that he would not identify them. Journalists watching the showdown were mindful of the historical responsibility of the press as an independent watchdog on government. If Caldwell testified, he in effect would become part of the investigative arm of the government. Tension mounted when a federal judge supported the grand jury, noting that all citizens are required to cooperate with criminal investigations and that journalists are no different.

A federal appeals judge ruled, however, that "the public's First Amendment right to be informed would be jeopardized by requiring a journalist to submit to secret grand jury interrogation." The government, said the judge, could command a journalist to testify only if it demonstrated "a compelling need." Meanwhile, journalists were running the risk of going to jail for contempt of court for refusing to respond to government subpoenas for their testimony, notes and films. In 1972 the U.S.

Earl Caldwell
Refused to reveal confidential news sources.

Supreme Court considered the issue and ruled that journalists "are not exempt from the normal duty of all citizens."

After that Supreme Court decision, several states adopted **shield laws,** which reorganized reporter-source confidentiality. A problem with shield laws is that they require government to define who is a journalist. This raises the specter of the government's deciding who is and who is not a journalist, which smacks of authoritarian press control. As an example, the Ohio shield law protects "bona fide journalists," who are defined as people employed by or connected to newspapers, radio stations, television stations and news services. Not only is it disturbing when government defines who is a journalist in a free society, but such attempts are destined to fail. The Ohio definition, for example, fails to protect freelance journalists and writers who do their work on their own in the hope that they will eventually sell it.

Defying a Subpoena. New York *Times* reporter Earl Caldwell faced jail for defying court orders to reveal the sources of his 1970 articles about urban terrorism. Caldwell argued that he had obtained his information on a confidential basis and that he would not break the covenant he had made with his sources. Others argued that journalists, like all citizens, have an obligation to tell all they know to officials who are investigating criminal activity.

Obscenity and Pornography

STUDY PREVIEW Despite the First Amendment's guarantee of free expression, the U.S. government has tried numerous ways during this century to regulate obscenity and pornography.

Import Restrictions

A 1930 tariff law was used as an import restriction to intercept James Joyce's *Ulysses* at the docks because of four-letter words and explicit sexual references. The importer, **Random House,** went to court, and the judge ruled that the government was out of line. The judge, **John Woolsey,** acknowledged "unusual frankness" in *Ulysses* but said he could not "detect anywhere the leer of the sensualist." The judge, who was not without humor, made a strong case for freedom in literary expression: "The words which are criticized as dirty are old Saxon words known to almost all men, and, I venture, to many women, and are such words as would be naturally and habitually used, I believe, by the types of folks whose life, physical and mental, Joyce is seeking to describe. In respect to the recurrent emergence of the theme of sex in the minds of the characters, it must always be remembered that his locale was Celtic and his season Spring."

Woolsey was upheld on appeal, and *Ulysses*, still critically acclaimed as a pioneer in stream-of-consciousness writing, remains in print today.

Postal Restrictions

Postal restrictions were used against a 1928 English novel, *Lady Chatterley's Lover,* by D. H. Lawrence. The book was sold in the United States in expurgated editions for years, but in 1959 **Grove Press** issued the complete version. Postal officials denied mailing privileges. Grove sued and won.

In some respects the Grove case was *Ulysses* all over again. Grove argued that Lawrence, a major author, had produced a work of literary merit. Grove said the explicit, rugged love scenes between Lady Chatterley and Mellors the gamekeeper were essential in establishing their violent yet loving relationship, the heart of the story. The distinction between the *Ulysses* and *Lady Chatterley* cases was

shield laws
Allow journalists to protect identification of confidential sources.

Random House
Fought against censorship of James Joyce's *Ulysses*.

John Woolsey
Judge who barred import law censorship of *Ulysses*.

Grove Press
Fought against censorship of D. H. Lawrence's *Lady Chatterley's Lover*.

that one ruling was against the customs service and the other against the postmaster general.

Communications Decency Act

The federal government's latest foray into systematically regulating media content were ill-conceived communications decency laws in 1996 and 1999. Without hearings or formal debate, Congress created the act to keep smut away from children who use the Internet. Although hardly anyone defends giving kids access to indecent material, the law had two flaws: the difficulty of defining indecency and the impossibility of denying questionable material to children without restricting freedom of speech for adults.

DEFINITION.   Through history the courts have found it impossible to define indecency clearly. Before a Philadelphia federal appeals court that reviewed the 1996 Communications Decency Act, witnesses from the Justice Department testified that the law required them to prosecute for certain AIDS information, museum exhibits, prize-winning plays and even the *Vanity Fair* magazine cover of actress Demi Moore nude and pregnant.

ACCESS.   When it reviewed the 1996 Communications Decency Act, the U.S. Supreme Court noted that the Internet is the most democratic of the media, enabling almost anyone to become a town crier or pamphleteer. Enforcing the law would necessarily inhibit a free expression of the sort that has roots in the Revolution that resulted in the creation of the Republic and the First Amendment, the court said. The 7-2 decision purged the law from the books.

How, then, are government bans of indecency on radio and television justified but not on the Internet? Justice John Stevens, who wrote the majority Supreme Court opinion, said the Internet is hardly as "invasive." The odds of people encountering pornography on the Internet are slim unless they're seeking it, he said. Underpinning the Court's rejection of the Communications Decency Act was the fact that the Internet lends itself to free-for-all discussions and exchanges with everybody participating who wants to, whereas other media are dominated by carefully crafted messages aimed at people whose opportunity to participate in dialogue with the message producers is so indirect as to be virtually nil.

Pornography versus Obscenity

Since the *Ulysses* and *Lady Chatterley* cases, much more has happened to discourage federal censorship. The U.S. Supreme Court has ruled that pornography, material aimed at sexual arousal, cannot be stopped. Import and postal restrictions, however, still can be employed against obscene materials, which the Court has defined as going beyond pornography. Obscenity restrictions apply, said the Court, if the answer is yes to *all* of the following questions:

- Would a typical person applying local standards see the material as appealing mainly for its sexually arousing effect?
- Is the material devoid of serious literary, artistic, political or scientific value?
- Is sexual activity depicted offensively, in a way that violates state law that explicitly defines offensiveness?

Censorship Today

STUDY PREVIEW Local governments have tried numerous ways to restrict distribution of sexually explicit material. Local libraries and schools also sometimes act to ban materials, but these attempts at censorship are not restricted to obscenity and pornography. Anything to which a majority of a local board objects can be fair game.

Local Censorship

Municipalities and counties have tried heavy-handed restrictions against sexually explicit publications and video material, generally without lasting success. Outright bans fail if they are challenged in the courts, unless the material is legally obscene. The U.S. Supreme Court spoke on this issue after Mount Ephraim, New Jersey, revised zoning laws to ban all live entertainment from commercial areas. The Court said the rezoning was a blatant attempt to ban lawful activities, and the decision was widely interpreted to apply to porn shops and other businesses that are often targets of local censorship campaigns. A federal court applied the same reasoning when it threw out a Keego Harbor, Michigan, zoning ordinance that forbade an adult theater within 500 feet of a school, church or bar. In Keego Harbor there was no site that was not within 500 feet of a school, church or bar.

Some local governments have been innovative in acting against sexually explicit materials. One successful approach has been through zoning laws to rid neighborhoods of porn shops by forcing them into so-called **war zones.** Owners of adult-oriented businesses generally have been pleased to go along. By complying, they face less heat from police and other official harassment. The courts have found that war zone ordinances are legitimate applications of the principle underlying zoning laws in general, which is to preserve and protect the character of neighborhoods. So just as local governments can create single-residence, apartment, retail and other zones, they also can create zones for adult bookstores and theaters.

An opposite zoning approach, to disperse these kinds of businesses instead of concentrating them, has also been upheld in court. In Detroit an ordinance insists that a 1,000-foot space separate "problem businesses," which include porn shops, adults-only theaters, pool halls and cabarets. This is all right, say the courts, as long as it does not exclude such businesses entirely.

Unlike the publishers in the landmark *Ulysses* and *Lady Chatterley* cases, in recent years book publishers have not taken the initiative against local restrictions aimed at pornography distributors and porn shops. Litigation is expensive, and major publishing houses do not produce porn-shop merchandise. Magazine publishers, notably *Playboy* and *Penthouse,* have fought some battles, but the issue has become fragmented since the Supreme Court's insistence that local standards be a measure of acceptability. Because what is obscene to people in one town may not be obscene to people in another, it is impossible for the producers of nationally distributed books and magazines to go after all the restrictive local actions.

Library and School Boards

Local libraries sometimes decide to keep certain books off the shelves, usually because of content that offends the sensitivities of a majority of the library board. This kind

war zones
Neighborhoods where pornography is permitted.

Media Abroad

Norway and Reprography

Since 1980 the tiny Nordic country of Norway, population 4 million, has led the world on copyright issues through an agency called Kopinor (pronounced KOH-pih-noor). Kopinor has agreements through which Norwegian businesses, governments and schools pay Kopinor a fee for the photocopying of copyrighted works by their employees. Kopinor then distributes these fees, $19.2 million in 1996, to publisher and author groups to which copyright owners belong.

While Kopinor still has some lapses in its collection mechanisms, including the Lutheran state church, which has stalled at paying reprography fees, no other nation has as comprehensive a collection system. The Norwegian government even pays Kopinor for the photocopying that citizens do on their own. Nor is any other country as faithful to the principle of copyright in returning reprography fees to the country where the copyrighted material originated. Kopinor typically returns about $1.2 million a year to the United States for U.S. works that Norwegians have photocopied.

At Kopinor the driving force is John-Willy Rudolph, who travels the globe with evangelical energy to encourage better systems for collecting reprography fees. As a result, countries as geographically and culturally diverse as Japan and Zimbabwe have established reprographic agencies. Slowly a comprehensive international network for collecting and distributing reprographic fees back to copyright owners is taking shape.

---

of censorship survives challenges only when legal obscenity is the issue, which is seldom. Also, the wide availability of banned books renders library bans merely symbolic.

Some school boards still attempt censorship, although there is little support in the courts unless the issue is legal obscenity, which is rare. Whatever latitude school boards once had was strictly limited in 1982 when the U.S. Supreme Court decided against the Island Trees, New York, school board after several members had gone into the high school library and removed 60 books. Among them were *The Fixer* by Bernard Malamud and *Laughing Boy* by Oliver Lafarge, both of which had won Pulitzer Prizes. School board members argued that the 60 books were anti-American, anti-Semitic, anti-Christian, and "just plain filthy." The Court did not accept that. School boards, said the Court, "may not remove books from library shelves simply because they dislike the ideas in those books and seek their removal to prescribe what shall be orthodox in politics, nationalism, religion or other matters of opinion."

Copyright

STUDY PREVIEW   Mass media people are vulnerable to thievery. Because it is so easy for someone to copy someone else's creative work, copyright laws prohibit the unauthorized re-creation of intellectual property, including books, music, movies and other creative production.

How Copyright Works

copyright
Protects intellectual property
from theft.

Congress has had a **copyright** law on the books since 1790. The law protects authors and other creators of intellectual property from having someone profit by reproducing their works without permission. Permission is usually granted for a fee.

Authors in a Dot.Com World. The National Writers Union, led by Jonathan Tasini, led a campaign for media companies to compensate freelance contributors when their works are recycled on web sites. Among writers' targets was the Boston *Globe*. The newspaper insisted that once it bought a freelancer's piece for the newspaper, it owned the piece for whatever further use it wanted, including posting it on the web—without the author's permission and without sharing additional revenue generated from the web site. The issue: who owns a writer's work under copyright law in the new age of the web.

Almost all books have copyright protection the moment they are created in a tangible form. So do most movies, television programs, newspaper and magazine articles, songs and records, and advertisements. It used to be that a creative work needed to be registered with the Library of Congress for a $10 fee. Formal registration is no longer required, but many people still do it for the fullest legal protection against someone pirating their work.

The current copyright law protects a creative work for the lifetime of the author plus 70 years. After the 70 years a work enters what is called the **public domain,** and anyone may reproduce it without permission.

The creator of an original work may sell the copyright, and many do. Authors, for example, typically give their copyright to a publisher in exchange for a percentage of income from the book's profits.

Copyright and the Web

Congress clarified numerous web legal issues in the Digital Millennium Copyright Act in 1998. The law gives specific protection to companies and individuals who post original material on the web. Other people cannot legally take it for commercial purposes. This is the same fair-use exception that applies in traditional media. One such fair-use exception is quoting from a book in a review of the book.

The law also exempted online providers, like American Online and telephone companies. They are not liable for copyright violations committed by subscribers who post material that belongs to someone else.

Music Licensing

Songwriters have a complex system to make money from their copyrighted works through music licensing organizations every time their music is played. These organizations collect fees from broadcast stations and other places that play recorded music, even restaurants, bowling alleys and scout camps. The licensing organizations

public domain
Intellectual property that may be used without permission of the creator or owner.

pass the fees on to their members. The largest licensing organizations are known in the trade by their abbreviations, the **American Society of Composers, Authors and Performers,** known as ASCAP, and **Broadcast Music Inc.,** known in the field as BMI.

ASCAP. For a commercial radio station to play ASCAP-licensed music, there is a charge of 2 percent of the station's gross receipts. ASCAP tapes six-hour segments from selected radio stations to determine whose music is being played. From the analysis a complex formula is derived to divvy the license income among songwriters, music publishers and other members of ASCAP who own the music.

BMI. The organization known as BMI, which licenses most country-western and soul music, checks radio station playlists every 12 to 14 months to create a formula for distributing license income.

American Society of Composers, Authors and Performers
Music licensing organization.

Broadcast Music Inc.
Music licensing organization.

chapter wrap-up

The U.S. mass media enjoy great freedom under the First Amendment, which forbids the government from impinging on expression. Even so, the freedom has limits. When the First Amendment guarantee of a free press runs against the constitutional guarantee of a free trial, there is a conflict of values that must be resolved. This is also true when the mass media violate someone's right to be left alone, which, although not an explicit constitutional guarantee, has come to be recognized as a basic human right. An understanding of mass media law and regulation involves studying how the U.S. judicial system, headed by the U.S. Supreme Court, has reconciled conflicting interests. In short, the First Amendment is not inviolate.

Questions for Review

1. Why is the First Amendment important to mass media in the United States?
2. In what situations may the government exercise prior restraint to silence someone?
3. Who can sue the mass media for libel?
4. Do the mass media face limits on intruding on an individual's privacy?
5. Do the mass media face limits in covering government meetings or the courts? Or digging into government documents?
6. How is obscenity different from pornography?
7. How did a U.S. Supreme Court decision pretty much end federal concern about pornography?
8. How does copyright law protect intellectual property from being stolen from its owners?

Questions for Critical Thinking

1. How can any restriction on free expression by the mass media or by individuals be consistent with the absolutist language of the First Amendment?
2. Define censorship. In a strict sense, who is a censor?

3. What lessons about prior restraint are contained in *Near v. Minnesota* (1931) and *New York Times Co. v. United States* (1971)?
4. How could Judge Herbert Blythin, who presided at the 1954 murder trial of Cleveland osteopath Sam Sheppard, have headed off the news media orgy that led to an appeal to the U.S. Supreme Court and an acquittal?
5. How do authors and creators of other intellectual property copyright their works, and why do they do it?
6. What kinds of meetings by public agencies can be closed to the public and the news media under the terms of open meeting laws? Are the public and the press barred from seeking any government documents under the U.S. Freedom of Information Act and sunshine laws?
7. What is the trend with local censorship by library boards and school boards?

Keeping Up to Date

Censorship News is published by the National Coalition Against Censorship.

Media Law Bulletin tracks developments in media law.

News Media and the Law is published by the Reporters' Committee for Freedom of the Press.

Media Law Reporter is an annual collection of major court cases.

Student Press Law Reports, from the Student Press Law Center, follows events in the high school and college press and broadcast media.

The *Wall Street Journal* has a daily law section that includes media cases.

First Lady and Governor Ventura. *In a foot-in-mouth magazine interview, Minnesota Governor Jesse Ventura said church-going was a weakness but nonetheless all right. His wife Terry did it, he said. With the First Lady's religious habits thus introduced into public dialogue, reporters began checking them out. "Outrageous!" said the governor in moral indignation. Was it a media ethics lapse?*

20

Ethics and the Mass Media

The motormouth governor of Minnesota, Jesse Ventura, proclaimed that his most embarrassing moment as governor occurred when news reporters, seeking an interview with his wife, staked out the church where she was attending Sunday services. It was an intrusion on the sanctity of worship, the governor said. He accused the reporters of unethical behavior.

Among ethicists, perceptions vary widely about what should be off limits to public inquiry. In the Ventura situation those who defended the reporters noted that Ventura himself, in an interview in the current *Playboy* magazine, had raised the issue of his wife's religious beliefs and practices. It was the governor who had made his wife's religion a public issue.

Some media people responded that the governor couldn't have it both ways. Either the Minnesota First Lady's religion was a public issue or it wasn't, and, these media people argued, the governor had made it one. A contrary view was that Mrs. Ventura hadn't talked about religion in *Playboy*, and it was her church-going, not the governor's, that was being intruded upon.

Like most ethics questions, the issue involving Mrs. Ventura has no slam-dunk answers. This chapter is intended to introduce you to types of ethics problems, many dilemmatic, that vex mass media people and show how you can sort your way through to answers you can be comfortable with.

The Difficulty of Ethics

STUDY PREVIEW   Mass media organizations have put together codes of ethics that prescribe how practitioners should go about their work. Although useful in many ways, these codes neither sort through the bedeviling problems that result from conflicting prescriptions nor help much when the only open options are negative.

Prescriptive Ethics Codes

The mass media abound with **codes of ethics.** The earliest was adopted in 1923, the **Canons of Journalism of the American Society of Newspaper Editors.** Advertising, broadcast and public relations practitioners also have codes. Many newcomers to the mass media make an erroneous assumption that the answers to all the moral choices in their work exist in the prescriptions of these codes, a stance known as **prescriptive ethics.** While the codes can be helpful, ethics is not so easy.

The difficulty of ethics becomes clear when a mass communicator is confronted with a conflict between moral responsibilities to different concepts. Consider:

RESPECT FOR PRIVACY.   The code of the Society of Professional Journalists prescribes that reporters will show respect for the dignity, **privacy,** rights and well being of people "at all times." The SPJ prescription sounds excellent, but moral priorities such as dignity and privacy sometimes seem less important than other priorities. The public interest, for example, overrode privacy in 1988 when the Miami *Herald* staked out presidential candidate Gary Hart overnight when he had a woman friend in his Washington townhouse.

COMMITMENT TO TIMELINESS.   The code of the Radio-Television News Directors Association prescribes that reporters be "**timely** and accurate." In practice, however, the virtue of accuracy is jeopardized when reporters rush to the air with stories. It takes time to confirm details and be accurate—and that delays stories.

BEING FAIR.   The code of the Public Relations Society of America prescribes dealing **fairly** with both clients and the general public. However, a persuasive message prepared on behalf of a client is not always the same message that would be prepared on behalf of the general public. Persuasive communication is not necessarily dishonest, but how information is marshaled to create the message depends on whom the PR person is serving.

Conflict in Duties

Media ethics codes are well-intended, usually helpful guides, but they are simplistic when it comes to knotty moral questions. When media ethicians Clifford Christians, Mark Fackler and Kim Rotzoll compiled a list of five duties of mass media practitioners, some of these inherent problems became obvious.

DUTY TO SELF.   Self-preservation is a basic human instinct, but is a photojournalist shirking a duty to subscribers by avoiding a dangerous combat zone?

Self-aggrandizement can be an issue too. Many college newspaper editors are invited, all expenses paid, to Hollywood movie premieres. The duty-to-self principle

---

code of ethics
Statement that defines acceptable, unacceptable behavior.

Canons of Journalism of the American Society of Newspaper Editors
First media code, 1923.

prescriptive ethics
Follow the rules and your decision will be the correct one.

privacy
Respect for privacy common in ethics codes.

timeliness
A virtue in most news ethics codes.

fairness
A virtue in most media ethics codes.

Media Abroad

Global Ethics Code

The World Association of Press Councils proposed an international code of ethics in 1998. The worldwide council, if it is indeed created, would hear public complaints about the media and measure them against the code. If media were found to be remiss, the council would issue a statement that might improve media performance in the future because of the embarrassment of a negative finding.

The association represents 16 regional and local news councils that take complaints in their localities. The new global council would take criticism on bias and inaccuracy in foreign coverage—issues that are seldom addressed by single-country and local news councils.

David Flint, of the World Association of Press Councils, said a global council would have more clout than in-country organizations to encourage news media freedom in authoritarian countries.

favors going: The trip would be fun. In addition, it is a good story opportunity, and as a free favor, it would not cost the newspaper anything. However, what of an editor's responsibility to readers? Readers have a right to expect writers to provide honest accounts that are not colored by favoritism. Can a reporter write fairly after being wined and dined and flown across the continent by movie producers who want a gung-ho story? Even if reporters rise above being affected and are true to conscience, there are the duty-to-employer and the duty-to-profession principles to consider. The newspaper and the profession itself can be tarnished by suspicions, no matter whether they are unfounded, that a reporter has been bought off.

DUTY TO AUDIENCE. Television programs that reenact violence are popular with audiences, but do they do a disservice because they frighten many viewers into also inferring that the streets are more dangerous than they really are?

Tom Wicker of the New York *Times* tells a story about his early days as a reporter in Aberdeen, North Carolina. He was covering a divorce case involving one spouse chasing the other with an ax. Nobody was hurt physically, and everyone who heard the story in the courtroom, except the divorcing couple, had a good laugh. "It was human comedy at its most ribald, and the courtroom rocked with laughter," Wicker recalled years later. In writing his story, Wicker captured the darkly comedic details so skillfully that his editor put the story on

Paparazzi. An ethics dilemma stems from the conflict that photojournalists face between their duty to serve their audience's interests and their duty to respect the rights of people they photograph. Before she died in a car wreck while being pursued by photographers, Princess Diana complained that media people go too far when pursuing a story becomes hounding a person.

Media People

Arthur Ashe

Tennis champion Arthur Ashe was glad but then leery to hear his old high school chum Doug Smith on the phone. Smith, tennis reporter for *USA Today,* wanted to see him for an interview. It was not unusual for reporters to call on Ashe. He was the first world-class American black male tennis player, and after his athletic prime he had campaigned vigorously against apartheid. But by 1992 he worried with every interview that the question of whether he had AIDS would surface.

Ashe, in fact, did have AIDS. He had contracted the virus apparently in 1983 during surgery. Five years later, when doctors found the infection, Ashe began therapy for the debilitating and inevitably fatal disease. He decided against going public with the fact that he had the disease, and his family and friends went along with what Ashe called "a silent and generous conspiracy to assist me in maintaining my privacy."

When Doug Smith showed up for the interview, he asked the dreaded question: "Do you have AIDS?" Although Ashe realized that some reporter someday would ask the question, it nonetheless caught him off guard. "Could be," he quipped. Then he recognized how much more revealing his words were than he intended. The secret was out.

Private Issue? Tennis hero Arthur Ashe objected that news media inquiries about his AIDS violated his privacy.

The next afternoon, before Smith's article could appear, Ashe called a news conference to announce that he suffered from AIDS. Although he was gentle on *USA Today,* Ashe criticized the mass media for intruding into the private lives of people. In the news conference, carried live by CNN, Ashe said, "I am sorry that I have been forced to make this revelation at this time. After all, I am not running for some office of public trust, nor do I have stockholders to account to. It is only that I fall in the dubious umbrella of, quote, public figure, end of quote."

Ironically, *USA Today* had decided against going with the story, but Ashe's news conference nonetheless epitomized one of the great media

ethics questions of our time: Who prevails when the mass media are at the intersection of the public's interest in knowing certain information and an individual's interest in preserving personal privacy? Like all vexatious ethics questions, people on both sides feel strongly and mount powerful arguments for their positions. Journalists themselves are hardly of one mind.

Among those supporting *USA Today*'s initiative was Gerry Callahan of the Boston *Herald.* Callahan said that the violation of Ashe's privacy was committed by whoever in his circle of friends tipped the newspaper anonymously. The newspaper, he said, merely was performing its function of checking out tips.

Not everyone saw it that way. *USA Today* received almost 1,100 calls, with 60 people canceling their subscriptions. Among journalists, there were negative reactions too: Mona Charen, a syndicated columnist, wrote that the fact that Ashe was a great athlete who had established a milestone for blacks was "no reason to treat his personal struggle as a peep show."

Page 1. Wicker was proud of the piece until the next day when the woman in the case called on him. Worn-out, haggard, hurt and angry, she asked, "Mr. Wicker, why did you think you had a right to make fun of me in your paper?"

The lesson stayed with Wicker for the rest of his career. He had unthinkingly hurt a fellow human being for no better reason than to evoke a chuckle, or perhaps a belly laugh, from his readers. To Wicker, the duty-to-audience principle never again would transcend his moral duty to the dignity of the subjects of his stories. Similar ethics questions involve whether to cite AIDS as a contributor to death in an obituary, to identify victims in rape stories and to name juveniles charged with crimes.

DUTY TO EMPLOYER. Does loyalty to an employer transcend the ideal of pursuing and telling the truth when a news reporter discovers dubious business deals involving the parent corporation? This is a growing issue as the mass media become consolidated into fewer gigantic companies owned by conglomerates. In 1989, for example, investigative reporter Peter Karl of Chicago television station WMAQ broke a story that General Electric had manufactured jet engines with untested and sometimes defective bolts. Although WMAQ is owned by NBC, which in turn is owned by General Electric, Karl's exclusive, documented and accurate story aired. However, when the story was passed on to the network itself, Marty Ryan, executive producer of the "Today" show, ordered that the references to General Electric be edited out.

DUTY TO THE PROFESSION. At what point does an ethically motivated advertising-agency person blow the whistle on misleading claims by other advertising people?

DUTY TO SOCIETY. Does duty to society ever transcend duty to self? To audience? To the employer? To colleagues? Does ideology affect a media worker's sense of duty to society? Consider how Joseph Stalin, Adolf Hitler and Franklin Roosevelt would be covered by highly motivated communist, fascist and libertarian journalists.

Are there occasions when the duty-to-society and the duty-to-audience principles are incompatible? Nobody enjoys seeing the horrors of war, for example, but journalists may feel that their duty to society demands that they go after the most grisly photographs of combat to show how horrible war is and, thereby, in a small way, contribute to public pressure toward a cessation of hostilities and eventual peace.

Promoting Self-Interest

It didn't surprise anybody much that the reviews from online book retailer Amazon.com were enthusiastic. Most were drawn from book jacket blurbs. Amazon.com, after all, was in the business of promoting books and sales.

When the Washington *Post* started an online bookstore in 1998, its credibility was jeopardized. The *Post* created an ethics problem for itself: Would the reviews be driven by the influential critical comment, sometimes negative, that had traditionally marked its arts section, or would the *Post*, like Amazon.com, gravitate toward upbeat, favorable reviews that were likelier to sell books?

To its credit, Amazon.com permits readers to post reviews, critical and otherwise. To find these reviews, however, you need to scroll through the sales pitch for the title.

Moral Principles

STUDY PREVIEW Concern about doing the right thing is part of human nature, and leading thinkers have developed a great number of enduring moral principles over the centuries. The mass media, like other institutions and also like individuals, draw on these

Media Timeline

Development of Media Ethics

400 B.C.	Aristotle laid out the golden mean.
20s	Jesus Christ articulated "Do unto others as you would have them do unto you."
1785	Immanuel Kant advanced the categorical imperative.
1865	John Stuart Mill proposed utilitarianism.
1903	John Dewey advanced pragmatism.
1919	Upton Sinclair exposed newsroom abuses in his novel *The Brass Check*.
1923	American Society of Newspaper Editors adopted a media ethics code.
1947	Hutchins Commission urged the media to be socially responsible.
1971	John Rawls advanced the veil of ignorance.

principles, but this does not always make moral decisions easy. The principles are not entirely consistent, especially in sorting through dilemmas.

Golden Mean. The Greek thinker Aristotle told his students almost 2,400 years ago that right courses of action avoid extremes. His recommendation: moderation.

The Golden Mean

The Greek philosopher **Aristotle,** writing almost 2,400 years ago, devised the **golden mean** as a basis for moral decision-making. The golden mean sounds simple and straightforward: Avoid extremes and seek moderation. Modern journalistic balance and fairness are founded on this principle.

The golden mean's dictate, however, is not as simple as it sounds. As with all moral principles, application of the golden mean can present difficulties. Consider the federal law that requires over-the-air broadcasters to give equal opportunity to candidates for public office. If one candidate buys 30 seconds at 7 p.m. for $120, a station is obligated to allow other candidates for the same office to buy 30 seconds at the same time for the same rate. On the surface, this application of the golden mean, embodied in federal law, might seem to be reasonable, fair and morally right, but the issue is far more complex. The equality requirement, for example, gives an advantage to candidates who hold simplistic positions that can be expressed compactly. Good and able candidates whose positions require more time to explain are disadvantaged, and the society is damaged when inferior candidates win public office.

Although minute-for-minute equality in broadcasting can be a flawed application of the golden mean, Aristotle's principle is valuable to media people when making moral decisions, as long as they do not abdicate their power of reason to embrace formulaic tit-for-tat measurable equality. It takes the human mind, not a formula, to determine fairness. And therein lies the complexity of the golden mean. No two human beings think exactly alike, which means that applying the golden mean involves in-

Aristotle
Advocate of the golden mean.

golden mean
Moderation is the best course.

dividuals making judgment calls that are not necessarily the same. This element of judgment in moral decisions can make ethics intellectually exciting. It takes a sharp mind to sort through issues of balance and fairness.

"Do unto Others"

The Judeo-Christian principle of "**Do unto others** as you would have them do unto you" appeals to most Americans. Not even the do-unto-others prescription is without problems, however. Consider the photojournalist who sees virtue in serving a mass audience with a truthful account of the human condition. This might manifest itself in portrayals of great emotions, like grief. But would the photojournalist appreciate being photographed herself in a grieving moment after learning that her own infant son had died in an accident? If not, her pursuit of truth through photography for a mass audience would be contrary to the "do-unto-others" dictum.

Universal Law. Immanuel Kant, an 18th-century German philosopher, urged people to find principles that they would be comfortable having applied in all situations. He called these principles *categorical imperatives.*

Categorical Imperatives

About 200 years ago, German philosopher **Immanuel Kant** wrote that moral decisions should flow from thoroughly considered principles. As he put it, "Act on the maxim that you would want to become universal law." He called his maxim the categorical imperative. A **categorical imperative,** well thought out, is a principle that the individual who devised it would be willing to apply in all moral questions of a similar sort.

Kant's categorical imperative does not dictate specifically what actions are morally right or wrong. Moral choices, says Kant, go deeper than the context of the immediate issue. He encourages a philosophical approach to moral questions, with people using their intellect to identify principles that they, as individuals, would find acceptable if applied universally.

Kant does not encourage the kind of standardized approach to ethics represented by professional codes. His emphasis, rather, is on hard thinking. Says philosopher Patricia Smith, of the University of Kentucky, writing in the *Journal of Mass Media Ethics,* "A philosophical approach to ethics embodies a commitment to consistency, clarity, the principled evaluation of arguments and unrelenting persistence to get to the bottom of things."

Utilitarian Ethics

In the mid-1800s British thinker **John Stuart Mill** declared that morally right decisions are those that result in "happiness for the greatest number." Mill called his idea the **principle of utility.** It sounds good to many of us because it parallels the democratic principle of majority rule, with its emphasis on the greatest good for the greatest number of people.

By and large, journalists embrace Mill's utilitarianism today, as evinced in notions like the *people's right to know,* a concept originally meant to support journalistic pursuit of information about government, putting the public's interests ahead of government's interests, but which has come to be almost reflexively invoked to defend pursuing very personal information about individuals, no matter what the human toll.

"Do unto others"
Judeo-Christian principle for ethical behavior.

Immanuel Kant
Advocated the categorical imperative.

categorical imperative
Follow principles as if they had universal application.

John Stuart Mill
Advocated utilitarianism.

principle of utility
Best course bestows the most good for the most people.

Utilitarianism. American journalists tend to like 19th-century British thinker John Stuart Mill's utilitarianism, which favors actions that result in the greatest good for the greatest number of people. This approach to ethics dovetails well with majority rule and modern democracy.

John Dewey
Advocate of pragmatism.

pragmatic ethics
Judge acts by their results.

John Rawls
Advocated egalitarianism.

veil of ignorance
Making decisions with a blind eye to extraneous factors that could affect the decision.

egalitarianism
Treat everyone the same.

Hutchins Commission
Advocated social responsibility as goal and result of media activities.

social responsibility
Making decisions that serve society responsibly.

deontological ethics
Good actions flow from good processes.

Pragmatic Ethics

John Dewey, an American thinker who wrote in the late 1800s and early 1900s, argued that the virtue of moral decisions had to be judged by their results. Dewey's **pragmatic ethics,** like other ethics systems, has problems. One is that people do not have perfect crystal balls to tell them for sure whether their moral actions will have good consequences.

Egalitarian Ethics

In the 20th century philosopher **John Rawls** introduced the **veil of ignorance** as an element in ethics decisions. Choosing a right course of action, said Rawls, requires blindness to social position or other discriminating factors. This is known as **egalitarianism.** An ethical decision requires that all people be given an equal hearing and the same fair consideration.

To Rawls a brutal slaying in an upscale suburb deserves the same journalistic attention as a similarly brutal slaying in a poor urban neighborhood. All other things being equal, a $20,000 bank burglary is no more newsworthy than a $20,000 embezzlement.

Social Responsibility Ethics

The **Hutchins Commission,** a learned group that studied the U.S. mass media in the 1940s, recommended that journalists and other media people make decisions that serve the society responsibly. For all its virtues the **social responsibility** system, like all ethics systems, has difficulties. For one thing decision makers can only imperfectly foresee the effects of their decisions. It is not possible to predict with 100 percent confidence whether every decision will turn out to be socially responsible. Also, well-meaning people may differ honestly about how society is most responsibly served.

Process versus Outcome

STUDY PREVIEW   The various approaches to ethics fall into two broad categories: deontological ethics and teleological ethics. Deontologists say people need to follow good rules. Teleologists judge morality not by the rules but by the consequences of decisions.

Deontological Ethics

The Greek word *deon*, which means "duty," is at the heart of **deontological ethics,** which holds that people act morally when they follow good rules. Deontologists feel that people are duty bound to identify these rules.

Deontologists include people who believe that Scripture holds all the answers for right living. Their equivalent among media practitioners are those who rely entirely on codes of ethics drafted by organizations they trust. Following rules is a prescriptive form of ethics. At first consideration, ethics might seem as easy as following the rules, but not all questions are clear-cut. In complicated situations the rules sometimes contradict each other. Some cases are dilemmas with no right option—only a choice among less-than-desirable options.

Deontological ethics becomes complicated, and also more intellectually interesting, when individuals, unsatisfied with other people's rules, try to work out their own universally applicable moral principles.

Here are some major deontological approaches:

- **Theory of divine command.** This theory holds that proper moral decisions come from obeying the commands of God, with blind trust that the consequences will be good.
- **Theory of divine right of kings.** This theory sees virtue in allegiance to a divinely anointed monarch.
- **Theory of secular command.** This theory is a nonreligious variation that stresses allegiance to a dictator or other political leader from whom the people take cues when making moral decisions.
- **Libertarian theory.** This theory stresses a laissez-faire approach to ethics: Give free rein to the human ability to think through problems, and people almost always will make morally right decisions.
- **Categorical imperative theory.** This theory holds that virtue results when people identify and apply universal principles.

Teleological Ethics

Unlike deontological ethics, which is concerned with the right actions, teleological ethics is concerned with the consequences of actions. The word **teleology** comes from the Greek word *teleos,* which means "result" or "consequence."

Teleologists see flaws in the formal, legalistic duty to rules of deontologists, noting that great harm sometimes flows from blind allegiance to rules.

Here are some major teleological approaches:

- **Pragmatic theory.** This theory encourages people to look at human experience to determine the probable consequences of an action and then decide its desirability.
- **Utilitarian theory.** This theory favors ethics actions that benefit more people than they damage—the greatest good for the greatest number.
- **Social-responsibility theory.** This theory judges actions by the good effect they have on society.

Situational Ethics

Firm deontologists see two primary flaws in teleological ethics:

- Imperfect foresight.
- Lack of guiding principles.

Despite these flaws, many media practitioners apply teleological approaches, sometimes labeled **situational ethics,** to arrive at moral decisions. They gather as much information as they can about a situation and then decide, not on the basis of principle but on the facts of the situation. Critics of situational ethics worry about decisions governed by situations. Much better, they argue, would be decisions flowing from principles of enduring value. With situational ethics the same person might do one thing one day and on another day go another direction in a similar situation.

m e d i a o n l i n e

Media Watch: A collection of online media-watch resources.
http://theory.lcs.mit.edu/
~mernst/media

Organization of News Ombudsmen: Formed in 1980, ONO is a nonprofit corporation that maintains contact with news ombudsmen worldwide.
www.infi.net/ono

Media Watchdogs: Links to media watchdog groups.
www.newswatch.org/
watchdog.htm

Project Censored: A collection of underreported stories.
www.projectcensored.org

theory of divine command
Proper decisions follow God's will.

theory of divine right of kings
Proper decisions follow monarch's will.

theory of secular command
Good decisions follow ruler's will.

libertarian theory
Given good information and time, people ultimately make right decisions.

teleology
Good decisions are those with good consequences.

situational ethics
Make ethics decisions on basis of situation at hand.

News Versus Taste. The carnage in the 2001 terrorist attack on the World Trade Center raised the perennial issue of how gruesome should news coverage be. CNN chose to show only quick snippets of people falling from the 110-story towers. Eason Jordan, in charge of newsgathering, said CNN didn't want "to shield viewers from the horrific reality." At the same time, CNN didn't dwell on the disturbing scenes. Video of falling bodies was confined to a correspondent's report and not replayed and replayed. Said Jordan: "If you show only the smallest snippet in the body of a story about the horrid, that's more appropriate than showing the person going to the ground." Video was available of the whole 10-second to 20-second descents of many victims. ABC decided against showing falling bodies but did show the horror on the faces of two women shrieking as their eyes followed the descent of one body. Neither NBC, CBS nor MSNBC showed bodies.

Ralph Potter
Ethicist who devised the Potter's Box.

Potter's Box
Tool for sorting through the pros and cons of ethics questions.

Consider a case at the *Rocky Mountain News* in Denver. Editors learned that the president of a major suburban newspaper chain had killed his parents and sister in another state when he was 18. After seven years in a mental hospital the man completed college, moved to Colorado, lived a model life and became a successful newspaper executive. The *Rocky Mountain News* decided not to make a story of it. Said a *News* official, "The only reason for dredging up [his] past would be to titillate morbid curiosity or to shoot down, maliciously, a successful citizen."

However, when another newspaper revealed the man's past, the *Rocky Mountain News* reversed itself and published a lengthy piece of its own. Why? The newspaper that broke the story had suggested that *News* editors knew about the man's past and had decided to protect him as a fellow member of the journalistic fraternity. *News* editors denied that their motivation was to protect the man. To prove it, they reversed their decision and published a story on him. The *News* explained its change of mind by saying that the situation had changed. *News* editors, concerned that their newspaper's credibility had been challenged, thought that printing a story would set that straight. Of less concern, suddenly, was that the story would titillate morbid curiosity or contribute to the destruction of a successful citizen. It was a classic case of situational ethics.

Flip-flops on moral issues, such as what happened at the *Rocky Mountain News*, bother critics of situational ethics. The critics say decisions should be based on deeply rooted moral principles—not immediate, transient facts or changing peripheral contexts.

Potter's Box

STUDY PREVIEW   Moral problems in the mass media can be so complex that it may seem there is no solution. While ideal answers without any negative results may be impossible, a process exists for identifying a course of action that integrates an individual's personal values with moral principles and then tests conclusions against loyalties.

Four Quadrants

A Harvard Divinity School professor, **Ralph Potter,** has devised a four-quadrant model for sorting through ethics problems. The quadrants of the square-like model called **Potter's Box** each pose a category of questions. Working through these categories helps to clarify the issues and leads to a morally justifiable position. These are the quadrants of Potter's Box:

SITUATION.   In Quadrant 1 the facts of the issue are decided. Consider a newsroom in which a series of articles on rape is being developed and the question arises whether to identify rape victims by name. Here is how the situation could be defined: The newspaper has access to a young mother who has been abducted and raped and who is willing to describe the assault in graphic detail and to discuss her experience as a witness at the assailant's trial. Also, the woman is willing to be identified in the story.

VALUES.   Moving to Quadrant 2 of Potter's Box, editors and reporters identify the values that underlie all the available choices. This process involves listing the positive and negative values that flow from conscience. One editor might argue that full, frank discussion on social issues is necessary to deal with them. Another might say that identifying the rape victim by name might discourage others from even re-

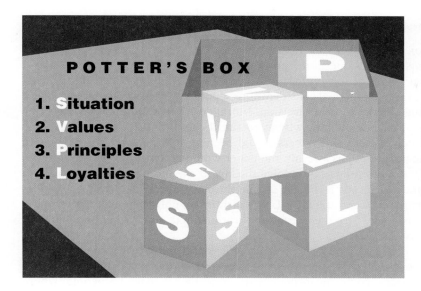

POTTER'S BOX

1. **S**ituation
2. **V**alues
3. **P**rinciples
4. **L**oyalties

Clarifying Process. Potter's Box offers four categories of questions to help develop morally justifiable positions. Ralph Potter, the divinity professor who devised the categories, said to start by establishing the facts of the situation. Then identify the values that underpin the options, recognizing that some values may be incompatible with others. Then consider the moral principles that support each of the values. Finally, sort through loyalties to all the affected interests. Potter's Box is not a panacea, but it gives people the assurance that they have worked through ethics issues in a thorough way.

porting the crime. Other positions: Publishing the name is in poor taste. The newspaper has an obligation to protect the victim from her own possibly bad decision to allow her name to be used. The purpose of the rape series can be accomplished without using the name. Readers have a right to all the relevant information that the newspaper can gather. An editor who is torn between such contrary thoughts is making progress toward a decision by at least identifying all the values that can be posited.

PRINCIPLES.   In Potter's Quadrant 3, decision makers search for moral principles that uphold the values they identified in Quadrant 2. John Stuart Mill's principle of utility, which favors the majority over individuals, would support using the victim's name because it could add poignancy to the story, enhancing the chances of improved public sensitivity, and perhaps even lead to improved public policy, all of which, Mill would say, outweighs the harm that might come to an individual. On the other hand, people who have used Immanuel Kant's ideas to develop inviolable operating principles—categorical imperatives—look to their rule book: We never publish information that might offend readers. One value of Potter's Quadrant 3 is that it gives people confidence in the values that emerged in their debates over Quadrant 2.

LOYALTIES.   In Quadrant 4 the decision maker folds in an additional layer of complexity that must be sorted through: loyalties. The challenge is to establish a hierarchy of loyalties. Is the first loyalty to a code of ethics, and if so, to which code? To readers, and if so, to which ones? To society? To the employer? To self? Out of duty to self, some reporters and editors might want to make the rape series as potent as possible, with as much detail as possible, to win awards and bring honor to themselves and perhaps a raise or promotion or bigger job with another newspaper. Others might be motivated by their duty to their employer: The more detail in the story, the more newspapers it will sell. For others their duty to society may be paramount: The newspaper has a social obligation to present issues in as powerful a way as possible to spur reforms in general attitudes and perhaps public policy.

Limitations of Potter's Box

Potter's Box does not provide answers. Rather, it offers a process through which the key elements in ethics questions can be sorted out.

Also, Potter's Box focuses on moral aspects of a problem, leaving it to the decision maker to examine practical considerations separately, such as whether prudence supports making the morally best decision. Moral decisions should not be made in a vacuum. For example, would it be wise to go ahead with the rape victim's name if 90 percent of the newspaper's subscribers would become so offended that they would quit buying the paper and, as a result, the paper would go out of business?

Other practical questions can involve the law. If the morally best decision is to publish the name but the law forbids it, should the newspaper proceed anyway? Does journalistic virtue transcend the law? Is it worth it to publish the name to create a First Amendment issue? Are there legal implications, like going to jail or piling up legal defense costs?

Is it worth it to go against accepted practices and publish the victim's name? Deciding on a course of action that runs contrary to tradition, perhaps even contrary to some ethics codes, could mean being ostracized by other media people, whose decisions might have gone another way. Doing right can be lonely.

Ethics and Other Issues

STUDY PREVIEW   Right and wrong are issues in both ethics and law, but ethics and law are different. Obedience to law, or even to professional codes of ethics, will not always lead to moral action. There are also times when practical issues can enter moral decisions.

Differentiating Ethics and Law

Ethics is an individual matter that relates closely to conscience. Because conscience is unique to each individual, no two people have exactly the same moral framework. There are, however, issues about which there is consensus. No right-minded person condones murder, for example. When there is a universal feeling, ethics becomes codified in law, but laws do not address all moral questions. It is the issues of right and wrong that do not have a consensus that make ethics difficult. Was it morally right for *USA Today* to initiate coverage of Arthur Ashe's AIDS?

Ethics and law are related but separate. The law will allow a mass media practitioner to do many things that the practitioner would refuse to do. Since the 1964 *New York Times* v. *Sullivan* case, the U.S. Supreme Court has allowed the news media to cause tremendous damage to public officials, even with false information. However, rare is the journalist who would intentionally push the *Sullivan* latitudes to their limits to pillory a public official.

The ethics decisions of an individual mass media practitioner usually are more limiting than the law. There are times, though, when a journalist may choose to break the law on the grounds of ethics. Applying John Stuart Mill's principle of "the greatest good," a radio reporter might choose to break the speed limit to reach a chemical plant where an accident is threatening to send a deadly cloud toward where her listeners live. Breaking a speed limit might seem petty, but it demonstrates that obeying the law and obeying one's conscience do not always coincide.

Accepted Practices

Just as there is not a reliable correlation between law and ethics, neither is there one between accepted media practices and ethics. What is acceptable at one advertising agency to make a product look good in photographs might be unacceptable at another. Even universally **accepted practices** should not go unexamined, for unless accepted practices are examined and reconsidered on a continuing basis, media practitioners can come to rely more on habit than on principles in their work.

Prudence and Ethics

Prudence is the application of wisdom in a practical situation. It can be a leveling factor in moral questions. Consider the case of Irvin Leiberman, who had built his *Main Line Chronicle* and several other weeklies in the Philadelphia suburbs into aggressive, journalistically excellent newspapers. After being hit with nine libel suits, all costly to defend, Leiberman abandoned the editorial thrust of his newspapers. "I decided not to do any investigative work," he said. "It was a matter of either feeding my family or spending my whole life in court." Out of prudence, Leiberman decided to abandon his commitment to hard-hitting, effective journalism.

Courageous pursuit of morally lofty ends can, as a practical matter, be foolish. Whether Irvin Leiberman was exhibiting a moral weakness by bending to the chilling factor of libel suits, which are costly to fight, or being prudent is an issue that could be debated forever. The point, however, is that prudence cannot be ignored as a factor in moral decisions.

Unsettled, Unsettling Issues

STUDY PREVIEW   When mass media people discuss ethics, they talk about right and wrong behavior, but creating policies on ethics issues is not easy. Many standard media practices press the line between right and wrong, which muddies clear-cut standards that are universally applicable and recognized. There is further muddiness because many ethics codes confuse unethical behavior and behavior that may appear unethical but is not necessarily so.

Plagiarism

Perhaps the most fiercely loyal media fans are those who read romance novels and swear by a favorite author. In an Internet chat room in 1997, romance writer Janet Dailey found herself boxed into an admission that she had plagiarized from rival writer Nora Roberts. There is no scorn like that of creative people for those who steal their work, and Roberts was "very, very upset." HarperCollins recalled *Notorious*, Dailey's book that contained the plagiarism, and Roberts' fans, many of them long-time Dailey detractors, began a hunt for other purloined passages.

What is **plagiarism**? Generally, it's considered passing off someone else's creative work as your own, without permission. It's still plagiarism if it's changed a bit, as was Dailey's loose paraphrasing.

The fact that Dailey's 93 books over 20 years had sold an average of more than 2 million each made the scandal all the juicier. In the end, Roberts proposed a financial settlement, and the proceeds went to promote literacy.

accepted practices
What media do as a matter of routine, sometimes without considering ethics implications.

prudence
Applying wisdom, not principles, to an ethics situation.

plagiarism
Using someone else's work without permission or credit.

Romance Plagiarism. Cynics think all romance novels are the same, but aficionados know the difference. It shook Janet Dailey fans in 1997 to learn that she had loosely paraphrased a passage from rival Nora Roberts. The publisher withdrew Dailey's book with the plagiarized passages, and the question was whether Dailey, whose 93 titles had sold more than 200 million copies, would ever recover from the tarnish. You decide how serious the transgression:

"Talk to me."

"It was just a dream as you said."

"You're hurting." He touched her cheek. This time she didn't jerk away, only closed her eyes. "You talk, I'll listen."

"I don't need anyone."

"I'm not going away until you talk to me."

—From *Sweet Revenge* (1989) by Nora Roberts

"Talk to me, Eden."

"It was only a dream, just as you said."

His fingers brushed her cheek. . . . She closed her eyes at the contact. "You need to talk about it. I'll listen."

"I don't need anyone," she insisted stiffly.

"I'm not leaving until you tell me about it."

— From *Notorious* (1996) by Janet Dailey

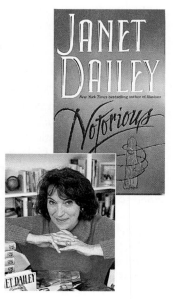

Nora Roberts   **Janet Dailey**

Everyone agrees that plagiarism, a form of thievery, is unethical, but the issue is not simple. The fact is that in many media, people draw heavily on other people's ideas and work. Think about sitcom story lines that mimic each other or the bandwagon of movies that follow an unexpected hit with an oddball theme that suddenly becomes mainstream. Journalists, most of whom consider themselves especially pristine compared to their media brethren, have standard practices that encourage a lot of "borrowing."

Among factors that make journalists uncomfortable when pressed hard on plagiary questions are:

- Institutionalized exchanging of stories.
- The role of public relations in generating news stories.
- Monitoring the competition.
- Subliminal memory and innocent recall.

SWAPPING STORIES. Some creative work, like scholarship, requires that information and ideas be attributed to their sources. Journalists are not so strict, as shown by story swapping through the Associated Press. The AP picks up stories from its members and distributes them to other members, generally without any reference to the source. Some publications and broadcasters do not even acknowledge AP as the intermediary.

Conditioned by 150 years of the AP's being a journalistic model and under pressure to gather information quickly, many journalists have a high tolerance for "borrowing." When the Chicago *Tribune* was apologizing for a story cribbed from the Jerusalem *Post,* for example, one of the writer's colleagues defended the story: "Everybody rewrites the Jerusalem *Post.* That's how foreign correspondents work."

In 2002 best-selling historian Stephen Ambrose found himself having explain the similarity of numerous passages in his books with earlier works. So did presidential scholar Doris Kearns Goodwin, whose works included numerous best-selling works on politics. Ambrose apologized, noting he had at least acknowledged his sources in the bibliographies. In effect, he said, he didn't let attribution clutter his breezy style. He promised to tighten up. Goodwin said her suspect works were done before she acquired a computer. Somehow, she said, her longhand notes from her sources got intertwined with her own hand-written drafts. It wouldn't happen again, she said. She had since switched to a computer, which, she said, would help her keep her working papers straight. Even so, Goodwin found herself under fire to resign from the Harvard faculty.

NEWS RELEASES.   In many newsrooms the plagiarism question is clouded further by the practice of using news releases from public relations people word for word without citing the source. Even in newsrooms that rewrite releases to avoid the embarrassment of running a story that is exactly the same as the competition's, it is standard practice not to cite the source. Public relations people, who are paid for writing favorable stories on their clients, have no objections to being plagiarized, and news organizations find it an easy, inexpensive way to fill space. Despite the mutual convenience, the arrangement raises serious questions of ethics to which many in the media have not responded. The practice leaves the false impression that stories originating with news releases actually originated with the news organization. More serious is that the uncredited stories are a disservice to democracy. Marie Dunn White, in the *Journal of Mass Media Ethics,* wrote, "In order for the reader to evaluate the information he or she is receiving correctly and completely, he or she must know which information came from a press release and, therefore, may be biased."

MONITORING THE COMPETITION.   Competitive pressure also contributes to fuzziness on the plagiarism issue. To avoid being skunked on stories, reporters monitor each other closely to pick up tips and ideas. Generally, reporters are not particular about where they pick up information as long as they are confident that it is accurate. For background, reporters tap newsroom libraries, databases, journals, books and other sources, and, in the interest of not cluttering their stories, they do not use footnotes.

SUBLIMINAL MEMORY.   Covering breaking events has its own pressure that puts journalists at special risk. Almost every journalist who writes under the pressure of a deadline has had the experience of writing a story and later discovering that phrases that came easily at the keyboard were actually somebody else's. In their voracious pursuit of information, reporters store phrases and perhaps whole passages subliminally in their memories. This happened to a drama critic at the St. Paul, Minnesota, *Pioneer Press,* who was horrified when a reader pointed out the similarity between his review of a play and an earlier review of the same play in the New York *Times.* Once aware of what he had done unwittingly, the critic offered his resignation. His editors instead moved him to the copy desk.

The muddiness on the issue of journalistic plagiarism is encapsulated in the fact that the Society of Professional Journalists' ethics code makes a flat statement that plagiarism is "dishonest and unacceptable" but then sidesteps the knotty part of the issue by declining to define *plagiarism.*

Misrepresentation

Janet Cooke's meteoric rise at the Washington *Post* unraveled quickly the day after she received a Pulitzer Prize. Her editors had been so impressed with her story "Jimmy's World," about a child who was addicted to heroin, that they nominated it for a Pulitzer Prize. The gripping tale began: "Jimmy is 8 years old and a third-generation heroin addict, a precocious little boy with sandy hair, velvety brown eyes and needle marks freckling the baby-smooth skin of his thin brown arms." Janet Cooke claimed that she had won the confidence of Jimmy's mother and her live-in man friend, a drug dealer, to do the story. Cooke said she had promised not to reveal their identities as a condition for her access to Jimmy.

The story, played on the front page, so shocked Washington that people demanded that Jimmy be taken away from his mother and placed in a foster home. The *Post* declined to help authorities, citing Cooke's promise of confidentiality to her sources. The mayor ordered the police to find Jimmy with or without the newspaper's help, and millions of dollars in police resources went into a door-to-door search. After 17 days the police gave up knocking on doors for tips on Jimmy. Some doubts emerged at the *Post* about the story, but the newspaper stood behind its reporter.

Janet Cooke, 25 when she was hired by the *Post*, had extraordinary credentials. Her résumé showed a baccalaureate degree, magna cum laude, from Vassar; study at the Sorbonne in Paris; a master's degree from the University of Toledo; abilities in several languages; and two years of journalistic experience with the Toledo *Blade*. Said Ben Bradlee, editor of the *Post*, "She had it all. She was bright. She was well spoken. She was pretty. She wrote well." She was black, which made her especially attractive to the *Post*, which was working to bring the percentage of black staff reporters nearer to the percentage of blacks in its circulation area.

"Jimmy's World" was published in September 1980. Six months later, the Pulitzer committee announced its decision and issued a biographical sheet on Janet Cooke. The Associated Press, trying to flesh out the biographical information, spotted discrepancies right away. Janet Cooke, it turned out, had attended Vassar for one year but had not been graduated with the honors she claimed. The University of Toledo had no record of awarding her a master's. Suddenly, doubts that had surfaced in the days immediately after "Jimmy's World" was published took on a new intensity. The editors sat Cooke down and grilled her on the claims on which she was hired. No, she admitted, she was not multilingual. The Sorbonne claim was fuzzy. More important, they grilled her on whether there was really a Jimmy. The interrogation continued into the night, and finally Janet Cooke confessed all: There were no confidential sources, and there was no Jimmy. She had fabricated the story. She resigned, and the *Post*, terribly embarrassed, returned the Pulitzer.

In cases of outright fabrication, as in "Jimmy's World," it is easy to identify the lapses in ethics. When Janet Cooke emerged briefly from seclusion to explain herself, she said that she was responding to pressures in the *Post* newsroom to produce flashy, sensational copy. Most people found the explanation unsatisfying, considering the pattern of deception that went back to her falsified résumé.

There are **misrepresentations**, however, that are not as clearly unacceptable. Much debated are:

STAGING NEWS. To attract favorable attention to their clients, public relations people organize media events, a practice known as **staging news**. These are designed to be irresistible to journalists. Rallies and demonstrations on topical issues, for

Janet Cooke
Classic case of representing fiction as true.

misrepresentation
Deception in gathering or telling information.

staging news
Creating an event to attract news media attention and coverage.

example, find their way onto front pages, magazine covers and evening newscasts because their photogenic qualities give them an edge over less visual although sometimes more significant events. The ethics question is less important for publicists, who generally are up front about what they are doing. The ethics question is more serious for journalists, who claim that their job is to present an accurate, balanced account of a day's events but who regularly overplay staged events that are designed by publicists to be photogenic and easy to cover.

RECREATIONS.   A wave of **reality programs** on television that began in the late 1980s featured **reenactments** that were not always labeled as such. Philip Weiss, writing in *Columbia Journalism Review,* offered this litany: shadows on the wall of a woman taking a hammer to her husband, a faceless actor grabbing a tin of kerosene to blow up his son, a corpse in a wheelbarrow with a hand dangling, a detective opening the trunk of a car and reeling from the smell of a decomposing body. Although mixing re-creations with strictly news footage rankles many critics, others argue that it helps people understand the situation. The same question arises with docudramas, which mix actual events and dramatic re-creations.

SELECTIVE EDITING.   The editing process, by its nature, requires journalists to make decisions on what is most worth emphasizing and what is least worth even including. In this sense, all editing is selective, but the term **selective editing** refers to making decisions with the goal of distorting. Selective editing can occur in drama too, when writers, editors and other media people take literary license too far and intentionally misrepresent.

FICTIONAL METHODS.   In the late 1960s many experiments in media portrayals of people and issues came to be called the **new journalism.** The term was hard to define because it included so many approaches. Among the most controversial were applications of fiction-writing methods on topical issues, an approach widely accepted in book publishing but suddenly controversial when it appeared in the news media. Character development became more important than before, including presumed insights into the thinking of people being covered. The view of the writer became an essential element in much of this reporting. The defense for these approaches was that traditional, facts-only reporting could not approach complex truths that merited journalistic explorations. The profound ethics questions that these approaches posed were usually mitigated by clear statements about what the writer was attempting. Nonetheless, it was a controversial approach to the issues of the day. There was no defense when the fictional approach was complete fabrication passing itself off as reality, as in "Jimmy's World."

Gifts, Junkets and Meals

In his 1919 book *The Brass Check,* a pioneer examination of newsroom ethics, **Upton Sinclair** told how news people took bribes to put stories in the paper. Today, media ethics codes universally condemn gifts and certainly bribes, but there still are many people who curry favor with the mass media through gifts, such as a college sports information director who gives a fifth of whiskey at Christmas to a sports writer as a gesture of goodwill. Favors can take many forms: media-appreciation luncheons; free trips abroad, known as **junkets,** for the experience necessary to do a travel article; season passes to cover the opera; discounts at certain stores.

reality programs
Broadcast shows with a nonfiction basis.

reenactments
Re-creating real events.

selective editing
Misrepresentation through omission and juxtaposition.

new journalism
Mixing fiction techniques with nonfiction.

The Brass Check
1919 book that exposed newsroom corruption.

Upton Sinclair
Author of *The Brass Check.*

junket
Trip with expenses paid by someone who may expect favors in return.

Despite the consistent exhortation of the ethics codes against gifts, favors, free travel and special treatment and privileges, there is nothing inherently wrong in taking them if they do not influence coverage and if the journalist's benefactor understands that. The problem with favors is more a practical one than one of ethics. Taking a favor may or may not be bad, but it *looks* bad. Many ethics codes do not make this important distinction. One that does is the code of the Associated Press Managing Editors, which states, "Journalists must avoid impropriety and *the appearance of impropriety* as well as any conflict of interest or *the appearance of conflict*. They should neither accept anything nor pursue any activity that might compromise or *seem to compromise* their integrity" [italics added]. The APME admonitions at least recognize the distinction between the inherent wrongness of impropriety, which is an ethics question, and the perception that something may be wrong, which is a perception that is unwise to encourage but is not necessarily unethical.

While ethics codes are uniform in prohibiting **freebies,** as gifts and favors are called, many news organizations accept free movie, drama, concert and other tickets, as well as recordings, books and other materials for review. The justification is usually that their budgets allow them to review only materials that arrive free and that their audiences would be denied reviews if the materials had to be purchased. A counterargument is that a news organization that cannot afford to do business right should not be in business. Many news organizations insist on buying tickets for their reporters to beauty pageants, sports events and other things to which there is an admission fee. A frequent exception occurs when a press box or special media facility is available. With recordings, books and free samples, some media organizations return them or pass them on to charity to avoid any appearance that they have been bought off.

When junkets are proposed, some organizations send reporters only if they can pay the fare and other expenses. The Louisville *Courier-Journal* is firm: "Even on chartered trips, such as accompanying a sports team, or hitchhiking on a State Police plane, we insist on being billed for our pro-rata share of the expense." An exception is made by some news organizations for trips that they could not possibly arrange on their own, such as covering a two-week naval exercise aboard a ship.

Some media organizations address the issue of impropriety by acknowledging favors. Many quiz shows say that "promotional consideration" has been provided to companies that give them travel, lodging and prizes. Just as forthright are publications that state that reviews are made possible through season passes or free samples. Acknowledging favors does not remove the questions, but at least it is up front.

freebie
Gift for which the giver may expect favor in return.

chapter wrap-up

Moral decision-making is rooted in conscience, which makes it highly individual. Attempts to bring order to moral issues in journalism and the mass media have included codes of ethics. These codes identify behaviors that are recognized as ethically troublesome, but because they are generalized statements, the codes cannot anticipate all situations. There is no substitute for human reason and common sense.

Questions for Review

1. Why cannot ethics codes anticipate all moral questions? And does this limit the value of codes for mass media people?
2. List and explain moral principles that mass media people can use to sort through ethics questions.
3. How can mass media people come to different conclusions depending on whether they use process-based or outcome-based ethics?
4. How is Potter's Box a useful tool to sort through ethics issues?
5. Is ethics the same as law? As prudence? As accepted practice?
6. Discuss dubious mass media practices that are inconsistent with many moral principles.

Questions for Critical Thinking

1. How are traditional libertarians deontological in their approach to ethics? How is the social responsibility approach teleological?
2. As someone who reads newspapers and watches newscasts, would you favor deontological or teleological ethics? Which is easier? Which system do you think most journalists prefer?

3. Can you identify the ethics principle or system most associated with Aristotle? Immanuel Kant? John Stuart Mill? John Dewey? John Rawls? Robert Hutchins?
4. How can codes of ethics help mass media people to make the right decisions? Do codes always work? Why or why not?
5. A candidate for mayor tells a news reporter that the incumbent mayor is in cahoots with organized crime. What should the reporter do before going on the air with this bombshell accusation? Why?
6. Can media people ever defend breaking the law as ethical?
7. Is there a difference between ethics and accepted practices?

Keeping Up to Date

Ethicists sort through moral dilemmas involving mass communication in the scholarly *Journal of Mass Media Ethics.*

Many trade and professional journals also deal with media ethics, including *Quill, Columbia Journalism Review* and *American Journalism Review.*

Index

Page numbers in italic and followed by the letter "w" refer to pages on the **www.abinteractive.com/login** web site.

Photo Credits

p. xxvi: Billy Tompkins/Black Star; p. 5: © AP/ Wide World Photos; p. 11: Juno and the Juno logo are registered trademarks of Juno Online Services, Inc. YellowOnline banner is © YellowOnline.com™; p. 13: AP/Wide World Photos; p. 15: Autowraps.com pays drivers to do their everyday commute. Reprinted by permission of Autowraps.com; p. 17: Hulton Getty/Archive Photos; p. 19, left: David M. Grossman; p. 19, right: Beacon Press; p. 22: Mike Segar/Reuters/Corbis; p. 23: Skidmore, Owings & Merrill and Acrimation; p. 26: AP/Wide World Photos; p. 28: Warner Brothers Pictures, Inc. HARRY POTTER, characters, names, and related indicia are trademarks of Warner Bros. © 2001; p. 29: North Wind Picture Archives; p. 31, left: Culver Pictures, Inc.; p. 31, right: The Granger Collection; p. 33: Oxford University Press; p. 38: Courtesy of the Library of Congress; p. 42, left: Copyright © 2000, The Chronicle of Higher Education. Reprinted with permission. This material may not be posted, published, or distributed without permission from *The Chronicle*; p. 42, center: Publishers Weekly; p. 42, right: New York Times Pictures; p. 45: Paul Souders/Liaison Agency, Inc.; p. 46, left: Bernard Boutrit/ Woodfin Camp/Picture Quest; p. 46, right: Courtesy of Gemstar/RCA/Thomson Consumer Electronics; p. 47, left: Capital Pictures, Corbis; p. 47, right: Shasti O'Leary-Soudant; p. 50: Tom Carroll/ Photographic International/Robert E. Petersen; p. 52: EMAP USA; p. 53: University of Illinois News Bureau; p. 55: Courtesy of Margaret Bourke-White Estate/Life Magazine. © Time Inc.; p. 56: Cover/ hologram photo-illustration by Tom Schaefges. Cover image used with permission of National Geographic Society. © National Geographic Society; p. 58: Ted Thai/TimePix; p. 59: Reader's Digest Association, Inc.; p. 60: The Granger Collection; p. 64, left: Newsletter & Electronic Publishers Foundation; p. 64, right: Reprinted with the permission of Mealey Publications; p. 65, top: Copyright © 1998 Watterson. Reprinted with permission of Universal Press Syndicate. All rights reserved; p. 65, right: Margaret Bourke-White/TimePix; p. 68: Reprinted by permission. © 1925 The New Yorker Magazine, Inc. Originally published in *The New Yorker*. All rights reserved; p. 72: Brian W. Smith/TimePix; p. 80, left: Reprinted by permission of the Wall Street Journal, © 2002 Dow Jones & Company, Inc. All rights reserved worldwide; p. 80, right: The Wall Street Journal; p. 82, left: Scott Maclay/The Freedom Forum; p. 82: Copyright 2002, USA TODAY. Reprinted with permission. Photos: top left, © Tami Chappell, Reuters; top right, © AP/Wide World Photos; center top, © Joe Raedle/Getty Images; bottom right, © AP/ Wide World Photos; p. 84, left: This cover page first appeared *in The Christian Science Monitor* on March 5, 2002 and is reproduced with permission. Copyright © 2002 The Christian Science Monitor (csmonitor.com). All rights reserved. Photos: top left, AP/Wide World center, © Susan Ragan/ Reuters; p. 84, right: The Granger Collection; p. 86, left: Copyright © 2002 by the New York Times Co. Reprinted by permission. Photo: © Paolo Pellegrin/ Magnum Photos, for The New York Times; p. 86, right: Copyright © 2002 by the New York Times Co. Reprinted by permission. Illustration: © C. F. Payne; p. 86, center: Copyright © 2002 by the New York Times Co. Reprinted by permission. Photos: top three, Department of Defense via CNN; bottom center, © Fred R. Conrad/The New York Times; bottom right, © Barton Silverman/ The New York Times; p. 96, left: Courtesy of the Library of Congress; p. 96, right: Courtesy of the Library of Congress; p. 97: Copyright © 2001 San Jose Mercury News. All rights reserved. Reproduced with permission; p. 98: The Tampa Tribune; p. 100: AP/Wide World Photos; p. 104: Lynn Goldsmith/Corbis; p. 106: AP/Wide World Photos; p. 108, top: UPI/Corbis; p. 108, bottom: Corbis; p. 112, left: Alain Benainous/Liaison Agency, Inc.; p. 112, right: UPI/Corbis; p. 114, top: Panasonic Consumer Electronics Company; p. 114, bottom: AP/Wide World Photos; p. 117: Corbis; p. 119, top: State Department photo by Mike Gross; p. 119, bottom: Credit: © Ethan Miller/CORBIS; p. 120: Ethan Miller/Reuters/TimePix; p. 121, left: Forrest Anderson/TimePix; p. 121, right: AP/Wide World Photos; p. 126: William Thomas Cain/Newsmakers/ Liaison Agency, Inc.; p. 128: Artisan Entertainment; p. 130: AP/Wide World Photos; p. 131, left: AP/Wide World Photos; p. 131, right: Culver Pictures; p. 134: Courtesy of Video Sound, Inc., NJ; p. 135: Sam Mircovich/Reuters/TimePix; p. 136, left: © AP/Wide World Photos; p. 136, right: Kobal Collection/ Dreamworks/ Universal/ Eli Reed; p. 138: Corbis; p. 141: Steve Allen/Liaison Agency, Inc.; p. 143: AP/Wide World Photos; p. 144: AP/Wide World Photos; p. 147, left: Ron Sachs/Corbis/Sygma; p. 147, right: Win McNamee/Reuters/Corbis; p. 148: Dennis Brack/Black Star; p. 152: Photopress/Corbis/ Sygma; p. 156, top: The Granger Collection; p. 157, top, center, bottom: AP/Wide World Photos; p. 159, left: Bettmann/Corbis; p. 159, right: Corbis; p. 160: Greg Smith; p. 161: Sal DiMarco, Jr./WHYY, Inc.; p. 162: AP/Wide World Photos; p. 163: Michelle Engel/KVMX Radio; p. 167, left:

Mark Richards; p. 167, right: Barry Staver/Time Inc. Magazines/Sports Illustrated; p. 172: UPI/Corbis; p. 178: Douglas Levere Photography; p. 180: Reuters/Jill Connelly/Archive Photos; p. 182: AP/Wide World Photos; p. 185: UPI/Corbis; p. 187: © 2000 TiVo, Inc. All rights reserved; p. 192: CNN Viewersource; p. 193: Cahners Business Information; p. 196, top: AP/Wide World Photos; p. 196, bottom: Fred Prouser/Reuters/Corbis; p. 199, left: NASA Headquarters; p. 199, right: AP/Wide World Photos; p. 200: Bill Swersey/Liaison Agency, Inc.; p. 203: AP/Wide World Photos; p. 205, left, right: AP/Wide World Photos; p. 206: AP/Wide World Photos; p. 208: Mike Maple/Woodfin Camp & Associates; p. 210, left: AP/Wide World Photos; p. 210, right: Frank Driggs Collection; p. 211: AP/Wide World Photos; p. 212: Everett Collection, Inc.; p. 216: © CERN Geneva; p. 224: AP/Wide World Photos; p. 230: AP/Wide World Photos; p. 231: UPI/Corbis; pp. 232–233: © 1998 Spaceshots/Living Earth, Inc. Reprinted by permission; p. 234: Corbis; p. 235: AP/Wide World Photos; p. 236: Ananova, Ltd.; p. 238: © Reuters/Lon Dematteis/Getty Images; p. 239, left: Diana Walker/TimePix; p. 239, right: Sigrid Estrada/Carl Bernstein; p. 240: Jeff Scheid/Liaison Agency, Inc.; p. 241: Nick Gunderson/HarperCollins Publishers, Inc.; p. 244: Kevin R. Morris; p. 246: Noel Quidu/Liaison Agency, Inc.; p. 248: North Wind Picture Archives; p. 251, right: Corbis; p. 253: The Granger Collection; p. 254: Corbis; p. 255, top: Culver Pictures, Inc.; p. 255, bottom right: Corbis; p. 255: bottom upper and lower left: Culver Pictures; p. 266: Amy Etra/TimePix; p. 268: AP/Wide World Photos; p. 269, left: Corbis; p. 269, right: Superstock, Inc.; p. 274: © AP/Wide World Photos; p. 276: © AP/Wide World Photos; p. 280, left: Colorado Historical Society; p. 280, right: AP/Wide World Photos; p. 283, top left: The Granger Collection; p. 283, top right: AP/Wide World Photos; p. 283, bottom: AP/Wide World Photos; p. 289, left: © Kevin Horan/Chicago; p. 289, right: Corbis/Sygma; p. 291: © AP/Wide World Photos; p. 292, left: Herb Schmertz; p. 292, right: © Van Bucher; p. 295: UPI/Corbis; p. 298: Mazola is a registered trademark of Best Foods. Used with permission; p. 300: The Bravo Group; p. 305: Pizza Hut; p. 313: Bamboo, Inc.; p. 315, left: Dr. Wilson Bryan Key; p. 315, right: From *The Clam-Plate Orgy* by Wilson Bryan Key; p. 317: Tom Wagner/Corbis/SABA Press Photos, Inc.; p. 319: Courtesy of Colon Cancer Detection and Prevention and the American Cancer Society; p. 324: Cliff Moore/Princeton Stock Photo; p. 330, left: © The Gallup Organization, 2000; p. 330, right: AP/Wide World Photos; p. 333: Broadcasting & Cable from Nielsen Media Research data; p. 334: The Arbitron Company, NY; p. 335: Roger Hutchings/Woodfin Camp & Associates; p. 339: Douglass Burrows/Liaison Agency, Inc.; p. 340, left, right: John C. Hilleary/Reuters/Archive Photos; p. 344, left: Courtesy of W. Joseph Campbell; p. 346: The East-West Center; p. 349: UPI/Corbis; p. 350, left: AP/Wide World Photos; p. 350, right: Sam Jones Photography; p. 356: Jacques Chenet/Woodfin Camp & Associates; p. 357: The Everett Collection, Inc.; p. 359: Reprinted from the Columbia Journalism Review, January/February 2001; p. 361: John Barnett/Globe Photos, Inc.; p. 426: © AFP/CORBIS; p. 364: Culver Pictures, Inc.; p. 371: AP/Wide World Photos; p. 374: David E. Dempster; p. 376: AP/Wide World Photos; p. 380: Evening Standard/Hulton Getty/Archive Photos; p. 381: Woodfin Camp & Associates; p. 384, left: Everett Collection, Inc.; p. 384, right: © 1998 SCi (Sales Curve Interactive) Limited. All rights reserved; p 385: Heikki Saukkoma; p. 386: AP/Wide World Photos; p. 392: Corbis; p. 396, left: © Fredrich Cantor; p. 396, right: Center for Media and Public Affairs; p. 397, left: © New York Daily News, L.P. Reprinted-reproduced with permission. Photo © Reuters/Archive News Photo; p. 397, middle: New York Times Pictures; p. 397, right: The New York Post. Photo © Reuters/Archive News Photo; p. 400: Steven Klein; p. 401, top: AP/Wide World Photos; p. 401, bottom: MADD; p. 402, left: Steve Liss/TimePix; p. 402, right: Mark R. Shughart/Corbis/Sygma; p. 404: AP/Wide World Photos; p. 405, left: AP/Wide World Photos; p. 405, right: AFP Photo/Sergey Chirikov/Corbis/Sygma; p. 408: Roslan Rahman/AFP Photo/Corbis; p. 411: PEPC Worldwide; p. 413: AP/Wide World Photos; p. 414: USCD Photo; p. 417: Freedom House; p. 418: John Merrill; p. 419: From Hiebert, Ungurait, and Bohn, *Mass Media: An Introduction to Modern Communication* (6th ed.). Copyright © 1991 by Allyn & Bacon. Adapted by permission; p. 426: AFP/Corbis; p. 427: Reuters/Luis Ramirez/Colombia Press/Corbis/Sygma; p. 430: AP/Wide World Photos; p. 436: AP/Wide World Photos; p. 438: AP/Wide World Photos; p. 440: CNN Cable News Network, Inc.; p. 442, left: UPI/Corbis; p. 442, right: Archive Photos; p. 445, left: AFP Photo/Timothy A. Clary/Corbis/Sygma; p. 445, right: AP/Wide World Photos; p. 450: Jeff Topping/Reuters/Archive Photos; p. 452: Electronic Frontier Foundation; p. 454: Justin Sullivan/Reuters NewMedia Inc./Corbis; p. 456, left: © Copyright The New York Times Co. Reprinted by permission; p. 456, both at right: AP/Wide World Photos; p. 457, left: Star Tribune; p. 457, right: From the collection of the Minnesota Historical Society; p. 461: AP/Wide World Photos; p. 463: George S. Mills; p. 469: AP/Wide World Photos; p. 473: Joel Veak; p. 476: Keri Pickett/TimePix; p. 479: Big Picture/Archive Photos; p. 480: AP/Wide World Photos; p. 482: Corbis; p. 483: North Wind Picture Archives; p. 484: North Wind Picture Archives; p. 486: © David Surowiecki/Getty Images; p. 490, top left: David M. Grossman; p. 490, bottom left: AP/Wide World Photos; p. 490, top right: David M. Grossman; p. 490, bottom right: Ed Lallo/Liaison Agency, Inc.; Microsoft Explorer browser frame reprinted by permission from Microsoft Corporation.